In this ambitious book, the author proposes a fundamental new approach to the study of one of the most central concepts in social analysis, that of social structure. He critiques the leading models and argues that each is inadequate to the task of explaining the complexity of structures that make up society and the processes by which these structures are formed and are interlinked.

A new conceptualization of the processes of societal formation is then presented, drawing on recent developments in the physical, biological, and cognitive sciences. This conceptualization allows for a multiplicity of processes of structuration, which the author refers to as logics, some of which function at the individual or "micro" level of society, others of which function at the organizational or "meso" level, and still others at the society-wide or "macro" level. The author terms this new conceptualization a theory of heterarchy, and it is the first truly comprehensive theory of societal structuration.

The logics of social structure

Structural Analysis in the Social Sciences

Mark Granovetter, editor

Other books in the series:

The series *Structural Analysis in the Social Sciences* presents approaches that explain social behavior and institutions by reference to *relations* among such concrete social entities as persons and organizations. This contrasts with at least four other popular strategies: (1) reductionist attempts to explain by a focus on individuals alone; (2) explanations stressing the causal primacy of such abstract concepts as ideas, values, mental harmonies, and cognitive maps (thus, "structuralism" on the Continent should be distinguished from structural analysis in the present sense); (3) technological and material determinism; (4) explanations using "variables" as the main analytic concepts (as in the "structural equation" models that dominated much of the sociology of the 1970s), where "structure" is that connecting variables rather than actual social entities.

The "social network" approach is an important example of the strategy of structural analysis; the series also draws on social science theory and research that is not framed explicitly in network terms, but stresses the importance of relations rather than the atomization of reductionism or the determinism of ideas, technology, or material conditions. Though the structural perspective has become extremely popular and influential in all the social sciences, it does not have a coherent identity, and no series yet pulls together such work under a single rubric. By bringing the achievements of structurally oriented scholars to a wider public, the *Structural Analysis* series hopes to encourage the use of this very fruitful approach.

Mark Granovetter

The logics of social structure

KYRIAKOS M. KONTOPOULOS
Temple University

 CAMBRIDGE
UNIVERSITY PRESS

Published by the Press Syndicate of the University of Cambridge
The Pitt Building, Trumpington Street, Cambridge CB2 1RP
40 West 20th Street, New York, NY 10011–4211, USA
10 Stamford Road, Oakleigh, Victoria 3166, Australia

First published 1993

Printed in the Printed in Canada

Library of Congress Cataloging-in-Publication Data
Kontopoulos, Kyriakos M.
The logics of social structure / Kyriakos M. Kontopoulos.
p.   cm. – (Structural analysis in the social sciences)
Includes bibliographical references and index.
ISBN 0-521-41779-1 (hardback)
1. Social structure.   I. Title.   II. Series.
HM131.K6931993   92-2470
301 – dc20   CIP

A catalog record for this book is available from the British Library

ISBN 0-521-41779-1 hardback

For Michael and Alexandra,
my eternal mentors in life

        and

For Ourania, Eirene, Michael, and Alexandra,
my Castalian springs of meaning
in an otherwise disenchanted world

Contents

Preface

This book is the result of ten years of measured thinking, adventurous reading over a wide spectrum, and accelerated, almost compulsive writing as I neared the completion of my goal. With some trepidation, I present here some provisional notions, taking stock of my progress at this first stop in my ongoing program of research. Since my graduate days at Harvard I have been bothered by the failure of sociologists to address the fundamental question of upward structuration, an issue to which I developed a special sensitivity there in the course of frequent discussions with George C. Homans, Seymour M. Lipset, and Gino Germani. I owe to the last, among many other things, the cultivation of a flexible, dynamic view of structural processes and collective agencies. At the time, although admiring it considerably in secret, I was an outsider to Harrison C. White's group, which was so successfully advancing network research. Having read Wittgenstein, Kuhn, and Lakatos, I was searching for a way to engage with the most fundamental issue of sociology in a postpositivist, nonfoundational manner. I have been working since then, in silence, exploring the borders of our discipline. I now feel that I have found an answer in what I would describe as the *heterarchical conception of structuration*. With this book, I stake a claim to new fields and conceptions and invite one and all to come and plow them together.

Given my rather heterodox trajectory, several influences on my thought were rather indirect and from a distance. I have never met Bourdieu, Boudon, Schelling, Edelman, or Hofstadter, whose work I both value and appraise. Also, I have missed the pleasures associated with the ongoing interaction with respected colleagues during the formative stages of my project. Mark Granovetter and Harrison C. White were the first to read my already completed manuscript and to give me extremely valuable comments on it. This has become a much better book as a result of their editorial advice, which I have tried to follow to the extent possible at this stage. I must also express my gratitude to Emily Loose and Andrée Lockwood, my Cambridge editors, for their personal encouragement and highly professional editorial suggestions. For all substantive problems, omissions, faux pas, creative misreadings, and the like, I alone, of course, must bear all responsibility.

I would also like to acknowledge the special contributions made by people in my own institution, Temple University. Here I must mention the philosophers Joseph Margolis and Chuck Dyke with whom I have shared a long association of labors on matters of postpositivist theorizing, the brain/mind, complexity, and emergence – many common themes are woven individually in our respective works. My colleague Leo Rigsby, a true alter ego, deserves my limitless gratitude for his indefatigable support and enthusiastic encouragement for so many years; without his trust and prodding, this project might not have taken off at all. Thanks also to Doug Porpora, David Kutzik, and Donald Eckard, who inspired me by their warm expectations, and to Maria Gasi, Chris Gannon, Kostas Markou, and Vassilios Alexopoulos, who helped me with the bibliographic checking and the completion of figures and graphs.

I also wish to express my eternal gratitude and sincere apologies to my beloved family for their understanding and ongoing support, their many sacrifices and accommodations so that my project could be completed. They – and the many others I have referred to above – are real coauthors of this work, as producers of its possibility, or as energizing partners and interlocutors affecting its development at different moments.

Introduction

In this book I propose to embark on an exploration of one of the most difficult yet fundamental concepts of the natural and social sciences, the concept of "structure." This will not be an easy voyage – many a tall ship has been wrecked in the course of such an enterprise. Nonetheless, the call of the open sea can be still heard and the time seems to be ripe for another daring undertaking. Let us then accept the challenge and investigate this much used and abused notion which, as Neil Smelser pointed out some time ago (1967), constitutes the chief conceptual focus of sociology and of numerous cognate fields as well.

Since the 1970s, under the stewardship of Robert K. Merton and Peter Blau, several conferences and ensuing publications have resulted in (a) increasing the visibility of the issue of "social structure," (b) mapping many previously held positions on the matter, and (c) heightening the realization that more progressive work was needed at both the conceptual and empirical levels (Blau 1975a and b; Blau and Merton 1981; Coser 1975). This was certainly facilitated by the dynamic influence of French structuralism, which at the time still reigned supreme. In the 1980s, this progress has been relatively halted, given the later misadventures of formal structuralism and the significant change of course in the social sciences away from the consideration of large social structures and more in the direction of presumed processes of "microstructuration." Giddens's attempted mediation became very attractive to many people for a short time; but his work now looks more and more like a diversion from the initial project and, certainly, as strategically exhausted.[1] Similarly, the equally heralded, more collective search for the missing "micro–macro link" (Alexander et al. 1987; Hechter 1983b; Knorr-Cetina and Cicourel 1981; Lindenberg et al. 1986; Wardell and Turner 1986) has been also proved – at least for the time being – to be a dead end, for it has failed to uncover any significant analytical mechanism(s) accounting for the processes of structuration from the micro- to the robust macro-level. So at this point, we seem to be at an impasse. Nonetheless all is not lost. Promising new ways of

---

[1] Sadly, I consider Giddens's work on social structure a walk in a blind alley. Its length is not a warrant of true theoretical elaboration and extension; it rather looks like a new language in search of some application, but unable to lead to a robust research program. I agree with Turner (1986a) and Elster (1985, 1989a) that we need to move from "verbosity" to "mechanisms" of structuration.

1

handling the issue of social structure do exist; but they are not available within the strict disciplinary confines of sociology. By expanding the search for new ideas to other relevant fields and to the exciting novel conceptions and empirical findings of current physical sciences, one may discover Ariadne's thread leading out of the labyrinth. There are no guarantees, of course – no absolutes or permanent foundations; only pragmatic, relative but robust promises inspiring such an exploration. Naturally, I intend to follow that route!

As the title suggests, my goal is to elucidate the logics of social structure – indeed, of social structures. Why logics? Why structures? This is not a simple matter to be resolved with a few explanatory strokes – this is the subject of this entire book. Nonetheless, some preliminary remarks are in order. To start with the notion of "structures," we would preemptively point out that the opposition of an abstract notion of structure (structure-type) to the many seemingly empirical structures (structure-tokens) seems erroneous. "Universal" notions of structure have been rightly opposed on both theoretical and empirical grounds. On the other hand, the naive presumption of the existence of "empirical structures" has been thoroughly contested as well: there are no empirical structures but interactional or social systems structured by particular structuring mechanisms. To make better sense of this, we will argue – and elaborate in later chapters – that any proper theory of social structure unavoidably must rest on a suitable metatheoretical notion of "level structure" populated by different "structural" entities (i.e., systems of interaction, systems involving externalities, social systems, and so on) exhibiting particular "structural" forms. This approach then pragmatically demarcates second-order questions about structure in general (the "structure of structures" as it were, the level structure, though not an abstract, universal conception of structure) from first-order questions about commonsensically presumed concrete structures (that is, structured systems that are taken to be "real" even when, defensively, they are construed as such only pragmatically or from an "internal realist" point of view).[2] There are many "concrete structures" inscribed in "structured systems" but their relations to each other and to the total "structure" one may have in mind is neither simple nor easily un-

---

[2] On the new pragmatic turn in the philosophy of science see Rorty (1979, 1982) and Margolis (1986). Putnam's notion of "internal realism" is explained in his 1981, 1982, 1987, 1988 (compare also Goodman 1978; Laudan 1977). I opt for a form of *intensional* realism (linguistic–conceptual) along lines suggested by Wittgenstein and Lakatos. In general, I believe that the scaffolding of Lakatos's notion of "Research Programmes" is very robust (though I dislike the narrow interpretation offered by Wagner 1984).

derstandable, nor does it exhibit perfect fit to a model of token-type inclusion.

The analytical difficulty of spelling out the relations obtaining among structures (not only among structured social systems) is compounded by the fact that for different concrete structures there exist distinct structuring operations or mechanisms. Thus the need to speak of the *logics* of structures: the various operative mechanisms in a multidimensional actional *and* structural topology that bring about structured systems exhibiting in a relative way an inscribed structural form. These are the treacherous reefs and shoals that have endangered many other efforts; namely, the realization that, if any serious advance is to be made, it is absolutely necessary to discover and elucidate these, as we shall see numerous, special structuring mechanisms producing, underlying, and animating the imputed structural forms of concrete structured systems. These are the logics of structuration from the micro to the intermediary and then to the robust macro levels (see their preliminary inventory in the Appendix), logics to which others until now have just alluded, and which must at this point become the focus of analysis. Consequently, in this book I have committed myself to the task of (a) articulating the progressive strategies fruitfully implemented in the study of social structure; (b) teasing out and elaborating significant forms of "structure" at different levels of size and complexity; and (c) analyzing the particular mechanisms involved in the production/emergence of these concrete structures.

The book is divided into five parts. Part I refers exclusively to the various epistemic strategies currently used in the physical and biological sciences and describes in more detail the new "emergentist" programs of research now flourishing in many scientific domains. This strategy may appear to many to be mistaken. Indeed, with the demise of the logical positivist model of science (see the story in Suppe 1977), the pendulum has moved in the opposite direction, to the point that once more one finds most sociologists arguing on behalf of the radical incommensurability of the respective explanatory models, if not for the outright rejection of the entire scientific enterprise. In the process, not much attention has been paid to the significant changes taking place in many scientific fields, changes which permit for the first time a real rapprochement of physical, biological, and social sciences on equal footing. In this sense, the study of current scientific and philosophical conceptions of "epistemic strategies," "emergence," and "structure" is extremely important for social theory. The message one gets from the recent developments in these domains is that the physicalist, Newtonian–Laplacean (dogmatic empiricist, mechanistic, equilibrium-based, atomistic) model of the world is superseded by a more robust, emergentist one, hospitable to the habitus of social scientists, who will find nothing offending their sensibilities in the current views favoring the ascription of semiautonomy and of a sui generis character to the social structural as well as the mental phenomena – indeed to all emergent phenomena. Since these positions are quite new and not widely known, a survey of the major advances in the physical, biological, and cognitive sciences, bearing on the issues at hand, seems indispensable. It could then be shown that a new convergent model has emerged – a nonreductive, nonequilibrium, multilevel conceptualization of phenomena, which is currently revolutionizing these sciences and which could provide support for a different and more successful recasting of the notion of social structure.

Therefore, we want first to focus on the strategies, proposals, and debates in the philosophy of science and the research practices of the scientists themselves. There are four chapters here addressing these issues: Chapter 1, "Epistemic strategies in contemporary science," presents five metatheoretical, second-order strategies guiding first-order theoretical research programs and low-level empirical research. These are called the reductionist, constructionist, heterarchical, hierarchical, and transcendent/holist epistemic strategies. Chapter 2, "The dynamics of emergence," reviews recent developments and debates in the physical, biological, and cognitive sciences, all of which seem to converge on the point that the world provides ample evidence of emergence, that it forms a level structure, and that the proper approach to the world should be based on a robust nonreductive materialist or "integrated pluralist" philosophy of science. As a result of this review of numerous scientific research programs I take it as a well-corroborated posit that the "emergentist epistemic strategies" of constructionism, heterarchy, and hierarchy are superior to the older and more extreme views of reduction and holism. Chapter 3, "The nature of hierarchical and heterarchical organization," focuses on clarifying the meaning of "hierarchy" and "heterarchy," the more robust as well as recent forms of emergentism. In this chapter the differences between hierarchical and heterarchical organization of phenomena are illuminated in a number of examples. I end by justifying my preference for the heterarchical approach, which I use to ground a metatheory of social structure in Parts IV and V. Chapter 4, "Some formal theses on hierarchy and heterarchy," specifies in a more formal way the differences between the two robust emergentist strategies. A number of theses are posited detailing and codifying the characteristics of these two strategies. After concluding this part, the reader ought to form the impression that, of the five candidate strategies, three (constructionism, heterarchy, hierarchy) are admissible as progressive metatheoretical research programs and, of these three, heterarchy is preferable on grounds of relative comparative merit.

In Part II we focus on the applications of the constructionist epistemic strategies to social phenomena in order to spell out what I call the constructionist or compositionist logics operative in the production of emergence. This strategy marks the first break with reductionism and, as argued in Chapter 2, is the preferred choice of many leading physicists and molecular biologists. In the domain of the social sciences, constructionism is represented by those research programs that begin to theorize the partly continuous, partly discontinuous emergence of social structure out of individual (intentional, rational, or other) actions and ensuing "systems of interaction." Usually, the emphasis falls on discontinuities and the emergent paradoxical effects. In any case, phenomena are explored that are said to be beyond the intentions, understanding, or control of the participating individual actors; and, of course, the higher the level and the more complex the systems of interactions, the more pronounced are the discontinuities presumed to be and the more complex the structural products. We pursue this strategy in three chapters, initially discussing several forms of the radical reductionist program. Chapter 5, "Methodological individualism," presents the archetypal versions of reductionism in the social sciences. Here we analytically demarcate four types of predicates (individual-, relational-, conventional/institutional-, and structural-) implicated and intertwined in the texture of human social phenomena. On this basis we critique the foundations and appraise the prospects of six forms of methodological individualism. Chapter 6, "Constructionism/compositionism: elementary notions," introduces the constructionist views as they apply to the case at hand. Here we briefly discuss the exchange and network models as well as the game theoretical logic, focusing on the work of Raymond Boudon, Thomas Schelling, Mancur Olson, and Jon Elster. Chapter 7, "Complex systems of interaction," is devoted to the further extension and elaboration of game-theoretical and other models to higher levels of structures. We look at "corporate" and "collective" actors, many-actor systems of interdependence, systems involving complex and compounded externalities, and more complex "entangled systems."

Part III focuses on the Logics of hierarchy for reasons of symmetry. Here the emergence of structure is seen not as a byproduct of aggregated individual actions but as derived from quasi-local, semiglobal, and global characteristics or macrovariables, such as size, phase-separated aggregate interactions, the coupling of lower-level structures, and new mechanisms of structuration and their ensuing structural effects. Furthermore, individual action is conceived as parameterized by the semiglobal or global characteristics of the structural systems, the latter said to have authoritatively superseded the former and to exert a downward influence over them. Chapter 8, "Hierarchy theory and postfunctional analysis," is intended as the antipode of Chapter 5: Here we present an analytical summary of the tumultuous career of the various forms of "functionalism," the backdrop for all "holist" versions of theory, and proceed to evaluate the prospects of holism on the basis of an extended articulation of changes that have taken place in the fields of physical chemistry, molecular biology, and ecosystem modeling. We then posit a "postfunctional" mode of analysis as the only viable form in the research program of former functionalists. Chapter 9, "The hierarchical theory of social structure," explores a number of previous conceptualizations of social structure along hierarchical lines (Bunge, Hernes) and details the extent to which the "received view of Marxist theory" is an exemplary instance of a hierarchical structural theory.

Part IV deals with Heterarchical logics, which I personally favor. This is the most complex type and is situated midway between the constructionist and the hierarchical logics. Here I build on Hofstadter's (1979) erudite, pathbreaking, analyses of heterarchical, tangled systems, placing emphasis on the *analytical* characteristics of the heterarchical model of social structure. Chapter 10, "Heterarchical thinking in social thought," presents various theories of "structuration," and attempts to go beyond the limits of the constructionist microstructuration programs (by introducing the dialectic between agency and structure). I also offer here my own basic views on the heterarchical organization of social structures as a positive heuristic of an ongoing research program on this subject. The ideas presented here are then further developed and applied in the next part. Chapter 11, "Neural networks as a model of structure," by far the most speculative section in the book, discusses the very novel conception of "neural networks" as a possible advanced model of social structure. Various parallels between the neuronal/mental and individual/social discontinuous connections are surveyed and appraised.

Part V addresses issues relative to the Phenomenology of social structures in accordance with the basic canons of the "logic of heterarchy." Here we offer a description of a matrix composed of structural types and structural levels and elaborate the relations obtaining not only between structures at a given level but, more importantly, between structures at adjacent levels; expectedly, these interlevel relations of structures are the more complex and difficult since, under the heterarchical canons, they are presumed to be entangled, not authoritatively subsumed under each other as in a hierarchy. Chapter 12, "Modalities and systems of interaction," posits various modalities of interactions implicated in the process of "emergence." We review several relevant proposals and then discuss the varieties of types of systems of interaction, the micrologics animating them, and the structural effects emerging out of them. Chapter 13, "Heterarchical levels of social structure," outlines a concrete description of upward heterarchical (entangled interlevel) structuration. We describe three levels of social structures: groupings, fields, and totalities. We then proceed to analyze the first two levels: We describe the distinct social structures populating them, establish the important intralevel as well as interlevel connections, and articulate the mode of their emergence. Chapter 14, "On structural totalities," posits several detailed examples of structural totalities (such as "class structures" or "the world system") and investigates the modes of their emergence and functioning, along heterarchical, not hierarchical or holist lines.

In Chapter 15, we reach some important conclusions, which we offer as recommendations to social theorists pursuing agendas relative to the study of social structures. We adduce certain preliminary results as guideposts for further development and we locate several issues in need of further clarification. Finally, we point out possible points of contestation and invite interested scholars to apply analytical scrutiny to these and to the rest of this work.

For reasons of proper closure we offer an Appendix and a Glossary. In the Appendix we inventory and briefly discuss numerous logics of structuration that need further elaboration. They are placed there in order to indicate their tentative nature as parts of an ongoing program of research into the character of such logics and their possible concatenations. I will focus on these logics in forthcoming work. The Glossary brings together brief explanations of philosophical and scientific terms. Readers will find the Glossary especially helpful for Part I. Words included in the Glossary appear in boldface in the text.

The reader should be advised that there are some rough waters in Chapters 2–4, 8, and 11. It may be sufficient, in the beginning, for one to focus on Chapter 1, then read Chapters 5–7, 9, 10, 12–14. Upon completion of these chapters one may then return to the more complicated "scientific" descriptions and arguments in the previously omitted chapters. In the end, I believe, it is important for understanding my argument that one cover the whole terrain.

In addressing this book to my professional colleagues in sociology and cognate disciplines, I do no more than offer my preliminary results as a starting point for appraisal and reevaluation of our thinking. I cherish the hope that it may be found useful to our fields in some meaningful way.

Part I
Metatheoretical considerations

Part I focuses on the recent developments in many scientific fields (physics, biochemistry, population ecology, neuroscience) where there has been a dramatic shift away from the dogmatic **reductionist** epistemic strategy and toward a dynamic and emergentist conceptualization of various kinds of phenomena along new – **constructionist,** heterarchical, and hierarchical – lines of thought. This informal introduction to current scientific issues and debates, prior to any consideration of the already available sociological approaches, will help us, I believe, to see the problem of social structure in a new light.

There are four chapters in this part and they address the following issues: the five basic **epistemic strategies** of reductionism, constructionism, **heterarchy, hierarchy,** and transcendence/**holism,** which provide a conceptual map within which subsequent discourses can be located (Chapter 1); the case against reductionism and in favor of emergence (Chapter 2); and the empirical (Chapter 3) and formal (Chapter 4) demarcation between the two higher forms of emergence, heterarchy and hierarchy.

As I stated in the introduction, the going here, especially in Chapter 2, may be unfamiliar for many readers, as it was for me when I started this research program. Because of our professional socialization most of us have built an aversion to "heavy" science, or have grown unaccustomed to its latest vocabularies and models. Yet, I have come to believe that the effort of investigating some of these models is very worthwhile. I would recommend to the wary colleague to first read this part quickly, and then proceed to the better known material of later chapters with a plan to return to this section for a second, more elaborate reading.

1 Epistemic strategies in contemporary science

One of the most puzzling issues among modern scientists and philosophers has been that of whether or not, for virtually all the domains of nature, higher levels of organization are determined – and therefore also explained – by lower levels of organization. Two obvious answers are available to this question informing two antithetical positions on the matter: (1) an epistemic belief in elementarism or microdeterminism holding that lower-level parts determine and explain the composition and behavior of higher-level wholes; or (2) an epistemic belief in holism and/or macrodeterminism, which asserts that higher level wholes are something distinct from the parts they incorporate and are, therefore, independent of them. Elementarism and holism, irreconcilable opponents, have been with us from the outset of philosophical inquiry. We saw them clash most recently when, in the 1930s and 1940s, the advancing armies of **logical positivists** and their allies attempted to enthrone elementarism, that is, behaviorism, **physicalism,** and **methodological individualism,** in the empires of science and philosophy. Today, in the **postpositivist** era, we still find ourselves entangled in and puzzled by the old dilemma – but now, at least, several new alternatives are open to us.

Epistemic strategies ← Start

Were one to complete a survey of contemporary science and philosophy of science, including the most recent and exciting work, one would discover five basic **epistemic strategies** that either have been already utilized in previous research or are currently proposed as more appropriate alternatives to previously-utilized strategies. I call these "epistemic strategies" with the understanding that they are, basically, *pragmatic* epistemic designs, rooted in provisional or permanent ontological commitments, and informing and guiding more specific methodological orientations. I believe that in actual scientific practice (but also in most of the less ethereal practices of philosophers) **ontological** and **epistemological** positions are intertwined and difficult to disentangle; the same is true of the relevant epistemological and **methodological** claims. In defense of these strategies, proponents claim that the orientation at hand is purely methodological; while at the same time stronger epistemological claims are allowed to surface for the purpose of augmenting the symbolic power of the given research program over its competitors and critics.[1] In many cases, therefore, this epistemic theorizing is a composite of interrelated ontological, epistemological, and methodological preferences and stratagems initializing a research agenda in philosophical discourse as well as in any local scientific practice.

We can call these five epistemic strategies:

> (1) the strategy of reduction (elementarism proper);
> (2) the strategy of construction or compositional emergence;
> (3) the strategy of heterarchy or heterarchical emergence;
> (4) the strategy of hierarchy or hierarchical emergence;
> (5) the strategy of systemic transcendence (holism proper).

We will start with a preliminary definition of these terms, before proceeding to their elucidation and the investigation of the dispositions and mechanisms they imply.

(1) We may define the strategy of reduction (**reductionism**) as adhering to a strict *microdeterminism;* that is, wholes are nothing more than their parts suitably combined to form a certain level of complexity and, thus, that higher levels of organization are determined and explained by their lower levels of organization, down to the most elementary level of quantum physics.

(2) In contrast, the strategy of construction or composition is rooted in a *partial microdeterminism,* but also pays significant attention to relational–interactional and contextual–ecological variables. That is, this strategy considers the higher levels of organization as products not merely of the aggregation or integration of lower level parts, but of the interaction of these parts and with the contextual–ecological "exigencies." The result is a constructionist, weak emergence of novel forms and properties practically irreducible to their constituent parts.

(3) The strategy of heterarchy (moderate emergence), the newest and, admittedly, least developed, strategy, is defined as *underdetermination* of the macrostructure(s) by the given microparts and as semiautonomous emergence of higher-level phenomena out of lower level phenomena. Therefore it is a strategy that supports a **nonreductive ma-**

---

[1] The notion that epistemic strategies compress ontological, epistemological, and methodological commitments into an overarching form of "strategic behavior" derives from Lakatos (1978) and Bourdieu (1977a, 1986b, 1988, 1990). There is a rhetoric of theory and research implicated in any epistemic strategy, because the latter is a form of argumentative discourse. A study of the texts and subtexts, say, of Elster would demonstrate this beyond any reasonable doubt (cf. 1985, 1986a, 1989, and in Roemer 1986). On my view, any research program incorporates many discursive apparatuses – conceptual, logical, pragmatically empirical, rhetorical, technical, inscriptive, and so on.

terialist position, explaining the emergence of novelty and higher-level properties and laws without falling into untenable dualist or idealist traps.[2]

(4) Hierarchy (strong emergency), is a full-fledged hierarchical emergence of more robust macroentities and *partial overdetermination* of the microparts by the dominant, organizing principles of the new higher entities. Hierarchy is a modified, and clearly more defensible, substitute for holism.

(5) Finally, the strategy of systemic transcendence (systemic functionalism, **vitalism, holism**) is defined as a downward, *strong determination* of the microparts by the macrosystem; the latter seen as an autonomous, higher entity superimposed on the lower systemic parts in a control-hierarchical manner that clearly supports the claims of a **dualist** metaphysics.

These five strategies, of course, have been unevenly developed. The two extremes, reductionism and holism, have been around since ancient times. The three intermediate types have more recent origins – evidence has been amassed on their behalf primarily in the last twenty or thirty years, and it is only in the last ten or fifteen years that arguments in favor of hierarchical epistemic claims have been provided at all. Even now the rhetorical debates in "normal science," especially in the social sciences, seem rather to be revolving around the extreme claims and countercharges of reductionism and holism, although the more advanced work of current "revolutionary science" is done and promoted by leading exponents of constructionist, heterarchical, and hierarchical strategies. Occasionally, proponents of extreme views manage to appear also to be speaking on behalf of the moderate views closest to their own. For example, reductionists have used a variety of constructionist arguments against the so-called "vitalists," and systemic functionalists have used the generalized rhetoric of emergence in the broadest possible sense to countenance the reductive efforts of "atomists" of all sorts. We will see later on in Chapters 5 and 6 how, for instance, Elster uses this rhetorical method on behalf of methodological individualism to attack all other types of theories as being inadmissibly and unscientifically "holistic." One must be quite careful not to fall for the rhetorical traps of either extreme view.

---

[2] Nonreductive materialism is an emergentist philosophy (see Margolis 1978) committed to the recent scientific and historicist talk of "emergence" and "integrated pluralism." It opposes reductionism as well as dualism, which is described as the philosophical view that the world is composed of at least two distinct, metaphysical substances, such as the Platonic matter and ideas, or Cartesian body and soul, or brain and consciousness (Eccles 1989; Popper and Eccles 1984; Sperry 1969, 1976).

In this chapter I proceed to demarcate the basic premises and claims of each of these analytically distinct epistemic strategies. This will enable us to eliminate a significant degree of conceptual fogginess in the social sciences. My goal is to provide a primary conceptual map, which will help us navigate through a large amount of social science material, both theoretical and empirical. At this stage, however, the examples I offer are drawn mostly from the recent literature of physical and biological sciences, so as to be domain-neutral to the social scientists. With these provisos in place, let us proceed to the strategies.

Reduction

Reductionists are reductive materialists, logical positivists, and, in the strictest sense, physicalists, elementarists, and atomists. Arguing that wholes are no more than their parts and that higher levels of organization of phenomena are fully determined and explained by lower levels of organization, they maintain the theory of an eventual reduction of all knowledge to that of elementary physical properties and their determinable relations. In a general sense, this implies a set of more special claims:

- that all *properties* of higher phenomena are reducible to other known properties of lower phenomena;
- that all *laws* and *regularities* of higher phenomena are also reducible to laws and regularities of lower phenomena; and
- that, perforce, all *conceptual novelties* and *theoretical terms* describing a higher-level domain are reducible to concepts and theoretical terms defined in the relevant lower-level domain.

Notice that the reductionist game can be played in an aggressive or a defensive way, that is, either by proving straightforwardly that reduction is possible in some specifiable steps, or by counterarguing that claims of emergence (in the broad sense of the term, especially as included in the 4th and 5th strategies) have been exaggerated and are unprovable, weak, or trivial. But what is the reductive claim itself? Basically, that certain key macroproperties can be said or shown to be the *direct result* of constitutive microproperties, which therefore are determining and explaining the former. This involves one of the following two claims:

(1) That the macroproperties of a system or entity are nothing but the mere aggregate of the properties of its microparts, so that one may say that microproperties and macroproperties are identical or, at least, that most of the microparts possess properties similar to and adding up to the macroproperties of the system. A typical example would be the

equivalence of the mass of a system with the sum of the masses of its microparts, by virtue of which a reductionist would say that an explanation of the former in terms of the latter is the only correct scientific procedure. In general, ceteris paribus, all questions of mass, size, extension, and quantity seem to avail themselves to this type of reduction, which has been called an "Empedoclean" type of microexplanation (Klee 1984).

(2) That the macroproperties of a system or entity, which appear to be different from the properties of its microparts, in fact result from the direct and complex integration of these microproperties. This so-called "Democritean" type of microexplanation is supposed to explain any macroproperty at a higher level of organization by reducing it to other (different) lower-level properties *in some complex integration.* The reductionist cites the explanation of the color of a system in terms of the absorption and reflection properties of its uncolored microparts. One could similarly microexplain the properties of water by reducing them to the different properties of oxygen and hydrogen, properly construed in a complex integration. However, this seemingly obvious explanation has been met with numerous objections supported by relevant counterexamples. Consider, for instance, the standard quantum-mechanical view of molecular structure, which challenges the simpler Empedoclean conception: "the space distribution of electrons in molecules, the set of the energy levels of electrons, and the probability of transition between them determine the optical, electric, and magnetic properties of molecules" (Vol'kenshtein 1970:4). Here reference is not made to the properties of the microparts as elementary units but to a stochastically behaving system having collective properties. Similarly, combining the light metal sodium with the poisonous gas chlorine results in salt, which has no metallic structure and is not poisonous (Rensch in Pattee 1973). Certainly, these counterexamples seem sufficient to disturb the lulling intuitiveness of the reductive arguments and leave us perplexed.

It appears, then, that the Democritean type of microreduction is more complex than it seems and cannot be accepted uncritically. Looking at the notion of integration in more analytical detail we can argue that it incorporates and conflates the following problematic and unduly unqualified commitments.

(1) The reductionist integration appears to be due to the *inherent potentialities and determinations* of the microparts themselves and nothing else – an unacceptable **essentialist** line (Margolis 1978; Popper 1966, 1974; Rorty 1979, 1982) – where bonding is but the enactment of this determination expressed through "affinities" and "valences"; but is this essentialism–immanentism (i.e., that matter deterministically includes in

itself all its future forms) scientific? Many leading physicists (P. W. Anderson, Bohm, Eigen, Prigogine, Feynman, R. Rosen, Wheeler, among others) would answer in the negative. Prigogine and Stengers, for example, referring to the paradoxical case of the **Bénard instability,** argue forcefully that, while the parameters describing crystal structures could be derived from the properties of the molecules of which they are composed, "Bénard cells, like all dissipative structures, are essentially a reflection of the global situation of nonequilibrium producing them" (1984:143–144). The emphasis is on context interaction, not on immanentist essence.

(2) The reductionist integration appears size- and quantity-independent, that is, the existence of different numbers of microparts and their quantitative magnitude are treated as rather irrelevant by the Democritean microreductionist. This assumes, for example, that physicochemical interactions among the many (say, many atoms of the same element) and different (say, many atoms of different elements) microparts follow a fixed order and that there are no uncertainties, instabilities, or nonequilibrium states that affect the integration process. Absent, too, is any consideration of the favoring of certain microparts that are quantitatively more abundant in the given natural or experimental setting. It is also assumed that integration is time-independent, in the sense that it is taken to be rather instantaneous and global, as if differential sequencing of bonding of different and unequal microparts has no bearing on the resultant form of integration. Yet, as the work of Prigogine and his associates in physical chemistry (Glasdorf, G. Nicolis, J. Nicholis), of Eigen and Stanley Fox and his associates in the biochemistry of life (see Matsuno et al. 1984, 1989; Wolman 1981), and several other leading researchers have demonstrated, *history* (due to **bifurcation branches, chaotic processes, template** specificity, prebiotic and biotic natural selection) is necessarily involved in integration leading to higher levels of phenomena. Indeed, integration involves a) various possible paths and sequences, and b) sequential reactions having their own history, which concurrently change the context of future reactions and structures.

The reductionist denigrates the significance of many types of mediating nonlinear processes and mechanisms of structuration, such as the several forms of **catalysis** and **hypercyclic** organization, and so on, simply because they do not fit the theory. In case after case, from physical chemistry to the development of **L-amino acids** (see Chapter 2), or in the case of **protocell** formation (in Stanley Fox's lab), the internalist, strict microdeterminist view proves indefensible.

(3) In addition to the contextualist arguments raised above, in the reductionist conception of the Democritean integration no reference is

made to the forces of selection and the post-selectionist articulation of the structured entities. For example, the philosopher Klee, a defender of reductionism, while making a passing reference to the "evolutionary view of the development of the universe" and accepting that "as matter arranges itself into increasingly complex locally stable systems, properties (particularly complex structural properties) are likely to appear that have not appeared before," still holds that "it does not follow that P (the novel property) was not determined by MS (the microparts)" (1984:51). The robustness of this claim necessitates a strict and complete determination of P by the MS. For the reductionist, given that microdetermination is an internal affair of the potentialities of the microparts, selection and evolutionary theory remain problematical if not outright antithetical. Ditto for the various **autopoetic processes,** grounded on all sorts of nonlinear dynamics and informing the various prebiotic and biological processes, such as coding, self-replication, and self-directed development (Jungck 1984; Weiss 1968, 1969; Zeleny 1980, 1981, among others).

We may conclude that a Democritean type of microdetermination may possibly be involved in some simple physicochemical instances, such as in simple compounds in conditions of context-free interactions, but it cannot be assumed to be directly operative in more complex cases, where *size, quantity, mediating nonlinear processes, history, context,* and *selection* introduce intervening and external components bearing directly on the mode of integration. For these reasons, Popper (1974, 1982) is undoubtedly correct in calling reductionism a necessary and partially successful, yet incomplete and, in principle, mistaken methodological strategy.

Construction/composition

Under the name of constructionism/compositionism we may classify all epistemic strategies that investigate the emergence of constructed novelty in nature. Two forms of constructionism have been discussed in the literature: a) formal or axiomatic constructionism and b) experimental (including computational) constructionism.

Formal or axiomatic **constructionism** is the strategy of logicomathematically producing a possible set of products or architectures derived from a set of elements related by a set of operators; the structures so generated are supposed to be formally exhaustive (were it not for Gödel's demon[3]) and include all actual and potential products. The

---

[3] Gödel's demon is the mathematical demonstration that any large enough system, such as arithmetic, can be shown to include or produce undecidable, i.e., potentially contradictory, theorems. To remedy this undecidability systems must be small and, therefore, incomplete. Such a demonstration hits hard any

trouble with formal constructionism is that it usually produces innumerable possible architectures, only a small fraction of which are actual or realistically possible; it does not incorporate causal efficacy in the production of these architectures so as to properly distinguish the actual, or the feasible, from the empirically unsustainable, or outright impossible. We have already seen how reductionism seems to partially fall into an equivalent trap. In the case of formal constructionism, too, the temptation is to regress into *structural reductionism,* according to which all higher-level phenomena can be explained by reference to lower-level phenomena forming their microparts together with a set of abstract, logico-mathematical operations which have universal validity. This neo-Kantian orientation conflates formal and efficient causes and, given its commitment to the sharp demarcation of form and content, concedes to the positivist microreductionist the identity of the material/ontic substrate of both the higher and lower levels of phenomena.

Experimental constructionism, by contrast, has been proposed by a variety of physicists, physicochemists and molecular biologists and has been strongly supported by their work. Support has come not only from the flamboyant work of Prigogine and Haken and associates, or the more austere work of the Fox group, but also the cautious work of P. W. Anderson (1972, 1983, 1984) on symmetry breaking and the spin-glass model of prebiotic evolution, and of A. J. Leggett on quantum mechanics and macroscopic realism (Leggett 1987; Leggett and Garg 1985). Experimental constructionism focuses on the actual and/or realistically possible products that may emerge in the laboratory setting under various theoretical and methodological conditions. For example, researchers might approximate the conditions that were most likely present, at specifiable times of prebiotic evolution on Earth, or they might construct feasible conditions for experimental or computational research in the physics of many-bodies, or BZ-like chemical syntheses,[4] or neural networks. In the case of prebiotic and protobiotic evolution,

rigorous logico-mathematical formalism supposed to operate on large-scale phenomena – e.g., game theory, or deductive theories of society suggested by Turner (1986b). On Gödel's proof see Davis (1965).

[4] The constructionist–ecological model of collective constraints, applicable to the physical and prebiotic evolutionary phenomena, seems to imply a weaker sense of externality: the environment provides possibilities for selection, somewhat biases the process, but does not select particular developmental paths. As P. W. Anderson remarked cautiously, symmetry-breaking is evident mostly in driven systems. On the other hand, Prigogine's arguments about dissipative structures indicate a strong sense of collective constraining. Too, some of the research in molecular biology on the origin of life indicates that "selection" is a short-hand term implicating a variety of specific biochemical mechanisms – hydrophobicity, light-absorption, oxidation, nucleation, lipidlike excitation, or membranicity.

for instance, the specification of parameters emphasized by experimental and computational constructionists is supposed to capture the real conditions and influences of the environment and the optimal number, kind, and quantities of the interacting, biologically important ingredients required to produce microspheres, membranes, protocells (*urzellen*), and the like (see Chapter 2). The emphasis here begins to shift, to a large extent, from the formally possible to the conditionally (relationally and environmentally) possible. This is true of most, if not all, **informational systems** – all nonlinear dynamical systems from physics to chemistry and, then, to biology. As Rohfling put it, "which option(s) a self-ordering, informational system takes depends very much on the surrounding (conditions) in which the system occurs. . . . [In] each case, the information content is present, but the expression of the content is mediated or constrained by the conditions" (1984:33). Clearly, this accords well with the comments I made earlier in my critique of reductionism. In a similar vein, Hsu summarizes the constructionist position of Fox and associates' work on the **proteinoid** model in the "origins of life" research program:

In considering simple chemical reactions, what theoretically can happen is essentially governed by the stereochemical state of the reactants and the thermodynamics of the system. Under a particular set of circumstances, however, only one of any number of theoretical possibilities is allowed to happen . . . The laws of physics and chemistry provide the guidelines (order) for a limited variety of possible interactions (limited variability). The environment at large then selects which particular reaction will actually take place. Natural selection does not determine what reactions are potentially possible, but dictates the direction of the change. When simple reactions are sequentially connected into pathways, patterns of molecular evolution become evident. (1984:402)

This clear statement sets straight the parameters of the compositionist–experimental constructionist strategy: It is an epistemic strategy pushing the "formal" constructionist results (i.e., the abstract set of all possible products) into the background and bringing into the foreground the concrete, limited set of actual experimental and historical (as well as computational–experimental) products, placing emphasis on particular circumstances, number, kind, and quantity of reactants, the Markovian history of interaction pathways, and other similar characteristics. Constructionism, therefore, is already an historico–ecological (nonlinear, irreversible, and field-theoretical) approach to the emergence of various categories of phenomena, even at the prebiotic level. However, experimental constructionism commits itself to a weak notion of emergence devoid of many characteristics that the more robust strategies of emergence emphasize in their discourse.

That interactionist–ecological lines of thought are prominent today in biochemistry and molecular biology (at the level of macromolecular structures) is not so strange. What is more challenging, especially if completely validated, is the work that shows that environmental externalities – collective–interactional and field forces – have a particular role even in physical chemistry (the more extreme Prigoginean arguments) and at quantum levels involving two, three, or many-body quantum systems (quantum chaos). Recent work has opened surprising new vistas in these areas and has indicated the existence of novel mechanisms explaining such occurrences (Leggett 1987; Pool 1989; Stewart 1989). We will return to these issues in the next chapter and throughout the rest of the book. The ideas of a continuous line of investigators have provided solid ground for constructionism/compositionism to compete successfully against the older views of reductionism.

There exist, however, both weak and strong constructionist arguments. Examples from quantum mechanics, many-body physics, and solid-state physics support the view that external fields and conditions exert an *interactional–ecological* influence on microentities (e.g., hydrogen atoms in microwave or magnetic fields [Pool 1989; Scadron 1985]) pushing the system to strange, weakly emergent behaviors. It is still disputed if at this level historicity (irreversibility) and dissipative structures are also produced in a sustained manner (P. W. Anderson 1984; Pagels 1985; Serra et al. 1986). On the other hand, examples from the **macromolecular** prebiotic domain have corroborated the claim of a stronger *interactional–selectionist* process taking place: several forms of pre-Darwinian adaptation to external conditions including new speciation (Matsuno et al. 1984, 1989; cf. Cairns-Smith 1986; Solla et al. 1986; Wicken 1987). These examples bring us closer to the Darwinian and stronger, post-Darwinian notions of irreversible adaptive selection and other forms of "aptation" (Gould and Vrba 1982; Vrba and Eldredge 1984; Weber, Depew, and Smith 1988), which push to the limit – and probably beyond – the compositionist program.

Heterarchical and hierarchical emergence

As a caveat, we must begin with the recognition that the concept of emergence is one of the most elusive, pluri-semantic, patently charged concepts in the current vocabulary of science and philosophy; the analytical elucidation of the term is still in progress and the task now looks to be richer yet harder and more controversial than originally thought.

As a first approach to the problem of definition, let us systematize the ideas suggested above – Empedoclean aggregation and Democritean integration, and the interactional–ecological and interactional–selectionist forms of constructionism. Discourses on "emergence" have appeared at different levels, for different reasons, on different grounds, and with differing degrees of success. These can be captured by a simple model, which will enable us (especially in Chapter 2) to demarcate more clearly emergence from reduction strategies, as well as from radical dualist (transcendence) strategies. The following notions of emergence have been proposed:

Level 0: the Democritean (though not the Empedoclean) notion of integration, subject to reduction.[5]

Level 1: two notions of *weak* emergence:

    1.1 an ecological–contextual notion of emergence at the prebiotic levels.

    1.2 an evolutionist–selectionist (stronger) notion of emergence in the neo-Darwinian and post-Darwinian sense.

Level 2: a *moderate* notion of emergence of semi-autonomous macrostructures heterarchically related to the microparts and underdetermined by them (see Chapter 3).

Level 3: the *strong* notion of emergence as a hierarchy based on applied **constraints** and a peculiar downward control.

Level 4: a transcending notion – if the hypotheses of group and species selection (Vrba 1984; Vrba and Eldredge 1984; Wade 1977; Wynne-Edwards 1986) find strong support – emphasizing holism, strong macrodetermination of microparts, vitalism, and mentalism. The notion of dualist control also belongs here.

The notion of emergence really begins at Level 1, in the case of ecological–contextual and evolutionist–selectionist novelty. A significant number of experimental and computational constructionist practitioners of science use the term to describe specific mechanisms and the unexpected properties emerging from them. Analyses of **symmetry-breaking** in **driven systems,** catalysis, **autocatalysis, hypercyclic** organization, **protohypercyclic** mutualisms, **allometry,** and various other nonlinear mechanisms in dynamical systems have all been re-

---

[5] A different version of a quasi-Democritean reductionism has been offered by Jaegwon Kim in a series of recent articles (1978, 1984a and b). It is grounded in the notion of supervenience, which intimates that there may be significant determinative connections between two families or classes of properties without the necessity for the existence of property-to-property connections between respective individual members of the families. As recent discussions have shown, a weak sense of supervenience (e.g., along neural network forms of connectionism) is acceptable in principle, but is quite distinct from Democritean reductionism (see Chapter 2, note 1;—see also Chapters 3, 4, 11).

ferred to as initializing or constituting mechanisms of emergence at Level 1. Similarly, as a result of recent studies on prebiotic evolution, as well as the post-Darwinian criticisms of the neo-Darwinian synthesis (see Chapter 8), an understanding of evolution along the lines of a nonreductive materialist epistemology has revitalized the concept of emergence at the upper limits of Level 1 (1.2).

However, it is the conceptualization of emergence at Levels 2 and 3 based on a variety of recent experimental findings that has attracted the interest of theoreticians across different scientific fields. Though the concept remains as yet incomplete given the revolutionary nature of the work, and the results are fuzzy at times, they do seem to point in the right direction and provide a tentative "working definition." What is, then, the meaning of emergence at these two higher levels?

Generally speaking, most of the significant contributors opt to explain emergence in terms of some particular notion of constraints superimposed on entities in a cumulative, successive mode. Intuitively, such constraints can be seen either as external – for example, constraints imposed on formal systems such as grammars or geometries, or internal – the view of matter or nature as self-constraining and self-organizing. We will examine these issues in some detail in the next chapter. For the time being it suffices to point out that the talk of "constraints" refers descriptively to the process of the restriction of a system's "degrees of freedom"; the existence of such constraints appears as, at least, the *necessary, if not sufficient,* condition for robust emergence to occur. Such a robust form of heterarchical or hierarchical emergence exists in case the novel higher-level systems attain a more or less significant degree of autonomy from the lower-level microparts. If this autonomy is moderate and interconnections between the higher and lower levels still obtain to a fair extent, we speak of heterarchical emergence. If, on the other hand, this autonomy is strong and the interconnections are biased in the downward direction of overdetermination, we speak of hierarchical emergence, in which case the **constraint hierarchy** is also, largely, a **control hierarchy.** To say that the higher levels are considerably autonomous is to say that they are to a certain degree "liftable" out of the lower levels, self-organizing, following a life history of their own.

The marks of emergence in their most telling form can be seen as:

(1) The emergence of a new domain of phenomena indicated by the appearance of a novel entity.
(2) The emergence of a new relational structure in or by this novel entity, which now appears as a boundary-maintaining, organized system.

(3) The emergence of local stability within this macrostructure (statistical stability, constancy, generation of order, etc.).

(4) The in principle (epistemic) or, at least, in practice (methodological) unpredictability of emerging properties, relations, and behaviors on the basis of knowledge of the lower-level microstates.

(5) The emergence of truly novel properties that the microstates fail to countenance to a significant extent.

(6) The emergence of new laws applicable at the new domain of phenomena – laws that are different than the lower-level laws.

(7) Arguably, the emergence of control and downward causation of the microstates by the macrostructure (macrodetermination) should be included, were the latter to be analytically articulated and empirically corroborated. But with this we may already have slipped into the next epistemic strategy.

We will discuss these issues in much more detail in the next two chapters.

Transcendence

Transcendence is used here to mean an epistemic strategy pursued mostly by vitalists in biology (Elsasser 1962, 1970; von Bertallanfy 1952; cf. Mayr 1982; Webster and Goodwin 1982) and collectivists in the human and social sciences (such as Durkheimians, group-selectionist sociobiologists, cultural historicists, and Marxist-structuralists). This approach utilizes quite often the vocabulary of systems theory or of the Hegelian notion of "totality" and usually allies itself in a more explicit manner with functionalist forms of expression and logic. For these reasons the paradigmatic exemplar of this strategy is that of systems functionalism.

Why, then, do we speak of "transcendence"? It is to emphasize the point that this epistemic strategy, even in its weakest, extreme emergentist form, stresses the full autonomy of the higher-level macrosystems and the control and macrodetermination that such systems exercise over the lower parts and components. There are two specific transcendence strategies, emergentist and non-emergentist. The emergentist version argues that the higher-level systems, though emergent in a diachronic sense, are radically distinct from lower-level systems that may appear as their parts or components and, indeed, macrodetermine all microstates, violating or cancelling lower-level laws. The nonemergentist version of transcendence rests on ontological dualist grounds, championing the "primacy" of the macrosystems in the relevant ontological and epistemological respects – for example, **demes** over individuals in group-selectionist theories, societies over individuals in the sociologistic tradition, structures "always-already-there" over "subjects" in the Althusserian structuralist-Marxist theory, and so on. In both emergentist and nonemergentist strategies the higher levels of organization *transcend* the lower levels on which they may have rested or to which they connect. In a parallel example, the mental rests on, yet supposedly transcends, the physical brain and the soul, being already distinct and autonomous, connects to the body and animates it. Full autonomy of macro or higher levels and subsequent determination of lower levels from above are the marks of the strategy of transcendence.

The view of transcendence as radical emergence leads one near the positions of ontological **dualists** and idealists, positions that have been thoroughly criticized in contemporary philosophy and science; yet, if one is careful, the distinction between an emergentist materialism and a dualist ontology can be made in principle. The second aspect of transcendence as control and macrodetermination is usually posited a bit more analytically though it still appears to produce several problems. Since the radical emergentism of the strategy of transcendence implies a total break of the emerging higher level from the lower levels, the necessary process of reconnecting to, relating to, and "controlling downward" the lower levels remains a mystery. Even at the level of hierarchical emergence, as we shall see, the clarification of such processes is slow and thorny; more so, of course, for the quasi-dualist arguments informing the strategy of transcendence. In any case, the scientific view of macrodetermination as the "violation" of lower-level laws remains largely uncorroborated.

At the beginning of this chapter we spoke of five epistemic strategies, yet from the brief presentation above one can maintain that the prominent contestants are the strategies of composition/construction, heterarchy, and hierarchy. Proponents of each of these strategies have labored to develop their own metascientific **logic** and to present their metamethodology of research programs as the only correct and progressive one. In the course of our subsequent efforts we will focus extensively on the metascientific "logics" of construction/composition, heterarchy, and hierarchy in the domains of both the physical and biological sciences, as well as – and more importantly – in the domain of the social sciences, given our very specific concern about the logics of social structure.

2   The dynamics of emergence: the case against reductionism

Several preliminary arguments were offered in the previous chapter countering the moves of reductive materialists and indicating possible meanings of the concept of emergence. In this chapter we will focus on the positive characteristics of emergence, and answer three basic questions:

(1) what exactly is emergent and how is it brought about;
(2) how could step-wise emergence be possible; and
(3) what are the results of emergence, which presumably appear as entities in the hierarchy of phenomenological levels.

Some preliminaries: emergence as irreducibility

As argued earlier, the size or quantity-, time-, context-, loop-, and selection-dependence of higher-level phenomena frustrate the purposes and efforts of microreduction. These forms of dependence demonstrate persuasively that contrary to the main reductionist argument, because of their history, evolutionary, emerging higher-level phenomena are *in principle irreducible* to lower-level phenomena. Instead, they show, at the very least, that microreduction cannot be done trivially – that even though diachronic reduction may be theoretically possible, synchronic reduction is *in practice impossible* (Simon's [1965] minimalist thesis on emergence).

The minimalist position is, perhaps, able to rebut extreme forms of **reductive materialism,** that is, a belief in the causally determinative power of microparts to bring forth by themselves alone, intrinsically and fully, higher-level forms of organization in our universe. Yet, minimalism may not be sufficient to counter more moderate reductionist programs such as that of **eliminative materialism,** which are actually based on a conflation of the reductive and constructionist strategies. For example, Paul Churchland, a leading eliminative materialist, in speaking of the mind–brain problem has argued that the case for the evolutionary emergence of mental properties through the further organization of matter is extremely strong; however, he still maintains that this does not mean the ultimate irreducibility of emergent properties to physical microparts (1984). Churchland's position lies somewhere between a radical reductionist program (such as

Klee's) and a pragmatic, minimalist emergentist program (such as Simon's).[1] His is a complex account that can be met only by reference to stronger emergentist arguments grounded in the strategies of heterarchy or hierarchy. So we must proceed to construct such a stronger case.

The process and character of emergence

Arguments for emergence are usually made on the grounds that higher-level phenomena appear to exhibit new "stabilities," or "boundary conditions," and, as such, form distinct or semidistinct domains of organization, in which novel properties and domain-specific laws emerge and apply. If correct, this sort of argument identifies emergence with new stabilities and regularities and treats novel properties and laws as their by-products. This is a very broad conceptualization covering all *aggregate* as well as properly *structural* emergent phenomena. An elementary example may be found in the field of statistical mechanics, where aggregates of gases or liquids are treated as collective entities behaving stochastically, having their own regularities and stabilities, exhibiting their own laws and novel properties – being in a sense distinct from the characteristics of the composing molecules taken in isolation. Ilya Prigogine (1980; Prigogine and George 1983; Prigogine and Stengers 1984; see also Haken 1978, 1984), the father of nonequilibrium thermodynamics, goes so far as to argue that free molecules in interaction behave individualistically, while molecules in a thermodynamic collective state behave synergistically. In his model, thermodynamic systems are at a higher level than are simple, mechanical dynamic systems; similarly, investigators now believe that nonlinear (chaotic) classical systems have different dynamics than their underlying quantum systems (Leggett 1987; Leggett and Garg 1985; Pool 1989). The most elementary notion of emergence is thus defined as "synchronized aggregation," that is, formation of higher collective quasi-entities exhibiting novel properties and new stabilities. By definition it is the weakest notion of emergence, for it cannot address the issue of the emergence of structured quasi-entities that become structuring modules of yet higher forms. However, the study of the mechanisms of emergence (nonequilibrium thermodynamics, chaos theory) has come mostly from the experimental analysis of the behavior of exactly this sort of constrained collective phenomena.

---

[1] Churchland's view comes very close to the conception of supervenience relations briefly discussed in Chapter 1, note 5. My heterarchical view is one level beyond: the relations between levels are parallel distributed (not simply global-to-global) implicating a complex, "tangled" form of "connectionism." Certainly, this would not help the eliminative materialist.

The notion of novel, higher systems emerging with new stability conditions has been also espoused by Herbert Simon (1965, 1981) who initiated the talk of "high, medium, and low frequencies" of phenomena. According to Simon, in any hierarchical order of phenomena there are events in the lower level occurring at high frequency (say, quantum mechanical events) which can be lumped or averaged together as a single, sufficient parameter for describing middle-level, middle-frequency events (say, statistical mechanical or other macromolecular systems). The transition from lower-level high-frequency to middle-level middle-frequency events involves a hierarchical jump indicative of the stochastic history of the middle-level system. On the other hand, there also exist events in the higher level occurring at low frequency; these are rare enough from the point of view of the middle-level system to be considered, according to Simon, only as exogenous variables to it.[2] Darwinian evolutionary processes, for example, are supposed to be of middle frequency, in contrast to high-frequency genetic events as well as to low-frequency geological and long-term climatological events. We will see later on that this concept is quite static; nonetheless, this general talk about levels and frequencies of phenomena, built around the notion of systems' characteristic **boundary** and **stability conditions,** constitutes the first line of emergentist defense against the objections of hard-line reductive materialists and, to a large extent, of the more moderate eliminative materialists.

The second line of defense supplements the first: the explanation of evolutionary emergence is predicated on the assumption that a variety of constraints are applied on the physical microparts that restrict their degrees of freedom and, through many constraint-dependent steps of **stochastic history,** produce emerging higher orders of phenomena. Broadly speaking, a "constraint" is a limitation applied on the possibility space of a set of phenomena, a restriction of the expression of possibilities associated with a microstate with a resulting bias favoring the production of a particular structured subset out of the larger set of all combinatorial possibilities. For example, we are given the letters O, P, and T, and asked to combine them to form all possible English words. The formal possibilities of combining these letters in three-letter strings are:

OPT, OTP, POT, TOP, TPO, PTO.

---

[2] This view has been contested by cosmologists (Hawking 1988; Waldrop 1988), mathematical ecologists (May 1976a; May and Oster 1976), and paleontologists (see the works of Vrba, Gould, Eldredge, and Stanley). The linkages are more active, to say the least.

However, not all of these strings form words in the English language. Opt, top, and pot are; the other three are not.[3] An admissibility constraint (possible English words) has been imposed on the basis of which only some of the formal strings are acceptable. This constraint has phase-separated the real words from the formal strings so that the real words appear to obey the rule of the constraint and not the broader rule of the formal permutation of the elements. The lower (combination) rule has been superseded by the higher (semantic) rule. Although the lower rule was restricted or receded into the background we cannot say that it was violated; it simply became less applicable to the new phenomena (of a defined language) that have emerged at a higher level. The difference was made by the application of a new constraint on top of the previous rule, as a result of which a meaningful demarcation of the higher from the lower order has been produced. The issue, then, for the microreductionist is this: can it be said that the linguistic meaning of the admissible words was already *inherent* in the formal possibilities of the letters and strings? This would be the much maligned essentialist line. It looks rather that the admissible words appear to have been "lifted" out and above the formal strings and "given" an extra meaning.

Now, obviously, this admissibility rule has been imposed from the outside, from a source external to the phonological or letter-string world, and quite arbitrarily at that! In any such case, there is an external imposition derived from the structure of the contingent – natural or cultural – world. Consider the case of amino acids and **tripeptide** formation. Biochemists have long established that the biologically most important molecules possess one very interesting property; they are asymmetric in the sense that they contain only a single left or right forming optical antipode – they are either left- or right-handed, mirror images of each other. Thus, all biologically significant amino acids – which are the building block substrate of proteins – are left-handed or **L-amino acids.** We see again that between formal possibilities (all left and right amino acids in free **racemic** mixture) and real structures (only left amino acids as a substrate of biologically important proteins) there is an indispensable stochastic history that accounts for the contingent emergence of macromolecular structures and of life.[4]

---

[3] The probabilities change with large numbers of letters: the larger the set, the lower the particular probabilities. See references to entropic and informational complexity: Bennett 1986; Gleick 1987; Landauer 1988; Nicolis 1986; Wicken 1987.

[4] Mason (1984) explains the origins of physicochemical chirality (one-handedness) on the basis of the weak-electric force interaction. In the amino acid case, left-handedness, L-amino acids, accounts for biomolecular behavior; right-handedness for the characteristics of nonbiological polymers or plas-

Let me press the point a bit further. Among the twenty-plus known amino acid residues one finds glysine (gly), glutamic acid (glu), and tyrosine (tyr). Combinations of these three amino acids produce several types of tripeptides. However, although the sequence (glu-tyr-gly and the sequence (glu-gly-tyr produce new tripeptide entities with specific characteristics and functions and, most importantly, with the first informational storage capacity, the sequence (tyr-glu-gly does not produce such a new entity.[5] This is a clear instance of the constraint-dependent elimination or restriction of expression of a possibility that otherwise was present (formally inherent, if the microreductionist pleases) in the amino acids themselves. These examples bring us closer to the notion proposed by Pattee (1973, 1978) and Polanyi (1968) that once a higher-level stability system appears with the selective formation of a new boundary (here, the tripeptide bonding), the stability conditions of that system will define new acceptability or selection rules restricting downward the "free" formal possibilities of relations of the microparts forming its substrate. In a sense then, constraints operate upward or forward (emergence of new boundaries, stability conditions) as well as downward or backward (restrictions of degrees of freedom, selection) in the specific context of a constrained system – though not in context-free situations.

Constraints themselves emerge as a result of the interface of processes operating (a) from below and pointing upward (**fluctuations** in space or time, instabilities, **molecular drive, genetic drift,** hypercyclic organization), (b) at the focal level (selection, **exaptation,** developmental structuration), or (c) from outside or above (prebiotic and biotic environment, the so-called downward causation). The study of these mostly nonlinear processes and their mathematical properties is currently one of the most exciting frontiers in science.

Constraints are of many different sorts. In the beginning, abstract mathematical structure generates a denumerable set of formal possibilities. When this very large set of so-called "necessary truths" is given a realism, a whole hierarchical sequence of constraints begin to apply:

(1) purely physical constraints of material properties, affinities, interactions, and laws;
(2) informational constraints giving rise to limits and possibilities of code formations;

---

tics. In all instances, constraints are imposed by the structure of the entities or compounds and the interfaces at the focal level (see Cairns-Smith 1986).

[5] See Matsuno 1981, Matsuno et al. 1984. On the meaning of "information storage" see P. W. Anderson 1983; J. J. Hopfield 1982; Nicolis 1986; Pattee 1979. On the origins of the genetic code see Jungck 1984; Küppers 1990; Woese 1967.

(3) molecular genetic constraints of replication, proofreading, and so on;
(4) genetic constraints;
(5) developmental constraints;
(6) selectionist constraints; and
(7) mental, social and cultural constraints as well.[6]

All these constraints shape the stochastic history of material phenomena in a cascading pathway so that the end result is some sort of an emergent hierarchy of phenomenological levels,[7] populated by novel, "structured" entities, which appear to us, at each focal level, as some kind of "individualities" (Ghiselin 1974; Vrba and Eldredge 1984).

Novel structures and their modular character

After new stabilities and regularities and a hierarchy of superimposed constraints, the third line of defense of the notion of emergence is the appearance of novel structures (individuated or quasi-individuated) modular structures which, once stabilized, become springboards for further evolutionary emergence. These are the heterarchical or hierarchical structures about which we have maintained (somewhat contra Simon) that their synchronous reduction is both in principle and in practice impossible. Their diachronic reduction is in principle conceded, though it is in practice nearly impossible, given the exigencies of their stochastic history. (The experimental constructionist is very active at this exact point, explicating diachronic discontinuous emergence. Indeed, the constructionist program shares with the heterarchical and hierarchical ones the first two defenses of emergence but not the third. This is the point of no return.)

The necessity of the modular character of these emerging structures (Fodor 1983; Simon 1965) certainly needs to be elucidated. For this, let us briefly examine some fascinating examples that indicate the extreme combinatorial explosion of evolutionary diversification and growth in aggregate size:

---

[6] Maynard Smith et al., 1985, and many references therein. Also Kauffman 1983; Levins 1973; Lewontin 1981.

[7] The main catalyst for the movement beyond the old logico-positivist doctrine was Feigl's problematic paper (1968 – discussed in Margolis 1978, Suppe 1977) on the two notions of the physical (the second being that of the biological world). Subsequently, we witnessed other lines of development: (a) Popper-Bunge-Bhaskar's "integrated pluralism," (b) Margolis's "attributional dualism" (1978), and (c) the scientific work on emergence (NET, neural nets), and so on.

- A cubic centimeter of a rarefied gas contains roughly 10 raised to the power of 18 [10^{18}] molecules at room temperature. Boltzmann has estimated the time required for the random reproduction of a particular microstate to be 10 raised to the power of 10, and that power raised to the power of 19 years, a figure beyond the bounds of our imagination and outside any physical materialization, as Eigen put it (1978).
- The space of the head of a pin could be occupied by one million cells. One cell has about 40 million molecules. So, in the space of a pin-head can be found 30–70 billion molecules.
- The genetic pattern of a colibacterium, transmitted from generation to generation in the form of a single giant DNA molecule, consists of about 4 million ordered symbols of a molecular four-letter alphabet in a linear chain. Transferred to the letter symbols of our language, such a sentence would have the scale of a book about 1,000 pages long. The symbol order is that of over 10 raised to the power of 2,000,000 alternative sequences.
- Hofstadter (1979) lists 10 billion neurons forming the cerebral cortex of the brain; Churchland (1984) states that there are roughly 100 billion neurons in the brain, each one making 3,000 connections with other neurons, so that the interconnectivity of neurons is from about 100 trillion to a quadrillion connections.

Given such enormous complexity, the world would not have been possible without the emergence of modularity and of level hierarchy. Evolution works through modular–hierarchical shortcuts. The converging views of most scientists today support this conclusion.[8] Recognition of this fact made also many philosophers (Bhaskar 1975, 1978a; Bunge 1969, 1973a, 1973b; Dyke 1988; Margolis 1977, 1986, 1987; Popper 1982) speak of an "open universe," of integrated pluralism, and of nonreductive materialism.[9] Even Churchland, a committed scientific realist and eliminative materialist, has introduced into his vocabulary the new conceptions of "semiclosed systems" – systems displaying complexity, order, and an unbalanced energy distribution – and speaks of "evolu-

---

[8] P. W. Anderson 1972, 1983; Edelman 1987, 1989; Eigen 1977, 1978, 1983, 1986; Fodor 1983; Pattee 1970, 1977; Prigogine 1980; Prigogine and Stengers 1984; Salthe 1985; Simon 1965; among many others.

[9] Popper's view of an "open universe" stresses the indeterminacy of large-scale transitions, from the Big Bang to galaxy formation, from matter to life, from brain to the mental. One may argue that his views have been more explicitly modified given the strength of the Quinean thesis on the indeterminacy of translation. See Popper 1974, 1978, 1982; also Margolis 1986; Quine 1953, 1960.

tionary emergence," although he is not ready yet to concede the epistemic irreducibility of that emergence.

For our purposes, modularity means that a would-be system can (a) achieve a degree of closure and can be seen as behaving independently or, at least, semi-independently of the surrounding conditions (semiclosed); and that (b) this system is seen as becoming a modular component of a larger semiclosed system, which itself may have achieved a degree of closure, and so on. Modularity, then, involves the notion of more or less efficacious composability or decomposability: either near decomposability (Ando et al. 1963; Simon 1965) or partial decomposability (Hofstadter 1979; Kontopoulos 1987).[10] The higher the degree of closure, of course, the more autonomous the modular structure, and the more nearly decomposable the higher system is (as in hierarchy theory); the lower the degree of closure, the less autonomous the modular structure, and the more partially decomposable the higher system is (as in heterarchy theory).

I personally put more emphasis on the fact that novel structures emerge, which are at least partially irreducible to the lower levels. I treat the degree of closure as a variable and, in any case, as something to be investigated empirically in the various sciences. I consider near decomposability as part of a simplifying strategy, against which I favor the more complex strategy of interlevel heterarchical multiple linkages. These matters will be analyzed more fully in later chapters.

Emerging structural entities

We must now look at the actual structures that the process of "constraining" has brought about. However, I must post a warning: In order to make sense of the notion of emergent novel structures and their specific characteristics I must briefly refer to recent developments in a variety of highly specialized scientific fields. The reader may find it helpful to consult the glossary for unfamiliar terms.

Let us take first the case of atomic molecules and look at their submolecular constitution. The factors accounting for atomic molecular stability, that is, for the emergence of the semiclosed, relatively stabilized, modular structure we call an atomic molecule, are: the space distribution of electrons in that molecule, the set of the energy levels of electrons, and the probabilities of transition between them; these factors determine the optical, electrical, and magnetic properties of molecules.

---

[10] Simon's hierarchical argument of nearly complete decomposability is *architectonic* in nature, while my heterarchical view of partial decomposability is *neuronic,* that is, it implies the tangledness of neural network models. The debate settled by 1982 against the "localization" thesis – also against Simon's view. Cf. J. A. Anderson 1983a, 1983b; Churchland 1984; Fodor 1983.

This elementary conception might lead one to believe that structure is defined by geometric location, quantitative difference, and mobility probabilities. In reality, particularly in polyatomic molecules, the stability conditions of the semiclosed system make it appear as if it were a physical ecology of sorts, as the molecule is defined in terms of non-localized electron orbitals extending over all of the nuclei (Vol'kenshtein 1970; Prigogine and Stengers 1984), a quantum mechanical notion following field theory as well as the new nonequilibrium thermodynamic conceptions. In this instance, the polyatomic molecule appears as a stochastically behaving system with collective properties, that is, a new module that cannot be fully decomposed to mono-atomic entities without a loss.

Yet, in order to understand real emergence, we have to begin getting away from "passive," that is, geometric, notions of structure that appear as so many permutations of mathematical relations or as accidents, as in the beautiful case of crystallography. We really should not call the structures of snowflakes emergent. In theory one could determine a snowflake's structure by knowing all the details about its approximately $10^{18}H^2O$ molecules; how many of them are incorrectly oriented, and in how many ways these misorders have been distributed within the lattice. In spite of the computational impossibility involved and the **frozen accident** character of each snowflake, this aggregate structure can, in principle, be thought of as reducible to its microparts. On the other hand, one cannot escape the thought that, if this is the easiest example of reduction, then reductionist strategies are in for a rough ride at higher levels of organization. Already, new discoveries of **quasi-crystals** and the novel mathematics of Penrose tiling have introduced elements of nonlocal influences on geometric structure implicating complex mechanisms of structural composition even at this lower level of crystallinity.[11]

Consider next the case of molecular compounds, more specifically the well-known **Belouzov–Zhabotinsky reaction** and its variations and extensions (Glasdorf and Prigogine 1971; Nicholis and Baras 1984; Nicholis and Prigogine 1977). Variations in the sequencing of materials used in chemical reactions and of the thermal conditions of interaction have been shown to give many different products and intermediary forms, a result strongly supporting the view that various experimental conditions may give rise to different modes of self-organization within

---

[11] Crystallinity implies the working of general physical laws of "packing" (see Appendix nos. 30 and 33), as in the honeycomb hexagons, but it is by no means simple. Consider the new notions of tiling and quasi-crystals (Davies 1988; Gleick 1987; Grunbaum and Shephard 1986; Nelson 1986; Penrose, 1989b; Steen 1988). For the transition beyond crystallinity see P. W. Anderson 1972, 1983, 1984, and Venkataraman et al. 1989.

the same system – a chemical clock, a stable spatial distribution, or the formation of waves of chemical activity over macroscopic distances (Prigogine and Stengers 1984). If we consider these forms as process structures or semistable structures, we can see the significance of this work for the onset of emergence (the notion of constraints, stability conditions, mediating mechanisms of symmetry-breaking and bifurcation, and so on).

From molecules and chemical compounds let us move now to macromolecules. It is written in textbook science that through polymerization, sugars, amino acids, and **nucleotides** become polymeric carbohydrates, proteins, and nucleic acids. Of these, proteins and nucleic acids are "informational macromolecules" or biopolymers, that is, they are the first foci of informational coding necessary for the emergence of life. The movement from amino acid to protein structure is done by specific amino acid sequence that constitutes the primary structure of proteins. The protein macromolecule appears as a text written with a twenty-letter alphabet, all amino acid residues, the particular character of any protein macromolecule being specified by the stochastic history of the transition from amino acids to tripeptides, from these to small **polypeptides,** and then to specific proteins. The emergence of primary protein structure comes closer to being a real emergence, for the primary structure contains a vast amount of expressed information, far beyond what one would ultimately find in the lower modules.

Notice that the primary structure (amino acid sequence) of each protein is a short or long book, that, on Eigen's and other new informational theorists' view, could not have been written even by accident, were it not for (a) the modularity or semimodularity of intermediate units (here, tripeptides and small polypeptides) and (b) the special processes and mechanisms of upward self-organization (e.g., through hypercycles). However, once emergent, the primary structure[12] of protein conditions the development of secondary structure (orientation of monomer units to one another, forming a helix, coil, folds, 3-D), tertiary structure (orientation of side chains accounting for the right three-dimensional configuration, e.g., globular, unitary, 3-D), and quaternary structure (subunit formation and relations) (Richardson 1981). Though from a causal point of view the existence of the primary structure is of the utmost importance, the secondary and higher structures of proteins are maintained by an entire ensemble of interaction forces: chemical

---

[12] The connections between primary, secondary, and tertiary structure are only stochastic; there is no deterministic closure. Grobstein 1973:45 singles out this reliance on "a successively altered and exquisitely regulated context." Kolata 1986 and Richards et al. 1986 explain the constructionist difficulties encountered in such structural transitions.

S-S bonds, hydrogen bonds, ionic bonds, Van der Waals intramolecular bonds, and especially hydrophobic interactions that are supposed to be the principal driving forces in the formation of protein globules (Bresler and Talmund in Vol'kenshtein 1970; Richardson 1981). Notice also that it is the particular three-dimensional structure of the protein that determines its biological function. In brief, we may reach the following conclusion: Proteins are emergent modular or semimodular structures with tremendously increased informational capacity and biological functions; every protein has sublevels of structure, each of which builds on its lower level for further structural configuration and for increased functional specificity, ending with the more important biological function.[13]

Many strange things happen to oligo- and polyamino acids under further experimental constraints, as the successes of the research program of Fox and associates (Fox and Dose 1977; Matsuno et al. 1984, 1989; Wolman 1981) have indicated. This constructionist program exclusively devoted to the biochemistry of the origin of life is built around the so-called proteinoid model of matter's self-ordering, replicating, and assembling into macromolecular and supramolecular structures. Proteinoids are experimentally produced thermal polyamino acids that, like proteins, have properties largely different from those of free amino acids. Rohfling, a constructionist/compositionist, readily argues that the proteinoid properties are *emergent*, because in the transition from one level of complexity to another, "properties result that were not shown by the starting materials and which would not be predictable without prior knowledge" (1984: 34). In the case of proteinoids, as Fox and colleagues have shown, the new properties consist in several specific catalytic activities, the ability to form microspheres in aqueous solutions, new stability conditions, and lipidlike properties. From proteinoids emerge proteinoid membranes, which are absolutely necessary for the further development of the cellular forms, and microspheres, called p-protocells. The p-protocells maintain all the properties of the proteinoids and exhibit many significant new properties, such as further stability, tolerance to extremes of pH, temperature and dehydration, selective permeability and osmotic properties. Combined with lecithin, these p-protocells become nervelike, excitable protocells. Notice again that this model of emergence remains thoroughly constructionist – though still antireductionist and antiformalist – emphasizing the self-assembly of matter under specific ecological and selectionist conditions.

---

[13] Stronger emergentist views are held by J. L. Fox (in Matsuno et al. 1984:334ff.). See also Sperry 1976a and b and 1983 for a strong emergentist view of the evolution of consciousness.

Constraints are also emphasized but it is not clear whether or not the notion of constraint is used as a new conceptual mechanism to support a stronger, hierarchical view of emergence. Finally, the concept of structure is used in a way contrary to structural reduction; indeed, it is already used in the sense of a "structured structuring structure" (to recall Bourdieu's strange but apt term) given that its emergence as well as its further possibilities and propensities are experimentally corroborated.

On the other side of the informational macromolecules ledger, nucleic acids emerge as polymers of nucleotides. The progeny goes like this: Compounds of the nitrogen bases with ribose (R) and deoxyribose (D) are called nucleosides (N), ribonucleosides (RN), and deoxyribonucleosides (DN). The phosphoric esters of these are called nucleotides, ribonucleotides, and deoxyribonucleotides. Nucleic acids are polymers of the above, now named nucleic acid, ribonucleic acid (RNA), and deoxyribonucleic acid (DNA). RNA and DNA, the basis of genetic structure and the genetic code, are thus another pathway in the emergence of biopolymers. The importance of this pathway consists in the fact that, as the hegemonic, Crick–Watson line of thought would have it (Crick 1962; cf. Jungck 1984), nucleic acids are the initial replicating macromolecules at the prebiotic level, giving rise to the genetic code and to the formation of living cells as we know them.

RNA forms are thought to be, at present, the first master replicative units that have appeared on earth.[14] They exhibit slow but high fidelity replicability. It is commonly accepted that RNA forms, better exploiting the resources found in the "prebiotic soup," became capable of higher rates of reproduction as compared to the spontaneous emergence and low-rate ecological reproduction of protein-based biopolymers of higher order (**urzellen** of the Fox line of research). Under suitable conditions, such as a more or less rich environment, a relatively efficient enzyme system, and a semiclosed membrane form, intermediate modular structures akin to an RNA virus have been probably evolved; the stochastic history of replications and impurities of such intermediate modules, coupled with various **autocatalytic** and **heterocatalytic** processes, are now believed to have given rise to the higher structure of DNA macromolecules. As it happens, DNA is a much better replicator than RNA, so that given differential rates of reproduction, we arrived at the present juncture of evolution where nearly all forms of life are DNA-based, except viruses, which are precellular molecular complexes of protein with RNA. The lesson here is that higher-level structures may be

---

[14] On the RNA world see Benner 1988; Woese 1967. Contrast Hoyle's arguments on the extraterrestrial origins of life (Hoyle 1983; Hoyle and Wickramasinghe 1981).

byproducts of lower-level modules or structures, but once they emerge, may restrict the range or even extinguish the existence of the previous generative modules – a sort of species selection. It is rather clear as well why DNA structures are code-informationally far superior to RNA structures. It is obvious then on these corroborating empirical grounds that reduction, at least synchronically – here, reduction from DNA to RNA – is, in effect, impossible.

Yet, the story is not yet complete because DNA structures are not by themselves primitive cells. Another step is necessary for the emergence of the cellular forms, a process that involves the coupling of proteins and nucleic acids. As we have indicated, there is a major difference between proteins (and ensuing proteinoid higher forms) and nucleic acids (RNA and DNA). The former are information rich but devoid of replicating machinery: they have to be produced constantly and randomly by an energy- and material-rich environment. The latter have the capacity and the initial machinery for self-replication (early t-RNA) but lack the informational resources to recognize and exploit the environment as well as the enzymatic abilities to promulgate large-scale reproduction. A "Catch-22" situation is therefore involved: Nucleic acids cannot replicate without the enzymatic activities of proteins, while proteins cannot replicate without the code-informational activities of nucleic acids. We find then, rather paradoxically, the need for complementary, collective action (Matsuno in Wolman 1981; Matsuno 1984, 1989; Vol'kenshtein 1970), which indeed emerges in the form of protohypercyclic and complex hypercyclic organization. Eigen (1977, 1978; Eigen and Schuster 1979) and Küppers (1990) have done the pioneering work on the hypercyclic integration of replicative systems. A prebiotic hypercycle is said to exist just in case it permits expansion of the limited informational capacity of one macromolecular structure (e.g., nucleic acids) by coupling with and integration of a second class of macromolecular structures with greater functional or informational capacity (e.g., proteins). Details of the hypercyclic organization and process cannot be given here, but it is this sort of organization incorporating, for example, P. W. Anderson's model of prebiotic evolution built on "spin glass" principles (1983; cf. Chowdhury 1986), that seems to explain the emergence of protocellular structures as new and higher modules incorporating replicative, translational, enzymatic, and membrane elements – in short, life itself.

Two preliminary conclusions

Many conclusions can be drawn from the previous discussion but we will limit ourselves to two basic ones. First of all, the moment one introduces into chemistry notions implicating nonlinear processes such as catalysis, autocatalysis, heterocatalysis, allostery, and hypercyclic organization, forces appear that are not trivial byproducts of the direct propensities of given microparts. On the contrary, though based on initial, lower-level affinities and valences in the prebiotic environment, such forces are the complex results of dynamic mechanisms – complementary, sequential, cyclical, collectively translational, or upward generative mechanisms – that constitute the very stuff of the process of emergence. Notice that we need to know more about these mechanisms to explain the irreversibility and irreducibility of the process of emergence and, thus, of the emerging macrostructures. An exponentially growing science of complex, nonlinear systems is making major strides at present in several domains of inquiry.[15] Already, we know enough to hold reliably that it is not the inherent capacity of free, individual microparts but self-organization processes and ensuing properties related to relational–structural and ecological–selectionist constraints that account for both the emergence of the mechanisms themselves and the emergence of higher (structured structuring) structures populating our multilayered universe.

The second conclusion we want to draw necessitates thinking again about the story of proteins and nucleic acids. Start first with the importance of membranicity, a lipidlike property we initially encounter in p-protocells. Proteinoids form membranes of spherical form or in the form of black bilayers. These appear to be "dumb" macromolecular special structures, semiautonomous transitional forms without the ability to reproduce or replicate. Next, we find membranicity in the viruses, composed as they are of RNA and protein, but devoid of a nucleus and a cytoplasm. Already in the viral structure we note (a) the coupling of RNA and protein and (b) the separation of this system from the environment via a semipermeable membrane of sorts. By the time we come to the living cell we find both of the above, augmented and strengthened by the inclusion of allostery and translation, properly amended and "smartly," that is, code-informationally, articulated. It now appears that a larger and higher structural unit has emerged incorporating the nucleic elements, the proteins, the needed membranicity, some form of RNA (t-RNA, mRNA), and several other

---

[15] The literature on nonlinear dynamical systems is already enormous. I have consulted, among others, Feigenbaum 1981, 1983; Haken 1978, 1984; Kirkpatrick 1981; Lundqvist et al. 1988; May 1973; Nicolis and Altares 1988; Prigogine 1980; Prigogine and Stengers 1984; Ruelle 1989; Serra et al. 1986; Solla et al. 1986; Tabot 1989; Vidyasagar 1978. On chaos theory and its applications: Crutchfield et al. 1986; Crutchfield and Huberman 1980; Cvitanovic 1984; Ford 1989; Gleick 1987; Grebogi et al. 1987; Hao Bai-Lin 1984; Richards 1988; Shaw 1984; Steeb and Louw 1986.

microstructures, such as organelles, lysosomes, centrosomes, and ribo-somes.[16] The important point here is that of incorporation or subsumption: A dominant, higher, emergent structure appears, subsuming fully or partially various previous modes of organization. This new structure re-organizes the possibility space, the resources and the processes, sets a new boundary for the emergent structure on the basis of which new laws and properties may appear, and ecologically asserts its new-found unity. This amounts to what Pattee and Polanyi have called a new **closure** property that operates as a new law of organization, the logic of the emergent structure. Henceforth, the relationship between a cell and an organelle or a membrane-like p-protocell or any particular form of RNA or even the nucleolus is one of subsumption and heterarchy or hierarchy, not of strict assembly implying structural reduction. From here it is only a jump to Darwinian evolutionary emergence.

The mental

From the brief consideration of the physical, chemical, and biological instances of emergence let us now turn our attention to the issue of emergent mental states. This is another complicated situation, which philosophers, cognitive scientists, and neuroscientists are still trying to disentangle under the general rubric of the "mind-body problem." The mind, to be sure, is not an entity; it is not an extensional phenomenon defined spatiotemporally.[17] Is it, then, nothing more than a category of **folk psychology,** a commonsensical, impure form of referring and naming? A number of theories, falling more or less under the umbrella concept of reductive materialism, or allied to it, have been proposed to explain the mental: philosophical **behaviorism,** the **identity theory** form of reductive materialism, **eliminative materialism,** and **functionalism.** Details of these doctrines and counterarguments relative to their claims can be found in the large body of relevant philosophical and cognitivist literature (see Churchland 1984; Margolis 1984) and brief definitions are given in the Glossary.

Is, then, the "mind" an emergent phenomenon? And is it a structure? The expected answer of philosophical behaviorists and identity theory followers would be negative on both counts. However, compelled by

---

[16] This may have happened by way of a larger cell-like structure in some sense eating small cell-like, viral, or organelle-like structures that were independent in earlier evolutionary times. See Fox and Dose 1977; Matsuno et al. 1984.

[17] On the dualist view, the mind may be considered an entity of a nonextensional order, i.e., without mass and extension in space. This Platonic view is approached asymptotically by Popper and Eccles (1984) and Elsasser (1966, 1970).

the evidence, eliminative materialists such as Churchland concede the evolutionary emergence of the mental but not the significant autonomy – relative as it may be – of its structure. Functionalists, such as Dennett or Fodor, have answered in the affirmative to both parts of the question: the mental is conceived as the relational system internal to the black box, a structure emergent though always connected to (in effect incarnated in and animating) the material substratum at hand. In a sense, then, the functionalist seems to argue for a many-to-one relation between material substratum – body, machine, silicon creatures – and the structure of the mind. In both eliminative materialism and functionalism the mental is viewed as diachronically emergent, novel in properties, organized somewhat autonomously (eliminative materialism) or fully autonomously (functionalism), and as a structure exhibiting its own organizing logic (though the eliminative materialist would accept the above on a tentative basis while still believing in the ultimate vindication of the full reductionist program).

Still, some functionalists, notably Fodor who is a leading member of the movement, came to rather tentative conclusions about the prospects of understanding the mind in a neat modular way: his summary of research in neuroscience and cognitive science indicates support for the modularity of the peripheral cortex, but points out the nonmodular, Quinean or indeterminate as he calls it, nature of the central high cortex (1983). Similar research findings by Eccles (1989) and Sperry (1969, 1976) convinced Popper to opt, unnecessarily, I believe, for an "interactionist property-dualism" (Popper and Eccles 1984), and Sperry to advocate a special "control hierarchical" organization of the mind. These views come close to those of Pattee (1970, 1973), Weiss (1969, 1970), and others, who were at work elaborating additional nuances of emergence such as distancing, self-loop, self-control, plasticity, or liftability on the basis of a full-fledged theory of hierarchy.

The work of Eccles (1989), Sperry (1969, 1976a, 1976b), Edelman (1987, 1989), Mountcastle (Edelman and Mountcastle 1978), and others has already demonstrated what even an eliminative materialist would now concede, namely, that the internal organization of the brain, particularly of the higher faculties, has achieved a more or less pronounced degree of plasticity and semiautonomy. We can use Churchland's own arguments and empirical references on the matter to clarify this point. He, too, finds plasticity and semi-autonomy expressed, among other things, in the fact that (a) "the functional properties . . . of a neuron are decidedly plastic, since the growth of new synaptic connections and the pruning or degeneration of old ones can change the input/output function of the cell" (1984:131); (b) even the most localizable module[18] privileged by reductive materialists is but "only one of several parallel systems" in interaction (140), which implicates redundancy, plasticity in neuronal connections, and loop processes; (c) as the brain monitors the extranervous world, "it also monitors many aspects of its own operations . . . and it also exerts control over many aspects of its own operations" (137).[19] Thus, even Churchland reaches the conclusion that "with the brain at the level of articulation and self-modulation found in humans, *a certain autonomy* has crept into the picture" (140; my emphasis). These points have been more recently amplified by the renowned neuroscientist Gerald Edelman in his books *Neural Darwinism, Topobiology,* and the more recent *The Remembered Present.* Using the newly developed logic of neural networks, Edelman espouses a theory of brain structure and development that provides the empirical underpinnings for a heterarchical conceptualization of emergence and interlevel connections. We will discuss his views in more detail in Chapters 3 and 11.

Conclusion

In the present chapter we have provided some solid grounds for accepting emergence, whether under a constructionist, heterarchical, or hierarchical construal of this term. We have discussed emergence at different levels and, according to the preferences implied in different emergentist strategies, emergence of varying strength and import (i.e., degree of implied relative autonomy). We have had a rough ride in the rapids of modern science to see the actual, contingent, and extremely complex production of emergence. We are now ready to move to an elucidation of the particulars of the heterarchical and hierarchical conceptions of emergence.

[18] On the older localization theories and their critiques see Edelman 1987, 1989; Fodor 1983; Gazzaniga 1970, 1984, 1988.

[19] These last remarks point clearly to why and in what direction Churchland is bound to abandon eliminative materialism in favor of a more complex heterarchical model – cf. his 1989.

3   The nature of hierarchical and heterarchical organization

The acceptance of emergence, under any of its weaker, moderate, or stronger conceptualizations, but especially in the case of the latter two, automatically commits one to the view that the world is differentiated not only horizontally in terms of phenotypes but vertically, in terms of different levels; that is, that it exhibits an *integrated pluralistic structure* (Bhaskar 1975; Bunge 1969, 1973a and b; Popper 1982). This view has been commonsensically expressed by authors writing in several fields: the phenomena of the world, they argue, cannot be either so randomly racemic or so globally interconnected as not to exhibit some differentiation from each other. Minsky, for instance, writing about the possibility of extraterrestrial communication, begins with the following argument: "There can't be any objects, things, or causes in worlds where everything that happens depends, more or less equally, on everything else that happens. . . . To deal with something complicated, you must find a way to describe it in terms of substructures within which the effects of actions tend to be localized. To know the cause of a phenomenon is to know, at least in principle, what can change or control it without changing everything else" (1985: 136). In a similar vein, our premiere social methodologist, Blalock, has asserted that "[T]he theorist must make the fundamental assumption that the real world can be approximated by a block-recursive model, in which the total set of variables can be partitioned into blocks in such a way that there is no feedback between blocks" (1969). His view then comes close to the earlier views of Ando, Fisher, and Simon (1963) who had argued that presuming the world can be conceptualized as a "system of simultaneous equations," there is nothing we can say or do about it unless we consider this system as nearly "decomposable" into a "hierarchy of subsystems" that have a causal ordering.

The above statements share a common insistence: if any knowledge of the world is to be had, we must, as Aristotle suggested, distinguish the essential features of the world from the inessential ones by focusing only on the essential (or stronger) connections obtaining in the world as against the inessential (or weaker) ones. This is equivalent to saying that we must partition the world again and again, until an acceptable number of units and subunits and subsubunits is found forming some sort of level structure; the world must be analytically separated exactly because it is presumed to be differentiated in reality both horizontally and vertically.

42

It so happens that this position accords rather well with the so-called state space or phase space approach to mapping the dynamics of the phenomena of the world (Garfinkel 1981; Primas and Mueller-Herold 1978), successfully applied to quantum mechanics and generalized by several philosophers of science (Lloyd 1984; Suppe 1990; van Fraassen 1980, 1990).[1] Thus, it is tempting to use phase-separation and frequency talk to support the talk about levels, in general to support the view of the hierarchy of systems and subsystems and of **integrated pluralism.** It appears that the concepts of emergence, constraint, modularization, and phase-separation are at minimum linked together and overlap, if they are not alternative descriptions of the same phenomena. The basis of each of these concepts, either implicit or explicit, is a reliance on a logically prior conception of "levels" and, thus, makes reference to and analysis of such a theory of levels inescapable.

Levels: initial conceptions

Working out a theory of levels is not a simple task – it must not be an arbitrary arrangement of levels arrived at by equally arbitrary procedures. There must be logic and reference involved, but not too idealized and rigid a logic because there cannot be any absolute reference.[2] These caveats having been stated, let us consider some instances of proposed level structures derived by the successive application of constraints on an initially unconstrained or minimally constrained field.

First, let us examine Chomsky's presentation of the types of formal grammars. Chomsky (1957, 1959; cf. Barr and Feigenbaum 1981; Hopcroft and Ullman 1969) considered four types of grammars (0–3) as forming a hierarchy on account of the number and character of restric-

---

[1] In the state or phase space approach, the world is conceptualized as composed of physical entities and entangled systems with many relations (the quantum mechanical view), or as fitting a mathematical model with many variables (the mathematical or semantic view). Any particular configuration of the values for these entities or relations is a *state* of the system, while *state space* or *phase space* is a collection of all possible configurations. States of the system have a temporal component so that the sequence of states manifests the deterministic or stochastic history of the system. The transition from a state or phase to another is usually not equiprobable; hence, the importance of knowing the Markovian-like, multidimensionally-specified transition probabilities from one state to another. Thus, also, the need to speak of "phase-separation" and differential "frequencies" in nonlinear systems, given that in such systems bifurcations and chaotic jumps bring about new boundaries, and, therefore, new stability conditions. On the general issues consult Garfinkel 1981; van Fraassen 1980, 1990; Suppe 1990.

[2] On reference in the internal realist and ontological pluralist conceptions see Goodman 1978; Putnam 1981, 1982, 1983, 1987, 1989. On the pragmatist notion of reference see Margolis 1986; Rorty 1979, 1982, 1989.

tions imposed on the form that algebraic or machinelike rewrite rules can take. Thus, Grammar Type O has no formal restrictions on the rewrite rules; the whole set of productions over a given vocabulary of symbols with no restrictions on the form of production can become a language if it can be recognized by a **Turing machine.** Type 1 Grammars have minimal restrictions and are called "context-sensitive" grammars; natural languages are usually of this Type 1 variety, exhibiting a lot of flexibility in construction and use with minimal formalities. Type 2 Grammars, called "context-free," have further restrictions on rewrite rules, are more formal, have less flexibility, and are usually instantiated in the area of programming computer languages. Finally, Grammar Type 3 has maximal restrictions, is rather rigid but very formal, logico-mathematical and is the prototype of what Chomsky and the structuralist linguists call model "regular grammar." So, in this case a *hierarchy of grammars* arises out of the successive restriction of rewrite rules, that is, the application of constraints on the generation of admissible syntactic structures.

The second example is offered by Peter Medawar and refers to the late nineteenth-century Erlanger program of formalization of geometries proposed by Felix Klein (Medawar 1974; cf. Yaglom 1987). Klein made the distinction between four types of geometry arranged in a *hierarchy of geometries* on the basis of the kind and number of constraints operating on each of them; thus, he distinguished geometries of higher abstraction and few constraints at the lower level of organization from geometries of lower abstraction and more constraints at the higher level. His system recognized topology with the fewest constraints (sidedness), projective geometry emerging with a few more constraints (linearity), affine geometry, even higher and with more constraints (parallelism, linear integral functions), and finally, Euclidean geometry with the most constraints (symmetrical magnification, on top of the previous ones) and highest specificity. Based on this Kleinian hierarchy Medawar has defined a level as the ensemble of properties of a domain's objects that remain unchanged or maintain invariance under the transformations of a given group. Medawar uses this insight to suggest that physics, chemistry, biology, and ecology/sociology can be analogically understood as a *level hierarchy* in the same way that Klein's geometries appear to be.

From a constraint-based theory of levels[3] let us move on to other formal views, such as those of Mario Bunge. In his paper "The Metaphysics, Epistemology, and Methodology of Levels" (1969; see also

---

[3] See Thom 1984; Zeeman 1974; and, especially, Atkin 1974, on the restriction of "possibility space."

1973a and b), Bunge defines a level structure as an ordered pair containing (1) a family of sets of individual systems and (2) a binary relation that is one–many, reflexive, and transitive, and represents a process of emergence or coming into being of novel or qualitatively new systems. Furthermore, a level is "a collection of systems characterized by a definite set of properties and laws," as "some of the emergent characteristics or nova are the exclusive property of the given level" (1969: 20). Bunge seems to accept the notion that the totality of systems forming the level structure is partially ordered (1973b:149), though he refuses to call it a hierarchy because the set is not equipped with a relation of domination. (His relation, E, of emergence is reflexive and not asymmetrical.) The rest of his formalization follows along the above lines.[4]

Bunge, notwithstanding his strongly realist rhetoric, comes surprisingly close to a heterarchical position. He argues that emergence brings forth novel properties and laws but that, in any case, newer does not necessarily mean higher or superior but just later in the game. On the one hand, he says, emergence is always an emergence from preexisting levels and, on the other, as in any evolutionary process, some new properties emerge while some other properties are lost. Given the above, and given also the definition of the emergence relation, E, as reflexive and not asymmetric, Bunge is ready to accept that there is no ordering involved here: "while some level structures are ordered sets, others are not (they could be only partially ordered or not linearly ordered at all)." How then does he conceive of this partial and/or nonlinear ordering? "The older levels," he says, "support the newer, without necessarily tyrannizing them. Moreover this dependence is primarily but not totally unilateral, as the new levels may *exert a secondary reaction* on the older ones" (1969:22–3). Here he has come upon something significant, which we will explore further later on.

Levels in computers

We may profit, too, from the work of many cognitive scientists, who have conceptualized the transitions in the level structure in terms of the notion of chunking (Cohen and Feigenbaum 1982; Miller 1956; cf. Schank et al. 1977, 1981, 1984). Let us again use Hofstadter as a guide: while at the lowest level of a computer's machine language any description appears "like the dot-description of a television picture," at the

---

[4] Bunge has a rather strong sense of realism of levels and, consequently, also of epistemic realism (1969). Bhaskar 1975 derives from him a "transcendental" argument about structural entities.

highest level the description is greatly chunked. "[T]he chunks on the high-level description are like the chess expert's chunks, and like the chunked description of the image on the screen: they summarize in capsule form a number of things which on lower levels are seen as separate" (1979:287–8). Now if we construct a computer language level structure, called by Hofstadter a "hierarchy of levels of description of programs," we will find four basic levels: that of machine language at the bottom, followed by the level of assembly language, then that of compiler language (compilers and interpreters), and, finally, the level of *operating systems* and higher-level programming languages. These levels are, obviously, artifacts of a particular simplifying description, while the truth of the matter is that the relationships between levels and within levels (at the sublevel domain, particularly in the intermediary levels) are neither so neat nor so equidistant. Indeed, as Hofstadter explains, the relationships are more tangled than that.

Machine language is as close as one can get to the hardware, that is, the physical and electronic constitution of the computer as a machine. The electronic hard-wiring of the computer involves a variety of modular or nonmodular networks built by incorporating numerous logical gates. Registration in and firing of the network is done in binary mode via the on/off switching and the (AND, OR, NOR, etc.) logical capacity of the gates. Machine language, therefore, consists of elementary – and rather formal – instruction of writing and manipulating "bit" sequences of binary (0,1) coding registered in the memory of the machine. On the other hand, assembly language consists of instructions that are "chunks" of machine language instructions, that is, abstracted summations of some of the latter, allowing the user to name them in plain natural language terms. Thus, instead of giving any address in memory in terms of binary representation, you can just refer to the word in memory by its "name." It is important to note here that this form of chunking involves a translation that preserves a one-to-one correspondence between assembly language instructions and machine language instructions, a correspondence which implies that, in this case, there is no real emergence.[5]

The movement from assembly language to compiler (or interpreter) language is of an altogether different nature. It is not a translation from assembly to compiler language and, a fortiori, not a transcription of the

[5] There is no true emergence in chunking except when we consider it as a gestalt switch, a change in the "order of parameters." Consider also in this context the hierarchical problem representations or abstraction spaces used in many artificial intelligence programs, such as in Newell's and Simon's GPS model of theorem-proving in logic or Sacerdoti's ABSTRIPS planner; in Cohen and Feigenbaum 1982.

former. It is not a form of chunking that involves reference to a contiguous area in memory, nor of one that involves simple (one-to-one or
many-but-contiguous-to-one) correspondence to assembly and, thus,
also to machine language. It is instead a sort of chunking that involves
many-to-many correspondence or mappings of contiguous or noncontiguous elements: algorithms, subroutines, and procedures emerge that
are higher modules or functions, operating as different modes of articulation of specific or equivalent parts or elements of the assembly/ma-
chine language. Different elements of the machine language map into
different modules or functions in the compiler language, so the units of
the compiler language appear to be special modes of articulation or
particular states of the system based on, but not trivially reducible to,
the elements of the machine language. This form of chunking begins to
manifest a real level emergence in a sense not found in the previous
example of the relationship between the machine and assembly languages. The same obtains in the case of operating systems and even
higher-level languages that become more liftable from the specific
machines on which they have been based, and, therefore, more portable and usable with other machines.[6]

Nonetheless, it is wrong to speak of complete liftability, because sta-
tistically not many hierarchical systems can be shown to possess this
property. It is more realistic to speak of a partial liftability, and abandon
or bracket the notion of portability or the alleged realizability of higher
levels of, say, mental states into alternative, machine or alien substrates
(as per **functionalism**). On my view, which is an extension and twisting
of Hofstadter's post-functionalist conception, across-level relations are
several-to-several or many-to-many mappings allowing the emergence
of semiautonomous modules or functions that are still supported by
(i.e., based on), yet are only partially liftable above the lower-level
substrates.

The brain/mind

On the basis of our discussion of the hierarchy of computer languages,
we may now confront the last example of a level structure – that of
mental phenomena (also see Chapter 11). Indeed, one may read afresh
accounts by Hofstadter (1979; Hofstadter and Dennett 1981), Dennett
(1981), Fodor (1983), or Churchland (1984), of the relationship obtaining between *brain* and *mind* and come to the following realization: A

---

[6] One may read in the context of liftability/portability the exciting, though possibly flawed, early essays of Putnam, "Minds and Machines" (1975a) and "The
Mental Life of Some Machines" (1975b).

partial ordering or level structure exists covering the domain of phenomena from the neurophysiology of the brain to the higher faculties of the mind. This level structure has at least four, maybe five, levels (from lower to higher):

(5) the level of agent;
(4) the level of the higher subsystems of the mind;
(3) the level of symbols and mental states;
(2) the level of the neuronic complexes;
(1) the level of neurons, the substrate of mind.[7]

The neurons are the real hardware of the brain, its electronic network. And this is, presumably, an inviolable level, in the sense that the higher levels cannot violate the physical neuronic substrate (and, thus, the physical, chemical, and biological constraints shaping it or, by derivation, the laws governing it). Or can they? Several neurobiologists have suggested, and Churchland concedes, that neuronic linkages are ever changing and, thus, are not like the stable logical gates of computers. Edelman's work (1987, 1989) and that of many other investigators has confirmed beyond any reasonable doubt that such change takes place constantly and not only randomly, but also as a result of competitive pruning and of influence from higher levels.

The level of neuronic complexes is even more intricate and intriguing. Neuron cells do not simply aggregate into neuronic complexes: if this were the case we would have found a perfect or near perfect correspondence between mental states and neuronic complexes (as per the extended localization theory).[8] But this is not so. Neuronic complexes could, to a certain extent, be thought of as fuzzy configurations of contiguous neurons, were it not for the fact that (a) different structures of neurons tend to be expressed, at least indirectly, and feed back onto one another; (b) particular neuron cells are differentiated as simple, complex, and hypercomplex, mapped into one another not only one-to-one but also many-to-one; (c) connections of neurons are not always contiguous, given the particular form of various neurons; indeed, a large number of connections are not localizable at all; and (d) mental functions do not appear to be fired via an exclusive pathway. Even if a so-called classical bundle of neurons is used, several alternate pathways seem to operate as well in parallel processing, giving rise to an astonishing number of Lashley-type paradoxes (see Churchland 1984, 1989;

---

[7] This is adopted from the work of Hofstadter and Dennett (1981). See also Arbib 1985; Dennett 1984, 1987; Edelman 1989.

[8] Churchland 1984 seems basically to subscribe to such a view of primary (though not secondary or tertiary) localization. See further exploration of this view in Edelman and Mountcastle 1978; Fodor 1983; and Gazzaniga 1970, 1984.

Edelman 1982, 1987, 1989; Edelman and Mountcastle 1978; Gazzaniga 1970, 1984, 1988; among others). Given these extremely significant violations of localization or one-to-one correspondence, neuronic complexes do not appear to relate as neatly and formally to their substrate as machine language relates to the electronic wiring of a computer. Rather, it looks as if these relations are already many-to-many mappings or, at least, closer to that model.

As we move from neuronic complexes to symbols and simpler mental states it becomes clear once again that the many-to-many mapping is more pronounced. Symbols, being quasi-hardware-based realizations of concepts and expressors of mental states, have a (semi) autonomy of their own: on the one hand, they are underdetermined by neurons and neuronic complexes carrying them because of the strong, many-to-many mappings; and, on the other, at their focal level symbols trigger other symbols (Edelman 1989; Hofstadter 1979:357) with which they are inevitably connected. Efforts in cognitive science to construct semantic networks (J. A. Anderson 1983a; Barr and Feigenbaum 1981; Winograd 1972, 1980, 1982) have had to face this problem squarely. In terms of our previous discussion, symbols are emergent and, as such (though based on it), irreducible to the neuronic level. The same holds true, a fortiori, for the higher functions of the mind, including conceptual cognition, agency, and self-consciousness.[9]

One arrives at the same conclusion by working through the implications of Gödel's incompleteness theorem (Davis 1965). Indeed, Gödel's proof suggests that a high-level view of a system may contain some explanatory power which is absent – even in principle – on the lower levels. There could be, therefore, some high-level way of viewing the mind/brain, involving additional concepts which do not appear on lower levels. If so, this would mean that "some facts could be explained on the high level quite easily, but not on lower levels at all" (Hofstadter 1979:707–8). This will be even more so in the still higher levels of mental subsystems or faculties (see Edelman 1989; Fodor 1983; Fodor and Pylyshyn 1988) and the so-called agent-level as well (Dennett 1987; Hofstadter and Dennett 1981). For reasons, then, having to do either with the formal consequences of the Gödelian theorem or with the empirical facts of the existing many-to-many mappings in both brains and computers, semiautonomous levels of structural organization seem to emerge almost inevitably – levels that are underdetermined by and partially liftable out of their supporting lower levels.

[9] Several examples of such many-to-many mappings can be cited. For instance, Levins (1973:120) relates that in genetics most significant traits are controlled by more than one gene and that most genes affect more than one trait. Levins explicitly mentions the importance of the several-to-several mapping function.

At this juncture, we need to derive some preliminary conclusions which will help us move on to another level of abstraction.

Level structures

The failure to demonstrate that any "higher" complex phenomenon is trivially and completely reducible to its constituent microparts justifies holding the presumption that the world, as we know it, is inescapably organized as a "level structure." This presumption is already widely held and increases to be so. This granted, however, the question of the character of that level structure gains greater importance and appears to divide opinions once more. What is the nature of the relationships between levels? What are the characteristics of the process of composition or relative autonomization of levels from each other? What sort of ordering obtains between the different levels?

In the previous chapter we disposed of two extreme possibilities, complete decomposability or the complete indecomposability of any complex system,[10] so we may now concentrate on the intermediate positions. Close to the extreme positions we find two moderate variants which make some concessions that, at least at the semantic level, appear to be significant. Thus, Simon in his early work introduced the pragmatic talk of "sealing off" various "phase-separated" "frequency" systems or "modules," and spoke of *nearly (completely) decomposable systems,* in which "(a) the short-run behavior of each of the component subsystems is approximately independent of the short-run behavior of the other components; and (b) in the long run, the behavior of any of the components depends in only an aggregate way on the behavior of the other components" (Simon 1965:69; cf. Ando, Fisher, and Simon 1963). According to Simon, near-decomposability implies that comparatively little information is lost by representing the systems as forming hierarchies, that is, as if they were completely decomposable. Here then speaks a methodological modular reductionist who is also, as we have seen, a pragmatic holist.

Elsasser (1966, 1975), Polanyi (1968), even von Bertalanffy (1952, 1968), on the other side, speak of *nearly (completely) indecomposable systems* and in so doing, are labelled by their opponents as **vitalists** because their argument refers basically to a nonreductionist conception of life. This line of thought tilts toward a "metaphysical dualist" phi-

---

[10] Any argument on behalf of complete or nearly complete indecomposability has hyperfunctionalist/vitalist overtones, as in the Romantic idea of an *Anima Mundi* or the current talk of Gaia. On the Gaia hypothesis see Lovelock 1979; on a similar cosmological anthropic principle, Barrow and Tipler 1986; Davies 1988.

losophy, strenuously championing the notion that the world is organized not only as a hierarchy but as a **control hierarchy** that is, in a way in which higher-level phenomena nearly subsume and control (Polanyi says "harness") the lower-level phenomena composing them. To this point we will return shortly.

Between the positions of complete or nearly complete decomposability or indecomposability, we find two variant views, very close together, which we may call positions of partial ordering. The first of these, partial indecomposition, can be thought of as a weakened Simonian view: though emphasizing the need for decomposition for knowledge, it considers the empirical successes and future prospects of decomposition limited or partial, resting on somewhat fuzzy differentiations that cannot exceed a certain threshold to become even nearly complete. This accords well with the Popperian talk of the open universe and the crucial failures of reductionism (Popper 1974, 1982) as well as the general line of development of constraint and hierarchy theory (Maynard Smith et al. 1985; Pattee 1973, 1979). The second view, partial decomposition, adds a further restriction to the possibility of partial decomposition by insisting that even such partial decompositions uncover multiple and different (e.g., parallel) modes of subsystem organization, interaction, or information processing that cannot be thought of as equivalently decomposable. A good example of this is that of the higher organization of brain/mind summarized above, which will be further developed in Chapter 11. My conception of partial decomposition involves the recognition that (a) though we may speak of pragmatically decomposable systems, the decomposition of such systems (b) sets forth a variety of nonequivalent, **polymorphous,** partially entangled subsystems and (c) still leaves over a host of nontrivial elements that cannot be simply ignored but must be considered as a set of externalities-to-decomposition (briefly, as externalities to the subsystems, including quasi-subsystems, free elements, strange animals).[11] Speaking in the language of many-to-many mappings in the brain/mind,

---

[11] For the dynamics of partial decomposability and its multilevel basis see Hopfield and Tank 1986; Kaufman 1969; Levins 1973; Lewontin 1970; Wills 1989; Wilson 1980. A different approach has been suggested by Simon (1973) and Hofstadter (1979), who see decomposability as a resultant of weak interaction within a system. Simon noted that while the interaction of protons and neutrons involves energies of some 140 million electron volts, molecular covalent bonds involve energies of the order of only 5 electron volts, and the bonds that account for the tertiary structure of large macromolecules involve just about one-half of an electron volt. Hofstadter has also distinguished the extremely strong interactions within proton and neutron particles (holding the invisible "quarks") from the strong interactions of protons and neutrons within the nucleus, and the weak interactions of nearly free electrons within the atom. This has suggestive but complex implications, undeveloped by the authors.

any decomposition of such mappings (1) would certainly be a partial one, (2) would only lead to a vague localization of symbolic activity in neuronal complexes, (3) would uncover a variety of indirect linkages, neuronal expressions, and parallel or multiple processing modes, and (4) would still leave unexplained a number of nonlocalizable paradoxes (Lashley effects; puzzles cited by Eccles, Sperry, and others) that would appear to be external to the localization-related decompositions.[12]

What on earth, then, is a level structure that is partially decomposable and possibly constitutes a partial ordering – that is, under certain restrictions and qualifications, a hierarchy of sorts?

Two-level relations

Consider the relations or mappings that obtain between any two levels of a proposed level structure. I distinguish four types of relations:

(1) a part/whole relation that affords the inclusion of parts in-to wholes in the form of nested structures on the basis of a several-to-one connection;

(2) a complex several-to-several or many-to-many relation between an emerging tangled system and an underlying micronet forming a tangled composite structure;

(3) a collective/individual relation that indicates a weak nesting of levels emerging by the application of some collective constraint; and

(4) an aggregate/individual relation that signals the rock-bottom inclusion of individuals to nonnested collections that are not structured.

These relations characterize different forms of orderings between levels. One way to look at these orderings is by distinguishing two basic forms, each one having two subtypes, as depicted in Figure 3.1.

Nested and nonnested levels

Any three contiguous levels of a level structure could be either nested or nonnested, where nesting implies successive, at least partial (if not complete) inclusion of lower levels into higher ones in the form of parts or wholes. However, in nonnested relations, there are no parts or whole relations across levels that make the structures of any particular level parts of the next higher level, but wholes relative to the level below. All we may have are relations between two levels that involve, in one

---

[12] On the nonlocalizable nature of neuronal processes see Churchland 1984; Edelman 1987, 1989; Fodor 1983; Gazzaniga 1984, 1988; Kohonen 1978, 1984.

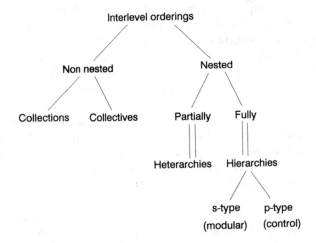

Figure 3.1. *Interlevel orderings*

instance (that of "collectives"), a weak form of inclusion and, in the other (that of "collections"), no inclusion whatsoever, so that at bottom, there is only one real level, that of the presumed ultimate elements. Of these two subtypes of nonnested relations, collections, on face value, are no orderings whatsoever. Collections of individual elements are exactly that – nominal aggregates. They are sometimes treated as if they involve a presumed form of inclusion that can lead to nesting, but in effect they appear as such only when taken metaphorically. So, for example, collections or aggregates of individuals have been posited as if they were individuals themselves to be included as members in another collection or as parts in a larger whole; but that is only commonsensically tolerable if one loosens up considerably the standards of analytical discourse. The appropriate relation in nonnested relations is an individual/aggregate or elements/collection relation, but never a parts/whole one. We will see later on that, in social theory, Homans's criticism of Blau (as well as Blau's inability to provide a cogent response) rests on the conflation of collections with collectives (see Homans 1975:56). Collectives are something more than a reducible aggregate of elements, though they are still based on a relation between only two levels (i.e., a nonnested relation). A collective exists (1) in a statistical sense, when collective constraints emerge spontaneously (as in **driven systems,** per P. W. Anderson 1984) as statistical properties on an underlying collection accounting for novel phenomena, such as cycles, oscillators, or spatial patterns; or (2) in a would-be control hierarchical sense, when a statistical closure property acting on the detailed dynamics of the given microparts constrains their degrees of freedom and redirects the functional performance of the system (as in "natural" systems **far-from-equilibrium,** per Prigogine [1980; Prigogine and Stengers 1984]). In both cases, however, some sort of a new (either semi-autonomous or dominant) boundary has emerged defining a new reference class, as a result of which we get a type of weak nesting and, perhaps, the formation of a true – three-level – hierarchical nesting.

Nested structures usually involve either (a) a more or less full inclusion of lower levels into the higher ones, spanning at least three levels, or (b) a partial inclusion of a similar sort. Full inclusion is indicated by a several-to-one or many-to-one relation between any couple of a lower and a higher level; in such a case, structures in a typical level of a nested structure are parts incorporated in the next higher level's whole(s) while, at the same time, they constitute such whole(s) relative to the structures of the level below them, of which they are presumably composed. On the other hand, partial inclusion between levels implicates a several-to-several or many-to-many relation, which makes the level structure considerably more complicated as it introduces significant degrees of autonomy at each level and a crucial form of **tangledness.**

Types of hierarchy

We will call the more or less fully nested structures "hierarchies." They are complete or nearly complete linear orderings with a straightforward relation of full inclusion applying at all levels. Now, it is true that any theory of levels necessarily involves the demarcation of any level as higher or lower relative to another level. A general theory of levels will define higher and lower levels in terms of some notion of "complexity" which may imply full inclusion, partial inclusion, or some other methodologically constructionist notion of emergent complexity. Not all level structures are hierarchies. The demarcation between higher and lower levels in a hierarchy proper is posited not merely on the grounds of a general increase in the scale and complexity of higher levels, but by full or nearly full inclusion of the lower levels into the higher as well.

There are two types of hierarchies. The stronger one we may call a control hierarchy or p-hierarchy (Pattee hierarchy), to honor the man who played a significant role in the development of hierarchy theory. This is a top-down view of hierarchy, resting on the assumption that the higher levels have a significant degree of authority over the lower ones. Such a view warrants the talk of "downward causation" (Campbell 1974) of the "harnessing" of the energy of the lower levels (Polanyi 1968), or the "constraining" of the degrees of freedom of microparts (Pattee 1973; Weiss 1969). In a control hierarchy, not only have the lower parts ceased to exert any important sort of control over the higher ones, thus leaving them more or less fully autonomous from the lower, but the higher levels have the power to determine the lower levels from above to a considerable extent; they have a relation of authoritative supersession with the lower levels.

The weaker type of hierarchy we may call a modular hierarchy or s-hierarchy (Simon hierarchy), to honor Herbert Simon, who first introduced the talk of modularity and pragmatic hierarchical chunking. Modular hierarchy is bottom-up; it accommodates the "in principle" originality of the microparts and of the lower-level hardware, while nonetheless recognizing nested structures and pragmatically irreducible emergence. This approach appears unwilling to restrict the broad notion of hierarchies to the more specific notion of control hierarchies, except when the latter are conceived in a strictly methodological, decisionist sense (e.g., for engineering, econometric, or artificial intelligence purposes). Still, modular hierarchies involve the notion of full or nearly full inclusion, a criterion demarcating hierarchies from heterarchies.

Heterarchies

We will call partially nested structures between three levels or more "tangled composite structures" or "heterarchies." They involve a theory of levels defined in terms of pragmatic criteria of scale and complexity, partial inclusion, and semiautonomy – partial determination from below, partial determination from above, partial focal-level determination, residual global indeterminacy – of levels, notions that admittedly are very complex. Tangled composite structures are the result of nonlinear orderings appearing to describe what I would call, following McCulloch (1945, 1965) and Hofstadter (1979), the patterns of a heterarchical ordering of phenomena. Heterarchies, either as programs having a structure or as pragmatically real structures, are level structures in which there is no single governing level; to the contrary, various levels exert a determinate influence on each other in some particular respect. This is possible by virtue of the fact that heterarchies involve multiple access, multiple linkages, and multiple determinations.

Again we will analyze a few meaningful examples. The best case is that of natural languages. We have seen Chomsky's hierarchy of grammars developed by the imposition of constraints on rewrite rules. In natural languages, admissibility criteria are of three sorts, phonological, semantic, and syntactical, all imposed as constraints by the pragmatic exigencies of sociohistorical life. Thus, for example, phonological constraints (species-specific, ethnic) must be imposed to restrict the admissibility of syllabic or other strings of characters; semantic constraints (historical, selectionist) must be imposed to account for the actual meanings attached pragmatically to words and expressions; and syntactical constraints must be imposed to formulate the formal and informal rules of grammar. From a more general point of view, that of scale and entropy-related "complexity,"[13] it appears that our language is a level structure produced by the additive application of a hierarchy of constraints: first phonological, then semantic, finally syntactical. However, on further inspection, given the pragmatic origins of natural languages – their grounding in *Lebensformen* – we find that it is not true that these constraints have been imposed in such a hierarchical order or that their effect is the production of a true hierarchy of language levels. Each constraint is autonomous and maintains its primacy in some particular respect, so that the interactive effect of all three constraints is not a true language hierarchy, but a tangled composite of interacting constraints forming language as an overall heterarchy. Indeed, phonetic constraints do determine and support characters but neither they nor the characters themselves determine the meaning of words or their syntactical functions in the sentence structure. Thus, we cannot speak of complete microdetermination (and, therefore, of reduction) to the character level as a reductionist may wish, nor of simple modularization as a structural constructionist may think. It is the historical–practical selectionist constraints that have given words their semantic–pragmatic meaning; so, in semantical terms, words are hierarchically "higher than" characters or sentence structures, in the former case appearing as meaning-producing "supersessions" of characters, while in the latter case appearing as determinative "modules" ascribing meaning to the sentence.[14] Syntactical constraints do raise the sentence level to the most important position when considering issues of grammaticality, but only then.

In brief, looking at the ordering of the level structure: though there is a sense of partial inclusion in terms of scale and complexity of characters–words–sentences which may, at first, make one think of a hierarchical nested structure, there is no way for us to say that sentences are authoritative supersessions of words and characters on all possible relevant criteria. Sentences may be higher-level phenomena in terms of macrosize or complexity and grammatical functions but not in

---

[13] For entropic and informational definitions of complexity consult Bennett 1986, Brooks and Wiley 1986, G. Nicolis 1987, Landauer 1988, J. Nicolis 1986, Wicken 1987.

[14] The issue, of course, is much more complicated. There are important differences between, among others: (a) the Saussurian-Chomskian/structuralist; (b) the Fregean/logico-semantic; (c) the neo-Wittgensteinian/language games as forms of life; and (d) the Austinian-Searlean/speech acts theories, which cannot be elaborated in the present context.

terms of determination of phonetic affinity nor, especially, of semantic and pragmatic meaning of words and expressions in a natural language, as Chomsky had thought. Natural languages, then, are tangled composite systems, heterarchical orderings, where semiautonomous levels and multiple differential determinations (complex feedbacks and self-loops) coexist and interact, allowing at best only a partial ordering of the phenomena involved and a relative hierarchy of overall importance. Natural languages are heterarchies.

The mechanisms that produce heterarchies are complex and have only recently begun to be investigated. We will analyze in later chapters the relevant mechanisms of heterarchical organization pertaining to social structures. For the moment, staying with the examples from the physical and biological sciences, we may point out that, in general, all forms of enzymatic catalysis, especially the cases of **cross-catalysis**, specifically the instances of interactive auto-catalytic and cross-catalytic modes of enzymatic activity at the macromolecular and supramolecular levels, are proto-exemplars of mechanisms of heterarchy formation. Furthermore, the complex and semiautonomous, higher-level byproducts of cross-catalytic interaction, the various forms of proto-hypercyclic (Matsuno 1981; Matsuno et al. 1984) and hypercyclic (Eigen 1977; Eigen and Schuster 1979; Küppers 1990) organization are exceptionally clear instances of heterarchical tangledness. So also is the complex genetic model of the relationships between DNA strands, RNA forms, and enzymes at the root of the genetic replicability of all eucaryotic cells and organisms.[15]

Another example of heterarchy is that of trophic structure, which emerges from the interaction of primary producers, herbivorous primary consumers, carnivorous secondary and tertiary consumers, and decomposers such as fungi and bacteria. Levins and Lewontin (1985; Levins 1968; and in Pattee 1973) have shown that interactions in a trophic structure are tangled and heterarchical because selection is multihierarchical; nonlinear fitness involves interactions among different loci and linkages, and so the result is a tangled composite system. As Levins, speaking of ecological heterarchies (or "open hierarchies") put it: "The dynamics of the system itself and the action of evolutionary forces on populations of subsystems produces structure, merges some subsystems, subdivides others, reduces total connectivity among parts, gives spontaneous activity and organizes [open] hierarchy" (in Pattee

---

[15] See Benner 1988; Dose et al. 1983; Dyke 1988; Küppers 1990; Woese 1967. The received view involves DNA strands, RNA forms (mRNA, tRNA), and enzymes, in a cross-catalytic process of "transcription," by enzymes, and "translation," by ribosomes containing ribosomal RNA.

1973:127). Similar conclusions have been reached by Allen and Starr (1982; Allen 1985), May (1976, 1987), and several other investigators.

The necessarily cursory presentation of the examples of language, brain/mind, computer languages, hypercyclic organizations, genetic replication, and of ecological systems suffices, I hope, to demonstrate the specificity of the heterarchical ordering of many categories of phenomena. In the next chapter, we will attempt to spell out the differences between hierarchy and heterarchy and, thus, to complete the metatheoretical task we have set ourselves in Part I.

4   Some formal theses on hierarchy and heterarchy

Our general discussion in the previous chapter has not yet prepared us sufficiently to enter the domain of social phenomena and spell out the basic characteristics of the competing epistemic strategies (or logics) of social structure. We still need to define the specific characteristics of **hierarchies** and **heterarchies** in a more detailed fashion; this will help us considerably later on, when we will attempt to articulate the contours of the relevant compositionist, hierarchical, and heterarchical theories of structural emergence in the social field.

The teleomatic, the teleonomic, the teleological

We begin, in a roundabout fashion, by offering a classification of various types of systems or structures – physical, biological, and socio-cognitive – following the suggestion of the biologist Ernst Mayr and of various other evolutionists after him (see also the last part of Chapter 8). Mayr describes in the form of a hierarchy three types of processes beyond the intuitively bottom level of physical existence (Aristotle's material cause). All three involve forward-directed processes. He calls them *teleomatic, teleonomic,* and *teleological.*[1]

Teleomatic processes are those that reach deterministically predictable end-states through ordinary physical processes (end-resulting; involving Aristotle's efficient cause). Mayr distinguishes two subcategories: mechanistic-causal and thermodynamic-statistical. Mechanistic processes obey the basic laws of nature, such as gravity. Thermodynamic processes – essentially of the nonequilibrium thermodynamic (NET) variety – obey the laws of entropy and dissipation and explain the occurrence of irreversible processes. Properly speaking, as Wicken (1985, 1987, 1988) has suggested, the concept of teleomatic process must be restricted to the thermodynamic-statistical subcategory which, because of the irreversibility of results, is a true case of the end-directed process.

Teleonomic processes are those guiding homonymous systems to end-states on the basis of internal end-directed programs (genetic devel-

---

[1] For these distinctions see Mayr 1969, 1982; O'Grady 1984; the latter speaks of the first two processes as end-attaining and subdivides them into end-resulting teleomatic and end-directed proper, teleonomic.

59

opmental programs, engrams, even equivalent computer programs; end-directed proper, they involve Aristotle's formal cause). These programs may be fixed or somewhat plastic, strictly directing to a prespecified end-state or stochastic in nature. The teleonomic involves "internal controlling factors" – exhibiting properties of internal representational and computational states – that guide homeostasis, ontogeny, and reproduction in biological organisms, primarily in stable environments.

Teleological processes take place in and by cognitive biological systems and are truly goal-seeking (involving Aristotle's final cause). They consist of "purposive behavior" and exhibit the properties of intentionality, beliefs, and cognition. By making this hierarchical classification Mayr suggests that a distinct level–order exists between physical, biological, and cognitive biological (human) phenomena. Implicit in this categorization is the belief in distinct boundaries, stability conditions, and modes of operation in these independent or, at least, semiindependent levels.

The explicit development of the specificity of these different boundaries, stability conditions, and operative mechanisms has been done by Prigogine and his associates, Brooks, Levins, May, Wicken, and other dynamically and thermodynamically sophisticated model-builders (see the Bibliography for specific references). As I see it, a good, realistic way of speaking about complexity and the different processes it involves would be to consider a horizontal coordinate with four types of systems characterized by their stability conditions: at equilibrium, near equilibrium, beyond equilibrium, and far-from-equilibrium. Systems corresponding to the above stability conditions have been called (a) causal systems (e.g., simple gravitational systems, such as a rock rolling down until it reaches the equilibrium point); (b) suppression systems, which are dynamical linear systems or linearized nonlinear systems near equilibrium involving disturbance and renormalization (e.g., linearly conceived pendulum systems, Stinchcombe's homeostatic functional model, arguably thermostats); (c) loop-cyclical systems, which are oscillating, circulating within, or traversing a limited phase-space and have a limited number of alternating states (e.g., chemical clocks, limit cycles, trophic systems); and (d) loop-autocatalytic systems or dissipative structures, which emerge far-from-equilibrium, involve nonlinear reactions and autocatalysis, evolve through bifurcations, and may attain a multitude of far-from-equilibrium steady states, some fragile, others robust (notably, organisms, ecosystems, socioeconomic systems, probably the mind).

One could draw the appropriate Cartesian coordinates and fill in the boxes with relevant examples and properties, but my goal here is more modest. For the present purpose it suffices to lump together the

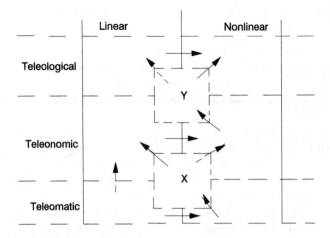

Figure 4.1. *The conceptual map of systems*

"causal" and "suppression" systems located at or near equilibrium and the "cyclical" and "dissipative" systems emerging beyond and far-from-equilibrium. The former are always *linear* or *linearizable,* the latter always *nonlinear.* We can use the simplified model in Figure 4.1 for pedagogical purposes.

Linear teleomatic systems, which are physical systems, are mechanical (Newtonian) and classical (equilibrium) thermodynamic. Nonlinear teleomatic, physical systems are based on nonequilibrium thermodynamics (NET). The more complex forms of NET are physical dissipative structures (convection cells, lasers, ferromagnets), as discussed by Prigogine (Prigogine and Stengers 1984), Haken (1978), P. W. Anderson (1979, 1984), and others. Nonlinear teleomatic processes give rise (via X) to teleonomic linear and nonlinear phenomena and processes, that is, account for the origins of biologically-relevant informational systems (proteinoids, RNA, DNA, chromosomal and genetic forms). The stability of linear teleonomic systems is the result of dissipative teleomatic processes. Something similar happens in the transition from nonlinear teleonomic processes, that is, biological dissipative structures (via Y), to linear and nonlinear teleological systems (intentional individuals, modes of social organization, modes of production). At this state of the progress of science we begin to know more about the black box marked X, thanks to the work of Prigogine, S. W. Fox, Wicken, Brooks and Wiley, and others; but we know precious little about the black box marked Y.[2]

---

[2] On the transition through black box Y see Campbell 1966; Popper 1978 and Popper in Pollard 1984. On my view, we must distinguish another level between

Dissipative structures need a bit more elucidation. We have already defined them as systems involving:

- nonlinear reactions (including chaos);
- autocatalysis (positive, even exponential loops);
- bifurcation regimes (arbitrary bipolar jumps);
- multiple far-from-equilibrium states (most of them with fragile stabilities).

The emergence of such dissipative structures can be explained only by nonequilibrium thermodynamics. As systems move beyond the equilibrium space as a result of changing thermal or entropic parameters, they go through bifurcation points and, in this irreversible sense, attain states in their potential phase-space unimaginable from the point of view of equilibrium or near equilibrium, narrow parameter values. Some of these phases are robust steady states while others are more fragile or even ephemeral.[3] Relatively steady dissipative structures are local forms of organization that draw or import energy from their environment and export or dump entropy into it as if it were a global sink. The ability to do this is based on complex processes that establish hierarchical (or heterarchical) organization by the superimposition of a variety of constraints on previous lower-level structures – as in the case of macromolecural forms, such as **proteinoids,** and, of course, cellular forms of organization. Here the combination of initial, both causal and generative-thermodynamic, and boundary conditions brings forth a hierarchy of levels, each one having more or less independence from the other either in the bottom-up or top-down sense, or in both senses equivalently.

Theses on hierarchy and heterarchy

Hierarchy theory has developed along a variety of lines and several key parts of the theory are still debated among self-proclaimed adherents to the hierarchical strategy. Heterarchy theory, on the other hand, is

the teleonomic and the teleological, which one may call teleopragmatic; I consider this in eminently sociohistorical terms along Hegelian-Marxist-Durkheimian lines.
[3] This is the basis of the P. W. Anderson–Prigogine debate. Anderson (Anderson and Stein 1984) is skeptical about physical "dissipative systems," although he recognizes that life itself is such a system; he speaks of dissipation only in "driven systems" (systems forced to move far beyond equilibrium) and searches for the appropriate mechanisms of the emergence of biological dissipative systems (e.g., the model of evolution in his 1983). Prigogine and his associates speak of physical dissipative systems without such caution (see G. Nicholis 1986 for a review).

still undeveloped and in need of articulation. I will try to capture the most important dimensions of hierarchy and elucidate the different concept of heterarchy by positing twelve theses; of these, the first eight relate to both concepts, while the remaining four address the distinct characteristics of heterarchy alone.

Thesis 1: the commitment to integrated pluralism

In a hierarchy, different levels of phenomena are formed, separated by different frequencies, rates, or time-scales. In general, higher levels are associated with slower rates and time-constants and lower levels with faster rates and time-constants. As contiguous levels interact, for any given focal level, lower-level processes, which have a fast dynamic, are smoothed out (averaged or lagged), while higher-level processes, with slow dynamic, appear as constants, partially translated into "critical parameters" of the focal level (Allen and Starr 1982; Eldredge 1985; Levins 1966, 1970; Prigogine and Stengers 1984; Salthe 1985). In this sense, hierarchy theory accepts the notion that "the world is a multi-level structure. Every level of complexity and organization has its peculiar properties and laws. No level is totally independent from its adjoining levels" (Bunge 1969:22; 1973a:173, 184). Levels are not juxtaposed layers; every level is rooted to lower levels, down to the chemical and physical ones. Therefore, same-level or intralevel analyses must be supplemented and enriched by cross-level or interlevel analyses. The world must be analyzed as a level structure. This postulate is also shared by heterarchy theory, but with the following provisos.

Hierarchical levels are characterized by complete (or nearly complete) ordering. On the other hand, heterarchies exhibit only a weak and partial ordering and, in some cases, even nonlinear partial ordering. Whereas one intuitively assumes that: (a) one level refers to microentities and another to macroentities and that, therefore, it must be the case that the microlevel is more fundamental and causally prior to the microlevel; or, the opposite, (b) that the macrolevel, emerging semiautonomously, must be more encompassing and causally superseding the microlevel. In both instances the reality of the situation is considerably more convoluted: As in the case of language, there is no bottom-up or compositional emergence nor top-down or hierarchical supersession of the lower levels. What we have instead is an entanglement of levels in which there is no way of telling once and for all that one level is superior to or causally more important or ontologically more basic. Hierarchy means *complete inclusion and supersession;* heterarchy means *partial inclusion and tangledness.*

Thesis 2: scale as a minimal criterion of a level structure

If they have physical realization, higher levels usually occupy larger volume. So, in the usual case, higher levels contain and consist of lower-level structures, phenomena, or processes, or at least of the information contained in lower levels. A distinction between scale and size is indispensable. Wimsatt (1980; cf. Salthe 1985) is certainly right when he points out that black holes and bacteria are different orders of things although they are the same size. Size is only one dimension of scale; the latter is better defined by rates of exchange, average time constants, and relative process isolation across levels. Membranes, for example, can be seen as boundary conditions which slow down exchange and decrease the rates of interaction across levels. However, enzymatic activity within membranes in cellular and organismic entities accelerates exchange, thus increasing the rate of exchange.

Sealing off, differential frequencies, and/or the application of constraints all account for the formation of levels. Indeed, in both hierarchy and heterarchy, scale, usually but not always inferred from the size of the relevant phenomena, is the basis for the emergence of the level structure. Hierarchy theory posits complete or nearly complete separation and inclusion of levels. Heterarchy theory, on the other hand, recognizes only forms of partial separation and inclusion – that is, a form of polymorphic and parallel distributive interlevel connectivity. Heterarchy theory also posits a variety of linkages, transitivities, and mappings across noncontiguous levels as we shall see below.

Thesis 3: the dynamics of focal levels

In a static, structural sense activity within any focal level implicates, besides its own specific laws of dynamics, "initiating conditions" (from the lower level) and "boundary conditions" (from the higher level). Hierarchical or heterarchical analysis must always proceed with the detailing of interactions between at least three contiguous levels: the focal "level of interest," the system; the "level without," the environment; and the "level within," the components (Patten 1981, 1982; Salthe 1985). Initiating conditions refer to the causal and thermodynamic processes intrinsic in the components of structures or systems at any focal level. Boundary conditions refer to the emergent properties of the next higher-level system as a result of self-organization, phase separation, and newly achieved stability; put differently, such boundary conditions are developed by the imposition of constraints on the faster dynamics of the lower level. At any given focal level the level within is a summation of all the lower levels for that system, in a decreasing order of importance; the level without, that is the environment, represents the summation of all the higher levels for that system, also in decreasing order.

This thesis as it stands is in agreement with heterarchy theory – however, to this minimalist platform, which is basically acceptable to all emergentists, proponents of heterarchy theory will add some "transitivities" from other levels non-contiguous to the focal level, on the basis of some other (non-additive) constraints. The outcome would be a tangled level structure. The bottom line is that heterarchy theory ascribes a more dynamic role to the focal processes given these complex transitivities operating therein.

Thesis 4: constraints involved in a scale hierarchy

Constraints themselves are determined by the amplitude and asymmetry of information exchange between any contiguous pair of constraining–constrained levels (cf. Allen and Starr 1982:20). A hierarchy, in fact, is nothing but a system of superimposed constraints on components at any given lower level. Constraints are "environmental referents" in the specific sense of an environment factored into levels that incorporate historical factors as well as immediately cogent ones (Salthe 1985:83; see also Patten 1982).[4] Levandowsky and White (1977) have described a number of mechanisms accounting for the emergence of higher level constraints, such as (a) spatial inhomogeneities emerging by virtue of the instability of homogeneous space, (b) complex wave patterns generated by the interaction or conflation of many phenomena at different higher levels having different periodicities, and (c) the specific nature of periodicities themselves as relevant, contingent, often nonlinear, temporal phenomena.

While in a hierarchy distinct hierarchical levels are said to emerge by the superimposition of new constraints on the faster dynamics of any focal level, in the case of heterarchies there is no definite hierarchy of constraints superimposed and implicated in the constitution of the respective (weak and partial) scale hierarchy. For instance, in the case of language, phonological, semantic, and syntactical constraints are not superimposed top-down; they are partially independent of each other. In the case of an organism, molecular, genetic, developmental, epigenetic, and other constraints seem to operate simultaneously and, in the usual instances, are not superimposed. This implies that at each particular focal level several different constraints may apply – a set of "tangled constraints" constitutive of the multidimensional character of

---

[4] Cairns-Smith (1986) speaks of such a "scaffolding" as "the invisible presence" in evolution. Atkin (1974) uses the "backcloth" metaphor. In both instances we recognize Elsasser's "semidefinite constructs."

entities or phenomena at each focal level.[5] What specifically defines such "tangledness" and to what effect we will see below.

One of the important results of the imposition of tangled constraints is the further uniqueness, or relative autonomization of each level vis-à-vis its contiguous levels. That is, the tangledness of constraints increases the probability of the underdetermination of the higher levels by the lower ones and, vice versa, the underdetermination of the lower levels by the higher ones.[6] The first would be an argument against reductionism and other similar forms of methodological individualism (MI); the second is needed as a corrective against functionalism as well as a point of demarcation of the heterarchical from the hierarchical views. An understanding of **Gödelization** will bear this out from a still different angle.

Thesis 5: historicity of levels

At any given level in the dynamic formation of hierarchies or heterarchies, systems or structures come to be as results of irreversible processes and, at least partially, historicity. By "historicity" I mean the long sequence of historical contingencies which, with a degree of bifurcational indeterminacy, account for any given form as – at least partially – a "frozen accident" (Prigogine and Stengers 1984; Salthe 1985). Given that historicity is implicated at all levels, the particular modes of behavior of the structures or systems at any focal level are dynamically defined at the point of intersection of initiating (generative), historical (irreversible), and boundary (higher-order constraining) conditions.

Historicity is involved in all emergentist forms of level structure. In fact, in a recent book British mathematician Roger Penrose (1989) has argued that the ongoing reevaluation of physical theories – partially as a result of the critical dialogue of relativity theory and quantum mechanics – will push the field toward a mathematics and a physics of time-asymmetric processes, the discovery of the most fundamental form of "time's arrow." If historicity seems to become the cornerstone of these new mathematical and physical conceptions, how much more important should it be in the domains of biological and human sciences! Heterarchical theory amplifies the general thesis on historicity by adding the notions of unique tangledness (the multiple determinations of the "concrete," as Marx put it in the *Grundrisse* [1973]) and of the co-evolution of tangled levels.

---

[5] This adds multidimensionality at each focal level, something akin to S. Wright's multidimensional depiction of "survival value" or the current view of "niche" as a hypervolume (Hutchinson 1978).

[6] Even though not as much as the functionalist theory of mind would have it; the older view of Dennett 1978; Putnam 1975 a and b; cf. Margolis 1978.

Thesis 6: asymmetry in interlevel influences

Hierarchy theory postulates the asymmetry of information exchanges between any pair of contiguous levels. The etymology of the term hierarchy – control from higher, sacred authorities – as well as the intention of most proponents of hierarchy theory often bias the meaning of the term in the direction of assigning more importance to the higher-level constraints than to the lower-level processes. For example, in a list that clearly reflects a distinct emphasis, Salthe (1985: 84) summarizes many conceptions as follows: "higher levels contextualize, inform (Muir 1982), select from among possible behaviors, dominate (Ashby 1956), coordinate (Weiss 1969), govern, regulate, or control (Grene 1966, Piaget 1971, Wilden 1972, Alexander and Borgia 1978, Koestler 1978, Bunge 1979), guide, harness (Polanyi 1968), organize (Grene 1966), or anticipate (Burgess 1975) the results of focal-level processes." Hierarchy in this stronger sense (p-hierarchy, as we called it in Chapter 3) is a relatively robust "control hierarchy." (The weaker version, s-hierarchy, may not subscribe to this thesis of asymmetry.)

In contrast, we must explain a certain heterarchical ambivalence regarding symmetry. Indeed, in heterarchies, given the tangledness of constraints and levels, there is no privileged way of knowing in principle if informational exchanges between levels are symmetrical or asymmetrical. There may be a prejudice toward symmetry as a composite, unstable equilibrium of all transitive and intransitive constraints involved. Asymmetry cannot be accepted in principle. On the contrary, the assumption must be that a number of constraints of differential significance may be operative in each particular case; so the final determination must be made empirically in each case after detailed analysis.

Thesis 7: transitivity and intransitivity across levels

Hierarchy theory postulates the intransitivity of information exchanges between noncontiguous levels. This means that only the level above and the level below, the proximate, contiguous levels, exert generative or constraining influence on the focal level under analysis. Allen and Starr, for example, posit this principle downward by arguing that the whole cannot know the details inside the parts. Salthe, more committed to the thesis of intransitivity, posits a "functional distance" between systems "two-levels-away" and argues that any system two-levels-below cannot be a "functional component" of any system at the focal level (1985:120). Given the asymmetry thesis cited above, one may argue for bottom-up intransitivity between levels but top-down transitivity. This has not been clarified in the relevant literature, but accords well with the built-in biases of a strong hierarchical program. My own position is closer to that of Lewontin (1981), who has accepted weak transitivities in the gene-culture noncontiguous level connection opposing E. O. Wilson's and others' (Dawkins 1976, 1982; Wilson 1975; cf. Lumsden and Wilson 1981) postulation of strong transitivities across such noncontiguous levels. The issue is very pertinent for sociology as I will argue later on, for example, in the case of Harrison C. White's analysis of firm profit center relations, and in any other mediated local–global exchange (White 1988; Eccles and White 1986, 1988).

While hierarchy theory posits the intransitivity of information exchanges across noncontiguous levels, heterarchy must posit weak transitivities given the notion of tangledness; the latter implicates an open and multidimensional sort of hierarchy, as a structure composed of several intersecting, possibly partial-level hierarchies. The postulate of weak transitivities stands in opposition to both the hierarchy theory postulate of intransitivity and that of strong transitivities proposed by hard-line gene selectionists favoring strong determination across levels (directly from "genes" to "culture"). The heterarchical posit of multiple and differential transitivities across levels introduces more dynamism into the system under analysis, as many transitivities from near/stronger or farther-lying/weaker levels, with different modes of constraining, may affect the behavior of any system at that focal level. The presumption that contiguous levels have relatively more influence than levels twice or more removed is, of course, held as indispensable.

Thesis 8: replicators and interactors

It may be the case that different and analytically separate hierarchies of levels may exist that are equivalent level-to-level or cross-cut each other at one or more levels. This thorny issue has emerged in reference to biological hierarchies. Biologists speak of a genetic or genealogical hierarchy, "replicators," and of an economic or ecological hierarchy, "interactors" (Eldredge 1985; Hull 1980; Salthe 1985; Vrba and Eldredge 1984). Though the ensuing classifications are highly contested, replicators are taken to include the levels of the gene, of the integrated genotype-phenotype, of the monophyletic lineage, of the deme, of species, of historical biota, and of the total biosphere; while interactors are taken to include the molecular, organismic, population, ecosystem, biogeographical-regional, and global levels. These hierarchies are presumably mutually dependent although it is said that "patterns in the genealogical hierarchy guide the processes characteristic of the ecological hierarchy" (Salthe 1985:178; but see Vrba and Eldredge 1984). Were we to generalize this thesis to the social level, we could talk of a generative hierarchy of transducers and replicators, forming what we usually – and poorly – conceive of as the "deep structure" of phenomena, and an ecological hierarchy of formed or structured interactors, which are the "objects of selection" and constitute what we usually term the "surface structure" of phenomena.

The distinction between replicators and interactors, which is so nicely drawn in hierarchical views of biology, is not so clear in heterarchical forms, presumably due to their complexity. On the other hand, heterarchical theory, in contrast to hierarchy theory, stands closer to molecular biology: it wants to pursue the "structuration" and "transactivation" of intralevel and interlevel connections, not the function of some homeostatic structure. Instead of generating entities, a more static concept, heterarchy joins the new nonequilibrium thermodynamic theories (NET) and their extensions in the biological and social domains in positing and analyzing specific nonlinear mechanisms generating the structural entities at each level. We may speak, therefore, of

(A) the generative mechanisms of structure (logics and mechanisms of structuration proper) and

(B) the phenomenology of structure (levels of organization of structured structuring structures),

with the special proviso that we construe those as complex intra- and interlevel entanglements, not as isolated and linearized mechanisms giving rise to simple and well-delineated phenomenological structures.

As I detail in the later parts of this book, my goal is to:

(1) set the topology or metatheory of the logics or mechanisms of structuration;

(2) make an inventory and suggest points of application of such logics or mechanisms;

(3) describe and explain the complex entanglement of such logics or mechanisms and their complex operation in the social field; and

(4) specify as well as possible the "fuzzy" phenomenological forms that appear as so many semidefinite instances of social structure.

One should keep in mind that although the distinction between "generative logics or mechanisms" and "phenomenology" better reflects the hierarchical position, the transition from the generative to the phenomenological level in the heterarchical mode involves (a) nonsmooth (abrupt, nonlinear) transitions and (b) equipotential transition branches. This matter is discussed below. (See also the "chaotic model of group formation" described in Chapter 11.)

Thesis 9: the dynamics of partial ordering

Theses 9–12 are specifically heterarchical theses, explaining the idiosyncrasies of heterarchies. Thesis 9 begins with the seminal axiom that the ordering of levels takes the mathematical form of "partial ordering." This means that, though a minimally scale-hierarchical level theory may be assumed, virtual levels in a heterarchy and, most importantly, phenomena associated with these levels form only a partially ordered hierarchy. To understand partial ordering one needs to first understand the notion of decomposition. Fully or nearly fully decomposable systems are those perfectly analyzed into constituent subsystems, with nothing or little left outside these subsystems, which in turn are also perfectly analyzed into their constituent sub-subsystems, and so on. Obviously, near-decomposability is more realistic to accept, and it simply defines the fact that within-subsystem interactions are quantitatively more, stronger and more pertinent, than interactions between subsystems. Now, heterarchical theory cannot accept full or near decomposability. It posits partial decomposability on the grounds that the historical dynamics of the focal level, the tangledness of constraints and weak transitivities, the ambivalence of symmetry, and the possible nonlinear dynamics involved in intra- as well as interlevel interactions simply prohibit full or nearly full decomposition. This means that: (a) all systems and subsystems are fuzzy; differential in scale, function, and causal powers; dissipative and concrete; or open to multiple tangled determinations; and, moreover, that (b) many "leftover" partial subsystems and sub-subsystems exist outside the main systems, as if they were externalities at every focal level.

This is, evidently, a more complicated picture of a level structure than the clear, unproblematic picture one gets from a theory of hierarchy. Yet, when the "new genetics" incorporates the work of molecular biologists and abandons altogether the relatively simple picture of singular genes lined up within the chromosome and accepts the more complex reality of genes splitting into pieces, jumping between chromosomes, slipping out of the genetic pool, "talking" to other gene families, and so on (see, e.g., Brandon and Burian 1984; Dillon 1981; Hull 1980; Lewontin 1970; Sober and Lewontin 1982; Wills 1989), does it not, in fact, move away from the hierarchical picture and toward the more dynamic heterarchical one? I would certainly argue so. The same can be said of the semantic partial composition or decomposition of language and the group and organizational partial composition or decomposition in the social domain. This new view of partial decomposability implies that relatively effective decomposition brings about a variety of differential and nonequivalent, partially entangled subsystems or substructures, still leaving over some impurities or externalities. The "nonequivalence" and "relative entanglement" of such substructures (usually dismissed by linear approximation) are irremediable; moreover, the component of impurities such as impaired flow or congestion within levels should not be underestimated.

Thesis 10: on the nonlinearity of focal dynamics

We would expect to find more complex forms of heterarchy in the event that the partial ordering between levels is a nonlinear ordering; in such a situation the overall tangled composite structure will involve nearly unsolvable, nonequilibrium dynamics. Put in more practical terms, an analyst will not be able to reach complete understanding of structures, due to a large extent to the unstable nature of most of their realizable states. Structures, then, will appear as relatively unstable, dissipative, or fuzzy, due to the gap between their model-like or algorithmic form and the various patterns of the form's realization. It is not possible in the present context to fully develop the forms and mechanisms that this nonlinear dynamics can take; this must be left for later elaborations (but see my relevant efforts in the Appendix). We may say that this discrepancy between model-structures and realized–structural forms may, but need not necessarily, involve an explanation of heterarchy in terms of a theory of "neuronal networks" as discussed below.

Thesis 11: heterarchy theory posits several-to-several mappings among levels

The strongest corroboration of heterarchical positions has come from the growing research program on neural networks (the basic tenets and applications of which are provided in Chapter 11). Considerations of neural networks in computer-electronic circuits, mathematical-computational random structure theory, and brain research have brought to our attention the notions of "parallel processing" and the complex forms of parallel process entanglement. The practical aspect of this work for our project regarding social structure is the demonstration that there exist numerous forms of several-to-several, many-to-many, several-to-many, and many-to-several connections or mappings within and across levels of phenomena. We can derive from that the postulate that across levels there exist multiaccess, multilinkages, multiple determinations and differential stabilities. What this means specifically for the theory of social structure will be explored in Chapter 11. For the time being, it suffices to point out that the notion of several-to-several mappings damages considerably the simpler picture of hierarchy as complete linear ordering involving one-to-one or many-to-one connections, that are the results of full or nearly full decomposition of relevant systems.

Thesis 12: higher heterarchical levels as partly hardware,
partly software realizations

If the view derived from the studies of neural networks is indeed generalizable to the social domain as it is to the domains of brain/mind and of computing machines, then a paradoxical result must be thought of as quite probable: the fact that higher levels of organization, being informationally richer, may be partly hardware, partly software realizable. This is an extremely thorny issue, to be sure. In the social sciences we still behave as if the social and the cultural spheres of human life were distinct, though no satisfactory theory of their demarcation has been proposed. We pretend, however, to know what the "social" and the "cultural" really are; and, for what it is worth, we even bring in the "mental" to round things off. Conceptual work in this fundamental area is mostly left to cognitive scientists, philosophers of mind, and neural researchers. In Chapter 11 I argue that the relationship between the social and the cultural – and, more important for our present goal, between social and cultural structure, or sociomaterial aspects and cultural-mental aspects of social structure – can be explained only on the basis of a complex and nonlinear connectionist theory of neural networks as applied to the brain/mind problem.

We now have a working understanding of the competing epistemic strategies, especially the progressive strategies or logics of constructionism, hierarchy, and heterarchy. In subsequent parts we will use this knowledge to describe the specific efforts of social theorists who exemplify one or another of these strategies, to develop research programs concerned with the formation and modes of operation of social structure.

Part II
Compositionist logics

Starting with this part we turn our attention to the issue of social structure, and spell out the constructionist/compositionist **logics** operative in
the emergence of an ascending order of social structures out of individual actions and ensuing **systems of interaction.** Given the discontinuities
involved and the emergent paradoxical effects, structural phenomena
appear beyond the initial realm of actions, interactions, and direct interdependencies.

In Chapter 5 I present the case of methodological individualism, the
archetypal version of reductionism in the social sciences and point out
its shortcomings. Chapter 6 introduces the constructionist views regarding the emergence of social structures, exemplified in exchange and
network models and the more ambitious game-theoretical logic. Part II
concludes with Chapter 7's investigation of complex systems of interaction, especially looking at further extensions and elaborations of
game-theoretical and other models to higher levels of structures, that
is, to complex, **entangled systems.** Overall, these three chapters present
the measure of the possibilities as well as the limits of the constructionist strategy when complexity increases.

5 Methodological individualism

Upon entering the domain of social sciences one is confronted with the perennial issue of the antagonism between the individualist and collectivist forms of explanation of human social phenomena. We have already encountered this dilemma in our earlier discussion of the epistemic strategies pursued at large in contemporary science; in this chapter we focus on the more specific formulations of the debate in social theory, between methodological individualists and the so-called "methodological collectivists" or "**holists.**"[1] It will clarify matters if we first elucidate the salient features of the two camps. Imagine, first, a political situation in which radical minorities of the Left and the Right frame the political discourse in preferred radical binary terminology, labeling their opponents as "communists" or "fascists." In such an environment the semantic cut of the population into two antagonistic camps is, of course, arbitrary and it is directed toward the absorption of the middle ground, based on the old strategic principle that those who are not friends of our enemies surely belong to our camp. "Anti-communist" or "anti-fascist" crusades would emerge putting pressure and, possibly, silencing the many other moderate voices. Apparently, something of that sort has happened in the debate between radical individualists and radical collectivists, an agon fueled by the foundationist, absolutist assumptions of the received positivist philosophy of science. The debate was framed primarily by the advancing armies of logical empiricists and other affine analytical philosophers (see Dray 1968; O'Neill 1973; Popper 1966; Suppe 1977; Watkins 1957; cf. Margolis 1977) who successfully labeled all those opposing epistemic individualism as "collectivists." Given the moral and political connotations of the labels and the commonsensical understanding and favoring of individualism in modern capitalist societies, the dice was loaded against all anti- "methodological individualist" epistemic arguments. As a result, a variety of possible positions between the radical individualist and collectivist programs did not develop in the earlier phases of the discourse and began to be articulated starting only in the 1970s.

Another qualification is also in order. Though the rhetoric of the combatants[2] makes use of the modest-sounding adjective "methodolog-

---

[1] For a discussion of various forms of holism in the general context of human studies see Margolis 1986. I describe the sociologically pertinent forms in Chapter 8.

[2] For the elements of the rhetoric of theory consult Lakatos 1978; for another

ical" (methodological individualism, methodological collectivism), as if to indicate that the choice is one of practical expediency and preference, there is an implicit agenda – stronger claims of ontological and epistemological significance are inscribed in the assertions made. Accordingly, we should view methodological individualism, not as a simple methodological view, but as a global – at once ontological, epistemological and methodological – strategy, and attempt to disaggregate the particular claims it makes. I have used the concept epistemic strategies (in the broad sense of the term "episteme") to indicate this complex of orientations postulated and followed by philosophico-scientific methodical movements. Sadly, although it is true that in the late 1950s, after the first rounds of the debate had somewhat settled, both sides began to realize that in the earlier conceptualizations many analytical meanings of individualism or collectivism had been conflated, this did not substantially alter the rhetoric of the discourse.[3] In view of this situation, some important distinctions are necessary to enable us to go beyond the previous impasses.

We may speak of "ontological individualism" in a strong or a weak sense. The strong sense is exemplified in the claim that only individuals (bodies, organisms and their assorted cognitive and behavioral capacities) are real, while society, structures, and collectivities are not real at all. It follows, therefore, that any reference to the latter is totally misplaced and the relevant terms should be eliminated from the explanatory vocabulary of the social sciences. The weak sense of ontological individualism rests on a defensive argument, that individuals are ineliminable from the human social ontology; to put it simply, "there is no society without people." This, however, appears to many as both unfair and unsuccessful; this particular issue has not been contested by many holists. People, one may concede, are necessary in any human ontology, but are they sufficient, if viewed as individuals, for the closure of that ontology? Most antimethodological individualists – who would not consider themselves as holists anyway – do not go as far as denying ontological status to individuals; it suffices for them that an extended ontology gives an equivalent, not even necessarily primary, status to other supraindividual entities or forms as well. Quite often, too, many theorists are prepared to accept the premises of ontological individualism though they would argue that this does not make them individ-

approach to the rhetoric of inquiry see Simons 1990. I have work in preparation that addresses the issue of rhetoric in sociological research programs.
[3] For a recent example see the debates between Jon Elster and G. A. Cohen on the proper, either rational choice/methodological individualist or functionalist, interpretation of Marxism (in Roemer 1986). Elster's work is replete with rhetorical claims, intonations, and devices.

ualists in other respects. Among the antimethodological individualists however, there is a minority of radical holists who deny ontological status to individuals and ascribe such ontological status only to supraindividual entities or forms, collectivities or structures (Althusser 1970; Althusser and Balibar 1970; Mayhew 1980, 1981, 1982).

"Epistemological individualism" attempts to avoid some of the problems posed by the ontological debate and advances several arguments for the superiority of individualism as an epistemological strategy of analysis.[4] Here, the claim is grounded on the commonsensically direct accessibility of individuals and their properties and the intelligibility of explanations involving individual human dispositions. The logico-linguistic pursuit of these claims has been articulated in terms of the normative canon of the old analytical school of philosophy, which demanded that all of the concepts used in social science be exhaustively scrutinized, reduced to, or at least translated into individualistic concepts, in terms referring to individuals and their properties – interests, activities, intentions and so on. Offending social scientific explanations would be considered imperfect, a sort of "half-way explanation" (Elster 1985; Homans 1967; Hummell and Opp 1968; Watkins 1976; Watkins in O'Neill 1973), on the way to true "bottom-line" explanations. As Elster readily concedes, "methodological individualism thus conceived is a form of reductionism" (1985:5).

Codifying the earlier ideas of Popper, Hayek and several antecedent thinkers – Menger, Schumpeter, von Mises, Watkins (1957, 1976; in O'Neill 1973) has given us the following formalization of methodological individualism based on the distinction between several kinds of **predicates:**

(1) An adequate description of S (Society) will essentially involve predicates – say, S-predicates – that are neither I- (i.e., Individual) nor R- (i.e., Relational) predicates.

(2) However, the explanans of an adequate explanation of the formation of S, or of the subsequent functioning of S or of changes in S, will essentially involve only I- or R-predicates. If S-predicates still figure in our explanans we have an "unfinished" or "half-way" explanation; we could proceed to a deeper explanans containing no S-predicates.

(3) Moreover, explanations of the formation of properties designated by the I-predicates in our explanans for S will in turn involve I-predicates but not S-predicates. (Watkins 1976:710)

It is obvious from the above that a reductive strategy is pursued here involving the liquidation of S-predicates into R- and I-predicates and, in turn, the liquidation of R-predicates into purely I-predicates. Homans

---

[4] Watkins 1976 presents and discusses the exact version of the "received view." For the abandonment of this view by Popperians see Wisdom 1987.

(1967, 1975) argued that any relatively enduring structure was indeed "created and maintained by the actions of individuals, actions of course taken under the influence and constraint of the actions of other individuals" (1975:64) and insisted that neither totalities nor collectives existed; only nominal "collections" of real individuals (1975:56). At the same time, by insisting that the propositions of behavioral psychology were the only general explanatory propositions needed in social science, Homans appeared to opt for the further reduction of R-predicates to I-predicates, that is, to fixed dispositions of a universal human nature conceived along Lockean-Smithian-Darwinian lines. The same reference to the dispositions of "anonymous individuals" was also made by Watkins (1976).

But the codified "received view" did not remain unchallenged or unmodified for long. Watkins himself realized that some important revisions were in order. In later work he suggested the following two changes:

(A) To (2) above: "if the conclusion of an individualistic explanation contains S-predicates while the premises do not, the deduction will not go through" (1976:711) unless some kind of bridging or coordinating assumptions are added. Such bridging assumptions would have, no doubt, to make concessions to situational factors and institutional contexts (cf. J.O. Wilson 1987, the other Popperian, for a similar change of view).

(B) To (3) above (a more fundamental revision): ascription of ultimate properties to individuals for the explanation of S cannot be made, because such individuals when placed in certain relations will engender something social as an unintended result of their actions and interactions. Only by a happy coincidence could the social consequence be said to correspond to the ascribed basic dispositions, because "there is no pre-attunement of the basic dispositions of individuals to collective needs" (1976:712). Watkins here recognized that group-selection has largely modified the fixed individualist dispositions of humans. Talk of "bridging" and "coordinating" assumptions has been also used by Lindenberg and Wippler (in Alexander et al. 1987) and other explorers of the so-called "micro-macro link."

Instead of introducing bridging assumptions into the methodological individualist terrain, Elster is willing to concede another issue to the opponents: "because and to the extent that people as a matter of fact have and act upon beliefs and desires which include references to social aggregates, the latter must be part of the explanation of their behavior" (1989:194). This is especially the case if, as Mandelbaum (1959) argued, beliefs with societal referents are ineliminable from social life; that is, supraindividual entities do occur irreducibly within **intensional** contexts, for example in language. In view of the fact that reduction of intensional contexts to an observational, extensional language is impossible,[5] one fails to see why Elster (1985, even 1987; but no longer in 1989) harbors the hardline belief that most social phenomena sooner or later will fall within the grasp of individualistic explanation. The recognition that a methodological individualist strategy necessarily incorporates references to social relations, situations, unintended consequences, and even beliefs in social aggregates makes one wonder about the robustness and prospects of this program.

The analytics of methodological individualism

An analytical but systematic presentation of the problems that face epistemic individualism is required. We must further modify Watkins's formalization, and develop a fine-grained model able to distinguish among the varieties and subvarieties of predicates characterizing human discursive practices. Indeed, any discourse on public human phenomena implicates at all times at least four distinct kinds of predicates:

> *Individual predicates.* I-predicates refer to purely individual characteristics; that is, physical, psychophysical and, arguably, psychological (nonsocial) properties of individuals.
>
> *Relational predicates.* R-predicates refer to essential features of interactional relations among individuals, to which we will return shortly.
>
> *Conventional/institutional predicates.* CI-predicates refer to institutional or organizational entities, conventional instruments, algorithmic rules or practices emerging out of or in reaction to relational interactions and regulating those interactions.
>
> *Social-structural predicates.* S-predicates refer to broader social properties, especially macrostructural properties, that on the argument of methodological individualists must be reduced or translated into an individualistic language of explanation that includes only primarily I-predicates.

The model then, looks like this:

Predicates involved in any social discourse:

(4) S-predicates

(3) CI-predicates

---

[5] For the impossibility of the reduction of the intensional contexts into extensional language see Dennett 1987; Goodman 1978; Margolis 1977, 1986; Putnam 1987, 1988; cf. Quine 1969; Dummett 1973 on the Fregean view.

(2) R-predicates
(1) I-predicates

A strong program of methodological individualism must claim in principle that not only S-predicates, but CI- and R-predicates are reducible, and must be so reduced to the bottom I-predicates. What sort of epistemic program would we have if it conceded not only that certain pertinent relational predicates are ineliminable, but that conventional/ institutional predicates are necessary as well? Or, if it further conceded that, in accord with the Elster–Mandelbaum argument cited above, the social stance (given ineliminative intensional contexts) is, to a large extent, unavoidable as well? Confusing as it may sound, there are methodological individualists who accept only I-predicates for social scientific explanations; others who accept, perhaps reluctantly, I- and R-predicates but, by defining R-predicates in special ways, try to play down their importance. Others, James Coleman or Raymond Boudon for example, have come to recognize the emergence of CI-predicates, of "bridging institutions" regulating interactions and managing the aggregation or composition problems of social actions leading to collective effects. So there is, indeed, a confusion of who – and what – on final count is a true methodological individualist (Elster [1989] now believes that social norms cannot be shown to derive from rational choice principles). The label is too broad and too ideological if it is meant to apply to anyone who is against any aspect whatsoever of radical ontological and/or epistemic holism.

The real defining point must be somewhere in the notion of relational predicates. It seems to me that there exist several distinct meanings associated with the term "relational predicates" as it is used by different theorists:

(A) The nominalist conception of relational predicates considers those predicates as mere epiphenomena of individual predicates. A strict nominalist view is radical in the sense that it claims the complete reducibility of *all* R-, CI-, and S-predicates into I-predicates, and considers that proper for establishing social scientific explanations. Homans, for example, can be said to hold a nominalist view of R-predicates. Like "collective effects," relational predicates are truly byproducts of individuals and their actions; they are atomic predicates, the property of individuals, and explainable by the propositions of behavioral psychology. So, for instance, the effect of the "other" on "ego" is nothing but an operant stimulus, no different from other stimuli.

As we survey the repertory of the various forms of the relational,[6] we see that the nominalist view is based on an **extensional** conception

---

[6] On this I have benefited from Elster 1985.

of R-predicates: external and extensional relations. What appears as a relation between individuals may be in fact the result of reference to some external, usually quantitative, criterion. Relations of that sort, involving the *more... than, better... than,* or similar comparison terms are reducible to the individuals if and only if they are based on criteria that are truly "extensional," not merely "external," to the relation; that is, if they are based on criteria of a physical and biological nature devoid of, or prior to the attachment of any, special sociocultural meaning. Thus, the relational statements "A runs faster than B," "C is taller than D," "E is physically stronger than F," exemplify truly extensional R-predicates by referring only to physical matters of fact without any important social relational quality.

(B) There are cases, too, which involve reference to external criteria that are not truly extensional: external but intensional relations. A statement such as "A is wealthier than B," although it refers to an external, quantitative measure like money, is not truly extensional, because it is implicitly connected to an intensional context–sociohistorical valuation, such as money as an institution, notions of private property, a special mode of production and distribution, a structure of inequality, differential marginal utilities, and so on – a context that is profoundly social. The criterion itself, money, may be both extensional and intensional – extensional on the surface but intensional in its conventional/institutional deeper role.[7] In other instances the criteria, though external, are not extensional at all. Take the statements "A is prettier than B," "C is a nicer person than D," or "E is a better actor than F." In all these instances the criteria for relation/comparison may be external to the relation (aesthetic or moral standards) but certainly not extensional. They implicate sociohistorically specific judgments of taste and culture which, though they may have become objectively codified, are nonetheless linked to irreducible intensional contexts – institutions, objectified cultural systems of valuation, underlying social structures.

(C) The final conception of R-predicates points to the existence of relational structures with explicitly intensional forms and contexts of reference: internal and intensional relations. Examples invoking the concept of *power* are classic. Certainly, one speaks of power not as (1) a property of individuals as individuals; but as something they have (2) *relative to others* and, more importantly, (3) *over others;* and, indeed,

---

[7] Marx writes in the *Economic and Philosophical Manuscripts:* "The antithesis between lack of property and property, so long as it is not comprehended as the antithesis of labour and capital, still remains an indifferent antithesis, not grasped in its active connection, in its internal relation, not yet grasped as a contradiction ... It does not appear as having been established by private property itself" (CW 3:293–4).

as something that (4) involves considerable *symbolic* (i.e., intentional/ intensional) components. Efforts by Homans to circumvent the third and fourth points went nowhere; on the contrary, the Emersonian version of power-dependence in exchange networks has recognized explicitly the irreducible relational components involved. Power relations and other more complex relations involving the concatenation of power with other CI- and S-predicates exhibit a strong relational predication that cannot be reduced in principle or in practice to individual characteristics.

Sometimes I have the sense that the real problem is a Quinean one of proper semantic analysis. The methodological individualist insinuates that all his opponents fall prey to totalitarian thinking and to the antiliberal denigration, nay abolition, of the human subject (in accord with Popper's early critique [in his 1966]). The truth, however, is that nobody seems willing to argue that the individual, or a population of individuals, is not involved in both social action and social phenomena (the ontological issue) and most thinkers – with the exception of a small number of radical collectivists, "sociologistic reductionists" such as Mayhew or Althusser – will also readily accept that individuals, however socialized, are ineliminably implicated as "agents" in any explanatory sequence of social phenomena (the epistemic issue). But, there is an important difference in treating individuals as necessary, yet not sufficient, components in a social explanation (i.e., conceiving social processes as *related* to and expressed through apparent individual actions) and treating them as exclusively sufficient for such an explanation (i.e., conceiving social processes as exclusive *functions* of the actions of transcendental individuals). In general, it seems to me that the second and, especially, the third meaning of "relational" defeat the prospects of a rigorous methodological individualism and constrain its proponents to plead at best for a weaker, pragmatic notion of social science that will concede an ad hoc preference to the individualist program; for the strong lines of methodological individualism do not persuade many. I find this epistemic strategy exceedingly self-inflated in importance, trying as it does to hold onto a Manichaean view of the world populated by radical methodological individualists or methodological collectivists. As I argued in Chapter 1, current epistemic strategies offer a number of other, more moderate and promising alternatives; methodological individualism need not be treated as the last line of defense against the radical version of the holist program. We will return to this in subsequent chapters.

In descriptions and explanations of social phenomena and in individual social action one finds a large number of conventional/institutional or CI-predicates. The Wittgensteinian example of "signing a check" is quite instructive. The explanation of a social action (not of a simple, observable behavior in the behaviorist–physicalist sense) implicates the prior existence of one or more institutions, such as banking, checking, credit, and a multitude of conventions – tacit agreements, rules and procedures, social arrangements, legal practices, and so forth – that are the institutional, organizational, practical antecedents and frameworks of the social actions and interactions involved. The institutions are at once enabling, constraining, and availing to the individuals. They enable them to function properly in the parameterized, ongoing, construction of reality; constrain them in the range and results of their actions; and avail them of – within the above constraints but beyond the known entitlements – opportunities for improvisation and innovative or trans- formative action. In some other instances the institutions appear more like fine-tuned or simplified ways of solving matching or composition problems that a simple aggregation process such as an "invisible hand" cannot resolve, or can resolve only in an imperfect and cumbersome way. Such is, for example, the case of the market-supplanting institu- tional procedure in which graduates of medical schools are matched with hospitals for their residency training.[8] The matching algorithm and the organization supporting and serving it introduce an institution that imposes a particular structure on the broad and vaguely bounded in- teraction system; in the language we have used in the previous chapters, this amounts to the imposition of a new "boundary condition" bringing about an emergent level of phenomena. Henceforth, the atomistic (free? market) game – its rules, strategies, and all – has ceased and a new institutional (organized? constrained? market) game has taken its place.

When speaking of CI-predicates I am referring to a broad range of institutions: (a) particular typified forms of so-called functional systems of interaction (per Boudon 1981a and b), such as families, markets, churches, schools; (b) all sorts of special-interest, mostly formal, organ- izations; (c) conventional institutional instruments (paper money, credit cards, checks, tax shelters, financial instruments such as CDs, com- modities or stock market indexes, futures or options, ARMs, etc.); (d) matching, sorting, or other algorithms applied socially or in-

---

[8] Hospitals submit rank-ordered lists of their choices for their residency positions and, at the same time applicants submit their preferences of hospitals, also in a rank-ordered fashion. Then, a computer algorithm matches hospitals and ap- plicants, in a way presumably optimizing the result. The initial work on this algorithm was done by Roth (1984). Coleman (1986) talks of a model of the institution contained therein, though he is aware of the issues of power involved in this matching. In any case, this and other more complex forms of "matching" are beyond the purview of methodological individualism (see, e.g., Mortensen 1988 and, especially, Sedgewick 1983; see also the Appendix, no. 13).

scribed in social processes; (e) social norms of all sorts; and (f) institutionalized or even semiinstitutionalized practices (manifested in carnivals, matrimonial exchanges, religious holidays, convict codes, and so on). In all such instances, one must properly speak of "bridging institutions" (Coleman 1987) or "covering institutions" (Margolis 1978) and consider these as emergent, discontinuous, independent and novel – in brief, as irreducible social forms.

No doubt, the emergence of institutions must be seen as a diachronic emergence out of either (a) population/species interactions along the lines of a neo-Darwinian or post-Darwinian group-selectionist theory (see Chapters 8 and 11) or (b) out of smaller interaction systems composed of, at least, minimally cognizing individuals. Indeed, the most likely case would involve the interaction of both of these processes. It does not make any difference to argue that enterprising individuals may be the creators of the institution; that someone had the idea of creating an institutional form, instrument, or algorithm. For it is not a question of origins. In all instances R-predicates are involved, which makes for complex and discontinuous results given the "unintended consequences" inscribed therein (as Watkins realized). The issue of the diachronic origins of the institution has no bearing on the matter of the synchronic structural import of already emergent institutions, given the discontinuities and the historicity associated with the concept of emergence. Seen diachronically the origins of institutions may be microexplainable in principle, though not so in practice. Seen synchronically this emergence is more or less irreducible: irrevocably so in the case of long-term institutions, which may have been produced by evolutionary or long-historical mechanisms; quite irreducible in the case of most sociohistorical institutions produced by the interplay of objective forces and large-scale collective actions; and, arguably, irreducible even when one comes to the sorts of explicit, synchronous institutions where no definite historical reentry has taken place as yet. One way or another, once in place, emerging institutions and related conventions significantly limit the prospects of microexplanation.

It is not necessary at this time to argue the further issue of the irreducibility of larger social structural forms and processes if the above were granted. Once CI-predicates have been accepted as ineliminable, the long-term and larger-scale institutions composing a society and their collective byproducts – its S-predicates – need only be conceived as conjunctures and developments of such lower-level institutions. In that sense, certainly, S-predicates are even more likely to be irreducible than CI-predicates or R-predicates. Having said that, I must add in all fairness that there is no reason to reject outright a strictly methodological individualist program, though one must reject its hegemonic epistemic claims. One could accept the premises of a weaker and modified methodological individualism favoring the investigation (to the extent possible) of social phenomena from the end-point of individuals, and proposing simplifying models for the understanding of such phenomena in terms of the ascribed perceptions and actions of the separate or collective individuals involved. A partial explanation of this type, modestly conceived and carried out without imperialist epistemic designs, cannot fail to provide important insights and a more robust explanation of social phenomena proper.

In general, epistemological and rhetorical claims of methodological individualism vary, from strongest to weakest, in roughly the following manner:

(A) The strongest bid, made by radical proponents, privileges exclusively individual actions and phenomenal – thus, reducible – interactions as the only requirements for scientific social explanations.

(B) Alternatively, a rather strong claim is made, if not for the exclusiveness, then at least for the ontological primacy of the individual in any social process and, thus, the epistemic primacy of methodological individualism as an explanatory model as well.

(C) Next comes the weaker claim that the import of individuals in social processes is a sine qua non, so that no explanation can be acceptable unless it incorporates and considerably valorizes such import. This view may prioritize methodological individualist explanations on pragmatic grounds, but cannot claim, let alone guarantee, their superiority.

(D) Finally, the weakest claim of all (which, once made, indubitably prohibits one from being a genuine methodological individualist and, in fact, as I will argue later, makes one, at least, a constructionist): Although most of the important social phenomena, in principle, cannot be synchronically reduced to or translated into microconstituent elements and, arguably, cannot, even in practice, be reduced to or translated into such microconstituent elements, no social phenomenon can exist without reference and relation to separate or collective individuals. This view has come to consider nearly all social phenomena above the level of social action and interpersonal interaction (even including a large range of phenomena associated with "interaction systems"), beyond the individual – beyond the individual's psychological make-up, motivations, subjective rationality, and so on – and thus as not amenable to strict methodological individualist analysis A or B.[9]

---

[9] I would imagine that Coleman, Boudon, and a host of micro–macro link explorers hold this view, in principle. See Alexander et al. 1987; Boudon 1981a; Hechter 1983b.

Important programs of methodological individualism

Presently, quite a few theoretical research programs qualify as instantiations of methodological individualism. I would like to briefly present six that are important in their own right as well as prominent in the social sciences. The first three represent the rationalist-instrumentalist cluster of MI programs (various versions of **utilitarianism**), while the other three represent the subjectivist-interpretative cluster. They are:

(1) the behaviorist program for sociology elaborated in the work of George Homans and, more recently, Karl-Dieter Opp;
(2) the rational choice theory of neo-classical economics, presented initially in the works of Menger, Schumpeter, von Mises, Hayek, and others associated with the Austrian school;
(3) the contemporary version of institutional economic theory, especially as developed in the works of Oliver Williamson;
(4) the eclectic microtheory of Randall Collins, known as the theory of "interaction ritual chains";
(5) all subjectivist-interpretive *verstehende* sociologies, including the European (Dilthey, Weber, and other) versions of analysis of social action as well as the symbolic interactionist program as formulated by Blumer; and
(6) the social phenomenological or ethnomethodological theories, to the extent that particular strands of them (such as the offshoots of Garfinkel's program) have achieved a new synthesis distinct from the previous set of theories.

All of these approaches to the study of social phenomena look to the individual (conceived either psychologically or in terms of a philosophical anthropology) and to the interactions of individuals to provide all the ingredients for the complete explanation of the processes of the social world. They therefore represent exemplary versions of the previously described "stronger" interpretations of methodological individualism.

Behaviorism

Behaviorism is a reductionist theory in two different senses. It involves a reductionism of mental properties (ontologically) and predicates (epistemologically) to physical properties and predicates, along the lines of a self-consistent empiricism or logical empiricism.[10] It also involves a second reduction of the social properties and predicates to psycho-

---

[10] On "physicalism" as the exemplar of extensionalism and its last defense by Feigl in 1968, see Margolis 1977; Suppe 1977.

logical properties and predicates. As Homans puts it, "all sociological propositions are reducible to psychological propositions" of the behaviorist variety.[11] A similar hard-line point of view has been advanced by Hummel and Opp (1968). Homans takes pains to explain his position. The object of study, the explanandum, is "social phenomena of simple or more complex form," phenomena toward which he seems to be, at times, ontologically ambivalent.[12] Most often, however, he has opted for more radical, nominalist positions. He writes, for example (1964a; cf. 1964b, 1971b), that "the institutions, organizations, and societies that sociologists study can always be analyzed, without residue, into the behavior of individual men. They must therefore be explained by propositions about the behavior of individual men" (1964a:231). Here the reductionist claim is both ontological and epistemological. Similarly, in *Social Behavior* (1974) Homans states that "we shall use propositions that hold good of the nonsocial behavior of single individuals to explain the social behavior of several individuals in contact with one another" (1974:12) – a proposal as strictly reductionistic of the social, at least epistemically, as one can get.

Occasionally, Homans seems to qualify the overall impression of what he is saying. For example, in several instances, he speaks of emergence as the appearance of social behavior, which goes beyond anything observed in the behavior of isolated individuals; but he is quick to insist that "nothing emerges that cannot be explained by propositions about the individuals as individuals, together with the given condition that they happen to be interacting. The characteristics of social groups and societies are the resultants, no doubt the complicated resultants but still the resultants, of the interaction between individuals over time – and they are no more than that" (1974:12). This is a very clear Democritean reductionist strategy, similar to that of Klee, as we saw in Chapter 2. Elementary social behavior and large-scale social institutions are governed, according to Homans, by identical fundamental social processes

[11] Homans writes: "The general propositions we shall use in explanation are psychological in two senses: they refer to the actions of individuals and they have for the most part been formulated and tested by persons who have called themselves psychologists. ... We shall use propositions that hold good of the nonsocial behavior of single individuals to explain the social behavior of several individuals in contact with one another" (1974:12).

[12] Homans is ambivalent on whether or not he is an ontological reductionist, although he is quite clear about being an epistemological reductionist. He writes: "I, for one, am not going to back into the position of denying the reality of social institutions. ... The question is not whether the individual is the ultimate reality or whether social behavior involves something more than the behavior of individuals. The question is, always, how social phenomena are to be explained" (1967: 61–2). In spite of this, I still do not share Turner's (1986b) spirited defense of Homans on epistemic as well as substantive grounds.

of behavior, although "in the institutions of society at large, the way the fundamental processes are combined are more complex" (1974: 358). The process of development from a society as a small group to a society as a complex organization is described in the last chapter of *Social Behavior.* "Emergence," "historicity," and "complexity" are recognized, but he reports his central explanation: despite many instances of imperfect knowledge about the matter, all such developments are explainable by the principles of behavioral psychology. The notions of emergence, historicity, or structure are not really given an autonomous or semiautonomous status – they are treated more or less as epiphenomena of individual behavior or as "noise" in the explanatory effort (paradoxically, much like Lévi-Strauss's conceptualization of history as residual contingency). Homans argues that the behavioral propositions at the top of the deductive system of a proper explanation are transhistorical; that is, they refer to human nature, "rooted in the nature of things, that is, in the nature of humanity," and, in an even more pervasive sense, they transcend human nature itself since they have been shown to refer to properties of very many animal life-forms. "The persons who will appear in this book," says Homans, "are, if you like, no less rational than pigeons. If it be rational of pigeons to learn and take the shorter of two paths to a reward, so it is of our men" (1974:49; cf. 1964b, 1971b).

Homans consistently declares that the reductive explanation of social phenomena, including social structures, involves general psychological propositions *in conjunction* with the given condition or conditions. Discussing the solidarity of the lower-class girls in his Hudson study, he cites different possible sets of such given conditions: failure to reward other members or even positively punish them by failing to conform to the norms of the group (deviance), geographical proximity of the girls in the dormitories, and similarity in background characteristics, such as belonging to the same ethnic group. Furthermore, referring to his "bank wiring" study, he cites the geographical layout, specializations, and flow of work. These givens he calls *parameters* or *boundary conditions* indicative of social organization. But are not, at least, several of these givens irreducible to individual characteristics? Are these not instances involving nonindividual predicates and other externalities?

In an explanatory sketch of social evolution in Chapter 16 of *Social Behavior,* Homans makes use of the notions of "power" and "resources" or "capital," which are – according to our earlier discussion – truly relational, intensional forms irreducible to individual predicates. For example, speaking of the emergence of hereditary chieftainship, he posits that the leader uses his "other resources," which might include some form of "capital" under his control, "such as hoards of food, perishable only slowly, which the members of the usual hunting-gathering band do not possess" (1974:360). Later, as in the case of kingship, capital takes the form of "unusually well-disciplined soldiers," of "a surplus of food or money," or of "a moral code, especially a code supporting trust and confidence between men" (361). "Conquering new territory" may result from the utilization of such capital. And so on. Now one may raise the thorny question: How are these notions of capital (especially, economic surpluses and resources), of an effective military, of conquest and enslavement, the world of coercive power, to be reduced to the activity of individuals as individuals? No detailed answer is forthcoming, presumably because, given a more robust notion of emergence, social phenomena are only partially determined (i.e., *under*determined) by individual behavior. Because no R- or CI- or S-predicates are given any degree of autonomy in its epistemic model – and in the human social ontology implied by it – behaviorism remains the strongest, fully reductionistic version of methodological individualism tending toward physicalistic conclusions.

Rational choice theory
Marginalist and neoclassical economists have developed a general theory of economic action that is the prototype of the rationalist–instrumentalist cluster of methodological individualist programs. The notion of methodological individualism was indeed explored for the first time by Carl Menger, although the term itself was coined by Schumpeter and extensively used and popularized by the Austrian school of von Mises and Hayek (Dray 1968; Elster 1987; Watkins 1976). MI primarily refers to the model of *homo economicus* postulated by modern microeconomics, more benevolently called rational choice theory.

Rational choice theory is built on a number of assumptions which may be classified for purposes of simplicity into three sets: (1) rationality and choice, (2) wants and preferences, and (3) alternative courses of action (see Chapter 6). There are both strong and weak programs of rational choice theory – we will explore the strong program of the Austrian school, which has been modified in the hands of human capital and institutional economists to yield the weak program.

The first set of assumptions posits that all, or nearly all, human actions are (a) rational, (b) profit maximizing, and (c) (notwithstanding a limited number of exceptions) self-interested. Thus, utilitarian principles are deemed to be foundational for the theory. In its orthodox economistic form, rational choice theory considers action as guided by a purely instrumental, selfish, and profit-maximizing calculus – the hyperrationality of *homo economicus* – which is ontologically grounded and transhistorical and is simply "revealed" in the choices and actions of individuals. In more moderate defensive–strategic accounts, such as the one offered by Elster (1985, 1986a and b), although a "methodological privilege" is given to the orthodox claims, they are suggested as a "heuristic principle" guiding researchers.

In the second set of assumptions, the notion of wants has a behaviorist flavor: it refers to deep-seated, natural, **essentialist** needs of individuals which are manifested in a variety of specific idioms in conjunction with variable opportunities and external constraints. Typically for the orthodox rational choice economist, these biologically grounded needs and wants are expressed as fixed preferences, which are similar for all individuals and stable across historical times. These preferences, then, have a purely exogenous formation. Fixed preferences in conjunction with the concrete constraints and opportunities given in a society define the actual revealed preferences of a population of individuals (Elster 1985; see also Sen 1970b, 1978, 1982). Each individual has subjective preferences, which manifest the application of fixed, revealed preferences in the concrete instances of individual decisions, fine-tuned but not changed by past behavioral history and current context.

Finally, the third set of assumptions refers to the existence of alternative courses of action, other possibilities of behavior having their own linkage with the wants and the preference schedules of the individual and presumably forming the total repertory of possibilities of action – the most rational of which the individual is bound to pursue. This assumption implies, therefore, the absence of "dictatorship" (Arrow 1959), that is, of any restriction of the repertory of choices to such an extent as to limit the applicability of the principles of rationality.

Under the above conditions, a strong program of rational choice theory formulates a universal model of explanation of economic and noneconomic rational actions that culminates with claims of microreduction of nearly all other social sciences (and all macrophenomena) to microeconomics. This is, obviously, an overly simplified model of action at the core of neoclassical economic theorizing – nevertheless, a highly regarded model on which the formal programs of academic economics have been grounded. In practice the model has been modified in numerous respects in the hands of more realistic thinkers and, as such, has provided different lines of theory-building (Becker [1976], Sen [1978, 1982], Simon [1961, 1978], Williamson [1975, 1981]). It is no accident that the ongoing revolution in economics seems to push toward more limited conceptions of rationality and intentional action. Ironically, economists become less economistic at a time when sociologists seem to become enamored with rational choice theory.

The neo-institutional model

Institutional economists have emerged in the vanguard of economic theory. The prodigious work of Oliver Williamson and several other associates in his program of "transaction-cost economics" (Oberschall 1986; Ouchi 1980, 1981; Williamson 1975, 1981a, 1981b, 1985; Williamson and Ouchi 1981) provides a good example of the new version of institutional economics. This theory begins with explicit microtheoretical statements and rhetorical exhortations ("look at the microanalytic detail," Williamson tells us [1985]) but moves toward an explanation of the emergence of various economic institutions as efficient organizations in an uncertain world. Transaction-cost economics, together with other relative microtheories such as the theory of teams and agency theory, constitutes an important subcase of the general "property-rights theory" (Pratt and Zeckhauser 1985; Winship and Rosen 1988). The work of Herbert Simon (1961, 1978) and James March (1978) on managerial behavior, with its emphasis on "bounded rationality" and its implications, is foundational for neo-institutional economics by giving it the grounds of a theory of human action that departs considerably from the extreme, hyperrational model of the neoclassical school. Three key revisionist notions are taken more or less for granted by neo-institutional economists: (1) the "satisficing" orientation to economic action, in accordance with which no ongoing effort at maximization of profit takes place once a certain satisfactory performance has been achieved (Simon) and no innovation is eagerly adopted unless profit falls below some comparatively critical level (Nelson and Winter 1982); (2) the principle of (inherent) objective "uncertainty" (as opposed to mere subjective "risk") in economic decision-making which, once taken as given, lowers the value of technical calculations and raises the value of pragmatic–experiential choices; and (3) the notion of opportunism in behavior, an opportunism inherent in the uncertainty conditions of the economic world and the ever-changing economic organizations, which invite the actors to exhibit the Machiavellian traits of *virtù* and *fortuna*. All three of these are obvious byproducts of the accepted belief that human action is more complex than the orthodox rational choice theorists would maintain and *is taken in an environment of imperfect knowledge, interdependent conditions, and objective uncertainty.* The complex issues that now surround economic action (information asymmetries, monitoring problems, incentive options, collective goods), account for the appearance of many distinct institutional practices and arrangements, which become the ways of filtering individual economic activity.

The concept of "institutions" is used quite broadly by these economists. For instance, Williamson refers to various types of contracts, to algorithms regulating transactions, to types of law (e.g., managing franchise settings), and to all types of complex organizations as institutions. This use of the term is closer to the loose sense I introduced above when speaking of the CI-predicates. Indeed, true to its microanalytical framework, transaction-cost analysis fares much better when referring to the least institutionalized arrangements than to highly institutionalized ones.[13] So, in spite of the seeming "institutional" character of the approach, the theory emphasizes the initial level of the emergence of such (least) institutions as efficient forms of operation given an uncertain world, but does little to explain the complexly interdependent mode of functioning of more established institutions. Too, the theory is more or less innocent of conceptions of relational power and large-scale structural constraints. For example, class effects or oligopoly power, or even technology as an external mover, are not recognized as independent forces; on the contrary, all economic institutions – entrepreneurial, collective, or capitalist – are explained as mechanisms of economizing on transaction costs, mechanisms created and manipulated by the managerial virtuosos concerned. "Asset specificity," particular fixed commitments of capital, and "uncertainty" are the primary parameters of economic action and they give rise to a "small-numbers opportunism." Even under these restrictive conditions, various institutional arrangements are created as the best possible ways to achieve satisfactory efficiency, which is defined not on the basis of a cost-benefit equation but of an opportunism–uncertainty reduction equation.

The basic trouble with transaction-cost analysis, in spite of its large number of significant analytical insights, is that in virtue of its priorities, it must totally ignore issues of power-asymmetries among economic actors as well as in the society at large and, thus, never come to grips with questions of social structure (see Granovetter 1985; Perrow 1979, 1981, 1986). It does have the potential to become a strong program along the constructionist/compositionist lines we will discuss in the next chapter, were it to pursue more systematically, in a broader sociological framework, the project of articulating the micro–macro links on the preferred transaction-costs grounds. Even in the form of postulated, if not analytically elaborated, micro–macro links, it remains for the time being confined within the general realm of methodological individualism,

---

[13] See Oberschall 1986 for the application of transaction cost analysis to least institutionalized agreements. Highly institutionalized cases such as the operations of reentry, legitimation, organizational friction and discretion, prohibit any rigorous transaction cost analysis. See also the similar problems Elster (1989b) faced in regard to a purist application of rational choice theory on real-life collective bargaining.

however ready to abandon ship. The general argument that institutional arrangements are always the direct results of the efforts of rational actors to economize on transaction costs (a post hoc imputation) has an uncritical "functionalist" flavor, as Granovetter has correctly observed. I doubt if sociology is ready to try once more this dangerous path.

Collins's microfoundations theory

Collins's significant theory, which is a Weberian-Goffmanian version of conflict sociology, has been presented in several forms and appears in addition to have shifted its own strategic focus once or twice. Initially, in *Conflict Sociology* (1975), Collins attempted to provide an elaborate analysis of a whole range of phenomena, starting from interaction ritual chains and moving to organizational and institutional macrophenomena, paying particular attention to the latter. Even in that work, however, in which Collins advanced dualist (or even cyclical-dialectical) arguments for the interactional constitution of social structures *and* the macro-dimensional effects of space, time, and size on interaction, primacy was given to the microprocesses. In his more recent collection, *Weberian Sociological Theory* (1985), Collins stresses once more the institutional – political, economic, and religious – order, staying very close to the Weberian texts. In the intervening years, however, he has offered us several papers focusing on microfoundations and advocating a more or less strong view of methodological individualism. It is this theory of "interaction ritual chains" that concerns us in the following paragraphs.

As a microsociologist, Collins defines all social phenomena, including social structure, as nothing but "microrepetition in the physical world" because such phenomena refer to "people's repeated behavior in particular places, using particular physical objects, and communicating by using many of the same symbolic expressions repeatedly with certain other people" (1981a:995). Strictly speaking, Collins asserts, there are no such things as a "state," an "economy," a "culture," or a "social class." "There are only collections of individual people acting in particular kinds of microsituations – collections which are characterized thus by a kind of shorthand" (1981a:998). One notices here Homans's (1975) line of argumentation about collections of individuals ("but if a collection, still individuals") with the difference that, instead of strict behaviorist propositions, a modified vocabulary of behavioral and emotive interaction rituals as well as symbolic strategic conflict terms is introduced. Collins, too, emphasizes the primacy of the individual element, not only in understanding but, especially, in the explanation of social relations, for he believes that "the dynamics as well as the inertia in any causal explanation of social structure must be microsituational"

(1981a:990). And he adds: "Social patterns, institutions, and organizations are only the abstractions from the behavior of individuals and summaries of the distribution of different microbehaviors in time and space. These abstractions and summaries do not do anything; if they seem to indicate a continuous reality it is because the individuals that make them up repeat their microbehaviors many times..." (1981a: 989). This statement is consistent with Collins's earlier assertion that social structure can be seen as the frozen residues found in an aerial time-lapse photograph (1975). But we notice here, once again, the confusion of the logical categories of "relation" and "function," that because individuals are necessarily implicated in social phenomena, it must be the case that individuals are the only causes of such phenomena. There is no other way of understanding his insistence that "A microtranslation strategy reveals the empirical realities of social structures as patterns of repetitive micro-interaction" (1981a:985). In such extreme statements Collins tilts toward a thoroughly antirealist view of the social world as being whatever is created by our informed actions or given to us through our perceptions. In many other instances, however, he seems to favor a peculiar dualist (to be precise, one and one-half) view of human social reality, according to which microprocesses constitute the *active side* of a more complex social world in which the macrodimensions of size, number, and time provide the *passive backcloth* of situational contexts. Indeed, he speaks of the actions and interactions of individuals as the "energizing" force in macrostructures: "structures never do anything; it is only persons in real situations who act" (Collins 1987:195; 1981:985; 1975:12; contrast this to Bhaskar 1975, 1978b, 1986). This conviction is reflected in his analysis of inequality and stratification consisting of nothing more than temporal chains of interaction rituals among varying numbers of people with different resources or in his analysis of organizations as structural forms created and sustained by people using resources in encounters (1981a, 1987).

Collins puts himself in a peculiar philosophical position by treating organizational and institutional macroreality in this sense. On the one hand, he does not want to argue that macrophenomena are not real at all and, on the other, he has no basis to ground their reality. Consider the following analytical possibilities available for adoption by a theorist:

(1) Only individual actions and interactions are real.
(2) Interactions properly extended in time, space, and numbers of people involved explain the "appearance" of macrophenomena (which, therefore, always have a provisional candidacy to the status of real phenomena).

(3) Complex forms of interaction implicating a variety of externalities including but not limited to time, space, and numbers,
compose structures that are diachronically reducible in principle (although not in practice) but are synchronically irreducible
to the actions of individuals.

(4) Complex forms of interaction are not only in practice irreducible; they also are ontologically real and epistemologically autonomous, producing their own novel phenomena and
necessitating new explanatory models.

(5) Moreover, these real structures condition, if not determine, the
actions of individuals.

(6) These structures do not emerge by way of composition (3) or
emergence (4 and/or 5), but exogenously, via mechanisms of a
biosocial – and, possibly, sociocultural – group-selection.

Now, it seems to me that Collins identifies with (2), although in moments of extreme rhetoric he sounds as if he were advocating (1) (a
strict MI approach) and, at times, on the opposite side, (4–5) (near to
a dualist position). We have seen above several instances in which he
is tilting toward (1). Let me give now some examples of his tilt in the
other direction. In *Weberian Sociological Theory,* Collins subscribes to
Weber's institutional or "structuralist" line of theorizing. Collins cites
approvingly, for example, the central Weberian theme that "the guiding
dynamic is a larger, international status system, not reducible to the
economic (or bureaucratic or other) internal interests and resources of
local political actors." Weber, he says, "was oriented towards the 'world
system' long before Wallerstein popularized the term" (1986:3). This
sort of argument, on the primacy of global phenomena, is reiterated
several times in the course of his analyses. In *Conflict Sociology,* we
find him trying, for example, to explain sexual stratification by reference
to a gender's control over the means of coercion; the existence of state
coercive powers; the level of economic surplus in a population; the inheritance of resources, and so on – certainly not obvious types of microprocesses. When he speaks of the state and the economy, we find
him using numerous macrostructural variables, such as the size and
scale of political organization, the productive capacity of the economy,
the level of technology, the level of natural resources, efficiency in the
organization of labor, and the level of wealth. What has happened to
his epistemic premise of microreduction and the primacy of action and
interaction? Do not these variables themselves need microexplanation?

Another point is more disturbing to me. While Collins tells us time
and again that the only macrovariables are time, space, and numbers,
in the course of his expositions he refers to and makes important use

of a fourth such variable, that is, resources, especially material resources – wealth, control of money, property, capacity to control spatial settings and people's place in them. Certainly here is an externality to action and interaction (the unequal distribution of resources in a population) absolutely irreducible to individuals. The same goes for power, which is also discussed as a form of unequal resource distribution. In brief, Collins I – the author of *Conflict Sociology* and *Weberian Sociological Theory* – extensively uses variables such as material resources, coercive power, and distributions that on any account are macrosociological. Collins II – the author of the microfoundations and microtranslation papers (1981a and b) – attempts to redefine resources *from inside out,* that is, from the point of view of individuals perceiving them, using them, or facing them. "Power" and even "social position" are conceived as mere abstractions from interaction rituals. "Property," "the state," and other such notions, which are in fact external, become internal to the individual and to the interactions in which these individuals are involved.[14] Collins calls this a "microtranslation," which operates as: (a) the ontological microtranslation of macroentities into microsituations; (b) the ontological microtranslation of external, material entities (material resources, economic surpluses, embodied technologies) into subjective, mental entities (a "sense" of property, etc.); and (c) the epistemic microtranslation of macrostructural descriptive terms into explanatory interactive terms. All these notions of microtranslation indicate rather strongly Collins's commitment to a nearly **antirealist** conception of macrophenomena; see (2) cited earlier.

In a more recent essay (1987), Collins amends his theory in an important way. Microtranslation aside, he now wants to concede that the macrophenomena are there, at least in a pragmatic sense (in counterdistinction to a properly epistemic sense?). "Macrostructures," he says, "are a distinct level of analysis on just this pragmatic level: One can make generalizations about the workings of the world system, formal organizations, or the class structure by making the appropriate comparisons and analyses of its own data. What I will argue, nevertheless, is that the effort to connect micro- and macrotheories is worth making. It is not absolutely necessary to do so; each level can proceed well enough without the other. I believe, however, that the power of ex-

---

14 "The underlying emotional dynamics, I propose, centers on feelings of membership in coalitions. Briefly put, property (access to and exclusions from particular physical places and things) is based upon a sense of what kinds of people do and do not belong where. This is based in turn upon a sense of what groups of people are powerful enough to punish violators of their claims . . . there is no inherent, objective entity called 'property' or 'authority', only the varying senses that people feel at particular places and times of how strong these enforcing coalitions are" (Collins 1981a:997).

planatory theory on either level will be enhanced if we can show their mutual penetration in a fairly precise way" (1987:195). Notice the dualist presentation of the micro- and macro- levels as independent though mutually interpenetrating, even though this is conceded on expedient and pragmatic rather than purely epistemic or proper ontological grounds. Collins continues to maintain that the only macrovariables are those of time, space, and number and that "every other macroterminology is metaphorical and ultimately it should be translated into these. Everything else in a theory is microprocesses" (ibid.:195). However, he still cannot avoid referring indirectly to resources as a part, I suppose, of the notion of space now loaded with them. To complicate matters further, he appears to agree that "the larger macrostructure seems to be primary in shaping microencounters" (ibid.:202), a point which, if taken seriously, would make one wonder about the merits of the proposed method of microtranslation. A clearer explanation would be helpful.

Notwithstanding the conflicting arguments and positions among parts of his various works, I believe that Collins's theory of microfoundations, to the extent that it does not propose a composition upward but a microtranslation downward, is a variant of methodological individualism (not a "microstructuralism" as Jonathan Turner [1986b; cf. Turner and Collins 1989] would have it).

Subjective–interpretive theory

Arguably, all *verstehende* sociologies fall into this category: symbolic interactionism, Dilthey's subjectivist-historicist hermeneutics, Weber's general interpretive theory of action, among others. We will focus, however, on symbolic interactionism, given its undisputed importance for a significant portion of American sociologists.

Symbolic interactionism, especially in the Blumerian rendition and the affine though amended program of social phenomenology and ethnomethodology, offers a mentalistic view of social action and interaction emphasizing the subjectively interpretive meanings that individuals attach to their actions and the actions of other interactants. The core of the theory consists in the treatment of an actor's meaningful action as an interpretive response to the subjectively meaningful action of another interacting individual, along the premises of the interpretation-stimulus-interpretation-response or I-S-I-R model. The bases of the theory are primarily individualistic and they lead directly to the conclusion that everything is microprocess.[15] Interactionist interdependence

---

[15] But consider the debate about the "social behaviorist" and (Blumerian) "sym-

(R-predicates) figures rather weakly and, insofar as it affects individual symbolic perceptions, is not a stepping-stone of "structuration" (notwithstanding the misuse of this term in the most recent efforts of Turner and Collins 1989; contra Maines 1977, 1979, 1981, 1982; Fine 1990).

For symbolic interactionists the physical environment never appears directly to the individual or to the interaction system; it is always mediated by symbols and makes its appearance in the communication process between actors through the interpretation of the symbols involved. It is twice mediated: translated from "physical environment" to "symbolic environment" and then inserted into the interaction by way of actors' meaning constructions and interpretations. Reality is constructed by the acts of individuals in interaction and, thus, always has a fragile, temporary character; "objects" figure only as internal elements of the situated interactions. Indeed, the theory seems to adhere to the notion that reality is not only individually and interactionally constructed but that it is also "in the mind" of individual interactants as well. This has been succinctly criticized by several other theorists: Bourdieu (1977a), Gouldner (1970), John Wilson (1983), Zeitlin (1978). The same applies more or less to all so-called macrophenomena – institutions, organizations, social structures, and the like, including society, the state, and culture. The program denies the true empirical and/ or analytic independence of any macroentity (cf. Stryker 1980). As Blumer emphasized, macroentities are not external forces that "play upon" the individual actors, but are at best already constructed phenomenal realities entering the situation of action and symbolic interaction through processes of interpretation and insertion, the interpretation itself in the given situational–interactional context being the constitutive element of reality. The definition of the situation, as Hewitt (1984:117) has put it, is an active process of reality construction in which individual interactants are "authors of their own experiences and of the realities they inhabit."

Given the creative nature of individual actors and their reflexive cognitive capacities, social interaction emerges as a continuous process, without evident beginning or end, with fragile agreements on shared meanings and ongoing redefinitions of self, act, and situation. In such a conceptual environment, macrostructures do not exist at all – they appear to the symbolic interactionist as false reifications or, at best, they assume "a much looser and less determinative character" (Maines 1981: 472); structure is ephemerally produced "in and through interaction" (Blumer 1975:60). Due to their tacit and precarious character, all mac-

bolic interactionist" interpretations of Mead: Fine 1990; Joas 1985; McPhail and Rexroat 1979; Warshay and Warshay 1986.

rophenomena are reducible to the ongoing microprocesses of symbolic negotiations. Power, material interests, organizational structures – all are fleeting emergences sustained only by the "organizing action" of individual interactants. It is evident then that the program follows consistently, or falls into, a microreductive/microinterpretive methodological individualism.

Phenomenology/ethnomethodology

As in the previous case, ethnomethodology, as the most systematic attempt to produce a consistent phenomenological sociology,[16] is an interpretative–cognitivist version of the general individualist theory. It shares with symbolic interactionism the belief that, as Garfinkel (1967) has said, actors are not "cultural dopes" acting out roles prescribed to them by structural positions, social facts, and cultural patterns; rather they are participants in a continuous process in which order and meaning are created in particular situations as an "ongoing accomplishment" of the concerted efforts of individuals. The definition of the situation is reflected in and created through the accounts actors give of their social world, accounts which themselves play a determinate role in the way they act in that world. This notion of "accounting" illuminates the contingent nature of interaction and context since it shows their indexical nature and the incessant reflexivities they involve.

What makes ethnomethodology different is its unique view of action itself:[17] Ethnomethodologists consider action as an order-producing and order-stabilizing activity. However, following the robust Husserlian program of phenomenology, they focus on the analysis of the formal properties and procedures constitutive of meaningful actions and interactions. The process of accounting is seen not as an activity that occurs after the completion of interaction – a recollective gathering of the meanings produced – but a constitutive process of the very interaction itself and of the meanings deployed in it. Ethnomethods, the fundamental components of action, interaction, meaning, and order, are deep interpretive methods that make up parts of human consciousness; the phenomenological basis of ethnomethodology permits it to speak of the basic processes of a transcendental consciousness that make pos-

---

[16] I consider ethnomethodology as the most systematic attempt to produce a consistent social phenomenology of the mental, at the intersection of cognitive science, the philosophy of mind, and microsociology. On this issue the work of Garfinkel and his students is, simply, superb – but I doubt if it can help us significantly to formulate a robust theory of social structure along pragmatic realist lines (see Garfinkel 1967, 1986; Heritage 1984; Mehan and Wood 1975).

[17] For the differences between ethnomethodology and symbolic interaction see Zimmerman/Wieder vs. Denzin (both in Douglas 1970) and Rawls vs. Gallant/Kleinman [*Symbolic Interaction* 6(1983):1-18; 8(1985):121–140].

sible all acts of interpretation and meaning creation at the surface level. (So, ethnomethodology is more idealistic and individualistic or, even, philosophicoanthropological, than symbolic interactionism, given the Husserlian views on transcendental consciousness.) These deep processes make possible all acts of reality construction, interpretative understanding, and cognitive deployment at the empirical, taken-for-granted level of the emerging and sustained roles, norms, and values.

Ethnomethods include various phenomenological rules constitutive and interpretive of actions, norms, and situations – deep-rooted, practical–cognitive, species-specific dispositions of sorts. The most important of these are (a) the reciprocity of perspectives; (b) the ascription of normalcy to events and situations or "normal forms"; (c) the et cetera principle; (d) the recognition of the indexical nature of expressions; (e) the constitutive use of social typing or typification procedures to identify and locate people in the accomplished order of things so as to make their conduct appear as meaningful; and (f) the forms of practical reasoning used by members to render social phenomena and settings recognizable and normal, especially the use of accounts and descriptions in a "documentary" fashion (Garfinkel 1967; Leiter 1980; Mehan and Wood 1975). Competent members use these ethnomethods to formulate and inscribe order to their actions, at the same time allowing the interaction process to "fill in" what is indexically implied, that is, the unstated but intended or possible significations of action. (Recall in this context Garfinkel's exemplary experiment involving an improvised pseudo psychotherapeutic procedure [Garfinkel 1967:79–94].)

The idealist–nominalist flavor of ethnomethodology is quite apparent: all social phenomena and macroentities are essentially mental productions and they may be said to be real in a mentalistic sense only insofar as the individual member's actions and interpretations accomplish their production and routine-like confirmation. Ethnomethodologists view the world – objects, order, institutions – as an accomplishment of members' practical reasoning, a constructed appearance. Thus, the ethnomethodologist is a social antirealist: Yes, an ontological or epistemological *sense* of social reality is microproduced as an accomplishment; but such constructed reality in itself has no independent, objective existence.

Summary

The methodological individualist programs we have surveyed converge, with some minor differences, on their consideration of social structure as a term that must be microreduced, microtranslated, microinterpreted or microproduced, in the specific sense we have attributed to these terms. In every instance, social structure is conceived, depending on the theoretical stance and rhetoric of the particular program, in a nominalist or a phenomenalist way, the latter defined as the view of macroreality as provisional, ephemeral, fragile. Given these assumptions, no robust notion of emergence could be tolerated.

While the discussion in this chapter centered on the varieties of methodological individualism, our real interest is to transcend this epistemic strategy and focus on the available alternatives suggested in the first part of this book. These alternative epistemic strategies rest on a philosophical conception of ontological monism but attributional, or integrated, pluralism (Bunge 1969; Bhaskar 1975; Margolis 1978). To put it simply and in the vocabulary that concerns us, they rest on the recognition that phenomena of emergence have appeared that, neither synchronically in principle, nor diachronically in a pragmatic sense, are reducible to individual mental or behavioral processes or to systems of action or interaction. We are, therefore, going to argue that the methodological individualist claims for the epistemic exclusiveness of reference to individuals or the epistemic primacy or centrality of any such reference – and, even, the more moderate but ad hoc and undialectical prioritization of the individual – are ill-advised. With this general premise in mind, let us consider the conceptions of social structure originating in other strategies.

6 Constructionism/compositionism: elementary notions

The limitations of methodological individualism have not deterred many analysts from searching for an individualistic framework for the explanation of social phenomena which, if cautious enough, would avoid the pitfalls we have cited in the previous chapter. For example, a number of contemporary students of symbolic interactionism, phenomenology, and ethnomethodology have argued that their approaches are not variants of MI but instead examples of "methodological situationism" or "methodological relationism" (cf. J. O. Wilson 1987), or something of that sort.[1] Examined analytically, these arguments do not seem to get us away from the field of individualistic micro-interactions since they fail to provide any operative mechanism of upward structuration. On the other hand, it is rather surprising that some of the most notable proponents of microstructural programs that have the potentials as well as some initial empirical support for moving beyond MI (e.g., game theory: Boudon, Elster, Hechter, among others), still conceive their approaches as being versions of strong, nearly orthodox methodological individualism. For it is clear that, as soon as one abandons the radical, reductive tendencies of MI, the scenery changes considerably as a result of the new assumptions and parameters introduced into the explanatory model. One then moves to the domain of compositionist or constructionist logics and is expected to investigate precisely these special constraints and emergent mechanisms. To these logics we turn now our attention.

The foundations of constructionism/compositionism appear on first inspection to be nothing more than those of the MI version of rational choice theory; however, this is deceptive in many important cases of constructionist strategies. The hard-line group of game theorists undoubtedly continues to hold to the pure model of rational choice founded on the older grounds of neoclassical economic theory. This model is based on a number of very important assumptions, the majority – if not the totality – of which must be strongly maintained and protected (as a Lakatosian core)[2] if one is to continue holding on to the theoretical language of rational choice. These assumptions are:

---

[1] On ethnomethodological claims of radical situationism see Attewell 1974; Heritage 1984; Mehan and Wood 1975; on the general interactionist attitude see Gonos 1977; in this spirit, even Durkheim has been called a "radical relationist" (Alpert 1939).

(1) the assumption of rationality: all behavior and any explanation of such behavior is guided by the rationality of individual actors, not by irrational or quasi-irrational social, cultural, or emotional forces. Thus, behavior is intentional, and rational at the individual level; all social phenomena are basically the direct, intended results of intended individual action.

(2) the assumption of rational maximization: all individuals operate with maximal, optimizing rationality in their efforts to realize their preferences in the best possible, most efficient and economic way (hyperrationality).

(3) the assumption of selfishness: individuals strive to maximize rationally the attainment of goals that are beneficial to them as individuals; ontologically, they are selfish profit-maximizers.

(4) the assumption of independence: individuals act rationally independently of others according to their set of preferences and the general logic of rational choice.

(5) the assumption of fixed preferences: individuals have a set of fixed and independent preferences, which are unaffected by the externalities of interaction contexts and of sociohistorical dynamics.

(6) the assumption of perfect information: individuals operate with full information in regard to the conditions, the generation, and the effectiveness of their choice.

(7) the assumption of "no dictatorship": no external power is imposed on individuals relative to the rational formation of their choice.

(8) the assumption of alternative courses of action: without this no real choice can be made.

A rational choice theorist, in principle, must hold fast to all of these assumptions if she is to be an epistemological purist. In practice, however, one can relax to some degree one or even several of these assumptions, while still advocating the necessity of the core propositions and their more fundamental relations. Of course, this process of relaxing assumptions cannot go too far; were it to be shown that most, if not all, of these propositions ought to be replaced or significantly modified, the program relying on them would be unwarranted, given the obvious degeneration of its core.

Criticisms of rational choice theory have come from many quarters,

---

[2] Lakatos describes the "metaphysical core" of a research program as the primitive beliefs, laws, or propositions that an adherent cannot give up, something like a sanctum or a citadel which is to be defended at all costs (Lakatos 1978; Lakatos and Musgrave 1970).

from those sympathetic and hostile to the enterprise. Sociologists, anthropologists and other scholars have raised counterarguments supporting the fact that quite a large share of human behaviors are "nonlogical" (Boudon 1981a,b; Geertz 1983; cf. Margolis 1986, Stinchcombe 1980); that no "pure" rational action exists unaffected by situational contexts, relational networks, sociohistorical structures, normative standards, or institutional conventions. Furthermore, most social observers (e.g., Merton and Boudon) have recognized that a whole range of social phenomena appear to be the simple or complex "unintended" and/or "unwanted" consequences of sometimes rational, sometimes less rational human action. Another line of attack has been directed against the assumption of hyperrationality, by sympathetic reformers such as Simon (1961, 1978), March (1978), Williamson (1975, 1981), Nelson and Winter (1982). These critics have made the point that real human beings, while acting more or less as rational agents, can be driven not by maximal rationality (profit maximizing), but by a "satisficing," limited, or pragmatic rationality and, at times, by perceived pragmatic necessity. Further reformist criticisms, such as those of Amartya Sen (1970 a and b, 1978, 1982), have been directed against the assumption of fixed preferences as an "overtly narrow view, underestimating the influence on choice other than the person's own preferences, i.e., group norms, culture of a class or community," thus bringing economic man close to being "a social moron," a "rational fool" (Sen 1982: 84–108). The individualist assumption of independence of choice has been discarded by numerous other *amici curiae* analysts such as Boudon (1981a), Coleman (1972, 1986, 1987), and Elster (1985), who still claim to largely follow the general framework of rational choice. The assumption of no dictatorship – in effect, of no differential coercive power distribution – has also been criticized as plainly unrealistic by Marxist, political conflict theorists (e.g., Tilly 1978, 1989), population ecologists (e.g., Boulding 1978), organizational analysts (e.g., Perrow 1986), and exchange network theorists (e.g., Emerson [1972b, 1981], Molm [1989]).

For any combination of these reasons, many contemporary proponents of rational choice theory (especially in sociology), have adopted a modified methodological individualism or MMI, and turned to the investigation of novel, more complex, or paradoxical effects produced by the qualification or abandonment of specific assumptions within the rational choice framework. Thus, current developments in game theory, collective action theory, public choice theory, and rational choice Marxism were triggered by the realization of the interdependence of individual actions, and in turn have given rise to variants involving further modification of the rational choice framework. These are the main theories with which we will be concerned in this chapter, the simpler forms of methodological constructionism/compositionism. All of these particular research programs share the belief that there is an important practical discontinuity between individual actions as postulated by a weaker model of rational choice theory (modified rational choice, MRC; or modified methodological individualism, MMI) and the variety of microstructural effects that emerge out of such individual actions in conjunction with specific contextualizing and constraining externalities. The understanding, then, in all constructionist programs is that individual actions, though necessarily posited as initiating conditions, underdetermine to a certain extent the structural effects, which thus appear as suboptimal, paradoxical, or weakly emergent and even liftable out of them.

A variety of research programs based on differentially modified rational choice principles (MRC/MMI) are currently active. These programs can be classified in one of the following categories:

(A) Programs attempting descriptively or analytically, to explain the emergence of institutional orders on utilitarian grounds.

(B) Programs attempting to explain the mechanisms implicated in the emergence of topologically based microstructures.

(C) Programs experimenting with the effects of network structure and network position (structural dependence) on exchange processes.

(D) Programs coupling MRC/MMI principles and network techniques to analyze emergent processes of upward structuration; these include the progressive programs currently focusing on mechanisms of market structuration and behavior.

(E) Programs following the general principles of game theory in the elaboration of strategic action, bargaining, the possibilities of collective action, political conflicts, or policy formation.

(F) Programs at the intersection of several of the above categories.

The following representative cases illustrate the specificity of the constructionist logics informing these programs, that is, the transition from individualist to relational and structural categories or the coupling of individualist MRC/MMI principles with social relational or structural processes. The operative micrologics of structuration are elucidated briefly here, in the next chapter, and in the Appendix.

Institutional constructionism

Consider first the issue of the development of institutions as conceived by the rational choice and exchange theories. Institutionalization is commonsensically said to occur whenever there is a "reciprocal typification of habituated actions by types of actors" (Berger and Luckmann 1967: 51–2); in that sense, institutionalization always refers to traditional practices. Homans (in the concluding chapter of *Social Behavior*) and Blau (in the now abandoned schema of *Exchange and Power*) made a valiant, though incomplete and unpersuasive, effort to derive institution-building from simple but foundational exchange principles. But institutionalization also signifies the emergence of novel arrangements to take care of difficulties, asymmetries, transaction costs, and the like, that appear as results of the uncontrollable combinatorial effects of aggregated individual actions.

We find a variety of rational choice–inspired theories attempting to explain the emergence of institutions. Chandler (1962, 1977; cf. Thompson 1967), for example, has argued that modern economic institutional formation and change is based on the prevailing or changing conditions of markets, which are themselves parameterized by technological development; the key then is efficient adaptation and control of markets through superior coordination within multidivisional firms. Williamson (1975, 1983) has argued that institutional formations (e.g., organizational hierarchies) emerge as a result of efforts by rational actors to economize on various transaction costs incurred in uncertain or not properly clearing markets. Arrow (1963, 1974) has argued, on the basis of his possibility theorem which shows that markets cannot aggregate smoothly and optimally, that economic institutions are created where market exchanges between individuals are insufficient to achieve collective action. He further explains that "when the market fails to achieve an optimal state, society will, to some extent at least, recognize the gap, and nonmarket social institutions will arise attempting to bridge it" (1963:947). Remember the example of the emergence of the matching institutional algorithm arranging the assignment of interns to hospitals throughout the United States (Coleman 1986b; Roth 1984; Sedgewick 1983): Here is a novel institution that can be explained as having emerged in order to economize on transaction costs and information, to guarantee efficient coordination, or as a result of a strategic cooperative game. In any case, it is obvious that behavior after the introduction of this matching algorithm is not the same as before. In the same manner, we may cite Simmel's discussion of the introduction of money into a barter-based economy as an example of efficient institutional innovation (Simmel 1978; cf. Shubik 1982).

Exchange networks

Let us next briefly examine the new ideas and experimental results derived from the research program on exchange networks. Richard Emerson successfully coupled exchange theoretical and network principles into a new approach involving interactional and structural interdependencies. The transition from psychological notions of exchange to structural exchange networks is, indeed, significant for the grounding of a properly conceived microstructuration, as the emphasis shifts from influence and balance to more robust notions of "power-dependence" and "structural asymmetries" based on structural location, access to goods, and unequal exchange opportunity (Emerson 1962, 1964, 1972a,b; Cook 1982, 1983; Molm 1987; Marsden 1983). In this program, the significant first step in the right direction of upward structuration has been taken. However, it remains to be seen how far one can go from here, and how well this program of research will invest or spend its credits in the future.

Coleman's program

James Coleman has proposed another form of coupling of individualistic and relational processes, a schema that makes the first step in the right direction of structural emergence.[3] Instead of starting from exchange-theoretical notions of interaction, Coleman adopts a rational choice approach, even though he rejects the extreme individualistic premises that often accompany it (1988:S95; cf. 1986b:364, 1986d, 1987). Coleman proposes a theoretical orientation which "accepts the principle of rational or purposive action and attempts to show how that principle, *in conjunction with particular social contexts,* can account not only for the actions of individuals in particular contexts but also for the development of social organization" (1988:S96; my emphasis). What Coleman has in mind is to describe the effects the social relational characteristics of actors have on their rational choices. Already the work of several scholars (Ben-Porath 1980; Bourdieu 1977a; Granovetter 1973, 1983, 1985; Hannan 1982; Coleman 1988; DeGraaf et al. 1988; cf. Olson 1986) have shown how preference formation, opportunities, and economic action can be affected by family, friends, weak ties, informal interpersonal strategies, and various institutional practices. Coleman (1988:S97) reintroduces the concept of "social capital" (see Bourdieu 1977a, 1986b) which "consist[s] of some aspects of social structures" (Granovetter's notion of embeddedness), "inheres in the structure of relations between actors and among actors," and "facilitate[s] certain actions of actors – whether persons or corporate

---

[3] I regret the fact that I cannot address here Coleman's *Foundations of Social Theory* (1990), which came out after the completion of my manuscript. It is not the type of work I can discuss lightly, and I must return to it at some other opportunity.

actors – within the structure." This seems to be another good "constructionist" way of getting, perhaps, to the notion of upward structuration via the typification of modal actions and social contexts, although much more work is needed for one to be able to assess its long-term prospects.

Network analysis

An even more rigorous constructionist research program has been that of network analysis. From the initial concerns of this program with dyads and triads, cliques, and the equivalence of persons and positions, some important steps have been taken in the direction of the analysis of structural equivalence and, the categorical partition of networks using blockmodeling techniques (Boorman and White 1976; White and Breiger 1975; White, Boorman, and Breiger 1976).[4] In addition to affecting other constructionist programs such as these of Emerson-Cook, Laumann, or Willer and Anderson, the network approach is moving fast in the investigation of further levels of upward structuration, especially with the recent work of Harrison White and others on current market structures and multidivisional firms (Eccles and White 1986, 1988; Wellman and Berkowitz 1988; White 1981a and b, 1985, 1988). This work is crucial for the prospects of constructionism (variably called relationism, analytical structuralism) and deserves a bit more scrutiny.

White's work on markets became known with the publication of two important papers (White 1981a and b), in which markets were treated as "induced role structures" maintained by mechanisms of "signaling"; this last concept derives from the intriguing though heterodox economic views of Spence (1974, 1976), put to use in White's network framework. "Markets" were said to be sustained by the "quasi-cooperative game" of oligopolistic firms watching each other's rational decisions and signals and acting accordingly. In more recent work (1988; Eccles and White 1986, 1988), White has focused more sharply on the firms themselves, locating himself squarely at the core of the concerns of realist management scholars rather than of idealizing economists. Considering the structure and behavior of multidivisional firms, White analyzes the networks of relations and decisionmaking within such "decentralized" institutions as well as across various markets. His resulting theory of "market and firm interfaces" does not explain the emergence of such firms as, arguably,

---

[4] For the network approach and its various applications see further Burt 1980; Marsden and Lin 1982; Wellman 1983; Wellman and Berkowitz 1988.

Chandler, Williamson, and others espousing the "principal-agent" theory have done (Chandler 1962, 1977, 1980; Jensen and Mechling 1976; Moe 1984; Pratt and Zeckhauser 1985; Williamson 1975, 1981b; but see White 1985); but it does offer invaluable insights on the coexistence of market and authority or hierarchy mechanisms of structuration and the dynamics that such an interplay produces. The notion of "interfaces" is an important one, which I will use later as a tool for understanding the heterarchical character of upward structuration. As a first result the theory shows that transaction costs considerations are not fully operative given the structural frictions at the points of intersection of these interfaces, and that other social (that is, less rational) processes affect the decision-making process, especially in matters involving "transfer pricing" (cf. Eccles 1985). In conclusion: A note of praise for White's work which is analytically superb – persistent in its pursuit of upward structurations within his overall relationist/structuralist/mathematical research program, and "progressive" in the Lakatosian sense.

These programs of microstructuration are quite successful, at least in their first steps, in going beyond the individual psychological level of action and interaction. They are also recent, with a way to go toward fulfilling the promise of providing the mechanisms of emergence of macrostructures. In contrast, the game-theoretical program has been around for quite some time and has been rather thoroughly developed; it is currently the most revealing, formal model of a constructionist nature. This program, while still based – however reluctantly[5] – on inappropriately extreme views of rationality, is posited as a model of the partially discontinuous transition from individual rational choice to the presumably limited forms of collective organization and action. We must explore it, therefore, with its extensions and affine formulations, in order to learn more about this partial discontinuity between the individual and the relational, structural, or collective types of phenomena. The historical development of game-theoretical thinking need not concern us here; neither need we dwell on the details and varieties of games as such.[6] We will concentrate instead on the basic forms in which game theory specifically has developed as a strong contender in the analytical conceptualization and explanation of social structure, the issue that is the central concern in this book.

---

[5] See the qualifications introduced by Boudon 1981a; Coleman 1986b, 1988; Elster 1989a,b; Lindenberg et al. 1986:123.

[6] For general overviews of game theory see Friedman 1986; Krass and Hammondeh 1981; Owen 1982; Shubik 1982, 1987. See also the classical work of Luce and Raiffa 1957; Rapaport 1966; Rapaport and Chammah 1965.

Elementary game theory

Basic game theory commits itself implicitly to all the assumptions of rational choice and puts forward three essential assumptions of its own:

(1) The *symmetry assumption,* according to which the agents are both equally rational and share the knowledge that both are equally rational.

(2) The *independence of choices,* exemplified in the Prisoner's Dilemma (PD) and other important games that constitute the core of the theory (although partially modified in other games where some limited informational interdependence is introduced).

(3) *Restriction of time* to one-shot games, for fear that any iteration of games may introduce pronounced interdependence and non-linearities, thus defeating the useful simplicity of game theory.

Game theory has proposed a number of simple games to model all behavior – simple or complex, individual or collective. Prisoner's Dilemma is the granddaddy of them all. The game is characterized by the following constraining assumptions: (i) there are two players in a situation (persons or agencies, such as governments or groups), in which they have to decide, independently of each other, to follow either (ii) a competitive or a cooperative strategy in a (iii) one-shot situation. Each must think and guess what the other player is likely to decide as a rational agent and take that into account in the formation of her rational choice. If A chooses the competitive strategy (acts in a selfish and mistrustful way, e.g., by confessing to a joint crime and turning state's witness) and B opts for the cooperative strategy (e.g., by refusing to confess on the assumption that A will do the same, which will bring about the optimal result), then A has made an individualistic rational choice – which is, however, suboptimal for their collective interest – while B, opting for the collective interest, has made an individualistic irrational choice. What is rational for the individual turns out to be irrational or suboptimal for the collective social interest (cf. Barry and Hardin 1982). This captures nicely the contradiction between social and individual interests, the suboptimalities inherent in and resulting from individualistic modes of thinking, and the fact that individualistic rational thinking in one-shot circumstances tends to favor and reinforce selfish and mistrustful orientations. As we have seen, these are elements that hard-line individualists take as the unchanging parameters of human nature and of all other life forms (but see Axelrod 1984, 1986; Axelrod and Hamilton 1981; Taylor 1982, 1987).

What are we to make of the PD game? Is all human life really a PD game and nothing but? (Stinchcombe 1980). A sociologist would most likely answer in the negative. The assumptions are too strong, too insulated from reality – idealized to the point of becoming Procrustean beds. People do not usually act independently of each other and in one-shot games; they do not assume an extreme symmetry of rationality, since no one operates with such an equally and highly elevated hyperrationality; they do not have sets of fixed preferences, formal logicomathematical rules of procedure, similar valuations, or such an extraordinary selfishness totally unaffected by socialization and social positions and cultural norms. Such a maximalist program remains unreflective of the complex realities of social life, making us truly look like "rational fools" and "social morons." Of course, no explanation of social behavior can exist without reference to some minimalist program of rational choice or of more complex quasi–game-theoretical situations. Such programs modify the assumptions of rational choice and of game theory but preserve the sense of "games" and "strategies."

Indeed, there are significant insights to be gained by adhering to a quasi–game-theoretical view of life, if only by turning a literal and formal conception of games into a pragmatic one, for example, along the lines proposed by Wittgenstein (1953) and Bourdieu (1977a). Game theory, like neoclassical economic theory, has rigor though not all that much realism. It is worth maintaining that rigor as much as possible while at the same time relaxing the unrealistic assumptions through a number of successive pragmatic adjustments. We can appreciate this point by focusing on the progressive complications emerging as we move from one-shot, two-person, hyperrationalist games to many-person (and collective agents), iterated, distributed and nonlinear, pragmatically rational games. But before doing that, let us look a bit closer at some other classic games.

Not all two-person games involve the same orientation of players, call for the imputed one-shot decision, or imply similarities of circumstances of the agents, as in the typical PD. Typically games may be:

(a) *cooperative* or *noncooperative,* according to whether or not they are admitting of binding, contractual agreements between the actors;

(b) involving *complete* or *incomplete information,* regarding the set of actors, the strategy sets, or the set of payoff functions;

(c) *single-period* (one-shot, one-stage) or *multiple-period* (many-phases), known as **supergames**;

(d) *two-person, few-person,* or *n-person,* the last being more difficult to handle;

(e) *constant-sum* (zero-sum) or *non-constant-sum* (non-zero-sum), distinctions that involve the closed or relatively open nature of the game.

The typical case of games that can be shown to have a unique solution (a so-called Nash equilibrium), and, therefore, to have both rigor and reasonable applicability, is that of *two-person, constant-sum, single-period, noncooperative games, with complete information*. None of the other categories admit of unique solutions; for example, even two-person nonconstant games, such as escalation and inspection involved in nuclear weapons or disarmament policy, are too dynamic to offer any firm solution, because the "max-min" strategy leads to unreasonable results. In general, the farther away one gets from the simplest model (say, the traditional PD game), the more dynamic and insoluble the games become. Some categories admit a variety of special solutions, usually under some restrictive assumptions. Other more complicated varieties have no solutions whatsoever and offer only limited insights as to their complexity. Various categories of supergames with time dependence and the set of **differential games** are too complex, uncertain, and without solutions to be helpful as models of mapping complex interdependencies in the real world. Caveat emptor!

Besides the PD game, the other most important category of games is that referring to oligopoly markets: bilateral monopoly, duopoly, noncooperative or quasi-cooperative oligopoly, auctions and bidding. Bilateral monopoly (Bartos 1967; Shubik 1975, 1982; cf. Elster 1985; Scharpf 1988) is a two-person game in which each agent controls a distinct variable, as in the case of collective bargaining between management and labor representatives where management controls the means of production (investments) and, thus, employment rates, while labor controls labor productivity and wage levels (the rate of profit), by possible unilateral action (firing in the case of management, striking in the case of labor). Clearly, this case has important applications in sociology and we will discuss it further. In contrast, noncooperative or quasi-cooperative oligopolies, as non-constant-sum games, do not provide unique game-theoretical solutions and can be handled better in other ways, such as by a theory of "signaling" and "induced role structures."

The more interesting cases of time-dependent supergames and differential games (Friedman 1986; Krass and Hammondeh 1981; Lancaster 1973; Shubik 1982) present us with a paradox: while these games reflect much better the conditions in the real world, because of their incorporated complexity and informational uncertainty, they lose the rigor of standard game-theoretical constructs and offer no determinate solution; in short, they do not resolve our problems. Game theory, therefore, appears very robust when one has in mind the basic formalism of the PD game and that of the bilateral monopoly, but has much less analytical and predictive power in these other complicated situations. For the purpose of understanding the complexities of the structuration process it is, of course, better to sacrifice formalist rigor for realistic depiction.

Olson's collective action game

The PD-like standard model has been extended in some other interesting directions. Imagine that, instead of two persons, the game is played by each one of us in a two-player situation in which any individual is A and all other anonymous individuals taken together as "others" are B. A PD game emerges that addresses the problem of "the logic of collective action" as Mancur Olson (1965, 1982, 1986), the originating force in this program, has presented and analyzed it. Under what assumptions would one join a group seeking the production of collective goods using rational choice and game theoretical criteria? In a typical PD matrix the dichotomous coordinates will become A and Others on one side, and a cost-benefit estimate of Joining and Not Joining, on the other. In the logic of collective action the rational outcome is calculated by reference to three variables: 1) the *gain from cooperation* that one would expect by joining an interest-based group; 2) the *gain from free riding,* that is, the gain that will accrue to A by the successful formation and functioning of a collective agency even though A did not participate in it and so had no costs of participation; and 3) the *loss from unilateralism,* that is, the costs that A will have to pay to join such a group early while most others will not join. The primary assumption in this logic of collective action is that, since collective goods are indivisible or unrestricted (e.g., getting the benefits from a collective bargaining agreement though one has not joined the bargaining union), a "free rider" is the optimally rational individual. As Olson writes: "A lobbying organization, or indeed a labor union or any other organization, working in the interest of a large group of firms or workers in some industry, would get no assistance from the rational, self-interested individuals in that industry" (1965:11). Following this, one is forced to assert that participation in a small group may be feasible but participation in any large group is irrational from the individual point of view. Where the group is large and the rewards from possible organization are public (i.e., collective goods) and cannot be restricted to particular individuals, the group is latent and likely to remain unorganized unless external force or other social or cultural incentives become the main parameters for such participation. Continuing the argument, in an apparent reference to Marxism, Olson argues that "class-oriented action will not occur if the individuals that make up a class act rationally" (1965:105). Notice also that, as a byproduct of the theory, one must accept that small groups have more power than larger ones because the former can easily organize and can act in unison while very large groups cannot. This leads to a straightforward oligarchical/ elitist theory of power and of interest groups; and indeed in his new work, *Rise and Decline of Nations*, Olson claims that the decline of nations is primarily due to the long-term accumulation of "distributional coalitions" of an obvious oligarchical nature that has led to pronounced inefficiencies; as he puts it "the longer a state has been settled and the longer the time it has had to accumulate special-interest groups, the slower its rate of growth" (1982:97). We shall return to critically evaluate Olson's and related arguments such as those of Hechter (1983, 1987). At this point we should note only that the further developments of game theory in the direction of **supergames,** structural time-dependent games, **differential games, oceanic** games, **two-level games, metagames,** and so on,[7] have weakened considerably Olson's position.

Arrow's work

A different line of development illustrating the partial discontinuity between individual and collective phenomena has been pursued by Arrow and a host of other analysts in the area of public choice theory. Historically, the analysis of the price system and the achievement of the competitive equilibrium in the markets has been a central concern of economists. Arrow (Arrow and Debreu 1954) was among the first to define "general equilibrium" from a game-theoretical point of view. However, Arrow is better known for his work on the production of collective goods, from a different angle than that of Olson, but with the same issue at heart: the disjunction between individual and public interests and choice. Since his seminal 1951 work Arrow has demonstrated that aggregations of individual choices are notoriously thorny and do not lead to optimal public choice. The starting point in Arrow's analysis is that market and other related systems, such as political voting markets, produce a joint result for many people, that is, a market price equilibrium or a majority rule. The system is presumed to start with

---

[7] For the definitions of complex games in the Glossary I have used the resources provided in the works cited in the previous note as well as: Axelrod 1984; Elster 1986b, 1989b; Lancaster 1973; Sen 1970a; Taylor 1976, 1982, 1987; and others.

many individual preferences (or better, individual preference schedules rankings) and to produce out of them one social preference or social preference ranking. This is what Arrow calls a "social choice function." Positing some elementary conditions derived from rational choice theory (rationality, Paretian aggregation, independence of irrelevant alternatives, nondictatorship) Arrow proved mathematically that no social function fulfilling these conditions could guarantee satisfactory results when there are more than two individuals in the society and more than two alternatives to choose from (Arrow 1959; Dyke 1979; Shubik 1982; among many others). The importance of this work has not received proper recognition in traditional social theory, especially among the versions of methodological individualism we have already discussed; yet, by demonstrating the impossibility of aggregating individual choices and preferences into a collective rational form, it defeats the more optimistic liberal arguments for a possible smooth transition from microchoices to macroprocesses via aggregation.

The message, however, has not been lost altogether; it has persuaded scholars to look for more discontinuous, although still quasideterministic, "constructionist" models of emergent structure. Several analysts, whose work we shall briefly describe below, working within the broad framework of game theory, have focused their attention on the "unintended consequences" and other complications of "bounded" rational action and have attempted to describe, if not fully explain, the particular ways in which social structural phenomena come about. Boudon decided to use the "logic of social action" to elucidate the "perverted" effects of systems of interdependence. Elster, though still holding to a seemingly hard methodological individualist point of view, embarked on a program of redescribing Marxism in game-theoretical terms. Schelling looked for algorithms that decipher the messy complexities of microstructures in a variety of everyday settings. All three have paid attention to the gray area beyond the consciously intended and monitored results of rational choice.

Boudon

Boudon begins his sociological analysis by insisting that sociology is the science of "non-logical actions" and of "social determinants." He predictably pays tribute to the Durkheimian tradition and gives special attention to the Paretian call for a proper analysis of the "logic of non-logical actions" (1981a, which I quote below). Boudon rejects the model of *homo economicus* and, with Dahrendorf, postulates that sociological analysis must proceed from a properly constructed model of a homo sociologicus; by which Boudon means a model that pays due attention to the constraining role of the social and physical environment, which helps to "determine two essential elements of the field in which the social agent is situated, namely the universe of choices offered to the agent and the value of the objectives that he is inclined to set himself" (1981a:154). Contrary to traditional rational choice theory Boudon argues that, "confronted with a choice, homo sociologicus can, in certain cases, do, not what he prefers, but what habit, internalized values and, more generally, diverse ethical, cognitive and gestural conditionings, force him to do" (ibid.:156). Moreover, contrary to the classical economic model which "supposes that, without exception, the notion of the best possible choice is defined," the model of homo sociologicus incorporates the fact that "numerous situations, by their very structure, are ambiguous. I mean that the notion of the best choice is badly defined here" (158), especially in the many cases in which the pursuit of possible short-term advantages invites long-term risks and discontent. Too, the economic model of rational action "treats the agent's preferences as states of affairs that one can either establish or deduce from an elementary anthropology" (160) as fixed preferences unaffected by historicosocial changes; on the other hand, the essential characteristic of the sociological tradition is the attempt "to make preferences internal to society" (160) by treating both "the objectives and preferences of the actors as variables partly dependent upon the environment and on the position of actors in the environment" (160). Finally, Boudon adds to this list of differences the sociological emphasis on the phenomena of pseudorationality or rationalization and the recognition that certain categories of action are explainable not by rational choice but in the normative context of "roles."

Given the above and the recognition of the long-run uncertainties of behavior and of the interdependencies of social actions, as evidenced even by the simplest PD game, Boudon argues that in most cases "the very notion of logical action would appear either to dissolve totally or to have the value of a simple limiting case" (163). The goal of modern microsociology, as he sees it, is to analyze the diverse classes of behavior and situations in order to understand the mechanisms by which unanticipated and perverse effects and structures are produced. This is the main reason for Boudon's insistence that a methodological individualist approach is required: he means, if I understand him correctly, MI in the most literal, weakest, sense, as a purely methodological choice for building up by the appropriate analysis and classification of micrologics of composition the complex "object" of social structure. On the other hand, Boudon understands that social actions, whose outcome is any macrosociological phenomenon, are themselves the outcome of the social environment of the actors, which is the outcome of macrosociological variables (1981a, 1987). It is obvious that Boudon does not follow the epistemological and psychological extensions of methodological individualism since he sees a causal loop where other, more extreme MIs see only a causal line from the individual to the social. I sense that Boudon, like many other theorists since the late 1960s, realizes the necessity of codetermination between action and structure but lacks – as much as Giddens (1984), Hernes (1976), Wippler and Lindenberg (1987), and a host of others – the proper analytical framework (that of heterarchy theory, as we shall see) to handle the problem. Nonetheless, he is very clear on the limited rationality of a creature that is partly homo economicus and partly homo sociologicus and in many passages in his work he argues in ways similar to those of Simon (1978), March (1978), and Williamson (1975).

Assuming the purposive character of action within the parameters of limited rationality, Boudon focuses on the varieties of systems of interaction within which social action is embedded and shaped. He distinguishes two categories of systems of interaction: functional (role-based systems involving "actors") and interdependent (non-role-based systems involving "agents") and, within the latter, two subcategories: systems of direct interdependence (face-to-face or otherwise direct strategic interactions) and systems of indirect interdependence (without purposive or, at least, accountable interaction, though still based on purposive individual action). Examples of functional systems are the customer–cashier, teacher–student, or mother–daughter interactions. Systems of direct interdependence, where the strategic element is paramount, are collective bargaining, state confrontations in war or peace, and other general PD situations. Examples of systems of indirect interdependence, which are more complex, include traffic jams, waiting queues, and other proximal systems, as well as systems at a distance, such as Marx's capitalists or de Tocqueville's landowners (1981a, 1981b, 1977). Boudon correctly perceives that functional systems are less strategic and, as I interpret him, cannot be modeled by game-theoretical schemes given the existence of a strong homo sociologicus mode of action. So, primarily, his project is to look at different examples provided in the social science literature and analyze them in game-theoretical, quasi-game-theoretical, or similar micro–macro compositionist terms, to the extent that this is feasible.

In other ways, though, Boudon's work remains somewhat tentative and analytically undeveloped. No convincing distinction is offered in it between game-theoretical, quasi-game-theoretical, and non-game-theoretical structural mechanisms. There is also a confusion inherent in many of his examples: like Blau, Boudon seems to conflate structural effects with structural mechanisms (for the resolution of this thorny problem see Chapters 12–14), a conflation that threatens his constructionist/compositionist program and weakens the import of his other, properly structural, cases. And there is also the circularism of micro-to-macro and macro-to-micro equivocations that marks all similar efforts of dualisms. All this being said, however, I find Boudon's strategy exciting in its attempt to do what molecular biology did to traditional systematic biology – not that it can reduce all explanations or the total explanation of social structure to microstructuring processes – but it can at least push the compositionist/constructionist program to its limit, providing on the way numerous insights and logical mechanisms for understanding the compositional continuities as well as discontinuities of structural emergence and for disclosing the gaps and insurmountable problems that this program will necessarily come across. I believe Boudon's theoretical research program is robust and progressive (even though he has not provided as yet a coherent presentation of the micrologics of structuration) and the general game-theoretical approach may well be proved to be the most exciting theoretical mistake in the social sciences (to borrow Haugeland's [1981] felicitous expression in reference to computationist cognitive science).

Schelling

Thomas Schelling is a highly respected social and policy scientist who, over the years, has elaborated a number of important social issues in terms parallel to those of Boudon, and he deserves greater attention on the part of theoretical sociologists. Schelling has argued that the most significant cases of behavior are those of contingent behavior, that is, behavior that depends on what others are doing usually within the same delimited phase space or topology. Since market economics are mainly concerned with voluntary exchanges while reality tells us that most contingent systems of interaction are mixed markets and authority systems (compare White's work on interfaces cited above), the economic models of action and exchange are only a subcategory of interaction systems and, indeed, usually model-like limit cases at that. Schelling seems to be thinking along lines similar to those of Kenneth Boulding (1978, 1981), who spoke of three "social organizers": threat, exchange, and trust. This is a point that we will explore fully in the last part of this book.

Schelling is a realist who has no great sympathy for highly idealized and, thus, unrealistic abstractions. For example, rational choice theorists would have us believe that in any case of exchange hyperrationality reigns supreme; Schelling posits that, in reality, even within the economic institutional order, the existence of "contrived" (for example, copyright) and "partial" (for example, neighborhood housing) markets indicate the near impossibility of using rational action and perfect market equilibrium models as realistic simulacra of the processes taking place in the social world (1971, 1978). Externalities (in my classification: interactional, social-institutional, political-economic, and topological) impinge on social action to make it contingent, rational in a limited sense only, and ensuing in complex entanglements. Furthermore, patterns and structures, or externalities, "impose a certain discipline on the variables, reducing the 'degrees of freedom' that related activities can enjoy" (1978:73). As a result, various microstructural systems (in Boudon's vocabulary, systems of interactional interdependence) emerge from such entanglements:[8]

- closed systems (circulating),
- semi-closed systems (forming a "transition matrix"),
- semi-open systems (such as turnstiles, bottlenecks, reservoirs, alternating systems), or
- fully open systems.

Presumably each of these categories of systems obeys different logical mechanisms of structuration (composition and articulation).

Schelling thinks of game theory as a useful tool in appropriate circumstances, not as a panacea or as "an apotheosis of rationality" (1984). He sees game theory as "vicarious problem-solving" and as showing the contradictions between individual and collective rationality. He acknowledges the point made by Rapaport "that a pair of cold-blooded rational individuals will (in these situations) come off worse than a pair of people both of whom are too obtuse to perceive their own incentives or two people both bound in conscience to behave the way they would like to be behaved toward."[9] He likes, however, game theory's contribution to what he considers a more general model of "strategic analysis" resting on the recognition of the multiple interdependence of decisions of a "small number of interacting decision units." This strategic analysis refers to situations or tactics, not personalities; it is "about the structure of incentives, of information and communication, the choices available, and the tactics that can be employed" (see Schelling, 1984:213–42). It is this emphasis on structured situations and the micrologics inscribed in them that make Schelling's program an important variant of constructionism.

---

[8] Cf. Boudon's definition of society as "complex entanglements of systems of interaction" (1981a:56) – a beautiful "orienting statement."

[9] Schelling 1984:209; Shubik 1982:294, who agrees on this point; see further Shubik ibid.:368. See further the critiques of Sen in his 1970a and b, 1977, 1978, 1982; and in Elster 1986b.

As I read Schelling's suggestive distinctions, I cannot help thinking that the goal of analysis should be to classify and articulate the logical operators at work in such types of interaction systems and "situations," as the latter are found in specific social environments (see the Appendix). These operators may possibly explain the various processes of reinforced polarization, chain reactions, exaggerated perceptions, lagged responses, and organized efforts that take place within the trajectory of a complex, situated interaction system, that is, a system entangled with externalities. In such instances, the intervention of nonlinear processes and of "self-enforcing conventions" (to use Coleman's expression) produces a condition in which the "systemic consequences of individual behaviors ... are not immediately and intuitively transparent even though the motivations have been postulated and the population characteristics specified" (Schelling 1978:182–3; the statement is almost identical to comments by Prigogine et al. cited earlier in Chapter 2). Hence, Schelling does not accept the dogma of smooth market aggregation and equilibrium reaching; he thinks, in the manner of Arrow, that "all the situations in which equilibria [have been] achieved by unconcerted or undisciplined action are inefficient – the situations in which everybody could be better off, or some collective total could be made larger [may] come about by concerted or disciplined or organized or regulated or centralized decisions."[10] For all these reasons, I submit that Schelling clearly argues on behalf of a strategy of "methodological constructionism," proposing to analyze the various mechanisms of structuration at the level of situated interaction systems in order to possibly arrive at a more global understanding of social structure. In doing so, he has offered us a considerable number of structuring mechanisms or micrologics, such as those of "tipping," "flows," "matching," cellular automata-like transitions, and so on (see the Appendix).

Elster

When examining the work of Jon Elster, it might be better off to follow what he does rather than what he says.[11] Elster's excessive zeal to cham-

---

[10] Schelling 1978:182–3, 225, where he also discusses the Multi-Prisoner Dilemma as a "truncated dual equilibrium." Shubik (1982:122–4) takes a position against Arrow's (1963:106) argument that actions are taken by society to remedy the effects of PD situations. Coleman (1988:117) seems to accept Arrow's view.

[11] Elster, most of the time, argues strongly on behalf of the mainstream model of rational choice/game theory, but modifies the model considerably in respect to several assumptions when discussing concrete cases. In 1989a he comes finally to recognize the inability of the model to explain the emergence of both social norms and non-(hyper) rational behavior.

pion the cause of methodological individualism should not disallow us to appreciate his real contributions to the constructionist logic. To my mind he follows still another parallel path to those of Boudon and Schelling, primarily investigating the implications of recasting the Marxist theory into a game-theoretical framework; hence Elster, together with the economist John Roemer and other sympathetic scholars, have introduced a new version of Marxist theory under the name of "game-theoretical" or "analytical Marxism" (Elster 1985; Roemer 1986 for a summation). Elster appeared forcefully on the theoretical scene with the introduction of his two books, *Logic and Society* (1978) and *Ulysses and the Sirens* (1979), in which he attempted to demonstrate, in the first, some basic social and mental contradictions and, in the second, the intentional and causal character of explanation in the human sciences as against the prevailing functional explanations in biology. Elster insisted that people adapt to their social and physical environment intentionally with a "generalized capacity for global maximization that applies even to qualitative new situations" (1979), since in the case of humans one finds a "strategic environment" affording the actors variable courses of action.

Starting from this basis of intentional action theory Elster then proceeded to accept the general premises of rational choice theory properly modified to serve as analytical tool for the understanding of social and mental contradictions. Although rhetorical at times and seemingly contradictory, Elster works with the following rather moderate premises:

(1) people are rational enough to pursue rational ends, as rational choice or game-theoretical framework postulates, although it is true that rationality is imperfect (1979:36; 1985);

(2) individuals possess a given "preference structure" although in the explanatory model we must accommodate sociohistorical processes that change preference, i.e., processes of "endogenous preference production" (1986b:193; 1985:116);

(3) in their day-to-day actions and interactions people apply a strategic (technical, formal, logical) calculus given that structural constraints do not completely determine the whole range of their choices (1985:9–10); and

(4) that this strategic calculus is primarily, although not exclusively, motivated by selfish considerations (1979:1; 1985:9).

To these premises Elster adds the realistic assessment already provided by Sen that, as against the PD's presumption of the independence of choice for each actor, social life manifests the multiple interdependence of actions.[12] Now, if the above premises are operative, then what emerges is a set of complex interdependencies (cf. Elster 1986b) with, as I believe, quasi-open dynamics, somewhat akin to dialectic. On the best reading of his work, that is what I believe Elster is after.

Anyone familiar with the PD game, its general criticisms and the associated criticisms of Olson's work (by Sen, Barry, Hardin, Taylor and others) will notice that Elster, however unhappily, must subscribe to the critical attitude toward the basic PD for at least two fundamental reasons – because of its assumption of the independence of actors' choices, and because of its closure as a one-shot game. We have briefly talked about the former criticism, but the latter must be presented as well. Elster, as others before him (Axelrod 1984; Axelrod and Hamilton 1981; Boulding 1978; Lancaster 1973; Sen 1967; Taylor 1976, 1982, 1987), has partially countered Olson's conclusions on the infeasibility of collective action on the grounds that, if one allows for the iteration of the PD game (i.e., transforming it into a supergame), cooperation will emerge as the dominant strategy due to the conditions of nearly-perfect information that the actors will develop stochastically relative to each other. (This is Sen's "assurance game," which would mean that as Rousseau had predicted, under an enlightened socialism, with perfect information, individuals would opt for "universal cooperation" over the "free rider" solution.) Even short of that, according to Elster, organizational leadership, iterative experience, and structural constraints may produce a weaker form of "conditional altruism" of the solidaristic variety with more or less similar results (1985:361–4; 1986a:12–13).

Elster's theoretical goal is to see to what extent the understanding of the extended game-theoretical interdependencies can lead to a partial reinvigoration of Marxist theory, so as to permit it to explain much better the social contradictions of "counterfinality" (by which he means the "fetishism" and "false naturalization" of social reality and the fallacy of composition) and of "suboptimality" (by which he means the inefficient social performance of the selfish, free-market, rational choice). In that direction Elster's work has contributed many promising insights, a plethora of good examples, and some very sharp analyses, though not a complete or transparent constructionist explanatory model.

What is to be done?

A tentative answer, derived from the work of the thinkers we have just reviewed as well as the previously presented research programs, would

---

[12] Elster (1985:10) cites four forms of interdependence between actors: one's reward on the rewards of others; one's reward on the choices of others; one's choice on the choices of others; and one's preferences on the actions of others.

be that we need, first, a comprehensive statement about the proper assumptions of rationality and social action and, second, a progressive spelling out, in terms of various analytical mechanisms, of the step-wise transition from simple strategic interactions and interdependencies to more complex interdependent systems and their higher-order entanglements. All of the scholars discussed in this chapter have contributed significantly to this goal; drawing on their work, we may attempt to systematize their assumptions and findings and push further the constructionist/compositionist program.

Let us begin with the model of "strategic social action" implied by all, which is at the heart of the constructionist program. Boudon, incorrectly I believe, praises too much the model of homo sociologicus. The Dahrendorfian concept is not immune to misarticulation and, for any refreshing view on the prospects of the homo sociologicus (such as Touraine's), there are other versions which cannot be accepted without some trepidation (the arguably misunderstood Parsonian model or the caricature presented by Wrong [1961] in his conception of the "over-socialized man"). Boudon has used the notion to his advantage, but without realizing the disservice done to clarity by the explicit ambiguity and implicit loadedness of its meaning. I think it appropriate to make the following distinctions, which go along with what I take Boudon, Schelling and Elster to say:

(1) The model of homo economicus implies perfect procedural rationality, fixity of preferences, independence of choices, and no import of power differentials. We have seen that all of these assumptions are to a large extent unrealistic.

(2) The model of homo sociologicus in its traditional form involves a normative view of social action; that is, implies a substantivist concession of an extremely limited individual rationality more or less thoroughly constrained by cultural norms, usually long-run social determination of preferences, significant overdetermination of choices, and various conceptualizations of power differentials. This will not do because "agency" has been squeezed out of the explanation altogether, as in the case of extreme structuralism and structural functionalism.

(3) A more realistic model – that is, a model that would seem to apply in most instances, allowing the other two models a supplementary role – could be constructed, a model of *pragmatic-strategic social action*. It would be based on a significantly modified set of assumptions related to the baseline rational choice or game theory. The new assumptions of this model would be:

(A) Bounded, imperfect, limited rationality given the uncertainty of the environment, the imperfect knowledge that agents have about the long term, and the indeterminacies produced by social inter-dependencies.

(B) Preferences that are species-specific as well as sociohistorical. An endogenous, pragmatic preference formation model is required that can explain the sociohistorical change of preferences and their differential politico-economic and cultural distribution. (Such a promising model has been suggested by Bourdieu [1977, 1980, 1984, 1985, 1986b, 1988].)

(C) In the cascading complexity of systems of interdependent interaction the agents usually lose track and cannot easily monitor the effects of their actions. The entanglement of systems of interaction with (social-institutional, politico-economic, and topological) externalities warrants the view that, although reference to pragmatic-strategic social action is necessary, it has no sufficient explanatory power in itself to properly explain the further emerging structural complexities. In lieu of a more appropriate model of pragmatic-strategic social action, a weakened form of methodological individualism (MMI), as a substrate of constructionism, could be tolerated only on methodological grounds so that the process of disentangling complexity may start from a presumed commonsensical point.

Armed with this pragmatic-strategic social action model, a constructionist (because the above represents the assorted interests of the constructionist program) may then proceed to describe the compositional process and explain the operating mechanisms that bring about more and more complex structures. This project involves a three-pronged attack.

First, one must move from the consideration of simple systems of strategic interaction to more complex systems. This will involve a systematic description, analysis, and classification of all micrologics implicated as one moves beyond the simple interactional systems, an area already partially explored by Schelling and Boudon.

Second, one must further investigate the mechanisms of emergence of corporate and collective actors, particularly in view of the many theoretical and empirical criticisms which have accumulated against Olson's baseline PD model. A realistic redescription of this field of possibilities would start from the new assumptions of pragmatic-strategic social action cited above.

Finally, one needs to investigate thoroughly the more complex mechanisms involved in later phases of composition. Indeed, beyond the interactional interdependencies it is likely that new combinatorial problems, nonlinearities and selective strange loops, possibly even chaos, will appear in the higher orders. We shall address these issues in the following chapters.

7 Complex systems of interaction

The micrologics we have discussed in the previous chapter are, in many respects, still quite simple, notwithstanding their relatively different degrees of complexity. On the other hand, the compositionist/constructionist logic must be able to demonstrate the emergence or construction of more and more complex, higher-level systems of structured interaction. Or, to wear our critical-evaluative hat, it is here that we find a telling weakness of most of the compositionist programs – their basic inability to spell out systematically the transition, translation, or aggregation rules or mechanisms leading to these more complex systems. It will be helpful to review some examples from the relevant microsociological literature.

The first example comes from structural balance theory and its extensions and modifications in the course of the formal study of clique and group formation (for a summation see Leik and Meeker 1975). The initial formalization of Heider's structural balance theory demonstrated that, if the possible relations in a pair of interactants were hypothesized to be *two* (like and agree; dislike and disagree), then, with the insertion of a third person into the relationship, *eight* possible triads were derived, of which only four were considered balanced (Heider 1958). In the further modifications of the theory's assumptions *sixteen* such triads were formally derived, of which eight or nine were considered balanced. Now imagine the results of the movement from three-person to many-person relations! We will be obliged to come to terms with unlimited open possibilities. For even when beginning with simple triads we encounter (a) a combinatorial explosion, which makes the formal constructionist aggregation procedure unmanageable and prohibitively costly; and (b) a discontinuity between formal possibilities, which include the so-called forbidden triads, and pragmatic realities, which presume the application of "constraints" on the formal possibility space, as we have said in the first part of this book. What we need, instead, is a hierarchy of constraining mechanisms, structuring the social space upward.[1] The constructionist must demonstrate step-by-step the transition from simple to complex systems of interaction and to more entangled formations of social structure – he cannot hide behind the et cetera clause.

[1] On this see also the instructive case of protein folding, which presents an extremely complicated combinatorial problem: Kolata 1986; Richards et al. 1986.

126

Consider, too, the case of exchange theory. As we have seen earlier, there has been a significant transition in this perspective from its older focus on interpersonal or dyadic behavioral exchanges (Homans 1974; Emerson 1972a) to the more recent focus on exchange networks (Cook, 1977, 1982; Cook et al. 1983; Emerson 1972b, 1976, 1981; Mardsen 1983; and others). Admittedly, this transition constitutes a "progressive problemshift" in the Lakatosian sense; but, somewhat contrary to Emerson's thought, it marks a discontinuity from the psychological to the sociological conception of exchange, and demonstrates the importance of *structural location, access to goods,* and therefore also of *differential power.* Now, how best to proceed to the second order aggregation of exchange networks into a higher structural entity? Given the *dis*continuities involved and the general problem of "embeddedness" eloquently presented by Granovetter (1985), no rules or detailed mechanisms of further aggregation, or admissible higher structure composition seem possible from the present version of the theory. The initial efforts of Homans (1974) and Blau (1964) (who was belatedly praised by Jonathan Turner [1986b]) to proceed from exchange principles to large-scale institutionalization and organization are rather sketchy and do not seem able to provide the needed detailed mechanisms of structural emergence without very significant amendations.

But the limitations of the constructionist program is not restricted to these two cases only. Several other efforts have also met with rather limited success. Boudon, for example, analyzing the conflict between England and Germany on the eve of World War I, suggested that the two players were engaged not in one but in *two games at the same time* – a more complex and unstable structure called by Boudon a "structure of structures" (an instance of a "supergame").[2] As elegant as this construction is, it is still limited in scope and complexity and cannot be helpful in conceptualizing the macrostructural levels.

More promising was the effort of mathematical sociologists Harrison White and students to aggregate network data using blockmodeling techniques. It now looks as if this work may have reached its limit; nevertheless, it has contributed greatly to our understanding of the categorial composition of larger groups (quasi-groups, Marxist "groups-in-themselves," or Olsonian "latent groups"). Redirecting our attention particularly to the sociological dynamics of markets in general (cf. Chapter 6) as well as the applicability of principles of cascading net-

[2] Boudon (1981a:24–32) describes the game between England and Germany as a dual Prisoner Dilemma and Chicken Game, played on two boards. But see also the more complicated cases presented by Scharpf (1988) and Putnam and Bayne (1984). For other notions of supergames see Friedman (1986), Krass and Hammondeh (1981), Shubik (1982).

works is very promising, and the payoff is beginning. I will discuss in later chapters and the Appendix how one can make use of the notions of firm–market "interfaces" and of the "cascade principle" to elucidate certain properties of heterarchies.

In brief, the burden of proof that there are further viable ways of aggregating or structurally constructing upward rests on the shoulders of the proponents of constructionism/compositionism. Despite the exciting but limited steps taken in the desired direction, much more is required to demonstrate the success of these programs without reservation.

What is required?

The answer is not simple; but I am going to offer a sketch of some basic issues that need to be investigated and resolved in future elaborations of constructionist/compositionist research programs:

In the case of general exchange theory: One needs a detailed examination of the emergence of institutional orders (organizations, practices, institutional algorithms, social norms, institutionalized instruments; for these see below) and the specific ways in which these orders are implicated in the production and change of macrostructures. The early efforts by Homans (1974) and/or Blau (1964) may provide the initial analytical framework, to be properly amended by detailed elaboration. Coleman's ideas of institutional emergence, Arrow's and Hirschman's Keynesian views of institution-building at the crossroads of failed markets, parts of Chandler's and Williamson's neo-institutional model of organizational hierarchies, and so on, may be used to beef up and detail this constructionist-emergent process. We will call this the *neo-institutional line* of compositionism.

In the case of the previously formal microstructuralist research program: The work should move away from purely formal considerations of triads, cliques, and free-forming groups, where no attention is paid to the **modalities** of relatedness, and toward the detailed study of such modalities and ensuing modal connectivities. Laumann's (1979) initial ideas on modalities implicated in networks could be a good starting point for further research. It is time we abandon the abstract possibilities in favor of the richness of the concrete local phenomenologies.[3] For instance, in the case of the diachronic production of "markets," of

---

[3] This is the area in which the recent ethnomethodological work (Garfinkel 1986, 1988; Garfinkel, Lynch, and Livingston 1981; Lynch 1985) has advanced considerable new insights. Cf. Latour 1987.

interest to all historical sociologists, one may focus on the analytical detail of emergent forms of productive or auxiliary relations, say, of the initial, post–guild-based economies. Or, one may do similar work on recently produced markets such as those of commodities and financial instruments, or the more informal markets of baseball cards, commemorative plates, or prints. The goal must be the detailed explanation of the processes of upward structuration by a combination of formal rules, preferred institutionalized practices, or opportunistic strategies, the latter two illuminating the bifurcation points of transition from the possible to the pragmatically emergent. What sort of connectivities account for the emergence of such relational markets? Knowledge of the modality of connection as much as of the form of connection is indispensable. Let us call this the *structural-phenomenological line* of compositionism.

In the case of exchange networks: The workup until now has been successful in demonstrating the microstructural constraints on exchange – network location, access to resources, differential power of positions – but once this phase is completed,[4] the research program faces the tough task of addressing the issue of *network aggregation* or *concatenation,* admittedly with little visible chance of success. However, there are a few avenues of worthwhile exploration: "Resource access" is an important **modal** characterization of the substantive value of a position and should be used together with other such modalities. The notion of "incomparable hierarchies of values" or "domains," introduced by Emerson in his posthumously published essay (1987), should persuade others to stay away from the economistic models of fixed preference. Marsden's (1983) incorporation of "unequal exchange" conditions into the exchange networks framework should be further developed and become standard in future studies. An effort should also be made to go beyond the individual experimental results and seek confirmation in historical materials indicative of group exchange networks, such as those between occupational categories or more structural class-fractions, along lines pursued by current historical sociologists (Aminzade, Calhoun, Hanagan, and others, cited below). I fail to see any other prospects for a next-step construction to the level of macrostructures – for the time being research in exchange networks remains the only experimentalist line of compositionism.

----

[4] Once this phase of power-dependency is completed the program must face the thorny issue of large-scale externalities, especially of the politico-economic variety. It should move beyond the good initial efforts of Marsden (1983) and Molm (1987).

In the case of network theory proper: Here the initial foundational work using graph theoretical and matrix algebra modeling tools has been surpassed by the progressive problem-shift from notions of interpersonal equivalence to those of structural equivalence proper decisively captured by the blockmodeling technique. This approach has opened the door to a fruitful appreciation of categories as "structural groupings," or quasi-groups, to which we will refer again in the last part of this book. Yet, the blockmodeling technique found no further stepwise application within the core of the research program or in affine domains. Currently, the positive heuristic of the program has shifted (a) to the promising analysis of markets (Burt 1988; Eccles and White 1986, 1988; White 1981a and b, 1985, 1988; and others) and (b) to the exploration of the possible applications of the mathematical notion of "cascades" to the intuitively understood problem of the cascading of social networks (Boorman and Levitt 1980a and b, 1987). Initial work on cascades has focused on applications in population genetics and policy issues; but a serious effort to apply cascade principles to network aggregation problems in mainstream sociology remains to be made. Nonetheless, this remains an exciting possibility in the ongoing development of this second area of the network research program. Let us call this the *mathematical line* of constructionism/compositionism.

In the case of topologically based microstructural analysis: Along the lines of research initiated by Schelling, Boudon, White, and others, one would expect a movement away from the local structures (jams, queues, microneighborhood transitions, and so on) toward the analysis of larger-scale structural ecologies. It would be profitable for the work here to move (a) in the direction of the inclusion of not only the topological but all varieties of "externalities" to the interaction systems, and (b) toward second- and third-order entangled systems; what is needed is some sort of analytical equipment or mechanism similar to the notion of interfaces introduced by White in his studies of markets. Progress is likely to come from the marriage of topologically based structural microsystems to the program on the "population ecology of organizations" (Aldrich 1975, 1979; Aldrich and Marsden 1988; Aldrich and Pfeffer 1976; Freeman and Hannan 1983; Hannan and Freeman 1977; Lauman et al. 1978; Pfeffer 1982), which has been stuck for lack of such a properly understood connection downward. Let us call this the *neo-ecological line* of compositionism.

In the case of the game-theoretical line of compositionism: This appears to be one of the dominant research programs in constructionist/

compositionist logics, and therefore its prospects warrant close examination. Most other constructionist programs appear to imply the foundational role of rational choice theory and have had explicit or implicit partial renditions in game-theoretical terms. This has been recognized by Arrow, Boudon, Coleman, Schelling, followers of Walrasian general equilibrium models, neo-institutionalists, and so on. We indicated earlier the limitations of the game-theoretical model in its elementary forms – the success of the research program utilizing the game-theoretical model rests on the feasibility of its extension and application in the direction of larger and higher structures, and for this several important transitions in scope and complexity are needed, in order to give rise to a "constructionist jump" to a new level of structural constitution and, thus, also of analysis. These transitions must presumably involve:

(1) A move from atomistic or individual actors to corporate and collective actors, based on a pragmatic theory of collective action.

(2) A move from one-person action systems and two-person interaction systems to systems with many actors – corporate and collective actors.

(3) A move beyond the consideration of simple externalities (for example, interactional interdependence) to that of complex and compounded externalities.

(4) A move from simple systems of interaction to "structures of structures," in Boudon's example, and then to entangled systems of such primary or secondary systems of interaction.

(5) At the intersection of the four above, a move from local, interactional systems to global, heterarchical and/or hierarchical systems and their complex dynamics, the recognition of which will certainly get us away from compositionist logics.

In the following we will examine in some detail what is involved in each of these transitions.

From individual to corporate and collective actors

There are three issues of importance here: (a) the emergence of institutions; (b) the emergence of corporate actors; and (c) the emergence of collective actors. All of these are rationally impossible in game-theoretical terms, though they may be explainable in terms of transaction-cost, impaired, or inefficient market theories, as well as in an array of other social science explanations. Recognition of corporate and collective actors may, in fact, be the death sentence for a rigorous game-theoretical strategy, so often it is resisted strongly. We investigate below several arguments and cases supporting the emergence of such corporate and collective actors.

Institutional emergence

As we have seen previously, one of the phenomena that appear to be emergent is that of institutionalization, defined in the context of a constructionist move from micro- to macrophenomena as: (a) a smooth transition from individual practices, interactions, and exchanges to institutional patterns of behavior (Berger, Blumer, Homans, and Luckmann, Schutz, among others), or (b) a discontinuous transition from the failing, imperfect, or transaction and information costs-plagued marketlike aggregation of presumed individual rational actions to organized institutional forms or practices which provide more efficiency, lower transaction costs, and better management for the same private or collective product (Arrow, Coleman, Levi, North, Oberschall, Oberschall and Leifer, Roth, Schelling among others). It is the second approach that at present seems to be dominant. Nevertheless, here too we find competing views focusing on transaction costs, game-theoretical solutions, general efficiency, public good production, political or economic entrepreneurship, or some combination of these.

An interesting example of the application of transaction cost analysis to explain institutional emergence is offered by Oberschall in his paper "The California Gold Rush." Oberschall accepts the central dogma of transaction-cost economics that "different modes of transacting, i.e., different institutional arrangements for interdependent actions and exchanges, are best understood from the point of view of minimizing all costs, including the very important transaction costs" (1986:111–2). This approach does not take for granted the existence of the agreed-upon conditions for cooperation in a society and the basic institutional arrangements which define the rights and obligations of each member or transactant. It instead explains them by reference to the underlying calculated motivations to economize on costs. Oberschall goes on to describe how the formation of self-governed assemblies and rules of conduct, including claims to property-rights and adjudication of disputes relative to such claims, can be seen as the spontaneous results of actions guided by a disposition for cost-economizing.

A telling instance of applying game theory to explain the emergence of a novel institution is found in the work of Roth (1984) regarding the previously cited case of the institutional arrangement for the assignment of interns to hospitals. Roth models this "matching algorithm" (see the Appendix) as a "cooperative game" whose outcome is in the core of the game – it is economically efficient. However, he provides insufficient reasons why it was the hospitals rather than the interns that initiated this algorithm, a question that introduces a power dimension into the analysis; for an answer one may have to construct a complementary model, for example, along the Olsonian lines of "privileged groups" (Olson 1965; cf. Coleman 1986b).

Welfare economists and other analysts of collective action and public goods have made different use of the general efficiency arguments. They have argued that (a) the failure of market mechanisms to provide stability and continuous efficiency (per the Keynesian and Marxist analyses of capitalist boom-and-bust cycles) as well as (b) the failure of marketlike mechanisms of aggregation of individual preferences to produce public goods (Arrow's (Im)Possibility Theorem and its implications), have forced society to intervene and provide various institutional solutions. Part of the problem, in this context, is the trouble of transaction cost or microeconomic efficiency theories to provide a proper theory of state development. The interesting efforts by Margaret Levi (1983; see also 1988) and Douglas North (1981) are still too tentative, relying on the simplified assumptions that the state is either a "utility-maximizing ruler" (North) or "predatory ruler" who is rational and self-interested (Levi). Both approaches, however, seem unable to reduce the basic structural and ecological parameters affecting state formation, such as, for instance, ecological pressures on the population, organizational boundaries among societies defining a state and its enemies, emigration opportunities and constraints, and power asymmetries.[5] A robust theory of state emergence would be found to rely on all three of these dimensions – predatory, social utility maximizing, and structural. Even a "max-min" approach (maximizing social utility, minimizing transaction costs), however, could provide some significant insights on the matter.[6] But it cannot reduce the motley of complicated relations between innumerable (collective, corporate, coalescing, or individual) actors to a simple formula involving only transaction costs or other

---

[5] The literature on state formation and state action is too large to cite in full, but see Alford and Friedland 1985; Levi 1983, 1988; Mann 1986; Poggi 1978; Skocpol 1979; Taylor 1982; and Tilly 1975b.

[6] Knut Wicksell's "unanimous consent" theory of taxation is cited briefly by Olson (1965). Wicksell recognized that the state could not finance the essential public services through the market system, since any citizen could get the benefits from these services, which are "indivisible public goods" (e.g., national security, police protection), whether he purchased any or not. Taxation then became an institutional arrangement facilitating the "unanimous" support of production and distribution of these public services. The state is also implicit in the workings of the market (per Karl Polanyi 1957) as well as in any exchange-theoretic transaction. Alford and Friedland consider the experimenter setting the parameters of exchange as such an implicit state (1985:46, n.11).

rational choice terms. The exceptional essay by Hamilton and Woolsey Biggart (1988) comparing "market," "culture," and "authority" variables in a comparative analysis of management and organization in the Far East demonstrates succinctly the limitations of rational choice models when applied to the real world. In any case, the emergence of institutional arrangements and orders and their subsequent constraining role is disputed by no one except the reductionist methodological individualists and the orthodox neoclassical economists.

Emergence of corporate actors

As Chandler (1977), Coleman (1974, 1982), Williamson (1971, 1975), and others have persuasively argued, in the contemporary social world the most important actors are not individuals as such but "corporate actors," corporations, public bureaucracies, and organizations of other kinds. Olson's (1965) distinction among different groups can also help us understand this new reality: groups range from small or "privileged" to "intermediary," to large or "latent." Of these, the "privileged groups" can easily become corporate actors, the "latent groups" can never become collective actors under rational choice assumptions, while in the case of "intermediary" groups Olson is more or less silent (a significant weakness given that most of the current organizational forms, for example, multidivisional firms, are of the intermediary variety). Olson does, however, recognize that privileged groups can emerge as corporate or collective actors without any outside force or noneconomic selective incentives. Indeed, in his second book on the subject (1982; but see also Kennedy 1987), Olson argues that the emergence of "distributional coalitions," the net effect of ongoing "cartelization" in more or less stable societies, accounts for those societies' long-term decline.

Transaction-cost economists, too, have argued that the desire to control opportunism, the need to economize on transaction costs and the necessity to reduce market uncertainties or inefficiencies in clearing would lead management teams to favor hierarchies (for example, mergers and acquisitions or development of internal production units) rather than markets (especially, subcontracting markets); enter, therefore, strategic power plays coupled with economic considerations of satisficing performance. However, this seems to refer more to smaller corporate entities, which are better integrated to the point that one can speak of a unified managerial policy.[7]

---

[7] A "market" and "authority" linked structure should be seen as *two* games, not one: for example, one with the options of subcontracting or market buying between producers and another of merger or a hostile acquisition. These are two different games linked together, and imply more complicated notions of

It is evident then, on whatever theoretical grounds, that corporate actors have become progressively more dominant in our fast-changing, complex, and strategic environment and that, in fact, we have also already moved beyond the smaller, integrated corporate units. The name of the game now is the complex, decentralized, multidivisional corporate entity, an Olsonian "intermediary group" if ever there was one. In such groups, principal–agent relations and decentralized firm–market interfaces give rise to many intra-organizational frictions that limit the efficiency and transaction cost-cutting efforts of these organizations (Eccles and White 1986, 1988; Pratt and Zeckhauser 1985; Oberschall and Leifer 1986; Vancil 1978; White 1988); and the problem gets worse in noneconomic organizations such as the state.[8] One may argue that, by now, within markets and across institutional orders, a system of multidivisional oligopolistic structures has developed, interfacing with respective (economic, political, medical, educational, and so on) markets and intersecting with each other in partly competitive, partly collaborative ways. This situation begins to look a bit like – although not yet identical to – a type of *corporatist representation*, in the limit case in which the constituent units are "limited in number, compulsory, noncompetitive, hierarchically ordered, and granted 'representational monopoly' by the state" (Schmitter 1977:9).[9]

The emergence of collective actors

Nothing I have said thus far seems unorthodox. However, as soon as one begins to talk of larger corporate actors, that is, truly *collective actors,* the argument becomes controversial. Olson was the first to forcefully make the point that latent groups, sociological categories such as classes, ethnicities, races, or genders, cannot become collective actors under any circumstances. The Olsonian PD presumably demonstrated, given its strong assumptions, that – barring the exercise of violence or significant social incentives, which in any case cannot work effectively at the global level – rational individuals will not find it optimal to join a collective effort and will become "free riders" in any such organizational endeavor. In the most recent rendition of his theory, Olson has

---

interfaces. Such interfaces – simple or linked to other considerations – are also evident in the linkages of national and international policies (Putnam and Bayne 1984), principals and agents (Pratt and Zeckhauser 1985), firms and markets (Eccles and White 1986, 1988), even economic and military powers (Olson 1982, Kennedy 1987).

[8] Levi 1983, citing Niskanen et al; cf. Hirschman 1970, 1981. One could possibly conceptualize the state as a multidivisional firm involved in a variety of economic, social, and political markets.

[9] On "corporatism" and the new talk of "concertation" see Alford and Friedland 1985; Scharpf 1988; Schmitter 1977.

softened his position and recognized more clearly that social incentives may prove to be very effective for the organization of collective action given proper group or subgroup interaction: "If the group does have its own social life, the desire for the companionship and esteem of colleagues and the fear of being slighted or even ostracized can at little cost provide a powerful incentive for concerted action" (1986:326). He now accepts that the existence of "organizational entrepreneurs" and of "social homogeneous membership" can explain the formation of collective goods.

While Olson seems to be approaching the sociologists, Michael Hechter (1983a, 1986, 1987) is moving closer to rational choice theory. Hechter has expressed serious doubts on the effectiveness of "selective incentives" to help in the formation of collective action groups and has countered that the provision of such incentives constitutes a serious additional cost minimizing even further the likelihood of collective action. He has added to this the costs of monitoring as well as the costs of properly allocating the collective incentives. On these basic grounds Hechter argues that the production of collective goods is even more difficult and rarer than Olson had thought. In the latest version Hechter sets the theory forth in terms of several core propositions and facilitating conditions. The main model postulates that solidarity rises to the degree that (a) the group produces immanent, exclusive collective goods, i.e., goods that directly satisfy members, are available to all members, and from which nonmembers are excluded; (b) members depend on the group for a wide range of goods; and (c) formal collective controls over noncompliance (previously called "monitoring capacity") are extensive. These conditions obtain better in situations "where individuals face limited sources of benefit, where their opportunities for multiple group affiliation are minimal, and where their social isolation is extreme" (1987:54). In addition, several other factors are also involved, such as weak markets or the possibility of low costs of control. Overall, the theory is well thought out and offers many analytical insights; however, Hechter has not come to terms with the endogenous, sociohistorical formation of individual preferences, the structural and cultural preconditions implicated in the variation across collective groups and societies in the provision of explicit or implicit collective goods, the simplifying role of ideology, the effects of political entrepreneurship, or the opportunities for nonlinear stepwise forms of organization provided by "asymmetrical groups."[10] The above make one

---

[10] Elster (1985), Roemer (1986), even Levi (1983) agree on the need to account for endogenous preference formation. But this will get them away from the "fixed preference" model and toward other views of different value systems (Hegel, Marx, Weber), social norms, or "irrationality." Elster has made con-

suspect that transaction costs considerations may be, after all, insufficient grounds for understanding collective movements.

Mechanisms conducive to collective action
Needless to say, numerous and significant criticisms of the rational choice or game-theoretical view of collective action are already in place. In the following, I will offer some comments on the causal contribution of these other factors in the formation of collective groups. "Solidarities" do emerge for one or more of the following reasons:

Structural opposition: external negative incentives. Some implicit mechanisms of structural interdependence seem to produce oppositional solidarity. As Offe and Wiesenthal (1980) have argued, following Marx,[11] labor is organized at first for purely defensive purposes, in what may be called a process of "negative escalation"; that is, facing a hostile and unified Capital the working class is forced to unite in order to countenance the threat. This, of course, involves an iterated game situation between classes but also within the working class (i.e., a **supergame**), contrary to Olson's or Hechter's one-shot PD. Even in the case of simply iterated PD games and without external negative escalation, a lot of empirical work has demonstrated that repetitive playing leads to the collectively optimal choice and to shifts in preference rankings and game types (from PD to Assurance Game/AG games), and thus also the formation of collective action groups. This accords well with Marx's expectation that class consciousness – here, the defeating of the individualist rational choice – will come after many years of trials and errors of the organizing proletariat. Of course, I am not arguing that what Marx describes as the "necessity" of proletarian organization for the reasons cited, or what E. P. Thompson (1963) or Tilly and Tilly (1981) describe as the "realities" of spontaneous "local" and "popular" collective mobilizations, are sufficient explanatory grounds to dismiss Olson's or Hechter's thesis; but they certainly weaken it, as Elster (1986b), for instance, has conceded.

cessions in the latter direction in his 1989a and b. Cf. Sen's critique of fixed preference, 1970, 1982.

[11] Marx's account of structural determination is as follows: "Large scale industry concentrates in one place a crowd of people unknown to each other. Competition divides their interests. But the maintenance of wages, this *common interest which they have against their boss,* unites them in a common thought of resistance – combination ... combinations, at first, isolated, constitute themselves into groups ... and, *faced with always united capital,* the maintenance of the association becomes more necessary to them than that of wages. ... In this struggle – a veritable civil war – are united and developed all the elements necessary for the coming battle. Once it has reached this point, association takes on a political character" (*Poverty of Philosophy,* my emphasis).

Internal processes. Several internal processes (i.e., within the latent group) also appear to countenance the free rider disposition; these may be negative (such as force), neutral (such as social-emotional ties), or positive (such as welfare incentives). Consider, for example, the candid statement made by Henry George regarding working class associations: "Labor organizations can do nothing to raise wages but by force; . . . they must coerce or hold the power to coerce employers; they must coerce those of their members disposed to straggle; they must do their best to get into their hands the whole field of labor they seek to occupy and to force other workingmen either to join them or to starve . . ." (cited in Olson 1965: 71). In the usual case, to use Boulding's language (1978), Threat, Exchange, and Grant practices are all mixed together in an effort to produce collective action. As Callon and Latour have aptly expressed it, leaders and vanguards use "all the negotiations, intrigues, calculations, acts of persuasion and violence" (1981: 279), thanks to which they "take authority" to speak or act on behalf of other actors as a unified force. This is, of course, more understandable if one concedes, as even Shubik does, the subconscious or semirational character of most human behavior.[12] This is a much more realistic account of collective organization in long trajectories compared to the one-shot, hyperrationalist accounts of Olson and Hechter.

Objective processes. Viewing the matter on a more abstract level one could argue that even social "objects" may be thought of as emerging randomly; there are significant developments in the mathematical and computational theories of random nets, random walk, random **fractals, percolation** clusters, clusters of correlated spins in **spin glasses, lattice animals** (P. W. Anderson 1983; Ërdos in Domb and Green 1972; Ërdos and Renyi 1960; Mandelbrot 1983; Rudnick and Gaspari 1987; Stauffer 1985) that develop this line of thought (on which admittedly I am an amateur). **Nucleation** is another phenomenon of similar import; on the logics of percolation and nucleation see the Appendix. Notwithstanding the caution with which a social scientist may look at suggestive similarities between social and natural processes (cf. Bhaskar 1978a and b; Elster 1985, 1986a; Giddens 1976, 1979; Habermas 1989), there is something intriguing in the thought that self-organizing principles lead to the formation of larger collectives (see Dyke 1988; Salthe 1985; Wicken 1979, 1987; Zeleny 1980, 1981; among others). In fact, some parallels – for instance, those between **cellular automata** (see Appendix, *Conway game*) and neighborhoods-in-

---

[12] See Shubik 1982:17.

transition (as per Schelling 1971) – are very tempting. However, the suggestion here is that we consider seriously that proximity and commonality of condition – as against a perceived common enemy – facilitate, although may not determine, the collective organization of some portions of classes, class fractions, ethnoraces, and other large social categories. We need to develop considerably more research on a variety of mechanisms that inform this more objective process. Granovetter (1978), for example, has discussed the utility of **threshold** models (see also Appendix no. 11) in several contexts, such as the dissemination of contraceptive practices in a population. We have also cited the example given by Schelling on the acceleration effect the perception of "how many unwanted families have moved into the neighborhood" has in determining the rate of transition in that neighborhood (Schelling 1972).

Many more examples can be produced of linear or nonlinear acceleration or **autocatalysis** in the production of similar, often paradoxical, complex effects. We may correctly argue, therefore, that some initial and slowly increasing participation in a collective movement would tend to increase the likelihood of further participation because of the threshold crossings, especially if nonlinearities are involved. Schelling (1978), speaking of "jaycrossing," has wittily called this the "there-is-safety-in-numbers" principle. On somewhat different grounds, conceiving the groups as asymmetrical, Schelling (1978) and Hardin (1982) have shown how a given subgroup k benefiting from the provision of a collective good even without cooperation from the rest of the members would produce that public good. A similar approach has been applied to the dominant behavior of a coalition of leading shareholders relative to the "ocean" of small shareholders (an **oceanic game** [Shubik 1982], which is clearly beyond the bounds of traditional game theory).

Leaders, vanguards, and cadres. There is also the role of leaders, vanguards, and significant category-fractions in negotiating, calculating, strategically persuading, even violently forcing potential members to join in the collective effort. The role of leaders in arousing the excitement and commitment of many members through charismatic persuasion or strategic manipulation and long organizational struggles is well known; the careers of Marx or Lenin, Gandhi or Martin Luther King, Jr., suffice to demonstrate the point. In these and other cases of collective movements (from consumers' unions to cultist groups), it is the vanguard of organized cadres who, under the mentorship of the leader(s), plays a very significant role in the formation of a movement and in the continuous mobilization of the would-be constituents (Kontopoulos 1973; Gouldner 1982). One may argue that these vanguard cadres participate in the collective organization for selfish rational reasons; however, it has been also shown that in numerous instances "value-rational" and "marginal" individuals become activist members carrying further the cause of the organization with a certain missionary zeal (Cable et al. 1988; Feinberg and Johnson 1988; Jenkins 1983b; Klandermans and Oegema 1987; Marwel and Ames 1979, 1980; Mc-Adam 1986; Oliver 1984; Oliver et al. 1985). Indeed, no collective organization can take place without leaders and vanguards, the first critical mass required for visibility, nucleation, and the autocatalytic ignition of participation by others.

Special fractions. Besides leaders and cadres, playing a significant part in the consolidation of any collective action-oriented entity is the activist orientation of certain significant fractions – those of class fractions, ethnoracial fractions, feminist professional women, students, intellectuals, officers' corps, and so on. Intellectuals and the intelligentsia played a well-known activist role in eighteenth-century France and nineteenth-century Poland and Russia as well as more recently in the many national liberation movements in Eastern Europe and the Third World. The army as a modern or semimodern collective actor has been credited with a similar role.

Recent scholarship has brought to focus the significant role played by artisanal or skilled workers in the formation of "solidarities" and the mobilization of the masses of semiskilled laborers for the collective benefit of the working class in nineteenth-century Western European collective actions. Calhoun (1981, 1983) has emphasized the significance of "communities" and "traditions" in bringing about the radicalism of artisanal labor. Aminzade (1981) has described the vitality of trade consciousness, the collective control of the workplace, and the richness of informal social networks, particularly evident in neighborhood coffee houses, that these skilled workers brought to the workers' movement. Katznelson (1985) has also emphasized neighborhood interaction and class segregation in his explanation of the formation of labor movements. Finally, Hanagan (1980, 1989; see also Hanagan and Stephenson 1986a, b) has brought vividly and persuasively to light the strategic significance of artisanal, skilled labor in mobilizing the semiskilled workers to forge a solid alliance with workers of other industrial plants and bring about a larger collective actor with solidarity and determination for action. Hanagan documents the formation of "common interest" on the issues related to the threats of technological obsolescence, overproduction, and industrial concentration.

Proactive collective action. Charles and Louise Tilly, in their important studies of popular collective action, have shown – by historical example though not analytically – how "ordinary people who share an interest, grievance, or aspiration band together to act in their common interest" and how these ordinary political struggles interact with larger events in the political center bringing about large-scale social change (Tilly and Tilly 1981:30). Elsewhere (1975a), the Tillys summarize their argument about the agents of collective action (which they call "collective violence"), pointing out that this is a set of actions by individuals, significant only insofar as it is a "formation," that is, "a group acting together" (1975a:313). The Tillys argue that group formations become progressively "bigger, more complicated, more bureaucratized" and more "oriented towards the state" (ibid.: 53). Thus, in the context of the European experience, with time, the character of collective violence changed from "reactive" (food riots, machine breaking, resistance to conscription) to "proactive" (most demonstrations and strikes), the latter being characterized by "deliberate attempts to seize control of the state" (50–1). Of course, organizations are "the mobilizers of collective action." In their view, Marx correctly favored "an analysis of collective action in which the making of claims by solidarity groups organized around articulated interests played the central part" (272–3). This is a rather telling summation of the broad historical record within the parameters of a realistic political "resource mobilization" perspective, which – in conjunction with the other studies cited – provides us with a robust understanding of the formation of collective groups.

In summation, there appear to be many mechanisms conducive to the transition from individualist considerations (as per Olson or Hechter) to the formation of collective, solidaristic groups. We have mentioned institutionalization processes, negative structural externalities (the "them" force "us" together argument), mobilizations by leaders and vanguards, superimposition of solidarity with a mixture of threat and persuasion, and various other objectivist mechanisms. All these make possible the actual emergence of collective actors in a model-like form of nested solidarities, that is, in a quasi-**synecdochical** mobilization of larger actors by smaller, embedded ones who are more organizationally apt, more articulate, and more committed.[13]

---

[13] This is not radically different from the common-sense understanding of the relations between, say, a faculty union's leadership, union members, and the faculty-at-large; or a government, politically active citizens, and the broad society. In such cases nationalist or liberationist "mobilization" is more or less successful on various grounds, which, in conjunction, override the free rider problem. This is logically blameless: a set of contributing factors operating in conjunction become an efficient cause of collective action.

From simple interactional systems to more inclusive ones

To a very large extent, rational choice theory and game theory in its standard forms refer to choices made by one actor in isolation, or two actors who are basically also in isolation but are taking into account the potential options and imputed rational choice ordering of the other. True, there is a part of game theory that deals with n-person games (Friedman 1986; Schotter 1981; Shubik 1982; cf. Coleman 1986a), but it has found no great application in social science given the combinatorial problems involved. The game-theoretical apparatus, as we have seen earlier, is applicable basically to two-person situations and all other kinds of situations translatable into that two-person form (the "I" vs. "All Others" form; or the "Us" vs. "Them" form). Because the complicated forms of **metagames, supergames,** and **differential games** do not have unique solutions, they lose their formalism and analytical rigor though they do gain in realism. Formalizing more complex social situations or processes into the standard game-theoretical types is a most difficult, perhaps insurmountable task, as Boudon, Elster, Shubik, and others have explicitly or implicitly recognized. This sounds like **Gödelization:** the basic, formal game-theoretical models are not large enough for reality, and to the extent that the theory of games becomes large (extended in the direction of supergames, differential games, and so on) it produces undecidable results. In the real world, of course, the situations where three, four, or many more players interact in systems of "direct or indirect interdependence" are not only common but predominant; and one must get away from all sorts of lulling but unduly restrictive binarisms to be able to map actual conditions.

A great deal of both theoretical and empirical import has been written on three-person systems and coalition formations. In this literature, the most obvious concern has been the investigation of the structural possibilities of coalition formation of the "two-against-one" type and the fundamental principles operating in the production and stabilization of such coalitions. From Simmel to Elster a number of principles have been investigated and codified in concrete sociohistorical instances. A good example is that discussed by Adam Przeworski in his *Capitalism and Social Democracy* (1985). Analyzing the two options available to the socialist parties of Europe, Przeworski makes clear that they have gone through an agonizing process of debate and trial and error to decide if an exclusive, workers only, or an inclusive, working peoples at large, strategy was most appropriate. The exclusive strategy would have kept the movement "pure" and its goals unadulterated but, at the same time, would have made the political movement a "permanent minority" with no prospect of conquering power by democratic-electoral means. On the other hand, an inclusive, populist strategy would have allowed the socialist parties to achieve democratic majorities and govern but substantially compromised their socialist goals so as not to alienate their allies and the voters at large in the open democratic contest. We have thus witnessed in the twentieth century the situation in which not only social democratic but "Eurocommunist" parties (such as the Italian one) have renounced their revolutionary character by way of a decisive *compromisso historico*. Note that each strategy involved in this case implies taking into account the presumed or imputed behavior of two other opposing actors – the capitalist class and the party (or parties) that express it as well as the petty bourgeois class and its political party or representatives – an uncertain game-theoretical situation, to be sure.

As soon as one moves from triads to sets involving relations of interdependence between four individual, corporate, or collective actors (a "tetradic system"), the situation becomes more uncertain and the possible games more entangled. Any tetradic system can be decomposed into four triadic systems and six dyadic systems. Suppose, for example, that we analyze the possible relations between two capitalists and two workers as individuals: (a) Each capitalist would relate to the two workers in such a way that, from each worker's point of view the games would be to enter into an agreement of joint production with the capitalist in competition with the other worker (atomistic solution) or to form a solidarity with the other worker and stand in opposition to the capitalist and the capitalist class at large; and (b) Each worker would relate to the two capitalists in such a way that, from each capitalist's point of view, the games would be to enter into an agreement of joint production with the worker in competition with the other capitalist (atomistic solution again) or to form a collective group with the other capitalist and oppose any wage demands of the worker and the working class at large. The combined analytical possibilities are the same for all four players: to work for intraclass integration and interclass competition or, the opposite, to work for interclass joint production even though it may involve intraclass competition.

There are numerous examples of this situation. The general Marxist case of the intraclass/interclass relations is prototypical, of course. Barrington Moore (1966) discusses more specifically the relationship between kulaks and small peasants on the one hand and traditional landowners and the autocratic state on the other, particularly as the configuration was seen from the point of view of the peasantry. Moore also discusses the relationship between monarchy and aristocracy, peasantry and bourgeoisie on similar triadic or tetradic terms. Wallerstein's (1974, 1984) way of understanding world systemic phenomena by reference to divided "national bourgeoisies" and an equally divided "peripheral" world is quite similar. Notice also the equivalent situation in foreign relations where politico-military antagonists (Western Europe–Eastern bloc, USA–China) behave as economic collaborators and where politico-military allies (USA, Japan, Europe) are, in fact, below the surface, economic antagonists. The model, indeed, has wide application.

Now, suppose one were to move to situations involving many more strategic actors, for example, different class-fractions across several classes operating simultaneously and in a complex interdependent way. In such a case, the multitude of relations obtaining will be mapped not as one-to-one (as in a triad presumably reducible to several dyadic relations) but as several-to-several, implying the effects of many more interdependencies on each other and a dramatic increase in uncertainty. A variety of diffused, distributed, or semisegregated systems would appear, the complexity of which is beyond the reach and formal analytical capabilities of game theory, transaction cost analysis, or of any currently espoused compositionist alternative. N-person games and Walrasian general equilibrium models offer no serious alternative, despite claims to the contrary (see the Olson-Coleman exchange in Lindenberg et al. 1986; cf. Shubik 1982:300). In brief, the transition from few to many players necessitates the abandonment of the formal strategic framework proudly invoked in the case of two-player games.

From simple externalities to complex and compounded ones

We have seen that one of the most important difficulties with rational choice theory is its inability to take into account the multiple interdependencies actors face every time they make a choice. It is true that many economists in the last two decades, especially institutional and welfare economists, have incorporated to some extent into their contractual and price-theoretical models rudiments of a theory of external social constraints under the general name of "externalities," but this is a compromise that falls short of the required complex model that must be developed for a realistic depiction and analysis of the social world. The standard economic models either neglect altogether to take into account such externalities or, as in the case of game theory and the various theories of "implicit contracts" and transaction-cost economics, treat such externalities as "perceived" by each actor (presumed fixed or merely imputed), not as dynamic variables implicated in the ongoing strategic interactions in the social world. The result is that, even in the most enlightened instances of recent economic theorizing such as transaction cost or collective choice, "externality" only refers to the case when an actor's preferences or opportunity set is a function of the choices of another actor (cf. Williamson 1975). The solution to the problems posed by such externalities is taken to be the control of these external effects of interaction by manipulation or agreement (i.e., "internalizing" them).

The economic understanding of externalities is still too narrow. By treating all social externalities as if they are the same, social complexity is reduced to a more manageable size at the expense of completeness and explanatory power. A better understanding of externalities requires a number of analytical distinctions between simple and more complex and compounded forms of externality along the following lines:

(1) The baseline notion of externality is what the economist has in mind: dependence of one's preferences and choice on the correlative choices of others. This may involve either the case of simple copresence, in which one player takes into account the imputed preferences of the other (as in the case of the PD) or the normal cases of direct or indirect interactional interdependence (as in the examples given by Boudon [1981a]). In any case, this must be characterized as a purely interactional type of externality and in its simplest form would be seen applying in all cases of cooperative or noncooperative behavior between equal or equivalent actors.

(2) A different analytical notion of externality could be said to involve the special cases where actors command differential powers – political, economic, cultural, or what have you – translatable into differential political effects on the other's preferences and choices. This must be properly understood as a political, especially politico-economic, form of externality; although taken very seriously by sociologists and political scientists, power-based externalities are denigrated by economists as so much unnecessary nonsense (even Williamson 1975, 1983; contra Perrow 1979/1986, 1981). Here we may also include the existing institutional orders as a subcase of political externalities (accounting for the CI-predicates described in Chapter 5).

(3) A third analytical notion of externality is that imposed by the environment, the physical and topological features of the natural and artifactual world in which humans live. Schelling would say that the parameters and contours of that environment are significant determinants of the processes of social structuration and affect any actor's behavior by constraining her opportunity set (Schelling 1978) – in this sense, for instance, traffic rules, traffic flows, and traffic jams are externalities imposing limits on and modifying the very grounds of rational choice of any automobile driver. Economists usually disregard this form of topological externality.

In reality, these three analytically distinct notions of externality may often be conjoined. We most often find externalities in which interactional and political elements are compounded. Games with differential power, such as the so-called survival games, class struggles, or the "organized crime" (OC) game, which Boulding (1978) has called the "threat organizer" ("you do something I want or I'll do something you don't want"; or simply, "your money or your life"). Other examples may include cases of "contrived" markets, state regulations, taxes, union dues, conscription, and so on. In the purely politico-economic sense, as social scientists understand it, the power to hold on longer in strikes, to impose a "take it or leave it" option, or to act as an oligopolist against weaker competitors, also involve such an externality. We also often find the compounding of interactional and topological externalities. Traffic flows and jams, all sorts of topological and physical systems' "matchings" with human flows, such as neighborhood (racial or ethnic) turnovers, ski-chair flows, assembly-line bottlenecks, and so on, are self-evident instantiations of this case (see the *logic of flows* in the Appendix).

The three externalities are, in fact, intertwined, forming systems that look like a "population ecology." Such, for example, is the case of the "urban structure" as various scholars of urban space describe it: a complex system of systems of interaction, a metastructure with obvious topological constraints; with political authorities, interventions, constrained markets, social forces, and fiscal crises; and with a myriad of individual, corporate and collective choices, actions, reactions and proactions. This metasystem of organized oppositions and joint productions, worrying eternally about urban–suburban asymmetries of income, costs and tax base, devoured by segregationist processes of gentrification and urban decay, and charged with a host of other contradictions and uncertainties – this is a structure too real and too complex to be explained by simple compositional means. Its many uncertainties, unanticipated and unmonitored consequences, and twice- or thrice-removed indirect interdependencies are, simply, impossible to be reductively understood. Here, indeed, is a clear instance of a truly complex form of structural externality.

A related commonsensical example is also illustrative. Consider the decision of a firm to leave the city: there are a number of direct effects due to the decision (loss of jobs by the individual workers, loss of business taxes by the city), several indirect effects (loss of taxes resulting from the loss of the jobs of individuals, loss of business by enterprises formerly catering to the now unemployed individuals) and "snowballing," or indirect effects two or three times removed (effects on other businesses' decisions, possible deterioration of city services, overall bad economic climate). It is the concatenation of these effects and their autocatalytic import that accelerate the process of deindustrialization in large metropolitan areas.

Or consider the economic condition of a nation with great trade imbalances, as the United States currently has. Such a nation may decide (a) to embrace protectionism, to close or restrict foreign trade at the risk of: bringing about trade wars, increasing internal inflation, deterioration of the employment picture, withdrawals or stoppage of new foreign investments, worsening international political relations, global market and currency realignments, internal social destabilization, and so on. Or, it may choose (b) to significantly raise its interest rates in order to attract much needed foreign capital to cover the deficits, at the risk of: precipitating a recession, increasing unemployment, increasing the payments required to service foreign debt, forcing the revaluation of currency, affecting the export market, and having a number of chain reaction effects such as social destabilization. Or, it may decide (c) to devaluate or allow the international currency market to devalue its currency at the risk of: increasing the likelihood of foreign buyouts of resources, the possible dumping of its currency by foreign states and capitalists, precipitating an international financial depression, affecting Third World countries' exports, thus worsening the debt problem of these countries and the internal banking system, igniting internal inflation with the immediate increase of import prices – all these with the promise of decreasing imports and increasing exports for a specific period of time. These economic strategies may or may not work effectively, but the one thing they make clear is the enormous complexity involved, the chain reactions and the structural externalities that are prohibitive of any thorough understanding, prediction, or "fine-tuning" of the enormously complicated overall structure. In short, it is indeed a nightmare to try to understand global economics at the level of individual action. Complex and compounded externalities are insurmountable obstacles to the implicit reductionist aims of elementary constructionisms.

From simple systems of interaction to entangled ones

The combination of complex and compounded externalities, corporate and collective actors, and many-person systems leads to what may be called "entangled interdependent systems." Boudon (1981a, b) advanced a relatively similar idea when he defined metastructure as "a complex combination of simple structures of interaction" or "a structure of structures," although his notion seems to refer only to second-order structures, not to higher-order ones, and paradoxically appears to be free of the further complications introduced by uncheckable indirect externalities or interdependencies. Boudon appears to limit his notion of complexity to the two-game situations between two actors, unwilling or unable so far to provide any more complex example.

The literature on differential games may allow us to somewhat map the process through which compounded externalities affect interactional systems. Differential games grew out of "search and pursuit," "evade," and "pursuit and engage" games, initiated by Paxton and Isaacs (see Shubik 1982) and further developed by Friedman (1986), Taylor (1982, 1987), and others (cf. Elster 1985). Differential games between two players are reminiscent of the tale of Achilles and the tortoise: Achilles chases the tortoise across the open field; Achilles attempts to minimize the time to capture or to pass, the tortoise to maximize it (Hofstadter 1979; Shubik 1982). In such a game, the numbers of moves, stages, and states as well as the number of time periods are infinite. Since the game is played over continuous time, strategies are chosen over time, and define the control functions of the players as functions of the state reached at a given moment of time. Thus, differential games are time-dependent and state-dependent, that is, at any moment, optimal strategies depend on the history as well as the previous and present state of the game. They involve discontinuous functions and can be described only by differential (Lancaster-type) equations (Krass and Hammondeh 1981). Because of this discontinuity and nonlinearity involved in differential games there is a disjunction between local and global optimality. The result is the *relative autonomy of the local and global levels,* a cardinal idea implicated in the "logic of heterarchy" as well.

Among neo-Marxists, in particular, differential games have been interpreted in collective bargaining or collective strife as if they were games involving "bilateral monopoly." Thus, following Lancaster (1973), Przeworski and Wallerstein have described the antagonism between capital and labor as such a bilateral monopoly, arguing that "given the existence of private property the relation between Capital and Labor can be modelled as a differential game in which the workers control the rate of profit and the capitalists (control) the rate of investment out of profit" (1982:217). Fritz Scharpf, in the insightful paper "The Political Calculus of Inflation and Unemployment in Western Europe" (1988), advances the model one step further. Using a game-theoretical interpretation along lines parallel to those of Korpi (1983) and Przeworski (1985) in their analyses of the European social democracies, he posits two intersecting games played in the European politico-economic arenas, (1) a "coordination game" in which the outcomes of macroeconomic policy are jointly determined by the government and the unions; and (2) a "politics game" in which the government responds to its anticipation of positive or negative voter reaction to these outcomes. This differential game, basically, is one between labor unions and government; for Scharpf – agreeing with Olson – does not consider capital as a collective actor. So here again, two separate games are linked together (Kelley 1984; Putnam and Bayne 1984) forming a payoff matrix in which the game of coordination is mapped on the binary choice between "aggressive" or "moderate" wage demands, while the game of politics is mapped on the binary choice of "Keynesian" (populist) or "monetarist" (nonpopulist) state economic policy. Scharpf then proceeds to analyze and explain the failures and changes in social democratic policies in the early 1980s. He does allow for the linkage of several other games (the game between union leaders and active union membership, or the game between different unions), although this is a peripheral concern in his paper.

A simple combination of games between capital and labor, labor and government, and government and capital (along lines indicated by Korpi 1983 and Maital and Benjamini 1979), gives a differential game of three monopolists, each controlling a particular resource – capital controlling rates of investment, government controlling rates of money flow, and labor controlling rates of profit. To that game-set one may add a fourth game played between governments in which currency rates are controlled. But as soon as one moves to such level of complexity the combinatorial possibilities increase dramatically; complex interdependencies make any would-be solution unstable and self-defeating, and structural results emerge that are radically different from the ones intended or foreseen.

Moreover, the complexity of game-like situations does not increase only in the already described directions, toward n-person games, n-period games (supergames), continuous-time games (differential games), and interlinked n-games. Interlinked games may also take the form of two-level, three-level, and n-level games. An important example of a two-level interlinked game is given by Putnam and Bayne (1984) in their work on Western summitry. The political leaders of any nation participating in a summit, such as a summit of the Western economic powers, play a game at two different levels.

At the national level, domestic groups seek to maximize their interests by pressuring the government to adopt favorable policies, and politicians seek power by constructing coalitions among these groups. At the international level, national governments seek to maximize their own freedom to satisfy domestic pressures, while minimizing the adverse consequences of foreign developments. (Governments may also pursue certain "state" interests, such as prestige or security, that are only indirectly related to pressure from their domestic constituencies.) (1984:3–5)

There are two game boards for each player and they are played simultaneously. The net result is that national policies derive to a large extent from both the domestic and the international "parallelograms of force." The authors then succinctly point out that "[T]he special complexity of this two-level game is that moves that are rational for a player at one board (such as raising energy prices or limiting automobile imports) may be quite irrational for that same player at the other board. Nevertheless, there are powerful incentives for consistency between the two games" (1984:3–5; cf. 202, 207). Summitry, international trade negotiations, international cartel summitry such as of the OPEC countries, all seem to conform to this complicated two-level game. It may appear that this two-level game is equivalent to White's firm–market interfaces in the sense that resultant efficiency also depends on two-level policies, those of the market and those of the multidivisional decentralized firm. Now imagine what would happen if the game is a *three-level* game, for example, where below the domestic national level a local or regional level is actively implicated (see, e.g., Logan and Molotch 1987; Molotch 1976). The connections across levels become heterarchical since the local, national, and international levels remain semiautonomous and interpenetrating, as in the case of letters, words, and sentences, which we discussed in Chapter 3. This is what I mean when speaking of "entanglements" of games and interdependencies – and I don't think that game theory, or any other constructionist version, has as yet dealt effectively with all of these entangled complexities simultaneously.

Having said that, I would wholeheartedly agree with Scharpf when he writes: "For my own understanding, I find it useful to conceptualize real-world events as 'intersections' of processes and factors whose separate 'logics' may be captured by specific explanatory theories, but whose interaction may only be accessible to historical description" (1987:9, n.4). This dual positive heuristic must be pursued relentlessly. We need to go beyond the intuitive microemphasis and the ideological microeconomic influences. One would hope that the leading proponents of the constructionist program will take on this or the other difficult challenges issued in this chapter. *Rhodus, hic salta!*

Part III
Logics of hierarchy

In this part we focus on the hierarchical **logics,** the symmetrical anti-pode of constructionism. Here the emergence of structure is seen not as a standard byproduct of properly aggregated individual actions, but as a complex derivative of other significant – quasi-local, quasi-global, and/or global – higher-level processes, involving different mechanisms of structuration, phase-separation, and nonlinear coupling of lower structures. Furthermore, individual action is now considered to be par-ameterized by the structural characteristics of higher levels, which are treated as autonomous and as exerting **downward causation** over such action.

Chapter 8 is intended as the opposite of Chapter 5: The focus is on "methodological holism" as opposed to the "methodological individu-alism" we discussed there. Here we present an analytical summation of various versions of functionalism, the mark of all kinds of holism, and proceed to appraise holism's prospects in view of the radical changes taking place in the fields of physical chemistry, molecular biology, ev-olutionary theory, and ecosystems modeling – fields out of which the original functionalist notions were derived. On the basis of these recent developments we posit a postfunctional mode of analysis as the only available path for former functionalists.

In Chapter 9 we explore a number of incipient hierarchical concep-tions of social structure (Bunge, Hernes), and then turn our attention to the "received view" of Marxist theory, which appears as an exem-plary instance of a dynamic hierarchical logic (with its emphasis on subsumption and on the logic of capital). It may be helpful at this point to refer to the theses on hierarchy presented in Chapter 4.

8 Hierarchy theory and postfunctional analysis

In this chapter we take up the issue of "methodological collectivism" and proceed to offer a criticism of its basic functionalist skeleton. I maintain the view that, when all is said and done, any collectivist theory is a variant of functional analysis, notwithstanding its special linguistic–conceptual transcription. I know of five basic versions of collectivist theory:

(1) *systems theory:* This includes the model of the "general systems theory" (Mesarovic and Takahara 1989; Weinberg 1975) as well as the more specific theories of social systems. Parsons's work, no doubt, remains the *locus classicus* in sociology, while in political science a similar value is assigned to Karl Deutsch's work. More recently, Niklas Luhmann has reworked this model in more imaginative ways.[1]

(2) *group differentiation theory:* From its Spencerian and Durkheimian origins, the differentiationist model, which places the emphasis on increasing size and complexity, has been advanced in slightly varying directions by systems theorists (Luhmann), structural evolutionists (Lenski), neo-functionalists (Alexander and Colomy), and so-called structural analysts (American structuralists such as Blau and Mayhew).

(3) *structuralist theory:* With roots in Saussure and the Bourbaki group (Gleick 1987; Halmos 1957) French structuralism – whether of the mentalist (Lévi-Strauss) or the sociologistic, Marxist variety (Althusser) – emerged as a collectivist version, the organizing principle of which was the construal of totalities on the basis of simple or complex binary oppositions.

---

[1] Luhmann's work is very interesting, but, I believe, still in the making. He has progressively modified his early traditional functionalism since his work on differentiation, especially, in his emphasis on the differentiation between community and society and the social and political systems. His subsequent focus on communication rather than interaction signals the beginning of a robust transition to a postfunctionalist program. In his later work on ecological communication, I detect a further shift toward a more dynamic conceptualization of social systems (complexity, autopoesis, self-referentiality); yet, the move is not complete at present (see his 1989, 1990). I have opted to omit any discussion of Luhmann's work on the belief that I cannot do it justice at present – I am sure another opportunity will arise for an appropriate, more attentive treatment.

153

(4) *group selection theory:* Biological versions of group selectionism – stronger (Wade, D. S. Wilson, Wynne-Edwards) or weaker (Boorman and Levitt, Maynard Smith) – appear to be gaining in importance. Edelman's work on neuronal group selection and the current interest in neural networks enhance the prospects of this orientation (1987, 1990). In sociology, group selectionism is represented by the still underdeveloped work on the population ecology of organizations and communities (Aldrich, Carroll, Hannan and Freeman, Pfeffer).

(5) *cultural holism:* Since Hegel (at least), cultural theories of humanity, of the *Volk/Ethnie,* of the *Zeitgeist,* of collective consciousness, and of all sorts of particular *Geistes* (capitalism among them) have been espoused with varying degrees of success. The emergence of such cultural wholes has not been properly explained, however; even now, the relevant disciplines prefer to take them for granted and focus only on gaining hermeneutical insights from their analyses.

I cannot help thinking that the fundamental question implicated in all these versions of methodological collectivism is the same: What holds a group together? In this sense, cultural dimensions (what representations maintain the group as a collective "subject"), social dimensions (what modal ties, incentives, and constraints form and maintain a social group), and biotic dimensions (what evolutionary–ecological constraints, selections, and **aptations** account for speciation and the focal specificity of groups in local ecosystems), all rely on functional characterization and processes. We need, therefore, to turn our attention to the language-game of "function" and "the functional" and examine our thoughts: What are, indeed, the current and future prospects of functional analysis, the exemplar of all forms of methodological collectivism?

Functional analysis

It has not been an easy matter to express an incisive opinion on functionalism, functional analysis, or on the more formal functional logic of explanation. Complications have usually arisen from either the lack of sufficient analytical rigor in the enterprise or the ideological dispositions and sensibilities of the scholars involved. I believe that significant transformations of the ground rules and technologies of functional analysis have taken place in the domain of evolutionary and ecological biology, the *urgrund* of functional explanation, that have radically altered our earlier conceptions. My goal, then, is not to fully address the issue of

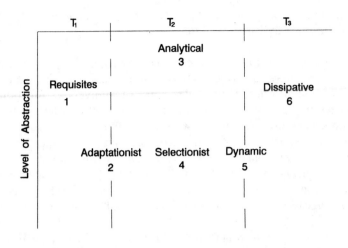

Figure 8.1. *Variants of functional analysis*

functional analysis, but to demonstrate how these important transformations lead to a hierarchical reconceptualization of social structure and, in so doing, redefine functional analysis along what I would like to call postfunctionalist lines.

We may start, first, with the description and elucidation of the following schema in which variants of "functional" analysis (where the term "functional" is defined in a neutral way, i.e., relationally) are designated in terms of (a) relative theoretical abstraction and (b) theory elaboration.[2]

There have been three stages in the post–World War II development of functional analysis, demarcated by T_1, T_2, and T_3. T_1 is the earlier and more simplistic phase during which the more traditional functionalist theories were proposed: variants 1 (the functional requisites program) and 2 (the adaptationist program). In the second phase, T_2, successfully elaborated in the 1970s, we find variants 3 (the abstract, analytical functional program) and 4 (the strict Darwinian/selectionist program) and, at the exact point of transition from T_2 to T_3, the hybrid variant 5 (the so-called program of dynamic functionalism). T_3 is the phase-space where, as I will argue below, we find variant 6, the emerg-

---

[2] The model I present utilizes the two dimensions of theoretical abstraction (degree of logical abstraction) and theoretical elaboration ("progressive problemshift" in the Lakatosian sense). In contrast to Wagner's (1984) and Wagner and Berger's (1985) unduly restrictive sense I interpret Lakatos in postpositivist, robust relativist terms.

ing postfunctionalist program of "dissipative structures" and its nonlinear (thermo)dynamic functions.

Variant 1: the functional requisites program

The earlier and more idealistic version of functional analysis began as a logico-conceptual quest for the discovery of "universal" functional prerequisites for the existence of societies by a sort of Kantian **transcendental argument.** "Functions" were logically prior to "structures" – indeed they were transcendental functions, that is, "conditions of the possibility of existence" of society. The *locus classicus* of this approach is the essay by D. F. Aberle et al., "The Functional Prerequisites of a Society" (1950), which prepared the way for Talcott Parsons's magisterial work *The Social System* published the following year.

The commitment to Kantianism (cf. Münch 1981) brought with it a variety of other logical, metaphysical, theoretical, and methodological consequences. On the logical level, the search shifted away from the establishment of *sufficient* explanatory conditions (from the **modus ponens** type of syllogism) and toward the positing of abstract, universal *necessary* conditions (in the syllogistic type of "asserting the consequent").[3] "Functional logic" was robust, at a par with other forms of logic, and most appropriate for the explanation of social phenomena.

The excess baggage associated with this functional variant has been detailed by several critics (Abrahamson 1978; Habermas 1989; Gouldner 1970; Turner and Maryanski 1979; among others) and conceded by sympathetic analysts as well (G. A. Cohen 1978; Faia 1982; among others). On the theoretical level, the undue emphasis on "social integration," "the equilibrium of the social whole," "survivorship," "homeostasis," and "the social order" have become easy targets. On the metaphysical level, the very idea of "universal requisites" was assailed as ahistorical and transcendentally idealist. On the methodological level, the difficulties of "analytic inductionism" (i.e., the neglect of studying negative instances such as extinct societies) were pointed out. More broadly, critics have assailed the conflation of the historical origin of structures or enduring patterns of behavior and of the actual function(s) they may currently fulfill, a conflation producing illegitimate social teleology. Most of these difficulties are the results of an extreme commitment to the transcendentalist view of social "function." If functions are transcendental, universal, prior to and unmitigated by history,

---

[3] The functionalist logical mistake involves the transition from *modus ponens* to the fallacy of asserting the consequent by way of an illegitimate reversal. Instead of the standard, correct form: if p, then q; p, therefore q, we now have: if p, then q; and $-q$, therefore $-p$. The mistake is quite obvious and irremediable.

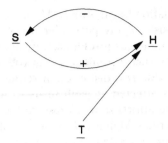

T=turbulence
   (environmental)
H=homeostasis
S=structure

Figure 8.2. *Stinchcombe's model*

then functions are logically prior to structures and the functors must have existed "always already there," created *illo tempore* at the primordial act of social constitution, and persisted ever since with minor modifications in structure. This is illegitimate teleology. Most scholars have come to the conclusion that this requisites form of functional analysis was overzealous and ahistorical, and therefore insupportable.

Variant 2: the adaptationist program
Many functional analysts were less sanguine (or perhaps less explicit), about the prospects of the "functional requisites" program. They heeded Durkheim's call for a separation of the issue of the causal origins of social facts from that of their functional role. In doing so, they put a wedge between "function" and "structure," allowing the latter to have an historically contingent character. The transcendentalist line of arguing has receded into the background, though it has never been explicitly abandoned; ditto the illegitimate teleology involved with it. However, an important overlap did exist between these two variants, centered around the core issue of "what a function is a function for." The older Newtonian notions of equilibrium or quasi-equilibrium and the notion of homeostasis derived from the privileged organismic metaphor remained central to the conceptualization of the *summum bonum* of society, that is, integration, stability, social order.

The logical form of the adaptationist model has been effectively captured by Stinchcombe (1968) as shown in Figure 8.2. Figure 8.2 posits that there are two systemic variables (or sets of variables), S and H, in reciprocal interaction, and one environmental variable (or set of variables), T. Variable S designates structures or persisting practices that have a functional relation to variable H. Variable H denotes the general state of "homeostasis" or any particular homeostatic aspect included therein. Variable T indicates turbulence introduced into the system by the environment. As such turbulence is introduced from the outside, the homeostatic variable H is disturbed or reduced, and, as a result, the structural variable is affected as well. In its turn, variable S adapts or increases its adaptive efforts so as to restore the homeostasis.

Stinchcombe describes Malinowski's theory of magic based on this model: Environmental uncertainty increases and, as a result, psychic homeostasis is reduced by the increasing anxiety. In its turn, anxiety and reduced homeostasis charge the structural variable S, in this case the practice of magical rituals, to increase its functional role so as to restore the previous psychic homeostasis. The adaptationist character of this "logic of functional explanation" is seen in the fact that "function" is conceived as *increased adaptational effort* to restore the pre-existing homeostatic condition. This implies an exclusive reliance on an Aristotelian model of final cause, an *entelechy* (i.e., having a set goal), which, of course, is inadmissible in today's neo-Darwinian and post-Darwinian climates of scientific opinion. The tyranny of equilibrium models and of the old organismic metaphor weighs heavily on this variant, burdening it with illegitimate teleonomy.[4] The devastating criticism of the adaptationist program in evolutionary biology – to which I will return below – can easily demolish this variant of functional analysis in the social sciences as well.

All this time I have purposefully spoken of "functional analysis" (or "functional explanation") rather than of "functionalism," intending to demarcate the two, more or less along the lines introduced earlier by Merton (1968), codified later by Cohen (1978) and, to a certain extent, taken for granted by Faia (1986). I do so without any further commitment to their particular views, which I will discuss shortly. As G. A. Cohen wrote, "functionalism" is the doctrine that affirms the following three basic theses:

(1) All elements of social life are interconnected. They strongly influence one another and in aggregate "form one inseparable whole" (interconnection thesis).

(2) All elements of social life support or reinforce one another, and hence, too, the whole society which in aggregate they constitute (functional interconnection thesis).

---

[4] By this I mean the ascription of a metarule to biological population systems to act adaptively in a global sense so as to maintain a goal-state; recall that in evolutionary theory adaptation exists only as local adaptation, i.e., adaptation to a "local ecosystem."

(3) Each element is as it is because of its contribution to the whole, as described in (2) (explanatory functional interconnection thesis). (Cohen 1978: 283–4)

Cohen argues (1978, 1982a, 1982b, 1986) that one can assert functional explanations without endorsing any of the above theses, that is, rejecting the doctrine of functionalism altogether, and with it its opaque implications of conservativism. What then remains in the residual category of "functional explanation" (per Cohen) we shall see shortly. A clue is given by Faia who promotes the compromising proposition that we can distinguish two types of functions, i-functions (that are "interest" based) and s-functions (that are "structure" based, as in the more traditional functional variants). This tactic, to shift the emphasis from s-functions to i-functions, may add vitality to functional explanation, but at considerable theoretical cost. In any case, as we move from T_1 to T_2, we notice that "functional analysis" and/or "functional explanation" abandon the excess commitments of "functionalist theory" and strive for respectability more or less along the lines sketched originally by Merton in his essay "Manifest and Latent Functions" (1968).

Variant 3: the abstract, analytical program

In his analytical treatment of Marxist theory, Cohen has provided a refreshing model of functional explanation based on "consequence laws" presumably underlying such explanations. Cohen has rejected the transcendentalist position, the three functionalist theses cited above, the conflation of causal origins and current functional roles, the homeostatic metaphor, and other paraphernalia of functionalism. His is a formal and minimalist sort of functional analysis, reduced to bare essentials so as to be both more defensible and broadly applicable to social phenomena by Marxists and conservatives alike. Using rigorous syllogisms, Cohen first argues that, even though it may be true that f (a function) preceded e (the existence of some practice or structure), that mere fact does not *guarantee* that f caused e (though that may in fact be the case).[5] Awareness of the fallacy *post hoc ergo propter hoc* simply cautions us to be careful in the above sense; that is, that something more is needed to support a correct functional explanation.

Cohen then proposes the backing up or the rendition of functional

---

[5] Cohen's syllogism applied to religion runs as follows: "One does not propose an explanation of the existence of religion by saying that (1) religion is required to sustain social order. Yet it might be true that (2) religion exists because it is required to sustain social order.

(2) may or may not be true, and if it is true, it is not true simply because (1) is true" (Cohen 1978:282, and in 1986). Notice the qualifiers *might, may or may not, not simply because.*

explanations by or in terms of "consequence laws." In general terms, a consequence law is a statement to the effect that whenever the explanandum would tend to produce the explanans, the explanandum is in fact observed. The logical form this takes is captured by the syllogism:

(1) if (if A, then B)
(2) B
(3) Thus, A.

Notice here the general Quinean view and, indeed, the Tarskian turn: rendering the major premise *empirical*, along the lines of the so-called "disquotational theory of truth:"[6]

> "if A, then B" is true if and only if A, then B is true (at least as a "contingent universal")

That is, the proposition (if A, then B) is true only if A, B, *and* the casual or functional connection between A and B are true, at least in a limited universal, pragmatic, or statistical sense. The proposition then "if (if A, then B)," which constitutes the major premise, describes a dispositional fact or property between or of two interrelated structures, for one to operate as functionally relative to the other. This rendition of functional logic is formally unassailable and less vacuous or tautological than the traditional functionalist forms.[7] However, it is not an applicable logic of explanation without a satisfactory case-by-case elaboration of what (and how exactly) constitutes a "functional fact." Such an elaboration is supposed to provide a fuller explanation by locating the functional fact within a parameterizing interpretive context which would specify its explanatory role more precisely.

Indeed, Cohen argues that there may be many possible types of elaboration of a functional explanation and lists four such types: purposive, Darwinian, Lamarckian, and self-deceptive elaborations. These may develop alone or in combination with each other, or with other elaborations, such as one based on a theory of "drift" (see below). Since Cohen intends his analysis as a defense of the functional explanation in Marxist theory, let us use his example of why "economies of scale" emerge and

---

[6] The general Quinean view is that issues of epistemology are, in fact, empirical in nature (see Quine's "Epistemology Naturalized" in his 1969); for the Tarskian "disquotational view" see Margolis 1986; Popper 1972.

[7] There are problems, of course, with the very definition of what constitutes a "dispositional fact" and of how such a fact comes about. Cohen's disquotational turn cannot simply explain away these two problems; the first seems to be temporarily relieved by the Quinean/Tarskian "aura" but the second must face reality in the form of a needed mechanism of aptation (see Appendix, no. 40) – or else it remains a "halfway house."

persist. On the basis of the purposive elaboration one would argue per Cohen that:

the industry's decision makers knew that increased scale would yield economies, and that they enlarged their producing units out of awareness of that functional fact. The functional fact would then play its explanatory role by accounting for formation of the (correct) belief that an increase in scale would be beneficial: that belief, together with a desire for the relevant benefits, being a more proximate cause of the expansion in size. (Cohen 1978:287)

In contrast, arguing on the basis of a Darwinian elaboration, one may hold that in a competitive economy it is not necessary for the managers in an industry to know that their firms would function more efficiently with increased scale.

Still, some firms increase the scale of their producing units, perhaps prestige is attached to size, or because the move is seen as a way of reducing tension between managers; or suppose that there is no intention to increase scale, but, in certain firms, [there is] an ungoverned drift in that direction. Then we could not say of any particular firm that its scale grew because of the associated economies. But the functional fact might still explain a change over time in the industry's scale profile, if only those firms which expanded (for whatever reason) would have succeeded, in virtue of having expanded, against the competition. Competition is bound to select in favor of firms whose practice is efficient, regardless of the inspiration of that practice. (Cohen 1978:288)

However, I find Cohen's analysis wanting. In the purposive elaboration of the above example neither the emergence or origin and persistence or proliferation of the practice of increasing scale in virtue of the postulated functional fact (production of efficient economies of scale) rely on or even need a functional explanation. If one puts under the microscope the "functional fact" involved, it will be clear under magnification that the relationship between increasing size and production, and thus decreasing fixed costs – hence also total costs – per unit of production is a technical-economic one, explained causally and metrically. The only sense of "function" involved is the mathematical one, to be a function of a variable. It is not enough to say that "scale is beneficial to economies" and leave it at that, when one can easily explain "why economies" or "why an increase in scale would bring about a more cost-effective regime of production." Moreover, consciousness of that so-called functional fact implies that the process is a teleological one, for in every case it involves agency and calculated action. If so, the "dispositional fact" indeed dissolves! Even under the Darwinian elaboration of this example, once scale has increased and economic efficiency resulted from such increased scale, the awareness, mental representation, and rational calculative acceptance of the functional fact would make its persistence and proliferation a teleological matter as well. The case looks rather like an "aptation" (Gould and Vrba 1982; Vrba and Eldredge 1984) transducing a "trial" or "drift" effect into an intentional-utilitarian choice. In both instances then, purposive and Darwinian alike, talk about "functional facts," "beneficial role," "adaptation," or "selection" is misplaced and analogical, and certainly not explanatory.

Cohen might be on firmer ground when discussing the Preface from Marx's *Contribution to the Critique of Political Economy*. He argues that the assertion that an economic structure (i.e., given relations of production) corresponds to a particular level of development of the productive forces simply means that: "the structure provides maximum scope for the fruitful use and development of the forces, and obtains because it provides such scope" (1978:278–9; cf. 1982a). Cohen also asserts more or less the same for the relations of superstructure (ideas, ideological forms) to infrastructure (political economy). Notice here that reference is made to large-scale phenomena, while in the previous example the reference was to firms, i.e., middle range phenomena at best. This explains to an extent why in the case of the economies of scale initial or later rational calculation was quite probable, while in the present case of the linkage between forces and relations of production or of infrastructure and superstructure purposive elaboration is much less likely – Cohen's analysis is more pertinent here. Nonetheless, even in this instance one must be cautious. Recall Faia's conceding distinction between interest-based i-functions and structure-based s-functions. In the case of Marxist theory, the larger part, if not all, of the explanation is constructed by reference to interest-based functions, an anomalous case of functional analysis, to say the least. Cohen follows this anomalous use:

Classes are permanently poised against one another, and that class tends to prevail whose rule best meets the demands of production. But how does the fact that production would prosper under a certain class ensure its domination? Part of the answer is that there is a general stake in stable and thriving production, so that the class best placed to deliver it attracts allies from other strata in society. (Cohen 1978:292)

To have "a general stake in stable and thriving production," to understand that "production would prosper under a certain class" and to became an "ally" to that class because of the above realizations – are these not mentalistic notions involving agency and intentional orientation to practice? We will see below that this very crucial problem of the conflation of the **teleological, teleonomic,** and **teleomatic** conceptual processes (see Chapter 4 for the distinctions) are at the root of many misconceptions about functional analysis in the social sciences as well as in biology. It is unfortunate that Cohen, despite the general analytical rigor of his work, has not escaped this confusion.

Variant 4: the Darwinian/selectionist program

The strict Darwinian program is characterized by its emphasis on three factors considered necessary and sufficient for biological evolution: (1) variation, (2) heritability of that variation, and (3) differential fitness of the inheritors of that variation, on the basis of which operates the process of natural selection (cf. Levins and Lewontin 1985). It is important to remember that "differential fitness" is defined by the degree of contingent adaptation of various organisms or species to local environments. In this strict reading there is no reference to general adaptability or to adaptation to any environment. The history of each species, that is, the totality of past **aptations** determines the field of possibilities for any new, more-or-less successful adaptation in conjunction with the specificity of environmental changes, that is, changes in the dynamics of the multidimensional local ecosystem. I mentioned these ideas as a preamble to my assertion that the strict selectionist program is considerably different, and more robust, than the adaptationist program discussed earlier.[8]

The type of sociological functional analysis based on the selectionist program is quite specific. In an attempt to avoid holistic and adaptationist traps it focuses on the levels of analysis just below the "systemic" or integrative level down to the middle-range level of organizational analysis; thus, even when the focus is on the higher levels, the larger unit of analysis is not treated as a systemic entity but as an aggregate (or statistical aggregate) of sorts. Starting with Hannan and Freeman's seminal paper "The Population Ecology of Organizations" (1977), the selectionist approach introduced into the older adaptationist model of "human ecology" the ideas of competitive relations between social units and potential instability or disequilibrium in the overall population ecology.

The typical Darwinian model applied to social phenomena, here the population ecology of organizations, has been modified along the lines suggested by Campbell (1966). It involves, not the usual trio of variation, heritability, and selection, but the new trio of *variation, selection,* and *retention.* Organizational variation may be exogenous or endogenous. Selection implicates mechanisms for the elimination of certain types of organizations (by dissolution, absorption, or radical restructur-

---

[8] For the sharp differentiation of the "selectionist" from the "adaptationist" program see Brandon 1978, 1985; Burian 1983; Ruse 1988; Sober 1984a, 1984b; Wimsatt 1972, 1976, 1980.

ing). Retention is the more tricky term, as it threatens to bring back the adaptationist line into the selectionist model. As the argument goes, retention is a structural problem: How is it possible to maintain advantageous traits in any organization threatened by incremental change or drift? Campbell posits an "inertial" basis of structural reproduction on the grounds that it ensures reliability. He suggests that this process operates more successfully in the case of large, core organizations than in small, peripheral ones, but this has been a highly contested point. In spite of this reference to inertia, however, the very mechanism of retention looks suspiciously teleological.

The problem with this approach is that it trades on the more or less robust – though currently contested – explanatory logic applicable in the domain of evolutionary biology, which it transposes rather uncritically to the domain of social phenomena. Thus, although the descriptive functional language is innocuous, the special elaboration of the mechanisms of variation, selection, and retention at the "colonized" domain is left, to a considerable extent, to the imagination. For example, we do know that in the biological domain variation takes place by genetic drift or substitution (at both the molecular and allelic levels); but in the approach under study variation is assumed exogenously. Furthermore, selection in evolutionary biology is based on "variable heritability" and on the "differential fitness" of organisms or species; in the approach under study, in spite of the significant introduction of the Lotka–Volterra logistic mode of analysis, the language remains a bit superficial, accounting primarily for the elimination of organizational forms through an ambiguous notion of aggregate mortality. Would it not be the case that, in focusing microscopically on the particulars, one would discover successful or failing managerial strategies and differential structural conditions along the lines proposed by Chandler (1962, 1977), Perrow (1979), Thompson (1967), Touraine (1977, 1988), H. C. White (1981a and b, 1988), Williamson (1975)? If so, this form of functional analysis is only halfway explanatory. The population–ecological research program has further to go, and one hopes that it will soon move in the direction of the fifth and sixth variants presented below.[9]

---

[9] Carroll (1984) described the field of organizational ecology as consisting of three subfields: organizational demography, population ecology of organizations, and community ecology. The first uses a "developmental," nearly embryological approach, the third one a macroevolutionary approach somewhat similar to that of ecological succession. The trouble is that both of these approaches rely to a great extent on adaptationist explanatory principles (adaptive differentiation, adaptation to internal and external constraints, deterministic adaptational succession as in the work of Lenski and Harris). As such, they still operate with an outmoded model and provide no better grounding of functional analysis.

Variant 5: the program of dynamic functionalism

Michael Faia is the author of a transitional set of arguments pointing beyond T_2 toward the new ideas of post-synthesis neo-Darwinians and other non-Darwinian evolutionists, which are exemplifying T_3. His position is transitional in the sense that in the exposition of his ideas (1986), several older positions are still defended in spite of intimations of what "dynamic theory" will do to functional analysis. For example, Faia maintains the use of functionalist terms although (a) he is critical of the "requisites" program, (b) quite properly suggests that the "stability" of a system is an empirical matter, and (c) wishes to redefine functional analysis along "dynamic" lines (with the use of time-series, curvilinearity, and so on).

The most important traditional elements in Faia's position are the following:

(1) a commitment to the adaptationist language;
(2) a preference for dynamic equilibrium models;
(3) a focus on "survivorship" and continuity.

What he attempts is to redefine these three elements dynamically and elaborate them methodologically so as to bring functionalism back to the mainstream of empirical research as a viable research strategy.

The adaptationist program is redefined by way of two methodological twists. Faia relies on the homeostatic model formalized by Stinchcombe (cited above) to demonstrate the dynamic character of "disturbances" and adaptive structural counterprocesses. He speaks of both negative as well as positive feedback processes that make the model more dynamic than initially thought. He is willing then to introduce *curvilinear* functions as representations of this new-found dynamism. The other twist is the reliance on *life-tables* to study and represent the time-dependent nature of dynamic functional process, as well as to support his new view of selective retention as methodologically demonstrable "survivorship." This is certainly a throwback; at one point he is forced to conclude that "perhaps Parsons was right" when he said that social equilibrium, that is, the continuity and maintenance of social patterns, is unproblematic and requires no explanation. Faia finds Campbell's model of variation–selection–retention more or less appropriate for functional analysis, and his explanation of how selective retention operates is given in terms of an exploration of the cited Stinchcombe model in terms of time-series analysis. This is an improvement over the less dynamic, one-shot or one-cycle, homeostatic model: here the reciprocal causation between the structural and the homeostatic variable, that is, the negative and positive feedback, is to be assessed through the use of lagged endogenous variables, hence the introduction and analysis of time-series data. The logic of functional explanation, writes Faia:

involves a nearly inescapable commitment to the use of time-series data. Because only those time-series variables that actually vary substantially over time are likely to play an important role in social research, we conclude that functional analysis is inherently dynamic in the sense of focusing on social variables that change (i.e., have temporal instability). (Faia 1986:87)

Temporal instabilities can be seen at work in every curvilinear process model: growth models, diffusion models, social movement stage models, ecological models of invasion–succession–dominance, or cybernetic control models (Faia 1986; Hernes 1976; Puccia and Levins 1985; Rosen 1970). Nonetheless, Faia is rather timid in the conceptualization of this temporal instability. He conceives it as a form of moving equilibria interrupted by disruptions, "a constant alternation between stability and disruption" (1986:90). He subtitles his major category as "Patterns of change within stability" (ibid.:58). He considers "oscillation" the essential process. He uses the stable population model (the theoretical basis of the "life-table") as a baseline, even though he realizes that it is deterministic and appropriate for closed systems only (88). He takes it, however, that the world is filled with "open systems" in which "equilibrium-seeking processes are subject to noise" (89) – a conservative attitude reminiscent of the premodern goal of "saving the phenomena." His own realistic model then posits that, if enough noise exists in time-series data, one could then proceed with a dynamic functional analysis of sequential stability and disruption patterns, of reciprocal and self-regulating relationships. The overall model that this alternation brings about is one of "cycles" or "chemical clocks," on the basis of which one studies functional adjustments to disturbance by analyzing the frequency and amplitude of such cycles to determine the amount of lag in a causal or functional process.

A bit more complicated, but still within the "change within stability" model, are the ecological examples Faia derives from the early formulation of the Malthusian theory (ibid.:61–6). Malthus's classical statement was that population growth produces pressure on resources (means of subsistence) of any given species, such as the human species, and that pressure on the means of subsistence brings about operations (famine, war, disease) that dramatically check, through increased mortality, the rate of natural increase, so that a state of stationary stability is maintained in the long run.[10] This notion, of course, derives from a

---

[10] This sort of circularity may be more complex, as in Darwin's cynical story (cited by Faia 1982:62) of the large "spinster" population and a large number of cats. As the story goes, the cats feed on field mice, which allows the larvae of bum-

view of ecological communities as self-stabilizing systems, a view which, as we will see shortly, is currently under severe attack.

Now, for the points that make Faia's work a progressive transitional step toward the more robust views of contemporary evolutionary biologists: Faia comes to rather pessimistic conclusions when assessing the prospects of Malthusian conceptions of societies.

> The trouble is that much of the time human societies do not seem to work this way, as Malthus discovered in the preparation of his second edition: There are too many sources of disturbance, too many instances in which a social transformation – for example, the invention of effective fertility control – disrupts a self-regulating system that otherwise might have retained considerable stability over time. (Faia 1986:62)

Here Faia refers to the global ecological model of the "Club of Rome" as a case of an advanced, neo-Malthusian model built on very complex realistic assumptions: a very large number of variables with very complex relationships between them – curvilinearity, multiple causation, a large number of causal loops, thus also many dynamic nonlinearities – leading to catastrophes and chaos rather than self-regulating cyclical stabilities. Several steps are still needed for the transformation of this form of quasi-dynamic functional analysis into a fully realistic model (steps only intimated by current adherents; cf. Alexander 1985; Alexander and Colomy 1985, 1990).

Notwithstanding a number of problems,[11] as I have already indicated I consider Faia's work a step in the right direction, which I would argue is represented by the final variant.

Variant 6: the postfunctional program

This last program has emerged as a result of the tremendous upheaval and transformation of the fields of evolutionary biology by a

---

blebees (the mice's food), to survive and pollinate the local crops, which enrich the local farmers who then marry local spinsters. The new wives get rid of the cats, the mouse population increases and eats the bee larvae, pollination declines, crops become scarce, farmers are poorer, divorce rates increase, and everything starts anew from the beginning.

[11] I see three major paradoxes in Faia's work: (1) he describes dynamic functionalism as involving processes of equilibrium-seeking, of cyclical stability, and – exceptionally – of possible catastrophic transformation. He apparently has no knowledge of the exciting developments in bifurcation theory and dissipative structures, the physicomathematical notion of "chaos," or the very dynamic, chaotic ecological models; (2) he is still prisoner of the "adaptationist" program, unaware of or unwilling to consider the new post-Darwinian theories of "drift" and "drivers," molecular biology, models of multilevel selection, and NET theories of self-organization and evolution; (3) he has not yet made up his mind whether his dynamic functionalism is a species of (a complicated) causal or of functional analysis, a confusion not relieved by modular views of microcausality (as in Hernes's case, 1976).

combination of many sets of interdisciplinary theoretical, modeling, methodological, and empirical work. Indeed, the revolution involves all the domains of physical and biological sciences: quantum mechanics and cosmology, many-body physics, nonequilibrium thermodynamics, constructionist physical chemistry and molecular biology, post-dynamic ecological models, neuroscience, models of neural networks, and distributed parallel processing in artificial intelligence studies. The message of this revolution for the social sciences is that we have been right all along to argue on behalf of the tremendous complexity of social processes. For the first time, models, tools, and metrics from the physical and biological sciences appear to begin to capture that complexity. All the more important for us, therefore, to be aware of these ongoing transformations in the scientific practices of these fields.

I will offer here only a summary of what I will detail later on. First, what comes out of the changes in evolutionary theory is (a) the clear rejection of the adaptationist program and (b) the complexification, questioning, rearticulation, and relative diminution of the role of selection in the dynamics of evolutionary change. One may immediately begin to wonder: What would happen to functional analysis if the older adaptationist and simpler selectionist lines of "defining the phenomenon" – in Merton's terms – are abandoned altogether? At present the field of biology is in disarray as it tries to reassess the earlier distinctions between teleology, teleonomy, and causality. A four-pronged attack on the neo-Darwinian synthesis has emerged since the 1970s and has produced a general belief that it needs significant modification or even wholesale sublation. The challenge has come from:

(1) the theory of "punctuated equilibria" in regard to matters of macroevolution and, especially, speciation;
(2) the divergent positions in the significant controversy over the "units and levels of selection";
(3) the development of dynamic, nonlinear models in the analysis of processes in local ecosystems;
(4) the growth of explanatory models based on the new nonequilibrium thermodynamics of **fluctuations, bifurcation branches, and dissipative structures.**

These challenges have considerably weakened the orthodox neo-Darwinian explanation of evolution and with it have nearly destroyed the premises of adaptationist and, to a large extent, of traditional selectionist groundings of functional analysis. As in the well-known transition from structuralist to poststructuralist modes of thought, we are witnessing here the transition from functional to postfunctional modes of analysis. One may argue *contra* Alexander and others that what lies beyond structural-functionalism is not a neofunctionalism of some half-baked sort but a robust theoretical method of such poststructural–post-functional analysis.

This dynamic mode of analysis must necessarily incorporate and rest on the gains already made in the fields cited above, namely:

(a) the multivariate character of phenomena (very many variables);
(b) the multidimensionality of social space and, thus, also of our analytical models;
(c) the superdynamic view of ecosystems and human dissipative systems;
(d) the nonlinear nature of relationships and structural processes, as a result of which the notions of fluctuation, chaos, bifurcation mechanisms, and processual instability must be central to any baseline model of the world;
(e) the recognition of the multiplicity of mechanisms involved in the evolution of any complex system, including thermodynamic generative processes, drift, drivers, developmental constraints, partially disjoint multilevel constraints, aptations, and dynamic selection;
(f) the characterization of any complex system as a multilevel hierarchy of relations and quasi-modular substructures with varying degrees of boundary stability; and
(g) the fact that complex "loop systems" are distinct and much more dynamic than the traditional "suppressor systems" of functional analysis. The former are dialectical in the richest sense – the sense of positive as well as negative feedbacks, of linear, curvilinear, and nonlinear relations, of a phase-space that is complexly differentiated into an intricate "patchwork," of multiple simultaneous processes operating, traversing, percolating through, interconnected in a cellular distributed parallel manner in that patchwork, and so on. To speak of these systems simply as "open systems" is, I believe, a form of conceptual violence: I would rather opt for the new term of "dissipative structures" which has captured the sense of the hyperdynamics to which I refer.

But, of course, simply saying so does not make it so. One needs corroboration of this new analysis and explication of the potential utility to be had from it. I now turn our attention to these matters.

The crisis in evolutionary biology

I have already made reference to the major transformations that have taken place (and continue to take place) in evolutionary biology and affine fields. I would like briefly to tell this story emphasizing, as I should, the parts that account for the demise of the traditional "functionalist" foundations and, by the same token, give grounds to the new conception represented by variant 6.

Critique of the adaptationist program

The old adaptationist program in evolutionary theory, which was the pillar of functionalist and earlier functional analysis, was built, in its essentials, on the following presumptions and beliefs: The simpler considerations were the positing and analysis of the relationships between two variables, *organism* and *environment,* and therefore also a given *population* and its *environment.* The commitment to the organismic principle was basic to the adaptationist program. The organism was the unit of selection: adaptation and selection operated only on individual organisms. This commitment also involved a reliance on the common sense perception of the homeostatic stability of organisms and, therefore, carried with it the further commitment to consider organisms and, analogically, organism-like systems, such as societies, as stable, equilibrium-based, or, at least, equilibrium-seeking systems. Too, the environment was considered more or less homogeneous and near-equilibrium, disturbed by temporarily occurring accidental physical forces of nature – the movement of tectonic plates, the action of volcanoes, climatic changes and their effects. After all, "Darwin's theory was an explicit extension of the Newtonian paradigm to the biosphere" (Depew and Weber 1985:252). Nature was seen as a closed system. Thus, the generalized model of "functional logic" offered by Stinchcombe did make sense under these assumptions. Organisms and populations were disturbed by environmental variables which exerted pressure on them, and the organisms or populations responded to that pressure with temporary or more permanent adaptive behavior. The mechanism explaining the degree of success of those adaptations was still undefined but the fact of such adaptation was secured.

This paradigm has come under severe criticism; I will briefly summarize some of the criticisms below, but here I will focus on the notion of adaptation itself. As cited earlier, the notion of adaptation is ambivalent when conflated with any sort of "illegitimate teleology," either of the intentionalist variety or the older Aristotelian variety of finalism ("entelechy"). It often has been the case that biologists commit this logical error when they infuse "adaptive functionalism" with one or another "finalist" expressions. The vocabulary of Darwinism is full of such interchanges between teleonomic and teleological modes of explanation. The concept of "teleonomy" was finally defined in a proper manner, that is, independently of the teleological, by several astute biologists. Teleonomy now implies that the function of a biological structure refers to the effect that the homologous structure in the ancestors had on survival in past generations, not to what that structure will do for the organism at present or in the future. Teleonomy refers to past effects, not present purposes.[12] Thus, there is no guarantee that past performance will be matched by similarly successful performance in present and future environmental states. This guarantee could exist, other things being equal, *only* if the specific ecology is conceived as stable or near-equilibrium.

Adaptationist notions also fail in many other respects. For example, as we will see below, as soon as one comes to the conclusion that organismic selection is not the only nor, indeed, the privileged locus of selection, the whole imputation of teleonomic-cum-teleological adaptedness to organisms seems to be part of a folk description. The question of what adapts cannot be so easily answered. The recent emphases on suborganismic loci or levels of selection (gene selection, multigene family, intergenic networks, genomic, and metagenomic[13]) and on the molecular subgenic level[14] have demonstrated that the concept of adaptation, even in the sanitized version cited above, is at once too complex, less significant in a formal logical sense, and of small substantive-explanatory value compared to the many nonselectionist and multiselectionist mechanisms posited currently.

Evolutionary speciation and punctuated equilibria

The older Darwinian and neo-Darwinian models were built on the assumption of gradualism; that evolution was a very long process of innumerable small variations and selections. Under such an assumption, however, the explanation of the processes of speciation becomes a nearly impossible task. In the 1970s the theory of "punctuated equili-

---

[12] Brandon (1985:88) defines adaptation explanations as follows: "An adaptation-explanation is a causal historical explanation that explains the presence and/or prevalence of an adaptation in terms of the selection forces leading to its evolution. An essential part of such an explanation is a citation of the effects of the adaptation that in fact increased the adaptedness of its possessors." But this, of course, is not predictive.

[13] For suborganismic forms of selection see bibliographic citations for Dawkins (gene), May (gene network), Lewontin (multiple genic foci), and J. Campbell (multigene families). Cf. also Wills 1989.

[14] For molecular subgenic selection see Dover (1982, Dover and Flavell 1982), Kimura (1979, 1982, 1985), Wicken (1987).

bria" was proposed (Eldredge and Gould 1972; Gould 1982; Gould and Eldredge 1977; Lewin 1986; cf. Vrba and Eldredge 1984) and was more or less immediately accepted because of its strong corroboration. Based on the reevaluation of the so-called "Cambrian explosion" in speciation, this new view suggested that, in macroevolutionary time-scales, periods of rapid evolutionary change did take place followed by periods of relative stability. Obviously, this position supported the perception that nature is not a closed system but a system with complex dynamics and many phases. Equilibria were temporary and recurrently punctuated under the influence of *infra*evolutionary (thermodynamic, geological, molecular) and *inter*evolutionary (global and local ecosystemic) forces. This way of positing the problem of speciation, though still within the parameters of sophisticated neo-Darwinism, was hospitable to other, more radical views held by thermodynamicists and molecular biologists who proposed teleomatic processes for the explanation of teleonomic phenomenologies (see below, non-equilibrium thermodynamics).

The debate about units of selection

The adaptationist–functionalist program and even the most sanitized version of selectionism were relying on the older notion that the process of selection operated at the organismic level. Since the thirties and, more particularly, in the last twenty years, a controversy has existed regarding the so-called loci of selection and levels of selection (Brandon and Burian 1984; Dillon 1983; Lewontin 1970; Vrba and Eldredge 1984). The distinction between genotype and phenotype had divided evolutionists into camps supporting competing theories of genotypic (genic) or phenotypic (organismic, ecological) selection. In both camps, further controversies also emerged relative to the privileged units or levels of selection (gene, complex genes, multigene families, intergenic networks, the whole genome; or organism, kin groups, demes, interdemic metapopulations, whole species) as well as the number of such points of selection from the allelic level upwards (one, two, or multiple loci of selection). The struggle is not yet over, as strict genic selectionists (such as Dawkins 1976, 1982) fight with multigene/multiloci selectionists (such as Campbell 1983, 1985; Lewontin 1970), and organismic and kin selectionists (such as Hamilton 1963; Maynard Smith 1964, 1986; cf. Boorman and Levitt 1980) fight against demic, interdemic and other group selectionists (such as Levin and Kilmer 1974; Wade 1977, 1978; Williams 1966; Wilson 1980; S. Wright 1956, 1969, 1980; Wynne-Edwards 1986). Nonetheless, the overall perception has emerged that strict genic, organismic, or even kin selectionists' arguments are not sufficient to explain many anomalous facts to the effect that selection indeed seems to operate (a) at a number of different levels, (b) on a number of different objects, (c) both at the genetic and the phenotypic-ecological fields, and that (d) even at the level of genes selection does not operate on mutually independent genes nor on genes considered to be passive (for a review see Wills 1989).

Once many levels and objects or loci of selection are accepted, the introduction of hierarchical or heterarchical thinking into evolutionary biology is unavoidable. As Gould stated, the study of evolution embodies "a concept of hierarchy, a world constructed not as a smooth and seamless continuum, permitting simple extrapolation from the lowest to the highest, but as a series of ascending levels, each bound to the one below it in some ways and independent in others" (Gould 1982a: 382; cf. Eldredge 1985, 1989; Salthe 1985; Vrba and Eldredge 1984). No doubt, one of the main factors for the emergence of such a hierarchy is selection operating at different levels and loci, giving more solidity to mutationally or generationally emergent new boundary conditions in the initially fragile hierarchy. Given that "selection" is a multidimensional dynamic process and that it operates on a whole hierarchy of levels and objects, any effort to define in persuasive, analytic terms the functional role of any adaptation or adaptive structure is next to impossible.

The dynamic modeling of ecosystems

Developments in the dynamic conceptualization and modeling of ecosystems have come to add support to the belief that biological systems may be "far-from-equilibrium." In general, an ecosystem is defined in terms of the physical environment and all the organisms in a given area, together with the web of interactions of these organisms with that physical environment and with each other. The physical element includes the thermodynamic energy of the sun, the climate, the soil, and other such elements. The biotic element includes the community of given populations of species, the food webs, the trophic levels, and so on. The older and simpler models of ecosystems, by theoretical myopia or pragmatic necessity, usually considered ecosystems in terms of the set of interacting populations in an otherwise stationary environment (see Allen and Starr 1982; MacArthur and Wilson 1967; May 1973; Pianka 1974). Within this closed system they then considered the various types of interactions at and across the trophic levels – symbiosis, competition, prey-predator and host-parasite relations, commensalism, and so on. Overall patterns of stability at least of the "cyclical" dynamic variety were then found at the ecosystem level. But, in recent years, the size of the ecosystem, the number of species in the community and/or the number of interactions, and the environmental perturbations were found to play a more significant role in the determination of the stability or instability of ecosystems.

It has become clear, for example, by virtue of recent cosmological theories, that nature is not a closed system. The environment is not near-equilibrium, but exhibits variable dynamic and even chaotic behavior, decays thermodynamically or physically and biotically, and is tremendously heterogeneous and, thus, for each particular species, constantly uncertain (Allen 1985; Brooks and Wiley 1986; Gleick 1987; Levandowsky and White 1977; Nicolis 1986a). The very notion of an ecological "niche" now is conceived multidimensionally, defined by Hutchinson (1978) as an n-dimensional hypervolume enclosing the complete range of conditions within which an organism can successfully reproduce itself. Emphasis has shifted from adaptationist considerations to complex ecosystemic interactions. Sewell Wright's topological simile of "an uneven 'adaptive surface' of hills and valleys, with contours to represent differences in the adaptive values of the numerous viable genotypes" has come to be seen as extremely valuable. On this surface, Wright conceives of populations as "structured into thousands of local units each subject to drift and sometimes to relaxed selection." Thus, in such complexity, the crossing of a single two-locus saddle is "only an elementary step in differentiation with respect to a multilocus interaction system" (Wright 1978:524; cf. also 1969, 1977, 1980).

The significant work of Robert May has provided us with dynamical models for single populations, for two interacting populations, and for multispecies communities (1972, 1973, 1976a and b, 1987, 1989; May and Oster 1976; see also Pool 1989). May considers the stability of many-species ecosystems not as given but as the sometimes very fragile result of a complex internal dynamics. Such stability is described by systems of differential equations, in which the signs and magnitudes of the interaction coefficients are varied randomly. On this basis May has shown that an increase in complexity, either in numbers of species, or in the number of interactions between them, tends to cause instability of the system as a whole. May calls systems which are only stable within a comparatively small domain of parameter space dynamically fragile: Such systems "will persist only for tightly circumscribed values of the environmental parameters, and will tend to collapse under significant perturbations either to environmental parameters or to population values" (1976a:160). Systems stable within a comparatively large domain of parameter space he calls dynamically robust. From his own more technical work and the empirical work of others May has formed the following two conclusions: (a) dynamical stability typically decreases with increase in the number or strength of interactions between species, and (b), as a mathematical generality, increasing complexity makes for dynamical fragility rather than robustness.

Others have more or less followed these lines, sometimes pushing the argument even further. Maynard Smith considers first the more orthodox neo-Darwinian line that, given May's results, one ought to conceive a model ecosystem as involving not random but systematic alterations of the magnitude of interactions (described by finite difference equations). The parameters describing the interactions between species must be highly nonrandom, the products of natural selection. On the basis of such an analysis he then concludes that "competition for resources at the lower trophic levels of an ecosystem leads to instability, but that competition between the top predators has a stabilizing effect" (1986: 115). Nonetheless, Maynard Smith ends by saying that models, such as those of May, "make it clear that stability is not a necessary or even a likely consequence of increased complexity" (ibid.). Other studies by Cracraft (1982), Halfon (1979), Levins (1970), Schaffer (1986), Schaffer and Kot (1985), Ulanowicz (1979), Ulanowicz and Platt (1985), Zeigler (1979), among others (see Pool's 1989 research note), have elaborated in more detail the hierarchical and nonlinear (quite chaotic) character of complex ecosystemic interactions. Puccia and Levins (1985), following the lead of Prigogine and his associates, offer a suggestive methodology for analyzing dynamic loop systems that operate and exhibit emergent properties both near-equilibrium and far-from-equilibrium (limit cycles, chaos). Levins and Lewontin speak of the latter as dialectical systems: "The dialectical viewpoint sees dynamical stability as a rather special situation that must be accounted for. Systems of any complexity – the central nervous system, the national and world capitalist economies, ecosystems, the physiological networks of organisms – are more likely to be dynamically unstable" (1985:283). We may agree to think of such systems as having, at best, a "dynamically fragile stability" and call them *dissipative structures*.

Non-equilibrium thermodynamics and evolution

Developments in this area of research are extremely significant for understanding the interface of "process" and "structure" but also extremely complex. Space and subject considerations require my summary to be brief and simplified; interested readers will profit from consulting the references cited in the text.

In a charming, whodunit-type book on the evolution of life, Cairns-Smith (1986) describes the evolutionary process as implicating a control structure ("what is needed to control what"), which is the focus of pre-Darwinian and Darwinian selectionism, and a supply structure ("what is needed to make what"), which is the focus of the newer views of compositionist structuralism or constructionism, of theories of drift and **drivers,** of views of self-assembly and self-organization, and of their more general underpinnings in current non-equilibrium **thermodynamics.** We have already said quite a lot on the compositionism/constructionist strategies in science and of the hierarchical/heterarchical role of structural and boundary constraints; so we only need now to briefly add some basic ideas about the rest of the package.

First, let us cite the growing importance of the work of molecular biologists who study the non-Darwinian or non-selectionist bases of evolution. Kimura's work (1979, 1982, 1985) on the so-called neutral theory of evolution is well known as the first systematic effort to propose a molecular basis for evolution with a secondary role assigned to natural selection and no significance attributed to the strong adaptationist program. Kimura and others have shown that the evolution of proteins and nucleic acids manifests a regular pattern of molecular substitutions that does not accord well with selectionist explanations. This work gave rise to the talk of drift and drivers in evolution: meiotic drive, chromosomal drive, gametic drive, mutational drive, and the more basic molecular drive (Brandon and Burian 1984; Brooks and Wiley 1986; Campbell 1983; Dover 1982; Dover and Flavell 1982; Gould 1982a; Ho and Saunders 1983; Jungck 1983; Küppers 1983, 1990; Milkman 1982; Wills 1989). Such drivers represent internal evolutionary forces driving the system in particular evolutionary paths within the existing possibility space.

This line of thinking is revolutionary. It is built on the new recognition that homogeneous spaces, states, or activities are inherently unstable (see the Appendix for the logic of the instability of homogeneity or "fluctuations"). If energy is supplied in increasing quantities, a homogeneous spatial field would become inhomogeneous. This is obvious at the moment of cosmological evolution (Davies 1988, 1989; Kauffman 1984; cf. Crutchfield and Huberman 1980), at lower chemical levels (Nicolis and Baras 1984; Prigogine and Stengers 1984), at the higher levels of enzymatic chemical activities (Cairns-Smith 1986; Dillon 1981; Kauffman 1969, 1983; Maynard Smith et al. 1985), at the level of ecosystems (Allen and Starr 1982; May 1972, 1973, 1989; Ulanowicz and Platt 1985; Wright 1969, 1977), as well as at the level of complex social systems (Allen and Sanglier 1978, 1983; Dyke 1988; Georgescu-Roegen 1971; Lösch 1954). Matter in space-time is now considered as active matter, generative of **fluctuations,** on the basis of which fragile structures and levels emerge more or less irreversibly with different probabilities of becoming self-sustaining **dissipative structures.** The new extensions of quantum mechanics in the direction of many-body physical phenomena exhibiting "broken symmetry" and emergent properties (Prigogine and his associates, Haken, Anderson, Leggett, among others) have given strong impetus to the search for the thermodynamic grounds of evolution.

The work of Wicken, of Brooks, O'Grady, Wiley, and others has moved in this thermodynamic direction. At the root of this effort is the new non-equilibrium conception of thermodynamics (NET) of Prigogine and the more recent developments in information theory (Gatlin 1972; Jantsch 1980, 1981; Nicolis 1986; Wicken 1979, 1987). There are some important differences, however, between Wicken's research program and that of Brooks, Wiley, Collier, and their associates. Wickens appropriates Prigogine's theory of "dissipative structures" at the lower chemical and macromolecular level, while Brooks and Wiley specify the particular biological character on the basis of a newly developed "hierarchical information theory" (HIT). Nonetheless, both programs agree on the fundamental non-Darwinian nature of evolution, which they explain starting with the principles of non-equilibrium thermodynamics.

Wicken's research program (1979, 1980, 1985, 1986, 1987, 1988) can be summarized as follows: Thermodynamic processes are **teleomatic,** that is, end-directed (see Chapter 4). The two-tiered hierarchy of causal principle involves mechanistic or quantum-mechanistic laws at the lower level and thermodynamic or statistical laws at the higher. A complete explanation of any natural process requires a specification of both the teleomatic *why* and the mechanistic *how*. When applied to evolution this will mean that "variation in all its aspects, from point mutations to chromosome rearrangements to sexual recombinations, occurs by virtue of the teleomatic drive toward configurational disorder" (Wicken 1988: 153). With regard to "mutation," the entropy principle forbids error-free replication in populations of biopolymers. "Selection" itself occurs via competitions for resources among thermodynamic flow patterns; "fitness" carries meaning only within specific contexts of resource utilization. Therefore, "the most general objects of selection are not individuals or genes or populations, but informed patterns of thermodynamic flow" (1988:156). An organism is such a pattern; so, too, are ecosystems and socioeconomic systems. "Emergence" then is consistent with the teleomatic principles. Finally, "speciation" also follows from breakdowns in reproductive cohesion resulting from the entropic drive to genome alteration. This is why it occurs, although how it occurs is explained by the particularities – isolating mechanisms, epigenetic constraints, ecological circumstances – of each case. "Evolution" in general involves entropic variation and self-organization, constraint, and selection. Neo-Darwinism has neglected the first two to a great extent; the new theories properly emphasize them. The fact is that most variations and constraints have considerable thermodynamic underpinnings. Natural selection itself is based on competitive success in autocatalytically converting resources into organization.

The Brooks and Wiley research program (1984, 1986) has been called an internalist version of NET evolutionary theory in contrast to Wicken's externalist version. The difference lies in the fact that Brooks and Wiley consider biological systems not only teleomatically but also teleonomically – as a very special case of proper biological dissipative structures. Their position is as follows: Evolution is a special case of the second law of thermodynamics (now named "Dollo's Law") because the irreversible behavior of certain biological systems has a quite different basis from that exhibited by purely physical dissipative structures. The order and organization of biological systems, such as organisms and species, is based on information that is carried by these systems in the form of genes, cytoplasmic organization, and chromosomal organization (see Brooks et al. 1988:222; Collier 1988:231–2). Thus, what specifically characterizes the order and organization of biological systems is that they have properties which are "inherent and heritable." In contrast, non-biological physical dissipative structures lack these characteristics. Of course, organisms do obey the second law of thermodynamics at the chemical level but this is of no relevance to understanding evolutionary organization. What is relevant are the implications of the second law at the biological level.

Biological information resides in biological systems and has a physical interpretation. Thus, the entropy of biological information must increase in irreversible processes, increasing the size and variety of the genome (increasing, that is, the genetic space of the system). This produces the need for a new theory explaining "expanded" dissipative structures, a need fulfilled by the hierarchical information theory (HIT). According to this theory, the "instructional information" of biological systems is inscribed in the molecular structure as potential for specifying various homeostatic and ontogenetic activities. Energy taken up by the organism from its environment forces the actualization of this potential. In ontogenetic time (short time-scale), the information expressed is only a subset of the potential. In evolutionary time (long time-scale), "the accumulation of variations on the molecular structure increase the realm of the potential and thereby the diversity of the actual. ... Over short time scales, biological systems, from cells to ecosystems, *behave like dissipative structures*. Over longer time intervals, they *behave like expanding phase-space systems*" (Brooks et al. 1988: 207; my emphasis). HIT, therefore, becomes a framework for understanding complex systems from a position intermediate between full reductionism (which insists that explanation proceeds from the lowest level in the hierarchy) and some variant of holism (which attributes significance only to the highest level). "HIT interprets the Second Law of Thermodynamics as a tendency toward disorder at low levels of a hierarchy that makes it possible for order to appear at higher levels" (Brooks et al. 1988:219). As a result, this internalist view suggests that evolution is *affected* by the environment while, primarily, other factors (e.g., Second Law, Dollo's Law) *effect* it.

A tentative conclusion

This review, although necessarily brief, of the important recent developments within evolutionary biology still enables us, I believe, to reach some tentative conclusions regarding the status of functional analysis and the prospects of the now emerging poststructuralist/postfunctionalist programs. In short, I see no payoffs coming from any redeployment of functionalism or of any other sanitized version of functional analysis. Such projects seem outmoded within the current intellectual environment in which "irreversible processes," hyperdynamic and NET thermodynamic principles and models, chaotic nonlinearities, multilevel modes of organization of "dissipative" – physical, biological, and social – structures, and so on, are considered seminal. It is time, therefore, to say farewell to functional analysis and to the rigid conceptions of holism and proceed to define and investigate in detail the new modes of analysis and explanation appropriate for such dynamical and complexly structured systems. In the next chapter we will consider the multilevel hierarchical mode of organization, applied to social phenomena. As we will see, hierarchical organization – unless improperly developed – need not be functionalist in any of the senses we have described previously.

9   The hierarchical theory
of social structure

The utility of a commonsensically conceived hierarchical theory in macrosociology is taken for granted by a large number of social theorists. The Marxian and Durkheimian legacies have given the social sciences foundational grounds and descriptive vocabularies that seem to breed hierarchical or straightforward collectivist modes of theorizing: It is intuitively grasped that any emphasis on the autonomy and explanatory primacy of societal phenomena necessarily rests on "group-theoretical" assumptions, namely, that macrophenomena have superseded their microconstitution and govern the microdimensions of social life in their own dynamic way.

We have already seen that any macrotheory may be defended from the usual reductionist attacks both as regards its diachronic constitution and its synchronic operations. In synchronic terms, proponents of a macrotheory are bound to argue defensively the nonreducibility of macrophenomena to microphenomena or microprocesses (the "holist" thesis[1]) and, possibly, take the stronger position that macrophenomena "reach down" causally and determine, constrain, parameterize, or condition the preferences, motivations, rationality, values, and so on, implicated in the actions and interactions of microagents (the thesis of "downward causation"). On the diachronic front, macrotheory advocates may also follow two distinct strategies to support their arguments on the autonomous status of macrostructures: they may either (a) refer to ecological-evolutionary and group-selectionist macroprocesses (Aldrich et al. 1986; Stanley 1979; Vrba 1984; Wynne Edwards 1986) that explain the autonomous development of macrophenomena; or (b) they may accept the notion of the diachronic emergence of macrophenomena out of microprocesses, adding to it the qualifying proposition that,

---

[1] Margolis (1988) distinguishes a variety of "holisms" within the respective domains of the sciences and human studies. Pertinent variants include: (a) collectivism: a priori positing of sui generis collective agencies; (b) functionalism: assigning functions to parts in a systemically linked complex; (c) structuralism: assigning properties to distributed elements as "relata" of an at least semiclosed, relational system; (d) hermeneutics: assigning interpretive claims as samples of an inexhaustible global meaning inscribed in any "text" or "textlike" system; (e) contextualism: positing that all meaningful actions, speech acts, and the like are intensional and "embedded" in their particular contexts; and (f) postpositivism: positing the theory-ladenness of facts, the overarching role of conceptual frameworks, and a weak (pragmatic, internal, intensional, global) form of scientific realism. See also the early part of Chapter 8.

180

once diachronic emergence takes place, the macrophenomena "super-sede" the prior and lower-order microphenomena or, at least, in a weaker sense, prevail and establish a "governance" over these micro-phenomena (Pattee 1973; Salthe 1985; Webster 1979). Having said enough about the first strategy of extreme collectivism in the previous chapter, I will now concentrate my efforts on the second, hierarchy theory proper.

Various hierarchical efforts

If we exclude the various collectivist readings of functionalism or group selectionism, we are left with very few examples of hierarchical theories of social structure.

The differentiationist tradition

Prime candidates for consideration, certainly, appear to be the "dif-ferentiationist" theories of Blau (1975a, 1977a and b, 1981), Mayhew (1973, 1974, 1980, 1981), and others (cf. Luhmann 1982a; Alexander and Colomy 1990b), theories that have distanced themselves from an overt commitment to the functionalist and culturalist Durkheimian strains.[2] These differentiationist theories imply – though they do not spell out explicitly – a hierarchical model of group formation and structure, a model which is based on a rank-ordered series of group-ings of increasing size, or a quantitative inclusion relation. Simply: as size increases, so do differentiation and organizational structure. This takes place in a rather inexorable manner, certainly independently of individual considerations of efficiency, interests, or values, since, if in-dividual intentional actions were required, one could not proceed with a proper hierarchical explanation (Mayhew 1980, 1981). These theories then maintain that they need no reference to micro–macro links. Nonetheless, I tend to think that they are rather vacuous, unable to provide in themselves the mechanism for structuration without linkage to either "relational" notions proper, or to diverse individual models of action (rational choice, transaction-costs, interaction rituals, and the like) taken as initial grounds of structuration within the varieties of constructionist programs we have already discussed.[3] It is only *in con-*

---

[2] Blau (1977b) has separated the structural from the cultural and the functional strains in Durkheim's thought; but I doubt if his effort can be considered suc-cessful. Ditto for those of Lenski and Mayhew, the latter following Blau in his strict insistence on structuralist-aggregate arguments. Tilly (1984) has criticized all similar quasi-functionalist efforts.

[3] Even Blau has recognized that size itself is not properly speaking a structural variable (1975a, 1977a and b). For a micromodular, complementary view of dual causation see Hernes 1976.

junction with other logics that the "differentiation logic" (see Appendix no. 19) can be inscribed with some explanatory power. So I do think that, despite the empirical nature of the differentiationist generalization, these theories constitute poor versions of a hierarchical theory of structure.

Lenski and social evolutionism

Lenski's theory is more complex but is an equally poor exemplar of hierarchy. Lenski's "evolutionary-ecological" program incorporates the differentiationist line together with a "population ecological" approach *and* a technological quasi-determinism. The result is less static than Blau's but also less rigorous, as allegiance shifts from the issue of population growth to ecological factors of natural or superimposed density and then to an implicit – and, at times, unpersuasive[4] – overvaluation of the role of technological factors. This shift also appears as a transition to a presumed, progressively more effective, causal mechanism, away from a strict population ecology and toward a more commonsensically acceptable model of human ecology. Nonetheless, a hierarchical population ecological theory for humans has not been yet successfully elaborated; bracketing for the moment the question of their explanatory utility, population ecological models or human ecology models (a) are not necessarily hierarchical and (b) need not be connected at all to the differentiationist principles.

Roy Bhaskar on integrated pluralism

A better conceptual effort has been suggested by Roy Bhaskar in several writings (1975, 1978a, 1982, 1983). Bhaskar, possibly following Bunge (1969, 1973a and b), has presented a neo-Popperian ontological and epistemological **transcendental realist** view of the world on the basis of what has been called the posit of an **integrated pluralism:** the world is composed of many levels, distinct from one another, and hierarchically integrated so as to form a "level structure." At each level entities exist that are real and these real entities are no Leibnizian "monads" (as liberal, Lockean-Kantian "individuals" are, as if they were "sovereigns"); they are "structures" emerging from lower levels and becoming ontologically and epistemologically autonomous. Thus, a hierarchical theory of structure is posited as the proper metatheoretical model for the social sciences. Bhaskar then proceeds to accept Marxism, slightly modified, as an exemplar of such a hierarchical struc-

---

[4] I still fail to see the presumed revolutionary significance of the "digging stick" for the transition to horticulture. Recent work on Upper Nile early habitations points out the smooth nature of the transition and the crucial role of other factors. See Henry 1989.

tural theory and sketches his own view of a transformative theory of social change. We will return to Bhaskhar's work later on, when discussing the Marxist theory, and in the next chapter, where several alternate views are analyzed as candidates of the competing strategy of heterarchy.

Gudmund Hernes on structural processes

A more elaborate theory of "social structure" and "structural change" has been proposed by Gudmund Hernes (1976) along what seem to be hierarchical lines of thinking. The importance of the model lies in its efforts to comply with several desiderata of what currently passes as a good theory and in the analytical distinctions it provides for an understanding of structural, both structuring and structured, phenomena.

There are three desiderata, Hernes argues, for the construction of an effective explanatory theory in social science: 1) it must explain both constancy and change; 2) it must incorporate intrinsic sources of change; and 3) it must see social change as being mediated through individual actors. First, no theory of social structure should be conceived of in static terms. Even a stable structure must be seen as a "process" in a presumed temporary equilibrium. The bias should not be in favor of a presumption of stability but against it; an explanation must be sought as to why the parameters governing the process are not themselves changing. Thus, instead of speaking of structure and change as two separate notions, presuming that structure implies stability, we should rather speak of "structural change" within which may appear any number of temporary equilibria. This follows on the lines suggested more than two decades ago by Dahrendorf (1968). On the second issue of the sources of change, Hernes closely follows Dahrendorf's lead in proclaiming the ubiquity of internal processes of change, although Hernes's argument is more defensive than offensive in nature. It is logically impossible, he argues, that all changes in or of systems are always exogenously generated. Intrinsic sources exist and should be accounted for. Certainly, these points are unassailable.

The final desideratum is to look at social change as mediated through individual actions. A great deal has been written on this issue by those scholars who, since the mid-1970s, have committed themselves to the proposition that micro and macro phenomena must be seen as interlinked (see Alexander et al. 1987; Hechter 1983; Knorr-Cetina and Cicourel 1981; Lindenberg et al. 1986; Wardell and Turner 1986). The trouble has been that when all is said and done, we still find these same people committed either to the primacy of the microprocess or of the macrostructures involved. Hernes is not different. He appears to favor the prioritization of the macrolevel – a requirement if his theory is to be considered as a hierarchical one. He gives the more or less standard neo-Simonian version of the individual as a satisficer: individuals are seen as purposive actors, having a set of preferences or priorities. They are seeking the best or, at least, a satisfactory way to realize their goals while operating under conditions of bounded rationality; their actions are "result controlled," that is, readjusted relative to any given deviation so as to reach the desired result. However, Hernes adds several provisos to this conception of actors: preferences, he says, are largely determined by socialization; and the individual's capacities are socially determined capacities (rights, abilities, competencies); so that, overall, it appears that macrovariables affect or determine individual motives and choices. Both the ends people pursue and the means at their disposal are decided largely by their past and present locations in the social structure. The macrostructure, consisting of an institutional or collective set (i.e., structural constraints on available alternatives) and the aggregative or distributive outcomes of choices of alternatives (i.e., properties of populations), provides a context for individual choices by its reward structure, incentives, and constraints. Hernes then turns the issue around and states that the choices individuals make in turn change the macrovariables; because in pursuing their goals people may modify the constraints under which they choose, and actions may change the parameters of choice by opening or destroying alternatives. This takes place via (a) a "cumulative series" of choices (e.g., in-cohort marriages progressively restricting the choice of latecomers), (b) as an "aggregate result" of independent decisions (as in hog cycles), or (c) by the "self-imposition of new constraints" in collective action or joint decisions (such as, I presume, in agreed-upon matching algorithms). However, Hernes does not speak so much of microactors per se as the conscious producers of these changes; the real force is beyond their reach and understanding since they have no control over the long-term cumulation series nor over the aggregate results, and they may have little control, if any, over the emerging institutional arrangements. Since preferences, resources, information, and capacities are "historically determined," and material conditions, social constraints, and cultural norms evoke and induce the interests that the members in various groups (not as individuals) seek to promote, there is not much left to individual autonomy or to individual rationality, strategy, and opportunism. Hernes provides some relief from the more extreme structuralist versions that propose the total dispensability of the actor but, nonetheless, remains firmly within the general structuralist camp. Now, of course, one *must* hold such a position when providing a theory of hierarchical supersession of the microprocess, and this is exactly the

point: given the ascription of a lesser importance to individual intentionality and agency, Hernes's theory appears to be rather heavily biased in favor of a hierarchical notion of structure implicating
downward causation.

Hernes's primary project is the definition of social structure and
structural change and the analytical explanation of the basic structural
processes. Hernes uses a very abstract, neutral definition of structure
as a "configuration of parts" (though a better definition would have
treated structure as a "configuration of *relations* between parts," which
are themselves also relational systems). Then, he proceeds along the
path suggested by the structuralists (Lévi-Strauss [1952, 1963] and Althusser [Althusser and Balibar 1970], for example; Bourdieu 1977a; or
Boudon 1968; cf. Homans 1975), of conceiving structure as a structuring
process ("structuring structure") as well as a structured outcome
("structured structure"). Hernes, too, favors identifying and constructing models of the generative process in order to explain the resulting
structure; the structure at one stage is the outcome of a process which
itself has a structure. Hence the distinction between process structure
(structuring structure) and output structure (structured structure).

"Process structure" is defined as the logical or functional form of
the process generating the results that constitute the output structure.
An "output structure," on the other hand, is defined as the distribution
of results produced by the operation of a process structure.[5] To the
process and output structures, Hernes adds the "parameter structure,"
defined as the structure of the parameter values governing the process
by taking definite values in concrete situations.[6] The main example
given by Hernes to illustrate the demarcation between process, parameter, and outcome structure is that of a population transition
model: Here, the process structure consists of the birth and death
process specifiable in a set of equations which represent its functional

---

[5] This follows the classical quantum mechanical view that treats the Hamiltonian
as an operator and the object on which it operates as a function (*eigenfunction*),
which is merely recovered after the presumed work of the given operator.

[6] Here I am not sure that Hernes has offered us anything of value: Do the
parameters form a "structure" of their own, or is that a definitional trick? In
the scientific conception of systems defined as mathematical functional forms,
the disctinction is not between process structure and parameter structure but
between the atemporal propositions defining the operative relations of the system in abstract-universal terms (a "formal structure") and the temporal propositions of the system, which *taken together with the atemporal ones* give us a
"realization" of that system in the space phase (a "realized structure"). The
timeless propositions characterize the system, while the temporal propositions
characterize the state of the system. See, for instance, the quantum mechanical
formalization offered by Primas and Mueller-Herold (1978); cf. Garfinkel
(1981).

form; the parameter structure is then defined by the age-specific fer-
tility and death rates in the population; finally, the outcome structure
consists of the population pyramid depicting the composition of population by age and sex. Hernes makes, perhaps, a good point in distinguishing the "operator structure" (formal process structure plus
specified parameter values) from the "output structure" – along the
lines of the "structuring"/"structured" distinction – but he is not persuasive in his attempt to conceive the parameter values as a structure
in itself. There is, I submit, a better scientific formulation: The postulate of a simple or complex formal process structure consisting of
abstracted relations (which may be "natural" or "historico-social."[7]
The temporal realization of that structure by specification of its parameter values – populational, ecological, material, historico-social –
brings about a realized operative structure. In its recursive ("linear
additive recursive" per Blalock 1969) operation this structure brings
about, and is inscribed in, an output, structured structure visible in a
number of distributional characteristics (e.g., distributions of powers,
material possessions, occupational stratification, ethnic or racial composition, rates of crime, and so on). Notice that the above three kinds
of structure – abstract, realized, output – form a "recursive" order of
realization from the deepest, formal level to the surface, empirical
level, at which survey analysis usually works. In this sense, the QM
Hamiltonian, the structuring structure of Bourdieu, the axiomatic
structure of Boudon, and the formal process of Hernes, all operate
similarly as deeper mechanisms structuring and, at the same time, inscribed into the structured or output structure. This rather distinct
mode of operation must not be compressed into a one-dimensional
view of structure, as is done by the empiricists (Blau, Homans, Lenski,
or Radcliffe-Brown).

Hernes's goal is to distinguish between different "structural processes," – simple and extended reproduction, transition, and transformation – and to demonstrate that a proper structural process
theory can encompass all of these processes at once. He considers the
question of whether or not the process structure, parameter values, or
output structure change as a result of the general functioning of the
operator; given all the possible answers, the following types of structural
processes emerge in a Guttman-like scale form:

---

[7] That is, implying exogenous (fixed, species-specific, universal) or endogenous
(historico-social, changing internally over time) relations. For the crucial nature
of the distinction see Elster (1985), but above all Marx's "Sixth Thesis on Feu-
erbach" – the individual is "the ensemble of social relations" (see McLellan
1977:157).

	Process structure	Parameter values	Output structure
Simple Reproduction	−	−	−
Extended Reproduction	−	−	+
Transition	−	+	+
Transformation	+	+	+

"Simple reproduction" exists when process, parameter, and output structures remain constant, in which case the output is a stationary state at equilibrium; examples are the equilibrium shape of the population pyramid, a stationary model of social mobility maintaining the given sizes of social strata, or the reproduction of a stationary economy, as in the case of traditional feudalism. "Extended reproduction" exists when the output structure changes but the process and parameter structures remain unchanged; here the relevant examples will be an expanding economy (with "growth" but no structural change), as when the means of production and, correspondingly, labor increase. Hernes's argument is unclear, however, when he claims that extended reproduction also exists in the case of dramatic changes in the time trajectory of the output, leading to "overshooting" or "reversal" (starvation) as well as in the case of cyclical fluctuations, as in the case of the hog cycles. "Transition" takes place when the changes in the output structure "feed back" on the parameter structure and change it while the process structure remains unchanged; illustrations include increasing crowding (output change), raising the death rate (parameter change), or the three-step theory of the "demographic transition" in Europe. Finally, "transformation" is defined as the structural process in which the process structure and the parameter structure change due to the feedback from the changing output structure; here Hernes cites the examples of "contagious diffusion" and, of course, the particular models of transformation of a mode of production proposed by Marx.[8]

Another important point in Hernes's work is his distinction among various structural systems in terms of whether they involve (1) one "singular" process structure, (2) a few "simple" transformations or combinations of one or two process structures, or (3), in more "complex" cases, many mutually implicated process structures. The singular case is, of course, unproblematic. The simple cases involve the following

---

[8] There are numerous difficulties in Hernes's model, for example, a failure to see that outputs do not always form a structure (toxic waste, pollution) or that "output structure" proper and "output effects" are not synonymous (to recall the correct judgment of Homans [1975] contra Blau). But this criticism cannot be extended in the present context.

variants: (a) two interacting systems, and (b) a set of process structures supplanting each other. I presume that, when speaking of two interacting systems, Hernes means two interactive process structures, such as that of the "forces of production" and the "relations of production." On the other hand, when speaking of process structures supplanting one another (as by a dialectic), he clearly refers to the Marxist succession of the modes of production and the models of "ecological succession" produced by population ecologists. The complex cases are the richest, in which a number of process structures are mutually implicated. Here Hernes leaves the range of possibilities unspecified but discusses the two limit cases, one in which process structures are "loosely coupled" and the other in which process structures are strongly integrated. I will state now and return later to critically evaluate the consequences implicit in this conception: the complex relations between several or many process structures necessarily give rise to (strongly or weakly realized) hierarchical systems.

Referring to the complex systems that involve at least several interacting process structures, Hernes points out the significance of focusing on the degree of coupling or uncoupling between those structures. If these structures are completely uncoupled they will operate as singular structures in uncomplicated ways. If they are loosely coupled or relatively tightly coupled (hence more or less integrated), different structural dynamics will ensue. A structural system that is "loosely coupled" will have decomposed into subsystems (here, the set of all process structures interacting), in such a way that the interactions or relations within each subsystem are stronger than the interactions or relations between subsystems. Nearly-decomposable systems, to use Ando, Fisher, and Simon's terminology (1963), such as those with loosely coupled subsystems, are hierarchical systems (s-hierarchies). In such systems, more or less independent stabilities exist at each level of organization (system, subsystem, subsubsystem, and so on), so that a change within a subsystem may not affect at all the overall stability of the system one level above it and, perhaps, vice versa – local change may not bring about global change; and global change may not bring about or imply local change in every component. Usually, the argument also states that loosely coupled systems are independent of one another in the short run, though in the long run, the influence of one on another may increase; this includes Marx's view of the short-term/long-term coupling of forces and relations of production as well as Simon's discussion of entropic dissipation of energy (1965). Notice also that in loosely coupled systems, as Hernes perceptively remarks, the differential rate of change among subsystems and subsubsystems creates "structural incompatibilities" or "structural contradictions" – the very stuff of any truly dynamical – must we avoid saying "dialectical"? – theory of society.

Alternatively, when systems (or subsystems, and so on downward) are "tightly coupled," what emerges is a strongly functional system, in which any change in one subsystem may be dampened by the rest of the subsystems to the point that a dynamic stability is maintained, or, if such a thing fails to occur or simply is overwhelmed by the disturbance, a holistic change in the overall system will take place. Thus, overintegration usually brings not only reproductive stability but exceptional change as well.

It seems at times that the more Hernes speaks of complex process structures, the more he moves his level of analysis to the larger macrostructure with the hierarchical or functionalist overtones associated with this kind of theorizing. I believe this shift is due to the fact that he has not considered "moderately coupled" systems that involve a stronger notion of hierarchy (p-hierarchy) – a proper hierarchical theory needs to posit an upward spiralling integration of phenomena, even if it is relative. Hernes's more effective examples are closer to this conception.

Hernes provides three major examples: (1) the "ecological succession" case; (2) the "population transition" case; and (3) the Marxist case of the transformative succession of "modes of production." Most of the other examples are secondary, supporting cases, or explainable on compositionist grounds. Of the exemplary cases two are derived from the ecological and demographic fields and the third is usually translated into functional terms (Cohen 1978). In short, Hernes's preferred focus is macrostructural and the underlying model for his theory of structural change is a thoroughly hierarchical one. This is quite evident in his extensive discussion of the demographic transition that took place in Europe in the last century, in which he says that the macrostructural demographic changes are describable as a transition model which explains the rates and how they have changed. One also needs to know why they changed; for which one can use one of the various microtheories operating as modules to complete the micro–macro link. Hernes seems satisfied with this connection, but a closer reading of the boundary conditions implied by his microtheories[9] reveals that the issue

---

[9] Hernes posits several microtheories as alternate modules, micro-explaining in a complementary fashion (a dualist view) the structural process: ideal number theory, no-split plot, cost-benefit analysis of the nth child, wage-labor theory. This, of course, leaves unanswered the question of the appropriate micro–macro linkage: What are the mechanisms of upward structuration that produce the large-scale structural processes? On the failure of this and other such approaches and the alternative see Chapters 10–14.

is not one of merely linking discrete micro- and macrotheories, but of articulating a series of levels (here, at least three levels) implicated in the connection. Hernes, then, intimates but does not fully develop, a true hierarchical theory of structural change.

Outline of a hierarchical social theory

In constructing a hierarchical theory of social structure, I believe it is essential for one to proceed on two fronts. First (in a proper hierarchical manner of course), to show how starting from some "initial conditions" of microchoices (species-specific notions of purposiveness, limited rationality, and a generic preference structure), various levels of increasing macrocomplexity emerge, becoming the "boundary conditions" of lower levels and of the rock-bottom microchoices and, therefore, exerting on them a certain reorganization or "governance," if not outright "control" (including endogenous transvaluations of beliefs and preferences). Second, to show that, as the emergence of higher-level boundary conditions proceeds, there is a convergence and coupling of "structuring structures," so that the higher levels become progressively more complex, multistructural, and thus also replete with more "structural contradictions." I believe these two very basic propositions exemplify the hierarchical logic of social structure.

Let us focus, first, on the hierarchical linkage of emerging levels of structure. Suppose, for the sake of the argument (which may, certainly, be rejected as a futile attempt to establish a so-called logic of origins[10] – an essentialist trap, to be sure), we begin with the (counterfactual) assumption of an initial state in which microchoices and microinteractions were exercised, presumably unaffected by any preexisting social or cultural context or tradition. We may assume that at this utopian state species-specific characteristics of individuals were antecedents of their perceptions, preferences, and choices. Thus, we may assume that generic individuals were (a) purposive actors, orienting their perceptions and activities toward the accomplishment of pragmatic goals; that they had, at least, (b) minimal rationality, that is, the ability to pragmatically evaluate – aided by whatever experience but severely limited by imperfect knowledge and uncertainty – presumed costs and benefits of choices and actions and opt for the more beneficial, "right" alternative(s); and, finally, that they had (c) a generic preference structure, which was not fully rational, hierarchical, and based on marginal utilities, but was basically oriented toward the pragmatic values of survival (see Harré et al. 1985; Heller 1976; MacIntyre 1981; Margolis 1977).

---

[10] For the critique of the logic of origins see Althusser and Balibar (1970), Derrida (1977, 1980), Foucault (1972); also Popper (1966), Prigogine and Stengers (1980, 1984).

Iterated behaviors based on these three assumptions would produce "realized" microstructures of different types, structural problems (impaired markets, blocked flows, contradictions), and local or semilocal institutional solutions (contracts, matching algorithm, conventions). These microstructures emerge as results of the initial microconditions of choice and interaction, but as soon as they emerge become "boundary conditions," reorganizing the field of possibilities and the particular contexts of any further choice or interaction – they "govern," if not outright "control," the parameters of choice. Local and semilocal structures and institutional solutions in their turn become coupled into higher-level structures, which represent the socioeconomic, historically specific, and cultural, contexts of future local and semilocal structures and institutional solutions – constraining their emergence, opening appropriate opportunities, and allowing relevant judgments to be made on the cultural propriety, rational character, or technical efficiency of any given set of such structures and institutions. So, in an organized hierarchical ordering involving governance or control, later and more complex structures become *more* significant than earlier and lower structures, and boundary conditions become *more* central than initial conditions. At this point, one can see why the quest for "initial conditions" is a utopian one, since the later boundary conditions have already altered the presumed initial ones.[11] This is the root dogma of hierarchy.

The second basic characteristic of hierarchical logic is that as levels emerge that are later, higher, and more complex, a process of relative convergence takes place: a multitude of microstructures couple to produce a system (or several such systems) at the next higher level. (In a *heterarchy* these will be only **polymorphously** coupled.) In turn these systems will themselves couple, forming even higher systems, and so on. This at least partial convergence implies that organizational micrologics couple to form more complicated intermediate and higher-level structural logics, which are variably integrated. Some contradictions will still exist and affect the dynamic trajectory of the system, but sufficient integration must also exist so as to demarcate the new boundaries of the system. Lack of such integration would imply unsuccessful boundary formation and the inability to sustain the autonomy of that level – boundaries are, after all, the "membranes of life."

If the above analysis is deemed correct, then it appears that the most important task for someone advocating a hierarchical theory of social structure is to demonstrate and thoroughly analyze this boundary for-

---

[11] This accords well with Marx's writings on method in the *Grundrisse:* "The so-called historical presentation of development is founded, as a rule, on the fact that the latest form regards the previous ones as steps leading up to itself . . ." (106).

mation process in the emergence and convergence of higher-level hierarchical "structuring" logics. In the rest of the chapter I will discuss the way in which Marxist theory appears to be an exemplary case of a hierarchical logic given that it focuses on the all-encompassing "logic of capital" as such a sufficiently integrative mechanism. (In later chapters I will dispute this interpretation and offer a reading of the Marxist theory along heterarchical lines.)

Is Marxism a hierarchical theory?

Marxism as a research program in the social sciences has given rise to a multitude of interpretations with distinct theoretical and political implications (Perry Anderson 1980, 1985; Bottomore 1988; Elster 1985; Roemer 1986). For the purposes at hand we may distinguish among these interpretations according to the emphasis they place on micro-foundations, intermediate scale processes, or structures and processes at the macrolevels and, therefore, the extent to which they prioritize compositionist, heterarchical, or hierarchical logics of analysis. It does not take a lot of thinking to realize that different "Marxisms" would emerge by simply following these distinct strategies. The question of which of the available or possible versions is the correct one is much more difficult to answer, especially since, in the current post-positivist environment, issues of "truth" and "correctness" have been either positively dismissed from the vocabulary of the philosophy of science and of epistemology or relegated to a more-or-less peripheral, relativistic status. Rather than speaking of the correct version we may ask pragmatically which version Marx's own texts support as evaluated quantitatively by relevant statements as well as by the logical centrality of specific arguments and examples. From this point of view the majority of Marxist scholars (including even Elster) agree that Marxism is an example of a hierarchical theory of social structure.

Compositionist Marxism?

It is not that compositionist proposals do not exist. Indeed, in the work of E. P. Thompson and Jon Elster we see two very interesting cases of reformulating Marxism along *nearly* methodologically individualist lines (in Elster, in particular). In his excellent book *The Making of the English Working Class* (1963) and his essays *The Poverty of Theory* (1978), Thompson commits himself to a conception of class as a process, not a structure. Class is a relationship and not a thing: "it" – say, the working class – does not exist as a solid, stable entity but is constantly made and remade by its constituent members and the political struggles in which they are relationally involved. Indeed, the question that must be answered is "how the particular social organization (with its property rights and structure of authority) got to be there" (1963:10–11), that is, how the whole relational system constitutive of classes has emerged. To quote Thompson's seminal expression. "Class happens when some men, as a result of common experiences (inherited or shared), feel and articulate the identity of their interests as between themselves, and as against other men whose interests are different from (and usually opposed to) theirs. The class experience is largely determined by the productive relations into which men are born – or enter involuntarily" (1963:9). The focus is on the actual experience of people as they enter local productive relations at the level of the small firm and of the specific community, not at an abstract national level of relations or a theoretically abstracted mode of production.[12]

Thompson's important contributions refer to the local and quasi-local levels of struggles and experiences: the development of small-scale organizations; the great leaders and reformers whose voices and proposals were heard and debated in workers' gatherings and debate societies; the camaraderie developed in working-class coffeehouses and pubs; and the variety of resistances and counterresponses produced in the course of living the antagonistic relationships between specific capitalist owners and the groups of workers related to them by virtue of the labor contract. Evidently, Thompson pursues what Granovetter (1985) has called the issue of "embeddedness," that is, the prioritization of concrete social relations over both individualist and collectivist–functionalist modes of theorizing.

The political and economic struggles, too, are seen always at the local and quasi-local levels. Even the "state" is recognized empirically at this same level, not as an external, grandiose, superimposed other, but through and in the actions of magistrates, members of parliament, and political leaders – that is, only in an internalist, relational sense, in the concrete, tangible, everyday-life world of workers and citizens. Thompson does recognize that "the exploitative relationship is more than the sum of grievances and mutual antagonisms. It is a relationship which can be seen to take distinct forms in different historical contexts, forms which are related to corresponding forms of ownership and state power" (163:203); nonetheless, he insists that these seemingly objective historical characteristics are operative only *through* people's daily experiences and responses, not in an external, deterministic way. "The working class made itself as much as it was made" (ibid.:194). The production of class is an ongoing process; class is not a ready-made entity.

Thompson notes that external forces are always locally mediated in

---

[12] Compare to this Olson's definition of class (1982:84).

their expression. I presume that it is in this sense that he agrees that the Industrial Revolution was truly catastrophic for ordinary people, who became "subjected simultaneously to an intensification of two intolerable forms of relationships: those of economic exploitation and of political oppression" (1963:198). This economic and political context was present in the form of the force of employers or the local representatives of the state against any resistance to exploitation made by the workers. Thompson despises abstractions, especially Althusser's formalist talk of abstract "levels," their "relative autonomy," or the "structural causality" they supposedly bring about. These he considers to be nothing more than armchair fictions. All these levels and instances, he says, are in fact human activities, institutions, and ideas. The real focus is on men and women, in their material life, their determinate relationships, their experience of those relationships, and in their self-consciousness of that experience (1978:97). In all of this, somehow, Thompson avoids any reference to the meaning of the "mode of production" within the Marxist problematic and the organizational objectivity of state power; he treats them as contexts but not as structural forces in their own right. Predictably, this has brought a battery of criticism from the neo-structuralist Marxist Perry Anderson who has reminded Thompson that, according to Marx, "classes are constituted by the mode of production and not vice versa" (1980:55).

We have already seen the basic principles animating the theoretical work of Jon Elster in our discussion of the utility of game theory (Chapters 6 and 7). Elster, we may recall, emphasizes the great significance of intentional explanation in the social sciences and the weaknesses of functional logic. His explanatory model uses Marxist theory as an exemplar and focus of his work. The game-theoretical or analytical Marxist proposals originating with Elster and with his fellow compositionist John Roemer are grounded on a view of social change initiated by active, purposive, calculative, rational agents in pursuit of their own self-interests. Thus Roemer, soaked in rational choice principles, has claimed that "micro-foundations for the formation of class can be provided by using more or less standard general equilibrium models" (1986:193). Elster also has strongly advocated the recasting of Marxism into a methodological individualist framework. In his more orthodox moments, Elster considers explanations of collective behavior in terms of the class positions of the individuals engaging in it, not as violations of methodological individualism but only as a convenient shorthand; "collective action should indeed be understood in terms of the propensities of individuals to engage in it," says Elster (1985:336n.1), proposing a variant of individual-level explanations.

Following in the steps of Olson, Elster readily concedes as highly problematic the formation of "collective actors." The only way he sees the formation of the working class as possible is (a) by iteration of the Prisoner's Dilemma game, (b) by a move from the visible material reward structure of rational individuals to the consideration of a broader "inclusive reward structure," or (c) by the recognition that actors do not behave in a fully rational manner (1986b:212). Roemer, more explicit on this point, considers the emergence of the working class and class struggle "as a kind of bargaining. Class struggle occurs when many agents in the working class, for example, learn to organize and act as one unit, so they can effectively set up a bilateral monopoly against capital" (1986:198). Elster, in his explanation of technical change, argues that "capital is not a collective actor with eyes that see and hands that move. On the assumption of methodological individualism, capital is only shorthand for the many individual capitalists," although in an attached footnote (1986b:210) he cites the "explicit denial of this view" by Marx (a point I will elaborate shortly). In summary, although there have been efforts to exposit Marxist theory as a species of microtheory, along more-or-less utilitarian grounds, this is still the minority opinion.

Marxist antireductionism; Marxist anticompositionism?

We all know that Marx did insist that collective or structural phenomena operate above the heads of individuals qua individuals. There are numerous references in his work indicative of his strong analytical intention to provide explanations at some macrostructural (though not necessarily global-collectivist) level beyond the individual will and consciousness. The so-called "functionalist" appearance of his explanations, references to "unconscious and reluctant" agencies, "unconscious tools of history," "characters who are but the personifications of the economic relations," the persons who act as "supports" (such as "the economic character masks of a capitalist"), and the plethora of other references to the determinative power of a class over its individual members – all these cannot be treated as peripheral to the Marxist theory. Marx is insistent that priority must be given to the macrostructures with or without reference to the dependent or, at best, semiautonomous strategies and actions of individuals and smaller groups.

In his writings, Marx discusses a number of distinct forms of "subsumption" or "subordination" of individuals and classes of individuals under capitalism, which gives us the proper measure of this antiindividualist stand. Thus, he elaborates on:

(A) the subsumption of individuals under classes, i.e., their subsumption under particular relations of production and the resulting effects;

(B) the subsumption of labor under capital, a central issue which he analyzes in extreme detail;

(C) the subsumption of smaller capitals under large capitals, i.e., the issue of capital concentration;

(D) the subsumption of the state under the capitalist logic, i.e., the rule of capital;

(E) the extension of capitalist control over the ideological apparatuses; and, in general, the totalizing effort of capitalism to penetrate and transform all spheres of production, circulation, and exchange of commodities, laws and political decisions, and ideas within national states as well as beyond them, at an all-encompassing, global level.

It is important to elucidate these notions if we are to properly support the argument that Marxism is a hierarchical theory of structure; the following includes numerous citations from Marx's work pertinent to the task at hand.

Classes over individuals. Several times, in the *Grundrisse* (and in other works, quoted below) Marx speaks of the "subsumption of individuals under specific relations of production"; but he is never as analytical as in the section on competition (*Grundrisse*:649–52; cf. 413–5) which provides several important points systematically corroborating his antiindividualist stand. There Marx explained that, given its particular historical emergence (as negation of feudal limits), "competition" was ideologically reinterpreted and elaborated as "the collision of unfettered individuals who are determined only by their own interests," and, hence, "as the absolute mode of existence of free individuality in the sphere of consumption and of exchange." This was an absurd and self-serving "mistake," according to Marx. While it is true that the barriers of feudalism were dissolved by competition, "it is by no means the case that it thereby suspended all limits, nor all barriers," except the limits not corresponding to it. Indeed, the so-called "free competition" is an affair of capital itself. "It is not individuals who are set free by free competition; it is, rather, capital which is set free." The competition among workers is only another form of the competition among capitals.

Hence, on the other side, the insipidity of the view that free competition is the ultimate development of human freedom; ... [it is] the most complete suspension of all human freedom, and the most complete subjugation of individuality under social conditions which assume the form of objective powers, even of overpowering objects – of things independent of the relations among individuals themselves. (*Grundrisse*:652)

Marx considers the possibility of an individual worker rising above the determinate conditions of his class position only as an exception from his class and from the general conditions of his existence. "If all or the majority are too industrious,... then they increase not the value of their commodity, but only its quantity; that is, the demands which would be placed on it as use value" (*Grundrisse*:286; cf. 164).

In *German Ideology*, Marx had already strongly maintained the view that "separate individuals form a class only in so far as they have to carry on a common battle against another class"; class, in its turn, "achieves an independent existence over against the individuals," so that the latter find their conditions of existence determined by class position – "become subsumed under it" (GI:77). This subjection can only be removed by the abolition of private property and of the class structure itself (ibid., 77 and *Grundrisse*:164).

Marx predicates the subsumption of individuals under classes on the subsumption of labor under the particular rule of capitalist production. We find this emphasis on macrosocial and, indeed, abstract structural notions in many other places in which Marx speaks of the functions of capital, the rule of capital, or of capital as a collective force. For example, in his long essay *Results of the Immediate Process of Production* (RIPP) Marx writes that "the rule of the capitalist over the worker is nothing but the rule of the independent conditions of labour over the worker," conditions that embrace both the objective conditions of the process of production (i.e., the means of production) and the objective prerequisites for the sustenance and effectiveness of labor-power (i.e., its means of subsistence).

The functions fulfilled by the capitalists are no more than the functions of capital – viz. the valorization of value by absorbing living labour – executed consciously and willingly. The capitalist functions only as personified capital, capital as a person, just as the worker is no more than labor personified. (RIPP: 989)

The sale and purchase of labor-power itself presupposes that the means of production and subsistence have become autonomous objects confronting the worker; these means, personified, negotiate as purchasers a contract with the workers as vendors. Therefore, the labor contract is a contract between "capital" and "labor," not an individual capitalist and an individual worker. Indeed, the labor process, in which "the means of production utilize the worker," is nothing else but "the self-valorization process of objectified labour through the agency of living labour" (RIPP 976, 989–90, 1006, 1008).

In the *Grundrisse*, Marx again discusses this objective and independent notion of capital as a "type," whose "tokens" are the various personifications, calling it a collective force. He writes that even "the collective powers of labour, its character as social labour, is therefore the collective power of capital." The very association of workers, as it appears in the factory, is "posited not by them but by capital. Their combination is not their being, but the being [*Dasein*] of capital" (*Grundrisse*:585).

Contrary to Elster's attempt at recasting it, these examples make it clear that Marx's view favors an understanding of the social process based on macrostructural considerations: Marx utilized and, at times, vacillated between relational, structural, and collectivist modes of analysis; but it is obvious to a systematic reader of his work that he placed emphasis on the structural mode of analysis.

Subsumption of labor under capital. The concept of the "mode of production" is fundamental in the Marxist theoretical agenda. Marx's authoritative presentation is found in the 1859 *Contribution to the Critique of Political Economy:*

In the social production of their existence, men inevitably enter into definite relations, which are independent of their will, namely relations of production appropriate to a given stage in the development of their material forces of production. The totality of these relations of production constitutes the economic structure of society, the real foundation, on which rises a legal and political superstructure and to which correspond definite forms of social consciousness. (CCPE:20)

Given these objectively determinate relations between people, no action or relation takes place in a purely voluntaristic manner in the absolute absence of some social constraints. For example, early bourgeois groups and practices were related to the older, feudal mode of production, they were "in the womb" of the old society. (Marx treats the "external" factors of development, such as geographical discoveries and their results, as facilitators, but not originators of capitalist development, contrasting the cases of Holland and Portugal to make his point [*Capital* III:333].) As the cited passages on competition indicate, the progressive strengthening of the bourgeoisie brought about the negative phase of "free competition," or the overthrow of the old barriers. The weakened structures of feudalism *under*determined the situation of the bourgeois class, permitting it to act in ways foundational of its future strength; the transitional structure availed to it a number of developmental possibilities.

Marx describes the emergence of the capitalist class, and of capital, quite extensively. He discusses the early phase (a) of independent *artisanal* production, prior to capitalism. Then, (b) *transitional forms,* in which capital emerged and pseudocapitalist forms of production were tried out. Following that, he details (c) the process of the emergence of capitalism proper, in its first, manufacturing phase in which the so-called "formal subsumption" or subordination of labor under capital took place. Finally, (d) he analyzes the second phase, that of industrial capitalism, in which, with the introduction of machinery, capital succeeded in bringing about the real subsumption or subordination of labor. Notice that in each and every instance, later forms of development are said to "subsume" the earlier form or, at a minimum, to replace it in terms of centrality, dominance, and hegemonic importance. This is definitely a hierarchical way of thinking about the historical process of emergence.

Weaker, transitional forms of capitalism emerged in the fifteenth and sixteenth centuries in connection with the activities of direct producers and merchants. For example, the merchant-clothier brought weavers, independent direct producers, under his control by selling them wool and buying their cloth; however, this merchant-manufacturer, said Marx, was only "nominally" a manufacturer. "In point of fact, he was merely a merchant, who let the weavers carry on in their old unorganized way and exerted only a merchant's control, for that was for whom they worked" (*Capital* III:334). This was an obstacle to the real capitalist mode of production: Without revolutionizing the older mode it only worsened the condition of the direct producers, turning them into mere wage-workers and proletarians under the old mode of production.

A similar situation developed in many handicraft industries of the old cities of Europe, in which artisanal establishments headed by master-artisans become more and more dependent on the owners of stores as buyers of their products: Under these circumstances the masters were really "only middlemen between the merchant and their own laborers. The merchant is the actual capitalist who pockets the lion's share of the surplus-value."[13]

Marx speaks of three basic processes bringing about and superimposing the specific character of the new capitalist mode of production

---

[13] Describing the origins of capitalism Marx writes:

There is, consequently, a three-fold transition. First, the merchant becomes directly an industrial capitalist. This is true in crafts based on trade, especially crafts producing luxuries and imported by merchants together with the raw materials and labourers from foreign lands, as in Italy or Constantinople in the fifteenth century. Second, the merchant turns the small masters into his middlemen, or buys directly from the independent producer, leaving him nominally independent and his mode of production unchanged. Third, the industrialist becomes merchant and produces directly for the wholesale market. (*Capital* I: 714–5)

On these "transitional" forms of protocapitalism see also *Capital* III:334–5, *Grundrisse*:586–7. On merchants' role: *Grundrisse*:855–6, 859; *Capital* I:750. On usurers' role: *Capital* I:750; RIPP:1023. On the medieval guild masters as limited capitalists: RIPP:1029–30. On artisanal developments (snail's pace): *Capital* I:750.

as a "logic" of a higher order. They are: (a) *in the transitional, early phase:* the accumulation of land on the agrarian side and the accumulation and concentrated investment of capital in the urban areas that produces "economies of scale"; (b) *in the formal, manufacturing phase:* the imposition of discipline and a capitalist division of labor in the growing manufactories; and (c) *in the real, industrial phase:* the increasing reliance on new machinery or on technical change in general for further capitalist development. These three processes appear as stepwise functions.[14]

The process of concentration, beginning with the emergence of manufacturers and moving to the subsumption of smaller manufacturing units under a larger capitalist enterprise, is documented by Marx in several places. In *Capital* I we read:

> The capitalist system pre-supposes the complete separation of the labourers from all property in the means by which they can realise their labour. As soon as capitalist production is once on its own legs, it not only maintains this separation, but reproduces it on a continually extending scale.... [This process then] transforms, on the one hand, the social means of subsistence and of production into capital, [and] on the other, the immediate producers into wage-labourers. (*Capital* I:714)

This point is elaborated further in the *Grundrisse* as one of the core notions of the Logic of Capital: Marx documents the process by which merchants made weavers and spinners dependent on them, as an example of the historic process of divorcing the objective conditions of labor from the laborers themselves.[15]

Thus, capital proceeded to deskill the artisan and to bring labor under its control. Marx speaks forcefully of the historical necessity for the dissolution of the artisanal world:

---

14 On the analogy between enclosurers and industry concentration see *Kritik 1861–3:* Marx compares "the separation of the earth from its industrious children" with the separation of small artisanal entrepreneurs from their means of production and their incorporation into larger industries (the translation is Elster's from his 1985).

15 In the *Grundrisse* (510, 511–2) Marx describes the transformation of "money" into "capital" in the case of merchants inducing various weavers and spinners from the countryside to come to the factories "under his command as wage labourers" making "their secondary into their chief occupation." The initial capitalist strategy is "to draw them away from their home towns and to concentrate them in a place of work." All that the merchant-emerging capitalist has done is "to restrict them little by little to one kind of work in which they become dependent, on the buyer, the merchant, and ultimately only for and through him." Then, after this "historic process which divorces the objective conditions of labour from the worker," capital proceeds to "conquer all of production and to complete the divorce between labour and property" by destroying all "craft and artisan labour, working small-landownership etc." as well.

Its annihilation, the transformation of the individualised and scattered means of production into socially concentrated ones, of the pigmy property of the many into the huge property of the few, the expropriation of the great mass of the people from the soil, from the means of subsistence, and from the means of labour, this fearful and painful expropriation of the mass of the people forms the prelude to the history of capital. (*Capital* I:762, where several powerful examples are given)

However, the destruction of the artisanal mode of production does not lead automatically to the mature phase of capitalist social relations. The first step in this direction, though absolutely necessary, is in itself incomplete. At first, "the subjection of labour to capital was only a formal result of the fact, that the labourer, instead of working for himself, works for and consequently under the capitalist" (*Capital* I:330). This formal subjection of labor under capital becomes possible with the advent of manufactories and the development and ossification of the division of labor therein.[16]

In the *Grundrisse* the so-called "formal subsumption" (subordination, subjection) of labor under capital is described from a somewhat different perspective: capital is said to presuppose concentration and accumulation of necessities, raw materials, and instruments – i.e., money – as well as accumulation and concentration of labor powers at a single point under the command of a capitalist.

The development proper to manufacture is the division of labour. But this presupposes the (preliminary) gathering-together of many workers under a single command.... [The individual capital] gathers them in one spot under its command, into one manufactory,... under overseers, regimentation, greater discipline, regularity, and the *posited* dependence ... on capital. (*Grundrisse:* 585–7; emphasis in the original)

A large number of pertinent insights on the issue of the subsumption of labor under capital are found in Marx's rather neglected piece *Results of the Immediate Process of Production*. After an analysis of the process by which the means of production and subsistence have become autonomous objects confronting the workers (i.e., their person-

---

[16] Manufacture, wrote Marx (*Capital* I:336–7), arises in two ways: "(1) By the assemblage, in one workshop under the control of a single capitalist, of labourers belonging to various independent handicrafts, but through whose hands a given article must pass on its way to completion. A carriage for example.... (2) Manufacture also arises in a way exactly the reverse of this – namely, by one capitalist employing simultaneously in one workshop a number of artificers, who all do the same, or the same kind of work, such as making paper, type, or needles...." In the second case a particular form of division of labor is imposed on these artificers on the basis of external pressures, for instance, to deliver large quantities on time, and advantageous "repartitions" of work, which "gradually ossifies into a systematic division of labour."

ification in the labor process as well as the valorization process (RIPP: 989, 1006–8), Marx writes:

> The subordination of the labour process to capital does not at first affect the actual mode of production and its only practical effects are these: the worker bows to the command, the direction and the supervision of the capitalist, although naturally only in respect of his labour which belongs to capital. The capitalist makes sure that he wastes no time and sees to it, for example, that he hands over the product of an hour's work every hour, that he only spends the average labour-time necessary for producing the product.... Lastly, the capitalist forces the workers to extend the duration of the labour process as far as possible beyond the limits of the labour-time needed to reproduce the amount paid in wages, since it is just this excess labour that supplies him with the surplus-value. (RIPP:1010–1, 1017; cf. 1019–23, 1025–34)

In *Capital* I we read more about the further effects of the subsumption of labor under capital in the manufactories: Manufacture produces a "hierarchic gradation" of workers:

> By decomposition of handicrafts, by specialization of the instruments of labour, by the formation of detail labourers, and by grouping and combining the latter into a single mechanism, division of labour in manufacture creates a qualitative gradation, and a quantitative proportion in the social process of production. (*Capital* I:360, 364)

But the formal subsumption of labor under capital, according to Marx, is incomplete and soon to become real subsumption in the specific capitalist mode of production, as the old manufactories give their place to modern, large-scale, machine-driven industries. In the *Grundrisse* Marx provides a contrast between formal subsumption, which refers to the manufacturing phase and involves "absolute exploitation" of labor-power, and real subsumption, which comes about with the introduction of machinery and involves "relative exploitation." Marx ascribes to this process a radical ontological significance: The subsumption of the worker under the machine transforms human beings into passive appendages of these machines; the more the machine is intellectually "humanized," that is, exhibits humanlike qualities of goal-oriented activity, the more are the workers "de-humanized" as simple appendages in the machine-based production process:

> But, once adopted into the production process of capital, the means of labour passes through different metamorphoses, whose culmination is the machine, or rather an automatic system of machinery ..., set in motion by an automaton, a moving power that moves itself; this automaton consisting of numerous mechanical and intellectual organs, so that the workers themselves are cast merely as its conscious linkages. (*Grundrisse*:692)

It is the machine that now possesses skill and strength in place of the worker; it is itself "the virtuoso, with a soul of its own in the mechanical laws acting through it."

In machinery, objectified labour materially confronts living labour as a ruling power and as an active subsumption of the latter under itself, not only by appropriating it, but in the real production process itself. (*Grundrisse*:693)[17]

This process of transition from the formal to the real subsumption or subordination of labor under capital is not an isolated phenomenon. It is a continuous process, exhibiting the tendency of capitalist production "to take over all branches of industry not yet acquired" (RIPP:1036) and expand "in other spheres" of production, including "the sphere of agriculture" (*Capital* I:383, 505).

Subsumption of small capitals under large capitals. As the transition from the early, less productive period of absolute exploitation of labor (extended working day, minimum wages) to the more advanced and productive phase of relative exploitation (expropriation of surplus-value under conditions of increasing productivity) proceeds toward its completion, another process is set at work. As Marx comments in *Capital*, after the real subsumption of labor under capital, the time has come for the expropriation of other capitalists:

That which is now to be expropriated is no longer the labourer working for himself, but the capitalist exploiting many labourers. This expropriation is accomplished by the action of the immanent laws of the capitalistic production itself, by the concentration of capital. One capitalist always kills many. (*Capital* I:763–4)

Once more we see here the workings of the capitalist mode of production as a system, according to Marx, arising and developing itself spontaneously. This particular issue of competition between capitalists, the necessity of technical innovation, ensuing concentration and centralization of capital, and the long-term negative implications of these processes to capitalist accumulation are thoroughly discussed by Marx in *Capital*, are quite well known, and seem less pertinent in the present context to be elaborated at length. Suffice it to point out that Marx, quite persistently, refers to a global level of processes that operate above and beyond the "subjective" will of individuals, who are actually "driven" by the "objective," interest-based and rationally compelling force of the Logic of Capital. Rhetoric notwithstanding, Marx's concern is

to consider ... the way in which the laws, immanent in capitalist production, manifest themselves in the movements of individual masses of capital, where they assert themselves as coercive laws of competition, and are brought home to the mind and consciousness of the individual capitalist as the directing motives of his operations. (*Capital* I:316)

---

[17] See further *Capital* I, chapter 25, "Machinery and Modern Industry," esp. pp. 379, 386, 418–20; also in RIPP:1023ff.; cf. RIPP:1034–5.

Speaking of the objectively compelling character of contradictions within the capitalist system of production, he argues that both possibilities and barriers are immanent in capitalism:

Capitalist production seeks continually to overcome these immanent barriers, but overcomes them only by means which again place these barriers in its way and on a more formidable scale. The real barrier of capitalist production is capital itself. (*Capital* III:250)

The Logic of Capital emerges as an objective, rational, compelling mode of desiring, thinking, planning, and then acting – a mode that imposes on the individual actor by its own force or modus operandi. Thus, we find here a process of subsumption under structuring principles of a higher and higher order – from simple labor exchanges in the guild-system to the initial "formal" subsumption in the early manufacturing phase, and to the more pronounced, "real" subsumption of labor under capital in the more advanced capitalist mode of production. The structures in each (diachronically) later and (synchronically) higher level are more organized and further expanded, transducing the local into global dynamics, and strengthening the power of macrostructure over the individual. On this last issue, Marx is quite clear, for he speaks of an "articulated hierarchy (*Gliederung*) within modern bourgeois society" put in place by the Logic of Capital (*Grundrisse*:28; cf. *Capital* I:489).

Both the level-ascending Logic of Capital (i.e., in its subsumption of labor) and the formation of classes at higher structural levels support the view that the Marxist theory is hierarchical.

Subsumption of the state. The other major project of this same Logic of Capital, according to Marx, is to see that all the basic societal institutions, especially the state, would fall under the realm of capital as well. (Here is where the functionalist tendencies of Marxism seem to be revealed, although I will argue in following chapters that this need not be so.) In the *Manifesto* Marx presents a picture of capitalism as the force that has revolutionized society, subjugated labor, rendered all previously honored professions as its employees, and controlled the state as "a committee for managing the common affairs of the whole bourgeoisie" (CW vol. 6:486). Though in later writings he qualifies his position by allowing for certain degrees of autonomy (a) in the organization and functioning of the state, (b) in the role of intellectuals and superstructural institutions, and (c) in the political mobilizations and coalitions of different collective actors, the bottom line remains that the Logic of Capital has tended, more or less successfully, to totalize the system under its hegemonic rule.

This totalizing project tends toward the direct control of the state in the long-term interest of the bourgeoisie, although this may at times involve policies seemingly against the short-term interests of the bourgeoisie as a whole or of certain factions of the bourgeoisie. "The bourgeois state," says Marx on another occasion, "is nothing more than the mutual insurance of the bourgeois class against its individual members, as well as against the exploited class" (CW 10:326ff.). From the very beginning Marx asserts:

the bourgeoisie, at its rise cannot do without the constant intervention of the State; it uses it to "regulate" wages, i.e., to depress them to the suitable level, to lengthen the working day and to keep the labourer himself in the desired degree of dependence. (*Capital* I:737)

Most often, this goal necessitates the use of brute force, the exploiting of the power of the state,

to hasten violently the transition from the feudal economic order to the capitalist economic order, and to shorten the transition phase. Indeed, force is the midwife of every old society pregnant with a new one. Force is an economic agent. (*Capital* I:751)

This direct and forceful pattern of action appeared, Marx argues, as soon as the bourgeoisie made its revolutionary presence in modern history. As such, the bourgeoisie either took over direct control of the state, or asserted a primary role for itself in a historical compromise with the previous rulers (see TSV I:300–1). This project of direct state control is only compromised under special circumstances, as that of Bonapartism.[18] Overall, however, whatever the form of its rule, direct, indirect, or even temporarily forfeited, the Marxist view is that the state has been brought more or less successfully under the rule of capital and never develops any "substantial" degree of autonomy to act against the – at least, long-run – collective interest of the bourgeoisie. (Notice that my interest here is not to evaluate the truth of this analysis, only to illustrate its implications within the parameters of a hierarchical theory of social structure.) In Marx's view, then, the state always remains a (more rather than less) subordinate structure relative to capital.

Subsumption of ideological apparatuses. The many relevant expressions and metaphors used by Marx to indicate the derivativeness and dependence of ideologies on particular relational locations in the mode of production are well known and need not be repeated here.

---

[18] The conditions of Bonapartism (the exemplar of a semi-autonomous state) are described in *The Eighteenth Brumaire* (129, 142–3): realizing its weakness to confront the angry subjugated classes, the bourgeoisie resolves to break its "political power" (destroy parliamentary democracy) in order to save its "social power" ("its purse"). The textual language here is extremely beautiful.

The claim of the *Manifesto* and of *German Ideology* that the dominant ideas in a society are always the ideas of the dominant class demonstrate the Marxist tendency to assert that capital has more or less successfully subsumed all other important institutions under its rule. One may recall the syllogism of Marx, already spelled out in the early *Economic and Philosophic Manuscripts* of 1843–44, in the section "On Money" – those who have money can buy the intellectuals, their knowledge, and their services (*CW* vol. 3:324).

In general, when Marx asserts that "the mode of production of material life conditions the general process of social, political and intellectual life" and that "it is not the consciousness of men that determines their existence, but their social existence that determines their consciousness" (CCPE:20–21), he signals that capital cannot but ultimately triumph over the state, the social institutions, and the ideological apparatuses of society. In *Theories of Surplus Value,* though in a different context, Marx suggests that "the various functions in bourgeois society mutually presuppose each other"; that "the contradictions in material production make necessary a superstructure of ideological strata, whose activity – whether good or bad – is good, because it is necessary"; and that "all functions are in the service of the capitalist, and work out to his 'benefit' " (TSV 1:287). Statements like these show clearly the peculiar quasi-functionalism of Marx: Under the domination of capital the most important institutions in a society are intentionally and strategically rendered functional, transformed in ways that make them subservient and helpful to the interests of the capitalist class to the greatest extent possible. According to Marx, to make the institutions functional for capital is a major "project" of capitalists, not something natural in society; a "task" to be realized, not a "fact" inexorably produced. One way or another, capital becomes the organizing principle and totalizing force in "bourgeois" society.

Concluding remarks on Marxism
This brings us to some tentative conclusions regarding Marxism.

(A) Notice, first, that Marxism operates primarily at a semi-global and/or global level of analysis. Its overarching emphasis on the Logic of Capital as the fundamental "structuring" principle strongly demonstrates the emergent "top-down" approach to social structure: recall Marx's argument that in every social formation there is one *dominant* mode of production and organizing logic (*Grundrisse* 27; CCPE:212; TSV 1:407). Capital is the totalizing principle, that is, the principle that attempts to, and pretty much succeeds in, making a "totality" out of the heterogenous and often contradictory elements and logics in a social formation. Thus, we have *a logic out of the many "logics" structuring modern society.*

(B) Alternative and potentially "contradictory" logics may exist in the social formation where the capitalist mode of production predominates, but they usually remain peripheral to the system and mostly subservient or functional to the capitalist organization – for example, "bureaucracy," "patriarchy," "simple commodity production," even "slavery." These alternatives have a minimum degree of autonomy within the parameters imposed by the Logic of Capital. This applies equally well to the state and to the ideological-reproductive apparatuses such as educational institutions, family, religion, and so on.

(C) The system's tendency is to reach an optimal level of direct, rather than indirect, hierarchical "control." A weaker "governance" will result in capitalism appearing to be in a crisis and unmask its internal contradictions. Strong control would be clearly visible in all attempts to determine the consciousness of individuals (through oppression as well as ideological hegemony) and produce a "false consciousness" in the proletariat.

(D) Given the imperatives of hierarchical control, no gray areas outside of the reach and control of capital are tolerated. There is no important institutional sphere that has not been made, to a large extent, "functional" for capital, no area on earth that has not been penetrated by capital, and no experiment in alternative, possibly inimical, organizations of production that has not been blocked, antagonized, or coopted.

In brief, the radical disposition of Marxism in the analysis and condemnation of the effects of the totalizing and hierarchically subsuming Logic of Capital make it a stunning example of a hierarchical theory of social structure.

Marxism is the exemplar of hierarchical analysis in the social domain. Other versions, such as those of Hernes or Bhaskar, trade on Marxism and are connected to it with invisible (and sometimes, quite visible) threads. Too, for a variety of neo-Marxist versions, the orthodox hierarchical form of Marxism remains a limit case against which they introduce a variety of modifications – for example, neutralizing the functionalist path, invoking the semiautonomy of the political or the ideological, and so on. In contrast, the differentiationist–evolutionist line of hierarchical theory is built on the diachronic emergence of higher, superimposed structures on unabashedly functionalist lines, such as the separation of "society" from "community" and population growth, and can be seen tilting toward holist or transcendent logic. Both of these theoretical strategies exemplify a robust hierarchical strategy regarding social structure.

Part IV
Heterarchical logics

The following two chapters focus on the Logic of Heterarchy, the basis of my own research program. Admittedly, this is the most complex type and is located – somewhat peculiarly – in the gray area between the constructionist and hierarchical logics. Here I build on Hofstadter's (1979) provocative initial analyses of "**tangled systems**" providing an elaborated transcription of the heterarchical talk into sociological talk. The emphasis is on the analytical characteristics of the heterarchical model of social structure, as described in the theses discussed in Chapter 4; the phenomenological description of social structures along the lines of this model follows in Part V.

Chapter 10 presents and appraises various theories of structuration, which have made an effort to go beyond the simpler constructionist models by introducing a certain dialectic between agency and structure; I also offer here my own positive heuristic on how a successful heterarchical research program can be fully developed.

In Chapter 11, which incorporates a considerable degree of speculation, I discuss the exciting developments in the area of neural networks as a possible, advanced model of social structure; this may seem to be an interruption of the sociological argument proper, but there is an important insight to be gained as we survey the parallel distributed connections between the neuronal/mental and the individual/social levels. By combining the discussion in Chapters 3 and 4 with that of Chapters 10 and 11, we can better understand the interlevel linkages between the numerous social structures to be described in Part V.

10 Heterarchical thinking in social thought

We have already pointed out that on the view of many theorists, the two extreme positions of methodological individualism and methodological collectivism seem fallacious and mutually implicated, functioning as the poles of an unsustainable dualism – the hallmark of "western metaphysics," to use Derrida's term. With the post-1960s demolition of "dualism," "objectivism," and the **metaphysical realist** conception of the certainty of knowledge brought about by the onslaught of attacks from a broad **postpositivist** coalition (Bernstein 1983; Kuhn 1970; Lakatos 1978; Margolis 1986; Suppe 1977), the focus in social theory has shifted from the previous binary and antinomial forms to a third, synthetic position that was introduced under the banner of theories of "practice," "the duality of structure," the "micro–macro link," and of "structural process" or "structuration." These views were offered as new claims or, at least, newly-insisted-upon old claims, to the effect that "action and structure" or "agency and structure" are innermostly connected and that to see them as completely distinct has been a terrible logical mistake and a theoretical dead end.

At this, even compositionist theorists began to hedge their bets and introduced into their model of explanation "structural" (or external) variables, to indicate that the line of causation is not only from individual actions and systems of interaction to larger structures but, somehow, also the other way around. For any compositionist to maintain this more moderate line, his or her best option is to argue that the causality operates diachronically from individuals to groups and structures, although synchronically at any given time; groups and structures and institutions are "always already there" and, thus, become the parameters of new actions and systems of interaction. Though not explicitly stating his view on this issue, Boudon clearly adopts such a compromised position; there is no other way to explain his adherence to the strategy of methodological individualism (compositionism, in my understanding of his work) and the recognition that any social action and, more importantly, any general theory of the large social process (theory of change) must by necessity include variables representing the "environment" of actions and interactions.

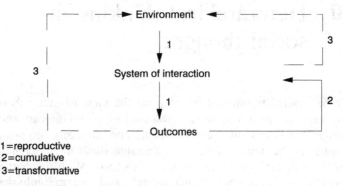

1 = reproductive
2 = cumulative
3 = transformative

Figure 10.1. *Boudon's structural schema*

Boudon on social change

Boudon's theory of social change includes three components or sets of variables illustrated in Figure 10.1: the "environment" as the parameter structure, the "interdependent system" (which is a "system of interaction") as the independent variable, and the "outcomes" or outputs or products of this interdependent system – actions, events, and distributed sets of actions which constitute the dependent variable (1981a; cf. 1984, 1987). Notice here Boudon's identification of the environment of an interdependent system as "parameter structure" and his clarity in locating the environment at the next higher level relative to that independent system (in contrast to Hernes's more confusing conception).

Processes of repetition or reproduction take place if there is no feedback between the components in Figure 10.1 Processes of cumulation take place if there is feedback of the outputs on the interdependent system. Processes of transformation develop when there is feedback to both the interdependent system and its parametric environment. Such a conception puts the inner workings of any interactional, interdependence system in a dependent position relative to the other two components of the above broader system. One must point out, however, that Boudon conceptualizes the environment of an interdependent system as primarily "social," that is, as composed of institutional, economic, and historical variables, and in that sense he could argue that this environment is the diachronic product of interacting microvariables; this will permit the theory to be, at least, logically coherent though not explanatorily as powerful (e.g., still unable to explain this environment, as "organized," rather than "perverted" structural emergence). By insisting on the dual, micro-to-macro as well as macro-to-micro, nature of causation, Boudon avoids committing himself to either a strictly compositionist or a strong hierarchical (p-hierarchical) view. On this ground

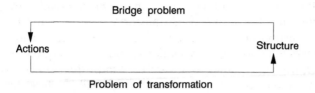

Figure 10.2. *Lindenberg's model*

alone Boudon's theory seems to be a heterarchical theory in the making.

Wippler and Lindenberg's dual model of explanation

A somewhat different approach, perhaps one step closer to the duality of action and structure, has been developed by Wippler and Lindenberg (1987). They have argued in support of a "dual structure of explanation" that is expressed in a two-step argument: (1) individual choices are made under institutional and structural constraints ("individual effects"); and (2) that the transformation of individual actions into collective phenomena is mediated by often complex constellations of institutional and structural conditions ("collective effects"). But what is the status of the "institutional and structural constraints"? Wippler and Lindenberg offer a peculiar argument to essentially bypass rather than resolve the problem of the relationship of action and structure. Making a distinction between "analytical primacy" (focus, context of explanation) and "theoretical primacy" (explanation proper), they agree with Homans that the correct method in sociology is one that ascribes analytical primacy to society but explanatory primacy to the individual. For example, they state, "profit maximization must not be seen as a motive [N.B.: which implies the analytical and explanatory primacy of the individual] but as an intermediate goal created by certain institutions given resourcefulness of human beings." Wippler and Lindenberg argue that rational choice theory with some modifications meets the requirements of the proper method. The modifications involve the addition of two mechanisms to resolve the "bridge problem" and the "problem of transformation" as shown in Figure 10.2.

The bridge problem consists of formulating propositions about the influence of social conditions on the three elements emphasized by rational choice theory – wants, subjective probabilities or preferences, and perceived alternatives – and of formulating propositions about under what conditions they are subject to individual initiative. Thus, bridge propositions together with rational choice theory explain individual behavior as social behavior in two ways: (a) as socially constrained behavior and (b) as resourceful behavior that is made possible by certain social conditions. The problem of transformation, on the other hand, raises the question of how institutions arise from social action as collective phenomena. For an explanation of this, "transformation rules" are needed, which, in conjunction with the "individual effects" (that is, rational choice *plus* the bridging assumptions), will produce the collective phenomena. In simpler cases these transformation rules will only be partial definitions connecting the individual to collective effects; in more complex cases, more assumptions are needed, such as models of "institutional rules." This is Wippler and Lindenberg's proposal. Though this may be a smart analytical exercise, it does not add any new insight on how exactly to posit, analytically describe, and explanatorily ground the institutional and structural conditions that are needed in Wippler and Lindenberg's scheme: where do they come from, what sort of mechanisms produce them, and what is their status, autonomous or dependent, in any explanatory model? Wippler and Lindenberg seem to opt for the "one-and-one-half" compositionist line[1] – they are absolutely silent on this most crucial point of the rules of transformation. Accordingly, their theory seems to be of the circular sort, for lack of any articulated theory of levels and of the genesis and characteristics of higher levels.

Giddens's theory of structuration

In the mid-to-late 1970s two theories that could possibly be described as heterarchical theories were proposed by Giddens (1976, 1979, 1984) and Bhaskar (1975, 1978b, 1982, 1983) more or less semi-dependently – one can presumably cite the Rom Harré connection. Bhaskar's views were first aired in *A Realist Theory of Science* (1975), Giddens's in *New Rules of Sociological Method* (1976). Both were proposing a theoretical elaboration of the Marxist discourse, especially on Marx's dictum that men make history but within given social-historical circumstances, i.e., the practices of previous generations. Starting from this fundamental notion of historical materialism, this entanglement of "praxis and structures," Giddens and Bhaskar delineated, incompletely in the beginning, pseudo-heterarchical theories of sorts, summarized below.

In his *New Rules* (1976:103–4, 118–21) Giddens introduced the notion of "the duality of structure" using the example of language: language is "mastered" and "spoken" by actors; it is employed as a medium of communication between them; and it forms a "structure" which is in

---

[1] On one hand, a solid compositionism is posited; on the other hand, a timid holism is also considered as (secondarily) necessary; but the illegitimate dualism still persists. I consider Wippler and Lindenberg's and Boudon's views as representative of this theoretical stance.

some sense constituted by the speech of a "language community" or collectivity. Language is both the product and the medium of communicative interaction; it is produced by the purposive practices of agents and, yet, as a structure also provides the means by which interactants make sense of what the others say and mean. In a more general fashion the same type of relationship between agency and structure is to be found in all cases involving structure. Indeed, "social structures are both constituted by human agency, and yet at the same time are the medium of this constitution" (121). So to study "structuration" is "to attempt to determine the conditions which govern the continuity and dissolution of structures or types of structure" (120). What Giddens understands as "agency" refers not only to the purposive actions of individuals but also the continuous, successful "monitoring" by the actor of his own activity (82). On the other side of the equation, Giddens makes an important distinction between structure and empirically given social entities, such as groups, interactions, or institutions. "A structure is not a 'group', 'collectivity' or 'organization': these have structures. Groups, collectivities, etc., can and should be studied as systems of interaction" (121). But structures are "subjectless," they can be described "out of time" and "impersonally" (127), even though they are constituted by human, "personal," and timely acts. In this sense, structures are not descriptive but theoretical and explanatory. They have three dimensions or aspects – signification, domination, and legitimation – each of which is important in structuration. Of these, "structures of signification can be analyzed as systems of semantic rules; those of domination as systems of resources; those of legitimation as systems of moral rules" (123–4).[2]

In the more mature rendition of his theory of structuration, several books and more than ten years later (esp. 1979, 1984), Giddens maintains the same vocabulary but sharpens his distinctions. Now a somewhat clearer definition of "structure," "structures," and "systems" is offered. In the early work Giddens did not properly define what he meant by structure. Now he tells us that structure refers to "rules and resources, recursively implicated in the reproduction of social systems" (1979:64–5; 1984:185) or "rules and resources, organized as properties of social systems; structure exists only as structural properties" (1979:

---

[2] Giddens's definitions of signification, domination, and legitimation introduce a number of problems. For instance, one cannot but notice the sloppiness in the equation "*structures* of signification = *systems* of semantic rules"; or the asymmetry between systems of semantic rules (signification) and moral rules (legitimation) and systems of resources (domination); or the circularity of defining resources as "structured properties of social systems" *and,* at the same time, positing them as characteristics of the most abstract definition of "structure" (as "rules and resources").

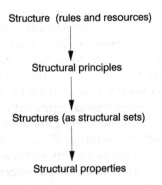

Figure 10.3. *Giddens's structural distinctions*

66). "Structural properties" are the "institutionalized features of social systems, stretching across time and space" (1984:185), giving structure its "solidity." "Rules" are "techniques or generalizable procedures applied in the enactment/reproduction of social practices"; and "resources" are defined as "the media whereby transformative capacity is employed as power in the routine course of social interaction; but they are at the same time structural elements of social systems as systems, reconstituted through their utilization in social interaction . . . but include (also) the means whereby the meaningful and the normative content of interaction is actualized" (1984:21; cf. Turner 1986a). This suggests that rules and resources are recursively implicated downward, to the level of the institutionalized features of systems of interactions and that they are implicit in these features; social systems exhibit structural properties but not the higher or deeper levels of structuring.

Next Giddens posits a recursive hierarchy of levels of abstraction/ concretization. The basic model of the structural hierarchy is depicted in Figure 10.3. First of all one must notice that these levels form a strong version of hierarchy – a control/governance hierarchy operating top-down in a recursive manner. Giddens calls this the "paradigmatic dimension" of the patterning of social relations in time-space and considers it involving "a virtual order of 'modes of structuring' recursively implicated" in the reproduction of situated practices (1984:17). Structure is defined abstractly, as "subject-less" and "time-less," as rules and resources in general. Yet, in an applied sense, "structure" refers "to the structuring properties allowing the 'binding' of time-space in social systems, the properties which make it possible for discernibly similar social practices to exist across varying spans of time and space and which lend them 'systemic' form" (1984:17). There are a lot of conceptual problems with these definitions which are supposedly resolved by this reference to the notion of recursiveness; I am puzzled by the fact that Giddens does not simply repeat Bourdieu's sensitizing notion of "structured structuring structure" (posited in the 1972 French publication of the *Outline*), which is remarkably similar.[3]

One level below the most abstract level of structure Giddens defines the concept of "structural principles." These are the "principles of organization of societal totalities"; "deeply embedded structural (properties) implicated in the reproduction of societal totalities"; the "principles of organization which allow recognizably consistent forms of time-space distantiation on the basis of definite mechanisms of societal integration" (1984:17, 181, 185). Here, at last, Giddens becomes historically more specific. He posits three types of historical societies, each structured by a dominant structural principle:

(1) Tribal societies structured "along an axis relating tradition and kinship" (1984:182).

(2) Class-divided societies structured "along an axis relating urban areas to their rural hinterlands" (ibid.: 182–3).

(3) Class societies (capitalism) structured as a result of "the disembedding, yet interconnecting, of state and economic institutions" (ibid.: 183).

How, specifically, this societal structuring is done Giddens does not say. He only alludes to the fact that these principles are inferred by "drawing upon a range of comparative and historical studies" (ibid.: 181). He postulates them as generative principles, though they appear to be simply empirical generalizations.

Giddens then moves to the third structural level, that of structures or structural sets, which, on his argument of recursion, are even more concrete. Structures (or "structural sets") are defined as "the rule-resource sets, involved in the institutional articulation of social systems." Giddens also argues that "[T]he study of structures (or structural sets) involves the isolating of distinct 'clusterings' of transformation/mediation relations implied in the designation of structural principles," "relations of transformation and mediation which are the 'circuit switches' underlying observed conditions of system reproduction" (ibid.: 24). "Structural sets" are elaborations of structural principles. At this focal level Giddens begins to talk of different structural sets related to different "modalities of structuration." Holding reflexively moni-

---

[3] The first, limited version of Giddens's theory appeared in 1976 without any reference to Bourdieu. In his 1979 volume Giddens remarks that Bourdieu's standpoint is "in some respects similar to that which I want to suggest here" (217); in his 1984 volume he cites Bourdieu only once and briefly, using an example from his Kabyle ethnographic work. The relationship would appear to be somewhat stronger.

tored social conduct in suspension so as to concentrate upon the analysis of the structural properties of social systems, he distinguishes three structural dimensions of such systems: *signification,* primarily inscribed in symbolic orders/modes of discourse; *domination,* primarily inscribed in political (authorizing) and economic (allocating) institutions; and *legitimation,* primarily inscribed in legal institutions (1984:31; 1979:97–103). Presumably, rules and resources transformed or mediated by structural principles produce various "structures of signification," "structures of domination," and "structures of legitimation." I say presumably, because Giddens gives the impression that, while rules are implicated in the dimensions of signification and legitimation, resources are so implicated in the dimension of domination. As Giddens wrote earlier, structures of signification are to be analyzed as systems of semantic rules and structures of legitimation as systems of moral rules, while, on the other hand, structures of domination are to be analyzed as systems of resources (1976: 123–4). He describes organizational authorization and material allocation of such resources as "capabilities" generating command over persons (the former) or objects (the latter) (1979:100). In both instances there is *no reference to rules.* This is certainly an anomaly.

Giddens's only example of a structural set is in the dimension of domination: it is the set of relations and transmutations in modern capitalism as analyzed by Marx:

private property : money : capital : labor contract : profit

Giddens might better have said that a structural set is something like "a mode of production" (here the capitalist mode), more specifically, the process structure that generates the relations and transmutations of capitalism.

Giddens is silent on the next lower level, that of the nonfundamental structural properties. The term operates like the Garfinkelian "etcetera rule": all *other* institutionalized features of social systems, except the structural principles and sets; else, *all* institutionalized features, large and small, important or less important, exhibit the recursive application of higher levels.

Finally, below the structural levels, "social systems" are defined as "reproduced relations between actors or collectivities, organized as regular social practices" (1979:66). We need add nothing more about them.

Two problems stand out in this summation of Giddens's linguistic redescription or modeling of social structure. One cannot fail to notice that all of the above concepts and definitions or distinctions are static, that is, offer no mechanism of structuration, of the power or force that accounts for the generation of specific structures. Compare Giddens's discussion, for example, to the efforts of myself and others cited throughout this volume and briefly inventoried in the Appendix, to initiate a research program on the specific **logics of structuration,** the conjunction of which could account for the emergence of empirical structured structures. Giddens's abstract and mostly definitional language cannot provide any real explanatory payoff as do these other efforts. The second basic problem in Giddens's conceptualization is the total lack of any theory of levels. The only time he cites the notion of levels, as we describe them above, is when he refers to structural properties as "hierarchically organized." This won't do. The important work is not to be done in the description or construction of a hierarchy of levels of (analytical) abstraction, but of either a hierarchy of levels of processes phase-separated from each other, or of levels of phenomena (systems, entities, structures) of different scale. There must be, therefore, more discussion of levels of social structure and, if needs be, of what is wrong with the more empirical, size-related, articulation of structural levels along the interpersonal, interpositional (organizational), and interorganizational continuum, which is the standard trademark of contemporary sociology (see Warriner in Blau and Merton 1981).

In short, the trouble with Giddens, besides the increasing abstractness and volume of his work, is that he has nothing to say about the specific mechanisms and logics that constitute the "structure" or, being the structure, operate "to structure" any social system. What are the nuts and bolts of this notion? How does it operate concretely, that is, in each and all of its instantiations? How exactly do we move up and down the levels of social phenomena (once such level-theory is established satisfactorily) and find their specific structural properties? Giddens does not say. In view of this crippling limitation I am not sure Giddens can go anywhere with the present form of his theory, for example, in terms of informing a robust research program on how to investigate in logical detail the structural properties he posits ex cathedra.

Bhaskar's view of structure

Both Giddens and Bhaskar theorize the issue of structure in reference to the well-known French "structuralist" definition, which has been formulated in more formal terms. The following quotations will serve to remind us of the conception of structure proposed by Lévi-Strauss: He defined "structure" as an order of relations that turns a set of bits, which have limited significance of their own, into an intelligible whole. "Structures are models, the formal properties of which can be compared independently of their elements" (Lévi-Strauss 1963:284). "If we want to understand religion or law, and perhaps even cooking and the rules of politeness, we must imagine them as being codes formed by articulated signs, following the pattern of linguistic communication" (Charbonnier 1969:151). Although both Giddens and Bhaskar remain closer to the structuralist conception than to the empiricist definition of structure, they offer some telling criticisms of Lévi-Strauss's notion, advocating the "reality" of structure, its processual character, and the implication of power in the structuring process (Giddens 1979:63–4). I find Bhaskar much clearer on the crucial philosophical aspects.

Bhaskar advocates a "realist theory" of science and a concomitant realist theory of structure, a view he calls "transcendental realism" or "theoretical realism" in quasi-Kantian phrasing. "Transcendental analysis of experimental (and applied) activity in natural science," says Bhaskar, "shows that the objects of scientific investigation are structures, not events, and that such structures exist and act independently of the conditions of their identification, in open or closed systems alike" (1982:277; cf. 1975). Those "structures are non-empirical but empirically identifiable, transfactually efficacious but only contingently manifest in particular outcomes, and they form the real ground for causal laws" (1982:277); in plain terms, this means that one cannot "see" structures directly, but instead must see them in the contingent outcomes they bring about through their "causal powers,"[4] and, therefore, their causal efficacy across various empirical events. The transcendental realist's view of science, in contrast to that of an empirical realist like Radcliffe-Brown or Blau, is that it is an enterprise moving deeper, from knowledge of manifest phenomena to knowledge of the structures that generate them. Society, then, may be conceived "as an articulated ensemble of . . . relatively independent and enduring (social) structures" (1975:14; 1978b:17).

Unlike Giddens, Bhaskar seems to be quite close to the Popperians in the conceptualization of an evolutionary emergence of phenomena and in the formulation of a theory of levels that is more or less heterarchical or weakly hierarchical (s-hierarchical). Popper himself (see Popper in Pattee 1973; Popper 1982) has pointed out the failures of reductionism in its effort to secure an explanation of the alleged "deterministically smooth" transition from the quantum mechanical notions of cosmology to the emergence of the human mind, and he has proposed a conception of the world that has been called "integrated pluralism." In his elaboration of this notion, Mario Bunge describes integrated pluralism as "an ontology that proclaims both the diversity

---

[4] For the sources and contours of the theory of "causal powers" see the work of Rom Harré (1972, with Secord 1979, 1980, 1985 with others, and Keat (1975 with Urry, 1981). See also John Wilson's *Social Theory* (1983) for a brief but very competent description of realist social theory.

and the unity of the world" (1973a:162). Bunge offers the following ontological hypotheses:

(1) That reality is a level structure such that everything existent belongs to at least one level of that structure.
(2) That in the course of every emergence process (self-assembly or evolution) some properties, hence also some laws, are gained while others are lost.
(3) That the newer levels depend on the older ones both for their emergence and for their continued existence.
(4) That every level has, within bounds, some autonomy and stability. And
(5) That every event is primarily determined in accordance with its set of specific laws that characterize its own level(s) and the contiguous levels.

Bhaskar, following in the footsteps of Bunge, argues that "reality consists of partially interconnected hierarchies of levels" and that in the human sciences ... "the most plausible form that integrative pluralism takes ... is that of a synchronic emergent powers materialism" (1982: 277–81). Bhaskar is willing to concede "diachronic reduction" but defends the "synchronic irreducibility" of the emergent higher levels of phenomena, the structures of which are causally efficacious (i.e., have material causal power) within each respective level. However, he defines the relationship between levels in a rather vague half-heterarchical/half-hierarchical way when he says that the form of the combination of elements into structures causally codetermines the elements; and the elements causally codetermine the form. This is right but does not get us far: we need to know more about (a) interlevel relations at several levels at once, and (b) the specific mechanisms that explain the posited or presumed codetermination. On this Bhaskar offers no help.

Given his commitment to emergent materialism or emergent realism, Bhaskar is obliged to accept only a modified naturalism when concerned with the human world. In this sense, he argues that "social structures" are different from "natural structures" in three respects:

(1) social structures, unlike natural structures, do not exist independently of the activities they govern;
(2) social structures, unlike natural structures, do not exist independently of the agents' conceptions of what they are doing in their activity; and
(3) social structures, unlike natural structures, may be only relatively enduring, so that the tendencies they ground may not be universal in the sense of space-time invariance (1978b:14).

However, in the corresponding footnote (1978b:25, n.36), Bhaskar notes that "the internal complexity and interdependence of social structures" does not mark a necessary difference with natural structures. These provisos regarding the difference between social and natural structures are shared by Giddens as well, and there is no way, as far as I can tell, of ascribing their origin to one or the other of these authors. As for the rest of Bhaskar's theory of social structure as a transformative theory of structuration, it seems to follow the Marxist theoretical framework rather closely (1982, 1983). By virtue of their explicitness, Bhaskar's formulations – integrated pluralism, intralevel and contiguous interlevel causality, semiautonomy of levels, irreducibility of structures to lower levels – are closer to the heterarchical model than are the less complete and more static ideas of Giddens on the same issues.

Bourdieu on structure and habitus

In 1972 Pierre Bourdieu published a book in French (English version, 1977) titled *Outline of a Theory of Practice*. It provided the first comprehensive effort toward a proper "theory of structuration" – a concept introduced, analyzed, and popularized earlier in the work of the (still underrated) great sociologist Georges Gurvitch (1958), who is the true father of dynamic structuration theory. This, then, is the other French tradition, established by Gurvitch's work and its continuation in the more current work of Alain Touraine (beginning in 1965 with his admirable dissertation), Michel Foucault, and Pierre Bourdieu, which views social processes as both structural and differentially dynamic, that is, opts for structurationist rather than structuralist theorizing. The British thinkers, Bhaskar and Giddens among them, did not start this discourse on structuration ex nihilo.

Bourdieu's work is significant in itself but also in the sense that, as far as I can tell, it was a seminal work (a) presaging the theories of Giddens and Bhaskar, (b) influencing their theories, and (c) far surpassing them in the richness of its insights and theoretical importance. Bourdieu started with a critique of the monological nature of the objectivist and subjectivist traditions of social science and advocated "a science of the dialectical relations between the objective structures to which the objectivist mode of knowledge gives access and the structured dispositions within which those structures are actualized and which tend to reproduce them" (1977:3).

As Bourdieu theorizes, the important explanatory concepts are, first, the "objective structures" generated in history, and, second, "habitus," or agents' dispositions durably inculcated by these objective conditions. **Habitus** (the basic form of which is "class habitus" and the habitus of "class-fractions") is defined as "the system(s) of durable, transposable dispositions" that act as "principles of the generation and structuring of practices and representations" (1977:72). These structured dispositions, as a "socially constituted system of cognitive and motivating structures," together with every "socially structured situation in which the agents' interests are defined" (habitus and situation forming together a "conjuncture"), would explain the "objective functions and subjective motivations of the agents' practices" (ibid.:76). Within this conjunctural context, provided by habitus and the specific situations, the agents would instantiate various strategies of exchange exploring and exploiting the "structural ambivalence which predisposes them to fulfil a political function of domination through the performance of the communication function" (ibid.:14). These strategies, conscious or unconscious, are "oriented towards the satisfaction of material and symbolic interests and organized by reference to a determinate set of economic and social conditions" (ibid.:36).

Since the habitus is a sort of "internal law," *lex insita* (ibid.:81), there is no need to refer to the "fitting" or "guiding" role of "rules," or for that matter to any other function of rules (ibid.:9, 17, 27–9, 75–6; 1986a for the latest version). The habitus provides the inventory of all cognitive and motivating principles appropriate to the situation and the situation has specified the objective context and the resources available to the agents in order for them to select and deploy their strategies. Bourdieu speaks of two sorts of strategies: "first-order strategies" geared directly toward the satisfaction of material and symbolic interests, and "second-order strategies" through which the agent seeks "to put himself in the right" by appropriating the advantages that lie in abiding by the rules. Strategic games, for example the matrimonial game, are "similar to a card game, in which the outcome depends partly on the deal, the cards held (their value itself being defined by the rules of the game, characteristic of the social formation in question) and partly on the players' skill: that is to say, firstly on the material and symbolic capital possessed by the families concerned, their wealth in instruments of production and in men . . . ; and secondly on the competence which enables the strategists to make the best use of this capital . . ." (1977:58). According to Bourdieu, "Only a virtuoso with a perfect command of his 'art of living' can play on all the resources inherent in the ambiguities and uncertainties of behavior and situation in order to produce the actions appropriate in each case" (ibid.:8).

Being temporally structured, the art of necessary improvisation, which defines excellence, is intrinsically defined by its tempo or "timescale." Given the different tempos of historical structures, conjunctural situations, and strategies, the objective structures, conjunctures, and strategies appropriate to them are always less than totally coordinated, being composed of "causal series" of different structural duration. There are, then, always some structural ambiguities and disjunctions, or a "hysteresis of habitus," and a semidependence of habitus and situations on the objective structure by which they are engendered (ibid.: 83). The result is a dynamics that provides considerable opportunities for strategic maneuvering (recall here the "opportunism" of Simon, March, or Williamson); by the same token, given these disjunctions and ambiguities of structures and conjunctures, no consistent systemic logic is possible, in spite of the existence of numerous "officializing" or "authorizing" strategies.[5]

Bourdieu arrives at the conclusion that there is a special "economy of logic" in the case of practices that operate on the principle that "no more logic is mobilized than is required by the needs of practice"; this economy of logic, by means of "polythesis" (ibid.:109–10), allows symbolic objects and practices to enter without contradiction into successive relationships set up from different points of view, making them subject to overdetermination through indetermination. This way the "fuzzy logic of practice works wonders," enabling the group to achieve as much social and logical integration as is compatible with the diversity imposed by the division of labor between the sexes, the ages, and the occupations (ibid.:163). Bourdieu here speaks of stability and diversity, the twin ingredients of any logic of structure (recall our references to "spin glasses" and the work of P. W. Anderson).

When discussing the general "economy of practice," Bourdieu develops the following scheme: There are, certainly, many differences between precapitalist, community or village-centered social formations and capitalist social formations organized around the market and other differentiated institutions. In both, the strategies of the agents are geared toward symbolic and material needs, but primarily the latter. Before the introduction of "objective mechanisms" of appropriation, "relations of domination can be set up and maintained only at the cost of strategies which must be endlessly renewed, because the conditions required for a mediated, lasting appropriation of other agents' labor, services, or homage have not been brought together." In that instance, the dominant classes "are obliged to resort to the elementary forms of domination, in other words, the direct domination of one person by another" (ibid.:190), by "winning" them personally or "tying" them – in short, creating a bond between persons. "By contrast, domination no longer needs to be exerted in a direct, personal way when it is entailed in possession of the means (economic or cultural capital) of appropri-

---

[5] *Outline*:38–40, 21–2. On this I agree with Bourdieu: there is no closure in the "totalization" process. See further Chapters 13–14 and Appendix 39.

ating the mechanisms of the field of production and the field of cultural production, which tend to assure their own reproduction by their very functioning, independently of any deliberate intervention by the agents" (ibid.:183–4). Indeed, once a system of mechanisms "has been constituted capable of objectively ensuring the reproduction of the established order by its own motion . . . , the dominant class have only to let the system they dominate take its own course in order to exercise their domination" (ibid.:190).

In the direct exchanges of early communities the domination strategies relied on economic violence brought about by the use of "debt" (and "slavery" at the limit cases). Later, symbolic violence was used, with the introduction of a variegated assortment of "gift" practices, which necessitated the softening of exchange relations into moral, affective obligations; the setting up, maintenance, or restoration of relations of domination was done through strategies expressly oriented toward the establishment of personal dependence, strategies which now had to be disguised and transfigured lest they destroy themselves by revealing their true nature – in other words, they had to be censored and euphemized (ibid.:191). All of this changed, of course, with the emergence of social formations "in which, mediated by objective, institutionalized mechanisms, such as those producing and guaranteeing the distribution of "titles" (titles of nobility, deeds of possession, academic degrees, etc.), relations of domination have the opacity and permanence of things and escape the grasp of individual consciousness and power" (ibid.:184). Bourdieu alludes to the fact that the transition from one mode of domination to the other (from debt to gift structures, and from these elementary forms to the organized institutional forms of domination) took place in order to economize on transaction costs and reduce instability: "The saving is a real one," he insists, "because strategies designed to establish or maintain lasting relations of dependence are generally very expensive in terms of material goods (as in the potlatch or in charitable acts), services, or simply time" (ibid.:184, 190).

Since our goal here is to discuss the extent to which Bourdieu's theory contains heterarchical ways of thinking about social structure, we need not extend this presentation further. What Bourdieu has tried to do – and does, I believe, quite successfully – is to talk about historically, that is, praxically, produced objective structures, as "determinate organizers of possibilities," within which specific social conjunctures are half-determined, half-emerging through the interaction of habitus and the situation at hand; furthermore, within these conjunctures, appropriate strategies are available and utilized by the purposive agents. (These agents are seen as culturally intentional and thus also situated and inculcated intentional agents, but not transcendentally so, as

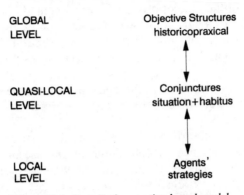

GLOBAL
LEVEL

Objective Structures
historicopraxical

QUASI-LOCAL
LEVEL

Conjunctures
situation+habitus

LOCAL
LEVEL

Agents'
strategies

Figure 10.4. *Bourdieu's practice-based model*

"souls" or as vehicles of a full-fledged phenomenological consciousness [ibid.:21, 79].) Figure 10.4 illustrates a commonsensically evident "hierarchy of inclusion" but no control hierarchy. The relationship between structures, conjunctures, and agents' strategies may seem to be hierarchical, ordered downward from the macrolevel to the microlevels, but, in fact, it is not: because there exist disjunctions and ambiguities (nonclosures, externalities, leftover degrees of freedom) at each level, the relationships across levels are not fully ordered in an asymmetrical, hence hierarchical, fashion. On the contrary, they are "entangled" with each other so, for example, the agents do not typically and homogeneously reproduce a limited set of practices by habit (as Giddens [1979: 217–8] implies, totally missing the point of Bourdieu's notion of habitus, which is a second-order, not a first-order concept), but generate a refreshingly large repertory of strategies that are at times contradictory and lead to a rather precarious reproduction but also, quite often, to change. Therefore, we recognize here the problem of the relationship between local and global dynamics, one that appears to relate to the heterarchical logic of explanation by theorizing the linkages across levels as semiindependent and entangled. Any theory that speaks of levels of phenomena that are semiindependent from each other and entangled with each other in other than totally ordered, asymmetrical ways, that is, levels that are partially ordered or nonlinearly ordered, is a heterarchical theory. Although Bourdieu never uses these logico–conceptual distinctions, he provides numerous approximating insights in his detailed discussion of the matrimonial strategies (1977a:58–71). Grounded in such heterarchical insights derived from a general economy of practices across levels, a proper heterarchical theory of social structure could be spelled out in detail and could be extremely robust as a research program.

Along these lines, it is instructive to refer to some other analyses of symbolic economies, affine to that of Bourdieu, such as the "generalized political economies" of symbolic/economic goods discussed by Baudrillard (1981), the "regimes of value" discussed by Appadurai (1986), or the regimes of appropriation discussed by Foucault. Foucault's work further elucidates the points made in the previous paragraph on the characteristic structure of heterarchies. Foucault focuses in his analysis on the discursive and nondiscursive practices of, essentially, corporate and corporate-to-be agents, practices that were invented and organized from the starting point of local conditions and experiences and were further developed in piecemeal fashion, prior to any bourgeois or state-based effort to weld them together into hegemonic ensembles (see 1980: 94–102). These local (actually, quasi-local) strategies of domination have included "disciplinary techniques," what Foucault calls techniques of "bio-power"; "discursive deployments," that is, stylized – and "euphemized" per Bourdieu – talks referring to the (benevolent) control of the body; and "subjectivizing practices," that is, practices that make, name, and recognize "subjects" and "sub-ject" them to disciplinary control. The local production of these strategies took place primarily in the interface between bodies in various institutional settings, like the asylum, the hospital, the panopticon, the army, and the school, where they attained a great degree of sophistication and stability. The objective of those strategies, initiated by aspiring professional bodies of medical doctors, mental health practitioners, criminologists, demographers, sociologists, and bureaucrats of all sorts, was "to produce docile, yet productive bodies, confessing bodies" (1979:271). Finally, the bourgeoisie, as the new dominant class, came in to take over and promote further these disciplinary achievements and incorporate them, by special mechanisms that need deciphering, into the contested regimes of legitimate social apperception and action through which a dominant class constitutes itself and its others. Thus, the contribution of the bourgeoisie was not to produce these practices but to appropriate them in a struggle, articulating systems of power relays and cross references that supported the process of class formation and, more importantly, of the rise of a hegemonic class (1973, 1977, 1978, 1980; on this mechanism see also my discussion of a similar example, that of the Aztec appropriation and incorporation of the local integrative practices of conquered people into their own system of rule, Kontopoulos 1980).

Foucault defines "bio-power" as "the new technology of administration, control, and direction of the accumulation of men"; as such, he says, "the economic system that promotes the accumulation of capital and the system of power that promotes the accumulation of men are, from the seventeenth century on, correlated and inseparable phenom-

ena" (1980:125). Throughout his work, Foucault presents and discusses
the effects of the alliance between the state and the bourgeoisie, or the
state and the *emerging professionals,* an emphasis that brings the previous programmatic – indeed, epigrammatic – statements considerably
down to earth. But there is no one final center! Power is a distributed
system, a non-denumerable and unaccountable network of powers inscribed in all the different institutional settings and social spaces. Power
must be understood, according to Foucault,

> as the multiplicity of force relations immanent in the sphere in which they
> operate and which constitute their own organization; as the process which,
> through ceaseless struggles and confrontations, transforms, strengthens, or re-
> verses them; as the support which these force relations find in one another,
> thus forming a chain or a system, or on the contrary, the disjunctions and
> contradictions which isolate them from one another; and lastly, as the strategies
> in which they take effect, whose general design or institutional crystallization
> is embodied in the state apparatus, in the formulation of the law, in the various
> social hegemonies. [In brief,] power . . . is the name one attributes to a complex
> strategical situation in a particular society. (1978:92–3; see also 1980:142)

On the other side of the equation, the popular side, Foucault speaks of
the many points of "resistance" to the various "projects of domination"
launched by these "totalizing" forces:

> Just as the network of power relations ends by forming a dense web that passes
> through apparatuses and institutions, without being exactly localized in them,
> so too the swarm of points of resistance traverses social stratifications and in-
> dividual unities. And it is doubtless the strategic codification of these points of
> resistance that makes a revolution possible, somewhat similar to the way in
> which the state relies on the institutional integration of power relationships.
> (1978:95–6; cf. Smart 1983, 1986; Walzer 1986)

For Foucault the tragic games of history are played between these various totalizing, global forces and the resisting, local individuals, groups,
and communities.

Local–global dynamics, and beyond

This theme of the unstable relations between local and global has also
been evident in the thought of many historical sociologists.[6] Their analyses, however, do not fully explain the mechanisms of the local–global
interchanges: they shed considerable light on the events, and indicate
some important factors, but they do not spell out completely the logic
of that connection – neither do the theories that speak of three levels
of structural organization and leave it at that. Alford and Friedland
(1985:16–7, and elsewhere), for example, advocate – and cite several

---

[6] See, for example, Moore (1966), Skocpol (1979:45), Tilly (1973), even Olson
(1965:67).

authors who advocate – an understanding of social phenomena on three distinct analytical levels: individual, organizational, and societal. This is reminiscent of the older distinction between "interpersonal," "interpositional," and "interorganizational" levels of analysis (Warriner 1981), levels which were kept forever apart for want of a proper way of bridging them. Even when Przeworski (1980) views the societal level as specifying the "basic constraints faced by actors," the organizational level specifying the "collective resources that are forged within those constraints," and the individual level specifying the "forms of rationality and strategies that are adopted using these resources within those constraints" (in Alford and Friedland 1985:340n) – a good variation on Bourdieu's themes cited previously – he does not explain the mechanisms involved, notwithstanding the usefulness and clarity of his conceptual distinctions. One needs to know more, go even deeper, see inside the "black box," as Elster would say.

Consider, for example, the kind of relationships involved between federal, state, and local government: certainly, this is a heterarchy of sorts. The federal government does not have authority over the state and local jurisdictions in every respect, nor does the state government over the cities and municipalities. And, of course, the opposite is also partially true; there is a certain degree of autonomy between these three levels but also a number of ambiguities and contestations of their relative domains. Here are three structures that depend partially on each other and are partially ordered, forming a "contextual" hierarchy (belonging) in geographical terms but a heterarchy in juridical and economic terms. Yet, even here we have to go deeper to understand the exact mechanisms and connections obtaining between them in dynamical rather than merely descriptive terms. The same can be said about the national economy, which is nothing but a heterarchical form of relating local, regional, and national levels of economic dynamics; also, the levels of firms, of industries (where one can speak of oligopoly or competition), and of interindustrial national economic relations. In each of these conceptualizations we are dealing with a heterarchical organization: it is at the level of the firm or the cities as "growth machines" (to recall Molotch's term) that we find the actual production dynamics; at the level of the industry or the regional interorganizational network that we find the power relations and the economic stratification of production, concentration, and competition; and at the level of the national economy that we speak of aggregate supplies and demands and, especially, of (federal) "state" and "federal bank" fiscal and monetary policies. Here is a trilateral monopoly. Each level clearly impacts on the other and no level by itself can be said to control the economic conditions of a society. In this particular case, however, we know more about the mechanisms of their interrelations, although not that much more. Here, at last, we have an intuitively clear understanding of a "heterarchy" as an entangled system of level-structures each of which imposes constraints on the workings of the others.

Yet, the relations between levels can be illuminated further. Keeping in mind the intuitive tripartite distinction of interactional-organizational-societal, let us investigate some other variations that may help us to arrive at an acceptable classification. For example, in a recent article in *Science* (1987) Bear and colleagues, working within a neural network paradigm, discussed the relationships and dynamic modifications of neurons at the levels of local, quasi-local, and global variables. Local variables are those affecting a particular synapse, jth, in the form of information available only through the jth synapse; quasi-local variables represent information that is available to the jth synapse through intracellular communication within the same cell; and global variables represent information that is available to a large number of cortical neurons including the neuron receiving the specific synapse. In other words, local variables are like "egocentric networks" and quasi-local variables like "sociocentric" (clique-like or serial) networks, while global variables are higher-level structures, or networks of networks. The specifics are not as relevant as are the broad similarities with the ideas of Harrison White, Foucault, and Bourdieu, although Foucault's notion of local and global, of course, is different from the one of Bear et al. Still another view can be found in the recent and exciting studies on the dynamics of "chaos" (Gleick 1987:45, 47, 70; Leggett 1987; Leggett and Garg 1985). But suppose that in the spirit of their conceptualization we decide to make distinctions between local and quasi-local as well as global and quasi-global levels of structure. We may then say that the "local" level is the level of individual actions and relations, the level of interactional modalities and their structural patterns, or the level of corporate and institutional actors embodied in individual representatives of authority, such as the policeman or the priest. The "quasi-local" level then will be the level of strategic exchanges within institutional contexts (the level of Bourdieu's strategies of pre-institutional domination, such as the matrimonial strategies; also, the level of Foucault's local bio-politics, the level of disciplinary techniques, discursive deployments, and subjectivizing practices, imposed as well as resisted, in asylums, hospitals, prisons, schools, or armies). The "quasi-global" level will be that of the interrelationships between *homomorphous* (say, among hospitals, the emergence of the medical profession at large) or *heteromorphous* (say, among different institutional orders in the same region or the nation at large, such as the offshoots of the conjunction of state-bureaucratic and professional interests, described by Foucault)

Figure 10.5. *Phenomenological levels of structure*

institutions or even competing classes and/or fractions of such classes. The "global" level, finally, will be the one in which a dominant or hegemonic collective agent (cf. the self/person in Dennett's mental/ neuronal hierarchy), such as an emerging dominant class or social category (e.g., the professional-managerial class), attempts to totalize its hegemony over society by transforming – to the degree that this is possible – the heterarchical societal organization into a pure "control hierarchy." We thus find more significance in Foucault's insistence that although there is a strong, quasi-local basis of the "microphysics" of power, there is an extra effort by the state or the bourgeoisie to totalize the system and consolidate the local and quasi-local structural differentials or differentials of domination into an overarching strategy leading to a global, dominating structure, whatever the success of that effort may ultimately be. I propose, then, that we pedagogically adopt the four-level structure depicted above, and analyze each of its levels. Figure 10.5 illustrates the levels and corresponding structures.

Local structures involve the patterns or forms of relationships between agents at or close to the individual level of analysis. However, interactions have to be described in terms of their different orienting principles, that is, in terms of different **modalities,** instead of being treated abstractly as if they were "unimodal." We will discuss modalities of interaction in detail in Chapter 12; however, I would argue here, more or less in accord with the interest-based theories of behavior, that the most central modality is that guiding "strategic" behavior geared toward broadly defined economic and political benefits (in the manner of Foucault and of Bourdieu). Boudon's generic notion of "systems of interaction" still belongs to this subinstitutional level. On the other hand, modalities of interaction do not explicitly or exhaustively describe the mechanisms of the formation of local structures. These mechanisms are of various forms, composing a vast inventory of micrologics (many of which are described in the Appendix) that are implicated in specific local and quasi-local interactions, structuring them and thus giving rise to (structured) structures.

Quasi-local structures are structures at the level of specific unit institutions – the firm or the factory, the local market, the prison, the hospital, and so on. They are also found in more diffused quasi-institutional contexts, such as that of matrimonial strategic exchanges, gift exchanges, and others. Here is the locus where "categories of interactants" relate to each other, not as individual actors, but as parts of phase-separated, entangled, institutionally bound "structured systems of interaction." Bourdieu's "conjunctures" are indeed primarily of a quasi-local form. Notice here again that the dominant modalities are strategic (with an economic and political thrust); the examples provided by Bourdieu and Foucault are quite sufficient – we need not refer at this point to other historical cases (for example, class-formation as construed by E. P. Thompson [1963] and others). Also note that we begin to perceive very clearly the differentials of power and of material and symbolic resources mobilized by the agents in their strategic pursuits. This also points to diverse, constraining-enabling-availing, causations from above, implicated directly, with direct structural effects, or indirectly, through the working of habitus, especially class-habitus.

Quasi-global structures: Here we are in the domain of "classes," "fractions of classes," and "social categories" or strata, operating in quasi-local or quasi-global "ecosystems," the intercorporate and intercollective level of analysis. Obviously, structural patterns of relations refer to and implicate – interactively, structurally, and aggregatively – these corporate and collective units and, therefore, the mechanisms of their dynamic structuration are appropriately more complex. An explanation at this level would focus on the rise of intercorporate institutional arrangements, federal groups or collective agencies, on the organizational and collective ecologies within which they operate, and on the macrologics of their structuration within the framework of the overall heterarchical theory. We move then from the hospital to the institutionalization of health and the rise of the corporate medical profession, from the local prison to the criminal justice system at large and the interlocking of state institutions and corporate bodies of professionals such as police, courts, social workers and probation officers, and, of course, most importantly, from the local firm or factory to the interlocking oligopolistic cliques, the capitalist class, and the assorted workers' organizations. Material and power differentials are even more visible at this level: Unilateral monopolies, dominating coalitions, or bilateral and trilateral monopolies are found among larger and fewer strategic agents, even if some of these agents are only **synecdochically** expressed. But the dynamics of this system will be unstable and distributive, because such agencies (in community ecologies) are not yet "totalizing."

Global structures: Here the prevailing characteristic is that of attempted and partially imposed structural **totalization** forced on the quasi-global system. An emerging dominant collective agent – a class or a state bureaucracy, or a vanguard acting synecdochically on behalf of a class or of "the nation" – imposes its own macrologic of organization and attempts to rebuild the global system in terms of that "logic," Logic of Capital or Logic of the State (one must distinguish these totalizing or structuring logics from the epistemic logics we have discussed earlier). I am not arguing, of course, that this agent's effort succeeds completely; only that it does succeed partially and in an imperfect way: totalizing efforts notwithstanding, the global system is never fully totalized, never perfectly rationalized, never smoothly operating. Thus, global structures are always riddled with structural contradictions – at least as many as the lower levels. In general, the transition from the quasi-global to the global level may take place only to a certain extent: a variety of possibilities exist ranging from (a) nearly "complete totalization" (centralization, totalitarianism), (b) the "dialectical," imperfect totalization I have mentioned above as the most likely outcome, (c) a "distributed" form (on which more in the next chapter) indicating a "hegemonic" mode of governance, to, finally, (d) an "anarchic" form of structural organization (with multilateral monopolies, such as in cases of "fluid" situations of civil or revolutionary strife).

I would also argue that the transition from the local to the quasi-local level is made by the intervention of various micrologics alone or in conjunction; correspondingly, the transition from the quasi-local to the quasi-global level implicates many mesologics, while that from the quasi-global to the global implicates one or more appropriate macrologics.

Interlevel transitions

We need now to make plain the difference between a *control-hierarchical* view of structural constraints (prioritizing the "top-down" influence of macrostructures on individual choice) and their *heterarchical* view (questioning any strong influence either way). This difference is due to the interlevel exchanges and multiple influences, since any focal level is a field in which many forces – from above, from below, focal-internal – operate simultaneously, giving the level its particular semiautonomy.

Suppose one starts from the level of global structures, leaving aside for the moment the problem of the generation of these structures themselves. One may posit that a direct influence is exerted by global constraints on the immediately contiguous level of quasi-global structures, say, institutional orders, and, through the mediation of the latter, on the level of quasi-local structures as well; and, once more, through the mediation of the quasi-local structures on the local level structures. This constraining influence is mediated and, then, twice mediated, so that it becomes more and more indirect. To be sure, these constraints restrict the possibility space of each lower level; although they are not superimposed in a linear additive sense (as when a straight control hierarchy exists), they accumulate in a *distributed parallel* (or polymorphous, or polythetic) sense accounting for a peculiar overdetermination which can be called – to use Bourdieu's wonderful expression – "overdetermination through indetermination" (1977a:110). The same would hold for the constraining of the quasi-local (directly) and local (indirectly, once mediated) by the quasi-global structures and, indeed, vice versa, from the local to the global levels as well (in the form of initiating conditions, the "laws" of phenomena in the typical physicalistic sense). As soon as one concedes that there are some degrees of indeterminacy in interlevel relations and, perhaps, a certain balance between the top-down and bottom-up indirect determinations, it is impossible to maintain a hierarchical view. The crux of the matter is the following: Hierarchy theory must posit global forces (constraints, logics) successfully or nearly successfully totalizing the fields below, subsuming them, integrating them, stabilizing them, "functionalizing" them. Heterarchy theory needs only recognize the possibility of "totalizing projects," partially successful at best, but never coming to a closure, always being replete with contradictions and generating resistances from below – structures that do not "clear," social forces that do not get integrated, societies that do not operate functionally.

Any ruling project, by a class, an army, a bureaucratic regime, a revolutionary vanguard, or an intellectual stratum (the "new class"), implies the mobilization of the society, the incorporation of most, if not all, of preexisting and perhaps independently developed quasi-local or quasi-global techniques and structures of domination, and a serious effort for the systematic rearticulation of society. That is the true mark of global regimes of power. In the *Manifesto,* Marx gave us a beautiful rhetorical account of the historical "project" of the bourgeoisie; so did Weber on the bureaucratic and Foucault (and Gouldner and the Ehrenreichs) on the professional project. The goal in these projects is always the same: to "handle" the unruly, unstable, and contradictory quasi-global relations among nonequivalent, semiinterdependent structures and complete a (material and symbolic) totalization that economizes on transaction and communication costs from the point of view and to the benefit of a more efficient "global regime of domination" and of the elites effecting it.

Now, lest my argument is misunderstood, I must clarify an important point: not all effects of a global structure on the quasi-global structures handled by it are constraining. This issue has become a battle cry for many theorists in their effort to distinguish themselves from extreme deterministic views of the Durkheimian or Althusserian, functionalist or structuralist, varieties. Bourdieu introduced the saying in 1972 – followed by Giddens – that structuring structures both *constrain* and *enable* strategic actions and exchanges. I would push this notion one step further and argue that, indeed, structures of a higher order do three different things on the structures of their contiguous lower level:

(A) they *constrain,* in the sense that they limit the possibility space of lower structural formations by prohibiting some structured states or, to put it in a more Darwinian manner, by differentially favoring certain forms and producing obstacles to the development of others;

(B) they *enable,* in the sense that the differential favoring of certain options is expressed through the favorite "returns" to and "endowments" of the corporate and collective actors who promote them, that is, the resources allotted to them, the roles assigned, the cultural capital possessed by them, the skillful development of their habitus. "Enabling," then, means to be given "capacities" and "powers," especially the class capacities and powers of the hegemonic class. Enabling also means to permit and support the development of quasi-global (and other lower) structures for the facilitation of the project of the hegemonic class.[7] Finally,

(C) the higher structures *avail* to the lower ones a labyrinthine web of unexplored opportunities, the "gray areas" of imaginative and exploratory, sometimes even counterintuitive, invention of new structuring logics, structured structures, or improvised strategies. While still operating within the constraining objective limits of the global regime's structuration efforts, these strategies nonetheless emerge and thrive in the periphery of the intended order of things, seen by the regime with indifference, as non-threatening and at times even complementary. I have in mind here the rise of bourgeois occupations and "free"

---

[7] Cf. Wallerstein (1984:154), where the development of the state machinery is seen as an alternative mechanism "whereby the owners of productive enterprises can try to affect the operations of the market to maximize their profit" or to control international aspects of capitalist growth and competition among national bourgeoisies.

cities in the margins of the feudal regime, or the rise of professional bodies complementing the modern state, beginning with the time of the French Revolution, along the lines persuasively argued by Foucault. The given global structures – the feudal order, the revolutionary state – had "availed," within their own project, the opportunities for such future collective actors to emerge, grow, and ultimately, challenge the overarching logic of the system within whose margins they had grown. This "availing" dimension of engulfing structures on the lower levels they influence is perhaps the most significant in specifying the characteristic form of heterarchy, in the sense of guaranteeing the "relative indeterminacy and independence" of each structural level from the one above it.

The combination of the dimensions of constraining, enabling, and availing makes it possible to see each level, at least in reference to the top-down aspect of interlevel relations, as semiindependent and yet interdependent with the others. And, as it must be clear by now, we can extend this notion of availing to all level connections, thus positing considerable "degrees of indeterminacy" or "degrees of creative discretion" evidenced (a) in the rise and differential strengthening of corporate and collective actors and forms of structures initiated by them at the quasi-global level; (b) in the formation of a variety of conjunctures and novel institutional forms, techniques of domination, technologies of invention and monopolization, and the various forms of bio-power developed within them; and (c) in the emergence, within these novel settings, of a number of improvised or unauthorized strategies and practices, articulated and used by virtuosic strategic agents. Bourdieu also spoke of the strategic manipulation of time and of conjunctural resources by competent agents (1977a:7–8; cf. Swidler 1986).

Levels below the global one

We have spent considerable time explaining the triple effects of higher structures on the contiguously lower ones; we now return briefly to the exposition of the other levels.

Quasi-global structures are structures in which no "dominant" (corporate or collective) force has emerged or currently exists. There is, therefore, no relatively successful totalizing effort, although such efforts are constantly initiated by aspiring classes (some successful, like the bourgeoisie, others unsuccessful, like the "aristocracy of office" in the *ancien régime,* the drama of which is beautifully described by Goldmann (1964) or political elites aspiring to the formation and control of a state (see Tilly on strategies of elite domination at the quasi-global level [1975b: 633]). Typically, the prominent collective agencies at this level – classes and their semiautonomous fractions, classlike strata or collective agencies, such as races or ethnicities, and social categories, such as state bureaucracies or strata of intellectuals – are located in some privileged institutional form such as the church, the state, or the universities, or have developed their own organizational forms such as parties, labor unions, and chambers. Between them there exist strategic antagonisms, more or less durable alliances, more or less intense struggles – all the ups and downs of multilateral monopolies of distinct resources or of differentially allocated or expropriated common resources. Here, "common situations" emerge and solidify as sets of interdependent, enabling, constraining, and availing structures of opportunity and choice under constant political, ideological and economic contention and rearticulation. The influence of the higher objective structure notwithstanding, within the constraints it imposes and the differential endowments ("empowerments") of agents it provides we still find a historical, not fully determined juncture, a delimiting opening as it were, within which subjects produce themselves (Mouffe 1979; Touraine 1988). And Przeworski (1985:70) would add, in the spirit of Gramsci, that exactly for that reason "the ideological struggle is a struggle about class before it is a struggle among classes." In this heterogenous field of nonequivalent, antagonistic agents and competing institutional and organizational fora numerous contradictions cannot but develop, and drive history to its march. It is precisely the dynamics within this level and the interlevel relations with the neighboring global and semi-local levels that is paramount for any understanding of history and social change (cf. Kidron 1974:88).

In the *quasi-local level* the above dynamics afford to the agents specifiable forms of quasi-local institutional entities, particular situations of strategic exchange (or domination), and differentiated types of habitus based on the quasi-global lines of group demarcation (class habitus, the habitus of class fractions, the habitus of classlike collective agents, such as races or ethnicities, and so on). The concrete institutions of the quasi-local level (hospitals, prisons, army units, schools, markets of agricultural commodities, and so on) become the contexts in which kin, familial, and individual agencies struggle to achieve maximum pragmatic benefits. It is here also that techniques of domination, discursive deployments, and subjectivizing practices (Foucault's domain) take place, forming people as "subjects" and "sub-jects," that is, as cognitive and motivated intentional agents and as individuals sub-jected to these techniques of domination – as controlled bodies, fingerprinted, catalogued, processed, inculcated, dissected and repaired, psychoanalyzed, taught, confessed, assembled, disciplined, trained to behave properly and be punctual, sanitized – in brief, "regimented" to peacefully and orderly reproduce the global and quasi-global structures. And, yet, it is also here that resistances flourish; alien strategies are improvised, rebellions are organized, and collective agencies geared to praxis are formed. (An instructive example of improvisation, though on the wrong side of morality, is the production of tax loopholes within the parameters of laws that in principle forbid them; another example is that of "creative financing.") Quasi-local levels once again are semi-independent, underdetermined by the higher structures.

Local structures are the level of individual agents, partly self-motivated and self-cognizing, and partly formed by the intersection of their habitus and the specific structure of the situation in which they operate (as Bourdieu has it, possessed by their habitus rather than possessing it [1977a:18]). These individual agents act as *bricoleurs,* using as well as improvising on the repertories of strategies and of styles of performance afforded them within the particular quasi-local structures; agents who can exploit the realm of ambiguities inherent in public rules and "officialized strategies" (1977a:38–40) and explore vague opportunities, in other words, agents who can resist and create new orders out of the old ones. These are the same agents then who become the indispensable, though never sufficient, microcauses of change and create new institutional forms and collective agencies as "political entrepreneurs" (as even Olson recognized).

Figure 10.6 illustrates the complex system of levels, time-lags, and connectivities of this overall heterarchical entanglement.

Logics of structuration across levels

The major problem that any satisfactory heterarchical theory of social structure has to resolve – and what a crucial problem it is! – is the discovery, elaboration, and classification of all the logics involved in these processes of more complex, intersected structurations. As a rule, shallow theories tend to be conceptually and verbally rich, but explanatorily poor, because they are unable to spell out the mechanisms of structuration in sequence and in conjunction. The goal in this last section of the present chapter is to selectively draw on the various logics described in the Appendix (where the foundations of an ongoing research program are laid down) and utilize them to underscore what is involved in the processes of structuration at various levels of structure.

We may begin with local logics. We can programmatically distinguish (a) *logics of modalities,* that is, the mode of orientation to, and the appropriate context of, interaction (such as communicative-interpretive, strategic, and others, which we will discuss in Chapter 12); (b) *logics of games* played within the framework of strategic – material as well as

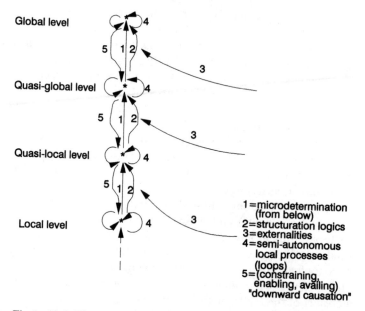

Figure 10.6. *The general form of heterarchical level structure*

symbolic – interactions; (c) *logics of packing,* which include "surface-to-volume" mechanisms of topological/ecological structuration; (d) *logics of flows,* which incorporate the various processes of movements of people through objectively constrained structures (such as traffics, assembly-line processes, flows of promotion along vacancy chains or otherwise, flows of races, ethnicities or classes through neighborhoods or sections of cities); (e) *logics of matching,* that is, logics that refer to the matching of people with other people (such as marriage logics) or the matching of people and positions (doctors and hospitals, army volunteers and each service, rank-based matchings of applicants and professional schools or law graduates and legal firms); and (f) *logics of exchange* (competitive market, unilateral monopoly, bilateral monopoly, and such). (Refer to the Appendix for more possibilities.) The elaboration of these logics satisfies the requirement imposed on theories of structuration to get down from ethereal concerns to the analysis of the structuring mechanisms.

Some of the combinatorial possibilities of local logics will be "selected" half-intentionally or half-functionally, that is, half-consciously and half-unconsciously (by virtue of the fact that agents are both "possessing" as well as "possessed" by their habitus), and thus they will appear under the new boundary conditions of the quasi-local level as distinct quasi-local logics. We can think here of three important types of quasi-local logics: (a) *logics of institution-building,* especially emerging as a result of "matching" mechanisms or for the sake of such matchings; here I have in mind all innovative mechanisms that emerge in order to economize on transaction and communication costs (such as Williamsonian hierarchies or long-term subcontracting), or typified systems of matching prospective spouses (preferred marriages and other systems of matrimonial matching), or job-applicant matching algorithms (in Coleman's example); (b) *logics of domination,* resulting from the deployment of quasi-monopolistic (material or symbolic) power, as the work of Bourdieu, Foucault, and Marx, and a host of contemporary Marxists has so aptly described. In addition there are the many mechanisms of material domination (land-compacts, personal compacts of service, debt compacts) and symbolic domination (professional "gaze" of doctors, bureaucratic or institutional "processing" of persons, educational "certification," techniques of institutional "disciplining" in armies, schools, mental wards, prisons, or monastic orders, and so on); and (c) *logics of accumulation,* or what Foucault has described as the twin project of the (i) "accumulation of capital" (the various techniques of "surplus" expropriation), symbolic (religious gifts, benefices, professional fees paid to experts) or material (surplus labor expropriation in the Marxist sense or price-expropriation under oligopolistic/monopolistic conditions); and (ii) the "accumulation of men" in its various forms – segregation under distinct institutional rules (for lepers, vagabonds, political prisoners, criminals, mental patients, the sick, soldiers, and so on, but also of "the dangerous classes" and oppressed races), and the "sectorization" (divisions, hierarchies, classifications) of these forms. These logics may operate as analytically distinct from one another or in combination.

Still different logics operate at the level of quasi-global structures. I want to briefly describe three types of such quasi-global logics. (1) *Logics of collective emergence* are those explaining the "formation" of macro, collective agents, despite and actually because of the "free rider" problem (strategic leadership games, critical mass "vanguard" logics [Lenin, Hanagan], threshold logics [Schelling, Granovetter], modularity logics [such as Olson's federal groups], and synecdochical logics [for which see Chapter 7], among others). (2) *Logics of relations of institutional orders* (coupling and uncoupling logics): At the quasi-global level there are several systems of logics of collective agencies – class logics, state logics, logics of professional bodies, the logic of patriarchy – operating simultaneously, antagonistically or in alliance as multilateral monopolies or as an oligopolistic clique. These systems act as **chaotic attractors** pulling and pushing the overall systems to unpredictable, metastable states by way of several bifurcations. In short, special logics of collective and institutional "coupling" or "uncoupling" are at work. Giddens alludes to something like these logics of coupling or uncoupling of institutional orders in the coupling of kinship and tradition in tribal societies, the coupling of urban and rural space and life in class-divided societies, and the uncoupling of economy and state in class society, i.e., capitalism. Of course, there is more going on than encompassed in these simplified notions: a whole range of simultaneous couplings, uncouplings, alliances, oppositions, struggles for hegemony and for imposing a "totalizing logic," be it the Logic of Capital, the Logic of the State, or some other logic – a flexible and changing, hence contradictory, dialectical, structure shaped by several "attractors" (Boulding's organizers, Bourdieu's structuring structures involving structuring strategies). There are, finally, (3) *logics of development and change:* these are "developmental constraints," in the sense elaborated by Maynard Smith and his collaborators (1985), that bias the likelihood of specific structures entering onto one developmental pathway rather than another; or quasi-global dynamic constraints, "tipping" (Appendix no. 11) the semiopen system of competitively entangled structures into biased structural states under changing stability conditions (cf. Garfinkel 1981). Logics of macrogames, logics of structural contradictions and of dialectics are exemplary in social analysis at this specific level. To finish with the quasi-global level, we should finally mention what is left over when we count out the workings of the above three sets of logics. What is left, indeed, is a variety of *secondary or peripheral logics,* describable as "eco-logics" of space (such as those presented by Lösch, Hägerstrand and his school, Mandelbrot and the latest chaos theorists) or of size, space, and niche (as in the work of population ecologists), or, finally, the logics of composition of the "pratico-inert" (Boudon's or Merton's "unintended collective effects"). These secondary or peripheral logics, operating at the margins of the primary logics referred to above, account for the "eco-logical" appearance of macrosocial structures.

As expected, the higher level exhibits its own logics of operation, *global logics.* Here we must seek to find the process of emergence of these global logics before listing their operative principles. Global logics have emerged diachronically simultaneously with the growing separation of the local and global properties of systems. That can be understood to mean that the distinctions between local and global characteristics have emerged at the time of separation of "community" from "society." In the beginning of human societies, the small size of the groups meant that society and community were identical; progressively, however, with the increase in size there was a concomitant separation of community from society, the latter engulfing the former, to an important extent giving rise to the "phase-separation" of global from local dynamics (Lenski, Luhmann). An historical, diachronic analysis would have to explain this emergence in terms of (a) *globalizing logics of transition* from one phase-state to the other, explaining the familial or communal control of lands, resources, and men, the transitions toward the first "logics of war and slavery" (Patterson 1981) the emergence of the first "logics of state" (Carneiro, Wright), and the further globalization of the techniques of accumulation of lands, capital, and men, until the modern stages of global structures were reached. The general mechanisms of global logics must be understood in terms of (b) the *logics of matching of humans and resources* or *distributive logics*, and the ensuing *logics of class* (or classlike) structuring (per the Marxists and the left Weberians, such as Parkin [1979]) – the unequal endowment of collective agents with material and symbolic resources that generate the objective parameters within which class-formation and class-contestation take place. Here is the intersection between ecological and social structural factors that for too long has raised the temperature of theoreticians. To complete our understanding of the global dynamics we also need to know (c) the *dominant logic of the articulation of societal structures* or *logic of totalizing*, the hegemonic logic attempting the totalizing of the structures so as to produce an organized structure of structures or a "system-structure." This is a role played in modern times by the Logic of Capital or the Logic of the State and, increasingly, by the progressing integration of these two formerly antagonistic logics into an Integrated Logic of State and Capital ("organized" capitalism, "concertation" social democracies, organized "state capitalism" of the collapsing Eastern European form).[8]

I contend that there is no progressive research program in the area of social structural analysis until these various Logics of Structuration have been conceptually elucidated, logically purified, and thoroughly investigated and applied (as we begin to do in the Appendix).

---

[8] On organized capitalism and its demise see Lash and Urry (1987). On concertation democracy see Scharpf (1988) for references.

11 Neural networks as a model of structure

In this chapter we are going to embark on a speculative journey – so, caveat emptor! There are some fascinating developments taking place in the fields of cognitive science and neuroscience that may hold the key to a radically new understanding of a host of fundamental problems in a variety of disciplines and provide new leads in philosophical thinking as well. I am referring to the exciting field of neural network research, which appears to be on the verge of revolutionizing our understanding of "dualisms" or of "dualities," such as the relationship between brain and mind. My intentions in this chapter are simply to explore some possibilities implicit in the neural network model for rethinking our conception of "structure" in general, and suggesting, more particularly, a new approach to the theory of social structure. The insights derived from the neural network literature are only orienting analogies at this stage of our research. I do not make the claim that they provide a coherent new theory, only that, if correct, they would add significant new lines of argumentation on behalf of the heterarchical model of structure as it was developed in the previous chapter (which stands on its own, without any need for reference to neural networks). There is a very serious assumption here – one that can be modified by analytical means as we shall see later – that in order for the model of neural networks to be useful, one must accept, at least temporarily as if by a phenomenological bracketing, that there is no significant discontinuity between natural and social phenomena and, thus, between "natural structures" and "social structures." Numerous theorists in sociology and the human studies in general have argued that such discontinuity does exist and that models of the natural sciences have no applicability in the human sciences (see Habermas's, Giddens's, and Elster's critiques of functionalism on these grounds and the cited critical distinctions made by Bhaskar). I will not contest these points; but, it seems to me, they are targeting the old and wrong notion of natural structures. If this is so, some important corrections will need to be made to the sociological models, if it is proven that neural network models are not isomorphic in respect to their assumptions with the previous models of natural science. This, of course, remains to be seen. All I am asking at this moment is the bracketing of disbelief and the suspension of the natural aversion that social theorists have toward novel "scientific/scientistic" proposals. With the above provisos in place let us now introduce the notion of neural networks.

Any social scientist of today knows enough about networks. There exist mathematical models of networks in sociology and models of exchange networks as well. Quite often these networks are conceived as "linear," that is, as one-dimensional strings or chains, but network connectivities may give rise to many other more complicated patterns as well, such as cliques, hubs, and so on. Linear connections between two points or positions also have a tendency to be conceived as "digital," that is, operating on an "on/off" or "1/0" digital logic; for example, it is usually the case that people are taken either to relate or not to relate to others, to like or dislike others in general, or to be similar or dissimilar in regard to some particular properties or features. Models of linear networks have shown robustness as conceptual tools as well as metrics, and they have given to the discipline significant analytical, computational, and empirical results. Alternatively, they have also shown us that they are of somewhat limited utility in the conceptualization and explanation of complex, global dynamics (say, Conway games, ecosystems, or large-scale social structures), although continuous refinements may still prove useful.

Neural nets: elementary notions

Neural networks are a different and more complicated business. I will offer here a simple descriptive definition and return later on to provide a fuller account. By "neural networks" we generally mean on first approximation something like a spider's web or a fisherman's net: a large number of points connected to each other both in "serial" *and* "parallel" fashions in what appears as an expanded web or net replete with multidirectional loops. This simple image will serve its purpose for now: imagine electronic computer connections and the neural connections in the brain as something similar, until we can make better sense of it.

The analogies of computers and brains is one that we must examine closely. To begin, what is the relationship between "hardware" and "software" in the computer or between "brain" and "mind" in higher animal forms? This is a notoriously thorny question, of course, and many philosophical, psychological, and scientific theories have been developed and fallen from grace trying to answer it. On first thought, what appears as the main difference between hardware and software, brain and mind is that computer hardware and brains are physical objects while software and minds are mental; a program, algorithms, and rules in the case of software, mental states, representations, or something of that sort in the case of the mind. They do look radically different from each other and the whole *wissenschaften* tradition has made the best of this distinction arguing for the radical discontinuity of the human sciences relative to the physical ones. And yet software and hardware, mind and brain seem to relate to each other in ways that justify a suspicion that they are connected, not in mystical ways, but in some (nonreductive, to be sure) materialist way. This analogy is of crucial importance to the understanding and the significance attributed to the work on neural networks. It may or may not be useful in social science, but I will dare to ask the scandalous question: Can society be conceptualized in terms suggested by the hardware/software and brain/mind analogies? Suppose that we are willing to say yes just for the sake of the argument. That may imply a willingness on our part to see a population of individuals (as bodies, as organisms with some "capacities") as forming the "social hardware" or "social brain," and what we call society or social forms as being the "social software" or "social mind." We recall that Durkheim had a similar vision, particularly in his discussion of "collective representations." We will discuss later the notion that were one to pursue this program to its conclusion using modern-day scientific views, a form of a heterarchical post-functionalism (as described in Chapter 8) may be possible and better defended.

To begin to formulate the problem we must start with some notions prominent in current physics. In the first part of this book we have discussed certain novel notions in physics and biochemistry relating to the issue of emergence, and cited works on instabilities and bifurcations initially introduced by some prominent European scientists (Eigen, Haken, Nicholis, Prigogine). The upshot of these proposals – some of which are still controversial – is that we have to get away from the notion of matter as something stable and entropic in all, including local, environments (although, of course, matter *is* entropic in the global sink, given the second law of thermodynamics) toward a notion of a dynamic and active matter operating in metastable and far-from-equilibrium conditions with paradoxical results. Similar, although more cautious, ideas have been progressively developed by a score of prominent scientists in the United States (and in the Soviet Union, e.g., the work of Landau), the exemplary case being that of P. W. Anderson, arguably the premier physicist in this country, at least in the area of many-body physics. Anderson's work pointed out the physical basis of "symmetry-breaking" (Anderson 1972, 1984; Foster 1990; cf. Gleick 1987; Pagels 1985) in the process of expression of matter in condensed matter forms and in higher macromolecular structures. Symmetry breaking involves the violation or breaking of the basic laws of parity by emerging new forms of organization: for example, while in their free (racemic) state larger molecules and inorganic macromolecules tend to be randomly equally left- or right-handed in their atomic connections, the one being a mirror image of the other. In organized "condensed matter" states, especially in their biologically significant macromolecular forms, they are predominantly either right-handed or left-handed. Anderson cites this as the ground for the emergence of complicated molecular systems, such as crystals, molecular liquids, ferromagnets, superfluids involving superconductivity, and so on. "Nature abhors symmetry." There is also the fact that all forms of biologically important macromolecules exhibit "chirality" (Mason 1984); for example, all biological proteins are built by left-amino acids. Anderson began with "symmetry breaking" and then further theorized that molecular forms have moved beyond the stage of mere "crystallinity" (that is, simple packing) to "information-ally rich" forms with emergent qualities such as selectivity, information storage (something like "coding" or "memory traces") and, later, mac-romolecular replicability (see also Venkataraman et al. 1989). A selec-tionist theory of pre-biotic phenomena is implicit in these arguments. Using the model of "spin glass," Anderson was able to formulate a theory of pre-biotic evolution and computer simulation models based on it (Anderson 1983; Chowdhury 1986). The key ideas here are those of "information-rich systems," "symmetry breaking," and the (**spin glass**) mechanisms of the emergence of an "informational" quality out of the older material substrate. The mechanism of the connection be-tween "substrate" and "information" raises questions similar to the hardware/software or brain/mind puzzle.

The "spin glass" is a system in statistical mechanics that has both the properties of stability and diversity; spin glasses are a category of mag-netic systems with ordering exhibiting the properties of (a) "quenched disorder" and (b) "frustration" due to contradictory constraints on parts of the system leading to higher degeneracy of the ground state of the system. These properties, Anderson argues, are absolutely neces-sary for molecular evolution and, thus, for biological evolution as well. The spin glass is similar to the model of "associative memory" which is the central dogma of neural networks. The behavior of the spin glass is such that a random charge of various nodes gives a variety of random values, some positive, some negative, some of which "frustrate" a part of the possible node interactions. This property of frustration (frus-trated cycles) makes it possible for the state of the overall system to become "degenerate" and many "metastable states" emerge exhibiting the properties of stability and diversity together (see also **cellular au-tomata,** and "percolation" and "Conway games" in the Appendix). I realize that it may seem at this point that we are "looking through a glass darkly," but the meaning of this will become clearer. For now we should know that there is an acceptable explanation in modern physics of the origins of the phenomena we are interested in, an explanation which solidly grounds the higher-level theories of neural networks.

Imagine networks not as one-dimensional strings with knots or nodes along their total length but as two-dimensional arrays, a net with both "serial" and "parallel" connections; a complex system of lines that cross, as in TV networks, telephone networks, computer networking, or the networks of roads or railroads. In such networks, the potential exists that all possible connections may be active, that is, have a positive value, or that they can be "activated," in which case they are given a positive value. That will involve global connectivity – a sufficiently strong activation of one node will produce the activation of all other nodes by entropic dissipation. What will happen, however, when not all nodes are interconnected but, instead, there is only "partial connectivity" in the network? In that case the active flow will move along the connected lines and be blocked when reaching an unconnected one. A "neural network" is a partially connected network in this sense, a network in which each node is connected with several or many other nodes: Thus, when a node activates, it excites many other connected nodes as well; and when a node is activated, it is not the only one so activated but only one among many other connected nodes. So the overall relations (or mappings) in any such network is neither "one-to-one" nor is it "all-to-all"; it is rather "several-to-several" or "many-to-many." This, as we shall see, has important implications. (Recall here that any notion of heterarchy by definition involves such many-to-many or several-to-several connections between levels.)

Suppose that an activation takes place starting from one or more neural nodes. Given a strong energy source, other nodes will be activated through their "synapses." This activation will proceed along the limited connectivities; it will be blocked when nonconnectivities are reached, and then change course and move further through other existing connectivities. Ultimately the excitation will stop because local energies will decline below the minima required due to entropic dissipation; then, the system will settle down to rest until the next activating energy jolt. Something like that happens to membranes and biological neuronal systems. But the process there is even more complex. For example, any neuron is connected to many other neurons both in excitatory and inhibitory modes; that is, certain connections between neurons act to excite the intraneuronic and interneuronic synapses but other connections act to inhibit excitation. This operation is explainable at the molecular level.[1] Also, neurons do not act in a binary mode, that

---

[1] On the molecular level connectivity in the excitatory or inhibitory mode is explained on the basis of special "self-adhesive molecules." See Edelman's groundbreaking work (1987, 1989).

is, get activated or not get activated all in the same way. On the contrary, there is a nonlinear "graded-response" mechanism at work: Neurons get activated above a certain threshold but not below it and there may be different thresholds for different neuron types. (This is reminiscent of Schelling's model of neighborhood change, where people decide to move out (get activated) or stay (remain nonactivated) at different threshold levels; or Granovetter's models.) The combination of excitatory (positive) and inhibitory (negative) modalities of connectivity, of "graded-response" mechanisms, and of partial connectivity in the overall two-dimensional (or high-dimensional) array which involves many-to-many connections – these are the elementary characteristics that properly define the realistic cases of neural networks (although many simplifying models exist that are linear rather than nonlinear, digital rather than of graded-response, and with fewer connections for each neuron).

Neurons may connect to many other neurons randomly; but in the course of their interactions, especially in biological systems, they may change their synapses to connect specifically to each other. This has been called "neuronal selection" (Edelman 1987) and we will return to it later. As a result of the initial random connections or the ensuing selective connections, relations between neurons tend to produce larger neuronal groups, which are – in a "fuzzy set" sense – the would-be outcomes of a partial "fuzzy" decomposition of the overall neural network into partially distinct, and at the same time partially overlapping, neuronal sets. So, neurons operate, not as individuals but as groups, like ferromagnets, organized in the case of brain into columnar collective entities and, at a larger scale, into neuronal brain subsystems. As a result, we are able to speak of the partial localization (Edelman 1987, 1982, 1989; Edelman and Mountcastle 1978; Fodor 1983; cf. J. A. Anderson 1983a; Fodor and Pylyshyn 1988) of brain functions in fuzzily specifiable subsystems and regions of such subsystems in the brain. This is only a "partial" localization, that is, a primary fuzzy localization complemented by secondary and tertiary "parallel" localizations that may support the functions on their own in case of a trauma in the primary area.[2]

What does this tell us? The nonconnections or negative connections with other neurons (Anderson's "frustrated functions") suggest that

---

[2] The old localization theory has been replaced by a more moderate partial localization theory positing fuzzy primary localizations, secondary and tertiary localizations in parallel modes, and degenerate replacement of functions. See Churchland 1984, 1989; Edelman 1987, 1989; Edelman and Mountcastle 1978; Fodor 1983; Gazzaniga 1970, 1984, 1988; on projections, substitutions, and compensations in brain functions.

many partially segregated systems may emerge with enough stability and diversity to become vehicles of information storage ("memory" if you like) in a "degenerate" manner; "degenerates" are systems with overlapping states or many more or less similar states, each of which may retain a sufficiently good, though never perfect, "trace of memory," i.e., stored information relating to that system.[3] This brings us to the concept of "associative memory" systematically explored by Kohonen (1978, 1984) and other investigators.

Kohonen on associative memory

Kohonen's interest was in the "intelligent" cybernetic functions as physical processes, realizable in computer information systems and biological information systems. In computer systems, starting from elementary relations consisting of a pair of items and a symbolic attribute linking them together, it is possible to create complicated structures of concepts and represent knowledge by such "relational structures." In the biological case, a computation-oriented organization does not exist but, nonetheless, we find "structured knowledge" or "memory" playing a prominent role. Focusing on the biological systems, Kohonen made a distinction between "local" and "distributed" memories. Local memories (like digital computer memories) exist when "every distinct data set is stored on its own piece of memory medium or set of memory elements," therefore becoming "localized." In distributed memories, which are primarily biological in nature, "every memory element or fragment of memory medium holds traces from many stored items," in a pattern of superimposed "representations," and, vice versa, "every piece of stored information is spread over a large area" (1978:11). Now it is necessary that changes in the type of memory storage obey (collectively, as it were[4]) specific transformations of the primary signal patterns which preserve their interrelationships without interference from the other stored items, otherwise information of one item will be lost in the storage by mixing with other items. What are stored are patterns distributed over many neurons in a larger area (and secondary areas as

---

[3] On "trace" memory see Hopfield 1982; Hopfield and Tank 1986; Kohonen 1978, 1984. On the information-theoretical and thermodynamic theories of "storage" see Nicolis 1986; Wicken 1987.

[4] On collectively changing patterns of memory storage see Kohonen 1978:128. Compare these to Conway games (Appendix no. 24) and the general transformations of cellular automata. Think also of Schelling's example of changing neighborhoods as such a case of structure inducing/mapping collective information: Each move changes the "information content" of the particular perceptual maps of the bounded neighborhoods, which from the individual's point of view become overdeterminations of his or her behavior – a case of "structurally mapped cognition" if you will. For another suggestive insight see Gleick 1987:339, n.314 (Farmer and Packard quotation).

well), patterns stored as "differential state changes," each neuron being the locus of parts of many such patterns. This represents the many-to-many mapping we have discussed previously. Because of this pattern registration in larger areas of the network, whole structures are registered overlappingly and they are also retrieved without any need for a "sophisticated control principle" as in control-hierarchical systems. The final exciting idea is this: in biological information systems neuronic synapses may be altered by a process of random competition and selection, a process that depends upon the global characteristics of the macrostate of the system (Edelman 1987, 1982; Edelman and Reeke 1982; Kohonen 1978:141, 145), so in fact, the brain is an adaptive distributed network.

Hopfield's models of neural networks

The pioneering work of J. J. Hopfield and his associates in the field of computational neurobiology is along these same lines of theory and experimental research (Hopfield 1982; Hopfield et al. 1983; Hopfield and Tank 1986). Using computational techniques, Hopfield embarked on a program of construction of neural networks in order to prove the point that memory, knowledge representation, and retrieval can take place in these networks without the need of an intelligent control subsystem (a "homunculus") or agent. In his seminal 1982 article, Hopfield argued that computational properties, that is, processes of memory and knowledge storage similar to those used by biological organisms, can emerge spontaneously "as collective properties of systems having a large number of simple equivalent components (or neurons)" (1982: 2554). These collective properties can be shown to produce a "content-addressable memory" (distributed memory) which correctly yields an entire memory from any subpart of sufficient size. (To connect this to Anderson's work: "Any physical system," says Hopfield, "whose dynamics in phase-space is dominated by a substantial number of locally stable states to which it is attracted can therefore be regarded as a general content-addressable memory" (ibid.; cf. P. W. Anderson 1983; Edelman and Reeke 1982). In his most recent work Hopfield has provided a simple model of nonlinear neurons organized into networks with effectively symmetric connections that has a "natural" capacity for solving even optimization problems (Hopfield and Tank 1986; and *Science*, March 1986 debate). Using from more than a hundred up to many thousands of neurons in computer-modeled "distributed systems," Hopfield demonstrated that self-organization would emerge under collective, associative, and distributive constraints, giving rise to many "intelligent" properties of memory, learning, problem solving, and attempts at "survival" (on the latter see also Anderson's work on the

"D-for Death-Function" in distributed, spin glass systems [1983] and Conway's "Games of Life" in the Appendix).

From the computational theories of Kohonen and Hopfield we may now turn to the actual brain studies of neuroscientists. It has come to be nearly universally accepted that the brain is like an advanced neural network (see the Bibliography for numerous citations). It consists of a very large number of neurons (some 50 billion nerve cells), each of which is directly connected to a large number of other neurons. A neuron can be in one of two states – "firing" or "not firing" – and, through its connections, is able to sense the states of its neighbors. During cerebral activation each neuron independently examines the current state of its neighbors and, as a result of this information, determines its own next state. This process is done by each and every neuron simultaneously and results in the sophisticated behavior of the neural network as a whole. The computational function, therefore, is done in a collective manner, that is, in a way in which thousands of neurons collectively and simultaneously influence the state of an individual neuron according to the application of simple rules. This process also allows information ("hardwired" to the appropriate [sub]net of neurons) to be encoded in the neural connections rather than in separate memory elements – in other words, across many neurons as a relational structured property. Each distinct piece of stored information is finally represented by a unique "pattern of connections" among neurons.

Gerald Edelman's work

The most fascinating and robust theory of brain development, structure, and function has been proposed by Gerald Edelman under the catchall name of "neural Darwinism," more analytically called "the group-degenerate selection model." Edelman theorizes that "an adequate brain theory must account for (a) the distributive nature of learning, (b) the associative nature of recall, (c) the adaptive reaction to novelty, and (d) the capacity to make highly abstract representations in a world model" (Edelman and Mountcastle 1978:94). Edelman rejects the hierarchical conception of mind which postulates a high "controller" organizing and directing the higher brain functions (the "homuncular" theories). Instead, following Mountcastle (Edelman and Mountcastle 1978), who has argued that higher brain functions depend on the "ensemble actions" of very large populations of neurons in the forebrain organized into complex interaction systems (through the multiply replicated local neuronal circuits constituting columns), Edelman suggests that "intracolumnar and intercolumnar connections are precisely arrayed, but they constitute distributed systems serving distributed functions" (1987:4).

Edelman views the brain as having been built through the following stages of development: First, during the development of the brain in the embryo a very complex but highly variable and individuated pattern of connections between neurons is formed; after birth, a specific pattern of neural connections becomes fixed in every individual but, through epigenetic processes, some combinations of connections are selected over others; selection is particularly strong in groups of neurons that are connected in sheets, called "maps," which once selected relate back and forth to one another to store, create, or retrieve categories of things or events. In the first part of the process, genetic forces are at work together with the developmental constraints imposed by the collective properties of the system at each state of its development. But after birth, a selectional process begins to work, in which the operational units are neuronal groups, each composed of hundreds or thousands of neurons which constitute the "local" units or *primary repertoire.* The repertoire of neuronal groups permits matching of repertoire groups to sensory signals in a degenerate manner, that is, with more than one way by which the repertoire can recognize given input signals (ibid.:5). Multiple signaling to primary repertoire groups leads to associative recognition and the formation of a *secondary repertoire* of neuronal groups having a higher likelihood of response than the cell groups of the primary repertoire. Changes that occur in the primary repertoire involve the change of "strength" but not the "pattern" of their connections; but the strengthening of connections in some groups may lead to the altering of their connections with other groups and, by *competing* with them, allow the incorporation of neurons from the other groups into their own, thus forming the secondary repertoires. As a result of experience, Edelman says, and the formation of secondary repertoires, *structures* are formed that discriminate between "self-inputs" and "external inputs." Thus, *consciousness* in the individual may result from "reentrant signaling" that involves associations between current sensory input and stored patterns of neuronal groups.

The result of the selectional formation of secondary repertoires is the emergence and stabilization of *distributed systems* (ibid.:40). Each large neuronal entity is fractioned into subsets, each linked by a particular pattern of connections to similarly segregated subsets in other large entities. The linked sets of modules of the several entities are defined as a distributed system. Figure 11.1 illustrates secondary repertoire connections.

Thus, according to Edelman, "major entities are parts of many distributed systems, contributing to each a property determined for the entity by those connections common to all of its modular subsets and by the particular quality of their intrinsic processing. Even a single mod-

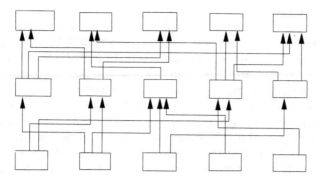

Figure 11.1. *Pattern of secondary repertoire connections – simplified model*

ule of such an entity may be a member of several (though not many) distributed systems." Distributed systems, therefore, are composed of large numbers of modular elements "linked together in echeloned parallel and serial arrangements" (40–42). Information flow through such a system may follow a number of different pathways, and the dominance of one path or another is a dynamic and changing property of the system. Such a system has many entries and exits and has access to outflow systems of the brain at many levels.

Overall, the brain's job is, of course, the processing and organization of (sensorimotor) stimuli in ways that will be meaningful and useful for the organism. This organization is achieved by the use of maps made up of neuronal groups. A "map," according to Edelman, is a collection of neuronal groups in the brain arranged in a way that preserves the pattern of relationships (a) between a sheet of sensory receptors and a sheet of neural tissue or (b) between two sheets of neural tissue in the brain. Groups arranged into maps seem to "communicate" with each other, affecting each other's extrinsic connections. In this manner, "maps become rearranged" due to the competitive selection of particular combinations of neuronal groups. Information in the brain is distributed among many such maps so, in order for perceptual categorization to be possible, there must be continuous reference back and forth between many maps.

But the operations are not restricted to a particular level; they also connect across levels in an exemplary heterarchical manner. In his books (1987, 1988, 1989) Edelman describes the full process by which vision and general perceptual knowledge takes place. He distinguishes between local mechanisms and global mechanisms performed respectively by local network circuits and by higher-order neuronal distributive organizations producing the higher-order maps. At the local level there are two distinct types of operations of "feature extraction" (specificity) and "feature correlation" (generality), the outcomes of which are interrelated at intermediate levels of abstraction (something akin to my conception of the quasi-local level). Context-bound, real intermediated outcomes are then stored across various neuronal groups forming particular maps. It is the further interconnectivity between these maps that forms "intelligent" subsystems (at the quasi-global level) and possibly gives rise to the emergence of "central system" notions of "selfhood" and "consciousness" (at the global level) (Edelman 1989:151–213; cf. Dennett 1984; Hofstadter and Dennett 1981). In Edelman's descriptions and theoretical postulates we see a heterarchical, "hardwired" neuronal system spontaneously bringing about, in conjunction with selectionist processes, intelligent "softwired" symbolic representations, i.e., mental states.

To summarize the pertinent issues involved in these recent scientific analyses: What we have here are models of heterarchical (many-to-many intralevel as well as interlevel) connectivity which, based on new analytical concepts such as associativity, distributiveness, degeneracy and group degeneracy, provide detailed "emergent but still materialist" explanations of higher-level symbolic, intelligent phenomena. This is, therefore, a strong version of heterarchy (a form of complex heterarchical "connectionism") in contrast to the more modest version we have presented in the previous chapter. We are nearly ready to discuss the possible implications of this strong version of heterarchy for the sociological conceptualization of structure, but not before we examine the outstanding and thought-provoking work of Hofstadter, who has contributed significantly to our appreciation of the logics of heterarchy.

Douglas Hofstadter's work

Hofstadter's preoccupation with tangled emergence originates with a nightmare (the Anteater): the "indescribably boring nightmare" of trying to understand a book on the letter level (1979:326, 570). For Hofstadter, since letters are the "medium," not the "message," the process of understanding must operate at higher levels which are, nonetheless, grounded on the lower level. Describing an ant colony's collective "intelligent" behavior, Hofstadter spells out – in an imaginative dialogue on "Ant Hillary" – the level distinctions that obtain therein between individuals and collectively-acting groups of ants. Like letters ants are conceived as senseless in their individual form. Teams of ants are one of the levels of structure falling somewhere between the single-ant level and the colony level and a special kind of team, which he calls a "signal," operates as a transporting device (much like "messenger RNA") moving ants of various specializations, primarily "information" and "expertise" to appropriate parts of the colony (much like a pattern of neuronal "firing"). Signal teams of a sufficiently high level, that is, teams of teams, which one can call "symbols," are active subsystems of a complex system and are composed of the lower-level active subsystems of "signals" (while the individual ants, the letters of the ant colony, are passive).

At the brain level, the counterpart of the caste distribution of the ant colony into teams and signals is the "brain state": individual neurons are like the ants of an ant colony; neuronal groups operate as teams, selectively, at the quasi-local level. Special processes of these teams, here self-organizationally emerging from the collective dynamic of teams (namely, from columnar organization), form patterns of "signals," that is, active "traces" of specific, distributed and associative, connections that are firing or not firing simultaneously, thus storing or recalling previously stored informational patterns. At the next level (the quasi-global one), connections between subsystems composed of several neuronal groups – indeed, connections between several neuronal groups across these subsystems – actively incorporate and recategorize "signals" into "symbols" (Pylyshyn's transducers) which are, according to Hofstadter, nothing else but partly hardware and partly software realizations of concepts. This is so because any particular large region of neuronal networks will be the locus of several, if not many, overlapping symbols superimposed on one another and distinguished from each other by specific modes of excitation: the relation to the neuronal network per se is a "hardware" realization, while the modes of excitation of each symbol are "software" realizations (Hofstadter 1979:357–9). So there is a certain "partial software isomorphism," that is, a certain correspondence of (1) the repertoire of symbols and (2) the triggering patterns of symbols (ibid.:371). It is because of this partial software isomorphism, I believe, that Hofstadter as well as Edelman, Hopfield, and others are willing to argue that the higher level (global dynamics) somehow "reaches downward" and reprograms some of the hardware underlying it (Edelman 1987; Hofstadter and Dennett 1981; even Churchland 1984).

The overall system of "symbols" and of their activities is strictly determined by the state of the full system in which they reside. Therefore, since the full system is responsible for how its symbols trigger each other, we may reasonably speak of the full system as the "agent." Hofstadter and Dennett (1981:200, 282) call the self-concept "a complex subsystem that is a model of the whole system."[5] What constitutes the

---

[5] For the notion of "self-concept" see also Hofstadter 1979:350. For a slightly different argument concerning "awareness" and "consciousness" see Edelman

"active" nature of symbols? That, when awakened, symbols send out "messages," or "signals," whose purpose is to try to awake, or trigger, other symbols (Hofstadter 1979:350; compare Edelman's description of the communication between maps). Obviously, each neuron is far from being a member of a unique symbol, as a hierarchical view will have it, but instead is a functioning part of hundreds of symbols; conversely, any symbol utilizes the registering, connecting, and firing capacities of hundreds or thousands of neurons for its emergence and activation.

Social structure and neural structure

We are now ready to turn our speculative gaze to social theoretical concerns. What is the relevance of these ideas to the domain of human phenomena, where individual cognitive and motivational agencies are admittedly – at least, in "folk-psychological" terms – implicated in their production, reproduction, or transformation? Obviously, the issue is not one of trying to "impose" one more model derived from physical science on the theories of the social domain; if there is any utility, it will be in the flexible exploration of the analogy, not in its use as a straight-jacket, for as Stinchcombe says, we learn a lot from analogical and comparative ways of thinking (1978).

Is it possible that social structure has anything in common with the way of thinking posited by neural network research? I would like to explore this question in the discussion of three examples representing, respectively, lower, middle-range, and higher scales of social phenomena.

Baker's crowds
Let us begin with the study done by Wayne Baker on the Chicago commodities and futures markets. In that study Baker challenged Blau's theory which, in the Durkheimian fashion, had asserted that increasing group size results in social differentiation in a monotonic way. Baker put forward the argument that markets differentiate in another way, curvilinearly, because large size and growth "outstrip the capacity of actors to communicate efficiently" (1984; cf. his 1981, 1983). Contrary to Blau's notion, empirical markets, said Baker, have no built-in limits or constraints on size, and they may expand virtually unabated, ex-

1987:74, 85, who argues that consciousness is not a property of the entire brain but rather is the result of processes occurring in certain defined areas; nevertheless, it still requires temporal processes that are both parallel and sequential, since there is "a constant shifting among cross-correlated multimodal signals phasically accessing a historically developed storage." This view is elaborated better in his 1989 (see p. 91 and elsewhere).

ceeding communication capacities and impairing performance. Baker
then embarked on a project to find out what would actually develop in
such "impaired markets." The commodities exchange he studied was a
closed system overall because trading status was conferred only to those
who were members and had bought the right to trade in the pits. Within
this closed system various "pits" operated, specializing in various individual markets – agriculturals, financials, metals, and so on. Each pit
is an open system in the sense that it can grow large or shrink according
to the interests of traders and the volatility of the market. In general,
an increase in one "crowd" means proportional decrease in another
crowd or several other crowds. Baker's question was to find out what
happened when one crowd became suddenly very large because of the
volatility of the commodity or other instrument involved. He describes
his findings as follows:

Under the assumption of bounded rationality and opportunism, actors would
be compelled to limit and restrict their trading. Participants' limited informa-
tion-reception and (information)-processing abilities force them to restrict their
search for partners to a trade. Furthermore, opportunism results in a reduction
as marketmakers curtail their participation. . . . One of the results of the cur-
tailment of trading in large groups is the formation of multiple subgroups.
These subgroups are truly emergent – they are the unintended outcomes of
human limitations on trading in the context of large aggregates. (Baker 1984:
783–4)

Baker also discussed the effects on these emergent phenomena in
dampening or exacerbating price volatility.

Notice the structure of this market: a fixed population of traders on
the exchange floor; subdivision of this population into many pits (as in
the "island" model of an ecology discussed by Boorman and Levitt
1980; see Appendix, for cascades, islands, percolation); swamping (see
Appendix) of a particular pit; and breakdown in that pit to multiple
subgroups exhibiting a fast dynamic and fragile stability.

This sounds rather similar to a "spin glass" or "neural network": when
a "crowd" increases in size, due to the limitations of communication as
Baker describes it, there develops only a partial connectivity (due to the
emergence of many "frustrated cycles" as Anderson [1983] would say)
between the individual traders, that is, traders related to a restricted set
of other traders. Restrictions are imposed by "proximity," "market making," or "old trading coalitions." Each individual trader cannot survey
the whole crowd to make the most lucrative contract; he has to restrict his
choice (on this see also Edelman [1987:146] on "disjunctive sampling")
by the above three constraints to a few contiguous traders, or to usual
partners, or to market makers (as against the so-called "locals"). So, different "signals" (that is, "firing" patterns) can be triggered within a lim-

ited context of several-to-several connections. It is in accordance with these rules of excitatory and inhibitory signaling that we can understand the emergence of "multiple subgroups." These are overlapping groups, not segregated and localized ones: They are **polymorphous sets,** that is, sets that define membership by the possession of some properties found in the overall set (such as black, or circular, or symmetric), characterized by the disjunction of the possible partitions, i.e., having between them a "nonexclusive OR function" (Edelman 1987:31, 261). Baker's multiple subgroups are polymorphous sets in this sense. This is a metastable state in which, if we recall Anderson, are found the twin requirements of (conditional) stability and diversity for dynamic evolution: The multiple groups compete against each other for space, attention/communicative efficiency (their notorious shouting), stability, and optimal trading size, analogously to the neuronal groups competing to strengthen their extrinsic synapses (per Edelman). And what are the patterns that register here as "signals" in Hofstadter's sense of the term? Not only the "flows" of trade through the "firing" of synapses (making a contract) but also the informational registration of a price (making a price, fixing a price, clearing) which is the software equivalent of a "memory." (I will return to this issue below.) I have a feeling that, were one to make a computational model of a neural network depicting the making and sustaining of any commodities market, a model would emerge similar to the ones proposed by Hopfield.

The fragmented ("island") model of population ecology
Local (biological or social) ecosystems are an example of an intermediary level of analysis. Attempts to characterize an ecology as a "stacked-up" or hierarchical system (Allen and Starr 1982) have been discredited upon the realization that any such system involves several "tangled" subsystems interpenetrating one another (as in the case of letters, words, and sentences). Thus the development of a new approach has been in progress.

In general, we see an ecology operating at many levels: interspecies, species, particular local population groups, small demes and ingroups, and individual organisms. The goal of individuals, if we follow the neo-Darwinian line, is to increase reproductive fitness of their inclusive group within the context of the community (interpopulation) ecological relations. Inhomogeneous ecological and reproductive space accounts for the relative isolation of local and regional ecosystems of particular sorts and for the fragmentation of local or regional populations of the various species. The ensuing free formation of multiple subgroups may take a form similar to Baker's "impaired market" (with several important differences between the two, to be sure) or similar to an "island" model on the basis of which a "cascading" process of genetic transformation may be launched (for details see the Appendix, "Islands," for Boorman and Levitt's work). "Polymorphous grouping" will be more apparent at the so-called "kin" (Hamilton 1964; Maynard Smith 1976) and "in-group" (Wynne-Edwards 1986) levels where "kin selection" and "intrademic selection" (small-scale group selection) operate. Particularly at the level of relations between "in-group" and "local population," the "synapses" (memberships and/or reproductive linkages) change in intensity for particular individuals and small groups, as described, for example, by primatologists and anthropologists (e.g., Colin Turnbull, in *The Forest People* describes such fragile synapses between family groups and affine marginal individuals). A "signal" at this level will be the successful stability conditions of such groups and/or of the reproductive rates achieved and stored in the social or genetic "memory" of the inclusive group. This may be thought of as analogous to Edelman's notion of primary or lower-level consciousness.[6]

This process is even more pronounced when one focuses on larger populations of a species: the increase in the population brings about a drift toward or a breakup into multiple groups that are "locally adapted populations" (demes, in-groups, or "trait groups"). At this level, in-groups relate to the overall population and the species in a clearly heterarchical, "federal" way. There is always a certain fluidity of individuals in and out of in-groups, of in-groups in and out of given populations (migration, invasion), and so on. "Demes" do compose a genetic or, in the human case, cultural polymorphous set. On the argument derived from the model of neural networks, the end result is that group-degenerate processes based on distributed and associative demic organizations of any population of a species seem to provide a working mechanism for the survival of these populations. Heterarchical organization facilitates performance and survival. In this sense, Anderson's ground-model of evolution (1983) and Boorman and Levitt's (1980) model of cascade process provide an important link between neural network (and advanced "cellular automata") and ecological models on the way to a full-fledged heterarchical theory.

A small detour: types of groups

The transition from local groups to macroentities cannot be a simple function of increasing size, the work of Durkheim, Blau, or Mayhew

---

[6] In Turnbull (1962) we get as close as one can to the "assembly language" of biotic (social-material) life: We find the "signal" to "symbol" transcription in the (partially hardwired) rules, "do not split the group," commit "no incest" (no serious transgression of threshold), make "no noise" (no continuation of fighting threatening the first rule). These rules are partly hardware, partly software.

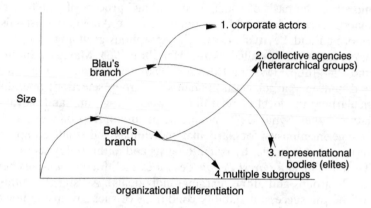

Figure 11.2. *Chaotic model of group formation (two-period chaos)*

notwithstanding. Models like the ones proposed by these theorists attempt to capture an independent function as a simplifying summation of a more complex process. As soon as one moves beyond the simplicity of the "compositionist fallacy" (Elster 1985), it is clear that some other, more complicated, at times chaotic, mechanisms are involved. Consider again Baker's analysis: In Blau's model, he says, communication and coordination problems are recognized, but they "feed back" and act to attenuate the rate of differentiation before the system malfunctions. But an empirical market has no such built-in limits or constraints on size, and it may expand virtually unabated, exceeding communication capacities and impairing performance, thus finally splitting into multiple subgroups (Baker 1984:783). Clearly, a bifurcation takes place: as the system progresses to larger sizes a point of instability is reached at which the system may go to any of two different states, one of which leads to organizational differentiation and the other one to the breakup into multiple subgroups. This is also the case with the population dynamics of a species ("island" divisions). Such bifurcations may be found to operate not as simple Markovian probabilistic transition paths (in fixed lattice-theoretical models) but as "chaotic dynamics," bringing about a variety of organizational possibilities representing local–global mapping transitions. Consider Figure 11.2's chaotic model of "group formation" with only two bifurcation periods.

As population increases, the "packing" rules change according to different modalities, each modality representing a push toward one particular bifurcation branch. The branches may be marked as implying, in our case, transitions toward more organized responses (hierarchy, organizational differentiation) or less organized responses (markets, and breakups into multiple subgroups). Within each bifurcation branch of period one, another bifurcation (period two) will take place along the same more or less organized transitions, giving rise to four possible formations with different stability (or instability) conditions. We can recognize the following stable forms within the second period bifurcation:

(A) strongly organized groups (corporate actors), instantiating "authoritative supersession" in true hierarchical form;
(B) moderately organized groups (representational bodies), exhibiting the property of "governance";
(C) lesser organized groups (collective agencies), operating as "federal" heterarchical groups; and
(D) groups with "impaired" organization (multiple subgroups), quite often forming "polymorphous sets."

Moving from the quasi-local to the quasi-global scales of organization we find: corporate actors in the form of strong hierarchical organizations in which decision-making authority is monopolized by top organizational elites (corporate business organization and state bureaucratic organization are the exemplary cases); representational bodies, which realize a weaker sense of hierarchy involving "governance," that is, more general representational authority, but not "authoritative supersession" or power to impose one-sided penalties on subordinates (professional bodies are the exemplary case); collective agencies, that as federal-heterarchical groups represent "synecdochical" and dynamic modes of organization (the paramount case being classes); and more unstable forms with minimal organization (markets in general, impaired or otherwise imperfect markets in particular). This transition, as we will see shortly, involves different modes of relation and organization. However, we should never lose sight of the fact that, while "corporate actors" and "representational bodies" are formally forms of hierarchy, essentially they operate as heterarchies, as Eccles and White (1986, 1988) have shown. In fact, corporate actors, representational bodies, and collective agencies all act as "federal," "heterarchical" groupings, as collective agencies *sensu lato*.

The heterarchical view of classes

Of the above, the case of (strict) "collective agencies" seems to be the pure heterarchical notion. The formation of classes, built on a "block-modeled" sort of relations (that is, the equivalence of persons occupying a position in the production structures relative to others), proceeds along heterarchical lines of emergence and "tangled" connectivities across levels. The relations between levels are not hierarchical,

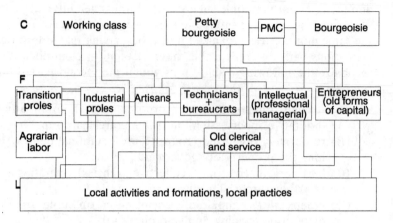

Figure 11.3. *A neuronal network model of classes, fractions, and local groups*

either in the strong or in the weak sense of this term, but federal-like, each level – class, fractions, local groups – maintaining a degree of autonomy and causative power vis-à-vis the others (interlevel processes) and having semiautonomous processes of their own (intralevel processes). The overall pattern of connections is a neuronal network structured as an associative and distributed system, along the heterarchical lines depicted in Figure 11.3.

Classes, then, are collective agencies organized out of "fractions." We can understand fractions in the following manner. Suppose that a set exists defining the member subsets by the sharing of five distinct structural characteristics. A subset may be found which includes all those individuals or groups that share all five of those characteristics; this may be called the exemplary fraction in the set and in the case of the Marxist conception of the working class this is the idealized "industrial proletariat." But it is more likely that five other subsets may also be found – forming a "polymorphous set" – each of which will share four of the five designating characteristics: these will be the core fractions of the class. Two steps removed from the exemplary fraction there will be ten other subsets sharing three of the five characteristics and forming another polymorphous set; for lack of any better name let us call them semicore fractions. Further, in the perimeter of the set's reaches there will be ten and five subsets – also forming two distinct polymorphous sets – sharing, respectively, two and one of those five characteristics; these are peripheral fractions of the class and we may take it that they are not true members. I contend that class is really the set of all those fractions and, most importantly, the set that includes the exemplary fraction together with the core and semicore fractions. So, class is not homogeneous in the strict sense of this term but, nevertheless, exhibits strong "polymorphic homogeneity." This process can be repeated within each class fraction to indicate the polymorphic nature of the quasi-local groups forming that fraction. The conclusion is that given the nature of this polymorphic overlap, the connections across levels can be only heterarchical, as the above simplifying figure represents. This fits rather well the picture of group-degenerate, distributed "neural network" systems drawn by Edelman.

Structure, informational structure, and culture

This brings us to the categorization problem and to the hardware-software part of the controversy. All of the proposed models of neural networks address the issue of a certain hardware organization working with internal processes (or external processes, in the case of computing machines) toward further self-organization and the development of internalized and/or purely internal knowledge representation and memory. Hopfield's models lead to "intelligent" behavior, learning or unlearning, memory, and even optimization solutions. Anderson's or Conway's models lead to realization of survival strategies and memory traces (information) of those strategies. Edelman's model leads to categorization, memory, and the development of higher cognitive functions (1989). All in all, these neural network models specify the conditions not only of further hardware structure modification (as in the so-called "synapse modification" commonly accepted by most neurobiologists) and upward structuration, but also, and most importantly, of the development and modification of software or representational structure – from presyntactic concepts to global maps, rules, language-based concepts – in short, culture. In Edelman's model, which is by far the most developed theory of brain structure and function and has been corroborated to a large extent by other research (see his 1989; Sacks 1990), there is an interaction of software and hardware processes and, to use Hofstadter's term, a "partial isomorphism." In simplifying terms, local groups, by the use of a "classification couple" of local feature detectors and local feature correlators and a reentry process coupling them, achieve the formation of "maps" which are related to each other as members in a polymorphous set. Some global feature correlators work on the basis on these maps and produce "global maps" which are registered, again, in a polymorphic sense, in various parallel, distributed systems of larger neuronal groups at the top of which stand the neuronal entities, i.e., functional regions of the brain. The local maps may be seen as "signals" in Hofstadter's sense and the global maps as "symbols" generated by these global correlators or transducers. The connections of symbols to signals is partially isomorphic to the connections of large neuronal groups (i.e., "chunked" networks of neurons registering or carrying information in a parallel distributed [PDP] process) to small ones: in both cases they are heterarchical and between the hardware–software transducing line heterarchical as well. Every symbol registers in several overlapping (and some not overlapping) large neuronal groups; and, vice versa, each such neuronal group triggers or is registering a variety of symbols which are superimposed on each other and distinguished by their specific (informationally rich) pattern of activation.

This complex system seems, therefore, to implicate the following:

(A) local-to-global groups of neurons linked heterarchically, here in many-to-several connections (hardware structures);

(B) local- (here-and-now, indicative of primary, lower-level consciousness) to-global maps (correlated, abstracted, elaborated via reentry signaling, indicative of higher consciousness); and

(C) somewhere dynamically between (A) and (B) a semi-isomorphic correlation (transducers, coupling of local feature extractors and global feature correlators) that generates semi-autonomous representational structures, such as internal conceptualizations of the individual or collective variety.

Having the above model in mind, let us now look at the notion of social (and cultural) structural formation. We can do so by positing all the relevant quasi-homologies between various domains, as shown in Table 11.1.

The "hardware" of society is bodies, a population of organisms with "bracketed" mental capacities. These are the neurons of the social system. Local-level connectivities, initially along biotic lines (see above discussion on Turnbull's work) and reinforced later on in interaction with "software" (socialized) modes, allow for the formation of neuronal groups (various modal social groups) which are numerous and act as conduits for the production of "local maps," which in our social case are (family, kin, and in-group) "representations" of the conditions and possibilities of the environment here-and-now, necessary for the species' survival. Local maps are active "signals": they register not as images of the environment but as organizational responses to the environment; therefore, they are "informationally rich," preserving in the mapping the counter-entropic history of the group-based, structural formation (Bennett 1986; Nicholis 1986a; Prigogine and Stengers 1984). This process gives rise to numerous low-level "software" maps, which I call modes of (local and semilocal) relations – group relations and

Table 11.1. *Heterarchical levels along the hardware–software distinction* (To be read from the bottom up)

Fourth (Top) Level: AGENCIES

    Agencies of any social form (corporate actors, collective actors, representational bodies, polymorphous groups, small groups, "persons"). Totalizing Logics.

    Genome, genetic engrams in the ant colony

    Self-concept in neural PDP terms (the mind of the brain)

    High-level languages and *operating systems*

    Authorial (authorizing) functions in language (the writerly, the speaking subject)

Third Level: SYMBOLS

    Modal norms, symbolic patterns, interlinked

    Symbols in the ant colony (jobs done, informationally coded "functions")

    Symbols, mental images/states, global maps in the brain

    Interpreters and compilers in computer languages

    Semantic, pragmatic, and grammatical meanings and patterns (words, speech acts, "grammars" of all sorts)

    [Between the second and third levels: *transduction of concepts, partly-hardware (signal-based), partly-software (symbol-forming)*]

Second Level: SIGNALS

    Modal networks of humans (egocentric and sociocentric)

    Signals in the ant colony (in Hofstadter's sense)

    Neuronal groups and complexes with *mapping* capacities

    Assembly language chunks

    Admissible *chunks* of letters forming words (before grammar: see Chomsky, Edelman 1989)

First (Bottom) Level: HARDWARE

    Networks of individual human organisms/human populations

    Ants in a colony (Ant Hillary)

    Population of *Neurons*

    Computer hardware/set of logical gates

    Letters, ideograms, or phonemes in a language

---

group-ecosystem relations – each one of which registers on various polymorphous groups and "structures" them into social groups, at the preinstitutional or the protoinstitutional level. When we speak of a dominance hierarchy or a local institution or a working group we do not basically refer to the number and volume of the bodies composing it but to the "principle" that organizes it, the "function" that it may have, or the "modes of relations" that structure it – in brief, its modal principle. In these cases, the characteristic is, primarily, a "chunked" (assembled) characteristic and the modes of local (or quasi-local) relations, their modality, are "signals" activating the connectivities between individuals. Ditto for the quasi-global and global structures: these exhibit software "symbols" (higher-level intentional logics, internal global mappings as visions, "projects"[7]) and "relational structures of such symbols," in a way preserving a partial isomorphism between the software and the hardware structures. Therefore, symbols remain partly-hardware, partly-software realizations of concepts (Hofstadter 1979) and, in an analogous fashion, culture and ideology remain partly-hardware, partly-software realizations of transduced "functions."[8] At the higher symbolic scales the structuring rules appear as progressively more conscious and globalizing modes of organization, as cognitive-political "projects" (those informing the Logics of Capital, State, Meritocratic Elitism, Democracy, Patriarchy, or what have you). In other words, populations of individuals are structured by the software structuring structures within the parameterized sphere of possibilities allowed by the hardware characteristics (in the "class" case, of course, these will be the structuring modes of expropriation of material resources intersecting with the modes of domination of the quasi-local and quasi-global levels). The process of "structuration" therefore is rather homologous to these other processes and relations we have depicted in Table 11.1. Social structures and increasingly conscious collective representations ("projects") seem homologous to neuronal structures and higher-level consciousness, to *intentional* personhood, to *intensional* language, and to high-level computer languages. On this

---

[7] In Chapters 13–14 I describe several "projects" as higher-level intentional (modal) logics. These are transcriptions from lower, partly-hardware, partly-software rules ("transcribed material interests"). See also Edelman's insightful analysis (1989:173, 186–192) on higher-order consciousness.

[8] Hofstadter has called "symbols" partly-hardware, partly-software realizations of concepts. This certainly can be extended to the notions of "culture" and "ideology," as systems of beliefs not merely reflecting but transducing various practices. The "symbolic" is not merely "functional"; it implicates transduced contingent functions. In other words, "functions" underdetermine "symbols" in the same sense that "facts" underdetermine "theories." For a similar view of the autonomy of "symbolic power" see Bourdieu 1977a and b, 1988, 1990.

reading, both ideas and social structures compose a software–hardware pair effecting various partly-hardware, partly-software realizations. Rerouting, reentry, iteration, recategorization of functions and operations are the dynamic tools that provide "informational" structure, not the sheer physical shape of the hardware body. As the mind is the nonlocalizable combinatorial heterarchy, as Edelman describes it, society, too, may be an embodied, yet nonlocalizable, combinatorial heterarchy of "primary" (biotic) and "higher-order" (sociocultural) social structures. Or is it?[9] I will address this issue more thoroughly in future work.

[9] Note the crucial homology between "mind" and "society" in terms of their (now discredited) view as "agents." See Edelman, Hofstadter, and Dennett on intimations of conceiving the mind and the self-concept in heterarchical terms: No need for an overarching "controller" or homunculus in mind or in society, although there may be "would-be totalizing agencies." Viewed differently, the sequence signals–concepts–symbols is homologous to the sequence informationally rich modal nets (patterned experience, micro-habitus)–"i-functions"–culture/ideology. On the difference between lower-order (primary) consciousness and higher-order consciousness see Edelman 1989; see also Chapter 15.

Part V
The phenomenology of social structures

In this final part we address issues related to the "phenomenology of structures" using our previous knowledge of heterarchical organization. We begin with the description of a matrix consisting, in one dimension, of structural types and, in the other, of structural levels; on the basis of this matrix we investigate intralevel as well as interlevel relations, especially between adjacent levels. Essentially, these relations are entangled, contrary to the hierarchical view. Figure V.1 illustrates phenomenological levels and structures.

In Chapter 12 we discuss various **modalities** of interactions implicated in the process of structural "emergence." We then review the different types of "systems of interaction," the structural micrologics operating on them, and the ensuing structural results.

With Chapter 13 we begin the concrete talk about upward heterarchical structuration. We distinguish three levels of social structure –

Figure V.1. *Phenomenological levels and structures*

groupings, fields, and totalities – and proceed to analyze the social structures situated in the first two levels.

Chapter 14 deals with the third level, that is, with the several examples of structural totalities ("class structures," "the world system"), whose modes of emergence we investigate in some detail in heterarchical terms.

12 Modalities and systems of interaction

In this chapter we focus our analysis on the different types of social action implicated in the production of corresponding "systems of interaction," capable of being "structured" in specific ways by appropriate **"micrologics"** (structuring principles, or structuring mechanisms). As in the general case of social structure, I would argue that, here too, we cannot speak of social action in the singular. Rather, our task is to specify the existential categories of social action in order to be able to link them properly to the relevant interaction systems they give rise to to and the possible structures they underdetermine. It is a tragedy for social science that no systematic analysis of the modalities of social action has ever been undertaken. Traditional interactional studies within the frameworks of the known symbolic and interpretative paradigms have always prioritized communicative action and understanding as the central mode and purpose of interaction and have shied away from alternative situations; alternatively, rational-purposive forms of analysis, particularly in economics, have attempted to show that the whole range of human behavior can be brought under the explanatory coverage of the instrumentalist-strategic paradigm. Consequently, a distinction has developed demarcating the sociological enterprise, with its emphasis on role-related, norm-related, and understanding-related considerations of social action, from the economic enterprise which prefers to build on utilitarian bases for the understanding of (instrumental) social action. Furthermore, the economistic tendency has many sympathizers within sociology and the other social sciences (Berger, Coleman, Elster, Hechter, arguably Zald, among others). The distinction between the sociological and the economic conceptions of social action has been presented in recent times in different terms by Boudon (1981a), Coleman (1986a, b and d), Dahrendorf (1958, 1959, 1968), Parsons (1937), Touraine (1977a and b), Wippler and Lindenberg (1987), among others.

The difficulties with the traditional sociological model must be noted first. One cannot simply refer to the communicative–interpretative interaction – including "normative" interaction – as the prototypical, if not singular, species of relatedness in the real social world. Even in the older studies in social psychology (such as the work of Bales [1950]), several categories of so-called "communicative acts" were distinguished – positive reactions, answers, questions, negative reactions; in brief, interaction was analyzed in positive, negative, or neutral terms. In

Homans's earlier work (1950), sentiment-relations and interest-relations were delineated as separate categories. In the plethora of studies that extended "balance theory" and produced a corpus of mathematical models and methods for the study of group and clique formation, the initial binary logic of positive linkage/no linkage progressively gave way to considerations of positive, negative, and absent relations. (For the trials and tribulations of this particular research program see the summation in Leik and Meeker [1975].) Finally, with the work of Laumann (1979), network analysis moved to recognize the "modal" nature of interaction. Granovetter's seminal work (1973, 1983) revealed that, besides the regular types, one must recognize the significance of "weak ties" as contributors or, even, underground operators in the structuring process. Going one step further, Aldrich (1982) has suggested the extension and application of social network analysis in the more specific processes of exchange, dependency, competition, and coalition, viewing these as important modalities of interaction. In the development of the so-called exchange-networks perspective, different types of relationships (sentiment relations, information-exchange relations, advice-giving relations, and material transfer or exchange relations) have been postulated and presumably will be analyzed in the ongoing elaboration of this research program (Cook 1982, Cook et al. 1983; Marsden 1983; Yamagishi et al. 1988). All these efforts signal a new interest in the modal conceptualization of social action and interaction.

What is the term "modality" supposed to mean, and what are modalities of social action and interaction? Certainly, we do not need to refer here to the traditional, primarily Aristotelian and Kantian philosophical conceptions of modality, or even to the more recent developments in modal logics (Hartmann; Hintikka). To keep matters simple, I suggest we use the term "modalities" to refer to *the necessary, contingent, possible, or impossible modes, manners, or ways of being and acting* – the last being of most interest to us in the present context. Jürgen Habermas has produced by far the most elaborate, although still programmatic, distinction among various modalities of action (1970:92–4; 1979:40–1, 208–9; and elsewhere). Based on his fundamental distinction between work and interaction (1970, 1975), Habermas has defined four modalities of social action: (a) "instrumental," (b) "strategic," (c) "communicative," and (d) "symbolic" actions. The first two presumably are types of actions implicated in work relationships (zweckrational forms); the other two are referring to meaningful interaction contexts (wertrational forms). By "work" or purposive-rational action, Habermas understands instrumental action and/or rational choice. Of these two, instrumental action is "governed by technical rules based on empirical knowledge," while rational choice is "governed by strategies based on analytic knowledge." Both imply deductions from preference rules (value systems) and decision procedures. On the other hand, by "interaction," Habermas understands communicative action or symbolic interaction. This type is "governed by binding consensual norms, which define reciprocal expectations about behavior and which must be understood and recognized by at least two subjects" (1970:91–2).

In subsequent work Habermas has further defined his modal types of action. He now speaks of strategic action (" 'oriented to the actor's success' – in general, modes of action that correspond to the utilitarian model of purposive-rational action") as well as of symbolic action (in general, "modes of action that are bound to nonpropositional systems of symbolic expression") as being different from communicative action; the difference consists in the fact that, in the former, "individual validity claims are suspended (in strategic action, truthfulness, in symbolic action, truth)" (1979:41). Habermas has come to recognize four modalities of action (instrumental, strategic, communicative, and symbolic), although he still cautions that his model remains underdeveloped. These four modalities of action would be, obviously, expected to produce different systems of interaction and characterize distinct forms of "structured structures."

Another relevant concept is that already implicit in network research, initially inspired by the Bourbaki classification of mathematical systems. According to the Bourbaki model, all mathematical conceptions fall in one of three categories: (a) "group"-like algebraic systems, (b) "linear" sequential systems, such as basic arithmetic, or (c) "topological" systems forming particular shapes and obeying canons of topological transformation. In general, a "group" is defined as a set of elements and (at least) one operation by which pairs of these elements can be combined to exhibit a variety of special characteristics by which the particular form of the group is determined (proper algebraic "group," "ring," "semi-group," etc). Usually, the relations between group elements are not linear (in the sense that they loop or produce dense interaction nets) and networks of such nonlinear pair-wise connections give rise to what we commonly understand as groups or cliques. These are usually depicted by graph-analytic or matrix-analytic techniques and obey the rules of group algebras. A network in which pair-wise connections produce a more-or-less linear-sequential pattern (with an insignificant number of loops) appears as a "linear series"; we usually think of railroad lines or telephone communications routing in such a linear fashion. Arithmetic and, I presume, complex number theory as well, with their sequential form of order and connectivities are prototypical here; but we know of other models as well. This notion is implicit in the conception of "weak ties," in studies of diffusion or dissemination of information (Coleman 1964; Leik and Meeker 1975), and in the "small world problem" as well (Milgram 1967). Finally, a "topology" is a group of elements and an operation of topological relations by virtue of which shapes, topological contiguities, and transformations are formed. Neighborhood structures, urban traffic structures, and so on, could be possibly mapped as topologies (as sorts of noninteractional or para-interactional externalities). Recall that Boudon's interactional systems of "indirect interdependence" are to a large extent topological in the above sense, as, too, are Baker's commodity "crowds," and other such examples. Network principles may, of course, be applicable to "group," "sequential-linear," or "topological" conceptualizations, perhaps equally well.

I propose that we link these two classificatory schemes and critically appraise the result – that is, estimate how good a general model it can produce for the understanding of the basic modalities of interaction. We can argue that any interaction can be categorized in terms of its *strength, modality,* and *quantity* (differential rate).

We may start with quantity, which seems to be the simplest. Interactions are rarely a one-shot business; they are iterated and the typifications they bring about as well as the intensity of relationships depend to a great degree on their quantity, that is, their differential rates of repetition. The emergence of "local" institutions is, at least partly, the direct outcome of such iterated interactions (remember the problem of game theory's limitations in this respect). We can understand strength as a variable, as referring to (1) "strong interactions" of the regular variety; to (2) "weak interactions" involved in (a) weak (more linear-like) ties of acquaintance and, broadly speaking, in (b) "possible ties" (to which I will refer shortly); or, finally, to (3) the "contingent," nearly "noninteractions" of the topologically constrained space (evident in waiting lines, traffic jams, the silent doctor's office, or, per Goffman, in congested elevators). Notice that these distinctions come rather close to the old philosophical notion of modality in referring to necessity (essential predication, the intended), possibility (networks of potential interaction), or contingency (accidental predication, the unintended). I suggest that different sorts of social structures are built out of these strong, weak, or contingent (very weak, constrained, impaired) interactions.

It is primarily, if not exclusively, in the area of strong interactions that we find examples of the Weberian–Habermasian modalities. First, an important difference is indicated when we distinguish interactional systems on the basis of the implicated "purposive-rational" (instrumental and strategic) or "communicative" (communicative proper and symbolic) orientations to or modalities of action. Boudon tried to capture this difference with the definitional distinction between "systems of interdependence" (especially of "direct interdependence") that are instrumental-strategic and "functional systems" that are, basically, normative-communicative. (Though Boudon also realized that within his functional systems there is a larger or smaller degree of strategic interaction taking place as well [1981a].) However, I would rather agree with Habermas who, by separating interactions geared toward reaching understanding from those interactions that follow already established "consensual norms," made clear that not all "communicative" modes of interaction involve "functional" interactional systems. We could argue that some communicative modes may lead to functional, role-based systems of interactions, while others may not. I see the modal distinction between "rational-purposive" and "communicative" modalities as a good one and intend to show that it leads to specific types of structured systems distinct from one another.

I therefore propose that we make the following modal distinctions of interactions:

(1) *interactive-strategic modalities:* involved in all strong interactions in which the purposive-rational (zweckrational) orientation is primary; here the primary element is strategic, although the strict instrumental element operates within organizations as well (on which more later).

(2) *interactive-communicative modalities:* involved in all interactions in which the communicative (wertrational) orientation is primary; here the communicative mode of reaching understanding and/or interacting under the guidance of (strongly or weakly accepted) consensual norms is primary, while the symbolic-expressive is subordinate.

(3) *quasi-interactive modalities:* involved in the cases of weak interaction and the broader sphere of possible interactions. Weak ties are ties of secondary acquaintance and information transfer in which each person involved need not and usually does not know the other persons located in other pairs of the mostly linear – from the perspective of any given individual – chain. This mode produces "potential" channels that may be activated in linear-parallel channels reaching outward.

(4) *nearly noninteractive modalities:* involved in the cases in which topological constraints and aggregated individual actions operating under such topological constraints produce systems of indirect interdependence where actual interaction is nearly nonexistent. These are contingent systems of indirect interdependence exhibiting logics of their own (as we have seen in earlier chapters) and further implicated with other interactional

systems in the production of higher-level structured structures. These are modalities in which "externalities-to-interaction" (topological or aggregate-topological) are primary.

Based on the above distinctions of modal interactions we are now able to describe the corresponding, emergent, "local" structures.

Strong interactions

Interactive-strategic modalities give rise to "antagonistic" (negative) interactions in which the purposive rationality of individual or corporate agents is guided by self-interest. It is proper to call these interactions "antagonistic" in the sense that utilitarian, strategic, and opportunistic behavior characterizes them and the agents are oriented, to the extent possible, toward profit maximization at the expense of other agents. Antagonistic interactions of this sort can be, more specifically, hierarchical or strategic proper (nonhierarchical): that is, geared (a) toward the production of "systems of domination" or, at a minimum, to "imperatively coordinated" (to recall Weber and Dahrendorf) "systems of governance," or (b) toward external "market systems" where the agents can partially exercise contingent control of their own choices and actions. Here once more reference must be made to the significant work of Oliver Williamson on "markets" and "hierarchies" already cited on previous occasions; recall that Williamson has defined the economic behavior of firms as strategic and opportunistic, oriented toward satisficing or maximizing behavior under conditions of uncertainty due to externalities and limited information. In such an environment, production firms have to strategically decide if, in terms of transaction-cost economic analysis, it is beneficial to them to acquire or merge with other firms, usually "subcontractors," in a hierarchical pattern of vertical integration, or to proceed with short- or long-term subcontracting practices. The first involves a policy of incorporation, the second, of subcontracting relations across firms. The idea is that when the markets do not "clear" easily across (for example, when subcontractors cannot guarantee the proper quantities or qualities of products desired, or their timely delivery, or when there is competition among major firms in securing access to technologically significant subcontracting firms), major firms would find it beneficial to buy out a subcontracting firm and organize production "within" rather than "across."

So the strategy of organizational hierarchies is posited as an alternative to external markets, given the latter's uncertainties of clearing. Organizational hierarchies ("organizations" in the commonsensical use of the term) and organized markets are the first "structured structures" emerging out of this different orientation. It is important here to also note that it is precisely within these organizations that we find as central the instrumental (technical, bureaucratic) rationality that Habermas discusses as one of the two variants of purposive-rational action. Notice, finally, that an extension of Williamson's argument would allow one to treat the "state" and any other bureaucratic entity as such an organizational hierarchy emerging as a result of social strategies relating to the nonclearance of "civil society's markets": the state is seen as an organizational alternative to the vicissitudes of unregulated private production and consumption markets of any variety. We recall that this has been the view of several liberal thinkers (Arrow, Hirschman, Schelling, among others cited earlier). Of course, a more radical, realistic point of view will also add that state formation is always originating in the "interested" efforts of organizing elites or classes to "totalize" a given social system.

We should also not forget Foucault's work on the emergence of systems of domination in the local institutional–organizational context of hospitals, schools, prisons, and so on. Here, too, the market (civil society) or hierarchy (political, organized society) dilemma is posited and the formation of hierarchies as an allied bourgeois, bureaucratic, and – for Foucault, especially – professional project is energized. A similar example can be drawn from the literature of societal evolution, in reference to the neolithic dilemma of familial land cultivation and interfamilial/intercommunal exchanges associated with it, versus the strategy of conquering other people for the control of their land and the exploitation of their labor to the detriment of any incipient local markets (Kontopoulos 1980; Lenski and Lenski 1987; Patterson 1981). From these examples one can adduce that hierarchies are instances of a double antagonism, at once economic and political.

Interactive-communicative modalities have an obvious "integrative" or positive quality and give rise to systems of interaction that involve much less antagonism and opportunistic behavior. Here I make a distinction between pragmatic interaction and integrative interaction. "Pragmatic" interaction involves a certain degree of competitiveness and opportunism afforded within well-prescribed social limits; "integrative" interaction properly speaking implies the nonexistence of any such antagonism. Pragmatic interaction is found, for example, in all instances of "social-cultural exchanges" (gift exchanges, marriage exchanges, systems of reciprocity at large) and brings forth the relevant "structured structures" of social exchanges implying "structuring structures" of a more or less formal character, such as the ones analyzed in the spirit of Lévi-Strauss by Harrison White in his intriguing book

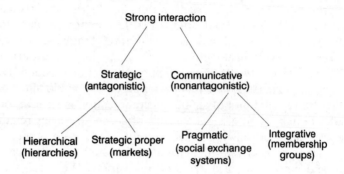

Figure 12.1. *Forms of strong interaction*

on the structures of kinship.[1] So one must argue, I submit, on behalf of the relative discontinuity between strategic "market" behavior and the pragmatic behavior involved in "social exchange systems."

Besides the pragmatic forms of interaction, in the non-antagonistic orientation involving strong interactions we also find integrative forms. "Integrative" interaction is the one usually referred to in the symbolic interactionist, ethnomethodological, social phenomenological, and hermeneutical traditions and described by Habermas as "interaction geared towards reaching understanding" and "interaction guided by consensual norms" (1970:92; 1979:209). It is based on the making, negotiating, interpreting, contesting, and following of presumably shared values, norms, expectations, meanings, deep interpretive procedures, and so on, and it gives rise to membership groups (e.g., "primary groups"), where cultural–communicative identification is of paramount importance. The structured structure of such groups has been the subject of analysis in the small group and sociometry research literature. One should stress the social–emotional rather than instrumental character of these groups to contrast them properly with the instrumental character of markets and hierarchies.

I do not propose to treat these categories as if they were ontologically distinct forms; instead I conceive a continuum from the most antagonistic/dominated to the least antagonistic/integrated orientations to interaction and treat the above four categories as "sensitizing" ideo-typical categories. Their connections are summed up in Figure 12.1.

We could also conceptualize these modalities in a slightly different

---

[1] Lévi-Strauss's work has been formalized by White (in his 1963). For a brief appreciation see Leik and Meeker 1975:76–85; see also further in this chapter. In this context also consult Bourdieu 1980 and Goffman 1959, 1963, 1972.

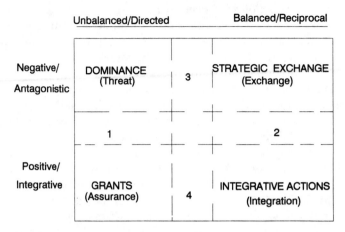

Figure 12.2. *Recasting Boulding's model*

form. Boulding (1978) has suggested that there are three "organizers" (or "structuring modal principles") of social life: threat, exchange, and integration; in the margin he adds to these a fourth, grant, which is a spin-off from integration. Threat produces aggressive behavior and "dominance" (dominance hierarchies) and initially takes the form: "You do something I want or I'll do something you don't want." Exchange is based on invitations rather than threats, in the form: "You do something for me and I'll do something for you." Finally, integration is based on each individual's image of his personal identity and of the identity of others and takes the form: "I will do something or I will ask you to do something because of what I am and because of what you are." Integrative benevolence, according to Boulding, tends to produce "grant behavior," i.e., one-way transfers of economic goods from the benevolent person to the person whose welfare she cherishes, unco-erced gifts that are not expected to be reciprocated. But grant behavior, with its unilateral character, appears to be the limit case of general integrative interaction. If we take seriously Bourdieu's analysis of gift exchanges, or pay closer attention to the economic consideration of grants as part of (collective or interpersonal) "implicit contracts," then we may have to treat several instances of grant behavior as reciprocal and, to an extent, strategic. Boulding's model is presented schematically in Figure 12.2.

One deduces from the schema in Figure 12.2 that dominance and grant behavior are unilateral, while strategic exchange and general in-tegrative or communicative behavior are bilateral. Too, the antagonistic (dominance, strategic exchange) or integrative (grants, communicative integration) distinction seems clearly marked. Now, obviously, there are several intermediary cases, represented by numerals. Thus, (1) refers to "status" or "authority" systems that are more or less unilateral but appear to have the dubious and highly contested character of being both good (or organizationally necessary) and bad (or symbolically dominating; e.g., Foucault's example of medicine); (2) represents the generalized social exchanges, such as the matrimonial exchanges, that are both strategic and integrative in Goffman's and Bourdieu's sense; (3) refers to "oligopolistic" strategic situations, where both power and strategic exchange are involved. Finally, (4) describes various forms of "symbolic," conceivably uneven, exchanges of expressive performance (in Habermas's as well as Durkheim's sense of the symbolic). I offer this as an alternative conceptualization of the modalities of interaction and to pay tribute to the ideas of Kenneth Boulding – I treat it as a sensitizing exercise or device rather than as an exhaustive formal classification, and suggest that it be taken as such.

Weak interactions

As soon as one moves to the realm of weak interactions some other particular properties appear and take center stage. The dyadic interactions are bringing about "weak ties," of the sort that one finds in casual interactions and acquaintance relations. But as they are linked together, weak ties with other weak ties, the result is not a group or a clique (something one would expect if the ties were strong and shared among many associates, intimates, and real friends) but a more-or-less linear series, starting from the position of any particular individual and radiating outward, with marginal crossings on the way. So, in general, beyond a particular weak tie, there is usually little, if any, knowledge of the further connections, though they are there as possible channels of communication, mobilization, and even potentially stronger interaction. Significant mediators (gatekeepers, professional middlemen in pre-industrial societies, brokers of all sorts)[2] are located at key junctions of these chains of weak ties; the story is too well known to be retold here. Beyond weak ties there is a whole world of potential ties to be made, available to middlemen and industrious individuals.

Granovetter presents a telling argument on the overall significance of these weak ties for information dissemination and potential mobilization for action – an argument that has withstood debate and empirical scrutiny. Milgram's (1967) study of the so-called small world problem

---

[2] For another form of social "brokerage" see, for instance, Miller 1973 on town–village brokers.

also demonstrated the structural peculiarity and organizational potentials of chains of weak ties and of activated possible channels of information transfer. In another interesting study, done by Mayer (1966), a large community was conceived as a "quasi-group," that is, as a potential rather than actual group, in which any individual's transactional linkages defined an "action-set," an individual-centered network of actual and potential linkages to other individuals. The overlap of the action-sets of many individuals represent the quasi-group. Politicians know very well how to play this game of mobilizing support through the further connections of other people, as Mayer's case study clearly illustrates.

I like this idea of quasi-groups, if for no other reason than because it places emphasis on the vast arrays of connectivities that lie beyond the grasp of individual interactants. In contrast to the commonsensical view that finds structure only in strong, intentional interactions, one recognizes here that various structures emerge as net byproducts of individual ties with others and are, because of that, beyond the monitoring or comprehension of these same individuals. Here again I expect the new directions in neural network research to bring about insightful, if not outright astonishing, results.

One may go a step further and speak of second-order quasi-groups, or structural groups, in the case of groupings of equivalent positions (occupied by individuals), as uncovered by blockmodeling techniques. Blockmodel algebras provide the tools (the "semi-group"-based modeling of role structures of social relations) that describe patterns, not in the network of relationships among individuals, but in the interrelationships between the social relations themselves.[3] Two individuals occupy the same position[4] in a social structure if and only if they are related to the same individuals in the same way, that is, if they are structurally equivalent. In reality, of course, allowance is made to consider the equivalence of positions if two positions themselves (that is, the associated pattern of relationships) are structurally equivalent to a great extent – if they are "nearly structurally equivalent." What I have called "second-order quasi-groups" or "structural groups" is more or less identical to the group of individuals occupying these nearly structurally equivalent positions. If we accept this description, then we may also agree that, for example, classes are groups-in-themselves composed

---

[3] On blockmodeled second-order groups see White et al. 1976; Boorman and White 1976. Nadel (1957) was the first to use the talk of network levels (relations of relations).

[4] On the distinctive definitions of the concept of "position" given by the blockmodeling (White; Boorman and White), residual graph (Emerson), and smallest space (Laumann) analyses, see Cook 1982.

of individuals in nearly structurally equivalent positions in the system of a given class society. We will return to this in Chapter 14; our examination of classes as polymorphous sets of different class-fractions in Chapter 11 is also very much related to the present discussion. Olson's "latent groups" may appear as somewhat equivalent to the above conceptualization, but he does not provide clear analytical insight on the issue.

Residual (constrained, impaired, contingent) interaction

The final category is that of "nearly noninteractive modalities." Clearly, this does not imply that in these instances there is no interaction whatsoever. Nor is it proper to suggest that these represent a specific intentional mode or orientation to interaction. One does assert, however, the residual, determined nature of interactions which take place merely (or nearly so) as a direct result of topological constraints on the aggregations of individuals. Some examples will illustrate the case. Remember Boudon's image of people planning to go to a movie theater to see a good movie on the rational expectation that they will arrive on time, buy their ticket, and enter the theater. Only, what do they find? That others having similar expectations are also there, as if only to produce the unintended result of a long waiting line. The relationship between these individuals may involve only residual, unintended but forced, nonchalant interactions, or may involve no interaction at all. Goffman's reference to the silent conduct of bus riders (1963, 1971), secretly scrutinizing each other without a word, epitomizes what I call "topologically constrained nearly noninteraction"; Goffman's example gives us a clue to the fact that, within the given topological constraints, the interactants are indeed intentionally reluctant or unwilling to produce a sustainable system of interaction – they do have a peculiar modal orientation toward each other; the result is impaired actions and interactions.

Another category consists of topologically constraining physical structures and distributions of people within them. Typical here is the example of "ecological communities," especially urban structures. It is not only size that differentiates the structural complexity of urban areas but organizational mode, historically "specific capital," and the topology of the region as well. Urban–rural differences but also metropolitan differences along the urban–suburban, residential–business, and so on, axes indicate structuring processes that are politico-economically, historically, and ecologically constrained.[5]

---

[5] For an important example see Logan and Molotch 1987 and the considerable bibliography cited there. For other, perhaps older but influential views see Castells 1979; Hagerstrand 1968; Hawley 1979; Lösch 1954; Park 1952.

What shall we call these preinteractional or non-interactional systems and their structured formations? It may be pertinent to distinguish between topological communities (urban settings) and topological congeries (from the Latin *congerere* which gives the neutral meaning of being "aggregated in space" as well as the negative meaning of being "congested"); both are agglomerations in the built environment, topological structured systems or topological distributions. They involve a "matching" of aggregates of individuals and of a given structured topology (customers in a bus or theater queue, skiers in front of a ski-chair installation, drivers in a road system, workers in an assembly line, neighbors living in or getting out of a neighborhood, residents stuck in an apartment complex, shoppers finding their way in parking lots or shopping mall corridors, and so on). In every case a perfect allocation or a smooth flow may possibly take place, like a clearing in a market or in the timely processing of people through places; or it may be that jams, bottlenecks, waiting lines, congestions of one sort or another may emerge indicating impaired clearing. Recall here the micrologics involved ("flows," "matchings"; see the Appendix) and the general pattern of these micrologics, that is, a proper or improper matching of people and places, of aggregates of individuals and structured topologies. These structured topologies themselves primarily represent "built environments" and they can be construed in Williamson's sense as social "specific capital" restricting the range of strategic actions available to the agents (1975). One cannot realistically think of social structure without implicating these usually underestimated structural externalities and mismatchings.

The result of the realization – in specific social practices – of the different modalities we have discussed is the emergence of local structured structures. To a certain, presumably large, extent, it is the aggregated, concatenated, and iterated actions of individuals that produce these structures. I say "to a certain extent" because in this case – as well as in any other case of heterarchy, such as, for example, in the data-theory relations as conceived by postpositivists[6] – the microactions of individuals "underdetermine" the emergence of local structures: the actions of individuals appear as the "initial conditions" of the emergence of structure; but, as we already know, besides these initial conditions one must also bring into the explanatory schema the "operative logics" of aggregation, matching, processing, and so on, as well as the "boundary conditions" within which these logics operate (such as the

---

[6] The issue of the undertermination of theory by data has been raised by Goodman (1978), Kuhn (1970), Lakatos (1978), Lakatos and Musgrave (1970), Putnam (1981, 1982, 1987, 1988), and Quine (1953, 1960, 1969), Suppe (1977), among many others.

topological or material constraints, the sociohistorical specificities of a concrete social state, and so on). Local structures are the results of the interrelationships of these initial conditions, operating logics, and boundary conditions taken together. Human actions, especially *current* human actions, though they may be "initial" and "necessary," are not "sufficient" to explain the emergence of structure.

The other issue that we should be clear about is that of the status of micrologics. There is a tendency, inherited from the formal-structuralist tradition, but also found in the so-called "realist" school of British so cial thinkers (Bhaskar 1975; Harré 1972, 1980; Keat 1981; Keat and Urry 1975) to assume that every "structured structure" has underneath it or logically prior to it – and internally connected to it – a "structuring structure" as the operator of its structuration. This may or may not be true. At the lower, local level of structured structures we are usually able to isolate the "structuring principles" and/or "structuring mechanisms" involved in the structuration process, but it is not that easy to find or presumptively pose the existence of structuring structures in every case. White's successful isolation of the deep structure of marriage exchange systems could not be duplicated easily, for example, in the case of Foucault's analysis of local domination processes.

Throughout this book I have used the term "logics of structuring" or "logics of structuration" to capture three distinct operative modes, as follows:

LOGICS OF STRUCTURATION

1	2	3
structuring structures (formal)	structuring mechanisms (semi-formal)	structuring principles (modal)

We are entitled to speak of "structuring structures" only in the case of formal mathematical or semiotic structures recovered by mathematical operations and established as the generative logics, or algorithms of structuration (structuring algorithms). We could use the concept of "structuring mechanisms" or "logics" properly speaking in the case of semi-formal, model-like descriptions and analyses of structural operators that have about them an "engineering character," i.e., operate as pieces of logico-conceptual equipment. I think most of the "logics" we have already presented (or summarize in the Appendix) have, at least, this special character. I propose – in contrast to Giddens's conception of structuring principles as the most fundamental structural properties – to call "structuring principles" the *modal logics of structuration* or *structuring modalities,* for example, the so-called logic of domination, that cannot easily be modeled as constructs of pure or applied mathematics (they have an intentional character about them, they involve a praxis-orientation, they add an element of intensity to the situation, and so on).

Hierarchies, markets, social exchange systems, integrative membership groups, quasi-groups, topological communities and congeries: these are the structured systems at the local level of analysis. In anticipation of our forthcoming analysis in the next chapter, we suggest further that these structured systems would be inserted and recategorized at the higher quasi-local level to yield heterarchically the determinate structural types of instrumentally organized structures (the "organizations" of markets and hierarchies), integrative structures (of "groups" and "group-coalitions"), implicit structures (of the distributed parallel networks of quasi-groups), and topological structures (of communities, congeries, distributions, and flows). All these, of course, must be viewed as analytical **semidefinite constructs** – to use Elsasser's suggestion (1975) – and, in reality, one would expect to find composite forms of structures implicating several of these analytical forms. But the only way to explain that is to proceed to the discussion of heterarchical structural levels.

Coda

Boudon has argued that due to the nature of "interdependent systems" the aggregation of individual actions may give rise to aggregated emergent effects not explicitly sought by the agents. There is, however, a major ambiguity in Boudon's expression concerning the nature of these aggregated emergent effects. In a different debate Homans has, rightfully I believe, criticized Blau for confusing aggregated or "collective effects" for "structural effects" (1975); in Blau's rather loose formulation the influence of the community's values (authoritarianism) were thought of as exerting external constraints on the individual, something that Blau considered as "structural effect." One must be careful here. On any logical reading, not all "social effects" are also "collective effects"; and, furthermore, not all "collective effects" are also "structural effects" – not all "structural effects" are "structured structures." The presence, intentions, and actions of another person are enough to produce social effects without these being collective. Collective actions and effects, such as a lynching mob or a cultural fad, are not by definition structural (or I beg someone to explain what exactly is structural about them). And what are "structural effects" if they are simple outputs of a given structure; for example, the level of air pollution is a structural effect in this sense but only by contrived means can we really call it a "structure" in its own right.

This ambiguity is evident in the many examples cited by Boudon in his *Logic of Social Action*. There he deals with aggregated emergent effects, most of which have the character of "collective effects," but, several times he talks about them as if they were "structures" or "structural effects" without any qualification. A few of his examples, indeed, imply real structuring structures (Marx's contradiction of the capitalist logic based on the change in the relationship of fixed capital to variable capital and necessitating the falling rate of profit, Lipset's and Bendix's example of the stability in the structure of intergenerational mobility, Schelling's example of neighborhood change). Other examples imply the operation of "structural mechanisms" in the sense I have qualified the distinction above (Parsons's explanation of nuclear family based on the distinction between home and work, the city-suburbs example, possibly Hirschman's example of the decline of the Nigerian railroads). A few others refer to the emergence of institutions that produce further structural effects (Simmel's example of the effects of introduction of money). Some refer to game-theoretical structures but not to social structures (for example, the nonemergence of collective groups, the nonaction of Tocqueville's landowners or, perhaps, of Marx's small peasants). Several more imply some "mechanism" of aggregation but it is not evident what this mechanism is or that a structural dimension is referred to (e.g., the run on the bank) – something I find disingenuous. We may say that a few examples truly refer to structural effects but for no apparent structural reasons, except, perhaps, some modal orientations (the growth of small towns in France under the *ancien régime*). And, finally, several examples refer to collective, but not structural, effects (Merton's explanation of racism, Blau's example cited previously). Boudon's work, therefore, remains undeveloped in these crucial respects.

13   Heterarchical levels of social structure

A theory of structures is, by necessity, a theory of levels. Different levels of structural analysis imply different units of analysis, which in an ascending order become dynamically different (in scale), larger (in size), and more complex (in information or entropic complexity). As we have already said, however, the relation between these units is not one of complete inclusion and supersession as one would expect in a hierarchical organization – something more complex takes place here, as the levels interrelate to each other in an "entangled" way.

We have suggested in the previous part that a distinction should be made between local, quasi-local, quasi-global, and global levels of organization. In the social world, we usually identify the local level as the interpersonal one, the level of "interpersonal interactions." Here is, for example, the locus of Boudon's various (functional, directly interdependent, and indirectly interdependent) "systems of interaction" which most often give rise to aggregated emergent effects. A variety of incipient structures always emerge at this level from the specific modalities and contingencies of interaction implicated; this is especially obvious, for example, in the case of systems of direct interdependence, organized by relevant elementary micrologics, such as the game-theoretical micrologics or the formal micrologics of coalition formation in triads. I call these "incipient structures" because they (a) involve rudimentary structuration (as in sociometric choices), (b) are quite often ephemeral (i.e., have a fast dynamic of emergence and extinction), and therefore (c) are not "institutionalized," at least not yet at this level. Moreover, as it has been suggested earlier (Chapter 12, Coda), not all aggregations of actions or interactions produce structural forms, even incipient ones. Such structures (structural systems), however, definitely emerge at the quasi-local level, which one may call the interpositional level (though not all structures here are positional structures strictly speaking, nor are positional structures restricted to this level alone; however, most of the basic interpositional structures are, indeed, located at this level, so that the attribution of this name is not basically wrong). One might also call it the local institutional level, in Foucault's usage of this term (local prisons, asylums, hospitals, army barracks, and so on). I would like to give it a more neutral label and call it the "first level of structural systems" or "level of groupings," and define it by reference to the structures populating it:

287

(1) organizational hierarchies,
(2) organized markets,
(3) social exchange systems,
(4) integrative (membership) groups,
(5) quasi-groups,
(6) topological communities, and
(7) topological congeries.

Each of these structures implies a different modality of interaction and different logical mechanisms of structuration or operation, an issue to which we will return shortly.

At the quasi-global level several more complex structures may be described, each one of which incorporates several first-level structures in different degrees of centrality. That is, each higher-level structure is, at rock bottom, a **polymorphous set,** which includes several structures from the next lower level more or less central to it. I would call this the "second level of structural systems" or "level of fields." In the previous literature this level has been usually referred to as the "interorganizational level" (Laumann et al. 1978; Negandhi 1975; Warriner 1981) but I believe that this designation is unduly restrictive. Indeed, I would posit that we should locate here not only: (a) the interorganizational field; but also (b) the field of collective agencies; and (c) the field of population ecologies; all three of which are analytically and, especially, dynamically distinct from each other. The attempt to integrate the interorganizational and population ecological field into an overarching theoretical model, namely, that of the "population ecology of organizations" (Aldrich 1975, 1979; Aldrich and Pfeffer 1976; Carroll 1984, 1987; Hannan and Freeman 1977; Pfeffer and Salancik 1978) has been, at least until now, at once very intriguing *and* unsuccessful. I will explain later on why these three structures must be kept analytically separate at this level.

The final, global level I would identify as the "third level of structural systems" or the "level of totalities." To this level belong class structures, national social formations (or societal structures), and the world-system, all of which are heterarchically linked "structural totalities." We will investigate this level in detail in the next chapter. At present our effort will be directed to the discussion of interlevel relations and the analysis of the structural systems at the levels of "groupings" and "fields." The overall conceptual framework we need to keep in mind is depicted in Figure 13.1.

Interlevel relations

One of the most difficult issues to face is the explanation of the actual process by which a higher level is said to emerge, then stabilize and

Level III: TOTALITIES : classes, formations, world-system

Level II: FIELDS   : interorganizational, collective agencies,
                         population ecologies

Level I: GROUPINGS : hierarchies, markets, social exchange
                     systems, groups, quasi groups, topological
                     communities, topological congeries

Level O   : "systems of interaction"; incipient structures

Figure 13.1. *Levels of social structural systems*

operate semiautonomously. We have seen that any straightforward argument to the effect that higher levels emerge from lower levels in a
direct causal sense is utterly wrong. In the case of the structural–organizational transformation of social systems we have also to consider the
fact (a) of the historico-dialectical nature of population growth (that is,
how, starting from smaller hunting and gathering bands, social systems
of large scale and size have come about by virtue of specific modes of
production and ecological insertion) and (b) of the simultaneous evolution of the "small" and the "large" social systems (the distinctiveness
of which are apparent first at the moment of the separation of "society"
from "community"). In the favored sense, micro and macro phenomena
are both *ab origine,* or they have emerged simultaneously from the
earliest (at once interpersonal and collective) communities. Evolutionary and historical perspectives may eventually provide a full account of
this diachronic development. On the other hand, when one is engaged
in synchronic analysis, as we are here, it is permissible to seek the
proper mediating mechanisms by which higher levels are said to emerge
and on the basis of which they are currently seen as underdetermined
and processually "sustained" (not straightforwardly produced, or created) by their lower levels. These mechanisms have to be seen as sorts
of transducers, in the apt expression of Zenon Pylyshyn (1984), a cognitive scientist who has addressed the homologous problem of interlevel
transitions as regards the brain/mind.

In any event, structures are not the direct and exclusive intentional
products of the intentional actions of intentional actors. Even if the
individuals are considered endowed with a species-specific intentionality, is it not really the case that their intentionality is primarily "**intensional,**" that is, expressed through and by language, and substantively
consists of a repertory of cultural embodiments of meaning and of the
dispositions of a "habitus"? And, is it not the case that not all actions
are purely intentional and that the results of such actions not always
are intended? Structures have inscribed in them various degrees of in-

tentionality in the practices of implicated agents as well as a variety of unmonitored processes and unforeseen structural results.[1]

How, then, are we to understand the "sustaining" underdetermination of structures by underlying systems of interaction? To be sure, we must begin with the intentional actions of individuals, however this "intentional" is to be understood; ultimately we must take the intentional stance, as even Daniel Dennett has conceded (1987). I take it that a person's dispositions are the "inten*t*ional" variations on the basic themes provided by the "inten*s*ional" culture, the "habitus" of intersecting individual and collective representations. Intentional × intensional actions are practices of purposive agents endowed with practical rationality and geared toward the satisfaction of a broadly defined set of interests, among which material–strategic interests may be relatively more important. Purposive action is a necessary condition for the emergence of *human* social structures, though not so for the emergence of social structures at large, as sociobiological studies have amply demonstrated. (This is why human social structures appear to be more like software structures.) For the emergence of social structures several other components are also necessary to jointly become the sufficient set of conditions bringing about structure. Besides (a) purposive (modal) actions, we must also account for (b) the particular micrologics and, in general, the structuring mechanisms, that transform one-shot or iterated, aggregated, and/or intersected actions into unforeseen collective or structural effects, (c) the externalities, material or topological, that constrain the process of micrologics in particular, providing different contours to the process and leading it to different realized states, and (d) the "self-looping" of the emerging structure (on the basis of which new boundary conditions appear at each new level), a certain degree of autonomization vis-à-vis the lower levels, new properties and specific laws, and a new organizing meso-logic. This is why we have argued that any lower level *only* underdetermines its next higher one, in the sense that the logic, properties, and laws of a higher level (for example, level I of structural systems) are not reducible to the logic, properties, and laws of the lower one (systems of interactions per se). The same, of course, holds true of the relationships between higher levels to one another. The general model of interlevel relations is graphically illustrated in Figure 13.2.

[1] I cannot accept Giddens's strong language on the monitoring capacities of individuals. With Bourdieu, Boudon, Merton, and others, I believe that such capacity is limited: collective effects, structural effects, social preference bundles, information packets, and the like, are only pragmatically, limitedly, or opportunistically perceived by the agents; thus, we speak of traffic jams, queues, collective bads, unintended consequences, "pervert" effects, frustration – phenomena exhibiting the relative *un*monitoring of agents' action effects.

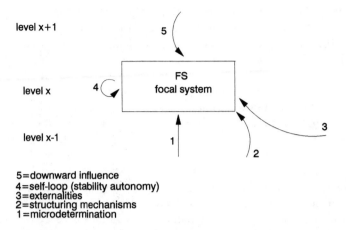

5=downward influence
4=self-loop (stability autonomy)
3=externalities
2=structuring mechanisms
1=microdetermination

Figure 13.2. *Interlevel relations*

What, then, is the set of conditions that give rise to the structural systems at level I ("groupings")? Let's take each one at a time and briefly indicate what is actually involved.

Groupings at the first structural level

(1) *organizational hierarchies:* here we can speak of (a) "dominance hierarchies," (b) complex, hierarchical, organizations masking the dominance process, and (c) "governance" organizational structures (i.e., regular organizations). Slavery, serfdom, or proletarianization are indicative of strong dominance; professional bio-power (per Foucault), state control, patriarchy, or workplace dominance are cases of moderate dominance; finally, a variety of other modern organizations exhibit the weaker form of an "authority hierarchy." Clearly, in the stronger first and second types, the organizing modality is not one primarily directed toward "efficient" organization, but one directed toward the direct or indirect control of people and resources with the added goal of achieving "satisficing" results. It has been argued that even the factory system – an exemplar of efficient production – was not introduced initially for the purpose of efficiency as much as for the long-term control of the working classes within the parameters of the long-term satisficing interests of the capitalist class (Calhoun 1981, 1983; Foster 1974). In these organized hierarchies then, as Foucault has insisted, there is a logic of domination at work. When, for example, during the neolithic period, extended families of farmers and landowners resorted to war with their neighbors or with other villages or valleys, one may presume

that they did so because the domination of others (taking their lands, putting them to work as slaves) appeared on balance as a preferable, more profitable project than toiling the land themselves (Cohen and Service 1978; Diakonoff 1969; Lenski and Lenski 1987; Patterson 1981).

Where do we find this logic of domination? In the "accumulation of men," in the making of dynamic coalitions, in the synecdochical (concentric) organization of support,[2] in the virtuoso application of the principles of *divide et impera* and *tertius gaudens,* in the transformation of material capital into social and cultural capital ("big men" in ethnographic studies, Foucault's "professionals," Bourdieu's strategic agents in general), and in numerous other organizing strategies. Notice that the externalities of material and physical power play a crucial role here, and that, once emergent, these hierarchies can be sustained indefinitely, semiautonomously, by improvised and improved techniques and processes of reproduction, transfigurations of discourses (bio-power into benevolence), by inculcation (external conditions becoming habitus), and internal circulations of capitals (from force to legitimation, from total institutions to the private couch, from authoritarian control of labor to "human resources" methods), and so on.

(2) *Organized markets:* here the strategic–utilitarian orientations of many actors in opposite market positions (capital–labor, producer–consumer, major producer–subcontractor, merchant–customer, creditor–debtor) define structures of direct interdependence with antagonistic interests, opportunistic strategies, and attempts to gain oligopolistic benefits. The logic of capital has certainly accelerated and reorganized in nearly totalizing ways – that is, in ways affecting all institutional orders – preexisting modes of antagonistic exploitation. For a realist, it simply is the case that the predominant orientation in economic markets consists in the pragmatic maximization of profits through the exploitation of opportunities and persons alike, to the extent possible. Adam Smith had his baker act on the basis of self-interest, not of benevolence. Slave-traders and slaveholders, robber-barons, and contemporary company-raiders certainly go a few steps beyond Smith's polite strictures – Wall Streeters are fond of repeating that "greed and fear" drive the markets. As far as the structuring mechanisms are concerned, we do not need

---

[2] In general, synecdoche is a form of reference in which a less inclusive term stands for a more inclusive term (or vice versa); a whole is expressed by a part. I use the notion to mean that smaller groups express larger groups in a more or less concentric fashion: central families in the conical clans (especially in early theocratic social formations), focal lineages in segmentary lineage organizations, central fractions within a (polymorphous) class-structure, elites and cadres in any collective movement, and so on.

to belabor the logics of the markets, which are exhaustively described in every textbook in economics; but we do need to keep in mind the many material and topological externalities involved in the making and sustaining of a market (ecology of materials and transport, capital distributions, state role). For better understanding of this last issue, the seminal work of Karl Polanyi (1957; cf. Hechter 1983b) remains indispensable. The new sociological theory of markets (Burt 1988; Eccles and White 1986, 1988; Wellman and Berkowitz 1988; White 1981a and b; among others), though still in the making, has already provided significant insights on markets as emergent structures, nearly along heterarchical lines.

(3) *Social exchange systems:* Gift, mutual aid, and matrimonial systems are, like markets, "systems of exchange," but they lack the obvious antagonistic and (less obvious) exploitative character of the latter. Micropolitics and strategies and interests do exist here as well, as Bourdieu's analysis of matrimonial exchanges in Kabyle (1977a), Joseph's analysis of the Rifi social organization (1987), and similar analyses of potlatch structures have illustrated (see also Ditton 1980; Goffman 1972). Yet, the structures per se are less the result of the purposive actions of individuals or families and more so of the structured collective perceptions, adaptive adjustments, ecological and demographic contingencies, and historically conditioned practices of "in-groups" and tribal populations. As such they appear to the interactants as sorts of requirements for good practical living (as if a very weak notion of "functional necessity" were involved, a necessity, however, which is satisfied by producing a whole range of equivalent structural systems, such as marriage systems, and which still gives enough room to negotiate, organize strategies, deploy resources, manipulate time – in brief, act as a virtuoso within the given structural limits). That there are many possible structures is indicative of the fact that no causal force operates in a determinative manner nor is there a strict mathematical necessity implicated in the range of realized variations; in brief, there is no full determination from below or from above, causal or formal. On the other hand, there is only a limited repertory of structural alternatives, a fact which, given the limits imposed by the externalities of population distributions and material resources, indicates the serious weakness of a rational choice explanation of such structures. The operating logics here are primarily (a) the logic of alliance/coalition formation, for mutual aid, supportive exchanges, and reproductive circulation, (b) the logic of gifts, which introduces a certain element of strategic behavior into this otherwise mildly integrative mode and, of course, (c) the formal (semigroup) logics, that capture the articulated systems of matrimonial exchanges.

(4) *Integrative (membership) groups:* these may be dedicated to a special purpose (task-oriented) or not so dedicated (social-emotional groups). A logic of participation is operative here indicating the integrative character of the underlying modality of interaction. Recall our previous analysis of the mechanisms of emergence of collective-action groups, as an antidote to Olson's and Hechter's radical positions on the near impossibility of such formation. There is so much work describing the formation of smaller structures of this type (small groups research, sociometry, formal studies of triads and of clique and group structures)[3] that any further discussion would be redundant. The "logic of participation" (or of "democracy") can be also seen operating in higher levels of structure; some scholars, notably Alford and Friedland (1985), Habermas (1970, 1971, 1985–9), Offe and Wiesenthal (1980), Przeworski (1985), treat it as an overarching logic with "totalizing" character – a genuine "totalizing logic" on a par with the logics of capital, of the state, or of the so-called professional project of the "new class."

(5) *Quasi-groups:* these are real but mostly invisible forms of grouping. They imply weak ties, hence a network pattern that is more likely to be linear; thus, knowledge of the quasi-group is not possible from the point of view of any actor. It extends in all directions, radiating outward, with criss-crossings that are impossible to monitor. The structure of the quasi-group can be sometimes given a formal expression by approximation, as in the formalization of the "small world problem" (White 1970) or the production of random graphs (Ërdos and Renyi 1960; Kauffman 1984). The organizing principle here is that captured by the algorithmic logic of network connectivities and it is inscribed in the phenomenological patterns given the constraints imposed on the combinatorial explosion of unrestricted connectivities by the limits of human communicative abilities (physical limits of the number of actual interactions for a person and limits of communicative attention – Miller's law, [Miller 1956]). The motivating (weak) modality is one of "broad inclusion," that is, the ability to outreach without any significant cost involved in the maintenance of these connections.

(6) *Topological communities:* From towns to metropolitan areas, aggregations of individuals in a particular space produce structures of various sorts that involve logics of matching of people and places, logics of topological differentiation (the inhomogeneity of space), neighborhood transition (threshold) logics, logics of flows, micrologics of comparative advantage, and so on (for all of these see the Appendix). Ecological communities in their simpler form are at the quasi-local

---

[3] For a review of the small group literature see Caplow 1968; Leik and Meeker 1975; Shepherd 1964.

level, although contemporary urban and metropolitan settings are to be considered as still higher structures located at the quasi-global level, for reasons we will discuss later. The externalities involved in such ecological communities are, of course, quite evident. We may say the same for the semiautonomous processes taking place at this level and setting limits to the individual preferences (center city or suburbs? which neighborhood?), choices (can I afford property taxes? car insurance? am I close to my job?), and patterns of use (residence, business, cultural activities). From the early Chicago school to today's studies in urban geography and sociology, we know a lot about the formation, ecological transition/succession, and ongoing dynamic transformations in such communities.

(7) Finally, *topological congeries,* by which I mean all aggregational impairments to flows of people through places. The linguists tell us that the Latin verb *congerere* implies both "aggregating" and "congesting" – hence, it is a perfect term for the intended sense. We have already cited many micrologics dynamically bringing about these congeries, the topological constraints, unwanted results and structures, and the semi-autonomous nature of the impaired process, so we need not repeat them here (see the Appendix for the logics of flows and matching).

A crucial, intervening point must be made at this juncture in reference to the ontological status of "social structures" such as the ones we have just presented. This is an important issue that I intend to address in the future. For now it suffices to state that we conceive the above phenomenological structures as **semidefinite constructs** (in Elsasser's terms) indicative of relatively stabilized structured systems of contingent practices. Let us now turn our attention to the further consideration of the status of these various levels and types of social structure.

Commonsensical considerations may make us initially believe that the movement from the level of interpersonal interactions upward to the higher levels of social structures is a movement *away* from the real. On this view, the "real" is the actions of concrete individuals, who are the only existing ontological entities; structures may "appear" to be real the closer they are to this primordial level of individuals. So, structural systems at level I, such as organizations, groups, and communities, appeal to our senses as visible entities of sorts, though, of course, that is not always the case with "congeries" or "quasi-groups." But what is one to make of the "interorganizational field" or of "ecologies" at the next higher level? There is a feeling that these terms refer to structures that are "constructed" and "posited" at the higher levels rather than "discovered" there, and that this construction is arbitrary and, therefore, contestable. But this is an empiricist trap, implying a view of reality still committed to foundationist programs of "Truth," now rejected by any post-positivist philosopher.[4] The great physicist Schrödinger (1944) compared our epistemic methods of knowing to fishing nets: they certainly are constructed and they get you a variety of fish, though never enough kinds to make you feel you know the world of the sea. This example, like any metaphor, has its shortcomings, but it certainly brings home the fact that theoretical constructions, such as those referring to structural systems at different levels of organization, may be more or less imperfect but are not necessarily empirically void. Theoretical strictures within research programs need as much corroboration as a boxer needs scoring points against his opponent – although no knockouts (i.e., falsifying, one-shot "crucial experiments") are to be found. Talk about "social structures" at different levels is just that kind of talk – not an arbitrary construction, but an imperfect theoretical articulation in search of corroboration (Lakatos 1978). I treat the distinctions offered in this part as phenomenological descriptions in relativized, and certainly fallible terms (a form of internal, intensional, modal realism).

At this time we must come back to this chapter's main concern and scrutinize the meaning of the heterarchical organization of social structures by working our way through the connections obtaining between levels I and II. In the schematic presentation of the case in Figure 13.3, the first thing we notice is the several-to-several connections between social structures at these levels. The "heterarchical" nature of these connections consists in the fact that they are several-to-several (or many-to-several) in the same sense as neural networks are. Furthermore, each of the level II structural "fields" is a polymorphous set prioritizing and accenting some specific properties of the relevant second-order structures. In this sense, the connections from level I to level II are more central or less central to each particular field. In Figure 13.3, we note the central connections with a double line, the average connections with a single one, and the most peripheral ones with a broken line. These fields have fuzzy boundaries: we explained earlier that any decomposition of levels is only a partial decomposition; it does not demarcate absolutely separated subsystems, only relatively demarcated ones. On the other hand, the decomposition is not basically arbitrary or capricious, capturing only different "slices" of the same reality. There is something more fundamental to the distinction; these fields seem to be complementary ways of constructing and analyzing

---

[4] The antiempiricist, antifoundationalist strains in post-positivist thought are expressed more radically by Goodman (1978), Kuhn (1970), and Rorty (1979, 1989). For the more robust forms of internal or intensional realism see references in note 7 of Chapter 12. I personally favor this robust form along neo-Lakatosian lines.

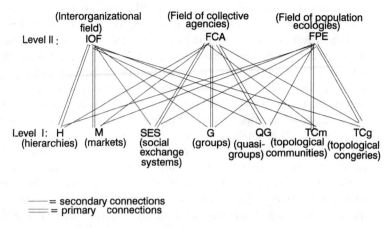

Figure 13.3. *Connections between polymorphous levels*

reality, each involving its own analytical and methodological apparatus; in brief, something akin to the particle and wave conceptions of quantum reality. The reality implied in our models is a constructed/corroborated reality. I have used the notion of fields to capture this sense of constructed/corroborated reality as an apt analogy to the notions of phase-spaces, state-spaces, Hilbert and other types of mathematical spaces, used in the more elaborate models of contemporary science. What, then, are these "fields" at level II? At this quasi-global level we may describe the following structures:

(A) An *interorganizational* structural system consisting of heterarchically interrelated quasi-local structures: related to this field are, primarily, hierarchical organizations (which give it the modal orientation), but also markets (aggrandized into a large interorganizational market), groups, even social congeries (producing organizational bottlenecks as well as interorganizational externalities, such as impaired markets). There are many subdivisions in the interorganizational field; for example, industries (including "institutional" service industries), firms or other organizational units, competitors, customer-supplier lines in subcontracting, and so on. The novel properties of this structure are the ones representing linkages and interdependencies (constraining, enabling, and availing at once) across organizations with all the new mechanisms and externalities they involve (market interdependencies; interrelated elasticities and substitutions of products or services; conversion strategies between markets and hierarchies; large-scale flows of capital, products, materials, and personnel; the formation of oligopolistic cliques or monopolies, cartels, and other such collusions; and so on). The animating logic in this field is a complex logic of both domination and exploitation. We have witnessed an explosion of activities involving many structural mechanisms serving this logic: organizational structurings and restructurings for the reduction of essentially competitive uncertainty and the better positioning in the field (for example, to gain market share as an oligopolist), "signaling" strategies indicative of a quasi-clique of oligopolists (see Spence 1974; White 1981a and b), absorption of other players through mergers and acquisitions, internal vertical reorganization of enterprises on the basis of different "modes of interfacing," ongoing concentration, and so on. The general structuring structure appears as a model of a rather highly stratified market, with a few strong oligopolists within as well as between different industrial branches, a number of (usually subcontracting) intermediate firms, and a large number of small, competitive businesses at the bottom. This is certainly the case in the industrial system, but it appears progressively also to be the case in several other organizational arenas such as health organizations or the news media. Neo-institutional models coupled with the new sociological models of markets and hierarchies should prove valuable in further understanding this basic field (but see also Lash and Urry 1987).

(B) A structural system involving *collective agencies:* collective actors organize on the basis of some structural parameter (in Blau's sense), such as class, race, ethnicity, religion, or profession, and posit themselves as potential powerful actors in the interagential struggle for recognition and predominance. I take this to be a very dynamic process, along the lines of analysis in Marx's work, or that followed by Foucault in his description of the "professional" project, or by Gouldner (1982), Konrad and Szelenyi (1979), and Kontopoulos (1973) on the alleged project of the "new class"– in contrast to the tame, matter-of-fact conception of Blau. The logic involved is the same as before: *dominance and exploitation* at once, here instantiated in the praxis of heterarchically or synecdochically organized "collective actors" competing oligopolistically and on a larger scale for advantages and hegemonic status in the larger society. Examples include mechanisms of coalition formation, inclusionary or exclusionary strategies aptly described by Parkin (1979) along left-Weberian lines, conversions of power capital into cultural-discursive capital and vice versa, techniques of physical and symbolic separation on a grand scale (such as class- and race-based, and certainly larger than the ones suggested by Foucault at the local level, e.g., his mechanisms of hospital and clinic separations, the "surgery" as against the reception room, the "gaze"), and other such mechanisms which structure the relationships among groups in this field. This is predominantly the field of large-scale groups mobilized out of categorial entities (class-fractions and classlike groups such as ethnoraces), or through the consolidation of smaller groups (hierarchical consolidation, for example, of unions), or by concatenation of similar forces across organizations and markets (such as associations). In brief, this is the field of "collective actors" performing the scripts described by historical macrosociology.

(C) *Ecologies* as structural systems: Here I have in mind the politico-economic and human–geographical ensembles of large cities and metropolitan areas (the "growth machines" of a nation, according to Molotch), as well as other rural, mountainous, or insular ecologies. In these, a variety of lower structures are entangled together – organizations and specific markets, regional systems of social exchange, simpler or more complex quasi-groups, and, certainly, a variety of communities and social congeries. Within an ecology (Braudel's Mediterranean world, the Mississippi world, the Gobi desert), material and topological externalities and populational distributions therein constrain, enable, and avail to the agents the repertory of strategies and practices to be used in the corresponding contingent or opportunity contexts to their benefit. Material and topological externalities constitute the parameters of "resource dependence" and "resource mobilization" of the larger organizations and groups competing within a given regional ecology. The semiautonomy of this field of "ecosystems" is indisputable.

However, I want to argue that, contrary to the hierarchical "partition" model, which implies complete or nearly-complete decomposability, these three interorganizational, intercollective, and ecological fields are not mutually exclusive. Indeed, as we have said above, in the heterarchical conception, all partitions are fuzzy and partial, producing polymorphous sets within a level and partial, heterarchical orderings between levels. Polymorphous sets imply that each single set shares with some other member sets some properties but not all properties and there is no single fundamental property (or, at least, no significant number of the total properties) that is shared by all of the sets. In our particular case the three structural systems at level II form such a polymorphous set; each pair of them shares some important properties brought to them by the lower-level structures involved (especially, the core ones), yet they are for the most part semiautonomous from each other. We could imagine a linkage of these three fields, but as soon as we do that we move one level up, to the level of totalities. Notice the different conceptions of "structure" associated with each field based on the dominant quasi-local structure(s) – structure of interrelated organizations, structure of interrelated collective agents, and structure of ecologically related groupings.

Since the connectivities (mappings) between the quasi-local and quasi-global levels are several-to-several or many-to-several, the emerging pattern or organization is that of a parallel distributed system. Individuals, their connections, and the material and topological externalities that necessarily match them are the "hardware" of a society or social formation. Indeed, an overall conception of social structure may be thought of as consisting of the "matching" of three kinds of distributions or aggregations: of people (populations), material resources, and ecological "basins" and niches; but these matchings are polymorphous and, thus, heterarchical. Our semidefinite constructs do exhibit this peculiar and fuzzy hardware quality of semi-distinct fieldlike entities that, given the nature of the parallel distributive matchings, cannot be fully localized and delineated with determinate, exclusive boundaries. Consequently, concept (i.e., software) realizations mapped on them cannot but be, like Schrödinger's fishing nets, incorrigibly imperfect. In these times of heterarchical neural network research, of the alchemy of superconductivity, and of the amazing discoveries of fractal and chaotic behavior (the peculiar fuzzy-stability of instabilities), all of which document the creative symmetry-breaking movements of nature; in these times of post-positivist nonfoundationalism we can certainly live with the corresponding uncertainties and imperfections unavoidably inherent in our sociological models of structure. If the heterarchical conception is robust and if heterarchy, indeed, sets incorrigible limits to modeling, then the only alternative left is, simply, a competitively better modeling of structural systems than the present one.

One last point must be made to counterbalance the impression given in the beginning of this chapter that we have given in to a compositionist strategy by the mere fact that we have proceeded from the lower to the higher levels. A correction is in order. We argued earlier that for the understanding of the emergence, stabilization, and functioning of each structural system at any higher level several component parts and processes are needed:

(1) the microactions and microinteractions of individuals in interpersonal or collective encounters which are the *under*determining instigators (it is clear that I try to avoid a term like creators or producers) and supports of social structures;

(2) the structuring mechanisms that transform individual or collective action, given material and topological externalities, into a determined structural system;

(3) the implicated externalities, both material and topological; and

(4) the semiautonomous processes of the structure once it has emerged (loops, self-organization, new properties, autonomous operation).

Now is the time to add a fifth and final component:

(5) the "downward influence" of a given structure as it heterarchically envelops and parameterizes (i.e., constrains/enables/avails) the possibility space of lower structures and of the assorted individual and collective agents. The heterarchical logic of level organization operates upward and downward and laterally at once, privileging neither a methodologically individualist nor a methodologically collectivist mode of level composition and relations. The semiautonomy of each level is the central dogma of heterarchy.

Totalities: classes

As we move from the quasi-global to the truly global level (level III) of structural systems the same sort of logical connections (heterarchical, parallel distributive, up and down and lateral) operate. Populations of individuals distributed into interorganizational, intercollective, and ecological fields and matched with political, material, and ecological externalities, form field-structures that are now themselves connected upward to the higher level of totalities. New structuring mechanisms and structuring structures become the midwifing operators bringing about these new higher structures. Several of these macrologics have been already presented or are described in the Appendix; some insights on their application will also be given in the next chapter. Furthermore, special processes of autonomization of these totalities become visible. And new downward influences "to totalize" the structures underneath begin to appear and be felt.

We can begin to understand this process by looking at the notion of class as a component of the totality of "class structures." Class is one of those constructions that is relatively corroborated in an internalist manner, that is, by its theoretical location and utility within a progressive research program and by relative empirical corroboration assessed intertheoretically, according to the new postpositivist (pragmatist or internal realist) models of science (see note 5). Class exists as part of a total system, a "class structure" generated by structuring principles, mechanisms, and structures known collectively as the "relations of production" within a given "mode of production." (We will return to class-structure in the next chapter.) A class is a semiautonomous structure, included as part of a class-system, and connected heterarchically with the lower levels of structures; in this sense a class is semi-incorporating – but not fully subsuming – various class-fractions and other semiautonomous strata or categories and is underdetermined by them as well.

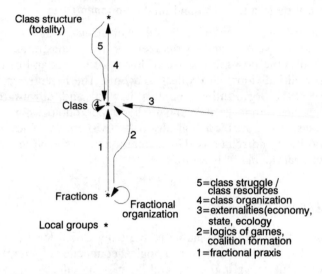

Figure 13.4. *Class determinations*

A class may appear as the collective or organizational result of an Olsonian game of class-fractions, or better yet, a more complex game of intragroup/inter-group relations as we have described in Chapter 7. A class may be seen through the lens of organizational and interorganizational relations, or through the lens of collective and intercollective agencies and practices, or through the lens of the populational ecological distribution of people to "places and functions," as Althusser put it, or to material resources, as Marx said (*Capital* II:385). Let us not forget, too, that since every level in a heterarchical structure of levels is only semiautonomous, the relative underdetermination of class (but though an underdetermination still a relative determination) reaches down, by virtue of weak heterarchical transitivities, to individual and group (intentional or compelled) modal orientations and practices which are always implicated and channeled through the higher levels according to the new boundary laws prevailing in these levels. A class may be said to be defined: (1) by the microactions, microelements and microstates deployed at lower levels, especially those channeled through organizational and group structures; (2) by mechanisms of class production and structuration linking or disjoining occupational categories and class-fractions, especially via game-theoretical and coalition-forming strategies and processes; (3) by the selective role of topological, material, and other externalities that favor one or another expression of class form (e.g., in class-segregated neighborhoods); (4) by its own "autonomized" logic of consolidation and counterdefinition in view of the concrete situations of this class and in conjunction with similar definitions of other classes; and, finally, (5) by the downward influence of the totality of class structures and of the other totalities (the historical moment of the social formation or the world-system and the intensity of class struggles in it). In this last sense, class is defined in terms of the contrasted interrelationships with the other classes and in the form and expression of the class struggle. Class is a thorough heterarchical concept interlinked simultaneously and affecting as well as being affected by (via differential transitivities) several structural systems at several levels of the heterarchy. A model of this complex situation is depicted in Figure 13.4.

Since class is a component part of a totality, rather than the totality itself (in this instance, a "class-structure"), we must proceed to the analysis of these totalities in the next chapter.

14 On structural totalities

The final level of structural emergence (level III) is that of structural totalities. Here the exemplary forms are those of class structures, national societal structures ("social formations" in general), and the world-system. These structures must be considered "global," in the sense that they are taken to be overarching, all-inclusive, organizing entities heterarchically constraining/enabling/availing to and, thus, relatively reorganizing more or less all the lower structures. I am using the term "totalities" to indicate two basic characteristics of the structural systems at this global level: First, their "inclusive" nature (since they include within them – though without absorbing or controlling – the lower-level structural systems; and, second, their "totalizing" nature, that is, the growth of several strong collective powers within them and the contestation and assumption by one or more of these powers of the hegemonic role of redefining and reorganizing the national societies – and, to the extent possible, the world-system – on the basis of their "vision" and their "project." I presume that these powers are, primarily, social "classes" and, secondarily, other "classlike" collective agencies ("social categories," such as bureaucracies or professionals).

Two different conceptions of totalities already have been advanced, one by Hegel and various neo-Hegelian versions (historicist, hermeneutical) (Gadamer 1975; Taylor 1975, 1979) and the other by contemporary structuralists, especially Althusser (1970a and b; in the following I cite Althusser and Balibar 1970 as Althusser 1970b).

(A) The Hegelian notion of totality posits a unifying essence behind the apparent multiplicity of phenomena. The *Geist* expresses and manifests itself in a variety of historical spatiotemporal forms and through its essential unity makes these phenomena meaningful, although imperfect, realizations of its own unfolding logic. Time, too, is conceived as both homogeneous and contemporaneous: homogeneous in the sense that it reflects the continuity of the unfolding Geist; contemporaneous in the sense that every "moment," every manifestation is a total expression of the Geist, an expression of the innermost structure of all possible objectifiable states, all past and future – summarized or prefigured, in any case indicated in the here-and-now – configurations. Therefore, the Hegelian notion of totality has an underlying real unity; it is "centered," to use Althusser's word (1970b:94–5). It is a unitary structure, the elements of which are always coexisting at any particular point in the continuity of time.

In contrast, (B) the Althusserian structuralist notion of totality, especially as exemplified in the capitalist mode of production, is said to be "decentered," that is, it "is constituted by a certain type of complexity, the unity of a structured whole containing what can be called levels or instances which are distinct and 'relatively autonomous', and coexist within this complex structural unity, articulated with one another according to specific determinations, fixed in the last instance by the level or instance of the economy" (1970b:97).

The Marxist–Althusserian notion of totality exhibits the following two basic differences relative to the Hegelian notion: First, it rejects the idea that an original unifying essence, such as a Geist or any other unitary Logic, exists behind the phenomena of the world, producing the latter by its own externalization, self-organization, unfolding, or self-discovery in evolution and history; for Althusser there is no such *Logos*. Second, the elements (levels or instances) composing this totality are neither fully integrated nor equivalent; they are relatively autonomous from each other, yet asymmetrically related in any particular state, the dominant element (structure in dominance) possibly being different from one state to the next. Yet, as regards any social formation, "in the last instance," it is the economic structure that determines which element is to be dominant in that social formation (ibid.:319). I don't want to belabor this point here (see my 1980). But it needs to be said that the Althusserian notion of totality – certainly an improvement over the Hegelian notion – is riddled with problems. Althusser still takes for granted the "systematicity" of the whole: the so-called whole is treated as always already "totalized," totalization ("integration" by another name) is seen not as an uncertain "task" or project but as a definite "fact," a conception that comes quite close to the structural–functionalist view. The "always-already-there" character of the whole also approaches Hegel's notion of the contemporaneity (though not the continuity) of the structural expression; the structure of the totality changes from one state to the next according to the overdetermination of contradictions and their uneven development, that is, for purely structural or formal reasons that operate only at the level of the totality and involve no lower levels, such as the activity of people (who are treated as mere "supports" of the structures). So the overall model has a strong control-hierarchical flavor – indeed Althusser speaks of the *Gliederung,* an "articulated, hierarchized, systematic combination," or an "organic hierarchized whole" (1970b:84, 98) – in contrast to the heterarchical view of totality we present below.

Totalities, in my sense of this concept, (C) are not fully organized, integrated, functional systems, as those have been conceived by the older "systems functionalist" theory or by the French structuralists. Totalities operate on two planes adjacent to one another – let us call them the oligopolistic and the monopolistic planes, the second being higher than the first. At the "oligopolistic" plane totalities are constituted by several competing "organizers" or "global structuring principles," each one more or less antagonistic to the other, striving to predominate within the totality as organizers of the possibility space of social life; a few competitors are above the others as an oligopolistic clique and their antagonisms, alliances, signaling processes, and so on, make up the repertory of structural mechanisms. At the next higher, "monopolistic" plane we see an emerging strong oligopolist taking the initiative of becoming a monopolist, whatever the success of this effort. Therefore, the characteristic here is the appearance of a hegemonic strategy to organize society on the basis of the structuring principles and mechanisms favored by the would-be monopolist (her "vision" of society, his "project") and, given some initial success of this effort, of a further attempt to expand this hegemonic strategy to all important institutional sectors. When we speak of the "global" level and of "totalities" we must keep in mind this ascent of a strong oligopolist and the totalizing effort following it (the attempt to impose an "organizing logic" on society). Otherwise, these oligopolists or monopolists are collective agencies.

Since there is always a jockeying for power to hegemonically totalize society, totalities are exemplars of the concrete. Marx (in the *Grundrisse*) has spoken of "the concrete" as the "totality of all determinations" and it is obvious to any serious reader of his work that he had in mind the dominant logics of primary determinations, which as such "constitute" reality. The concrete is concrete exactly because it is structurally constituted by one or several would-be dominant modes of totalizing. Were one to simply posit a fully successful monopolist, then the mode of dominance would be certainly simpler and analytically more pure, and the overall level structure would be "control hierarchical." On the other hand, in the heterarchical way of conceptualizing totalities, the intersection of several modes of totalizing make the structure of the totality more complex, dynamic, and contradictory. There exist several would-be monopolists but no secure, fully successful, totalizer in the long term. We may say, indeed, that there is a predominant collective agency, but not a really dominant one.

In modern times, totalizing projects have been undertaken by the bourgeoisie, various political-bureaucratic elites and vanguards acting through the state, and the professionals (the so-called New Class) oriented toward symbolic–cognitive modes of domination. At which point, one may ask, did the bourgeoisie become the hegemonic organizer? At which point and under which historical conditions did the states elite ("bureaucracy" as a social category) bid to become a dominant organizing power? To what extent is the New Class successful in the implementation of a similar project? What are the specific "concrete" relations between these three modern organizing logics – together with older ones, such as the logic of patriarchy – at each and every stage of development of different national societies? These are fundamental questions for understanding the precise structure of a totality.

Within each totality there are several interlacing modal orientations implicated in any specific organizing mode:

(a) a modality directed toward *domination,* either explicit or symbolic, of the other collective agents and the various institutional structural systems, exhibited by capitalists, state elites, or groups of professionals; there is also

(b) a modality directed toward *exploitation,* especially the production-based exploitation of labor, if one takes Marx seriously, but also other forms of such exploitation, such as that of "women's labor," or the exploitation by "experts"; then, there is

(c) a modality geared toward the *organized mobilization* of people, in the broader sense elaborated by Foucault, as citizens, as productive laborers, or as modern subjects (this last exemplified in the advancement of hygienic, reproductive, or intellectual education); and, finally there is

(d) a modality directed toward the *integration/reproduction* of the structural totality at hand, implemented more or less successfully by the intellectuals and institutional guardians functioning in the given totality (Bourdieu's "dominated sector of the dominant class").

These modalities are usually intersected and more or less consolidated, for as we have said above, an effort at least is made by the predominant organizing collective agency to consolidate them, largely in accordance with its own project and, of course, with differing degrees of success.

I have mentioned collective agencies – a neutral word encompassing class, classlike, and categorial collective entities that are not organized groups in the usual sense. In general, collective agencies are large groups that are (1) rarely organized into collective "agents" proper; or (2) are organized only synecdochically, that is, heterarchically connected across scale-levels and mobilized for a common purpose by some core fraction in a nonlinear, iterative, threshold-based way; or (3) are mere categorial quasi-groups mobilizable in similar ways by political entrepreneurs. There are specific structural systems of collective agencies that include several similar agencies together: class structures, classlike (exclusionary) structures of race or ethnoreligious groups, and classlike strata structures (structures of "social categories,"[1] such as those of intellectuals–managers–professionals and of the state, civil or military, bureaucracies). Within each of these systems one or more dominant agencies, such as the capitalist class or the state elites in modern times, and to a lesser extent particular fractions of the New Class, engage in their own organizing, totalizing project. The accumulated powers of these agencies (capital, state power, knowledge-power) vary across space and time; so that here and now it may be the capitalist class that has the hegemonic role, there the state (or party) bureaucracy, with the professional strata holding usually – at least, until now (cf. Gouldner 1982; Konrad and Szelenyi 1979; Kontopoulos 1973) – the junior position. Given the predominance of any one of these, or any other agency in any particular contemporary society, the overarching structuring principles will also tend to be those of capital, of bureaucracy, or of the New Class. I treat these three as the primary *Logics* of the global systems in our time: the Logic of Capital, the Logic of Bureaucracy, and the Logic of the New Class. One could easily add to these the Logic of Race (today in South Africa and less so in other racially mixed societies, but in the past in all colonized areas) and the long-enduring Logic of Patriarchy, both of which, however, have become progressively weaker. Each one of these Logics (and several of them combined together) organize the structural totalities we are analyzing in a dual sense: (a) on the basis of a favored modal orientation (domination, exploitation, knowledge-power) and (b) with the use of particular logics for achieving hegemonic status, that is by organizing social relations on some "rational" grounds (techno-economic efficiency, legal-bureaucratic rationality, expert knowledge).[2] We will describe these Logics further in the latter part of this chapter.

A structural totality, as we have said earlier, is never a fully integrated system. Even when only one agency organizes the global terrain, there are always failures, contradictions, disjunctions, and the praticoinert world of externalities. This is especially true in the (rather usual) cases in which several Logics operate competitively at once. In a sense,

---

[1] There are two meanings of the term "categories" – one based on blockmodeling results (on a par with the mathematical theory of categories), the other referring to corporate or semicorporate bodies or strata, such as the army, the bureaucracy, the professional-managerial strata or the intellectuals (along the lines of historical political sociology).

[2] Here, "logics" and ideology may coexist: technocratic efficiency, legal-bureaucratic rationality, expert knowledge – all of these are power/knowledge claims, "projects" with structuring capacities, modalities of structuration. In this sense, I speak of Logics (such as the Logic of Capital or of Technobureaucracy) at the higher levels of level-structure.

the hallmark of structural totalities is the permanent existence of structural contradictions.

Contradictions arise at three distinct levels. They emerge as (1) *contradictions between the basic Logics* of Capital, of Bureaucracy, of the New Class, of Race, of Patriarchy; in this sense they appear as disjunctions (amidst the efforts of consolidation) due to the competition for predominance between the agencies activating these Logics (e.g., contradictions between State and Capital, the New Class of symbolic capital and the older class of economic capital, the state elites and the adversarial intellectuals, and so on). They emerge also as (2) *contradictions between the modal orientations (*or *projects) of* one or more of these Logics; that is, as contradictions between the interests of "domination," of "exploitation," of "mobilization/participation," and of "integration/ reproduction." Here, too, there are numerous disjunctions, disarticulations, conflicts in orientation, unintended results, costs of conversion, and so on; the examples of economic disarticulation, of the adversarial role of intellectuals signaling their reaction to the reproductive role expected of them, the costs of conversion of economic troubles into bureaucratic solutions and of state inefficiencies into legitimation crises (for which see Habermas 1975) are indicative of these sort of disjunctions. Finally, they emerge even as (3) *contradictions within the dominant modal orientation* (and any other orientation) of a particular Logic due to internal and implicit nonlinear structural instabilities and bifurcations (e.g., mood fluctuations such as those described in the Appendix,[3] or of the Marxist variety, such as the structural transition from "variable capital" to "constant capital," initiating the process of "the falling rate of profit"). To the above structural contradictions we must add (4) the *contradiction between the totalizing project of some elite or class and the contesting projects and collective actions of subjected agencies* (for example, of labor, of minorities, of women). In a heterarchical sense, these contesting projects, the revolutionary movements and the many rebellions and local resistances – to recall Foucault – that take place against the totalizing efforts of any Logic of politico-economic or symbolic domination and/or exploitation, are an important and permanent fixture of totalities. For, as we have already said, no totalizing effort is ever completed or becomes fully accepted by the dominated or exploited collective agencies.[4]

[3] "Loss of nerve": see Trotsky's beautiful description (cited in Stinchcombe 1978) of such loss of nerve by the czarist army. See also Richardson (1960) and Watt (1989); consider Christiansen (1988) for such loss of nerve by the aristocracy in the eighteenth century.

[4] Elster (1985 and in previous work) speaks of psychological and social "contradictions" (the latter involving counterfinality and suboptimality) generated within capitalism. See especially 1985:43–48 and passim.

A totality, then, is a precarious system of precarious stabilities, a dynamic and always imperfect realization of a predominant "totalizing" Logic: "Stability" in the system is produced by the powers and mechanisms at the disposal of the given Logic and, to a lesser extent, by other intersecting Logics now deployed or remnants of older Logics in use; "instabilities" are produced by the various forms of contradictions we have mentioned. In this tug-of-war, totalities travel through many states in the phase-space and these transitions are in principle *under*determined and, therefore, rather unpredictable in their long trajectories. We must not lose sight of the fact that we need to know the detailed dynamics of the structural instabilities involved in each specific structural process (Gurvitch's destructurations and restructurations). With this goal in mind, I now turn to the consideration of "class structure" as a totality and offer an initial exposition of its dynamics.

Class structures as totalities

Marxist theory usually begins with the analytical distinction of the concepts of the "mode of production" and of "social formation." In the canonical interpretation, a politico-economic or, simply, a "social formation" is "a definite, historically concrete society, constituting a system of social phenomena and relations in their organic unity and interaction on the basis of a given mode of production, and developing in accordance with its own specific laws" (Althusser 1970b:108; Kelle and Kovalson 1973:43). A "mode of production" is defined as the unity of two coexistent sides; those of the "productive forces" and of the "relations of production." Both of these express relations among humans: the productive forces referring to the relations of social agents to nature and the relations of production referring to the relations of social agents to each other. Althusser specifies the double articulation of the mode of production more precisely as follows: "The productive forces constitute the connection of real appropriation of nature or the 'possession' connection, while the relations of production are the relations of expropriation of the product or the 'property-ownership' connection" (Althusser 1970b:317; cf. G. A. Cohen 1978). Put differently, the productive forces imply the real material appropriation of the means of production by the direct producers in the labor process, the individual appropriation of natural objects the laborer controls himself, and the relations of production imply the appropriation of surplus labor by nonproducers. For example, the capitalist appears as the expropriator of the means of production and, thus, organizer of production as well as the expropriator or exploiter of labor-power. Overall, the mode of production, as Marx said, is "a definite form of activity of these individuals, a definite form of expressing their life. . . . The nature of individuals thus depends on the material conditions determining their production" (*GI,* CW 5:32).

Starting with the productive forces, the Marxist view posits that classes and individuals heterarchically located in them come up with special "endowments" (Elster, Roemer) or "powers" (G. A. Cohen) as "effective capacities to do something" (Cohen 1978:220) that are determinative of their productive engagement. The most basic of these powers is the disproportionately large or small "access to property" or economic resources, especially in the form of the means of production (land, a herd of animals, capital, an industrial plant). The effective control of the means of production may come about in several ways, as we have already seen in Chapter 9 in the case of the emergence of capitalism and as we shall see shortly in earlier historical cases. The decisive step in most instances is the "separation" of direct producers from the means of their labor; for example, in capitalism, the expropriation of land (through the enclosures) from the peasants and the destruction of the independent artisanal producers. As soon as this expropriation takes place, the "released" peasants and the "proletarianized" artisans find themselves compelled to sell their labor-power to the capitalist. On this point, if we can bracket his individualistic bent, Elster is most assuredly right when he says that "a class is a group of people who by virtue of what they possess are compelled to engage in the same activities if they want to make the best use of their endowments" (1985: 331). This is obvious in the case of the exploited class but also holds true of the exploiting class, which must engage labor in the production process if it is to come up with any material benefit. This mutual necessity of involvement permits the relations of production to exist as the locus of the expropriation of surplus labor of the exploited class by the exploiting one. A mode of production exists as the interplaying of the productive forces and the relations of production, showing this double feature of the expropriation of the means of production and of surplus labor, as the central mechanism of structuration.

We may pursue this line a bit further by looking at some empirical examples documenting and corroborating the emergence of class structures and of class-based modes of production. Quite a lot of recent evidence from archeological excavations makes it possible to reconstruct in a robust relativistic sense the sequence of events that have brought about class systems (Diakonoff 1969; Kramer 1981; Lloyd 1978; Mellaart 1975; Patterson 1981; Redman 1978; Trigger et al. 1983). In general, there may have been three basic ways – theocratic, military, and economic – of bringing about the unequal distribution of resources and the ensuing unequal access to the control of larger social resources in a growing community. The first case seems to be the oldest, as it appeared in the earlier agricultural communities of Mesopotamia at least by 4000 B.C.E. Differentiation had already proceeded at a rather fast pace in the communities of Catal Hüyük in Anatolia (between 6500 and 5600 B.C.E), of Yarim Tepe I and the Samara Phase settlements in Northern and Southeastern Mesopotamia (6000 and 5000 B.C.E.), and of Warka and Eridu in Southern Mesopotamia (5000 and 4000 B.C.E). By about 3000 B.C.E, in these and other communities in Egypt, the Near East, and the Mesopotamia region, but also in Turkmania, the Susiana Plain of Iran, the Indus Valley, and various Far East locations, full class systems had begun to develop. (Similar patterns also appeared in the Meso-American societies. See Patterson and Gailey 1987.) In these early communities the increasing population size did not lead immediately to functional organization but to fragmentation into segmented lineages of descent. Population differentials in these lineages made certain groups more successful, allowing them to translate their success into claims of being closer to the direct line of descent stemming from the divine or an "elect" ancestor. As a result communities were now organized into a social form that anthropologists call a "conical clan": All relations of social rank were defined in terms of genealogical proximity or distance from the higher unity that stood above the larger community. The particular group that occupied the higher position in this rank order was endowed with the power to control a greater portion of the community's labor by requiring tribute and labor payments from the other lineages in return for its mediation to the god for the well-being of the community. This is the source of the (a) *theocratic systems* figuring prominently in most instances of the Asiatic mode of production, that is, in social formations in which the palace and the temple corporation become the state authorities for organizing water control systems, public works and granaries, and the production and distribution of commodities.

The further development of this process led directly to class stratification. The ruling noble-theocratic families severed the kinship relations that had once existed between the various descent groups and assumed titles of kingship – via the consolidation of the office of the "lugal" (Patterson 1981:153–4) – and officiating nobility. The class structures that emerged included in a descending order (besides the ruling royal and noble families), a class of commoners who owned land as members of kin groups, a class of clients attached to and supported by the temple corporations or noble households, and an exploited class of captive slaves, "debt" slaves, and dependent producers, such as women working in public artisanal workshops. With this class structure in place, the natural population growth accelerated by the production of surpluses, and the dynamics of competition between neighboring settlements (attested to by the emergence of walled towns and observation towers), protracted wars over disputed lands became common: The war between Lagash and Umma lasted for more than five generations; that between the kingdoms of Upper Egypt and Lower Egypt in the Old Kingdom period was quite protracted as well. As a result, (b) *politico-military* elites came to power supplanting (or at least surpassing in importance) the earlier purely theocratic powers of temple corporations. Ensuing empire-forming wars solidified a class structure in which slaves and other dependent working groups became the machinery of surplus production.

Another means of development of class systems was prominent in the outward areas of the neolithic revolution, noticeably in Greece, especially during the Minoan and Mycenean periods, where contiguous populations were relatively separated into smaller city-states and developed confederate systems of relations. In these conditions, neither strong theocratic nor imperial modes of organization took hold. Rather, class structures emerged more naturally along the lines of descent groups but without the strength of temple organizations. Inequalities emerged from the interplay of population differences between various descent groups and their strategic practices of production and exchange – in general, the larger the group, the larger the number of adult males,[5] the stronger the physical and material powers of the group, the more the surplus produced, the more likely for that group to support other groups and receive in return tribute and labor, the higher its military capacity, the more likely to end up as a ruling group. This (c) *economic* way of the formation of the ruling class was still capable of producing a class of in-group ("debt") slaves that carried out the most demanding tasks of production. (In Athens this was a rather large class of people finally liberated as a result of rebellions and the Solonian legislation in the early part of the first millennium B.C.E.) Needless to say, these three analytically distinct mechanisms of class production were in reality intersected and consolidated with one another in several overlapping variations; but they all ended up producing class systems led by imperial/ theocratic or oligarchical ruling classes and relying more and more on the work of captive, debt, and service slaves as exploited primary producers.

The genesis of the early class structures provides us with a good opportunity to sharpen our understanding of the "structuring" process per

---

[5] For the pragmatic valuation of males as productive workers, defenders, or members of armies see Lenski (1975, 1987), Mamdani (1972), or Patterson (1981). All works on the Yanomamo stress the same point.

se; it is a sort of relatively controlled laboratory in which one can work to isolate the involved mechanisms of structuration and try out the synthetic mode of their operation. First, let us begin with the modal structuring principles, that is, the general modalities of action and interaction orienting the structuration process toward a particular structural form. In the early class systems these structural principles may or may not have involved clearly defined, *conscious* strategic–purposive actions geared toward domination and exploitation. It seems rather that the initial orientations were not antagonistic but broadly integrative (group-oriented or oriented toward social exchange) as they were primarily based on kinship relations. But with the increasing size of the communities and the differentiation in the fortunes of the now "decentered" descent groups (multiplied into so many extended families that the aboriginal center or common ancestor had receded into the mythological realm), antagonistic, strategic relations became more prominent. At this point the gaining of strategic advantage, the successful deployment of the powers and resources controlled by each group, and the acceptance of strategies of domination and exploitation become the structuring principles of the kin, familial, and individual agents. Class structuring mechanisms are produced by the proper understanding of the interrelations and possibilities of use of physical, social, and cultural powers and resources: the recognition of the importance of family size, of the preeminent role of adult males, of increased surplus production, of social exchange strategies of gift-giving and support-providing in exchange for labor obligations and mobilization, of matrimonial strategies and alliances, of strategies of converting physical power to control over others in neighboring territories, of converting from systems of personal labor to systems requiring the exploitation of the labor of other groups (slavery), or of converting economic success into cultural capital (the theocratic way, the lugal, the big man) – all of these became "structuring mechanisms" of separation, elevation, domination and exploitation – in brief, mechanisms of class structure formation. Once a class structure had emerged, it operated as a structured structuring structure, that is, as a "dissipative structure" or a "process structure" operating on its own laws, following structural forms of simple or extended reproduction or of transformation (see Chapters 9 and 10), semi-independent from the mechanisms of its own structuration and conditioning (constraining/enabling/availing) the further strategic practices of the agents distributed inside it heterarchically. Concomitant with, but (contra Blau and Lenski) not, strictly speaking, as a result of (i.e., related to but not a function of) the increase in the size of the community, we witness the emergence and demarcation of a level structure, built on the progressive separation of family, community, and society, but analytically incorporating distinct structural systems: groupings (extended families, temple corporations, nonfamilial work units, matrimonial systems), fields (community settlements, urban–rural systems, interkin and protocaste markets of labor and commodities, water control-related human ecologies) and totalities (class structures, kingdoms and empires). Even in these smaller-scale, earlier totalities, then, we find evidence corroborating the heterarchical nature of social structural organization.

As we move from these early modes of production and class structures to subsequent modes we cannot but be struck by an important paradox of discontinuity, a thorn in the side of developmentalist interpretations of history, including the corresponding form of Marxism. What one comes to recognize, for example, is the fact that, although modes of production share several fundamental characteristics, their particular channeling of the structuring principles that animate them produces a number of different structural processes and distinct transitions into the next mode. We have basically agreed that the transition from the earliest mode of hunters and gatherers living a communal or associative life with a vague and limited conception of property to the neolithic settlements and their more developed kingdoms was initially due to population ecological pressure, drift, and the recognition of relative advantage, while the later developments were possible under noncooperative structuring principles. The next transition from the Asiatic and Ancient modes of the early civilizations to the Feudal mode seems to have taken place primarily as a result of two operating forces: (a) the breakdown of empires, which, at least on the surface, involved external invasions and resettlements (the movements of Goths and Germanic tribes in general, of Anglo-Saxons, Slavs, Mongols, Ottomans) and/or (b) the conversion of brute force into a culturally or ideologically sanctioned corporatism. In general, any transition may involve a combination of causal factors. It may imply populational or ecological changes, demographic drifts, or invasions – factors which appear descriptively to be external to social structure per se. It also usually involves the existence and dynamic playout of internal contradictions which, in the long run, may bring about a weakening or breakdown of the old organizing mode (productive stagnation, military weakness, elite dilution, moral decadence) on the one hand, and on the other, new structurally emerging groups that would potentially impose a new structuring order on the societies. For example, numerous studies have shown that the breakdown of the Roman Empire in the West due to internal contradictions considerably preceded the domination of these areas by the invading peoples. Moreover, Charlemagne's dynastic order became legitimate only with the massive Christianization of the new ruling groups and the reconversion of the old, Romanized, now captive populations into allegedly coequal Christian subjects or serfs.

The transition from feudalism to capitalism repeats some parts of this sequence but is different in some other important respects. It has been a transition under relatively peaceful conditions in the European theater (meaning that no major external invasions took place with the containment of the Arab and, later, Ottoman threats; to the contrary – colonial invasions by the European nations have speeded up tremendously the internal structural processes). Internal contradictions relating to the economic inefficiency of feudalism (Brenner 1977, 1982; Moore 1966; Wallerstein 1974) were complemented by the complex structural effects of colonialism (population release, imports of species and commodities, enrichment of importing/exporting and shipping groups, increase in inflation and conspicuous consumption, relative decline of the economic basis of landowners). A third force of increasing importance, described by Adam Smith, was the growth of bourgeois groups, production units, and markets in the towns, in what I take to be the "margins of feudalism." The historical record is providing us with a clear picture of (a) the emergence in the margins of feudalism (playing a lesser functional role and more of a parasitically symbiotic role) of towns and, within them, of bourgeois groups as *dritte personen,* who achieved (b) their relative autonomy within the feudal order by royal writs (cf. Moore 1966), became (c) structural operators in their own domain in the periphery (through growth, differentiation, primitive accumulation, new work-structures), and, when stronger, midwifed (d) the transition to capitalism (imposing their newly redefined instrumental–strategic modality as the paramount structural principle, imposing new mechanisms of structuration – for example, the labor contract, the separation of work from home, and so on – and becoming totalizers in the modern order of things). It may be said that a new attractor had appeared that became the new gravitational point or center, bringing to its basin all other social entities and reorganizing them as far as it could by its own structuring principles. The end product, of course, was due to the nonlinear dynamic interplay of external factors (colonial expansion and commerce), internal contradictions that weakened the old system (increasing absolute exploitation of peasants, declines in productivity, stagflation in the relatively fixed incomes of the ruling aristocratic class), as well as of the important developments occurring at the margins of feudalism (bourgeois towns); all of these contributed, in arguable degrees of importance, to the transition out of feudalism and into capitalism.

The capitalist mode of production emerged on the basis of the "structuring principles" of utilitarian/strategic behavior that turned capitalists, ideotypically, into self-interested, highly rational maximizers of private profits. In Elster's view, as stated earlier, the capitalists were *compelled* to act in the particular ways they did if they were to make the best use of their endowments (powers) and they had to make a working class that was also compelled to sell their labor-power to them, if they were to survive. Among the first "structural mechanisms" employed, therefore, were the separation of the peasants from the land (especially, via the enclosures) and their subsequent "subsumption" under the organizing power of the industrial capital. We have described this process rather thoroughly in Chapter 9, but here we must reconceptualize it along heterarchical lines. Indeed, Marx makes a comment to the effect that the former (i.e., separation of peasants from the land) will not lead automatically to the latter (i.e., subsumption of labor), citing the case of Ancient Rome, where the separation of peasants from the lands led to the formation of an idle proletariat, living parasitically at the expense of society (*The Letters of Karl Marx*: 321). On Marx's argument, in the case of capitalism three distinct steps were taken: (1) proletarianization (release) of the peasantry (marginalization, mobility, uneven growth of urban areas), (2) formal subsumption in the larger artisanal workshops and early factories (social production by still independent artisans, separation of workplace from home, gender stratification), and (3) real subsumption under the industrial capital (expropriation of the artisans' means of production, proletarianization, absorption of former peasants, and division and control of the labor force). These structural mechanisms applied at the level of production brought about the structured structuring structure of the capitalist mode of production. The numerous logics and mechanisms which, linked together in dynamic ways, bring about the special "system" of capitalist production and relations cannot be described here in more detail.

What, then, is the capitalist class structure considered as an already developed totality? It is a *Gliederung,* that is, an "articulated combination" of material forces and relations forming a structured structuring structure and, furthermore, an articulated combination of this structure and other instances or structures coexistent in a social formation. The Marxist theory of totality posits the existence of three structuring structures of relations: (1) that between the "productive forces" and the "relations of production," which is the most fundamental structure; (2) that between "base" and "superstructure," in whatever more or less sophisticated sense this connection is to be understood; and (3) that between the "dominant" mode of production and other "subordinated" (e.g., petty commodity production), remnant (family farming, semifeudal mode), or emerging (socialist? bureaucratic? New Class?) modes occupying a certain niche in the modern social formations. These structures are truly entangled in ways that preclude their hierarchical classification or decomposition in terms of analytical or causal importance (somewhat as in the letters–words–sentence entangled system). On the heterarchical argument, then, it is not true that the "forces of production" determine the given "relations of production," although they do constrain/enable/avail those relations – that is, shape the possibility space on which they would develop. Similarly, the relationship between "base" and "superstructure" is not a causal-determinative, but a constraining/enabling/availing one. In both cases, the heterarchical argument goes against (a) the reductive economistic version of Marxism, which advocates a causal-determinative relation, as well as (b) the functionalist version of Marxism (Cohen's), which advocates a functional-optimizing relation. In our heterarchical version, (c) the relation involved is one of *constraining/enabling/availing:* It restricts the possibility space of compatible relations or superstructural forms, enables certain possibilities to appear as commonsensically "satisficing," indeed as approaching a perceived quasi-optimal limit, and still avails to the totalizing as well as to the countermobilized players many strategic moves and creative improvisations, able to bring about novel structures within the broader, constrained or permitted degrees of freedom. If there is any determination, therefore, it certainly is a weak and relative one. Furthermore, as we have already seen, the heterarchical view of classes themselves, not only their relations, prohibits their consideration as fully organized and conscious collective agencies, allegedly subsuming all lower levels (i.e., classes, fractions of classes, local laboring groups, and individuals are considered as semiautonomous). The whole complex game of class formation, class relations, and class contestations is very dynamic, considerably implicating important political and ideological moves. Given this entanglement of separate levels and structures, any class structure – and more so the capitalist one – is fraught with contradictions and the equilibria it may reach are only temporary and dynamically fragile.[6]

Marx also specified two "structural mechanisms" that, within his research program, are essential to understand the actual dynamics of capitalism (Marx spoke of "mechanisms" in a large number of places

---

[6] Like any other class system, capitalism exhibits – on the Marxist argument – the contradictions (a) between forces and relations of production, (b) between base and superstructure, (c) between the currently dominant mode and other institutional forms, (d) between the primary antagonistic classes of the dominant mode, (e) between the dominant (economic) elements within a mode and the representatives of the political and ideological institutions, and (f) between the organizers of the dominant mode and other would-be organizers of alternative modes (bureaucratic-political, professional-managerial, or New Class elites).

using the words machinery [*Triebwerk*], mechanism [*Mechanismus*], and construction [*Getriebe*]). The first refers to the analysis of capitalism as the pure state in which "objectified labor" or "dead labor" in the form of constant capital emerges as a force and comes in conflict with "living labor," representing for the capitalist variable capital. Hence the paradox of capitalism: *ceteris paribus,* the more the capitalists compete in cost-cutting measures, the more their investment, primarily, in labor-saving machinery, the larger the share of constant capital over variable capital, the less the surplus-labor expropriated from living labor, the greater the fall in the rate of profit. This logical–structural sequence may or may not be right, but it is part of the central dogma in Marxist theory. The second structural mechanism is the effect of the first one, an effect that in its turn further structures the basic classes: It is – it was for Marx – the quantitative and qualitative growth of the proletariat, not least via the proletarianization of the older middle classes, and the polarization of the class conflict around the primary antagonists, Capital and Labor. Again this is fundamental to Marxist theory, even though it has proved to be a premature inductive statement relying on observations and extrapolations that were in the long run more or less wrong.[7]

The previous analyses, without regard to their actual (strong or weak) corroboration by the historical record, have demonstrated, I believe, the character of a class structure as a "totality" and the complex structuring principles, mechanisms, and structures implicated therein. The argument has been a theoretical one, of course. It has addressed the issue of the conceptualization (by Marx) of class structures as totalities involving the interplay of several entangled structures and mechanisms, in a more complex heterarchical way than the one we have presented in Chapter 9. Moreover, from the point of view of a contemporary – even if amended – reading of Marx, the case remains that a heterarchical recasting is not only possible but desirable, compared to the previous hierarchical work that ends up denying any importance to human agents. Recall in this context the Althusserian dictum that "the structure of the relations of production determines the places and functions occupied and adopted by the agents of production, who are never anything more than the occupants of these places, insofar as they are the 'supports' (*traeger*) of these functions.... The true subjects are these definers and distributors: the relations of production (and political and ideological social relations)" (1970b:180). Althusser blocks any move

---

[7] Abercrombie and Urry 1983; Bechofer and Elliott 1981; Poulantzas 1975; see also Marx's comments on the "new middle class" in the McLellan reader (1977). The question whether or not Marx is right or wrong in the *very long run,* that is, presuming a truly global capitalist system, still remains open.

to talk about the diachronic emergence of these structures, that is, the historical production of these selfsame relations of production. On our argument, however, the rejection of the historical-transformative consideration of structures is a regrettable mistake. Diachronic structuration as well as synchronic interlevel relations can be analyzed equally well by the heterarchical Logic. Too, the fact that not only abstract structuring structures, but also more concrete (intra- and interlevel) structuring mechanisms and underlying structuring principles (modal orientations of agents/agencies) determine a system's states and transformations demonstrates the necessity of a heterarchical, synchronic as well as diachronic, conceptualization of class structure. The mechanisms of structural emergence cannot be presumptively thought of as having been fully absorbed and nullified by the totalizing structured structuring structure (say, the capitalist relations of production) they give rise to; this is as absurd as saying that the laws of physics or biochemistry have been thoroughly and definitely annulled by "life" and "consciousness," too idealistic a dogma for any serious science to espouse. (In reality, we may speak of "local" violations, say, of the laws of thermodynamics, but certainly not of "global" violations.) Instead, as we have said before, they are partly superseded, partly supporting, and always entangled in complex heterarchical ways to the semi-inclusive structure.

National societal structures ("formations") as totalities

A societal system is also a structured structuring structure – a totality. In the Marxist sense such a system is a concrete "social formation" composed of (wholes or parts of) competing modes of production and more or less organized under the hegemony of one dominant mode. A more flexible view would consider these competing modes to be general "organizing Logics" making efforts to "totalize" the societal system on the basis of their structuring principles and mechanisms. We have already cited as such competing Logics in the modern world, besides the Logic of Capital, those of State Bureaucracies and of the New Class; we must, of course, add here the Logic of Labor or of Socialism, or of (an ideotypical) Democracy (Alford and Friedland 1985; Offe and Wiesenthal 1980; Przeworski 1985) that has also been inserted into our contemporary organizing practices. These Logics, as indicated, have their own distinct structuring principles and mechanisms, which we may briefly describe as follows:

The Logic of Bureaucracy, especially State Logic: This Logic's structuring principle may be called "hierarchical instrumental"; it is geared toward the establishment of an impersonal bureaucratic-managerial order that operates on the grounds of instrumental technical rationality (effectiveness, efficiency, technical ways of problem-solving). Its primary structuring mechanisms are (a) the separation of commoners from the role and means (including expertise and information) of decision making and the appropriation of these roles and means by an expert techno-bureaucratic category, and (b) the formation of a dominance hierarchy within that category that expropriates the decision-making powers of lower-placed agents by higher-placed ones. The structure of a state then emerges as a structured structuring structure pursuing its own State Logic in partial accommodation, partial competition with the capitalist class. (On this, see the extensive literature on the "relative autonomy" or independent development of the state.[8]) This State Logic is informed by the material interests of the elites involved as a "corporate agency," but also by the general interests of the state as an organism of sorts in competition with other states, as well as by the broader interests of the civil society as a whole (the specific political function of the state) reflected in the state's interests for relative integration and social peace. The institutional structures of the state develop as strategic adaptations (in the sense of Chandler 1962, North 1981, Thompson 1967, Williamson 1975) to the environmental uncertainties – as "structures for performance," as it were.

The Logic of Professionals/Intellectuals (of the experts, the New Class): This Logic refers to the specific efforts of the "professionals" (managers, experts, free professions, the professoriate) – to the extent that, as the argument goes, they form a relatively unified New Class – to become definers and organizers of a new mode of societal structure where powers and resources would be distributed and utilized according to (ideologically?) proposed criteria of competence and meritorious performance. Since "intellectuals" are in fact a "flawed universal class," to use Gouldner's expression (1982), their rhetoric of meritocracy seems both positively promising as well as suspect (on some readings, masking their long project of class dominance); recall here Foucault's major analyses of the negative dominating logics of all (old and new)[9] intellectuals, their bio-politics affording them in previous regimes a prominent role or in modern times, junior partnership roles within capitalism

---

[8] See, among others, Alford and Friedland (1985); Evans et al. (1985); Skocpol (1979).

[9] Contrary to conservative New Class critics (P. Berger, Bruce-Briggs, Kristol) Foucault (1965, 1973, 1977, 1978, 1980) attacks *all,* old and new, intellectuals – the priests, cultural elites, medical doctors, sociologists, all at once. A more pronounced ambivalence is found in Gouldner (1982).

and/or the state. The structuring principle of this Logic is the dubious notion of a benevolent, lateral (that is, nonhierarchical and seemingly nonexploitative) yet superior "expert practice" that leads to the establishment of a loose hierarchy or a heterarchy of merit symbolically topped by an "aristocracy of the spirit." The structuring mechanisms involved in this Logic are (a) the separation of the common people from the means of expert practices and discourses (educational capital, licenses and professional certifications, access to specific means, such as doctors' use of instruments and drugs, distribution of powers, such as those of attorneys, the esoteric nature of scientific discourse, among others) and (b) the subjugation of these peoples under the jurisdiction of professionals, even against their will (hospitals, mental institutions, children's welfare agencies, processing agencies of the state, and so on). Foucault speaks extremely eloquently about this logic of symbolic (and, at times, not so symbolic) domination and the historical context and process of its emergence – one should read his work for further erudition.

The Logic of (ideal) Democracy: This has been also called the Logic of Labor or the Socialist Logic, or the Logic of "the people"; it is the project of equality and cooperation ascribed to the earliest communities and posited as a realizable task by Rousseau and Marx. We see elements of this Logic in the demands of labor, minorities, women, and a significant portion of intellectuals – groups that have no effective power of totalizing this project except by collective movements, resisting and challenging the more successful projects of capital, bureaucracy, and the professionals. But resist and challenge they do, and in this respect, offer still another strategic agency in the already complicated arena of societal structures. At present we see expressions of this Logic in (a) collective movements of dominated minorities (black civil rights, poor people's movements, feminism, and others) and (b) in the organizational practices of labor unions (especially so in the national union movements of European societies). Maybe these players do not appear as powerful as capital or the state elites, but they do enter the equations of the national structural totality as class or classlike agencies (especially Labor) as well as units in the political struggles in every society. Recall the trilateral monopoly we mentioned in Chapter 7 in which Capital (controlling the flow of investments), the State elites (controlling to a large extent fiscal and monetary policy), and Labor (controlling to some extent the rate of profit for capital by actions, e.g., radical wage demands, or omissions, e.g., lower productivity) jointly determine the well-being of the national economy, not counting the effects of the international forces. In cases like these, Labor enters if not as a primary force in terms of direct Capital–Labor games, at least as an indirect, third force in the potential antagonism between a semiautonomous state and capital. Similarly, all sorts of social movements enter into consideration in the political arena, as forces potentially supporting or opposing the ruling state elites and with the potential to damage the "implicit social contract" of the national society (for example, via rebellions and criminal acts).

To the above Logics one may add the *Logic of Patriarchy* and the *Logic of Ethnorace*. These continue to be quite important in the contemporary world, rhetoric to the opposite effect notwithstanding. The Logic of Patriarchy is, of course, very old, patriarchal relations having emerged nearly at the onset of the neolithic revolution with the rise of advanced horticulture and of pastoralism. The Logic of Patriarchy was rearticulated in the early phase of the industrial period of capitalism, when the separation of workplace from home, the subsumption of artisanal and proletarian labor in factories, the prohibition of child-labor, and the reestablishment of moral economy in the modern communities once more forced women to engage exclusively in household activities (mothering, nurturing, service, possibly piece-work). In the Victorian era, therefore, patriarchy was more or less redefined and reactivated by the capitalist organization of production and of the broader social and political relations. The Logic of Ethnorace, of race relations and ethnic relations conceived as relations between collective agencies in antagonistic terms of "exclusion" and "usurpation" (Parkin 1979) or, in terms used in similar contexts, of "domination" and "resistance" (Foucault), or "exclusion" and "contestation" (Tilly), is also visibly applicable in quite a few instances. However, an argument can be made to the effect that both of these Logics are currently in relative retreat.

In general, a national societal structure is another "quasi-articulated combination" of "entangled structures" with a relatively and temporarily dominant Logic at the would-be core, and several other competing, allied, subordinated, or challenging Logics around it, all meshed together into a dynamic "totality." Consistent with the heterarchical model, these Logics are also entangled downward with the lower-level structural systems interconnected with them and upward with the corresponding international division of labor and the world system that heterarchically incorporates them.

The world system

Here one may repeat the process of analysis offered above. The world system can be conceived, in a manner more or less compatible (though heterarchically recast and thus upgraded) with that of Wallerstein

(1974, 1984), as an entangled structure including various Logics, the capitalist and socialist Logics being the dominant ones at this time. It incorporates heterarchically many organizations (States) and interorganizational blocs, a number of collective agencies (capitalist classes and state elites, but also nationalist and liberation movements), and a variety of human ecologies and economies (industrial/agrarian, urban/rural, developed/underdeveloped, resource-rich/resource-poor, capitalized/debt-owing, etc.). Within these parameters States and Capital usually operate competitively and their strategies toward markets or hierarchies (colonialism or neocolonialism, multinational corporate control or indigenous control of local resources, dependence or independence, isolation or capitalist incorporation, and so on) match to an extent the complex game-theoretical practices we outlined briefly in Chapters 6 and 7 and more appropriately befit the heterarchical mode of analysis. That the Logic of Capital, the twin principle of domination and exploitation, has become the paramount structuring principle needs no further detailing. The examples of the British destruction of preexisting "local" industrial structures in India, or in Greece and the Ottoman Empire, the restriction of industrial development in the colonies, such as the indigenous development of shipping (American colonies), the destruction of other states' fleets (Spain) and effective blocking of their external shipping trade (Holland), the restrictions of any shipping from the colonies other than through London and via British ships – these certainly add up to such a strategy of domination and exploitation. The recent talk of a "new world order" betrays again the significant degree of entanglement of all smaller collective entities in such a "world system."

Totalities

We may sum up our investigation of totalities by pointing out their defining elements: First, that they are the highest level of structures related heterarchically; that is, partially incorporating and partially being semiindependently supported by lower levels down to the level of direct human, individual agency. Second, since every level in a heterarchy is semiautonomous from both the level above it and the level below it, totalities have their own operative structuring principles, mechanisms, and structures expressed through competing Logics of totalization. Third, each totality is a member of a polymorphous set and, therefore, the three totalities we have discussed are overlapping in several (but not all and not the same) respects; they are entangled with each other, not subsumed in a true control-hierarchical order. Fourth, within each totality various structures are also entangled, accounting for a multitude of contradictions and dynamic disequilibria and conflicts that, in the longer run, push the system to sometimes moderate and manageable, other times radical and unmanageable, transformations and new states. Finally, fifth, it is the combination of the above, of conflicting Logics and contradictions, of collective struggles and new strategic emergences, of "places and functions" (per Althusser) as well as "strategic practices" (per Bourdieu and others), that accounts for the irreducible "historicity" of totalities. Heterarchy is jointly the production and the producer of necessity and freedom, structure and agency, stability and transformation – in brief, the fragile solidity of societies and the historicity of their forms.

15 In conclusion

We have reached the end of this volume, and I feel the pressure to provide some closure to the multiple arguments. But how can this be done? Having been so much concerned with nonlinear dynamics, emergence, and structuration, how do we reach any definite conclusions, or, dare I claim, gains from the enterprise? In the postpositivist/postmodernist discursive mode, the belief of the Greeks that "the beginning is already half the whole story," gives me little relief. With Bachelard and Lakatos, I, too, consider it important to maintain that the intellectual game consists not in giving all the right answers but, at least in part, in posing and grounding the historico-pragmatically "proper" questions which will, in turn, raise even more questions of an important sort. Thus, instead of "In conclusion" I am tempted to offer "An inconclusive unscientific postscript."

But perhaps that won't do. We have reached, after all, several tentative (semireal) landmarks or, to put it in an alternative idiom, we have committed ourselves to several tentative posits (semiconstructed in an "internal realist" sense). Honesty dictates that I sum up these investments and claimed payoffs for public display and appraisal; by the same token, a prudent attitude also suggests that I display some of my further (perhaps essentially "promissory") markers, to stake a claim to new fields that will be mined at a later time. For this heterarchical research program of social structure has a long way to go. The issues we have addressed have only been outlined in broad strokes and suggestive examples. The details of the patterns and of the production process, even if they have been intimated at times, need much more elaboration.

What has been done so far? We have distinguished five epistemic strategies – reductionism (methodological individualism), constructionism, heterarchy, hierarchy, and holism (methodological collectivism/systems functionalism) – which form the competing tracks for the development of respective, self-consistent research programs addressing the issues we usually consider under the rubric of "social structure." A variety of arguments have been raised regarding the serious weaknesses of the extreme reductionist and holist strategies: we have discussed in some detail the new scientific and philosophical developments favoring an emergentist conception of the world in accordance with the three intermediate epistemic strategies (Logics); and we have presented several arguments and examples as to why the Logic of Heterarchy seems to be the most promising of the three as it addresses in a very sophisticated manner the complex, nonlinear nature of structural emergence, level structure, and structural relations. We have attempted as objectively as possible, given our human frailty, to describe and appraise various sociological research programs or partial theories dealing with the issue of social structure in an explicit, or an implicit but pertinent way; and we have praised or criticized various specific views from what I consider (fallibly to be sure), a relatively better theoretical position (more robust, having excess theoretical and empirical content, specifying structuring mechanisms and modalities, converging with novel scientific views, and so on).

In the deployment of my arguments I have tried to enlist a variety of fascinating insights and provocations making the rounds in the many frontiers of current science and philosophy: nonlinear dynamics and chaos, dissipative structures, diverse mechanisms implicated in emergence, informational biological and cognitive biological theory, the beauty of modern mathematics (say, fractals and tilings), the high complexity of the current hyperdynamic ecological models, the sophisticated connectionist models of brain/mind and computers, "internal realist" notions in postpositivist philosophy, and so on. I apologize to my colleagues in the social sciences for these necessary insertions; I do believe, however, that the payoffs far outweigh the investment in this extended process. At a minimum, I hope the reader has seen that a new convergence is emerging between philosophical, scientific, and social scientific views, a convergence steering us away from the Scylla of reductionism as well as the Charybdis of collectivist functionalism toward more robust, intermediate, complex but self-consistent conceptualizations of the world and, in the present context, of social structure.

I call my own theory *heterarchical* in the complicated sense I have tried to explicate throughout this volume. It is a species of structuration theory, but quite different from what now passes as such (in the versions of Giddens, Turner, and Collins). In contrast to their views, I have insisted on two fundamental posits: (1) that a proper theory of structuration must elaborate – both separately and in conjunction – the numerous logics of structuration operating in the social space and time (see the Appendix for a preliminary inventory); and (2) that a successful theory of structuration must explain in detail upward structuration, that is, provide a proper level-structure scaffolding for the location, partial ordering, complex heterarchical networking, and dynamic transactivation of particular structured structuring structures. I can see no other serious way of producing the so-called micro–macro link to which others allude by way of often magical incantations.

A final example, even at this late stage, may serve to illuminate the

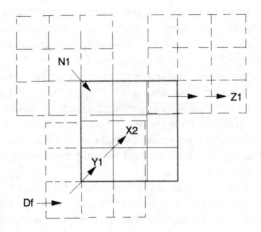

X2=2/8 Threshold
Y1=1/8 Threshold

Figure 15.1. *Transitions in polymorphous "neighborhoods" (eight-house model)*

complexity and multiple structural embeddedness of individual actions. Consider the already cited case of neighborhood transitions. Schelling suggested that an eight-house bounded neighborhood in the mind of each individual homeowner operates as a context of reference for deciding, according to a given threshold level, the likelihood that this homeowner may get out if one or more person(s) with some given characteristics move in one (or more) of the houses in (his or her) bounded neighborhood. The decision may involve, to recall Blau (1977b), some vague cultural preference of the like over the unlike, although – unfortunately – in reality it involves biases with discriminatory overtones (along religious, ethnic, or racial lines) which we as sociologists find offensive. Let us examine this case, bracketing any implicated value judgment for the sake of illustration. (The same process operates in the opposite direction as well, as a gentrification process [for which see, for instance, Sassen-Koob 1984].)

Each neighbor has a "neighborhood" overlapping with the "neighborhoods" of his eight neighbors, as depicted in Figure 15.1. This gives rise to a really dynamic (quasi-local and quasi-global) situation. The decision of each agent (neighbor) to leave, is, at least, based on the following considerations:

    (1) his or her provisionally "fixed" tipping threshold, or habitus in several appropriate concerns (cultural, ethnic, racial, and/or class preferences, values, and biases; status considerations; util-

itarian considerations of the housing market). This may come to be seen as a preference principle that "if ⅛ (or ⅖, and so on) of my neighbors are not to my liking I will leave." This threshold point is, of course, itself the result of past cycles of experience and socialization.

(2) his or her conception of the bounded neighborhood itself, which defines the points of entry (this and/or that neighboring house changing) triggering the tipping threshold.

(3) the unmonitored process by which the "unwanted" (semi-local) entry to the neighborhood has been itself triggered (in some other neighbor's neighborhood and before that, and so on).

(4) the semiglobal (cellular-like) relations among all outwardly extending neighborhoods, operating simultaneously to trigger (in an excitatory or inhibitory mode) the transitions inside each of the personal neighborhoods (cells), as if they were parts of a (Conway) game of Life or a percolation process (see the Appendix).

(5) the more complicated "cellular automaton" emerging by the realistically expected different tipping thresholds for neighbors in any given neighborhood, accounting for different tempos and frustrated transitions.

(6) the global effects that may further excite or inhibit the thresholds or the dynamics of the process (such as the effects of economic downturns, rapid social change, structural dislocations, etc.).

Where is agency in all of these? Surely, agency is there! But it is a bruised agency, a manipulated, heroic, limited, improvising, "possessed," monitoring, confused, strategic, compromised – in brief, a struggling agency, a self-conceiving and situation-construing agency, partly (structurally) made and partly (modally) making its social practice. Agency, habitus (here, the threshold points), the semi-local cellular structure, the semi-global percolation or "life" process, the global constraints parameterizing habitus, all come together simultaneously to define a structural situation and the process involved therein. This is the only real game in town.

Structuration theory must most assuredly develop along such heterarchical (interlevel) lines. I have already shown, I hope, in the present work and will further elaborate and corroborate in forthcoming endeavors that the heterarchical research program has the required robustness to progressively proceed with (a) the thorough elucidation of the logics of structuration, (b) the explication of upward structuration and interlevel relations, and (c) the investigation of the metatheoretical underpinnings of the Heterarchical Epistemic Logic and their consequences for a proper postpositivist philosophy of science and scientific practice. In this latter direction we have already seen the foundations and contours of the heterarchical conception and its probable affinity to the sophisticated "connectionist" (neural network) approach of current neuroscience and cognitive science.

This talk of science is bound to arouse some curiosity, if not mild irritation, in many readers with a humanistic disposition and/or a political-moral engagement. I should know; I am one of them. Is there no distinction between natural structures and social structures, as Bhaskar, Habermas, or Giddens have suggested? Of course there is! Such is the distinction between brute letters and meaningful words or speech acts, between computer hardware and artificial intelligence, between brain and mind. Why not between population structure or social networks and culture or narrative construals of social and/or personal life? Notwithstanding our commitment to a postpositivist, internal realist view of philosophy, the important work lying ahead *must* address this connectionist question.

My own ongoing agenda in this regard includes a direct attack on two major issues: (1) the elucidation of the analogy between hardware/software, brain/mind, and social structure/cultural–mental structure along the lines of an advanced and sophisticated noncomputational "connectionist" (PDP-NN) model (for which see my suggestions in the latter part of Chapter 11); and (2) the contrasting of such a noncomputational connectionist (PDP-NN) social–mental (social structural/cultural mental) model to the already sufficiently developed brain–mental model, which is conceived to be insufficient to explain its own origins. This requires some special elucidation.

The PDP-NN model (Parallel Distributed Processing-Neural Networks) implies an interlevel form of mappings (categorizations) and subsystemic parallel interchanges (no need for a control agent) as sufficient for the emergence and operation of the mental process. In Gerald Edelman's sophisticated PDP version (especially in his 1989 book) there is the additional dimension of memory (recategorization) "reentry" from the corpus of a brain/mind's past experience, especially as mediated by language. This, on the one hand, introduces the social–practical dimension of life into the very brain/mind process itself while, on the other, breaks down the alleged computationality of the process. We are back, once again, to the social–mental roots of brain/mind cognition, the very grounds of the sociology of knowledge of Marx and Durkheim. There is an increasing need on the basis of the PDP-NN model to explore the historical-praxical ways in which "life worlds" get *transduced* into "language games" (per Wittgenstein), prudential (even "local" functional) experiences, or contingencies, and requirements get *transduced* into narrative versions of the world (per the internal realists) – in other words, how a "set" of presumably real conditions of life get *transduced* into a "hyperset" (here, a set of all possible subsets) of narrative interpretations. This social–mental PDP-NN process will also explain the focal implosion we call the emergence of human "consciousness" (individual agency or "self") by way of the **hypercyclic** organization of the brain–mental and the social–mental, of individual capacities and collective representations. I view this as the beginning of an exciting era for social theory, a real move to a truly post-classical era of social theorizing. It is, of course, only the beginning. It is a new opening in the possibility space. But I expect that time will indeed show the robustness of this program, which I will pursue diligently in the years to come.

Instead of closing, therefore, I speak of opening. I offer these views to my colleagues requesting not their approval but their engagement with them. I do hope, nonetheless, that I have contributed a little something to our common efforts in understanding our frustratingly opaque social world.

Appendix
The logics of structuration

Micrologics

1. The logic of organizational hierarchies
2. The logic of flows and impaired flows
3. The logic of self-selection and segregation
4. The logic of "constraining identities"
5. The logics of comparative advantage and comparative exclusion
6. The logic of oligarchy and oligopoly
7. The logic of gaming
8. The logic of federalism
9. The logic of social frustration
10. The logic of market (price) reversals
11. Tipping rules (thresholds)
12. Sorting rules
13. Matching rules
14. Traveling (graph traversing)
15. The logic of interfacing
16. The logic of voting

Mesologics

17. The logic of fluctuation
18. The logic of nucleation (catalysis, autocatalysis)
19. The logic of differentiation
20. The logic of allometry
21. The logic of allometric speciation
22. Islands and the logic of fission
23. The logic of percolation
24. The logic of Conway games of life (cellular automata)
25. The logic of fractals
26. The logic of mixing and merging
27. The logic of waves
28. The logic of branching/uncoupling
29. The logic of cascades
30. Packing rules
31. Surface-to-volume ratios

333

32. Rules of unpacking (partitioning)
33. The logic of informational packing
34. The logic of parsing

Macrologics

35. The logic of swamping
36. Rules of pruning
37. Eco-logics: the entropic form
38. Eco-logics: the heterarchical form
39. Totalizing logics
40. The logic of metaptations

We have argued that the fact that individual actions and interactions underlie all social processes and emerging macrophenomena has, in most instances, a rather limited explanatory value. Agency is *necessary,* to be sure, but *not sufficient* to explain the production, reproduction, and transformation of social structures. Given the interactional complexities, varieties of externalities, and nonlinearities involved, individual agents – presumably being less than gods – cannot effectively monitor the global course of events and eliminate the multitude of unwanted, unanticipated, or unnoticed consequences of different social or collective actions. Indeed, much more is involved in the generation of higher-level structural phenomena. For a more complete explanation one needs to add to the microcausal powers *the detailed dynamics of mediating mechanisms of structuration,* i.e., the specific aggregative or transformative role played by numerous local "micrologics," various quasi-local and quasi-global "mesologics," and even several global "macrologics," all of which transform and transpose or transduce a phenomenon from a lower level (e.g., individual action, molecular behavior) into a higher one (e.g., collective situation, social structure, chaotic dynamical system, sentence structure, life forms, and so on).

One may, of course, wish to start from the lower level of the numerous, local micrologics of structuration: these are the many logics of aggregation of individuals or their actions and interactions into local systems of structure, that is, "systems of interdependence" involving one or more "externalities." Here the analytical possibilities are too numerous to catalog and describe in detail; but since the matter is of great importance I cite below briefly – given the limits of space – some significant instances that exhibit the work of particular microstructuring mechanisms. To be sure, in the more complex cases of structure there exist further mechanisms of structuration, interconnecting these micrologics in particular ways and producing more complicated, higher-order structures. The process may involve two, three, or more steps and thus may also span several levels of structuration. Mesologics do the work of interconnecting several local structures and translating the results of this structural work into intermediary structural fields. Furthermore, several macrologics operate simultaneously with (and on) the previous levels and produce global systems of structure (structural totalities) at the higher level.

As stated earlier, I use the term "logics of structuration" to capture the essential characteristics of particular processes or operations of structuring, which can be formal (algorithms), semi-formal (mechanisms), or nonformal (modalities). For present purposes I propose to use these terms in a general manner, as indicative of a "transformative operation of upward structuration." This basic, minimal definition will therefore apply to all micrologics, mesologics, and macrologics of structuration.

Happily enough, the process of locating and studying such mediating dynamical mechanisms has already started in most – including the social – sciences and quite a few good, paradigmatic cases of such logical mechanisms have been isolated, described, and analyzed. In the following sections I will try to present my first efforts to pinpoint, though by no means exhaustively, various types of such mechanisms operating at different levels, starting from the local level, the domain of micrologics. I provide examples, drawn from various literatures, that instantiate these various logics and point out the implications of this desirable, detailed focus on analytical mechanisms of structuration. A note of caution before we begin: I am not an accomplished modeler and so, especially given the preliminary nature of this analysis, my bookkeeping is neither exhaustive nor formally developed. I make no claim that these logics cannot be reworked in some way so as to yield a better classificatory system; moreover, it may indeed be the case that some of these logics are marginal to the social sciences. So be it! I consider this a progressive challenge from within the positive heuristic of my research program, a promissory note that more work shall be done in that direction.

MICROLOGICS

Sixteen micrologics are described in this section – all apply to individual-type data (individual preferences, choices, practices, interactions, and (individual or group) distributions, and transform them into mostly discontinuous structural situations. Some of these micrologics apply *only* to this local level of structuration; others that are more abstract or formal conceivably also apply to the intermediary and global levels as mesologics or macrologics; these are indicated in each particular case.

(1) The logic of organizational hierarchies

The basic case of "purposive structures" or "authoritative organizations" is, of course, the bread and butter of sociology and management schools. Williamson (1975) has given an insightful explanation of the origins and growth of organizational hierarchies in transaction-cost analytic terms. Levi (1983, 1988), North (1981), Oberschall (1986), and several others have used transaction-cost analysis or similar notions to explain the emergence of the state or of public order. Moreover, Boudon (1981a) has argued that, in general, the passage from an unorganized system to an organized one is often due to the desire shown by the social agents to eliminate undesirable ("frustrated" or "pervert") emergent effects, that is, (a) suboptimalities and (b) counterfinalities, to use Elster's useful distinction. Along the same liberal lines, Arrow (1963:947), Hirschman (1970:18–19), and Schelling (1978) understand the emergence of the modern interventionist state as a collective "purposive structure" supplanting the failing markets of public goods. This *logic of organizational efficiency* leads to the formation of particular structures, brainchildren of some "visible hand" (Chandler 1977).

(2) The logic of flows and impaired flows

To understand the structuring *logic of flows* and *impaired flows* one must make a distinction between four categories of systems: closed, semi-closed, semi-open, and open. Schelling (1978) gives several examples of such systems.

"Closed systems" are by necessity "circulating systems"; that is, the flowing elements of the system travel through the same networks, states, or topological (or social) spaces. Matrimonial exchanges ("circulation of wives"), discussed by Lévi-Strauss and formalized by Harrison C. White (1963), and elite replacement ("circulation of elites"), per Pareto and Mosca, are pertinent examples. A special case of closed systems is that of "clocks," in which flows alternate between two states – switching systems, chemical clocks (Prigogine and Stengers 1984), alternation of moods, such as in the arms race (Richardson 1960), in war and peace sentiments (Watt 1989), in optimistic or pessimistic attitudes toward markets, and so on.

"Semi-closed" systems involve a "transition matrix" with feedback and considerable viscosity (cf. Schelling's example of waiting lines for ski-chairs). Arguably, such a semi-closed system of flows is the structural system of intergenerational mobility, especially if one considers class-to-class (origins–destination) flows. The remarkable overall stability of intergenerational mobility indicates the relative closure of class flows (cf. Boudon 1981a; Lipset and Bendix 1959).

"Semi-open" systems involve more fluidity in their transition matrix; that is, they are processing systems with considerable differential input–output transitions. Schelling cites the cases of turnstiles, bottlenecks, reservoirs, alternating tunnels and bridges, the age profile of a population, flows through the criminal justice system, and free migration. These are the typical cases of flows and, at times, impaired flows with which we are all familiar: traffic flows, material flows in assembly lines (Sedgewick 1983 for more complicated network flows; see *waves* no. 27), organizational promotion flows, student flows through the educational system, client processing in businesses, hospitals, and public agencies, neighborhood transitions (cf. *tipping* no. 11), cohort transitions in the population, etc. The flip side of these are also semi-open: queues, bottlenecks, traffic jams, personnel congestions, impaired markets, and so on.

Finally, there are "open" systems, which involve significantly perforated, nearly open boundaries, multiple inputs, complicated network flows, nonlinear internal dynamics, and other such characteristics. The classical case of an open – and indeed "chaotic" – system is, of course, that of the weather. A national economy with open international flows of goods and capital, especially in today's interdependent world, approaches the model of an open system as well. So, too, does a regional/metropolitan economy involving urban/suburban/rural flows of people, residences, jobs, capitals, and markets.

Speaking of closed, semi-closed, semi-open, and open systems is not enough in itself; it describes the parameters within which different types of flows can occur, but it does not tell us everything we want to know about the mechanisms themselves. The *logics of flows* are properly specified by the interactive effect of (a) the system's parameters (boundary conditions), (b) its initial conditions, (c) its phase-space (network connectivity, states, topological contours, currents, or what have you) and (d) the situation-specific operative algorithm (e.g., a Lorenz attractor in the case of weather). At least, the logic of flows involves the processing of people or any other material through (organized or not organized, physical or social/bureaucratic) space. This process logic attains specific values as a result of the underlying structure of that space (e.g., a network of streets and a traffic system), the quantities and properties of flowing materials (e.g., number of cars, driving patterns), and the external contingencies (e.g., traffic accidents or light malfunctions).

The *logic of flows* can be formally algorithmic, but this is not usually the case in complex social instances. Consider, for example, the case of the system of higher education analyzed by Boudon (1981a) as involving "priority tickets" of varying value. In a centrally organized system as that of France, where the structure of available positions (students accepted in each program) is determined exogenously and that of the flow (population of candidates) is determined endogenously, a "meritocratic waiting-list process" becomes necessary. A "congestion" (swelling of the queue) is, therefore, engenic in such a model, resulting in the discounting of these "priority tickets." Add to this flow the next-stage flow of graduates through occupational positions (e.g., in the bureaucracy or teaching jobs) and the specific pressure this further swelling of the queue exerts on the educational flow; the result is that the complexity and changing nature of the concrete situation is bound to limit the applicability of any efficient algorithm. Moreover, such "congestions" in flows most often produce a variety of unanticipated byproducts. For example, a tendency to resort to conspiratorial organizations and to seek political interventions is associated with lower-middle ranks in the military hierarchies of less advanced nations, a tendency that has been shown to be, to a large extent, the result of engenic or contingent promotional congestions (Kontopoulos 1976).

(3) The logic of self-selection and segregation

A special case of flows is that of neighborhood transitions and the quite similar urban/suburban form of transitions. Schelling is credited with the most competent algorithmic analysis of neighborhood transition, which we will present below under the *logic of tipping (thresholds),* no. 11. Here we focus on one ingredient of that logic – the structuring principle of self-selection, which is at the root of the problem. By *"self-*selection" I mean the principle of the selection of "similar" rather than "dissimilar" neighbors, associates, lifestyles, environments, or what have you, according to the prevailing sociohistorical notions of similarity and difference. As a result of this preference, practices will develop – staying in or moving out of a given neighborhood, or moving in another self-similar neighborhood – which have an indirect collective consequence of ethnoracial or class segregation (more or less pronounced heterogeneity between neighborhoods and homogeneity inside each neighborhood). This logic is applicable to the microstructural level (clique formation in groups) as well as the mesostructural level (neighborhood transitions, urban/suburban transitions).

(4) The logic of "constraining identities"

The term is Schelling's (1978). The logic is similar to the previous one in many respects, only here it is eminently *relational.* Moreover, while the operative structuring principle before was the selection of "like," now the relevant principle is the effect of the joining in or withdrawal of the unlike – a principle of *dissimilarity,* if you will. In this case, identities change relationally by a process of elimination of the upper or lower populations deviating from the mean. Consider the following case: What happens to a city when the economically poorest 10 percent of a regional population joins the city to use its social services and cheaper housing, while at the same time the economically richest 10 percent of the city population makes a countermove to the gentrified suburbs? The influx of the poor (or their *in situ* marginalization) constrains the identity of the city, changes the parameters of city life, the nature of expenditures and services, and hastens the flight of the upper middle classes to the suburbs. Or vice versa: the exodus of the middle classes due to suburban development leaves the city poorer in many ways. Boudon (1981a) has offered an analysis of the educational process (the "investment" model) in similar terms.

(5) The logics of comparative advantage and competitive exclusion

Let us begin with the principle of "competitive exclusion" posited by evolutionary ecologists. As a rule, two highly similar species cannot occupy the same niche; inevitably, one will displace the other (Boulding 1981; Wilson 1975; cf. Maynard Smith 1974). This is the usual result of the ecological interaction of "mutual competition": sharing the same territory, food supplies, or nesting sites, the species are tangled in a system of interdependence in which the success of the one reduces the niche of the other – a zero-sum game.

The logic of competitive exclusion is very common in the economic domain: the larger a company's market share becomes, the higher its "competitive advantages" (partially due to "economies of scale") and the more likely that it will begin to dominate its competitors (as an oligopolist or monopolist). This applies across industries as well: Hirschman (cited in Boudon 1981a) has documented the progressive decline of Nigerian railroads from the moment they were exposed to the competition of road transportation. Something similar had happened earlier in the railroad–canal competition, only that time the railroads had the comparative advantage. Robert Fogel (1964) has assessed the advantages offered by the railroads in the American economy by counterfactually reconstructing how railroads were to perform with an extensive canal system.

The same processes seem to operate on ecological regions as well: suburbs vs. cities, sunbelt vs. frostbelt, core vs. periphery, and so on.

When the highest social stratum begins to move outside the dense city perimeters to avoid the congestion, noise, and other harmful elements, and separates itself from the lower strata, a deterioration of the inner city sets in through, among other things, loss of receipts, jobs, and tax base (Boudon 1981a). This same process works in the opposite direction in the European cities and in cases of gentrification of select areas in inner cities (Sassen-Koob 1984): When the highest social strata begins to bid up prices in select neighborhoods, the cost of living goes up (e.g., property taxes), pushing the poorer dwellers out of their homes. The examples can be multiplied at will. Boudon cites the example of elite schools which, by attracting as magnets the elite of students, relegate all other schools to the second or third tier. Braverman (1974) speaks of "upskilling" and "deskilling" in somewhat similar terms. In most of these cases a tier-structure is formed: first-, second-, and third-tier universities; oligopolistic enterprises, competitive firms, and mom-and-pop shops; core, semi-periphery, and periphery; and other such dominance hierarchies.

An affine but more tamed logic is that of *comparative advantage,* according to which nations, regions, or enterprises are presumed to be better off developing their own areas of relative economic advantage to the fullest while conceding to others the rest (Adam Smith's example has England sending industrial products to Portugal in return for port wines). This is certainly correct to an extent; yet, competitiveness is largely the result of different national, organizational, or other strategies and conditions implicating a broader political-economic system of relations (cf. Adam Smith on the exploitation of colonies). In brief, uneven economic development, implicating a whole package of entrepreneurship, inventions, human exploitation, structural dependencies, and cultural capital differentials, is at the root of most of the given cases of comparative advantage. We now come to a structuring logic somewhere between these two notions of comparative advantage and competitive exclusion.

(6) The logic of oligarchy and oligopoly

We spoke above of the development of oligopolies as the result of the logic of comparative advantage or competitive exclusion. However, there is another logic that deals differently with the same case. Following the rational choice and public choice models we may formulate it thus: Michels's "Iron Law of Oligarchy" can be seen as the result of communication limits (Mayhew 1973; Mayhew and Levinger 1976; Miller (1956), difficulties of aggregation (Olson 1965), differential organizational mobilization due to transaction costs (Williamson 1975), and resulting corporatism, growing indirectedness of representation, and so on. Thus, "members" or "voters" form a baseline "latent group" in relation to their party or to the party system, or their national union or federation of such unions. On this argument, even in a formally democratic institutional environment where people "choose" their representatives, candidates are screened, credentialized, and offered by the oligarchy itself to the mass of members or voters who must accept them, or at best select mainly among the offered candidates (the second best, or the next second best, and so on).

Harrison White (1981b) has argued that this condition also prevails in today's production markets, in which dominant firms operate not according to laws of supply and demand but as members of an oligopolistic production clique "signaling" to each other appropriate modes of behavior so as to sustain the oligopolistic market at hand. Buyers are considered as more or less passive (loyal, manipulated by advertising, or held captive by the competitive balance among clique members), only indirectly relevant to each firm's decisions on prices and quantities of production. This model, however, is neutral regarding the issue of the origins of oligopolies.

In a similar case we can see at work both the abdication of representation (from below) and the demobilization of any such possible representation (from above). Consider the example of representation of small shareholders in today's heavily capitalized oligopolistic corporations – a typical Olsonian world; at times, the costs of participation exceed the total value of investment, as when the holder of 100 shares of a low-priced stock XYZ is invited to attend the three-day annual shareholders' meeting, say, at the Honolulu Sheraton! At the same time, oligopolistic shareholders and the management team thrive in actively manipulating and paper-mobilizing via proxies this mass of small shareholders. This is an instance of an uneven, differential, "oceanic" game, as we have seen in Chapter 7.

(7) The logic of gaming

We have already spent considerable time in Chapters 6 and 7 discussing the merits and various forms of games, so there is no need here for long elaborations. The catalog of games (Prisoner's Dilemma, chicken, battle of the sexes, bilateral monopoly, assurance), their particular form (e.g., basic PD, Olsonian PD, Schelling's n-person PD), and their extensions and generalizations (supergames, metagames, differential games, and so on) have been thoroughly analyzed in the relevant literature. Besides the examples we have already provided (Boudon, Elster, Olson, Schelling), one may cite numerous applications proposed by

Baechler, Bartos, Harsanyi, Shubik, M. Taylor, and others. In brief, the logic of games is *one* of the most important of micrologics; yet, it is neither all-encompassing nor the most important of logics, as its proponents would have it (for a frustrated conversion see Elster 1989b).

(8) The logic of federalism

Recall Olson's argument that a large group is always a "latent group" unless it is organized as a "federal group" composed of local "privileged groups." The federal model of organization is somewhere between the models of global (centralized) and local (totally decentralized, dispersed) ways of group formation. Conceive the latter as a loosely connected island model and compare it to the *logic of islands* (below, no. 22) and *cascades* (below, no. 29). The characteristic of Olsonian federations is, presumably, the balance between global and local authorities; if there is a bias, it is in the direction of the local groups (a confederacy rather than a federal group per se). The best example is the relationship between local unions and their national or international agglomerations. The other example of federal government–state government relations indicates a bias in favor of the federal over the state and, thus, it is a top-down rather than a bottom-up model of organization. Federalist models, such as that of unions, exhibit strong local collective action but weaker global collective action possibilities; nonetheless, they are admissible forms of collective organization even under the Olsonian restrictions. More recently, this logic is promoted by the proponents of a postmodernist politics for the Left and for feminism.

(9) The logic of social frustration

The logic of frustration is at the core of all constructionist programs in sociology with its twin emphasis on the indispensability of individual rational action and, on the discontinuities and, indeed, opposition between individual intentional action and collective results. Boudon has used the term "frustration" as an umbrella concept to include all such instances of discontinuity and opposition between individual actions and collective effects. Others, notably Elster (1985), make a distinction between the invisible hand and counterfinality (cf. suboptimality, too): the former refers to the *positive* aggregate outcome of similar individual actions while the latter refers to the *negative* aggregate outcome of such actions (cf. Elster 1978:106). Counterfinality and frustration are more or less indistinguishable terms and refer to the emergence of "pervert," anomalous, or counterintended effects as a result of the "fallacy of composition." In this respect sociology can indeed be defined as the study of nonlogical negative aggregate effects of masses of individual (logical or nonlogical) actions; these effects, the results of relational and other externalities, subsequently become social determinants constraining future individual action.

Frustration may involve one, two, or many agents. The notions of "diminishing returns" and of "discounting" are instances of the working of the logic of frustration at the individual level. Furthermore, "overgrazing," as we shall see below, is also possible at this individual level, as when one fisherman or fishing company overexploits and thus eliminates the fishing population, of a given area. But in the most important cases frustration involves two or more agents acting similarly but independently of each other and bringing about negative results.

I propose that we distinguish four basic types of frustration:

(a) frustration of possibilities prohibiting the growth of expectations;
(b) frustration resulting from high or rising expectations;
(c) frustration in the production of a collective good (collective action); and
(d) frustration in the avoidance of a collective bad (the core notion of frustration).

The first type refers to the set of cases where relational externalities restrict either the opportunities to pursue a specific course of action or the expectations associated with such a course, or both. These cases involve high "reward/risk" ratios. Boudon's (1981:77–8) already cited conceptualization of schooling and educational achievement as an investment offers us, perhaps by default, a good example of type (a) frustration. It is also evident in the case of destabilizing, rapid economic growth: the more aggressive take the higher risks and may reap the highest rewards, bypassing the older and more conservative strata as well as the poorer or less aggressive risk-takers.

The second type of frustration, that resulting from unfulfilled or less rapidly fulfilled rising expectations, is well developed in the literature (cf. Tocqueville's description, cited in Stinchcombe 1978:34). Many promising political programs of progressive governments have failed as a result of this exacerbation of expectations and their impatient pursuit. (Compare also Davies's theory of revolutions.)

The third type of frustration refers to the relative inability of various latent groups to engage people in collective action. We have already discussed Olson's initial theory on the matter and the variations on it (such as Hechter's). The logic of the Olsonian PD presumably explains these difficulties and failures. Boudon seems to follow this logic, providing an example of the difficulties landowners would face in pursuing an effort to collectively pressure for the lowering of property taxes. We argued in Chapter 7 that this logic may be countered in several ways. Nonetheless, when special facilitating circumstances do not exist, it is difficult to bring about collective action in latent groups. This is especially so in the case of the existence of further inhibitory factors (such as dispersion in the case of "small peasants," according to Marx).

The last type of frustration is the most fundamental one. It describes and explains situations in which individual rational actions lead to unintended *and* unwanted consequences: suboptimal or catastrophic results for all the actors and unavoidable production of some collective bad. The most crucial cases could be mapped on an n-person PD game form. What is rational from the individual point of view, if pursued by n-persons, would produce a catastrophic effect for all; yet, unless a common agreement is reached for a collective solution, each individual's rational behavior cannot be altered because it is still maximizing and dominant. Examples abound: I will list a number of them to indicate the range and importance of this logic.

(i) Garrett Hardin has popularized this frustration logic by an analysis of "the tragedy of the commons" (1968): the short-run individualistic interests of any actor run counter to the long-run collective interests of the group and thus also of the individual itself. A peasant may add one cow to graze in the commons because this accords with his private interest; once all others add their cows the commons get overgrazed to the detriment of all. In this same way, seas get overfished, forests get overcut, and so on (Boulding 1981; Parfit 1985; Taylor 1987).

(ii) Pollution is another important case. Producers (e.g., of emissions which cause acid rain) and consumers (e.g., car drivers) pollute for convenience and to avoid various costs: The environment deteriorates to the detriment of all.

(iii) Falling rate of profit: Firms or capitalists have a common interest to get a higher price for their products; but they also have antagonistic interests relative to the amount of output each one of them will produce. Consider the OPEC cartel: Each member wants to produce and sell more oil at an agreed-upon higher price and at the same time wants the other members to produce and sell less, because if they also increase their production the price of oil will be forced down. All members get to be worse off as a result, although each one *had to* behave in that way. Marx analyzed in similar terms the condition of each capitalist (profit maximizing by minimizing labor costs) and the ultimate frustration of the overall capitalist class. Joan Robinson has noted this paradox: Every capitalist wants his or her workers to get a lower wage, but also wants the workers of the other capitalists to get a higher wage in order to allow them to buy products as well as to provide an edge in cost differentials. Every capitalist wants to hire more labor in periods of expanded production, and so all together drive the price of labor higher. Every capitalist, just when the price of labor gets higher, wants to introduce new technology in the production process to increase productivity; that means, according to Marx, that workers will be kicked out of work with the effect that the capitalist profits will decline as well. Finally, as capitalists appropriate ever more profits and as the composition of capital shifts, that is, as the proportion of "fixed" capital (especially, machines) to "variable" capital (essentially, wage labor) increases, capitalists get the unwanted result of the "falling rate of average profit" that becomes the central tendency in the capitalist system.

(iv) The "cobweb" problem: When a product is in demand and commands a premium price, new firms enter the market and established firms increase output. The collective result is overextension of production, higher inventories and, by necessity, lower prices. This often goes to the extreme of such lowered prices that many firms will lower or abandon production so that prices and production will form a base and begin to rise, and so forth. Business cycles are thus unavoidable in capitalist production. The process obeys the logic of chemical clocks (Nicolis 1987; Prigogine and Stengers 1984).

(v) The example of government requisitions is a similar case of type (d) frustration. Tilly (1973) discusses in detail the case of the French revolutionary government requisitioning grain from the peasantry in order to avoid city and army scarcities during the period of revolutionary mobilization. As a result of such actions or stated intentions, the peasants withheld considerable quantities of grain in the hope of higher prices and the scarcity became worse. Supermarkets undergo a similar process (hoarding) in cases of inclement weather conditions.

(vi) Financial panics: Rumors of a bank's troubles or of the deterioration of the banking system make rational people want to rush to their bank in order to withdraw their savings. The aggregate result brings each bank to a virtual state of insolvency. No one wants the failure of the banks but the aggregation of individual rational actions brings it about anyway.

(vii) Another good example is provided by Mamdani (1972) in his analysis of population control and family patterns in rural India. In the special conditions of class and caste structures parameterizing village life, having four sons is a necessity for any relatively poor family seeking better chances of survival. But four sons imply on the average having four daughters as well – and thus a family of ten. This certainly is bound to lead to a great population expansion that further impoverishes all peasant families – a Malthusian tragedy.

In each of these and other cases (noise, jaywalking, standing up to see better, jumping queues, cheating on taxes; see Parfit 1985, Schelling 1978) frustration arises as a result of rational action geared toward the achievement of short-term gains. As the number of instances indicates, the logic of frustration is at the foundation of social analysis.

(10) The logic of market (price) reversals

A regulative ideal for investors in the financial and commodities markets prompts them to always buy low and sell high; yet, in reality most investors do the exact opposite, that is, sell at market bottoms and buy at market tops. This certainly has to do with the overshooting effects of mood changes and the "herd instinct" exacerbating rapid trend following; so, savvy investors tend to follow a contrarian logic. But why is it that market reversals take place at certain "limit" price-levels? A good explanation is offered by those who follow *sentiment indicators* and/or *volume indicators* that tend to precede price changes. In both instances an underlying logic seems to exist that explains the whole set of phenomena. Consider, for example, sentiment. Analytical services (in the U.S., *Investors Intelligence,* Hadady's *Market Vane,* Infodata's *Institutional Investors Report*) provide statistics – now weekly reported in *Barron's* – reflecting the sentiment of advisors, commodities traders, and institutional investors relative to the markets. When the sentiment is excessively bullish, it indicates that all players (advisees, traders, and institutions) not only believe that the markets are moving higher but have invested their monies on the basis of this belief. As a result, the more bullish the sentiment, the more likely that most of the available liquid reserves have already been committed to the market and prices cannot move higher for lack of other buyers. At that time, of course, investors who have been committed in the market earlier and at lower prices usually realize that it is time to take a profit – selling exceeds buying, and prices fall to the detriment of the latecomers, of the weak hands, and of the wrongheaded speculators. A price reversal takes place. This situation resembles the now famous case of the instability of Bénard cells or the "iceberg effect": in both instances we see a catastrophic overturn (Boulding 1981; Prigogine and Stengers 1984).

Mood changes following a cyclical pattern (reminiscent of chemical clocks) can be explained accordingly. Analyzing the arms race and war involvement Richardson (1960; cf. Blalock 1969) sees two moods co-existing simultaneously in every population; (a) a willingness to engage in war and (b) an unwillingness to do so. The first rises as a result of perceived provocations, felt insecurities, or actual hostilities, the push of the arms race, and the mutual suspicions (the so-called defense coefficients). The second rises as the cost of war increases, budgetary constraints are visible, or other mitigating factors are felt (the so-called fatigue coefficients). In any case, these war moods alternate in a nation, going through reversals on the basis of the analytical mechanism described above. A very interesting account of the mood changes of the government leaders and the public in England between 1936 and 1939 – from an extreme antiwar to an extreme pro-war mood – has been recently given by Donald Cameron Watt (1989).

(11) Tipping rules (thresholds)

Tipping logics have been analyzed by Schelling, especially in reference to the issue of neighborhood transitions (Schelling 1971, 1978). Recall that these transitions involve the workings of some initial mechanism of selection of "likes" (above, no. 3) and subsequent amplification. Schelling discusses egocentric ("eight homes around my own") and sociocentric ("bounded neighborhood") models, implicating fixed or variable rules. A fixed rule (implying homogeneous population), for example, could be that any person will leave his or her neighborhood if four out of eight surrounding homes are occupied by people of another ethnicity or race. Such a move will tip the balance for several other homeowners in the vicinity and, as a result, a neighborhood transition may ensue. Or, it could be the case that each homeowner operates at distinct threshold levels of tolerance, say, $2/8$, $3/8$, $4/8$, or $5/8$ (in which case the population is heterogeneous, having different thresholds). Then the transition is more complicated and uncertain as to its speed or form (a veritable "cellular automaton").

Granovetter and others have pursued this program in further applications (1978; Granovetter and Soong 1986). Threshold logics have been seen at work in the diffusion of, say, information about contraceptives as well as in the production of collective action and the formation of solidaristic groups. The work of Oberschall (1980, 1986), Oliver (1984), Oliver, Marwell, and Teixeira (1985), among others, has shown the importance of different forms of production function and of heterogeneity in the emergence of collective outcomes (cf. Chapter 7).

Schelling's examples, seen from a particular perspective, seem to come close to what is nowadays called a *Conway game of life* (below, no. 24) or its variants (such as P. W. Anderson's "spin-glass" model of evolution resting on the twin characteristics of diversity/heterogeneity and viscosity). Tipping models have been also expressed in the formal conceptual machinery of bifurcation theory (Ruelle 1989) and of catastrophe theory (Thom 1984).

(12) Sorting rules

The logic of sorting applies as much to nature as to society, controlling for the specific characteristics of human purposive structures. The simpler notion of sorting implies a selective process of separating certain elements from others. This "sieve" model is exemplified in the work of membranes, the osmotic structure of which permits the selective passing through of some molecules and not others. Elimination of defective products from the production line, selection of college students, and personnel screening of job applicants rely on such simple sorting mechanisms. Here we can also put Schelling's simple puzzle of sorting people into two dining rooms (1978:184).

Another type of sorting involves classification by size. Calvin (1986) cites the example of the downward flow of the river in the Grand Canyon sorting the rocks by size. *Sorting by size* in humans is more complicated as it involves a constant process of matchings among individuals (a "compare-exchange" sorting algorithm). Sorting by performance (such as educational achievement) is even more complex and inefficient given the multiple sets rank-orderings involve and the Condorcet-Arrow paradoxes associated with it (for which see *voting*, no. 16, below).

Sorting to a meaning order is still another case. Consider as such the process of unscrambling a set of letters into a meaningful word, or the more complicated forms of cryptography. Here we see an important instance of what P. W. Anderson has called the structures of "informational strings." In this sense, order is a structure of *im*probability already achieved by natural selection at the macromolecular level. Certainly, the whole business of protein and nucleic acid structures is extremely significant for understanding the natural transition from (a) crystalline structure (molecules, crystals, solid objects) via (b) linear informational strings and their conformations (say, the DNA structure) to (c) nonlinear, information-processing complexes (such as the brain/mind, or society/culture).

Coming to purposive structures we find many sorting mechanisms involved in the processing of materials and people through organizations, a kind of *sorting of flow* in (a) queues, (b) stacks, and (c) priority queues. *Sorting in queues* involves "first come/first served" sorting mechanisms (implemented in deli sections of supermarkets, in routine visits to doctors, or in public bureaucracies). *Sorting in stacks* involves the different mechanism of moving newer rather than older stacked durable products (e.g., in warehouses). The more complicated case of *sorting in priority queues* is seen in the processes of the criminal justice system where, presumably, the most serious cases are dealt with on a priority basis; in police, fire, or ambulance responses to emergency calls; and in structural–strategic networking in military conspiracies, in which sorting coconspirators through the reassignment process to more strategic positions useful for an intended coup d'état is a priority (Kontopoulos 1976).

Sorting logics may be applicable at the microlevel as in the case of the "compare-exchange" form and, in general, all instances of "match-sort," but they are also applicable at the meso- and macrolevels. In effect, processes of intergenerational mobility are as much sorting processes as flow processes. At the macro-level one could, indeed, speak of class-sorting, especially in view of the noticed remarkable stability of the overall process.

(13) Matching rules

Matching could be viewed as a synonym for sorting but that would be a mistake. Matching involves not a simple sorting of incoming elements into and/or out of a data structure, but a mapping of a differentiated set of elements into another differentiated set. There are, of course, several types of matching processes. In certain cases we speak of the *matching of people to places,* as in Schelling's example of the game of musical chairs, in matchings of skiers and ski-lifts, or in restaurant sittings. In other cases we speak of the *matching of people and positions* in organizations, in job vacancy chains as analyzed by White (1970), or in the more commonsensical conception of structure; here also belong the algorithm of matching interns to training hospitals (Roth 1984) and the similar though nonalgorithmic processes of matching college applicants and colleges as a result of mutual preferences. The most obvious cases of this logic, needless to say, are those involving *matching people to one another,* in friendship circles, dating, marriage, or voluntary organizations of all sorts.

A number of important matching processes – possibly, the "true" matching processes – involve not a simple but a quite complicated mapping of elements. For example, in a simple matching/mapping process a Catholic archdiocese may assign priests to parishes without consideration of any preference by these priests or the parish representatives. In a more complex case of matching, such preferences held by the elements of both sets are thoroughly implicated. Consider the matching of interns to hospitals: The algorithm is to make the match according to or as close as possible to the preferences of both sides. This is a true matching. Much less efficiency and much more uncertainty exists in the process of accepting students, say, to graduate schools: Here the brightest candidates are accepted by many schools, make their pick according to their order of preference, and so a match is made; on the other hand, many of the schools that have accepted these candidates will learn later or presume that these candidates are not coming to them, and thus proceed to their next choices, who meanwhile are awaiting an answer. Or are they? It may be that the second-choice candidate have already accepted another offer (perhaps from middle-rank institutions) and are no longer available. In short, there is no efficient equilibrium of matched choices (stable pairings) here. In this context one could also consider the even more complicated case of marriage matching rules for individuals in a group when personal preference schedules are to be respected (Mortensen 1988; Sedgewick 1983). Those who have played, as I have for several Christmases now, a gift-picking "white elephant" game, will understand these biases quite easily. Stable matchings are produced only by imposing some closure rule to the game. Given such complications more pragmatic solutions have emerged, involving group partitions and quick-sorting or matching techniques.

Complicated matchings give rise to different logics as well. We will see below (*interfacing*, no. 15) that such forms are very useful in the analysis of the multidivisional organizations of our time.

(14) Traveling (graph traversing)

Try to unravel the so-called problem of the traveling salesman: given a set of cities, and known distances between any pair of them, find the shortest tour of these cities without a second visit to any of them. The problem, as far as I know, cannot be solved by any deterministic algorithm though it can be satisfactorily handled by nondeterministic ("guessing") algorithms in polynomial form. This particular problem seems to have enormous theoretical importance, although not many applications are visible at the present time.

On the other hand, relaxed traveling salesman-type puzzles, or traveling rules, are intuitively important in several cases. I will cite two for illustration: The first refers to the definition of a "niche" in ecological theory as "a multidimensional bundle of interactions" of a species with particular spaces, resources, and other populations in that environment. One key element in this conception is the characterization of interactions as "trips" to resources for the completion of important species tasks. We see the same conception in the second example, the case of urban ecologies, in which issues of "location" choice have been described as determined by the bundles of "trips" specifying the lifestyle preferences of individuals (work, shopping, cultural events, and so on). Certainly, more work is needed on the range of applications of this logic.

(15) The logic of interfacing

In the examples of marriage matching or graduate student placement we recognized a more complex pattern of matching with expressed preferences by elements of both sets. Now imagine an even more complex situation in which preferences are expressed *simultaneously* and in an iterated fashion; by that I mean that the elements of each set are, to a certain extent, *interdependent* on each other and thus the matchings of any pair of elements between sets (one from each set) is also interdependent on the other matchings of the same sort. I would call this structuring logic "interfacing," borrowing the term from the important work of Eccles and White (1986) on multidivisional firms.

Eccles and White consider the interrelationship between markets and present-day multidivisional firms as relying on such processes of interfacing. The new organizational formations are quite distinct from the traditional (centralized, even if vertically integrated) firm. The growth of multinationals, the experiments with conglomerate forms, and a certain fear of excessive "asset specificity" evident in older industries have pushed the contemporary corporations to multidivisional forms of a semidecentralized, federal, even feudal-like, character: Firms are now composed of divisions with positions in different markets and divisions consist of more or less compatible "profit centers," i.e., local production units, which operate relatively autonomously at their level. One can conceptualize the relationship in terms of a grid, one dimension of which lists the different multidivisional firms, and the other the different markets in a production system. Each point in the grid represents a profit center and each profit center interfaces one firm and one market.

What is important about this conception? Eccles and White point out the semiindependence of "profit centers" from the top echelons of the "firms": the profit centers have *local* discretionary power on production and day-to-day operation as well as the ability to become obstacles to the implementation of top-down decisions; the "firm," that is, top management, has *global* power; it allocates assets for research and development or for upscaling production and it even has the ultimate authority to dispose of any of its profit centers. This sharing of power, to whatever degree, is a new phenomenon associated with size, market knowledge, and local technologies of flexible production. The result is that firms and markets interface through these rather loosely connected intermediate structures in such a way that firms, profit centers and markets, though still interconnected, maintain a degree of relative autonomy vis-à-vis each other. The connection of one firm to another is now more **polymorphous** as it implicates various pathways through different profit centers and markets.

This is, of course, what heterarchy is all about. What the logic of interfacing presents is a system of interpenetrations of local and global levels that, like the relational system of letters, words, and sentences, cannot easily be considered as a hierarchical ordering (see Chapter 3).

The utility of this redescription of interfacing is immense. We need to apply it to other instances of interlevel connections and to actual historical contexts. Zeitlin (1981), for example, in his work on Chilean conflicts among different class segments, seems to refer to such (semi-autonomous) interfaces between agrarian sectors, urban sectors, and the state: patron–peon relations were indirectly interdependent with the dynamic prospects of the urban bourgeoisie. In this particular case the interfaces were with "impaired markets" that could not clear; hence a civil war ensued.

(16) The logic of voting

Perhaps one should speak of the logics of voting, since voting implicates many different processes and can be modeled in several different theoretical ways: single voting or logrolling, voting as group choice with or without the implication of true utility aggregation (collective preference), voting modeled as a market process with prices for votes, as a noncooperative game, or as an explicit cooperative game (Shubik 1982: 386). The elaboration of the famous "Condorcet Paradox" by Arrow and others (Arrow 1959; Elster 1985; Shubik 1982) has shown that there is no optimal aggregation procedure to translate individual votes into efficient public choices. Hence, "majority rule" is always suboptimal.

A special case is that described as the "selection of the second best," by a process of mutual elimination of the first choices. It has become progressively more significant to notice not only how many voters like a candidate but also how many dislike him or her as well; the latter indicates the limits of future conversion of votes and of coalition formation. In our cynical times, we easily form the opinion that the less specific candidates are in their platforms and statements, the more acceptable they are to the voters.

Blau's theory of structural differentiation rests on a similar, generalized notion of preference (1977). According to Blau, any person has a preference order of (a) interacting with likes, that is, in-group, (b) interacting with unlikes, that is, out-group, and last (c) not interacting at all. Blau's argument is a probabilistic rather than a rational choice one, but it has the same result: The larger the population size, the more the heterogeneity, the less the in-group interaction, and the more the options of interaction with the out-group, that is, the second-best choice.

All the previous logics may be considered to be primarily operative at the microlevel, that is, to be *micrologics of structuration,* though they may apply to the meso- and macrolevels as well. The defining characteristic is the fact that all micrologics involve individual actions or mappings of small numbers of individuals to other sets (positions, material objects, topologies). The next set of logics begin their application at the mesolevel and extend it to the macrolevel as well. Their defining characteristic is that they operate on a collection of individuals as a collective, or on a topology as a collective of points, and so on. At the macrolevel the collectives could be populations, or ecologies, or what have you. Let us turn now to these logics.

MESOLOGICS

(17) The logic of fluctuation

Those who are acquainted with recent developments in cosmological and physical theories will already know that fluctuation theories ("turbulence" due to radioactive decay, weak electric interactions, or quantum chaos) are posited *ab origine* as the preconditions of cosmic order out of chaos (Gleick 1987; Hawking 1988; Leggett 1987; Waldrop 1988). Furthermore, in recent advances in physics and dynamical systems (Nicolis 1987; Nicolis and Baras 1984; Prigogine and Stengers 1984), fluctuations have been analyzed as the grounds of self-organization. The postulated mathematical mechanisms are too complex to be summarized here and, quite honestly, as in the case of several other advanced mathematical conceptions, I am not confident I understand them fully myself. The realization of these mechanisms may also vary from domain to domain. However, the logic is definitely intriguing, and interested explorers will find many examples easily available.

Sociologists know Spencer's famous expression that evolution proceeds from a state of "incoherent homogeneity" to a state of "coherent heterogeneity." Lösch (1954), in his geo-economic work, has developed the Spencerian saying into an elaborate theory regarding the "instability of homogeneous economic activity," that is, of evenly spaced actors pursuing similar economic activities. Underlying fluctuations of kinetic energy, however conceived at the human level (motivation? opportunism? *fortuna* in the Machiavellian sense?), make some of these actors collide, thus increasing the dynamics of their combined system, changing its parameters and throwing it into new spins and bifurcation branches, into new phase transitions. The development of cities (cf. Allen's cited works), the differential growth of firms ensuing in oligopolies (Marx), and the emergence of new universes (Wolf 1988) have been analyzed in terms of this logic.

Calvin (1986), in his discussion of volcanoes and the movement of tectonic plates, provides some important insights on the mechanisms potentially involved. Tectonic plates are spread all around the planet forming its crust. But there are "weak spots" in the earth's crust beneath the drifting plates. There, kinetic fluctuations bring to the surface magma, squeezing it out of the crust as an extrusion. The result is volcanoes and volcanic islands that interrupt the homogeneity of the space and produce new topological structures (for example, a cluster of islands). This whole business is of the utmost concern for the new theories of thermodynamics. Whether or not kinetic energy flows are the results of "symmetry breaking" in nature (Anderson), of thermodynamic instabilities (Prigogine), or of some deeper cosmic fluctuation mechanisms in the void (Waldrop 1988) is beyond our context. It suffices that in each instance energy flows account for the breakdown of homogeneity and symmetry as a result of which a variety of "islands" are formed; the latter become new forces in structuration as we will see below (*differentiation*, no. 19, *islands*, no. 22, *cascades*, no. 29).

(18) The logic of nucleation (catalysis, autocatalysis)

Boulding (1981:49–50) has summarized the gist of the notion of catalysis or heterogeneous nucleation of objects and I will rely on and extend his presentation. A "catalyst" is an extraneous substance which becomes a "template" to a collection of molecules, individuals, or data, sorting them into separate positions and permitting them to interact. This implies that the template has a particular surface configuration or structure that facilitates sorting or interactions of the elements of a collection: It conveys information to molecules to nucleate about it (as in the case of catalyzed chemical reactions [cf. raindrops]); to individuals to nucleate in a particular space (early port or fort towns); or to data to be sorted and analyzed on the basis of the template (as in the case of computer software, for example, spreadsheet templates).

We use this logic in common parlance speaking of this person or group, or this event or situation, as being catalysts to something important. Stinchcombe (1978:46–7) insightfully speaks of "strategic groups" as such catalysts, citing Tocqueville's view of the nobility or Trotsky's analysis of the role of the army in the Russian Revolution as examples. In both cases, he says, these strategic groups played "the role of opening up or cutting off the sense of possibilities for the revolutionaries."

An *autocatalysis* involves the production of further quantities of an already catalyzed product by the powers of the critical mass already produced, endogenously so to speak. Notable is the case of protein production on the basis of such an autocatalytic mechanism (see emergence, Chapter 2). Here, the results of early nucleation may strengthen and further accelerate the process. This could be seen, for instance, in the simple example of jaywalking where, as Schelling said, the "safety in numbers" attitude of individuals produces more jaywalkers. In general, in every case of threshold processes (see Granovetter's work cited above in no. 11) autocatalysis seems to be at work.

(19) The logic of differentiation

We already know almost too much about this logic from the work of Adam Smith and Durkheim on the division of labor, Ricardo's notion of comparative advantage, and Blau's and Mayhew's more recent work (compare also Alexander and Colomy 1990b; Luhmann 1982a). The general argument is that, whether operating at the individual level or the collective level, an increase in the size of an interactive population will trigger (geographic, functional, or hierarchical) differentiation and its assortments ("As size increases, so does differentiation"; "The concentration of power is an increasing function of group size"; and so on). This is undoubtedly true at the phenomenological level and, perhaps, also at a somewhat deeper level, as Mayhew's baseline models imply (1974; Mayhew and Levinger 1976). Still, the explanation is not quite satisfactory in view of the fact that some other, even deeper mechanisms are applicable as well (the logics of fluctuation and allometric fission, the neoclassical calculation of comparative advantages, or the neo-institutional process of economizing on information and transaction costs). Tilly's criticisms of the view that "differentiation is a progressive master process" (1984) seem to me much to the point. Besides, Baker's work on commodity markets has shown quite clearly that the process of differentiation is not monotonic, as the received view would have it. In view of these important weaknesses, it is amazing that this logic as well as the sociological theory championing its paramount importance remain overvalued – a result of general complacency, I believe.

(20) The logic of allometry

The biological notion of allometry (cf. von Bertalanffy 1952) tells us that every particular structural organization has a theoretically optimum size below and above which it functions inefficiently. Boulding (1981: 214) suggests that this may have to do with the differential, subtle relations of length, area, and volume (*surface-to-volume ratios,* no. 31). In any case, the most important example one can cite is the economist's description of the benefits of "economies of scale" as well as of the dysfunctions of "diseconomies of scale." On the argument, scale of production implies lower costs of per unit production; this is so because, though the variable costs, such as labor and raw materials, are proportionate to the size of production, the fixed costs, such as infrastructural investments and machinery, decline per unit with increasing production. So a large corporation, other things being equal, is more efficient than a smaller one – up to an optimum size.

In diseconomies of scale an organization is too big to be efficient. Inefficiencies may emerge as a result of endogenous or of exogenous causes. Endogenous causes emerge primarily in large hierarchical structures from the sheer informational and practical distance of top managers from the details of day-to-day operations of production units at the bottom ("profit centers"). It is because of this reason that, as we have said above, contemporary multidivisional firms have moved toward a semidecentralized form of organization (Chandler; Eccles and White). In other cases, exogenous cases produce diseconomies of scale when a sudden increase in size disturbs the already existing balance of exchange and communication. Baker (1983, 1984) has shown that this is commonly the case in the "pits" of the commodity exchanges where a sudden shift of traders to a volatile pit transforms a clearing market into an impaired one. Baker derives from this several strong arguments against Blau's monotonic view of differentiation (according to which increasing size leads to increasing differentiation and scale of organization, *without upper limits,* as it were).

(21) The logic of allometric speciation

Somewhere between the optimal size and the point at which an allometric breakdown may occur we find the following situation: A population spills over beyond the core of an ecology or of a given societal structure. Suddenly, some people find themselves in the margins: hunters beyond hunting grounds, cultivators in low-yielding lands, species in harsher or rapidly changing environments, competitors pushed out of contested niches, and so on. Evolution is primarily operating at these margins of a metapopulation: here, the harsher the living, the higher the failure rate, but also the more significant the adaptive changes of the marginal populations. Speciation takes place in such allometric, "allopatric" (May 1982) environments (see Loren Eiseley's beautiful description [1967]). Novelty emerges in the periphery; new centers emerge at the margins of previous centers.

We can see the workings of this *logic of allometric speciation* in numerous social instances as well. Industries and entrepreneurs operating in the periphery of an established market often emerge as the producers of significant technical innovations (the Apple vs. IBM phenomenon).

We know, too, that many early medieval towns were port or fort sites
in the margins of a diffuse agricultural organization. Along these same
lines I have argued elsewhere (Kontopoulos 1980) that the growth of
the early bourgeois sectors took place in the margins of the feudal system; Barrington Moore (1966) also has cited the self-interested way in
which towns became "chartered" as free areas with the consent of the
monarchy. One may also suggest that, contrary to Marx, any new dominant class appears in the periphery or comes from the outside – new
ethnic groups as conquerors, the bourgeoisie in feudalism, the intellectuals in capitalism.

We will also see below (*islands,* no. 22, *cascades,* no. 29) that, given
allometric speciation, a process of takeover of the center by the periphery may develop as well.

(22) Islands and the logic of fission

Baker's studies (1983, 1984) describe how the breakdown of normal
patterns of market making led to the formation of many small residual
groups of interacting traders. Such "fissioning" is also evident in several
historical cases, notably the establishment of "colonies" by ancient city-
states: A part of the population moves away and establishes a daughter
colony elsewhere maintaining the basic pattern of smaller community
size. Barrington Moore, speaking of China's extensive past empire, has
described how warlords emerged in the periphery of the empire (see
no. 21, *allometric speciation*) and attempted to wrestle power away from
the central government; similar cases could be easily found in the his-
tories of the Roman and Byzantine empires. The possibility of fissioning
as a result of excessive size has been raised by Moore (1966) and Boulding (see especially 1981:322) in the case of India as well.

In larger societies, as has been argued since Montesquieu, the government has to be centralized or else the society will break down to
smaller regional entities. A weakened monarchy in a large feudal territory will be unable to counter the territorial claims of local or regional
principals: Germany before Bismarck's unification drive was broken
into a large number of smaller kingdoms, principalities, duchies, and
free cities exactly because of this. Weakness of the center (here, political center) allows the breakdown of the system (country) into smaller
units.

Fission leads to island structures. Evolutionary biologists are fond of
pointing out that "islands" are breeding laboratories of population adaptation and normal evolutionary development (Boorman and Levitt
1980; Calvin 1986; MacArthur and Wilson 1967). As a rule, "in-
tra-island" inbreeding is more successful than is "inter-island," which

explains the successful growth of initial founder populations in islands. There are numerous arguments claiming the importance of the Danakil peninsula (formerly island) in the story of the emergence of the human race (Calvin 1986:290–7; Morgan 1982). For the dynamic implications of this see below (*cascades*, no. 29).

(23) The logic of percolation

We noted earlier (*fluctuation,* no. 17) that homogeneous spaces are unstable and, sooner or later, give rise to heterogeneous formations (heterogeneity, islands, cities) due to some sort of inherent fluctuation of kinetic energy. Recall Calvin's example of the movement of tectonic plates as a result of underlying thermal changes: In a sense, lava flows through the perforated areas where the plates meet and its deposits account for the formation of islands or volcanic mountains. Lava percolates (perks) upward.

Percolation means, simply, forcefully passing through a porous medium, a permeable barrier, such as perforated plates or landscapes, coffee filters, or any other passable barrier. But this is in itself a complicated matter exhibiting significant formal properties elaborated by a special branch of mathematics called percolation theory (Stauffer 1979, 1985).

The simplest example used by mathematicians is that of a forest fire: How long does a forest fire take to either penetrate the forest or to be extinguished? Forests are not homogeneously thick. Trees are found in patches. Little woods are separated from each other. Mountains, rivers, and roads traversing a forest make it somewhat discontinuous. Suppose we superimpose on a forest a square lattice, or large two-dimensional array of small squares; it would appear that patches of trees occupy some of those squares while some other squares remain unoccupied. Clusters are formed in this lattice composed of neighboring squares that are thus occupied and separated from other such clusters by interposed nonoccupied squares. The whole terrain looks structured in peculiar ways as smaller clusters appear to connect to others producing strange configurations called "lattice animals." Now a fire starts and pretty soon each square in the lattice will be color-coded: green if the tree has not caught fire; red if it is currently burning; black for trees already burnt; and white for squares that are not occupied. As a fire starts in one occupied square the question arises as to what its next move will be and its overall course in the forest. Each square has four neighboring squares with which it shares a side. The fire can move randomly in any of these neighboring squares if they are occupied; if not, the move is stopped. These rules may, of course, change. Prevailing winds may determine that the sweep will go from top to bottom or from the top left to the bottom right of the lattice. Or it may be that the neighbor is affected only if two trees burn in a given square; or that the fire travels to the next-nearest neighbor if three or more trees are burning in that square. Variations of this sort will obviously affect the penetration speed, the range, and the multiple pathways or sweeps that compose the lifetime of a fire. These variations define the so-called percolation threshold of any particular forest fire.

The transition from one site in the forest to another can be simply conceived as a "shortest path" network transition (see above, *graph traversing*, no. 14) and be mapped as a "directed acyclic graph" (DAC) (see Sedgewick 1983); but this will not do justice to the complexity of the percolation problem. We can also conceptualize the problem as one of "diffusion" or "conduction" with the proviso that we speak of conductance in *random, differentiated* resistor networks and of difusion *in disordered media,* such as hydrogen atoms diffusing through solids, which are usually disordered structures. As in our forest lattice, not all sites are occupied or are penetrable. Like an "ant in a labyrinth," any moving force will find numerous dead ends.

Random percolation sweeps produce an (incipient) infinite cluster with a very complicated structure: Not a simple one-dimensional channel of occupied sites, say, as in the case of a maze; but a complicated structure looking like a complex urban network of different-capacity roads ("links"), crossing points ("nodes"), multiply connected parks or parking lots ("blobs"), dead ends ("dangling ends"), and the like. There then comes the first payoff. Percolation theory can help us remodel social mobility along structural rather than aggregative lines, an important project that, admittedly, cannot be properly addressed here. There is more value in the logic of percolation than in traditional diffusion, flow, or "transition matrix" models. Percolation logic, therefore, can help us understand better the "firing" or activation of social structures and the ensuing results, and give us exciting insights regarding their dynamics, much as the firing of the brain has inspired recent advances in neuroscience and cognitive science.

(24) The logic of Conway games of life (cellular automata)

In the percolation case transitions through disordered media are still conceptualized, primarily, in linear terms, or at least sequentially. The fire passes from tree to tree and cluster to cluster and traverses the forest possibly in many sweeps. The focus is, at each moment, local. What would happen, though, if the "local" result was dependent on the "context" of each square? (Recall here Schelling's work on neighborhood transitions, above, no. 3.) Conway (Poundstone 1984) produced simulated "games of life" in which survival in a square (cell) happens under a simple "context rule," such as, for example, that a cell survives if and only if two or three of the adjacent cells are occupied at each particular moment. If less than two neighboring cells are occupied or all four of them are occupied, then the particular cell under consideration does not survive. From the point of view of each cell, "context" is semilocal; but since for each neighboring cell there exist other neighboring cells twice-removed from the original one, the overall pattern changes according to the semiglobal configuration of the grid. Change then is *simultaneous and nonlinear,* not sequential and linear – though it is not purely global, given that the basic rule operates at the semilocal level.

The "game of life" is one type of two-dimensional cellular automaton (Kauffman 1984; Wolfram 1983a and b; see also Rucker 1987). Conway's analysis of this automaton has uncovered structures that exhibit coherent movements, reproduce themselves in specific life cycles, confront, modify, or destroy other configurations, and bring about several other intriguing results. In this context, see also P. W. Anderson's (1983) model of a complex cellular automaton which, like a Conway game, demonstrates dramatically the conditions, mechanisms, and phase-transitions leading toward the emergence of life.

What do all of these have to do with the social domain? For one thing, the "population ecology of organizations" could learn a trick or two from this linkage and simultaneous operation of local and global transitions. I will show in future work how Schelling's "neighborhood transition" models may be extended along these structural lines.

(25) The logic of fractals

Fractal geometry is a recent revolutionary advance in mathematics and in the way we view the world. The logic of fractals is quite simple in its basic rules. It rests on three basic posits: (a) *fractional dimensionality,* (b) *embeddedness,* and (c) *self-similarity* (Mandelbrot 1983; Stewart 1989). By fractional dimensionality, Mandelbrot, the originator of fractal geometry, means the existence of innumerable dimensions between the commonly assumed 0, 1, 2, 3, and so on, dimensions. Consider, for example, a snowflake. As Koch has shown, one can draw a snowflake starting from a triangle of equal sides, then adding at the middle third (⅓) of each side a smaller triangle one-third the size of the first. After four or five repetitions a snowflake (Koch snowflake) is formed. The length of the perimeter increases after each repetition by a factor of ⅓, tending toward infinity. The dimensionality of the snowflake's perimetry – something more than a line, yet less than a plane – is 1.2618, that is, a fractional dimension, or *fractal*. The second posit of fractal geometry refers to the idea of embeddedness. In the example of the snowflake, the structure involves a basic triangle and then more and more – and smaller and smaller – triangles of the same shape attached to each other, all embedded in the snowflake perimetry. This relates to the third posit in a straightforward manner: if we disregard size and focus on (structural or process) form we will immediately recognize the self-similar character of all the units. Each unit may be regular, as the cited triangle, or irregular, even randomly constructed; but the rule of self-similarity (or near self-similarity) will produce the fractal result. In any case, the same fractal rule of construction underlies all units as if it operates simultaneously at all levels. In the actual geometry of nature (coastlines, tree branches and leaves, galaxies, and so on) we have indeed discovered the remarkable fit of Mandelbrot's fractal set.

We can derive from this a number of results; for example, (a) it provides points to criticize reductionism, (b) lends support to the quest for basic rules of structuration operating simultaneously at all levels, and (c) illustrates the grounding of a proper theory of interlocked levels, and so on. But the primary issue is to find areas of direct application in the social domain, similar examples of structuration of actions and interactions. Mandelbrot himself was astonished by the near perfect fit to the fractal geometry of cotton prices since 1900, indicative of the fact that mood changes, even if random, represent a "regular irregularity," i.e., they appear irregular until their fractal dimensionality is discovered. There seem to exist many affine notions in market movements (Fibonacci points, Elliot waves) that are presumed to describe in a lawlike fashion complex mood oscillations; it will be useful someday to investigate their application to the cultural/mass psychological domain (amending the older work of Spengler and Sorokin).

(26) The logic of mixing and merging

Computer programmers often use sophisticated merging algorithms (two-way merging and multiway merging, recursive mergesort, polyphase merging, and a host of such notions) to handle a very complex problem. Consider only the merging of two rivers or any two flows and the vortices and turbulence they produce to intuitively realize that the problem is indeed complicated.

Complex and dynamical forms of merging or mixing have now become important in the new theories of nonequilibrium thermodynamics and of chaos. One cannot but be impressed by Prigogine's description of the workings of his group's so-called "Brusselator" (Prigogine and Stengers 1984). This is a machine in which thermal chemical reactions are permitted to be produced by manipulating the mixing or merging of different kinds and quantities of chemical elements and compounds in different sequences and under different thermal conditions. Prigogine and his associates have observed strange dynamic processes (stable equilibria, chemical clocks, bifurcation regimes, and chaotic behavior) that open the door to a new physics of broken symmetries and nonlinearities undreamed of before.

Now imagine merging different network connections. Edelman (1987) has provided a dynamic model of neural network connectivity in the brain along Darwinian selectionist lines. In this sense it will not be farfetched to use a similar language in the case of social network connectivity. We need to describe network connectivities as "shifting over time." This may be the result of the interaction of local strategies of agents and of semilocal dynamics. In this context, the work of Bourdieu on social and cultural capital strength, uses, and conversions (1977a, 1984, 1988; see also Coleman 1988) is promising, although still semilocal. We need to go one level up (to the semiglobal mechanisms) to make the effective transition to large-scale structures.

(27) The logic of waves

We have described earlier the logic of flows at a rather simple level. Yet, the "network flow problem" is much more complex. In a network of oil pipes, for instance, the flow is not always from source to destination; there are lateral flows and counterflows, in short, flows in the wrong direction, that complicate the matter considerably. Something of that sort happens in any type of waves as well. Waves are a special subtype of flows. They involve the simultaneous advance of mass at two different speeds, in two different directions, or in even more complex ways. Take the case of regular ocean waves. Here a faster flow and a slower flow interact to produce novel effects: faster wave and slower wave, cresting wave and receding wave, straight wave and sidewave or back-eddy, straight flowing waves and cascading whirls.

Where do we see applications of wave principles in the social domain? In crowd behavior in stadia, parades, demonstrations, festivals, subway exits, overcrowded trains, even elevators, or in war, where – as depicted in the *Iliad* – men fight "mixing their cries of victory and pain with their movements of pushing and being pushed."

Of considerable significance, too, is the type of phenomena composing *backlash politics*. At the root of any backlash situation we find wave processes: first two movements, one faster and the other slower; then reversal of directions. Consider the case of fascism: It seems to be the result of the reaction and countermobilization (properly used by the dominant classes) of the petty bourgeoisie against the mobilization and political visibility of the working class (Germani 1978). We agree in this instance that the slower economic growth and political representation of the petty bourgeoisie relative to the faster growth and (union and party) representation of the working class precipitated fascist organizations. On a smaller scale, in the United States we speak of the backlash reaction of lower-middle-class conservatism against the seeming gains of minorities (affirmative action, welfare state, housing projects). Here we see the differential waves at work. On the international scene, too, we keep hearing the talk about "fast locomotives" and "slow locomotives" of growth bearing on each other – a wave notion once more.

(28) The logic of branching/uncoupling

We spoke earlier of the processes of bifurcation as analyzed by Prigogine and mathematically elaborated by Ruelle. Bifurcation may also be seen as based on fractal rules as the famous Bethe lattice (or Cayley tree) illustrates (Gleick 1987). Boulding also suggests that bifurcations may emerge as a result of heterogeneous nucleation; such as when a church spins off a college that becomes independent; but this argument, as any matter-of-fact argument about differentiation as an inexorable process, is relatively vague. Branching may have a mathematical form in nature but uncoupling in the domain of social phenomena seems either more purposive or more chaotic.

Giddens, speaking of "structural principles," names three of them: the relating of tradition and kinship in tribal societies; the relating of urban areas to their rural hinterlands in class-divided societies; and, finally, "the disembedding, yet interconnecting, of state and economic institutions" in the class capitalist societies (Giddens 1984:181–3). However, there is no discussion of any specific mechanism involved in this structuration process. Marx, in *German Ideology*, previously defined these divisions of urban from rural areas, mental from manual labor, and economic institutions from the state and the older corporatist order.

A special notion of uncoupling is the following. Imagine the following fractal rule: Draw a certain line; then delete the middle third section of that line; continue deleting the third middle sections of the leftover parts one and three. The result is what is known as Cantor's set. Now the social application: Imagine the branching of the bourgeoisie out of the old feudal system; as the uncoupling proceeds, middle grounds, such as the traditional gentry, are weakened or eliminated. Then it happens again, when the bourgeoisie fights for power in its revolution and cries

"We the People"; then uncouples itself from the lower classes to begin its rule. From the first (populist) to the second (Gironde) wave of the French Revolution, and from the February struggle (with the populace) to the May–June struggle (against the populace) in the Revolution of 1848, we see the uncoupling and deletion of the middle ground (Marx, *Eighteenth Brumaire*).

(29) The logic of cascades

Cascades appear thoroughly irregular to us and yet they are the products of a mathematical process much like the one described above for the creation of a Cantor set.

In a paper published in *Nature,* Argoul et al. (338[1989]:51–53) provided the first experimental geometric evidence for the fractal composition of cascades. As summarized by Ian Stewart in the same issue, if a drop of ink is placed in a jar of water, it creates a vortex ring as it falls. The ring acquires corners, from which smaller vortices break off, and so on. Each stage is geometrically similar to the previous one, but on a smaller scale. After many subdivisions the total energy is reduced by viscous friction, slowly in the beginning, but more rapidly later as the sizes of the vortices decrease, until they are dampened out by viscosity. The cascade principle, then, is based on fractal subdivisions and the dampening effects of friction and viscosity, a coupling of mathematical and physical rules. The process starts with subdivisions and ends with "self-erasure."

The first application of the logic of cascades that I am aware of is that of Boorman and Levitt (1980; cf. 1987) in their work on the paths to sociality. They sum their proposals and research in the following three statements: (1) In the beginning, social evolution is blocked by a selection threshold B_{crit}, rising in a randomly mixing population and inhibiting reciprocity selection, i.e., the emergence of cooperative traits; (2) however, this barrier is not absolute and the cascade principle becomes a recourse for "crossing" the barrier in the presence of an appropriately subdivided population; (3) finally, as the boundaries between subpopulations may themselves be erased in the course of the evolutionary sequence (self-erasure), a limit is put on the cascade principle. The cascade principle itself is conceptualized by the authors as follows: "In the presence of an appropriately viscous population structure (obstacles to random mixing), a local concentration or "pocket" of the social gene may be able to spread out and capture a much larger metapopulation, even though the initial fraction of social genes may be far below B_{crit} in the species gene pool as a whole" (1980: 339). The key words here are "an appropriately viscous population structure," that is, an optimally subdivided population forming "pockets" or islands. The *structure* seems extremely close to Anderson's notion of the "spin glass" which also allows for an optimal diversity and viscosity for the evolutionary process to begin; the *process* seems close to the "percolation" process.

Can it be that the growth of urban "islands" and industrial "pockets" have played a similar role in the emergence of the modern capitalist system? As one reads studies of urban growth (compare, for example, the cited work of Peter Allen) and industrial development, the strong forces of hegemonic radiation and attraction exerted on the countryside are plainly evident (cf. Moore [1966] on the adoption of bourgeois ideas of entrepreneurship by the British gentry).

(30) Packing rules

Packing may mean: (a) efficient packaging so as to ensure maximum storage; (b) efficient packing in the sense of maximum value as in the tricky problem of dynamic programming called the "knapsack problem" (Sedgewick 1983), or in preparing for backpacking (Dyke 1979); (c) packing optimal to a functional task, such as the hexagonal cross-sections of honeycombs that are optimal for a society of bees (Calvin 1986:360); it may even be (d) a metonymy for the packing of space itself as Einstein envisioned it (see Wheeler's felicitous description cited in Calvin [ibid.: 399]).

Quantity packing is what we usually do when we place our food in the refrigerator or in cabinets, our clothes in drawers, our traveling necessities in luggage, or ourselves in crowded buses or elevators; *value packing* and *functional packing* are more complex. In any case, packing may produce exquisite crystallinity (P. W. Anderson 1983; Venkataraman et al. 1989), which is the exemplary form of static structuring. Other times it produces functional perfection as in the case of the honeycomb hexagons, produced inevitably by "the mathematical law governing the behavior of spheres packed together at even or random pressure from all angles" (Calvin 1986: 360). In still other instances, such as the columnar and hypercolumnar organization of the cortex, packing seems to operate on the principle of "degeneracy" (redundancy): there is high packing density and more neurons configuring redundantly the neural/mental message (Edelman and Mountcastle, 1978). In each case, different packing premises and rules give different packing structures.

For an intuitive example of the application of packing principles in society consider the packing of populations that takes place in the "built environment" of the cities – urban designs, home styles, places of aggregation, traffic systems (Allen 1981b, 1983; Hägerstrand 1968). Organizational packing, packing of military units especially in war theaters, classroom packing, and hospital packing are some other examples. Goffman's work on public spaces is replete with references to packing principles.

(31) Surface-to-volume ratios

Stephen Jay Gould (1977:171–98) has thoroughly analyzed the importance of the relationship between size and shape, perimeter to area, and surface to volume. He points out that, simply by growing larger, "any object will suffer continual decrease in relative surface area when its shape remains unchanged." This happens because volume grows more rapidly than surface (volume increases as a cube of length, while area increases only as the square of length). In living creatures this may lead to the formation of internal process (lungs) or structure (skeleton) – organs which sustain the organism in spite of a relatively unfavorable volume-to-surface ratio. This line of investigation gets us to *structural differentiation,* one of several available options.

Consider now the human brain, this exquisite instrument of intelligence: the brain is pleated so much so as to increase the surface-to-volume ratio and maximize its exposure to external stimuli and parallel linkages. Something similar seems to happen in the case of DNA and protein folding (helices, b-sheets, and so forth) where secondary connectivities are maximized not by compactness (as in the case of crystalline structures) but by meanderings and other supporting connectivities. This is a different sort of *structural heterarchical extension.* It seems to me that "weak ties," as described by Granovetter (1973), are of this variety: They are informationally rich exactly because they increase the surface of human connections to a larger set of outsiders; surface (weak ties) far exceeds volume (strong ties). But it is not only humans who increase their surface connectivities. Trees do the same by extending their branches in all directions and growing leaves (high surface-to-volume ratio) to be able to photosynthesize.

(32) Rules of unpacking (partitioning)

A variety of logics implicate some form or another of efficient partitioning. We saw above that extension of surface may be done in several ways, some involving continuous, others discontinuous extension. Partitioning is always related to the latter. In some instances partitioning is done by fractal rules, as in the case of the Cayley tree (Bethe lattice) or of tree branching. In other instances the process involves more complicated, diverse rather than self-similar operations.

In sociology, partitions have been primarily used in the study of networks. The "blockmodeling" method has been quite successful in illuminating the problem of comparing structural positions across networks and organizations. Yet, as we have seen, this program of unpacking structure has not advanced much beyond the initial step to help us understand better the nature of larger structures. The shift from blockmodel partitions of smaller networks to larger interfaces among firms and markets marks a certain discontinuity in this constructionist program; or so it seems to me. In operations research and decision theory similar thorny problems are said to exist as a result of the difficulty of relating deterministic and nondeterministic polynomial-time algorithms (while the "divide-and-conquer" methods seem pragmatically satisfying). For structuralists in sociology the unpacking/partitioning logic still remains "the philosopher's stone."

(33) The logic of informational packing

Informational packing is a distinct and superior form of packing. It implies "coding" as well as "transmittability." Now it could be maintained that any structure, including crystalline structures, involves coding in one sense or another; students of thermodynamics, who treat "entropy" as hard currency, have long maintained that any structure, any orderly arrangement, implies "improbability" and gives in the quantitative value of its so-called "negative entropy" a value number of structure: Order is the reverse of entropy. Other scholars, more interested in informational development and evolutionary theory, have argued that structure is the informational repository of its history, a stepwise description of Markovian transitions; as such, it involves not only "improbability" but also "historicity" and "irreversibility" as Prigogine has put it. At a still more advanced level we can make the further distinction of certain structures which are not only (a) improbable and (b) historical and irreversible, but also (c) instructional: that is, structures that become codes for meaningful informational transmissions and interactions (coding for messages and meanings) rather than simple codes of an improbable and/or irreversible state (on these issues see Anderson and Stein 1984; Bennett 1986; J. Nicolis 1986; Prigogine and Stengers 1984).

The primary form of informational packing is, thus, the *sequential ordering of elements into informational strings.* RNA, DNA, protein – in fact, every macromolecular (polypeptide, polynuclease, even oligopeptide) structure is a case of informational packing. Informational packing in the form of distributed systems takes place in neural networks too (J. Anderson 1983b; Edelman and Reeke 1982; Hopfield

1982; Kohonen 1978). In human terms, of course, language is the primary system of information packing. With the use of language we also develop collective memory systems and more complex forms of packing (dictionaries, encyclopedias, databases, and so on).

(34) The logic of parsing

Parsing is the operation of recognizing information-rich sequences (languages, computer programs, other codes) and the subsequent attempt to decompose their structure into a form suitable for deeper understanding and compositional manipulation. Parsing plays an important role in understanding and translating natural languages, in the recognition of particular case relations (agent of, goal of) and grammatical functions (subject of, object of), in constructing and learning high-level computer languages intuitively closed to humans, or in translating such "high-level" languages into "low-level" assembly or machine languages suitable for machine execution. A parser functions (a) in the production of parse trees subdividing any informational string, such as a sentence, into fundamental grammatical forms and, then, (b) in the selection of these informational strings as acceptable products within a meaning structure.

We can see the work of parsing in the selection roles or positions and, subsequently, of social actors to fit these roles or positions. Propp (1968), for example, did a formalist parsing of folktales into such a "parsing tree." Structuring functional roles in the theater, in the family, in kinship groups, and so on, is a form of such parsing. "Tracking" candidates, mainly through schooling, to emerge in such a way as to more or less fit a structure of distributed positions is another. Parsing people and positions sociometrically or, perhaps, even by blockmodel techniques may be still another.

MACROLOGICS

Logics 17–34 discussed above seem to apply more appropriately at the mesolevel of social phenomena: They do not start from individual action (as the micrologics do) nor do they primarily refer to large-scale structures (as the following macrologics do). This categorization, I admit, is a bit vague and needs conceptual elaboration in the future. For the time being, however, it serves the purpose of changing our focus in terms of scale. I will discuss six mechanisms as examples of macrologics. The focus here shifts to the production of the global characteristics of a structural system, which then appears to us, in some fuzzy sense, as *the* social structure.

(35) The logic of swamping

Let us begin by citing the case of swamping at the level of species reproduction, the so-called r-selection: species under r-selection have high birth rates and high infant mortality. Reproductive swamping permits survival under conditions of extreme selection at the critical postnatal stage. We have also seen another form of swamping in our discussion of the packing density of the cortex. Such forms of swamping may be the results of the Law of Large Numbers (LLN), another version of the size-related algorithms; but we need to investigate the particular responses and ensuing structural patterns generated by a system under such conditions. The most interesting form of swamping involves both redundancy and degeneracy, as a special subcase of the outcomes of large numbers.

The most telling example of a redundant and degenerate swamping is the brain. In the brain, redundancy implies the availability of myriads of neurons dedicated to particular sets of mental functions. That means that a large number of "dumb" elements networking together can produce some "smart" mental results, such as memory, vision, or calculations; they work as a "loose committee" (Calvin 1986), as a "society of mind" (Minsky 1985), as a "republic of schemata" (E. O. Wilson 1978), as a "repertoire" (Edelman 1987), as an organized "neural network" (Hopfield 1982; Hopfield and Tank 1986). On the other hand, degeneracy signifies the parallel and distributed ways these neurons are connected to map complex mental events and processes. For instance, vision is accomplished by the cooperation of simple, complex, and hypercomplex cells organized in the primary visual cortex and, *more than a dozen secondary visual centers* outside the primary visual cortex. All these centers, sequencers and parallel processors (J. Anderson 1980, 1983; Calvin 1986; Edelman 1987, 1989; Kohonen 1978, 1984; Marr 1982; Reeke and Edelman 1984), operate simultaneously to produce the exquisite forms of human vision. Each cell has a limited, imprecise, and overlapping role but the swamped "parallel distributed processing" produces coherent and precise results. The structural system that emerges is a complicated, multilevel, multidimensional neural network – a heterarchical structure.

(36) Rules of pruning

Every so often librarians go about reviewing their inventories of books in the stacks. They then take out books that have been abused by extensive use and other books with dated materials. They analogically call this the "weeding" process. Natural selection and human organization share these basic rules of pruning or weeding. Ebbesson (1984) has pointed out that neuronal connections in the brain are wired up widely at first, then get selectively reorganized to define the functioning human brain. Edelman's more detailed work (1987) discriminates the stages of this pruning process at the levels of the "primary repertoire" of genetically unfolding wild connections, of the "secondary repertoire" of developmental pruning and, finally, of the postnatal pruning lasting throughout an organism's life. Edelman considers these prunings the results of a competitive process among neurons and their columnar and hypercolumnar organizations.

Pruning sharpens performance but, of course, does not produce the effects "swamping" has on collective precision in mental functioning. However, pruning eliminates weaker connections, strengthens the already strong ones, and permits their further extensions. How exactly this is done is not entirely clear, although the work of Edelman on "self-adhesive molecules" may be seminal in this respect. On the more formal level, several algorithms of pruning a database instead of doing exhaustive searches have been suggested (removing symmetries, cutting labyrinthine paths, producing minimal spanning trees) but this type of work has not provided any better insights.

Competitive pruning of connections, needless to say, are very common in systems of social interaction and in extended networks of weak ties: forgetting friends, losing lovers, making new, stronger connections. The whole business of developing and deploying "social capital" (cf. Bourdieu, Coleman) is built around this strengthening of winning hands and pruning losing ones. Eccles and White (1986) have discussed the way in which top managers decide to strengthen or prune various profit centers they control: they certainly sell off the "dogs" (i.e., profit centers with small market share in markets with low growth rates) and strengthen the "stars" (i.e., profit centers with significant presence in high growth markets). "Cash cows" (providing profits without further capital outlays) are maintained as such and "question marks" (small exposure to high growth markets) give them many a headache.

(37) Eco-logics: the entropic form

Simple Malthusian ecological models conceive of an ecosystem as an entropic sink of sorts. Recall the strict Malthusian rule: The growth of human population far exceeds the growth of food and, as a result, natural pruning takes place – the starvation of the weak. Wynne-Edwards, since his early studies, has shown that, given increased quantities of food and more space, a species such as *drosophila* will increase its population; but, as the food supply decreases, the species will begin to lose members and genetically adapt to a new level of reproduction. This is not exactly the same with humans. Certainly, as population increases and food supplies decrease, there will be a Malthusian effect, *other things being equal.* When a hunting group increases in size, animals are killed at a faster rate, and fruits, nuts, and vegetables are consumed faster too; it is only a matter of time before the hunting and gathering population will feel the impact. Yet, as we all know, there are still quite a few options – nomadism, increasing attention to cultivation, reorganization of production, new technologies – open to the inventive human group. We do have starvation in Eritrea, Sudan, or Bangladesh, to be sure, for which we must all feel ashamed; and we do have a significant number of self-produced "tragedies of the commons" (see above, *frustration,* no. 9). Nonetheless, somehow, in spite of the increasing risks, the global human ecology is not necessarily a "sink," at least not yet; entropic eco-logics act, therefore, as limit cases for the human species.

(38) Eco-logics: the heterarchical form

We have already discussed this logic quite extensively, so not too many words are necessary here. Briefly put, a controversy has erupted among evolutionary biologists on the so-called loci of selection, and the current wisdom is that selection takes place at various levels (individual, kin, sib, deme, and so on). But, if this is so, an ecology is not only composed of many species but of many levels as well, levels which maintain a relative autonomy from each other by virtue of the independent selection forces acting on them. Different ecological relations obtain among as well as within species, recursively embedded at different levels and implicated in the overall ecological game of life. This is obviously a heterarchical notion of an ecology. The sociological form this takes has been presented in Chapters 11–14.

(39) Totalizing logics

The logic of totalizing is arguably the most important macrologic in human societies. Although one (a) may readily accept that entropic eco-logics fall easy prey to the functionalist fallacy (Bhaskar 1978b; Elster 1985, 1986a; Habermas 1989) and (b) cultivate an element of doubt vis-à-vis heterarchical eco-logics and sophisticated forms of connectionism (Ballard 1986; Edelman 1987, 1989; McClelland et al. 1987; Pylyshyn 1984; Reeke and Edelman 1985; Rumelhart et al. 1986), it is plainly the case that the totalizing logic addresses the issues of sociohistorical structuration and transformation in a straightforward manner. By totalizing logic I do not mean to imply something already denoted by the notion of "system" or "system-structure" as evidenced in the work of systems theories, structural functionalists, or French structuralists. I treat "totalizing" as a process resulting from particular "projects" of politico-economic and/or politico-cultural entrepreneurs. Therefore, my sense of the term implies a *process of totalizing without totalization,* something compatible with the Hegelian–Marxist, Nietzschean, neopragmatist conceptualizations dominant in current philosophy. I have presented several totalizing logics (those of Capitalism, Bureaucracy (State), the Professional Class, and Patriarchy) in Chapters 13 and 14. Totalizing logics may start at the mesolevel (even if quasi-local) of social phenomena (for example, the strategies of transition from family work, to the employment of the work of others, and then to slavery or serfdom; or the strategies of professional institution building described by Foucault); but they apply most particularly at the macrolevel (quasi-global and global) where the organization of work on a grand scale, the proactive control of the state, and cultural hegemony inspire persistent totalizing efforts on behalf of the ascending classes or categorial strata.

(40) The logic of metaptations

Sidesteps in evolution may sometimes lead to "jumps into hyperstates" (Calvin) or "quantum leaps" (L. Hsu 1984). The result is the emergence of a new trait that makes possible the reorganization of the organism or of life around it and, therefore, the emergence of more special traits. These have been called "metaptations" (Vrba and Eldredge 1984). One can cite a series of such metaptations, from the first composition of macromolecular informational strings, to RNA and DNA replicative codes, the monocellular formation of life, speciation, the brain, the growth of sociality in hominids, the emergence of "symbols" out of "signals," and in the human case, the development of language and culture, that is, the intensional and intentional world. We usually speak also of metaptations in the case of major catalytic events in our history, such as the Neolithic evolution, the development of writing, or significant transitions in science, technology, and systems of production and government. Metaptations in any of these cases implies the emergence of some peculiar novelty that catalyzes the preexisting order of things and sets forth a new order, be it a paradigmatic shift in science, a technological transformation of warfare or of production, or what have you. One needs to know more about (a) the conditions of emergence of such metaptations, (b) their relations with the previous structure of things, and (c) their transforming influence on that structure.

As one looks back on this inventory of the logics – algorithms, mechanisms, or modal principles of structuration – bear in mind our initial caveat: The list is not exhaustive, the logics are complementary rather than exclusive, and indeed it may be that several of them may be conceptually parasitic or logically reducible to one or more of the other logics. There is no closure. Furthermore, the applications are not always visible, or central to structuration, or outright influential in sociology. The task is not complete. What I present here is a preliminary compilation of such logics in need of further analytical purification, theoretical extension, and paradigmatic corroboration. Much more is to be done in forthcoming works, now that this initial effort has been presented. As Lakatos would have said, charity and time must be extended to any beginning research program.

Glossary

adaptation: refers to properties of organisms resulting from past instances of natural selection; such properties are acquired as solutions to given problems in local ecosystems.

affirming the consequent (fallacy of): a logical fallacy reversing the *modus ponens* form into an invalid form of the following structure: if *p*, then *q; q*, therefore *p*. The correct *modus ponens* form is: if *p*, then *q; p*, therefore *q*. An effort to salvage the "fallacy" was made by G. A. Cohen in terms of a theory of dispositional facts.

allometry: the presumed principle that any particular kind of structure tends to have an optimum size; the further below or above that optimum size a structure gets the more difficult its function, especially above that optimum size; the structure tends to break into various smaller structures available for allometric speciation (Boorman, Levitt), cellular automata-like transitions (Baker), or other such nonlinear processes.

allopatric: living in different regions; populations or species are said to be allopatric when occupying local ecosystems separated from each other. Allopatric speciation, that is, new species formation, may result from such conditions. (See also Appendix nos. 22 and 29 – the island model, cascades.)

allostery: stepwise synthesis of a metabolite with the participation of a number of enzymes, often ending with an allosteric inhibitor which stops the process.

aptation (Gould and Vrba): the capacity of organisms or species to relate aptly to the continuing features of their environment regardless of the origins of that capacity. Aptation includes both adaptation and exaptation.

attractor: a topological point or small region that appears as the source of local (local attractor) or global (global attractor) stability. Chaotic attractors exhibit asymptotic stability with respect to nearby initial conditions and instability of motion on the attracting set itself, that is, they show a movement away fron their basin and in random directions as well as a continuous return near their source.

authoritative supersession: higher-level autonomization and downward control; see **control hierarchy.**

autocatalysis: the process of changing the speed of a chemical reaction by crossing particular thresholds in quantity or energy of the selfsame catalyzing substance.

autopoesis, autopoetic processes: the process of self-emergence of higher levels of phenomena by nonlinear mechanisms (fluctuations, drift, mutational substitutions, thermodynamic branching) at lower and faster dynamics, properly aggregated, driven, frustrated, or constrained.

behaviorism, logical or philosophical: holds that "mental talk" is simply "behavior talk." Any sentence describing a mental state can be translated, without loss of meaning, into one or more sentences about observable behavior within observable contexts. Untranslatable "mental" statements are simply greatly ambiguous – i.e., nonsense.

Beluzov-Zhabotinsky reaction (also transcribed as Belousov-Zhabatinski): a chemical reaction in which chemical waves, chemical clocks, and even chemical chaos were observed. A reaction thought to demonstrate processes corroborating the new nonequilibrium thermodynamics. Cited consistently by Prigogine as an example of dynamic process. In brief, when quantities of elements, insertion sequences, and thermal energy were varied, strange processes and phenomena were observed.

Bénard instability, Bénard cells: instability resulting from convection; see also **percolation;** when a fluid is heated from below and the temperature at the bottom is raised quickly, a threshold is crossed and the liquid becomes unstable, giving rise to chemical waves, new hexagonal structures, and chaos. Similar examples in meteorology, forest fires, lasers, and ferromagnets bring to light the transition from local to global instability.

bifurcation branches: possible paths in nonlinear dynamical processes selected randomly by a driven system as if by a choice or jump; they may implicate the influence of different attractors.

bilateral monopoly: a two-person game-theoretical situation in which each agent controls a distinct resource; for example, Capital controls investments (job production) and Labor controls wages (labor cost, rate of profit).

blockmodeling: a mathematical method (algorithms) aggregating individuals who are in structurally equivalent positions (or nearly so) because of their similarity of ties to third parties (i.e., because they have the same local network pattern). Properly construed, such aggregations give rise to categorial identities (the "in-itself" ground of collective agencies, such as a class-in-itself).

boundary conditions: the values of various global characteristics of a system; the magnitudes of such values appear as parameters describing relationships obtaining within a given system; boundary conditions may also be described as higher-level constraints imposed on and restricting lower-level processes with high frequencies (or fast dynamics).

bounded rationality: agents experience limits in formulating and solving complex problems and in processing information, yet they otherwise remain "intendedly rational."

Bourbaki: a group of French mathematicians working under this pseudonym; they have classified mathematical systems into three categories: (a) group-like structures, (b) linear series, and (c) topological systems.

bridge problem (Lindenberg): formulating propositions about the influence of social conditions on individual action.

cascades: nonlinear systems of propagation exhibiting both instabilities and bifurcation regimes; involved in physical cascading systems (flows), genetic and ecological transitions, and potentially in social network propagations; may be thought of as waves of forward propagation; for example, ion chain propagation in an electrical discharge; in population genetics, takeover cascades explain how "a genetic trait facing frequency-distribution selection with a threshold may take over a large viscous population even though starting at a sub-threshold initial frequency" (Boorman and Levitt). In sociology cascades may help us move from (static, additive) "aggregations" to (dynamic, multiplicative) "propagations" of networks. (See Appendix no. 29.)

cascading hierarchy, cascading hierarchical pathway: a hierarchy of constraints superimposed on each other and defining a level structure (in structural emergence) or a developmental-morphological path (in ontogenesis).

catalysis: the process of starting or changing the speed of a chemical reaction by the presence of another substance that acts as a catalyst (see also **auto-catalysis, cross-catalysis**).

catastrophe theory: an earlier topological transcription of chaotic processes (Thom).

cellular automata: bounded structures of cells, each of which can assume a limited number of states; at each time interval, these states change simultaneously according to "transition rules" that govern the passage of information to a cell from a specified set of "neighbors." Therefore, individual behavior becomes affected by values attained in neighboring cells, and the result is a highly unstable structural system exhibiting many phase transitions. Examples: the famous Conway Game of Life as well as neighborhood transitions (Schelling).

chaos, chaotic processes: nonlinear, aperiodic processes in dynamical, not strictly deterministic systems; described by nonlinear orbits, bifurcations, and semiglobal basins of attractors; chaotic systems appear as systems under constant and severe random shocks exhibiting abrupt transitions. In such systems, stability conditions, identity-defining properties, and functional characteristics are too fragile to be of any significant analytical value; in this sense, chaos renders obsolete the older vocabularies of function, adaptation, homeostasis, structural stability, and the like.

chaotic attractor: an object, space position, or "basin" which attracts chaotically (nonlinearly) given moving objects or behaviors.

chunking: summation of a number of collective features which on lower levels are seen as separate; for example, a TV picture "chunked" out of dots, or a computer-generated dot-matrix printed image made of distributed points; one no longer sees the many dots but instead the image or picture.

closure: given boundary conditions, a system is said to have a closure property, such that interactions within the system (i.e., between its parts) are more (or more dynamic) than interactions with elements outside the boundary. Systems have degrees of closure: they are always at least partially open.

co-evolution: evolution of two species or populations in conjunction with each other, that is, by active reciprocal modification of the characteristics of the co-evolving groups; each species or population is an important active part of the other's environment, exerting some significant selective pressure. Example: bees and flowering plants.

community (biological): the set of all species having populations in any given local ecosystem; they are presumed to have some important ecological relations (several-to-several, at least).

complexity: complication in structure and dynamics obtaining in more inclusive systems; usually, the case involves emergent structures along constructionist, heterarchical, or hierarchical lines; in any case, complexity involves interaction of dynamics with constraints (Pattee), historicity (Prigogine), informational specificity (Atlan, Gatlin, Küppers), thermodynamic branching (Wicken), and so on.

compositional hierarchy: a hierarchy of parts and wholes; implies perfect modularity; affords structural reduction if perfect or, at least, nearly complete decomposition (Ando, Simon).

conical clan: intracommunal relations of social rank defined in terms of genealogical proximity or distance from the divine or an elect ancestor. Potential antecedent of theocracies.

connectionism: the view that higher-order phenomena are due to increasing volumes of elements and the density of their connections. Simple connectionism has only an aggregative notion of the connections obtaining (Galton on brain connections, Durkheim, and Blau, on social connections). Sophisticated connectionism focuses on the structure itself; thus, hierarchical connectionism emphasizes the semi-localization of mental faculties in brain regions, while heterarchical connectionism, based on the recent advances in cellular automata and neural networks, emphasizes the partial, interlevel connectivity of the brain and (in the present work) of social structure.

constraint: a restriction or limitation imposed upon some process or the products of such process; a limitation applied on the possibility space of a phenomenon; a restriction of the degrees of freedom of lower-level dynamics; a restriction or regulation of microscopic processes by collective states; a restriction of the expression of possibilities associated with any microstate, microentity, or microprocess; imposition of admissibility rules on microentities exapting (lifting out) a new "bounded" system of value.

constraint hierarchy: a level structure formed by the superimposition of constraints (contrast **control hierarchy**).

constructionism: a synonym of **compositionism;** it is used in the present context to denote the strategy or Logic of deriving – mostly experimentally – complex forms of organization at higher levels of phenomena out of particular lower-level interactants, but in a discontinuous, nonlinear, emergent way.

context: a particular sort of boundary or constraint with the power to regulate, restrict, or influence the forms and/or results of processes taking place within it.

control hierarchy: a level structure formed by the superimposition of constraints *and* exhibiting "downward causation" or control (contrast **constraint hierarchy**).

conventional/institutional predicates: predicates specific to institutional or cultural forms, irreducible to individual or interactional characteristics.

critical parameters: select causal relations that directly limit the rate of production of various so-called events at the focal level; the small subnetwork of critical variables (B. Wright).

cross-catalysis (or heterocatalysis): catalysis of two substances operating on each other. At the root of the amino acid–nucleic acid chemical reactive cycles.

deme: a local group of genotypically related organisms of a species (a subpopulation) potentially mating with each other in any given generation. Interdemic relations at some larger scale form what we call a species.

diachronic: the temporal dimension; system changes over time; temporal transformations in structure.

diachronic reduction: presumed reduction to the origins and the diachronic mechanisms and contingencies that give rise to the emergent high levels; in principle possible, in practice improbable.

differential games: situations of conflict or cooperation in which players choose their strategies over time; in such games the numbers of moves, stages, states, as well as time periods are infinite – they are governed by systems of differential equations. Furthermore, the strategies of the players depend entirely on the given state of the game at any particular, discontinuous moment of time; these games therefore have no solutions.

dissipative structure: a structure or pattern of force relations produced in some material system under particular conditions of energy flow through it; some of this flowing energy dissipates in the process of producing the pattern, while some is stored in the structured pattern so produced; a dissipative structure is established far from the original equilibrium, becomes irreversible, and exhibits novel properties. The term has been coined by Prigogine. According to Nicolis (1986a), dissipative dynamical systems are characterized by irreversibility, contraction of phase space, and the ability to possess attractors.

downward causation: (D. Campbell): is said to imply that the higher levels reach down and influence (regulate, restrict, determine) the lower levels; emphasizes the active, event-producing nature of constraints; implies a stronger notion of constraint.

downward control: the strong case of **downward causation** supporting an equally strong form of hierarchy.

driven systems (P. W. Anderson): systems driven beyond equilibrium by thermodynamic branching or other thermal means; they may thus produce sustainable or unsustainable dissipative structures (Prigogine).

drivers: all sorts of "push" factors at the subgenic and genic levels that are said to produce particular genetic distributions before any selection.

dualism, dualist: a philosophical position that posits the independent existence of at least two distinct ontological realms, such as those of the metaphysical (spiritual, religious) and the physical, the ideal (logic, ideas) and the material, or the mental (soul, mind) and the bodily (body, brain).

ecological hierarchy of nature: hierarchy of phenotypes, or economic hierarchy; that aspect of the natural hierarchy concerning energy exchanges in ecosystems.

ecosystem: the system of total energy flows over a region, which includes biotic (cf. biological populations) and abiotic (cf. physical structures) entities.

efficient cause (Aristotle): the particular, proximate, diachronic cause that gets something going (changing state) or stops it from going (not changing).

eliminative materialism: the view that our commonsense psychological framework ("folk psychology") is incorrigibly false and radically misleading; and, thus, it must be eliminated altogether. The new language to replace it would be neuroscientific.

entangled systems: systems at different levels of a heterarchy interacting in complex ways; the notion of tangledness implies many complex relations between adjacent levels and some such relations across nonadjacent levels; the result is, at best, a partial ordering with only a relative hierarchy of inclusion in terms of size (though not scale proper). Even Foucault has defined his chief notion of an "archaeology" as the systematic description of a discourse-object itself on a horizon "entangled in unique interrelationships of relations" (called interpositivities).

entropy: energy flowing from particular sources to the universal "sink" so as to equalize (e.g. heat dissipation). Such entropic energy may pass through particular systems, get partially dissipated, and partially stored; as a result, such systems exhibit new states, novel properties, special processes, and maintain an (irreversible, historical) informational record of these energy flows. This notion of entropy then can be used as a measure of complexity; it indicates the number of possible states of a system preserving a given information-carrying capacity. Social structures (e.g., urban structures, firms, social formations) may be conceived along these lines as dissipative structures – on a par with informational macromolecular structures.

epistemic strategies: see **Logics (Epistemic).**

epistemological: referring to questions about the possibility and character (truth status) of knowledge; addresses issues of the correspondence of our knowledge to a presumed objective world.

essentialism: a deep-seated disposition to find the "essence" of things; the belief that such a project is possible; a quest for origins; any form of metaphysical realism or foundationalism; any theory or philosophy referring to constant (Plato) or unfolding (Hegel) universals.

exaptation (Gould and Vbra): capacity for aptation derived from one set of circumstances of organismic–environmental relations and aptly applied to another such set.

experimental constructionism: the empirical program of constructionism; especially evident in the works of Stanley Fox and his students and associates and in the Belouzov–Zhabotinsky-type of chemical reactions.

extensional description: a description presumed to rely exclusively on reference to "objects" (mass extended in space) and "facts" about these objects (properties, displacements); an impossible feat, since all descriptions are linguistic (statements, propositions) and, as such, implicate *intensional* contexts. Besides, "pointing" to objects is itself an *intensional* and *intentional* act.

far-from-equilibrium: systems pushed beyond their normal stability conditions. See **dissipative structure.**

fields, structural: structural forms at the second level of a phenomenological level structure; they include the interorganizational field, the field of collective agencies, and the field of population ecologies.

final cause (Aristotle): the goal-state ("entelechy") for which processes or events occur; a diachronic telic (teleomatic, teleonomic, or teleological) aspect or form of causality.

fluctuation: a seminal concept in new physics; spontaneous, wavelike, random deviations in the output function of a system, implying a pulsating, energy-unstable, inhomogeneous conception of matter/energy.

focal level: that level in an emergent (compositional, heterarchical, or hierarchical) level structure which is being examined in an investigation (or at which particular processes, constraints, properties, or relations are examined).

folk psychology: denigrating expression used by eliminative materialists and reductionists when referring to philosophical, psychological, or interpretive theories which utilize natural language (mental) terms (see **eliminative materialism**).

formal cause (Aristotle): the synchronic, structural aspect of causality; the idea or pattern that is realized (gives shape, is inscribed) in the produced thing.

formal constructionism: the strategy of seeing the real as an approximation of a model, i.e., as an expression of an underlying (say, algebraic) formalism. Models are constructed by the application of some mathematical relation onto some elements. In such a case, of course, the formal products far exceed the real ones (see our discussion of protein formation).

formalism, formal structuralism: the strategy of ascribing value only to mathematically formulated structural forms.

fractals: geometrical forms obeying mathematical rules of scaling, proportionality, and self-similarity or near self-similarity (Mandelbrot); the infinite self-embedding of complexity (Gleick).

frozen accident: in crystallography; the accidental, contingent, and irreversible process giving rise to crystalline forms, such as snowflakes.

functionalism (philosophy of mind): the view that mental states are not fully reducible to structural-material states. Mental states are rather *logical* states, such as languages or software, or, at least, *global* states involving internal representations, not only sensory inputs and behavioral output. On Putnam's old account, functional states are "portable" (i.e., defined independently of any physical realization), potentially realizable in many structural-material media, and have *sui generis* attributes.

genealogical hierarchy of nature: hierarchy of genotypes or replicators; that aspect of the natural hierarchy referring to the reproduction of biotic informational components (genes and such).

genetic drift: aggregated sampling errors in genetic replication, especially from generation to generation; affect gene frequencies; they tend to be exacerbated by small size and homogeneity in genotypic pools.

global: referring to the totalization process initiated by collective agencies and giving rise to the Logics of Capital, State, the New Class, and others; characteristic processes of class systems, societal formations, and the world system.

global description: any higher-level description in relation to a lower focal level; such a description emphasizes the collective properties of a total system or the environmental constraints imposed on it; more specifically, global descriptions may refer to higher levels as the focal level in itself.

Gödelization: the effect of Gödel's demon. Implications of Gödel's "incompleteness theorem," namely, that no system that is sufficiently large is formally tight; in any axiomatic system theorems exist that are undecidable.

group selection: any selection at the group level; it includes, for example, multigene family selection, in-group selection, demic selection, interdemic selection, and species selection (Vrba, Wade, Wynne-Edwards).

groupings, structural: structural forms at the first level of a phenomenological level structure; they include hierarchies, markets, social exchange systems, membership groups, quasi-groups, topological communities, and topological congeries.

habitus: "systems of durable, transposable dispositions; . . . a socially constituted system of cognitive and motivating structures; . . . the durably installed generative principle of regulated improvisations" (in Bourdieu 1977a).

Hamiltonian: a function not of positions and velocities of Newtonian (atomic, individual) objects but of coordinates and interrelated momenta. The Hamiltonian is now seen as a mathematical operator applied to an object – a function (its "eigenfunction") – which attains values as a result of the application of the operator (values recovered as "eigenvalues" of the operator). Data then are seen as process-based and operational, not as objectivist data to be merely "discovered" by the scientist.

heterarchy: a level structure formed by a process of partial ordering; especially, if it involves complex multilevel interactions (not only across adjacent levels); a structure involving at least several-to-several connections between adjacent levels and, potentially, projections of such connections to other nonadjacent levels; in brief, a partially ordered level structure implicating a rampant interactional complexity (Wimsatt).

heterocatalysis (cross-catalysis): mutual catalysis of two substances, each needing the other for different reasons.

hierarchical jump: said to take place in the transition from lower-level high-frequency phenomena to higher-level low-frequency phenomena; it implies a rather strong discontinuity between levels consistent with the strong hierarchical view.

hierarchical system: an ensemble of interacting parts that is composed of (and is analyzable or decomposable into) successively nested sets of interacting subunits (J. S. Nicolis).

hierarchy: a level structure formed by the superimposition of constraints in an additive or multiplicative way; it implies processes of supersession of lower levels by novel higher levels; it rests on a relatively strong notion of constraint and of closure; it flirts with **holism.**

hierarchy of nature (Pattee, Bunge, Bhaskar): a representation of the world in "integrated pluralist" terms, i.e., as composed of entities or structures occupying a hierarchy of levels of organization; it presumes that the world is indeed hierarchically structured (**transcendental realism**).

holism: the doctrine or, at best, epistemic strategy that prioritizes the global level of phenomena; it considers as most important systemic relations that are presumed to transcend the microparts or microprocesses operating at lower levels.

hypercycle, protohypercycle: hypercyclic or protohypercyclic organization takes place when two different structures cooperate cross-catalytically to produce higher forms; a proposed method of informational co-evolution at the macromolecular level; the hypercyclic (Eigen) and protohypercyclic (Matsuno) organization at the root of the co-evolving interaction of proteinoid and nucleic forms that give rise to high-capacity proteins and DNA.

identity theory: considers mental states as physical states of the brain, plain and simple. Thus, mental and physical states or processes are treated as identical.

incompleteness (logical), undecidability: the restrictive condition imposed upon any sufficiently complicated formal/logical system if it is to be self-consistent (per Gödel; see also **Gödelization**); this cannot be relieved as Carnap realized; incompleteness necessitates the undecidability of certain theorems or statements within a self-consistent formal/logical system. Alternatively, any attempted remedy of incompleteness or undecidability defeats the self-consistency of the system (see Davis 1965).

informational macromolecules: biopolymers; the first foci of informational coding (proteins, RNA, DNA) necessary for the emergence of life forms.

informational systems: systems of a physical nature that are able to store, reproduce, and/or process information. They may exist even at the molecular level (see discussions of the issue of "complexity"); they definitely begin at the macromolecular level before the emergence of life (see Fox, Matsuno). We refer to such systems every time we speak of a "code" – genetic, linguistic, or cultural.

initiating (or initial) conditions: conditions reflecting lower-level constraints and the ensuing lower-level dynamics; they intuitively appear as immediate causative factors at the focal level and as representing the intrinsic properties of focal entities; this is, of course, only partially correct.

instability of homogeneity: if energy is supplied, a homogeneous spatial field tends to become inhomogeneous (Lösch).

integrated pluralism: the view that there exists a level structure of different ontological structural forms, for example: physical, biological, mental; may be said to rest on ontological monism (materialism); but attributional pluralism (hierarchical, heterarchical, or constructionist emergentism).

intensional (description): a sequence or list of descriptive statements on the basis of which one seems warranted to assign to (or exclude from) a token a membership relation to a class or set. However, such statements and the assigned memberships are neither symmetrical nor transitive; thus, they do not permit one-to-one translation, adequation, or extensional fixing (e.g., "I move my hand" is not equivalent to "my hand is moving"). Thus, the *intensional* character of language and of any linguistically expressed conceptual system, program, or theory prohibit a direct extensional description, a straightforward correspondence to "objects" or "facts."

intentional: as distinct from *intensional;* exhibiting intentionality, that is, conscious and/or cognitive goal-seeking behavior; the distinction between the *intentional* and the *intensional* is only relative in the human case because, as linguistically qualified, the *intentional* always implicates beliefs, that is, *intensional* contexts.

interactive-communicative modalities: involved in interactions in which value-rational (reaching understanding, participation, normative consensus) communication is primary.

interactive–strategic modalities: those involved in strong interactions in which the purposive–rational orientation is primary.

interactors (Hull): entities (such as organisms or species) in the ecological hierarchy of nature involved in energy flows; entities in ecosystems.

interdemic selection: selection with demes as units; it implies differential survival and differential dispersion within an interdemic population. Differential dispersion implicates an island model.

interfacing (White): a matrix of firms–markets connections; as I see it, it implies several-to-several connections as in a heterarchy; it is reminiscent of a simpler neural net or a cellular automaton of some sort.

internal realism (Putnam), or **intensional realism** (Kontopoulos, Margolis): in contradistinction to external or *extensional* realism (any form of metaphysical realism, including not strongly qualified forms of scientific realism); it rests on the new (postpositivist) philosophical view that there is no direct correspondence between statements of language and natural objects; it asserts that all "factual" information is *intensionally* described, that it is internal to language systems (including scientific research programs), that theory is underdetermined by "facts," and that, so construed, "factual" information corroborates in a robust relativist way but does not guarantee the "reality" of statements internal to any linguistic version of the world.

L-amino acids: left-handed amino acids, especially of the alpha-amino acids group forming proteins (by way of peptides and oligopeptides), which are absolutely necessary for biological formation, catalytic processes, membranicity, and – arguably – informational storage and replicability.

lattice animals: strange configurations of complex mathematical objects in random graphs or in the process of percolation.

level: a representation of scale and sealed-off processes in a hierarchical or heterarchical structure; it involves considerable closure of the focal phenomena; it implies the operation of focal constraints and, therefore, the emergence of new boundary conditions, new properties of focal structures, and novel processes.

linear dynamics: involve processes describable by additive models and represented by linear graphs; typical mechanistic models.

local: referring to individual modal orientations, actions, and interactions.

local description: a description of processes or the behavior of entities at lower levels; a description of processes of some small part of a system; it focuses on microparts and microprocess.

logical positivism: the previously dominant philosophy of science now demised; a formalized form of neo-positivism/neo-empiricism proposed as the foundation of (the unity of) "Science"; it rested on the strong assumptions of direct (isomorphic) correspondence of statements to observations and of the demarcation of the analytic from the synthetic. Plagued with serious logical problems, this "Received View of Metaphysical Realism" gave way to various forms of postpositivism.

logics, logics of structuration: various operative mechanisms in a multidimensional actional and structural topology; they bring about "structured systems" (phenotypes/interactors) exhibiting in a relative way an inscribed "structural form" (genotypes/replicators). I use the term as a shorthand to refer to three different types: *structuring algorithms* (the most formal); *structuring mechanisms* (special pieces of equipment not amenable to full formalization); and *structuring modalities* (actional orientations in structurable space giving rise to "projects" or, at a minimum, constraining the possibility space of interactors).

Logics (Epistemic): more general metatheoretical (second-order) analytical orientations toward the phenomena; they imply a set of ontological, epistemological, as well as purely methodological commitments to theorizing or to the research enterprise. In this volume, five such Logics or Epistemic Strategies are discussed: reductionism, constructionism/compositionism, heterarchy, hierarchy, and holism (systemic transcendence).

Logics (Structuring): overarching logics of structuration starting from the semilocal level of structures and moving toward the global level; especially emerging as projects of collective agencies (capitalist class, bureaucratic state elites, the professional-managerial category); referred to sometimes as the Logic of Capital, the Logic of Bureaucratization or State Logic, the Logic of Patriarchy, and so on; they emerge as conscious or opaque collective "projects" (Foucault) with particular modal orientations; they become totalizing, tending (without complete success) toward the formation of a strong hierarchy of material and/or mental control.

macrologics: logics of structuration between the quasi-global and global levels.

macromolecular structures: large molecular structures such as those of proteins and nucleic acids; these two are biologically significant for replicability (amino acids, peptides, proteins) and high-fidelity information storage (nucleic acids, nucleotides, RNA and DNA); there also exist numerous inorganic macromolecules (such as polymers).

material cause (Aristotle): ascription of causal importance to the substance out of which something is made or to the entities generating it; this usually involves reference to the potentialities of that substance or entities.

mesologics: logics of structuration between the quasi-local and quasi-global levels.

metagames: noncooperative games which include the possibility that players may rely on higher-order expectations (second-order scenaria) regarding the dependency of the choice of one on the behavior of the other(s); this exacerbates the "lack of unique solution" problem already inherent in noncooperative games in general.

metaphysical realism: the view that *there is* a differentiated real world and that *it is* knowable by us (especially by science).

methodological: related to pragmatic or technical aspects of knowing, i.e., knowing for all practical purposes, or to the best of our ability. It raises questions about adequacy and pragmatic (global) validity; it avoids foundationalist commitments.

methodological individualism: an epistemic strategy in human studies positing that all social and cultural phenomena are, at bottom, individual phenomena and that all social and cultural explanations are reducible to individual explanations.

micrologics: logics of structuration at the local and quasi-local levels.

modalities, modal: necessary, contingent, possible, or impossible modes, manners, or ways of being and acting; in the present context they indicate modal orientations to action and interaction and structuring modalities ("projects") at higher levels.

modularity: resulting from nearly-perfect-decomposition; a hierarchy of structures that are modules or composites of such modules (a modular hierarchy).

modus ponens: a valid mode of inference in the following form: if p, then q; p, therefore q. This mode should be distinguished from the invalid form of affirming the consequent as well as from the intermediary form of *modus tollens* (if p, then q; $-p$, therefore $-q$).

molecular drive: changes occurring at the molecular level as a result of thermodynamic instability (quantum and aggregate fluctuations); such changes affect the rates of gene mutation.

natural selection: the result of the differential reproduction of genotypes in a deme. The selective process at the demic level with organisms as presumed basic units of selection. Currently under serious debate (units of selection controversy, nonselective processes of evolution controversies).

near (or nearly complete) decomposability (Ando, Fisher, Simon): the property of hierarchical (but not of heterarchical) systems to be decomposed into a nearly completely ordered hierarchy of scale, that is, into hierarchical levels.

nearly noninteractive modalities: involved in topologically constrained orders of interdependencies, for example traffic jams or elevators and buses; involves residual interaction.

nestedness, nested inclusion: the characteristic of hierarchies, which have entities of smaller scale (lower levels) enclosed within those of larger scale (higher levels).

neural networks: the very complex and dynamic networking of neurons in the brain; the modeling of such connections in parallel distributed computational systems; multilevel several-to-several or many-to-many connections capable of degeneracy, accurate massive reproduction of memory schemata and learning, and other more advanced functions; corroborating the heterarchical mode of analysis.

nonequilibrium thermodynamics: the study of energy and entropy relations of open and nearly-open systems; such systems implicate rapid transition phases, bifurcations of branches, randomness, irreversibility, and historicity; they also give rise to more complicated nonlinear behaviors (chemical clocks, waves and cascades, percolation, and chaos). Some thermodynamic systems far-from-equilibrium attain the status of dissipative structures (see Landau, Prigogine).

nonlinear dynamics: involve processes describable by multiplicative and even more complicated models and represented by nonlinear (for example, chaotic) graphs.

nonreductive materialism: an emergentist form of materialism, committed to "integrated pluralism," that is, the view that the world exhibits diachronic emergence and it appears synchronically as a level structure (along constructionist, heterarchical, or hierarchical lines); such a view opposes both **reductive materialism** (which is inimical to any notion of emergence, or of active matter) as well as **dualism** (which posits two or more metaphysically distinct substances, for example matter and spirit or soul).

nucleation, heterogeneous nucleation: the process by which structures or complex entities are formed. Heterogeneous nucleation involves the fact that the process takes place around a special object or place.

nucleotides: nitro-based (phosphoric) compounds at the root of nucleic acids, known to us in their RNA or DNA forms – the basis of our genetic code.

oceanic games: games that include an "ocean" of minor players; for example, corporate stockholders. They have very complicated, open dynamics.

ontological: pertaining to questions about the nature of reality; it has quite often, therefore, an objectivist (or quasi-objectivist) flavor; it addresses issues of reference.

p-hierarchy (Pattee): strong version of hierarchy theory.

packing rules: rules of spatial arrangement guided by considerations of (goal-related) efficiency and economy; they apply in numerous settings, from crystal formation, tiling, hexagonal honeycombs, transport, and species packing, to organizational packing in schools, restaurants, offices. (See Appendix no. 30.)

parallel distributed systems (Hopfield, Kohonen): systems of neural networks with "content-addressable memory," that is, patterns of (mental) global mapping distributed over a large range of neurons; many neurons carry a pattern collectively and every neuron carries a bit of many such patterns.

partial localization: a primary fuzzy localization of brain functions complemented by secondary and tertiary "parallel" localizations; mental functions project in several of these fuzzily specifiable subsystems and regions.

partial ordering: this interlevel structure obtains when relations between systems or entities at different levels show a strong degree of interactional complexity, i.e., they exert influence on adjacent as well as nonadjacent levels, upward or downward. Example: the relations between letters, words, and sentences; in such a case modularity and nestedness do not obtain.

peptides, tripeptides, polypeptides: compounds of amino acids, which become the basis for the building of proteins.

percolation theory: a mathematical theory of nonlinear transitions, named after the surprising, complex behavior of common percolation which exhibits Bénard instability. It is applicable in **cascade** models, in several forms of cellular automata, and possible in spin-glass-like models of evolution; forest fires are examples of percolation through space.

phase space: an abstract, theoretical, multidimensional space defined by the critical variables of a system whose dynamic trajectory one is studying.

phase-separation: phenomena of different frequencies get sealed off or relatively lifted out of other phenomena due to application of certain constraints. Phase-separation establishes the semiautonomy of different levels. For example, "life" is phase-separated from simpler informational macromolecular forms.

physicalism: the ultimate form of reductionism; the view that all phenomena, including the biological and the mental, are in fact physical phenomena plain and simple; the basic version of **reductive materialism.** Examples: Humans are mere physical bodies. Psychological attributes are fully reducible to physical attributes and, ultimately, to the language of physics (radical reductionism).

polymorphous (sets): imply several-to-several or many-to-several connections; sets composed of overlapping subsets; the set of overlapping Vennian diagrams; the set of structures sharing several critical substructures; the set of neural networks sharing some important neuronal groups of network substructures.

postfunctional analysis: the analysis of interdependencies and dynamic open systems in nonlinear, far-from-equilibrium models; it rejects the use of the old vocabularies of equilibrium, homeostasis, function, adaptation, or similar terms.

postpositivism: the recent set of theories of science that share a hostility to foundationalism, i.e., to metaphysical realism (along the older lines of logical positivism). There exist many varieties of postpositivism, which could be profitably classified into two sets: robust relativist (critico-pragmatism, dialectical historicism, pragmatism) and extreme relativist (all theories accepting the notion of the radical incommensurability of paradigms or theories and, therefore, the impossibility of appraisals or, indeed, of any claim to knowledge).

prebiotic natural selection: selection operating on physicochemical elements on the basis of constraints of different sorts (collective, ecological, structural, thermodynamic). Examples: chirality, i.e., right- or left-handedness of chemical compounds; abiotic template formation; thermal transitions in reactions (like Beluzov-Zhabotinsky); accounts partially for autopoesis; it is evident as well in the emergence of macromolecular forms (RNA, DNA) and of protocells (in Stanley Fox's sense).

predicate: logical or linguistic elements that designate attributes or qualities of given subjects. In epistemological terms, that part of the sentence which serves to identify what is being discussed or designated as a property of a subject (including the subject's activity, expressed by a verb). The usual simple form is "s is P," i.e., the subject has such and such characteristic properties. Here we speak of predicates of social or cultural-institutional types of subjects and their relata. In our context, the subject may or may not be an individual organism or person; it may be an institution, group, or society; thus, the talk of relational, institutional, or structural predicates. The last refer to a nonindividual subject of predication and are irreducible to individual predicates.

problem of transformation: the question of how institutions as collective phenomena arise from social action.

proteinoids: prebiotic or protobiotic entities experimentally constructed by Fox and his associates in their work on the origins of life. They exhibit types of behavior found in more advanced protobiotic forms (see **protocells**).

proteinoid model: a model advocating the protein-based origin of life; it rests on extensive experimental constructionist work by Stanley Fox and his associates. It is opposed by those who advocate the nucleic-based origin of life (Watson, Crick). The truth may be somewhere in between, in the so-called hypercyclic model (Eigen, Matsuno, Küppers) and its thermodynamic underpinnings.

protocells (urzellen): further developed proteinoid microspheres produced in the laboratory along experimental constructionist lines; they exhibit properties such as irreversibility, membranicity, neuronal-like excitability, information storage; said to be the "origins of life."

punctuated equilibria (Eldredge, Gould): suggested pattern of evolution whereby species remaining structurally nearly constant over long periods of time exhibit rapid speciation, or are suddenly replaced by other, quite different species.

quantum chaos: potential chaotic processes operating at the quantum level (Leggett, Pool).

quasi-crystals: possess orientational order (parallel orientation of edges and faces of the composing atoms) but not translational order (building units may shift sideways without change in the lattice), while regular crystals possess both; square or hexagon tiling formations are crystalline lattices, while pentagon tiling formations are semi-crystalline (Penrose).

quasi-global: referring to the interrelationships between homomorphous (same kind) or heteromorphous (different kind) institutions, collective agencies, or regions.

quasi-group: the set of all overlapping egocentric networks of people. Consider, for example, a large neighborhood as the set of all "bounded neighborhoods" (in Schelling's sense of "eight houses surrounding my house"); such bounded neighborhoods form overlapping (Vennian) sets.

quasi-interactive modalities: involved in weak interactions (weak ties) and possible interactions (the small world); imply potential "channels" of networks.

quasi-local: referring to exchanges or strategic behavior within and across institutional, collective, and topological contexts.

racemic mixture: a random and equivalent mixture of elements; for example, equal amounts of right-forming and left-forming chemical elements or compounds are admixed.

recursion (iteration): stepwise movement involving continuous return to previous steps and then running forward again.

reductionism: the doctrine or epistemic strategy of interpreting any phenomenon in terms describing its parts or processes implicated among its parts, down to the ultimate microlevel.

reductive materialism: the view that all higher-level phenomena are reducible to lower-level phenomena, down to the elementary physical laws.

relational predicates: predicates specific to interaction or interdependence systems, irreducible to individual properties.

replicator (Hull): entities (such as genes) in the genealogical hierarchy of nature, involved with informational reproduction.

s-hierarchy (Simon): weaker, modular version of hierarchy theory.

scale: the ranking and separation of phenomena based on size, dynamic frequencies of energy flows (time scales), and scope of influence. Size alone is not enough as the case of black holes demonstrates.

semiclosed (or semiopen) systems: systems exhibiting complexity, relative order, and an unbalanced energy distribution or exchange.

semidefinite constructs (Elsasser): "combinations of contingencies with mathematical order"; that is, per Kontopoulos, pragmatic constructs that have achieved a sufficient degree of logical elaboration within a given, broad research program; constructs with theoretical elaboration and an adequate, if not excessive, empirical content.

spin glasses, spin-glass model: phenomena in many-body physics exhibiting random spin properties and collective properties of differentiation coupled with redundancy; central in the work of P. W. Anderson; presumed to provide a basic quantum/thermodynamic model of chemical and biochemical evolution.

stability conditions: conditions under which a system (i.e., any bundle of related phenomena) achieves some sort of – fragile or sustained – stability at particular points in the phase space (at equilibrium, near equilibrium, or far-from-equilibrium). Such stability is required for the emergence of any would-be "novel" phenomenon or level exhibiting its own laws or characteristics.

stereochemical type: a chemical form that is left-handed or right-handed, involving one or the other of the "optical antipodes"; see L-amino acids.

stochastic history: the contingent history of an entity's or a system's evolution; implies specific context, historicity, and irreversibility; transitions in phase-space resulting from the imposition of constraints; a system's contingent developmental trajectory.

structural effects: predictable or unpredictable (and/or unintended or unwanted) results of structuration; to be distinguished from mere collective or social effects.

structural predicates: predicates of a complex character involving interactional, material, political, and topological externalities; they are irreducible to conventional/institutional, interactional, or individual predicates.

structural stability: relative constancy of certain crucial (structural) relations even in the face of numerous changes among elements; macrostability in the face of microchange.

structuration: the process of structural generation, of the generation of structural forms and structured systems; the operation of the logics (algorithms, mechanisms, and modalities) of structuration.

structure (per Giddens): "rules and resources recursively implicated in the reproduction of social systems."

structured structuring structures: structured structures predisposed to operate as structuring structures (in Bourdieu 1977). Emergent structures, which, once stabilized, become irreducible and function as springboards for further structural emergence.

structured systems: "systems of interaction" or "systems of interdependence" (phenotypes, interactors) structured by the operation of one or more logics of structuration (genotypes, replicators). Of course, the replication is never exact.

structuring algorithms: formal (logico-mathematical) operators structuring a social space; the formal rules, equations, and ensuing formal transformations are presumed to give the exact number and form of social relations observed (minus some noise). Examples: formalizable matrimonial systems of exchange (Lévi-Strauss, H. C. White), sorting rules, solutions to the traveling salesman problem. Also called structuring structures in the text.

structuring mechanisms: moderately abstract mechanisms of structuration developed (consciously or not) as better solutions to problems related to "systems of interdependence" or signaling the onset of such problems; these mechanisms cannot (or cannot easily) be brought to complete formalization. Examples: matchings and impaired matchings, market mechanisms and impaired market clearings, traffic rules and jams, queuing, flows. A considerable part of social space is structured by such structuring mechanisms.

structuring modalities: existence-bound (*intentional* and *intensional*), critical modal orientations giving rise to different structural systems; especially important are the strategic and collective modalities which give rise to "projects" of a totalizing nature (for example, the Logics of Capital, of the State, of the Professional–Managerial Class). Also called structuring principles in the text.

structuring structures: see structuring algorithms.

structuring principles: see structuring modalities.

substrate: a substance modified by the action of a certain catalyzing enzyme, i.e., protein.

supergames: sequences of static games that are not contingent on the past actions of the players; for example, an iterated PD-game. Such repetition brings about a stochastic change of attitude (according to Sen, the transition from individual to collective rationality, from a Prisoner's Dilemma to an Assurance Game context). Supergames can be even more complicated, when they have structural-time dependence or strategic-time dependence at higher levels.

surface-to-volume ratios: structural mechanisms accounting for the stability of cathedrals and bodies, the behavior of schools of fish, evolutionary rates, or the pleatedness of informational macromolecules, or the brain.

symmetry-breaking: processes of a nonlinear thermodynamic nature producing paradoxical results (systems or behaviors); at the root of lasers, ferromagnets, superconductivity, and other novel phenomena (P. W. Anderson, Haken, Prigogine). At rock-bottom, broken symmetry is due to the parity violation and time asymmetry characterizing the weak nuclear force; resulting electro-weak interactions are said to explain the polarity (up-down) and chirality (left-right) of biological macromolecules (Mason).

synchronic: occurring or considered at the same point in time; for example, different levels produced diachronically but now linked synchronically.

synchronic reduction: alleged reduction of high-level phenomena to low-level processes; impossible according to the emergentist Logics (constructionism, heterarchy, and hierarchy).

synecdoche, synecdochical: a mode of expressing the whole by one of its parts; used here to indicate the expression of the interests of a larger group by one of its mobilized subgroups.

systemic transcendence, systemic functionalism: see holism.

systems of interaction: a generic term used by Boudon to describe all functional and interdependence systems.

systems of interdependence: a term used by Boudon to describe nonfunctional systems of interaction; such systems may involve direct (essentially face-to-face) or indirect interdependence (not face-to-face).

tangled systems, tangledness: see entangled systems.

teleological: processes taking place in and by "cognitive biological systems" and exhibiting true purposive behavior; they are ascribed the properties of intentionality, beliefs, and cognition; they are highly plastic in the selection of goals and in the improvised formation of goal-seeking paths.

teleomatic: processes that deterministically reach some predictable end-state through ordinary physical processes; end-directed or end-resulting; arguably the mechanistic–causal processes but especially the thermodynamic–statistical processes.

teleonomic: processes guiding some systems to end-states on the basis of internal end-directed programs (genetic developmental programs, engrams, computer programs); the end-states are usually prespecified at some level; thus the teleonomic involves internal controlling factors implicating a sort of internal representational and computational state.

template: a substance with a surface configuration that conveys particular information and catalyzes other elements of its environment (i.e., shapes them on the basis of its own configuration).

tertius gaudens: for a third party to benefit from the already existing conflict of two others.

thresholds: points at which a critical mass has been reached tipping the behavior or preferences of a system, agency, or individual; examples: neighborhood transition thresholds, innovation thresholds, collective participation thresholds, chemical catalytic thresholds, and so on.

totalities, structural: structural forms at the third level of a phenomenological level structure; they include class structures, (national, societal) social formations, and the world system.

totalizing logic: a modal macrologic operating between the quasi-global and global levels attempting to organize the global level on its basis (for example, Logic of Capital).

transaction-cost analysis: a neo-institutional economic theory resting on the following three assumptions: (a) that human agents are subject to bounded rationality; (b) that the world in which they live exhibits considerable uncertainty; and (c) that at least some agents are given to opportunism.

transcendental argument (Kantian): an argument focusing on the a priori "conditions of possibility" of real or cognitive objects, the preconditions of existence. The typical form is: For such and such to exist, this or that prior condition must exist or be satisfied – or, usually, must be postulated. The functional requisites program had an underlying transcendental structure; so do now Habermas's or Karl Otto Apel's theories.

transcendental realism: the view that the world forms a level structure populated by distinct structures; the latter are perceived as transcendental in character, that is, as individuals with "causal powers" of their own; this seems a bit arguable (Bhaskar, Harré, Keat).

transducers (Pylyshyn's term): a transition device said to systematically link in some complicated bottom-up process physical or biological phenomena and emergent cognitive phenomena; (Kontopoulos): pieces of equipment transforming some focal-level phenomena to phenomena of the next higher level; mechanisms of upward structuration; thermodynamic, chaotic, and other processes bringing about new stability conditions (new boundaries); automata operating on principles of partial isomorphism and effecting the transduction of hardware rules to software rules; mapping hierarchies transcribing signals into symbols and concepts.

tripeptides, oligopeptides: See **L-amino acids, peptides.**

Turing machine: a mathematical abstraction in the form of a device that can perform computer-like procedures (read, write, process formal information).

two-level games: games played concurrently at two levels; two different games – played at different levels – linked together so that the strategies of a player at one level depend not only on the state of the game at the focal level but also on the state of the other game; example: political games at the (intra)national and international or summit levels (Putnam and Bayne).

urzellen: See **protocells.**

vitalism: an older doctrine conflating the teleomatic, the teleonomic, and the teleological; a view of life as "entelechy" (as having specific ends); a collectivist conception of the metaphysical independence of life from matter.

Bibliography

Abercrombie, Nicholas, and John Urry. 1983. *Capital, Labour and the Middle Classes*. Boston: Allen and Unwin.

Aberle, D. F., A. K. Cohen, A. K. Davis, M. J. Levy, and F. X. Sutton. 1950. "The Functional Prerequisites of a Society." In N. Demerath and R. Peterson, eds. *System, Change and Conflict*. New York: Free Press, 1967, pp. 317–31.

Abolafia, Mitchell Y. 1984. "Structured Anarchy: Formal Organization in the Commodities Futures Markets." In Patricia Adler and Peter Adler, eds. *The Social Dynamics of Financial Markets*. Greenwich, CT: JAI Press, pp. 129–51.

Abraham, Farid F. 1974. *Homogeneous Nucleation Theory*. New York: Academic Press.

Abraham, Ralph. 1985. *Complex Dynamical Systems*. Santa Cruz, CA: Aerial Press.

Abrahamson, Mark. 1978. *Functionalism*. Englewood Cliffs, NJ: Prentice Hall.

Adams, R. N. 1975. *Energy and Structure: A Theory of Social Power*. Austin: University of Texas Press.

1982. *Paradoxical Harvest*. Cambridge University Press.

Adler, Patricia, and Peter Adler, eds. 1984. *The Social Dynamics of Financial Markets*. Greenwich, CT: JAI Press.

Akerlof, George A. 1976. "The Economics of Caste and the Rat Race and Other Woeful Tales." *Quart. J. Ec.* 84:599–617.

1984. *An Economic Theorist's Book of Tales*. Cambridge University Press.

Akerlof, George A., and J. L. Yellen. 1985. "Can Small Deviations from Rationality Make Significant Differences in Market Equilibria?" *Am. Econ. Rev.* 75:708–20.

Alba, R. D. 1982. "Taking Stock of Network Analysis: A Decade's Results." In S. B. Bacharach, ed. *Research in the Sociology of Organizations*. A Research Annual. vol. I. Greenwich, CT: JAI Press.

Alchian, A. A., and H. Demsetz. 1972. "Production, Information Costs, and Economic Organization." *Am. Econ. Rev.* 62:777–95.

Aldrich, Howard. 1975. "Ecological Succession in Racially Changing Neighborhoods: A Review of the Literature." *Urban Affairs Quarterly* 10: 327–48.

1979. *Organizations and Environments*. Englewood Cliffs, NJ: Prentice-Hall.

1982. "The Origins and Persistence of Social Networks." In Peter V. Marsden and Nan Lin, eds. *Social Structure and Network Analysis*. Beverly Hills, CA: Sage.

Aldrich, Howard, and Jeffrey Pfeffer. 1976. "Environments of Organizations." *Ann. Rev. Soc.* 2:79–105.

Aldrich, Howard, E. Auster, U. Staber, and C. Zimmer, eds. 1986. *Populations Perspectives on Organizations*. Stockholm: Almqvist and Wiksell/Uppsala University.

Aldrich, Howard, and Peter Marsden. 1988. "Environments and Organizations." In N. S. Smelser, ed. *Handbook of Sociology*. Beverly Hills, CA: Sage.

Alexander, Jeffrey, ed. 1985. *Neofunctionalism*. Beverly Hills, CA: Sage.

Alexander, Jeffrey, and Paul Colomy. 1985. "Toward Neo-Functionalism." *Sociological Theory* 3:11–23.

Alexander, J., B. Giesen, R. Münch, and N. Smelser, eds. 1987. *The Micro-Macro Link*. Berkeley: University of California Press.

Alexander, J., and P. Colomy. 1990a. "Neofunctionalism Today: Reconstructing a Theoretical Tradition." In G. Ritzer, ed. *Frontiers of Social Theory*. New York: Columbia University Press.

    eds., 1990b. *Differentiation Theory and Social Change*. New York: Columbia University Press.

Alford, Robert R., and Roger Friedland. 1985. *Powers of Theory: Capitalism, the State, and Democracy*. Cambridge University Press.

Allen, Peter M. 1975. "Darwinian Evolution and a Predator-Prey Ecology." *Bul. Math. Bio.* 37:389–405.

    1976. "Evolution, Population and Stability." *Proc. Natl. Acad. Sci.* 73, 3:665–68.

    1981a. "The Evolutionary Paradigm of Dissipative Structures." In E. Jantsch, ed. *The Evolutionary Vision: Toward a Unifying Paradigm of Physical, Biological and Sociocultural Evolution*. Boulder, Co: Westview Press for the American Association for the Advancement of Science.

    1981b. "Urban Evolution, Self-Organization, and Decision-making." *Environment and Planning* 13:167–83.

    1983. "Self-Organization and Evolution in Urban Systems." In Robert Crosby, ed. *Cities and Regions as Nonlinear Decision Systems*. Boulder, CO: Westview Press.

    1985. "Ecology, Thermodynamics, and Self-organization: Towards a New Understanding of Complexity." In Robert Ulanowicz and Trevor Platt, eds. *Ecosystem Theory for Biological Oceanography*. Ottawa: Department of Fisheries and Oceans.

Allen, P. M., and M. Sanglier. 1978. "Dynamic Model of Urban Growth." *J. Soc. Biol. Structures* 1:265–80.

Allen, T. F. H., and Thomas B. Starr. 1982. *Hierarchy: Perspectives for Ecological Complexity*. Chicago, IL: University of Chicago Press.

Alpert, Harry. 1939. *Emile Durkheim and His Sociology*. New York: Columbia University Press.

Althusser, Louis. 1970. *For Marx*. New York: Vintage.

Althusser, Louis, and Etienne Balibar, eds. 1970. *Reading Capital*. London: New Left Review Books.

Aminzade, Ronald. 1981. *Class, Politics, and Early Industrial Capitalism: A Study of Mid-Nineteenth Century Toulouse, France*. Albany: SUNY Press.

Anderson, J. A. 1980. *Cognitive Psychology and Its Implications*. New York: Freeman.

    1983a. *The Architecture of Cognition*. Cambridge, MA: Harvard University Press.

    1983b. "Cognitive and Psychological Computation with Neural Models." *IEEE Transactions on Science, Man, and Cybernetics* 13: 799–815.

Anderson, Perry. 1980. *Arguments within English Marxism*. London: New Left Review Books.

1985. *Considerations of Western Marxism.* London: R. Chapman and Hall.

Anderson, P. W. 1972. "More Is Different: Broken Symmetry and the Nature of the Hierarchical Structure of Science." *Science* 177: 393–6.

1983. "Suggested Model for Prebiotic Evolution: The Use of Chaos." *Proc. Natl. Acad. Sci. USA* 80: 3386–90.

1984. *Basic Notions of Condensed Matter Physics.* Menlo Park, CA: Benjamin/Cummings.

Anderson, P. W., and D. L. Stein. 1984. "Broken Symmetry, Emergent Properties, Dissipative Structures, Life: Are They Related?" In P. W. Anderson, ed. *Basic Notions of Condensed Matter Physics.* Menlo Park, CA: Benjamin/Cummings.

Ando, Albert, F. M. Fisher, and H. A. Simon. 1963. *Essays on the Structure of Social Science Models.* Cambridge, MA.: MIT Press.

Appadurai, Arjun, ed. 1986. *The Social Life of Things: Commodities in Cultural Perspective.* Cambridge University Press.

Arabie, P., S. Boorman, and P. Levitt. 1978. "Constructing Blockmodels: How and Why." *J. of Math. Psych.* 17:21–63.

Arbib, Michael. 1985. *In Search of the Person: Philosophical Explorations in Cognitive Science.* Amherst: University of Massachusetts Press.

Arbib, Michael, and Allen R. Hanson, eds. 1985. *Vision, Brain, and Cooperative Computation.* Cambridge, MA: MIT Press.

Arbib, Michael, and M. Hesse. 1986. *The Construction of Reality.* Cambridge University Press.

Arnold, A. J., and K. Fristrup. 1982. "The Theory of Evolution by Natural Selection: A Hierarchical Expansion." *Paleobiology* 8:113–29.

Arrow, Kenneth. 1959. *Social Choice and Individual Values.* New York: Wiley.

1963. "Uncertainty and the welfare Economics of Medical Care." *American Economic Review* 53(Dec):947.

1967. "Values and Collective Decision-making." In P. Laslett and W. G. Runciman, eds. *Philosophy, Politics, and Society.* Oxford: Blackwell.

1974. *The Limits of Organization.* New York: Norton.

1975. "Gifts and Exchange". In E. S. Phelps, ed. *Altruism, Morality, and Economic Theory.* New York: Russell Sage Foundation.

1985. "The Economics of Agency." In J. W. Pratt and R. J. Zeckhauser, eds. *Principals and Agents.* Boston, MA: Harvard Business School Press, pp. 37–51.

Arrow, Kenneth J. and G. Debreu. 1954. "Existence of an equilibrium for a competitive economy." *Econometrica* 22:265–90.

Atkin, Ronald. 1974. *Mathematical Structure in Human Affairs.* London: Heinemann.

Atkins, P. W. 1984. *The Second Law.* New York: Freeman.

Atkinson, J. Maxwell, and John Heritage, eds. 1984. *Structures of Social Action.* Cambridge University Press.

Atlan, H. 1981. "Hierarchical Self-Organization in Living Systems." In Milan Zeleny, ed. *Autopoiesis.* New York: Elsevier North-Holland.

1985. "Information Theory and Self-Organization in Ecosystems." In R. Ulanowicz and T. Platt, eds. *Ecosystems Theory for Biological Oceanography.* Ottawa: Department of Fisheries and Oceans.

Attewell, Paul. 1974. "Ethnomethodology Since Garfinkel." *Theory and Society* 1:179–210.

Axelrod, Robert. 1984. *The Evolution of Cooperation.* New York: Basic.

1986. "An Evolutionary Approach to Norms." *APSR* 80:1095–1111.

Axelrod, Robert, and William D. Hamilton. 1981. "The Evolution of Cooperation." *Science* 211:1190–96.

Ayala, Francisco, and Theodosius Dobzhansky, eds. 1974. *Studies in the Philosophy of Biology.* Berkeley: University of California Press.

Badie, Bernard, and Pierre Birnbaum. 1983. *The Sociology of the State.* Chicago, IL: University of Chicago Press.

Baechler, Jean. 1979. *Suicides.* New York: Basic Books.

Baker, Wayne. 1981. "Markets as Networks." Unpublished Ph.D. Dissertation. Evanston, IL: Northwestern University.

1983. "Floor Trading and Crowd Dynamics." In Patricia Adler and Peter Adler, eds. *Social Dynamics of Financial Markets.* Greenwich, CT: JAI Press.

1984. "The Social Structure of a National Securities Market." *AJS* 89:775–811.

Bales, Robert. 1950. *Interaction Process Analysis.* Cambridge, MA: Addison-Wesley.

Ballard, Dana H. 1986. "Cortical Connections and Parallel Processing: Structure and Function." *Beh. Brain. Sci.* 9, 1:67–120.

Barbano, F. 1968. "Social Structures and Social Functions: The Emancipation of Structural Analysis in Sociology." *Inquiry* 11:40–84.

Barr, Avron, and Edward Feigenbaum. 1981. *The Handbook of AI.* Vols. I and II. Stanford, CA: Heuristech Press.

Barrow, J., and F. Tipler. 1986. *The Cosmological Anthropic Principle.* New York: Oxford University Press.

Barry, Brian. 1980. "Superfox" (Review of Elster 1978). *Political Studies* 28:136–43.

1988. *Sociologists, Economists, and Democracy.* Chicago, IL: University of Chicago Press.

Barry, Brian, and Russell Hardin, eds. 1982. *Rational Man and Irrational Society?* Beverly Hills CA: Sage.

Bartos, O. J. 1967. *Simple Models of Group Behavior.* New York: Columbia University Press.

Baudelot, Christian, R. Establet, and J. Malemont. 1975. *La Petite Bourgeoisie en France.* Paris: Maspero.

Baudrillard, Jean. 1975. *The Mirror of Production.* St Louis, MO: Telos Press.

1981. *For a Critique of the Political Economy of the Sign.* Telos Press.

Baumol, William J. 1952. *Welfare Economics and the Theory of the State.* Cambridge, MA: Harvard University Press.

1972. "On Taxation and the Control of Externalities." *Am.Econ.Rev.* 62:307–22.

Baumol, W., J. Panzar, and R. Willig. 1982. *Contestable Markets and the Theory of Industry Structure.* New York: Harcourt Brace Jovanovich.

Bear, Mark, L. N. Cooper, and F. F. Ebner. 1987. "A Physiological Basis for a Theory of Synapse Modification." *Science* 237:42–8.

Beatty, J. 1981. "What's Wrong with the Received View of Evolutionary Theory?" *PSA 1980,* vol. 2. East Lansing MI: Philosophy of Science Association.

Bechofer, Frank, and Brian Elliott, eds. 1981. *The Petite Bourgeoisie: Comparative Studies of the Uneasy Stratum.* New York: St. Martin's.

Bechtel, W. 1988a. "Connectionism and the Philosophy of Mind: An Overview." *The Southern Journal of Philosophy* XXVI (Suppl.) 2:17–41.

1988b. *Philosophy of Mind: An Overview for Cognitive Science.* Hillsdale, NJ: Erlbaum.

Bechtel, W., and A. Abrahamsen. 1990. *Connectionism and the Mind: An Introduction to Parallel Distributed Processing.* Oxford: Blackwell.

Becker, Gary S. 1976. *The Economic Approach to Human Behavior.* Chicago, IL: University of Chicago Press.

1981. *A Treatise on the Family.* Cambridge, MA: Harvard University Press.

Beckner, Morton. 1974. "Reduction, Hierarchies, and Organization." In Ayala and Dobzhansky, eds. *Studies in the Philosophy of Biology: Reduction and Related Problems.* Berkeley: University of California Press.

Ben-Porath, Yoram 1980. "The F-Connection: Families, Friends, and Firms and the Organization of Exchange." *Population and Development Review* 6:1–30.

Benner, S. A., ed. 1988. *Redesigning the Molecules of Life.* New York: Springer-Verlag.

Bennett, Charles H. 1986. "On the Nature and Origin of Complexity in Discrete, Homogeneous, Locally-acting Systems." *Foundations of Physics.* 16 (6):585–92.

Berge, Pierre, Yves Pomeau, and Christian Vidal. 1984. *Order Within Chaos.* New York: Wiley.

Berger, P., and T. Luckmann. 1967. *Social Construction of Reality.* New York: Doubleday.

Berk, R. A., and S. F. Berk. 1983. "Supply-side Sociology of the Family: The Challenge of the New Home Economics." *Ann.Rev.Soc.* 9:375–95.

Berkowitz, S. D. 1982. *An Introduction to Structural Analysis: The Network Approach to Social Research.* Toronto: Butterworths.

Bernal, J. D. 1967. *The Origin of Life.* Cleveland, OH: World Publishing Company.

Bernstein, Richard. 1983. *Beyond Objectivism and Relativism.* Philadelphia: University of Pennsylvania Press.

Berry, Jeffrey. 1978. "On the Origin of Public Interest Groups: A Test of Two Theories." *Polity* 10:378–97.

Bhaskar, Roy. 1975. *A Realist Theory of Science.* Sussex: Harvester.

1978a. *The Possibility of Naturalism: A Philosophical Critique of the Contemporary Human Sciences.* Atlantic Highlands, NJ: Humanities Press.

1978b. "On the Possibility of Social Scientific Knowledge and the Limits of Naturalism." *J. Theory Soc. Behaviour* 8, 1:1–28.

1982. "Emergence, Explanation, and Emancipation." In Paul Secord, ed. *Explaining Human Behavior.* Beverly Hills, CA: Sage, pp. 275–310.

1983. *Dialectic, Materialism, and Human Emancipation.* London: New Left Review Books/Verso.

1986. *Scientific Realism and Human Emancipation.* London: Verso.

Bienenstock, E. L., L. N. Cooper, P. W. Munro. 1982. "A Theory for the Development of Neuron Selectivity." *J. Neurosci.* 2 (1):32–48.

Blalock, Hubert. 1969. *Theory Construction: From Verbal to Mathematical Formulations.* Englewood Cliffs, NJ: Prentice-Hall.

Blau, Peter. 1960. "Structural Effects." *ASR* 25:178–93.

1964. *Exchange and Power in Social Life.* New York: Wiley.

1972. "Interdependence and Hierarchy in Organizations." *Soc.Sci.Research* 1:1–24.

1975a. "Parameters of Social Structure." In Blau, P. ed. *Approaches to the Study of Social Structure.* New York: Free Press.

1975b. *Approaches to the Study of Social Structure.* New York: Free Press.

1977a. "A Macrosociological Theory of Social Structure." *AJS 83,* 1:25–54.

1977b. *Inequality and Heterogeneity: A Primitive Theory of Social Structure.* New York: Free Press.

1981. "Introduction: Diverse Views of Social Structure and Their Common Denominator." In P. Blau and R. K. Merton, eds. *Continuities in Structural Inquiry.* Beverly Hills, CA: Sage.

1982. "Structural Sociology and Network Analysis: An Overview." In P. Marsden and N. Lin, eds. *Social Structure and Network Analysis.* Beverly Hills, CA: Sage.

Blau, Peter, and Robert K. Merton, eds. 1981. *Continuities in Structural Inquiry.* Beverly Hills, CA: Sage.

Blim, Michael. 1990. *Made in Italy: Small Scale Industrialization: Its Consequences.* New York: Praeger.

Block, Fred. 1977. "The Ruling Class Does Not Rule." *Socialist Revolution* 33: 6–28.

1988. *Revising State Theory.* Philadelphia, PA: Temple University Press.

Block, Ned. 1978. "Troubles With Functionalism." In *Cognition: Issues in the Foundations of Psychology.* C. W. Savage, ed. Minnesota Studies in the Philosophy of Science, vol. 9, pp. 261–325. Reprinted in N. Block, ed. 1979. *Readings in Philosophy of Psychology.* Cambridge, MA: Harvard University Press.

1980. *Readings in the Philosophy of Psychology,* vols. 1–2. London: Methuen.

Bluestone, Barry, and Bennett Harrison. 1984. *The Deindustrialization of America.* New York: Basic.

Blumer, Herbert. 1969. *Symbolic Interactionism: Perspective and Method.* Englewood Cliffs, NJ: Prentice-Hall.

1975. "Exchange on Turner's 'Parsons as a Symbolic Interactionist.'" *Sociological Inquiry* 45:59–62.

Boden, Deirdre. 1990. "The World as It Happens: Ethnomethodology and Conversation Analysis." In G. Ritzer, ed. *Frontiers of Social Theory.* New York: Columbia University Press, pp. 185–213.

Boden, Margaret. 1981. *Minds and Mechanisms: Philosophical Psychology and Computational Models.* Brighton, England: Harvester Press.

1987. *Artificial Intelligence and Natural Man.* New York: Basic.

Bohm, David. 1980. *Wholeness and the Implicate Order.* New York: Routledge & Kegan Paul.

Bonner, J. T., ed. 1982. *Evolution and Development.* New York: Springer-Verlag.

Boorman, Scott and Harrison C. White. 1976. "Social Structure From Multiple Networks: II. Role Interlock." *AJS* 81, 4:730–80.

Boorman, Scott, and Paul R. Levitt. 1980a. "The Comparative Evolutionary Biology of Social Behavior." *Ann.R.Soc.* 6:213–33.

1980b. *The Genetics of Altruism.* New York: Academic Press.

1987. "The Cascade Effect: An Essay in Disequilibrium Theory." In L. Freeman, A. K. Romney, D. R. White, eds. *Research Methods of Social Networks Analysis.* Chicago, IL: Nelson-Hall.

Bosserman, Phillip. 1968. *Dialectical Sociology: An Analysis of the Sociology of Georges Gurvitch*. Boston, MA: Porter Sargent.

Bottomore, Tom. 1988. *Interpretation of Marx*. Oxford: Blackwell.

Boudon, Raymond. 1968. *A quoi sert la notion de structure?* Paris: Gallimard.

1971. *The Uses of Structuralism*. London: Heinemann.

1977. *Effet pervers et ordre social*. Paris: Presses Universitaires de France.

1981a. *The Logic of Social Action*. New York: Routledge & Kegan Paul.

1981b. "The Undesired Consequences and Types of Structures of Systems of Interdependence." In Peter Blau, ed. *Continuities in Structural Inquiry*. Beverly Hills, CA: Sage.

1982. *The Unintended Consequences of Social Action*. London: Macmillan/ New York: St. Martin's.

1984. *La Place du Désordre: Critique des théories du Changement Social*. Paris: Presses Universitaires de France.

1987. "The Individualistic Tradition in Sociology." In J. Alexander et al., eds. *The Micro-Macro Link*. Berkeley: University of California Press.

Boulding, Kenneth 1978. *Ecodynamics: A New Theory of Societal Evolution*. Beverly Hills, CA: Sage.

1981. *Evolutionary Economics*. Beverly Hills, CA: Sage.

Bourdieu, Pierre. 1977a. *Outline of a Theory of Practice*. Cambridge University Press.

1977b. "Symbolic Power." In D. Gleeson, ed. *Identity and Structure: Issues in the Sociology of Education*. London: Nafferton Books.

1980. *Le sens pratique*. Paris: Minuit. Translated as *The Logic of Practice*. Stanford, CA: Stanford University Press, 1990.

1984. *Distinction: A Social Critique of the Judgement of Taste*. Cambridge, MA: Harvard University Press.

1985. "The Social Space and the Genesis of Groups." *Soc.Sci.Info.* 24, 2:195–220.

1986a. "The Forms of Capital." In John G. Richardson, ed. *Handbook of Theory and Research for the Sociology of Education*. Westport, CT: Greenwood.

1986b. "From Rules to Strategies." *Cultural Anthropology*. 1:110–20.

1987. "What Makes a Social Class?" *Berkeley Journal of Sociology* 32:1–17.

1988. "On Interest and the Relative Autonomy of Symbolic Power." *Working Papers and Proceedings of the Center for Psychosocial Studies*, no. 20: 1–11.

1990. *In Other Words: Essays Towards a Reflexive Sociology*. Stanford, CA: Stanford University Press.

Bourricaud, Francois. 1975. "Contre le sociologisme." *Revue Fr. de Soc 16*:583–603.

Bowman, J. 1982. "The Logic of Capitalist Collective Action." *Soc. Sci. Info.* 21:571–604.

Boyd, R., and P. J. Richerson. 1985. *Culture and the Evolutionary Process*. Chicago, IL: University of Chicago Press.

Brandon, Robert. 1978. "Adaptation and Evolutionary Theory." *Stud. Hist. Phil. Sci* 9:181–206.

1981. "Biological Teleology: Questions and Explanations." *Stud. Hist. Phil. Sci* 12:91–105.

1985. "Adaptation Explanations." In David Depew and Bruce Weber, eds. *Evolution at a Crossroads*. Cambridge, MA: MIT Press.

Brandon, R. N., and R. Burian, eds. 1984. *Genes, Organisms, Populations: Controversies Over the Units of Selection.* Cambridge, MA: MIT Press.

Braudel, Fernand. 1980. *On History.* Chicago, IL: University of Chicago Press.

Braverman, Harry. 1974. *Labor and Monopoly Capital.* New York: Monthly Review.

Breiger, Ronald. 1974. "The Duality of Persons and Groups." *Soc. Forces* 53: 181–90.

Brenner, Robert. 1977. "The Origins of Capitalist Development: A Critique of Neo-Smithian Marxism." *New Left Review* 104:25–92.

1982. "The Agrarian Roots of European Capitalism." *Past and Present* 97: 16–113.

Bresnan, J. 1978. "A Realistic Transformational Grammar." In M. Halle, J. Bresnan, and G. A. Miller, eds. *Linguistic Theory and Psychological Reality.* Cambridge, MA: MIT Press, pp. 1–59.

ed. 1982. *The Mental Representation of Grammatical Relations.* Cambridge, MA: MIT Press.

Bresnan, J., and R. M. Kaplan. 1982. "Introduction: Grammars as Mental Representations of Language." In J. Bresnan, ed. *The Mental Representation of Grammatical Relations.* Cambridge, MA: MIT Press.

Brittan, A. 1973. *Meanings and Situations.* New York: Routledge & Kegan Paul.

Broadbent, D. 1985. "A Question of Levels: Comment on McClelland and Rumelhart." *Journal of Experim. Psych.: General* 114:189–92.

Brodbeck, May. 1968. "Methodological Individualisms: Definition and Reduction." In M. Brodbeck, ed. *Readings in the Philosophy of the Social Sciences.* New York: Macmillan.

Bronowski, J. 1970. "New Concepts in the Evolution of Complexity: Stratified Stability and Unbound Plans." *Zygon* 5.

Brooks, D.R., D. Cummings, and R. LeBlond. 1988. "Dollo's Law and the Second Law of Thermodynamics: Analogy or Extension." In Weber et al., *Entropy, Information, and Evolution.* Cambridge, MA: MIT Press, pp. 189–222.

Brooks, D., and E. Wiley. 1984. "Evolution as an Entropic Phenomenon." In J. W. Pollard, ed. *Evolutionary Theory: Paths into the Future.* New York: Wiley, pp. 141–71.

1986. *Evolution as Entropy: Toward a Unified Theory of Biology.* Chicago, IL: University of Chicago Press.

Bruce-Briggs, B., ed. 1979. *The New Class.* New Brunswick, NJ: Rutgers: Transaction Publishers.

Bruner, Jerome. 1986. *Actual Minds, Possible Worlds.* Cambridge, MA: Harvard University Press.

Buchanan, Allen. 1982. *Marx and Justice: The Radical Critique of Liberalism.* London: Methuen.

Buchanan, James, and William Stubblebine. 1962. "Externality." *Economica* 29:371–84.

Buchanan, James, and Gordon Tullock. 1962. *The Calculus of Consent: Logical Foundations of Constitutional Democracy.* Ann Arbor: University of Michigan Press.

Bunge, Mario. 1969. "The Metaphysics, Epistemology and Methodology of Levels." In L. L. Whyte, ed. *Hierarchical Structures.* New York: Elsevier.

1973a. *Method, Model and Matter.* Dordrecht: Reidel.

1973b. *Philosophy of Physics.* Dordrecht: Reidel.

1974. "The Concept of Social Structure." In W. Leinfeller and E. Kohler, eds. *Recent Developments in the Methodology of Social Science.* Dordrecht: Reidel.

1972–79. *Treatise of Basic Philosophy.* 4 vols. Dordrecht: Reidel [vol.3:1977 *The Furniture of the World.* vol. 4: 1977 *A World of Systems*].

Burawoy, Michael. 1979. *Manufacturing Consent.* Chicago, IL: University of Chicago Press.

1985. *The Politics of Production: Factory Regimes Under Capitalism and Socialism.* London: New Left Review Books.

Burger, Thomas. 1977. "Max Weber's Interpretive Sociology, The Understanding of Actions and Motives, and a Weberian View of Man." *Sociological Inquiry* 47:127–32.

Burian, Richard. 1983. "Adaptation." In M. Grene, ed. *Dimensions of Darwinism.* Cambridge University Press.

Burt, Ronald. 1976. "Positions in Networks." *Soc. For.* 55:93–122.

1977a. "Positions in Multiple Network Systems." *Soc. Forces* 56:106–31, 551–75.

1977b. "Power in a Social Topology." *Soc. Sci. R.* 6:1–83.

1980a. "Models of Network Structure." *Ann. Rev. Sociol.* 6:79–141.

1980b. "Autonomy in a Social Topology." *Am. Soc. Rev.* 85:892–925.

1988. "The Stability of American Markets." *AJS* 94, 2:356–95.

Burt, Ronald, and M. Minor. 1983. *Applied Network Analysis: A Methodological Introduction.* Beverly Hills, CA: Sage.

Cable, S., E. Walsh, and R. Warland. 1988. "Differential Paths to Political Activism: Comparisons of Four Mobilization Processes After the Three Mile Island Accident." *Social Forces* 66: 951–69.

Cairns-Smith, A. G. 1986. *Seven Clues to the Origin of Life: A Scientific Detective Story.* Cambridge University Press.

Calabresi, G., and P. Bobbitt. 1978. *Tragic Choices.* New York: Norton.

Calhoun, Craig. 1981. *The Question of Class Struggle: Social Foundations and Popular Radicalism During the Industrial Revolution.* Chicago, IL: University of Chicago Press.

1983. "The Radicalism of Tradition: Community Strength or Vulnerable Disguise and Borrowed Language?" *AJS* 88: 886–914.

Callon, M., and B. Latour. 1981. "Unscrewing the Big Leviathan: How Actors Macro-structure Reality and How Sociologists Help them to Do So." In K. Knorr-Cetina and A. Cicourel, eds. *Advances in Social Theory and Methodology: Toward an Integration of Micro- and Macro-Sociologies.* New York: Routledge & Kegan Paul, pp. 277–303.

Calvin, Melvin. 1969. *Chemical Evolution.* Oxford University Press.

Calvin, William H. 1986. *The River That Flows Uphill: A Journey from the Big Bang to the Big Brain.* New York: Macmillan.

Campbell, Donald T. 1966. "Evolutionary Epistemology." In P. A. Schlepp, ed. *The Philosophy of Karl Popper.* La Salle: Open Court.

1974. " 'Downward Causation' in Hierarchically Organized Biological Systems." In F. Ayala and T. Dobzhansky, eds. *Studies in the Philosophy of Biology.* New York: Macmillan.

Campbell, Jeremy. 1982. *Grammatical Man.* New York: Simon and Schuster.

1989. *The Improbable Machine: What the Upheavals in Artificial Intelligence*

402   Bibliography

Research Reveal About How the Mind Really Works. New York: Simon and Schuster.

Campbell, John. 1982. "Autonomy in Evolution." In Milkman, ed. *Perspectives in Evolution*. Sunderland, MA: Sinauer Associates.

——— 1983. "Evolving Concepts of Multigene Families." *Isozymes* 10:401–17.

——— 1985. "An Organizational Interpretation of Evolution." In D. Depew and B. Weber, eds. *Evolution at a Crossroads*. Cambridge, MA: MIT Press.

Caplow, Theodore. 1968. *Two Against One: Coalition in Triads*. Englewood Cliffs, NJ: Prentice-Hall.

Carello, C., M. Turvey, P. Kulger, and R. Shaw. 1984. "Inadequacies of the Computer Metaphor." In M. Gazzaniga, ed. *Handbook of Cognitive Neuroscience*. New York: Plenum, pp. 231–48.

Carneiro, R. L. 1970. "A Theory of the Origin of the State." *Science:*733–8.

Carrithers, Michael, Steven Collins, and Steven Lukes, eds. 1985. *The Category of the Person*. Cambridge University Press.

Carroll, Glenn R. 1984. "Organizational Ecology." *Ann. R. Soc.* 10:71–93.

——— 1987. *Ecological Models of Organizations*. New York: Harper Business.

Carroll, Glenn, and Jacques Delacroix. 1982. "Organizational Mortality in the Newspaper Industries of Argentina and Ireland: An Ecological Approach." *Admin.Sci.Quarterly* 27:169–98.

Carse, J. P. 1986. *Finite and Infinite Games*. New York: Free Press.

Cartwight, Nancy. 1983. *How the Laws of Physics Lie*. New York: Oxford University Press.

Castells, Manuel. 1979. *The Urban Question*. Cambridge, MA: MIT Press.

Causey, R. 1969. "Polanyi on Structure and Reduction." *Synthese* 20: 230–7.

Cerf, Walter. 1969. "Hartmann, Nicolai." *Encycl. Phil.* Vol. 3. New York: Macmillan, pp. 421–6.

Chalmers, Alan F. 1982. *What is This Thing Called Science?* New York: Humanities Press.

Chandler, Alfred. 1962. *Strategy and Structure*. New York: Macmillan.

——— 1977. *The Visible Hand*. Cambridge, MA: Harvard University Press.

——— 1980. *Managerial Hierarchies: Comparative Perspectives on the Rise of the Modern Industrial Enterprise*. Cambridge, MA: Harvard University Press.

Charbonnier, G. 1969. *Conversations with Claude Lévi-Strauss*. London: Cape.

Charon, Joel. 1985. *Symbolic Interaction: An Introduction, an Interpretation, an Integration*. 2nd ed. Englewood Cliffs, NJ: Prentice-Hall.

Chernavskaya, N. M., and D. S. Chernavski. 1984. "On the Problem of Origin of Biological Information." In K. Matsuno, ed. *Molecular Evolution and Protobiology*. Dordrecht: Reidel.

Child, John. 1972. "Organization, Structure, Environment, and Performance: The Role of Strategic Choice." *Sociology* 6: 1–22.

Chomsky, Noam. 1957. *Syntactic Structures*. New York: Norton.

——— 1959. "On Certain Formal Properties of Grammars." *Information and Control*. Reprinted in R. D. Luce, R. R. Bush, and E. Galander, eds. 1963. *Handbook of Math Psychology*. Vol. 2. New York: Wiley, pp. 137–67.

——— 1965. *Aspects of a Theory of Syntax*. Cambridge, MA: MIT Press.

——— 1966. *Cartesian Linguistics*. New York: Harper and Row.

——— 1972. *Language and Mind*. Extended ed. New York: Harcourt Brace.

——— 1980. *Rules and Representations*. New York: Columbia University Press.

1986. *Knowledge and Language: Its Nature, Origin, and Use.* New York: Praeger.

Chowdhury, Debashish. 1986. *Spin Glasses and Other Frustrated Systems.* Princeton, NJ: Princeton University Press.

Christiansen, Rupert. 1988. *Romantic Affinities.* New York: Putnam.

Churchland, Patricia S. 1986. *Neurophilosophy: Toward a Unified Science of the Mind-Brain.* Cambridge, MA: MIT Press.

Churchland Paul. 1984. *Matter and Consciousness.* Cambridge, MA: MIT Press.

1986a. "Cognitive Neurobiology: A Computational Hypothesis for Laminar Cortex." *Philosophy and Biology* 1, 1: 25–52.

1986b. "Some Reductive Strategies in Cognitive Neurobiology." *Journal of Philosophy* 78, 2: 67–90.

1989. *A Neurocomputational Perspective: The Nature of Mind and the Structure of Science.* Cambridge, MA: MIT Press.

Clark, A. 1989. *Microcognition: Philosophy, Cognitive Science, and Parallel Distributed Processing.* Cambridge, MA: MIT Press.

Clark, John W., Jeffrey V. Winston, and Johann Rafelski. 1984. "Self-organization of Neural Networks." *Physics Letters* 102A: 207.

Clark, Priscilla P., and Terry Nichols Clark. 1982. "The Structural Sources of French Structuralism." In Ino Rossi, ed. *Structural Sociology.* New York: Columbia University Press, pp. 22–46.

Clawson, Dan, Alan Neustadt, and James Bearden. 1986. "The Logic of Business Unity: Corporate Contributions to the 1980 Congressional Elections." *ASR* 51:797–811.

Clawson, Dan, and Alan Neustadt. 1989. "Interlocks, PACs, and Corporate Conservatism." *AJS* 94, 4: 749–73.

Cohen, G. A. 1973. "Bourgeois and Proletarians." In S. Avineri, ed. *Marxist Socialism.* New York: Lieber-Atherton, pp. 101–25.

1978. *Karl Marx's Theory of History: A Defense.* Princeton, NJ: Princeton University Press.

1982a. "Functional Explanation, Consequence Explanation, and Marxism." *Inquiry* 25:27–56.

1982b. "Reply to Elster, 'Marxism, Functionalism, and Game Theory'." *Theory and Society* 11:483–96.

1986. "Marxism and Functional Explanation." In John E. Roemer, *Analytical Marxism.* Cambridge University Press.

Cohen, Kalman, and Richard Cyert. 1975. *Theory of the Firm: Resource Allocation in a Market Economy.* Englewood Cliffs, NJ: Prentice-Hall.

Cohen, Paul R., and Edward A. Feigenbaum. 1982. *The Handbook of AI.* Vol. 3. Stanford, CA: Heuristech Press.

Cohen, R., and E. R. Service, eds. 1978. *Origins of the State.* Philadelphia: ISHI.

Cohen, Stephen, and John Zysman. 1987. *Manufacturing Matters.* New York: Basic.

Coleman, James. 1964. *Introduction to Mathematical Sociology.* New York: Free Press.

1971. "Collective Decisions." In Herman Turk and Richard Simpson, eds. *Institutions and Social Change.* Indianapolis, IN: Bobbs-Merrill.

1972. "Systems of Social Exchange." *J. of Math. Soc.* 2:145–63.

1974. *Power and the Structure of Society.* New York: Norton.

1975. "Social Structure and a Theory of Action." In Blau, ed. *Approaches to the Study of Social Structure.* New York: Free Press.

1980. "Authority Systems." *Public Opinion Quarterly* 44:143–63.

1982. *The Asymmetric Society.* Syracuse, New York: Syracuse University Press.

1986a. *Individual Interests and Collective Action: Selected Essays.* Cambridge University Press.

1986b. "Micro Foundations and Macrosocial Theory." In S. Lindenberg, J. Coleman, and S. Nowak, eds. *Approaches to Social Theory.* New York: Russell Sage Foundation.

1986c. "Social Structure and the Emergence of Norms Among Rational Actors." In Andreas Dickmann and Peter Mitter, eds. *Paradoxical Effects of Social Behavior: Essays in Honor of Anatol Papoport.* Heidelberg/Vienna: Physica-Verlag, pp. 55–83.

1986d. "Social Theory, Social Research, and a Theory of Action." *AJS* 91, 6:1309–35.

1987. "Actors and Actions in Social History and Social Theory: A Reply to Sewell." *AJS* 93, 1:172–75.

1988. "Social Capital in the Creation of Human Capital." In C. Winship and S. Rosen, eds. *AJS Supplement: Organizations and Institutions,* pp. S95–S120.

1990. *Foundations of Social Theory.* Cambridge, MA: Harvard University Press.

Colinvaux, Paul. 1980. *The Fates of Nations: A Biological Theory of History.* New York: Simon and Schuster.

Collier, J. 1988. "The Dynamics of Biological Order." In Weber, Depew, Smith, eds. *Entropy, Information, and Evolution.* Cambridge, MA: MIT Press, pp. 227–42.

Collins, Randall. 1975. *Conflict Sociology.* New York: Academic Press.

1979. *The Credential Society.* New York: Academic Press.

1981a. "On the Microfoundations of Macrosociology." *AJS* 86, 5:984–1014.

1981b. "Micro-Translation as a Theory-building Strategy." In K. Knorr and A. Cicourel, eds. *Advances in Social Theory and Methodology: Toward an Integration of Micro- and Macro-Sociology.* New York: Routledge & Kegan Paul.

1983. "Micro-Methods as a Basis for Macro-Sociology." *Urban Life* 12:184–202.

1985. *Weberian Sociological Theory.* Cambridge University Press.

1987. "Interaction Rituals, Power and Property." In J. Alexander et al. *The Micro-Macro Link.* Berkeley: University of California Press.

Collins, S. 1982. *Selfless Persons.* Cambridge University Press.

Colomy, Paul. 1986. "Recent Developments in the Functionalist Approach to Change." *Sociol. Focus* 19:139–58.

Cook, Karen. 1977. "Exchange and Power in Networks of Interorganizational Relations." *Sociol. Quarterly* 18:62–82.

1982. "Network Structures from an Exchange Perspective." In P. Marsden and Nan Lin, eds. *Social Structure and Network Analysis.* Beverly Hills, CA: Sage.

ed. 1987. *Social Exchange Theory.* Beverly Hills, CA: Sage.

Cook, Karen S., R. M. Emerson, M. Gillmore, and T. Yamagishi, eds. 1983. "The Distribution of Power in Exchange Networks: Theory and Experimental Results." *AJS* 89:275–305.

Cornman, James. 1962. "Intentionality and Intensionality." *Philosophical Quarterly* 12, No. 46:44–52.

Corrigan, Philip. 1980. "Towards a History of State Formation in Early Modern England." In P. Corrigan, ed. *Capitalism, State Formation, and Marxist Theory*. London: Quartet, pp. 27–48.

Coser, Lewis A. ed. 1965. *Georg Simmel*. Englewood Cliffs, NJ: Prentice-Hall.

ed. 1975. *The Idea of Social Structure: Papers in Honor of Robert K Merton*. New York: Harcourt Brace Jovanovich.

Cowan, T. D. 1982. "Nonlinear Phenomena in Physics and Biology." *Science* 217:G24–G25.

Cracraft, J. 1982. "A Non-equilibrium Theory for the Rate-control of Speciation and Extinction and the Origin of Macroevolution." *Evolution* 36: 474–98.

Creutzfeldt, Otto. 1990. "Brain, Perception, and Mind." In *Visual Perception: The Neurophysiological Foundation*. New York: Academic Press.

Crick, Francis. 1982. *Life Itself: Its Origins and Nature*. New York: Simon and Schuster.

1989. "The Recent Excitement About Neural Networks." *Nature* 337:129–32.

Crouch, C. 1982. *Trade Unions: The Logic of Collective Action*. London: Fontana.

Crow, J. F. 1969. "Molecular Genetics and Population Genetics." *Proc. XII Int. Congr. Genet.* 3:105–13.

Crow, J. F., and M. Kimura. 1970. *An Introduction to Population Genetics Theory*. New York: Harper & Row.

Crutchfield, J. P., and B. A. Huberman. 1980. "Fluctuations and the Onset of Chaos." *Phys. Lett.* 77A, 407.

Crutchfield, James P., J. Doyne Farmer, Norman H. Pachard, and Robert S. Shaw. 1986. "Chaos." *Scientific American* December 1986, Vol. 255, no. 6:46–57.

Cullen, J., and S. Novick. 1979. "The Davis-Moore Theory of Stratification: a Further Examination and Extension." *AJS* 84:1424–37.

Cummins, R. 1983. *The Nature of Psychological Explanation*. Cambridge, MA: MIT Press.

1989. *Meaning and Mental Representation*. Cambridge, MA: MIT Press.

Cummins, R., and G. Schwartz. 1988. "Prospects for a Radical Connectionism." In T. Horgan and J. Tieson, eds. *The Southern Journal of Philosophy* XXVI (Suppl.) 26:43–61.

Cvitanovic, Predrag, ed. 1984. *Universality in Chaos*. Bristol: Hilger/Taylor and Francis.

Dahrendorf, Rolf. 1958. "Out of Utopia: Toward a Reorientation of Sociological Analysis." *AJS* 64:115–27.

1959. *Class and Class Conflict in Industrial Society*. Stanford, CA: Stanford University Press.

1968a. "Toward a Theory of Social Conflict." *J.Conflict Resol.* 2:170–83.

1968b. "Homo Sociologicus." In his *Essays on the Theory of Society*. London: Routledge and Kegan Paul.

Darden, L., and N. Maull. 1977. "Interfield Theories." *Phil.Sci.* 44: 43–64.

Davidson, Donald. 1971. "Agency." In R. Binkley, R. Bronaugh, and A. Marras, eds. *Agents, Action, and Reason*. Toronto University Press.

1980. *Essays on Actions and Events*. Oxford University Press.

1984. *Inquiries Into Truth and Interpretation*. Oxford University Press.

Davies, James. 1962. "Toward a Theory of Revolution." *ASR* 27:5–19.

Davies, Paul. 1988. *The Cosmic Blueprint: New Discoveries in Nature's Creative Ability to Order the Universe.* New York: Simon and Schuster.

ed. 1989. *The New Physics.* Cambridge University Press.

Davis, M. ed. 1965. *The Undecidable.* New York: Raven.

Dawkins, R. 1976. *The Selfish Gene.* New York: Oxford University Press.

1982. *The Extended Phenotype: The Gene as the Unit of Selection.* New York: Oxford University Press.

1986. *The Blind Watchmaker.* New York: Oxford University Press.

DeGraaf, Nan Dirk, and Hendrick Derk Flap. 1988. "With a Little Help from My Friends: Social Resources as an Explanation of Occupational Status and Income in West Germany, The Netherlands and the United States." *Social Forces* 67:452–72.

De Groot, S., and P. Mazur. 1962. *Nonequilibrium Thermodynamics.* Amsterdam: North-Holland.

De Jasay, Anthony. 1989. *Social Contract, Free Ride: A Study of the Public Goods Problem.* New York: Oxford University Press.

Delbrueck, M. 1985. *Mind from Matter.* Boston, MA: Blackwell Scientific.

Dennett, Daniel. 1978. *Brainstorms.* Montgomery, VT: Bradford Books.

1984. *Elbow Room: The Varieties of Free Will Worth Wanting.* Cambridge, MA: MIT Press/A Bradford Book.

1987. *The Intentional Stance.* Cambridge, MA: MIT Press.

Denzin, Norman. 1970. "Symbolic Interactionism and Ethnomethodology." In J. Douglas, ed. *Understanding Everyday Life.* Chicago, IL: Aldine.

Depew, David, and Bruce Weber. 1985. *Evolution at the Crossroads.* Cambridge, MA: MIT Press.

1986. "Non-equilibrium Thermodynamics and Evolution: A Philosophical Perspective." *Philosophica* 37:27–57.

Derrida, J. 1977. *Of Grammatology.* Baltimore, MD: Johns Hopkins University Press.

1980. *Writing and Difference.* Chicago, IL: University of Chicago Press.

1983. *Dissemination.* Chicago, IL: University of Chicago Press.

1984. *Margins of Philosophy.* Chicago, IL: University of Chicago Press.

Dewdney, C., P. R. Holland, A. Kyprianidis, and J. P. Visier. 1988. "Spin and Nonlocality in Quantum Mechanics." *Nature* 336, 6199, 536–44.

Diakonoff, I. M. 1969. *Ancient Mesopotamia: A Socioeconomic History.* Moscow: Nauka Publishing House.

1974. *The Structure of Society and State in Early Dynastic Sumer.* Los Angeles, CA: Undeno Publ.

Dietrich, E., and C. Fields. 1988. "Some Assumptions Underlying Smolensky's Treatment of Connectionism." *Behavioral and Brain Sciences,* 11:29–31.

Dillon, L. S. 1981. *Ultrastructure, Macromolecules, and Evolution.* New York: Plenum.

1983. *The Inconstant Gene.* New York: Plenum.

DiTomaso, Nancy. 1982. " 'Sociological Reductionism' from Parsons to Althusser: Linking Action and Structure in Social Theory." *ASR* 47:14–28.

Ditton, Jason, ed. 1980. *The View from Goffman.* New York: St. Martin's.

Domb, C., and M. S. Green, eds. 1972. *Phase Transitions and Critical Phenomena.* London: Academic Press.

Dore, Ronald. 1976. *The Diploma Disease*. Berkeley: University of California Press.

Doreian, P. 1979. "On the Evolution of Group and Network Structure." *Social Networks* 2:235–52.

Dose, K. ed. 1983. *Origins of Life*. Kluwer Academic.

1984. "Molecular Evolution and Protobiology: An Overview." In K. Matsuno, ed. *Molecular Evolution and Protobiology*. New York: Plenum.

Dose, K., S. W. Fox, G. Deborin, T. Pavloskaya, eds., 1974. *The Origin of Life and Evolutionary Biochemistry*. New York: Plenum.

Douglas, Jack, ed. 1970. *Understanding Everyday Life*. Hawthorne, NY: Aldine.

Douglas, Jack et al. eds. 1977. *Existential Sociology*. Cambridge, MA: University Press.

Dover, G. A. 1982. "Molecular Drive: a Cohesive Mode of Species Evolution." *Nature* 299: 111–17.

Dover, G. A., and R. B. Flavell, eds. 1982. *Genome Evolution*. New York: Academic Press.

Dray, W. H. 1968. "Holism and Methodological Individualism." *Encycl. Phil.* vol. 4. New York: Macmillan, pp. 53–8.

Dreyfus, Hubert, and Paul Rabinow. 1982. *Michel Foucault: Beyond Structuralism and Hermeneutics*. Chicago, IL: University of Chicago Press.

Dreyfus, Hubert, and Stuart Dreyfus with Tom Athanusiou. 1986. *Mind Over Machine: The Power of Human Intuition and Expertise in the Era of the Computer*. New York: Free Press.

Dummett, Michael. 1968. "Frege." *Encycl. Phil*, vol. 3. New York: Macmillan, pp. 225–37.

1973. *Frege: Philosophy of Language*. London: Duckworth.

1987. *The Interpretation of Frege's Philosophy*. Cambridge, MA: Harvard University Press.

DuPlessis, R., and M. C. Howell. 1982. "Reconsidering the Early Modern Urban Economy: The Case of Leiden and Lille." *Past and Present* 94: 49–84.

Dyke, C. 1979. *Philosophy of Economics*. Englewood Cliffs, NJ: Prentice-Hall.

1988. *The Evolutionary Dynamics of Complex Systems*. New York: Oxford: University Press.

Ebbesson, Sven. 1984. "Evolution and Ontogeny of Neural Circuits." *Behav. Brain Sci.* 7(3):321–31.

Eccles, John. 1989. *Evolution of the Brain: Creation of the Self*. New York: Routledge & Kegan Paul.

Eccles, Robert. 1981. "The Quasifirm in the Construction Industry." *J. of Ec. Beh. and Org.* 2:335–57.

1985. *The Transfer Pricing Problem*. Lexington, MA: Lexington Press.

Eccles, Robert G., and Harrison C. White. 1986. "Firm and Market Interfaces of Profit Center Control." In S. Lindenberg, J. S. Coleman, and S. Nowak, eds. *Approaches to Social Theory*, New York: Russell Sage Foundation, pp. 203–20.

1988. "Price and Authority in Inter-Profit Center Transactions." In C. Winship and S. Rosen, eds. *AJS Supplement: Organizations and Institutions*, pp. S17–S51.

Edel, Abraham. 1959. "The Concept of Levels in Social Theory." In Llewellyn

408   Bibliography

Gross, ed. *Symposium on Sociological Theory,* Evanston, IL: Row Peterson, pp. 167–95.
Edelman, Gerald M. 1982. "Through a Computer Darkly: Group Selection and Higher Brain Function." *Bulletin of the American Academy of Arts and Sciences,* vol. 38, 1:20–48.
   1987. *Neural Darwinism: The Theory of Neuronal Group Selection.* New York: Basic.
   1988. *Topobiology: An Introduction to Molecular Embryology.* New York: Basic.
   1989. *The Remembered Present: A Biological Theory of Consciousness.* New York: Basic.
Edelman, Gerald M., and Vernon B. Mountcastle. 1978. *The Mindful Brain: Cortical Organization and the Group-Selective Theory of Higher-Brain Functions.* Cambridge, MA: MIT Press.
Edelman, G., and G. N. Reeke, Jr. 1982. "Selective Networks Capable of Representing Transformations, Limited Generalizations, and Associative Memory." *Proc. Natl. Acad. Sci.* 79:2091–5.
Edwards, Richard. 1979. *Contested Terrain: The Transformation of the Workplace in the Twentieth Century.* New York: Basic.
Ehrlich, Paul R. 1986. *The Machinery of Nature.* New York: Simon and Schuster.
Eigen, Manfred, 1977. "The Hypercycle: Principle of Natural Self-Organization." *Naturwissensschaften* 64:541–65.
   1978. "How Does Information Originate? Principles of Biological Self-Organization." In S. A. Rice, ed. *Advances in Chemical Physics 38:* 211–62.
   1983. "Self-Replication and Molecular Evolution." In D. S. Bendall, ed. *Evolution from Molecules to Men.* Cambridge University Press.
   1986. "The Physics of Molecular Evolution." In H. Baltscheffsky, H. Jhornvall, and R. Rigler, eds. *The Molecular Evolution of Life.* Cambridge University Press.
Eigen, M., and P. Schuster. 1979. *The Hypercycle: A Principle of Natural Self-Organization.* New York: Springer-Verlag.
Eiseley, Loren. 1967. "Man and Novelty." In *Time and Stratigraphy in the Evolution of Man.* US National Academy of Science, publ. 1469, pp. 65–79.
Ekeh, Peter. 1974. *Social Exchange Theory: The Two Traditions.* Cambridge, MA: Harvard University Press.
   1982. "Structuralism, the Principle of Elementarism, and the Theory of Civilization." In Ino Rossi, ed. *Structural Sociology,* New York: Columbia University Press, pp. 122–48.
Eldredge, N. 1983. "Phenomenological Levels and Evolutionary Paths." *Syst. Zool* 33 (4):338–47.
   1985. *The Unfinished Synthesis.* New York: Oxford University Press.
   1989 *Macroevolutionary Dynamics: Species, Niches, and Adaptive Peaks.* New York: McGraw-Hill.
Eldredge, Niles, and S. J. Gould. 1972. "Punctuated Equilibria: An Alternative to Phyletic Gradualism." In T. J. M. Schopf, ed. *Models in Paleobiology.* New York: Freeman, pp. 82–115.

Elias, Norbert. 1978. *What is Sociology.* London: Hutchinson.

Elsasser, Walter. 1962. "Physical Aspects of Non-Mechanistic Biological Theory." *J. Theoret. Biol.* 3:163–91.

1966. *Atom and Organism: A New Approach to Theoretical Biology.* Princeton, NJ: Princeton University Press.

1970. "The Role of Individuality in Biological Theory." In H. Waddington, ed. *Towards a Theoretical Biology,* vol 3, pp. 137–66.

1975. *The Chief Abstractions of Biology.* New York: Elsevier.

Elster, Jon. 1978. *Logic and Society: Contradictions and Possible Worlds.* New York: Wiley.

1979. *Ulysses and the Sirens.* Cambridge University Press.

1983a. *Sour Grapes.* Cambridge University Press.

1983b. *Explaining Technical Change.* Cambridge University Press.

1983c. "Reply to Comments." *Theory and Society* 12: 111–20.

1985. *Making Sense of Marx.* Cambridge University Press.

1986a. "Marxism, Functionalism and Game Theory." In John Roemer. *Analytical Marxism.* Cambridge University Press.

ed. 1986b. *Rational Choice.* New York: New York University Press.

1989a. "Marxism and Individualism." In M. Dascal and O. Gruengard, eds. *Knowledge and Politics.* Boulder, CO: Westview Press, pp. 189–206.

1989b. *The Cement of Society: A study of social order.* Cambridge University Press.

Emerson, Richard M. 1962. "Power-Dependence Relations." *ASR* 27:31–41.

1964. "Power-Dependence Relations: Two Experiments." *Sociometry* 27:282–98.

1972a. "Exchange Theory, Part I: A Psychological Basis for Social Exchange." In Joseph Berger, Morris Zelditch, Jr., and Bo Anderson, eds. *Sociological Theories in Progress,* vol. 2, pp. 38–57. Boston: Houghton-Mifflin.

1972b. "Exchange Theory, Part II: Exchange Relations and Networks." In Joseph Berger, Morris Zelditch, Jr., and Bo Anderson, eds. *Sociological Theories in Progress,* vol. 2, Boston: Houghton-Mifflin, pp. 58–87.

1976. "Social Exchange Theory." *Annual Rev. Soc.* 2:335–62. Palo Alto, CA: Annual Reviews.

1981. "Social Exchange Theory." In Morris Rosenberg and Ralph H. Turner, eds. *Social Psychology: Sociological Perspectives.* New York: Basic, pp. 30–65.

1987. "Toward a Theory of Value in Exchange." In Karen Cook, ed. *Social Exchange Theory.* Beverly Hills, CA: Sage.

Ennis, James G., and Richard Schreuer. 1987. "Mobilizing Weak Support for Social Movements: The Role of Grievance, Efficacy, and Cost." *Social Forces* 66, 2:390–409.

Ërdos, P., 1973. In Joel Spencer, ed. *The Art of Counting: Selected Writings.* Cambridge, MA: MIT Press.

Ërdos P., and A. Renyi 1960. *On the Evolution of Random Graphs.* Hungarian National Academy.

Evans, Peter, D. Rueschemeyer, and T. Skocpol, eds. 1985. *Bringing the State Back In.* Cambridge University Press.

Faia, Michael A. 1986. *Dynamic Functionalism: Strategy and Tactics.* Cambridge University Press.

Falk, A. E. 1981. "Purpose, Feedback, and Evolution." *Phil. Sci.* 48:198–217.

Farmer, Doyne, Tommaso Toffol, and Stephen Wolfram. 1984. "Cellular Automata." *Physica* 10D. Amsterdam: North-Holland.

Faulkner, Robert. 1983. *Music on Demand.* New Brunswick, NJ: Transaction Publishers.

Feigl, Herbert. 1958. "The 'Mental' and the 'Physical.' " *Minnesota Studies in Phil. Sci.* vol II:370–497.

Feigenbaum, Mitchell J. 1980. "Universal Behavior in Nonlinear Systems." *Los Alamos Science* 1:4–27.

    1983. "Universal Behavior in Nonlinear Systems." *Physica* 7D, 16.

Feinberg, William E., and Norris R. Johnson. 1988. " 'Outside Agitators' and Crowds: Results From a Computer Simulation Model." *Social Forces* 67, 2:398–423.

Feldman, J. A. 1985. "Connectionist Models and Their Applications: Introduction." *Cognitive Science* 9:1–2.

Feldman, J. A., and D. H. Ballard. 1982. "Connectionist Models and Their Properties." *Cognitive Science* 6:205–54.

Feynman, R. 1967. *The Character of Physical Law.* Cambridge, MA: MIT Press.

Field, A. 1981. "The Problem With Institutional Neoclassical Economics." *Explorations in Economic History* 18:174–98.

Field, R. and M. Burger, eds. 1985. *Oscillations and Travelling Waves in Chemical Systems.* New York: Wiley.

Fincher, Jack. 1981. *The Brain.* Washington, D.C: U.S. News Books.

Fine, Arthur. 1984. "And Not Anti-Realism Either." *Nous* 18. Reprinted in Janet Kourany, ed. 1987. *Scientific Knowledge.* Belmont, CA: Wadsworth.

    1986. *The Shaky Game: Einstein, Realism, and the Quantum Theory.* Chicago, IL: University of Chicago Press.

Fine, Gary Alan, 1990. "Symbolic Interactionism in the Post-Blumerian Age." In G. Ritzer, ed., *Frontiers of Social Theory.* New York: Columbia University Press.

Fine, Gary Alan, and Sherryl Kleinman. 1983. "Network and Meaning: An Interactionist Approach to Social Structure." *Symbolic Interaction* 6: 97–110.

Finkel, L. H., and G. M. Edelman. 1987. "Population Rules for Synapses in Networks." In G. Edelman, W. E. Gall, and W. M. Cowan, eds. *Synaptic Function.* New York: Wiley, pp. 711–57.

Fireman, Bruce, and William Gamson. 1979. "Utilitarian Logic in the Resource Mobilization Perspective." In Mayer N. Zald and John McCarthy, eds. *The Dynamics of Social Movements: Resource Mobilization, Social Control and Tactics,* Cambridge: Winthrop, pp. 8–44.

Fodor, J. A. 1981. *Representations: Philosophical Essays on the Foundations of Cognitive Science.* Cambridge, MA: MIT Press.

    1983. *The Modularity of Mind.* Cambridge, MA: MIT Press.

Fodor, J. A., and Z. W. Pylyshyn. 1988. "Connectionism and Cognitive Architecture: A Critical Analysis." *Cognition* 28:3–71.

Fogel, Robert. 1964. *Railroads and American Economic Growth.* Baltimore, MD: Johns Hopkins University Press.

Ford, J. 1989. "What is Chaos, That We Should Be Mindful of It?" In P. Davies, ed. *The New Physics*. Cambridge University Press, pp. 348–72.

Foster, Dieter. 1990 *Hydrodynamic Fluctuations, Broken Symmetry, and Correlation Functions*. Redwood, CA: Addison-Wesley.

Foster, J. 1974. *Class Struggle and the Industrial Revolution*. London: Methuen.

Foucault, Michel. 1965. *Madness and Civilization*. New York: Random House.

1972. *The Archaeology of Knowledge*. New York: Pantheon.

1973. *The Birth of the Clinic*. London: Tavistock.

1977. *Language, Countermemory, Practice: Selected Essays and Interviews*. Ithaca, NY: Cornell University Press.

1978. *History of Sexuality*, vol. 1. London: Allen Lane.

1979. *Discipline and Punish*. New York: Vintage.

1980. In Colin Gordon, ed. *Power/Knowledge: Selected Interviews and Other Writings*. New York: Pantheon Books.

Fox, Stanley W., ed. 1965. *The Origin of Prebiological Systems and of Their Molecular Matrices*. New York: Academic Press.

1988. *The Emergence of Life*. New York: Basic.

Fox, S. W., and K. Dose. 1977. *Molecular Evolution and the Origin of Life*. New York: M. Dekker.

Fox, T. D. 1981. "Evolution Evolving." In Y. Wolman, ed. *Origin of Life*, Dordrecht: Reidel, pp. 387–96.

Frank, Robert H. 1987. "If *Homo Economicus* Could Choose His Own Utility Function, Would He Want One with a Conscience?" *Am. Econ. Rev.* 77:593–604.

Franklin, I., and R. C. Lewontin. 1970. "Is the Gene the Unit of Selection?" *Genetics* 65:707–734.

Freeman, C. Robert. 1980. "Phenomenological Sociology and Ethnomethodology." In Jack Douglas et al., eds. *Introduction to the Sociologies of Everyday Life*. Boston: Allyn and Bacon, pp. 113–54.

Freeman, Jo. 1983. *Social Movements of the Seventies and Eighties*. New York: Longman.

Freeman, John, and Michael Hannan. 1983. "Niche Width and Organizational Populations." *Am.J.Soc.* 88, 2:1116–45.

Freeman, L., D. R. White, and A. Kimball Romney, eds. 1989. *Research Methods of Social Network Analysis*. George Mason University Press/University Press Association.

Freifelder, David. 1976. *Physical Biochemistry*. New York: Freeman.

Fried, Morton. 1970. "On the Evolution of Social Stratification and the State." In E. O. Laumann et al., eds. *The Logic of Social Hierarchies*. Chicago, IL: Markham.

Friedman, Debra. 1983. "Why Workers Strike: Individual Decisions and Structural Constraints." In Michael Hechter, ed. *The Microfoundations of Macrosociology*. Philadelphia, PA: Temple University Press, pp. 250–83.

Friedman, James. 1986. *Game Theory with Applications to Economics*. New York: Oxford University Press.

Fullbrook, Mary. 1978. "Max Weber's 'Interpretive Sociology'." *Brit. J. Soc.* 29:71–82.

Gadamer, Hans-Georg. 1975. *Truth and Method*. New York: Seabury.

Gagliani, Giorgio. 1981. "How Many Working Classes?" *AJS* 87:259–85.

Galaskiewicz, Joseph. 1985. "Interorganizational Relations." *Ann. Rev. Soc.* 11: 281–304.

Galaskiewicz, Joseph, and Deborah Shatin. 1981. "Leadership and Networks Among Neighborhood Human Service Organizations." *Admin. Sci. Quarterly.* 26:434–48.

Galenson, David W. 1986. *Traders, Planters and Slaves: Market Behavior in Early English America.* Cambridge University Press.

Gallant, Mary J., and Sherryl Kleinman. 1983. "Symbolic Interaction and Ethnomethodology." *Symbolic Interaction* 6:1–18.

    1985. "Making Sense of Interpretations: Response to Rawls and the Debate between Symbolic Interactionism and Ethnomethodology." *Symbolic Interaction* 8:141–5.

Gamson, William, Bruce Fireman, and Steven Rytina. 1982. *Encounters With Unjust Authority.* Homewood, IL: Dorsey.

Gardner, H. 1985. *The Mind's New Science: A History of the Cognitive Revolution.* New York: Basic.

Gardner, M. 1979. *The Ambidextrous Universe: Mirror Asymmetry and Time-Reversed Worlds.* New York: Scribner.

Garfinkel, Alan. 1981. *Forms of Explanation: Rethinking the Questions in Social Theory.* New Haven, CT: Yale University Press.

Garfinkel, Harold. 1967. *Studies in Ethnomethodology.* Englewood Cliffs, NJ: Prentice-Hall.

    1986. *Ethnomethodological Studies of Work.* New York: Routledge & Kegan Paul.

    1988. "Evidence for Locally Produced, Naturally Accountable Phenomena of Order." *Sociological Theory* 6:103–9.

Garfinkel, H., M. Lynch, and E. Livingston. 1981. "The Work of a Discovering Science Constructed with Materials from the Optically Discovered Pulsar." *Philosophy of Soc. Sci.* 11:131–58.

Garrioch, David. 1986. *Neighborhood and Community in Paris, 1740–1790.* Cambridge University Press.

Gatlin, Lila. 1972. *Information Theory and the Living System.* New York: Columbia University Press.

Gazzaniga, Michael S. 1970. *The Bisected Brain.* New York: Appleton-Century Crofts.

    ed. 1984. *Handbook of Cognitive Neuroscience.* New York: Plenum.

    1985. *The Social Brain.* New York: Basic Books.

    1988. "The Dynamics of Cerebral Specialization: Modular? Intersections." In L. Weiskrantz, ed. *Thought Without Language.* New York: Oxford University Press.

Geertz, Clifford. 1973. *The Interpretation of Cultures.* New York: Basic/Harper.

    1983. *Local Knowledge.* New York: Basic.

Gellner, Ernest, ed. 1973. *Cause and Meaning in the Social Sciences.* New York: Routledge & Kegan Paul.

Georgescu-Roegen, N. 1971. *The Entropy Law and the Economic Process.* Cambridge, MA: Harvard University Press.

Germani, Gino. 1978. *Authoritarianism, Fascism and National Populism.* New Brunswick, NJ: Transaction Publishers.

    1981. *The Sociology of Modernization.* New Brunswick, NJ: Transaction Publishers.

Ghiselin, M. T. 1974. "A Radical Solution to the Species Problem." *Syst. Zool.* 23:536–54.

    1981. "Categories, Life, and Thinking." *Beh. Brain Sciences* 4:269–313.

Giddens, Anthony. 1976. *New Rules of Sociological Method: A Positive Critique of Interpretative Sociologies*. New York: Basic.

1979. *Central Problems in Social Theory: Action, Structure, and Contradiction in Social Analysis*. Berkeley: University of California Press.

1984. *The Constitution of Society: An Outline of the Theory of Structuration*. Cambridge, MA: Polity Press.

Giere, R. 1968. "Structure of an Organism." *Science* 162:410.

Giesen, Bernhard. 1987. "Beyond Reductionism: Four Models Relating Micro and Macro Levels." In J. Alexander et al., eds. *Micro-Macro Link*. Berkeley: University of California Press.

Glasdorf, P., and I. Prigogine. 1971. *Thermodynamic Theory of Structure, Stability, and Fluctuation*. New York: Wiley-Interscience.

Glasersfeld, E. von. 1984. "An Introduction to Radical Constructionism." In P. Watzlawick, ed. *The Invented Reality*. New York: Norton, pp. 17–40.

Glass, Leon, and Michael Mackey. 1988. *From Clocks to Chaos*. Princeton University Press.

Gleick, James. 1987. *Chaos: Making a New Science*. New York: Viking-Penguin.

Godelier, Maurice. 1970. "Structure and Contradiction in *Capital*." In Michael Lane, ed. *Introduction to Structuralism*. New York: Harper.

1972. *Rationality and Irrationality in Economics*. New York: Monthly Review.

1988. *The Mental and the Material*. London: Verso.

Goffman, Erving. 1959. *The Presentation of Self in Everyday Life*. New York: Doubleday.

1963. *Behavior in Public Places*. New York: Free Press.

1971. *Relations in Public: Microstudies of the Public Order*. New York: Basic.

1972. *Strategic Interaction*. New York: Ballantine.

Goldbeter, A., and S. R. Caplan. 1976. "Oscillatory Enzymes." *Ann. Rev. Biophysics and Bioengineering* 5:449–73.

Goldmann, Lucien. 1964. *The Hidden God*. New York: Routledge & Kegan Paul.

1967. *The Human Sciences and Philosophy*. London: Cape.

Goldstone, Jack. 1986. "State Breakdown in the English Revolution: A New Synthesis." *AJS* 92:257–322.

Gonos, George. 1977. " 'Situation' Versus 'Frame': The 'Interactionist' and the 'Structuralist' Analyses of Everyday Life." *ASR* 42:854–67.

Goodman, Nelson. 1978. *Ways of Worldmaking*. Indianapolis, IN: Hacking.

1983. *Fact, Fiction, and Forecast*. Cambridge, MA: Harvard University Press.

Gorman, Robert A. 1977. *The Dual Vision: Alfred Schutz and the Myth of Phenomenological Social Science*. New York: Routledge and Kegan Paul.

Gorz, A., ed. 1976. *The Division of Labor*. New York: Longman.

Gould, Carol. 1978. *Marx's Social Ontology: Individuality and Community in Marx's Theory of Social Reality*. Cambridge, MA: MIT Press.

Gould, Stephen Jay. 1977. *Ever Since Darwin: Reflections in Natural History*. New York: Norton.

1980. "Is a New General Theory of Evolution Emerging?" *Paleobiology* 6: 119–30.

1982a. "Darwinism and the Expansion of Evolutionary Theory." *Science* 216: 380–87.

1982b. "The Meaning of Punctuated Equilibrium and Its Role in Validating a Hierarchical Approach to Macroevolution." In Roger Milkman, ed. *Perspectives on Evolution.* Sunderland, MA: Sinauer Associates.

Gould, S. J., and N. Eldredge. 1977. "Punctuated Equilibrium: The Tempo and Mode of Evolution Reconsidered." *Paleobiology* 3:115–57.

Gould, S. J., and E. S. Vrba. 1982. "Exaptation – A Missing Term in the Science of Form." *Paleobiology* 8:4–15.

Gouldner, Alvin 1970. *The Coming Crisis of Western Sociology.* New York: Basic.

1982. *The Future of Intellectuals and the Rise of the New Class.* New York: Seabury.

Granovetter, Mark. 1973. "The Strength of Weak Ties." *AJS* 78:1360–80.

1978. "Threshold Models of Collective Behavior." *AJS 83*:1420–43.

1979. "The Theory-Gap in Social Network Analysis." In P. Holland and S. Leinhardt, eds. *Perspectives on Social Network Research.* New York: Academic Press.

1983. "The Strength of Weak Ties: A Network Theory Revisited." In *Sociological Theory* 1:201–33.

1985. "Economic Action and Social Structure: The Problem of Embeddedness." *AJS 91,* 3:481–510.

Granovetter, Mark, and R. Soong. 1986. "Threshold Models of Interpersonal Effects on Consumer Demand." *Journal of Economic Behavior and Organization* 7 (1):83–99.

Grant, Michael. 1987. *The Rise of the Greeks.* New York: Scribner.

Grebogi, C., E. Ott, and J. Yorke. 1987. "Chaos, Strange Attractors, and Fractal Basin Boundaries in Nonlinear Dynamics." *Science* 238, 632.

Grene, M. 1967. "Biology and the Problem of Levels of Reality." *The New Scholastic* 41:427–49.

Grobstein, Clifford. 1973. "Hierarchical Order and Neogenesis." In H. H. Pattee. *Hierarchy Theory.* New York: Braziller.

Grossberg, S. 1980. "How Does the Brain Build a Cognitive Code?" *Psychological Review* 87:1–51.

Grossman, Siegfried, and Gottfried Mayer-Kress. 1989. "Chaos in the International Arms Race." *Nature* 337:701–04.

Grunbaum, Branko, and G. C. Shephard. 1986. *Tilings and Patterns.* New York: Freeman.

Gurvitch, G. 1958. *Traité de Sociologie.* Paris: Presses Universitaires de France.

Habermas, Jürgen. 1970. *Toward a Rational Society.* Boston, MA: Beacon Press.

1971. *Knowledge and Human Interests.* Boston, MA: Beacon.

1973. *Theory and Practice.* Boston, MA: Beacon.

1975. *Legitimation Crisis.* Boston, MA: Beacon.

1979. *Communication and the Evolution of Society.* Boston, MA: Beacon.

1985. *The Theory of Communicative Action.* Vol. I: *Reason and the Rationalization of Society.* Boston, MA: Beacon.

1989. *The Theory of Communicative Action.* Vol. II: *Lifeworld and System: A Critique of Functionalist Reason.* Boston, MA: Beacon.

Hacking, Ian. 1981. *Scientific Revolutions.* Oxford University Press.

1983. *Representing and Intervening.* Cambridge University Press.

Haferkamp, Hans. 1987. "Complexity and Behavior Structure, Planned Associations and Creation of Structure." In J. Alexander et al., eds. *The Micro-Macro Link.* Berkeley: University of California Press.

Hägerstrand, Torsten. 1968. *Innovation Diffusion as a Spatial Process.* Chicago, IL: University of Chicago Press.

Haines, Valerie. 1985. "From Organicist to Relational Human Ecology." *Sociological Theory* 3:65–74.

Haken, H., ed. 1978. *Synergistics: An Introduction: Nonequilibrium Phase Transitions and Self-Organization in Physics, Chemistry, and Biology.* New York: Springer-Verlag.

1984. *Advanced Synergetics.* New York: Springer-Verlag.

Halfon, Efrim, ed. 1979. *Theoretical Systems Ecology.* New York: Academic Press.

Hall, Peter. 1987. "Interactionism and the Study of Social Organization." *Sociol.Quart.* 28 (1):1–22.

Halmos, Paul R. 1957. "Nicholas Bourbaki." *Sci.Am.* 196:88–9.

Hamilton, Gary G., and Nicole Woolsey Biggart. 1988. "Market, Culture, and Authority: A Comparative Analysis of Management and Organization in the Far East." In C. Winship and S. Rosen, eds. *AJS Supplement: Organizations and Institutions,* pp. S52–S94.

Hamilton, W. D. 1963. "The evolution of altruistic behavior." *Americ. Natural.* 97:354–56.

1964. "The Genetical Theory of Social Behaviour." I, II, *J. Theor. Biol.* 7(1): 1–52.

Hanagan, Michael P. 1980. *The Logic of Solidarity: Artisans and Industrial Workers in Three French Towns, 1871–1914.* Urbana, IL: University of Illinois Press.

1989. *Nascent Proletarians: Class Formation in Post-Revolutionary France.* Oxford: Blackwell.

Hanagan, M., and C. Stephenson. 1986a. *Confrontation, Class Consciousness, and the Labor Process.* Westport, CT: Greenwood.

1986b. *Proletarians and Protest: The Roots of Class Formation in an Industrializing World.* Westport, CT: Greenwood.

Handel, Warren. 1982. *Ethnomethodology: How People Make Sense.* Englewood Cliffs, NJ: Prentice-Hall.

Hannan, M. T. 1982. "Families, Markets, and Social Structures: An Essay on Becker's *A Treatise on the Family." J.Econ.Lit.* 20: 65–72.

Hannan, Michael, and John Freeman. 1977. "The Population Ecology of Organizations." *Am.J.Soc.* 82, 5:929–64.

1986. "The Ecology of Organizations: Structural Inertia and Organizational Change." In S. Lindenberg et al. eds. *Approaches to Social Theory.* New York: Russell Sage Foundation.

Hao Bai-Lin, ed. 1984. *Chaos.* Singapore: World Scientific.

Haraway, Donna. 1983. "Signs of Dominance: From Physiology to a Cybernetics of Primate Society." *Studies in the History of Biology* VI:129–219.

Hardin, Garrett. 1960. "The Competitive Exclusion Principle." *Science* 131: 1292–7.

1968. "The Tragedy of the Commons." *Science* 7, 162:1234–48.

1974. "Living on a Lifeboat." *Bioscience* 24, 10:561–67.

Hardin, Russell. 1971. "Collective Action as an Agreeable n-person Prisoner's Dilemma." *Beh.Sci.* 16:472–81.

1982. *Collective Action.* Baltimore, MD: Johns Hopkins University Press.

Harnad, S. 1982. "Neoconstructivism: a Unifying Theme for the Cognitive Sciences." In T. Simon and R. Scholes, eds. *Language, Mind, and Brain.* Hillsdale, NJ: Erlbaum.

1989. "Minds, Machines, and Searle." *Journal of Experimental and Theoretical Artificial Intelligence* 1:5–25.

Harré, Rom. 1972. *The Philosophy of Science.* New York: Oxford University Press.

1980. *Social Being: A Theory for Social Psychology.* Totowa, NJ: Littlefield.

Harré, R., D. Clarke, and N. de Carlo, eds. 1985. *Motives and Mechanisms: An Introduction to the Psychology of Action.* London: Routledge & Kegan Paul.

Harré, R., and Paul Secord. 1979. *The Explanation of Social Behaviour.* Totowa, NJ: Littlefield.

Harris, Marvin. 1979. *Cultural Materialism.* New York: Random House.

Harsanyi, John. 1969. "Rational Choice Models of Political Behavior vs. Functionalist and Conformist Theories." *World Politics 21:*513–38.

1977. *Rational Behavior and Bargaining Equilibrium in Games and Social Situations.* Cambridge University Press.

Hartley, J. B., and S. W. Hawking. 1983. "Wave Function of the Universe." *Physical Review* D28:2960–4.

Hartmann, N. 1975. *New Ways of Ontology.* Westport, CT: Greenwood.

Haugeland, John. 1981. "Semantic Engines: An Introduction of Mind Design." In J. Haugeland, ed. *Mind Design,* Montgomery, VT: Bradford, pp. 1–34.

1989. *Artificial Intelligence: The Very Idea.* Cambridge, MA: MIT Press.

Hawking, Stephen. 1988. *A Brief History of Time.* New York: Bantam.

Hawley, Amos, ed. 1979. *Societal Growth: Process and Implications.* New York: Free Press.

Hayek, F. A. 1967. "The Results of Human Action but Not of Human Design." In F. A. Hayek, *Studies in Philosophy, Politics and Economics.* New York: Routledge & Kegan Paul.

Heap, James L., and Phillip A. Roth. 1973. "On Phenomenological Sociology." *ASR* 38:354–67.

Heath, Anthony. 1976. *Rational Choice and Social Exchange: A Critique of Exchange Theory.* Cambridge University Press.

Hechter, Michael. 1983a. "A Theory of Group Solidarity." In his, ed. *The Microfoundations of Macrosociology,* Philadelphia, PA: Temple University Press, pp. 16–57.

ed. 1983b. *The Microfoundations of Macrosociology.* Philadelphia, PA: Temple University Press.

1986. "Comment [on Olson]." In Lindenberg, *Approaches to Social Theory.* New York: Russell Sage Foundation.

1987. *Principles of Group Solidarity.* Berkeley: University of California Press.

Heider, Fritz. 1958. *The Psychology of Interpersonal Relations.* New York: Wiley.

Heller, Agnes. 1976. *The Theory of Need in Marx.* New York: St. Martin's.

Henry, Donald. 1989. *From Foraging to Agriculture: the Levant at the End of the Ice Age.* Philadelphia: University of Pennsylvania Press.

Heritage, John. 1984. *Garfinkel and Ethnomethodology.* Cambridge, MA: Polity Press.

Hernes, Gudmund. 1976. "Structural Change in Social Processes." *AJS* 82, 3: 513–47.

Hess, B., A. Goldbeter, and R. Lefever. 1978. "Temporal, Spatial, and Functional Order in Regulated Biochemical Cellular Systems." *Advances in Chemical Physics.* Vol. 38:363–413.

Hewitt, John. 1984. *Self and Society: A Symbolic Interactionist Social Psychology.* 3rd. ed. Newton, MA: Allyn and Bacon.

Heydebrand, W. "Marxist Structuralism." In Blau and Merton, *Continuities in Structural Inquiry.* 1981. Beverly Hills, CA: Sage.

Hilmy, S. Stephen. 1987. *The Later Wittgenstein.* Oxford: Blackwell.

Hindess, Barry. 1986 "Actors and Social Relations." In Mark L. Wardell and Stephen P. Turner, eds. *Sociological Theory in Transition,* Boston: Allen and Unwin, pp. 113–26.

Hintikka, J. 1963. "The Modes of Modality." *Acta Philosophica Finnica* 16:68–82.

Hinton, G. E., and J. A. Anderson, eds. 1981. *Parallel Models of Associative Memory.* Hillsdale, NJ: Erlbaum.

Hirschman, Albert. 1970. *Exit, Voice, and Loyalty: Responses to Decline in Firms, Organizations, and States.* Cambridge, MA: Harvard University Press.

——— 1981. *Essays in Trespassing.* Cambridge University Press.

——— 1982. "Rival Interpretations of Market Society: Civilizing, Destructive, or Feeble?" *J. Econ. Lit.* 20, 4:1463–84.

——— 1986. *Rival Views of Market Society: And Other Recent Essays.* Baltimore, MD: Viking-Penguin.

Ho, M. W., and P. T. Saunders. 1983. *Beyond Neo-Darwinism.* New York: Academic Press.

Ho, Mae-Wan, Peter Saunders, and Sidney Fox. 1986. "A New Paradigm for Evolution" *New Scientist* 1497:41–3.

Hockett, C. F. 1960. "The Origin of Speech." *Sci. Am.* 203:88–108.

Hodgson, Geoffrey. 1988. *Economics and Institutions: A Manifesto for a Modern Institutional Economics.* Philadelphia: University of Pennsylvania Press.

Hofstadter, Douglas R. 1979. *Gödel, Escher, Bach: An Eternal Golden Braid.* New York: Basic.

——— 1981. "Mathematical Chaos and Strange Attractors." *Scientific American,* November 1981. Reprinted in his *Metamagical Themas.* New York: Basic. 1985.

——— 1985. *Metamagical Themas.* New York: Basic.

Hofstadter, D., and D. Dennett. 1981. *The Mind's I.* New York: Basic.

Holden, Arun, ed. 1986. *Chaos.* Princeton, NJ: Princeton University Press.

Holland, Paul, and Samuel Leinhardt. 1979. *Perspectives on Social Network Research.* New York: Academic Press.

Holloway, J., and S. Picciotto, eds. 1979. *State and Capital: A Marxist Debate.* Austin: University of Texas Press.

Holzmueller, Werner. 1984. *Information in Biological Systems: The Role of Macromolecules.*

Homans, George C. 1950. *The Human Group.* New York: Harcourt, Brace and World.

——— 1964a. "Commentary." *Soc. Inquiry* 34:225–31.

——— 1964b. "Bringing Man Back In." *ASR* 29:809–18.

——— 1967. *The Nature of Social Science.* New York: Harcourt, Brace and World.

——— 1971a. "Commentary." In Herman Turk and Richard Simpson, eds. *Institu-*

tions and Social Exchange. Indianapolis, IN: Bobbs-Merrill, pp. 363–74.

1971b. "Reply to Blain." *Sociol. Inquiry* 41:19–24

1974. *Social Behavior: Its Elementary Forms.* New York: Harcourt Brace Jovanovich.

1975 "What Do We Mean by Social 'Structure'?" In P. Blau, ed. *Approaches to the Study of Social Structure.* New York: Free Press.

Hooker, Clifford. 1981. "Towards a General Theory of Reduction." *Dialogue* 20:496–529.

Hookway, C., ed. 1985. *Minds, Machines and Evolution.* Cambridge University Press.

Hookway, C., and P. Pettit, eds. *Action and Interpretation.* Cambridge University Press.

Hopcroft, J. E., and J. D. Ullman. 1969. *Formal Languages and Their Relation to Automata.* Reading, MA: Addison-Wesley.

Hopfield, J. J. 1982 "Neural Networks and Physical Systems With Emergent Collective Computational Abilities." *Proc. Natl. Acad. Sci. USA* 79: 2554–8.

Hopfield, J. J., D. I. Feinstein, and R. G. Palmer. 1983. " 'Unlearning' Has a Stabilizing Effect in Collective Memories." *Nature* (July):158–9.

Hopfield, John J., and David W. Tank. 1986. "Computing With Neural Circuits: A Model." *Science* 233:625–33.

Hoyle, Fred. 1983. *The Intelligent Universe.* London: M. Joseph.

Hoyle, F., and C. Wickramasinghe. 1981. *Evolution from Space.* London: Dent.

Hsu, Cheng-Kuang, R. M. Marsh, and H. Mannari. 1983. "An Examination of the Determinants of Organizational Structure." *AJS* 88:975–96.

Hsu, Laura. 1984. "Concepts of Prebiological Evolution." In Matsuno Koichiro, *Molecular Evolution and Protobiology.* New York: Plenum.

Hubel, David. 1988. *Eye, Brain, and Vision.* New York: Scientific American Library. Distributed by W. H. Freeman.

Hubin, Donald C. 1986. "Of Bindings and By-Products: Elster on Rationality." *Philos. and Publ. Affairs,* Winter, Vol. 1, 15:82–95.

Hull, David. 1974. *Philosophy of the Biological Sciences.* Englewood Cliffs, NJ: Prentice-Hall.

1980. "Individuality and Selection." *Ann. Rev. Ecol. Syst.* 11:311–32.

Hummell, Hans J., and Karl-Dieter Opp. 1968. "Sociology Without Sociology." *Inquiry* 11:205–26.

Hunnings, G. 1988. *The World and Language in Wittgenstein's Philosophy.* Albany: SUNY Press.

Hutchinson, G. E. 1978. *An Introduction to Population Ecology.* New Haven, CT: Yale University Press.

Hylland, A., and J. Elster, eds. 1985. *Foundations of Social Choice Theory.* Cambridge University Press.

Israel, Joachim. 1971. "The Principle of Methodological Individualism and Marxian Epistemology." *Acta Sociologica* 14:145–50.

Jacobs, Jane. 1984. *Cities and the Wealth of Nations.* New York: Random House.

Jantsch, Erich. 1980. *The Self-Organizing Universe.* Elmsford, NY: Pergamon.

ed. 1981. *The Evolutionary Vision.* Boulder, CO: Westview Press.

Jay, Martin. 1984. *Marxism and Totality: The Adventures of a Concept from Lukacs to Habermas.* Berkeley: University of California Press.

Jeffrey, R. C. 1978. *The Logic of Decision*. Boston: Houghton Mifflin.

Jencks, W. P. 1969. *Catalysis in Chemistry and Enzymology*. New York: Mc-Graw-Hill.

Jenkins, J. Craig. 1983a. "Resource Mobilization Theory and the Study of Social Movements." *Ann. Rev. Soc.* 9:527–53.

1983b. "The Transformation of a Constituency into a Movement: Farmworker Organizing in California." In Jo Freeman, ed. 1980. *Social Movements of the Sixties and Seventies*. New York: Longman.

Jensen, Michael, and William Mechling. 1976. "Theory of the Firm: Managerial Behavior, Agency Costs, and Ownership Structure." *Journal of Fin. Econ.* 3:305–60.

Jessop, Bob. 1982. *The Capitalist State: Marxist Theories and Methods*. New York: New York University Press.

Joas, Hans. 1985. *G. H. Mead*. Cambridge, MA: MIT Press.

Johnson, Michael. 1988. *Mind, Language, Machine: AI in the Poststructurist Age*. New York: St. Martin's.

Johnson-Laird, P. N. 1983. *Mental Models: Towards a Cognitive Science of Language, Inference and Consciousness*. Cambridge, MA: Harvard University Press.

1988. *The Computer and the Mind*. Cambridge, MA: Harvard University Press.

Joseph, Roger. 1987. *The Rose and the Thorn: Semiotic Structures in Morocco*. Tucson: University of Arizona Press.

Jungck, J. R. 1983. "Is the Neo-Darwinian Synthesis Robust Enough to Withstand the Challenge of Recent Discoveries in Molecular Biology and Molecular Evolution?" In P. Asquith and T. Nickles, eds. *PSA 1982*, vol. 2. Lansing, MI: Philosophy of Science Association.

1984a. "The Adaptationist Programme in Molecular Evolution." In K. Matsuno, ed. *Molecular Evolution and Protobiology*. New York: Plenum, pp. 345–64.

1984b. *On the Origins of Genetic Codes*. New York: Dowden/Academic Press.

Kadanoff, Leo. 1983. "Roads to Chaos." *Phys. Today,* 36n, 12:46–53.

Kahneman, Daniel, Paul Slavic, and Amos Tversky. 1982. *Judgment Under Uncertainty: Heuristics and Biases*. Cambridge University Press.

Kantor, Brian. 1979. "Rational Expectations and Economic Thought." *J. Econ. Lit.* 17:1422–41.

Katchalsky, A. 1971. "The Isodynamics of Flow and Biological Organization." *Zygon* 6.

Katchalsky, A., and P., Curran. 1975. *Nonequilibrium Thermodynamics in Biophysics*. Cambridge, MA: Harvard University Press.

Katznelson, Ira. 1985. "Working-Class Formation and the State: Nineteenth-Century England in American Perspective." In Evans et al., eds. *Bringing the State Back In*. Cambridge University Press, pp. 257–84.

Katznelson, Ira, and A. R. Zolberg, eds. 1986. *Working-Class Formation: Nineteenth-Century Patterns in Western Europe and the United States*. Princeton, NJ: Princeton University Press.

Kauffman, Stuart. 1969. "Metabolic Stability and Epigenesis in Randomly Connected Graphs." *J. Theor. Biol.* 22:437–67.

1983. "Development Constraints: Internal Factors in Evolution." In B. Goodwin, N. Holder, and C.G. Wylie, eds. *Developmental Evolution*. Cambridge University Press, pp. 195–225.

1984. "Emergent Properties in Random Complex Automata." *Physica* 10D (1–2):145–56.

1985. "Self-Organization, Selective Adaption and Its Limits: A New Pattern of Inference in Evolution and Development." In D. Depew and B. Weber, *Evolution at a Crossroads.* Cambridge, MA: MIT Press.

Kaufman, Michele. 1969. "A Possible Mechanism for the Origin of the Sequence of Cosmic Bodies." In L. L. Whyte, ed. *Hierarchical Structures.* New York: Elsevier.

Keat, R. 1981. *The Politics of Social Theory.* Chicago, IL: University of Chicago Press.

Keat, R., and J. Urry. 1975. *Social Theory as Science.* New York: Routledge & Kegan Paul.

Kelle, V., and M. Kovalson. 1973. *Historical Materialism.* Moscow: Progress.

Kelley, Harold. 1984. "Theoretical Description of Interdependence by Means of Transition Lists." *J. Person. Soc. Psychol.* 47:956–82.

Kelly, J. 1978. *Arrow Impossibility Theorems.* New York: Academic Press.

Kemper, Theodore. 1978. *A Social Interactional Theory of Emotions.* New York: Wiley.

Kennedy, Paul. 1987. *The Rise and Decline of Great Powers.* New York: Random House.

Kenny, Anthony. 1986. *The Legacy of Wittgenstein.* Oxford: Blackwell.

Kessler, S., and W. McKenna. 1978. *Gender: An Ethnomethodological Approach.* New York: Wiley.

Kidron, Michael. 1974. *Capitalism and Theory.* London: Pluto Press.

Killian, Lewis M. 1984. "Organization, Rationality, and Spontaneity in the Civil Rights Movement." *ASR* 49:770–83.

Kim, Jaegwon. 1978. "Supervenience and Nomological Incommensurables." *Am. Phil. Quarterly* 15:149–56.

1984. "Concepts of Supervenience." *Phil. Phenom. Res.* 45:153–76.

Kimura, Motoo. 1979. "The Neutral Theory of Molecular Evolution." *Scientific American* 24, 5:98–126.

1982. *Molecular Evolution, Protein Polymorphism, and Neutral Theory.* Tokyo: Japan Scientific Societies Press.

1985. *The Neutral Theory of Molecular Evolution.* Cambridge University Press.

Kimura, M., and T. Ochta. 1971. *Theoretical Aspects of Population Genetics.* Princeton, NJ: Princeton University Press.

Kirkpatrick, S. 1981. *Disordered Systems and Localization.* Lecture Notes in Physics, vol. 149. C. Castellani, C. Dicastro, and L. Peliti, eds. New York: Springer-Verlag.

Klandermans, Bert, and Dirk Oegema. 1987. "Potentials, Networks, Motivations, and Barriers: Steps toward Participation in Social Movements." *ASR* 52:519–31.

Klee, Robert. 1984. "Micro-Determinism and Concepts of Emergence." *Phil. Sci* 51:44–63.

Knoke, David H. 1988. "Incentives in Collective Action Organizations." *ASR* 53:311–29.

Knorr-Cetina, K., and A. Cicourel, eds. 1981. *Advances in Social Theory and Methodology: Toward an Integration of Micro- and Macro-Sociologies.* New York: Routledge & Kegan Paul.

Koestler, A. 1967. *The Ghost in the Machine.* New York: Macmillan.

Kohonen, Teuvo. 1978. *Associative Memory: A System-Theoretical Approach.* New York: Springer-Verlag.

1984. *Self-Organization and Associative Memory.* New York: Springer-Verlag.

Kolata, Gina. 1986. "Trying to Crack the Second Half of the Genetic Code." *Science* 233:1037–9.

Kondepudi, Dilip 1988 "Parity Violation and the Origin of Biomolecular Chirality." In Weber, Depew, Smith, eds. *Entropy, Information, and Evolution.* Cambridge, MA: MIT Press, pp. 41–50.

Konrad, G., and I. Szelenyi. 1979. *The Intellectuals on the Road to Class Power.* Sussex: Harvester.

Kontopoulos, Kyriakos M. 1973. "Marxism and the Intellectuals." Unpublished monograph.

1976. "The Making of an Authoritarian Regime: Greece, 1944–1974." Unpublished Ph.D. Dissertation, Harvard University.

1980. *Knowledge and Determination.* Amsterdam: Grüner.

1987. "Near or Partial Decomposability?" Unpublished paper.

Korpi, Walter. 1983. *The Democratic Class Struggle.* London: Routledge & Kegan Paul.

Kotarba, Joseph. 1979. "Existential Sociology." In Scott McNall, ed. *Theoretical Perspectives in Sociology,* New York: St. Martin's, pp. 348–68.

Kotarba, Joseph, and Andrea Fontana, eds. 1984. *The Existential Self in Society.* Chicago, IL: University of Chicago Press.

Kourany, Janet, ed. 1987. *Scientific Knowledge.* Belmont: Wadsworth.

Kramer, Samuel. 1981. *History Begins at Sumer.* Philadelphia, PA: University of Pennsylvania Press.

Krass, Iosif, and S. Hammondeh. 1981. *The Theory of Positional Games: With Applications in Economics.* New York: Academic Press.

Krassilov, V. A. 1980. "Directed Evolution: A New Hypothesis." *Evol. Th.* 4: 203–20.

Kuhn, Thomas. 1970. *The Structure of Scientific Revolutions.* 2nd ed. Chicago, IL: University of Chicago Press.

Küppers, Bernd-Olaf. 1983. *Molecular Theory of Evolution.* New York: Springer-Verlag.

1990. *Information and the Origin of Life.* MIT Press.

Lakatos, Imre. 1976. *Essays in Memory of Imre Lakatos.* R. S. Cohen, P. Feyerabend, and M. W. Wartofsky, eds. Boston: Reidel.

1978. *Philosophical Papers.* 2 vols. Cambridge University Press.

Lakatos, Imre, and Alan Musgrave, eds. 1970. *Criticism and the Growth of Knowledge.* Cambridge University Press.

Lancaster, K. 1973. "The Dynamic Inefficiency of Capitalism." *J. Pol. Econ.* 81:1092–1109.

Landau, L. D., and E. M. Lifschitz. 1969. *Statistical Physics.* Elmsford, New York: Pergamon.

Landauer, Rolf. 1988. "A Simple Measure of Complexity." *Nature* 336, 6197, p. 306.

Langton, C., ed. 1988. *Artificial Life.* Santa Fe Institute Studies in the Sciences of Complexity. Reading, MA: Addison-Wesley.

Lash, Scott, and John Urry. 1984. "The New Marxism of Collective Action: A Critical Analysis." *Sociology* 18, 1:33–50.

1987. *The End of Organized Capitalism.* Madison: University of Wisconsin Press.

Lashchyk, Eugene. 1986. "Heuristics for Scientific and Literary Creativity: The Role of Models, Analogies, and Metaphors." In Joseph Margolis et al., eds. *Rationality, Relativism, and the Human Sciences.* Dordrecht: Nijhoff.

Latour, Bruno. 1987. *Science in Action.* Cambridge, MA: Harvard University Press.

Latour, Bruno, and Steve Woolgar. 1986. *Laboratory Life: The Construction of Scientific Facts.* Princeton, NJ: Princeton University Press.

Laudan, Larry. 1977. *Progress and Its Problems: Towards a Theory of Scientific Growth.* Berkeley: University of California Press.

Laumann, Edward O. 1973. *Bonds of Pluralism: The Forms and Substance of Urban Social Networks.* New York: Wiley-Interscience.

1979. "Network Analysis in Large Social Systems: Some Theoretical and Methodological Problems." In Holland and Leinhardt, eds. *Perspectives on Social Network Research.* New York: Academic Press, pp. 374–423.

Laumann, E. O., J. Galaskiewicz, and P. Marsden. 1978. "Community Structure As Interorganizational Linkages." *Ann. Rev. Soc.* 4:455–84.

Laumann, E. O., and David Knoke. 1986. "Social Network Theory." In S. Lindenberg, J. Coleman, and S. Nowak, eds. *Approaches to Social Theory.* New York: Russell Sage Foundation, pp. 82–104.

1987. *The Organizational State.* Madison: University of Wisconsin Press.

Laumann, E. O., P. Siegel, and R. Hodge, eds. 1970. *The Logic of Social Hierarchies.* Chicago: Markham.

Lazarsfeld, Paul, and H. Menzel. 1964. "On the Relation Between Individual and Collective Properties." In A. Etzioni, ed. *Complex Organizations.* New York: Holt, pp. 422–40.

Leary, D. E., ed. 1990. *Metaphors in the History of Psychology.* Cambridge University Press.

Lecourt, Dominique. 1975. *Marxism and Epistemology: Bachelard, Canguilhem, Foucault.* London: New Left Books.

Lefebvre, Henri. 1982. "La notion de totalité dans les sciences sociales." *Cahiers Intern. de Soc.* 18 (1):55–77.

Lefort, Claude. 1974. "What is Bureaucracy?" *Telos* 22 (1974–5).

Leggett, A. J. 1987. "Quantum Mechanics at the Macroscopic Level." In his *The Problems of Physics.* New York: Oxford University Press, pp. 188–98.

Leggett, A. J., and Anupam Garg. 1985. "Quantum Mechanics Versus Macroscopic Realism: Is the Flux There when Nobody Looks?" *Physical Review Letters* 54, 9:857–60.

Lehman, E. 1975. *Coordinating Health Care: Explorations in Interorganizational Relations.* Beverly Hills, CA: Sage.

Leifer, Eric M. 1985. "Markets as Mechanisms: Using a Role Structure." *Social Forces* 64:442–72.

Leik, Robert, and Barbara F. Meeker. 1975. *Mathematical Sociology.* Englewood Cliffs, NJ: Prentice-Hall.

Leinfeller, W., and E. Kohler. 1974. *Recent Developments in the Methodology of Social Science.* Kluwer Academic Press.

Leinhart, Samuel. 1977. *Social Networks: A Developing Paradigm.* New York: Academic Press.

Leiter, K. 1980. *A Primer of Ethnomethodology.* New York: Oxford University Press.

Lenski, Gerhard. 1975. "Social Structure in Evolutionary Perspective." In: P. Blau, ed. *Approaches to the Study of Social Structure.* New York: Free Press.

Lenski, G., and Jean Lenski. 1987. *Human Societies.* 5th ed. New York: McGraw-Hill.

Leplin, Jarrett. 1984. *Scientific Realism.* Berkeley: University of California Press.

Lerner, Abba. 1973. *Flation: Not Inflation of Prices, Not Deflation of Jobs: What You Always Wanted to Know About Inflation, Depression and the Dollar.* New York: Quadrangle Books.

Levandowsky, Michael, and B. S. White. 1977. "Randomness, Time Scales, and the Evolution of Biological Communities." *Evol. Biol.* 10:69–161.

Levi, Margaret. 1983. "The Predatory Theory of Rule." In M. Hechter, ed. *The Microfoundations of Macrosociology.* Philadelphia, PA: Temple University.

1988. *Of Rule and Revenue.* Berkeley: University of California Press.

Lévi-Strauss, Claude. 1952. "Social Structure." In A. L. Kroeber, ed. *Anthropology Today.* Chicago, IL: University of Chicago Press.

1963. *Structural Anthropology.* New York: Basic Books.

Levin, B. R., and W. L. Kilmer. 1974. "Interdemic Selection and the Evolution of Altruism: A Computer Simulation Study." *Evolution* 28: 527–45.

Levine, Donald, ed. 1971. *Georg Simmel: Individuality and Social Forms.* Chicago, IL: University of Chicago Press.

Levins, Richard. 1966. "The Strategy of Model Building in Population Biology." *Am. Scientist* 54:421–31.

1968. *Evolution in Changing Environments.* Princeton, NJ: Princeton University Press.

1970. "Complex Systems." In C. H. Waddington, ed. *Towards a Theoretical Biology.* Edinburgh University Press.

1973. "The Limits of Complexity." In H. H. Pattee, *Hierarchy Theory.*

Levins, Richard, and Richard C. Lewontin. 1985. *The Dialectical Biologist.* Cambridge, MA: Harvard University Press.

Levy, David. M. 1985. "The Impossibility of a Complete Methodological Individualist: Reduction When Knowledge Is Imperfect." *Economics and Philosophy* (April) 1:101–8.

Lewin, Roger. 1986. "Punctuated Equilibrium is Now Old Hat." *Science* 231: 672–3.

Lewontin, R. C. 1967. "The Principle of Historicity in Evolution." In P. S. Moorehead and M. M. Kaplan, eds., *Mathematical Challenges to the Neo-Darwinian Interpretation of Evolution.* Philadelphia, PA: Wistar Institute Press.

1970. "The Units of Selection." *Ann.Rev/Ecol.Syst.* 1:1–16.

1974. *The Genetic Basis of Evolutionary Change.* New York: Columbia University Press.

1981. "On Constraints and Adaptation." *Behav. Brain Sci.* 4:244–5.

Lewontin, R. C., and Richard Levins. 1980. "Dialectics and Reductionism in Ecology." *Synthese* 43:47–78.

Lin, N. 1981. "Social Resources and Strength of Ties." *ASR* 46:363–405.

Lind, Joan. 1983. "The Organization of Coercion in History: A Rationalist-Evolutionary Theory." *Social. Theory* 1:1–29.

424   Bibliography

Lindblom, Charles E. 1977. *Politics and Markets: The World's Political-Economic System.* New York: Basic.
Lindenberg, S., J. S. Coleman, and S. Nowak, eds. 1986. *Approaches to Social Theory.* New York: Russell Sage Foundation.
Lipset, S. M., and R. Bendix. 1959. *Social Mobility in Industrial Society.* Berkeley: University of California Press.
Lloyd, Dan. 1989. *Simple Minds.* Cambridge, MA.: MIT Press.
Lloyd, Elizabeth. 1984. "A Semantic Approach to the Structure of Population Genetics." *Phil. Sci.* 51:242–64.
Lloyd, Seton. 1978. *The Archaeology of Mesopotamia.* London: Thames and Hudson.
Lockard, Joan S., ed. 1980. *Evolution of Human Social Behavior.* New York: Elsevier.
Lockwood, D. 1981. "The Weakest Link in the Chain? Some Comments on the Marxist Theory of Action." In R. Simpson and I. Simpson, eds. *Research in the Sociology of Work,* Greenwich, CT: JAI Press, pp. 435–81.
Logan, John, and H. Molotch. 1987. *Urban Fortunes.* Berkeley: University of California Press.
Logue, Dennis. 1975. "Market Making and the Assessment of Market Efficiency." *J. of Finance* 30:115–23.
Lomnicki, A. 1988. *A Population Ecology of Individuals.* Princeton University Press.
Lösch, A. 1954. *Economics of Location.* New Haven, CT: Yale University Press.
Lovelock, J. E. 1979. *Gaia: A New Look at Life on Earth.* New York: Oxford University Press.
Luce, Robert D., and Raiffa, H. 1957. *Games and Decisions.* New York: Wiley.
Luhmann, Niklas. 1974. "Sociology of Political Systems." *German Pol. Studies* 1:3–29.
    1979. *Trust and Power.* New York: Wiley.
    1982a. *The Differentiation of Society.* New York: Columbia University Press.
    1982b. "The World System as a Social System." *Intern. J. Gen. Systems* 8: 131–8.
    1984. *Soziale Systeme.* Frankfurt: Suhrkamp.
    1987. "The Evolutionary Differentiation Between Society and Interaction." In J. Alexander et al., eds. *The Micro-Macro Link.* Berkeley: University of California Press.
    1989. *Ecological Communication.* Chicago, IL: University of Chicago Press.
    1990. *Essays in Self-Actualization.* Chicago, IL: University of Chicago Press.
Luke, Timothy. 1987. "Methodological Individualism: The Essential Ellipsis of Rational Choice Theory." *Phil. Soc. Sci.* 17:341–55.
Lukes, Steven. 1973. "Methodological Individualism Reconsidered." In A. Ryan, ed. *The Philosophy of Social Explanation.* New York: Oxford University Press.
    1977. "Power and Structure." In his *Essays in Social Theory.* New York: Columbia University Press.
    1980. "Elster on Counterfactuals." *Inquiry* 23: 145–56.
    1983. "Can the Base Be Distinguished From the Superstructure?" In D. Miller and L. Siedentorp, eds. *The Nature of Political Theory.* Oxford University Press, pp. 103–20.

Lumsden, C. J., and E. O. Wilson. 1981. *Genes, Mind and Culture: The Co-evolutionary Process.* Cambridge University Press.

Lundqvist, Stig, Norman H. March, and Mario P. Tosi, eds. 1988. *Order and Chaos in Nonlinear Physical Systems.* New York: Plenum.

Lynch, Michael. 1985. *Art and Artifact in Laboratory Science.* London: Routledge and Kegan Paul.

MacArthur, Roger, and Wilson, E. O. 1967. *The Theory of Island Biogeography.* Princeton, NJ: Princeton University Press.

MacDonald, Glenn. 1984. "New Directions in the Economic Theory of Agency." *Can. J. Econ.* 17:415–40.

MacFarlane, Alan. 1978. *The Origins of English Individualism.* Oxford: Blackwell.

MacIntyre, A. 1981. *After Virtue: A Study in Moral Theory.* South Bend, IN: Notre Dame University Press.

MacNeil, Ian R. 1980. *The New? Social Contract: An Inquiry Into Modern Contractual Relations.* New Haven, CT: Yale University Press.

Maddox, John. 1989. "Complicated Problems – Not Yet Soluble." *Nature* 338: 457.

Maines, David R. 1977. "Social Organization and Social Structure in Symbolic Interactionist Thought." *Annual. Rev. Soc.* 3:259–85.

1979 "Mesostructure and Social Process." *Contemporary Sociology* 8:524–27.

1981. "Recent Developments in Symbolic Interaction." In G. Stone and H. Faberman, eds. *Social Psychology Through Symbolic Interaction.* 2nd ed. New York: Wiley, pp. 461–86.

1982. "In Search of Mesostructure." *Urban Life* 11:267–79.

Maital, Shlomo, and Yael Benjamini. 1979. "Inflation as a Prisoner's Dilemma." *J. of Post-Keynesian Econ.* 2:459–81.

Mamdani, M. 1972. *The Myth of Population Control: Family, Caste, and Class in an Indian Village.* New York: Monthly Review.

Mandel, Ernest. 1987. *Late Capitalism.* London: Routledge, Chapman & Hall.

Mandel, Michael. 1983. "Local Roles and Social Networks." *ASR* 48:376–85.

Mandelbaum, Maurice. 1957. "Societal Laws." *Br. J. Phil. Sci.* 8, 31:211–24.

1973. "Societal Facts." In Alan Ryan, ed. *The Philosophy of Social Explanation.* New York: Oxford University Press. Published earlier in P. Gardiner, ed. 1959. *Theories of History.* New York: Free Press.

Mandelbrot, Benoit. 1983. *The Fractal Geometry of Nature.* New York: Freeman.

Manicas, Peter. 1980. "The Concept of Social Structure." *J. Theory Soc. Behaviour* 10, 2:65–82.

Manis, Jerome, and Bernard Meltzer, eds. 1978. *Symbolic Interaction: A Reader in Social Psychology.* 3rd. ed. Newton, MA: Allyn and Bacon.

Mann, Michael. 1973. *Consciousness and Action in the Western Working Class.* New York: Macmillan.

1986. *The Sources of Social Power,* vol. 1. Cambridge University Press.

Mansfield, Edwin. 1975. *Microeconomics: Theory and Applications.* New York: Norton.

March, James. 1978. "Bounded Rationality, Ambiguity, and the Engineering of Choice." *Bell J. of Econ.* 9:587–608.

Marglin, Steve. 1976. "What do Bosses Do." In A. Gortz, ed. *The Division of Labor.* New York: Longman.

Margolis, Joseph. 1978. *Persons and Minds: The Prospects of Nonreductive Materialism.* Dordrecht: Reidel.

1984. *Philosophy of Psychology.* Englewood Cliffs, NJ: Prentice-Hall.

1986. *Pragmatism without Foundations.* Oxford: Blackwell.

1987. *Science without Unity.* Oxford: Blackwell.

1988. *Texts without Referents.* Oxford: B. Blackwell.

Margolis, Joseph, M. Krausz, and R. Burian, eds. 1986. *Rationality, Relativism, and the Human Sciences.* Dordrecht: Nijhoff.

Marr, D. 1982. *Vision: A Computational Investigation into the Human Representation and Processing of Visual Information.* New York: Freeman.

Marr, D., and T. Poggio. 1977. "From Understanding Computation to Understanding Neural Circuitry." *Neurosciences Research Program Bulletin* 15, 3:470–88.

Marsden, Peter. 1983. "Restricted Access in Networks and Models of Power." *AJS* 88:686–717.

Marsden, Peter, and Nan Lin, 1982. *Social Structure and Network Analysis.* Beverly Hills, CA: Sage.

Martindale, Don. 1988. *The Nature and Types of Sociological Theory.* 2nd ed. Waveland Press.

Marwel, Gerald, and Ruth Ames. 1979. "Experiments on the Provision of Public Goods. Resources, Interest, Group Size and the Free Rider Problem." *Am. J. Soc.* 84:6, 1335–60.

1980. "Experiments on the Provision of Public Goods. II: Provision Points, Stacks, Experience and the Free Rider Problem." *Am. J. Soc* 85:4, 926–37.

Marx, Karl. 1967. *Capital I, II, III.* New York: International Publishers.

1971. *Contribution to the Critique of Political Economy.* [CCPE]. London: Lawrence and Wishart.

1972. *Theories of Surplus Value.* [TSV]. vol 1. London: Lawrence and Wishart.

1973. *Grundrisse.* New York: Vintage.

1976a. *German Ideology.* [GI]. In Marx-Engels, *Collected Works [CW]* 5, New York: International Publishers.

1976b. *Eighteenth Brumaire.* In Marx-Engels, *Collected Works.* New York: International Publishers; and in McLellan, *Karl Marx: Selected Works.*

1977a. *Results of the Immediate Process of Production.* [RIPP]. Appendix to *Capital I.* New York: Vintage.

1977b. *Selected Writings.* Ed. by D. McLellan. New York: Oxford University Press.

1979. *The Letters of Karl Marx,* Ed. by S. Padover. Englewood Cliffs, NJ: Prentice-Hall.

Marx, Karl, and F. Engels. 1976. *Collected Works.* [CW]. New York: International Publishers.

Mason, Stephen F. 1984. "Origins of Biomolecular Handedness" *Nature* 311, 6:19–23.

Matsuno, Koichiro. 1984. "Protobiology: A Theoretical Synthesis." In K. Matsuno et al, eds. *Molecular Evolution and Protobiology.* New York: Plenum, pp. 433–62.

1989. *Protobiology: Physical Basis of Biology.* New York: RCR Press.

Matsuno, Koichiro, Klaus Dose, Kaoro Harada, and Duane L. Rohlfing, eds. 1984. *Molecular Evolution and Protobiology*. New York: Plenum.

Maull, N. 1977. "Unifying Science Without Reduction." *Stud. Hist. Phil. Sci.* 8: 143–62.

May, R. M. 1972. "Will a Large Complex System Be Stable?" *Nature* 238:413–4.

1973. *Stability and Complexity in Model Ecosystems*. Princeton, NJ: Princeton University Press.

1976a "Simple Mathematical Models with Very Complicated Dynamics." *Nature* 261:459–67.

1976b *Theoretical Ecology: Principles and Applications*. Oxford: Blackwell.

1987. "Chaos and the Dynamics of Biological Populations." *Proc. Royal Soc. Lond.* A 413:27–44.

1989. "Detecting Density Dependence in Imaginary Worlds." *Nature* 338:16–7.

May, Robert M., and George F. Oster. 1976. "Bifurcations and Dynamic Complexity in Simple Ecological Models." *The American Naturalist* 110: 573–99.

Mayer, Adrian C. 1966. "The Significance of Quasi-Groups in the Study of Complex Societies." In M. Banton, ed. *The Social Anthropology of Complex Societies*. London: Tavistock.

Mayhew, Bruce. 1973. "System Size and Ruling Elites." *ASR* 38:468–75.

1974. "Baseline Models of System Structure." *ASR* 39:137–43.

1980. "Structuralism versus Individualism, Part 1." *Social Forces* 59:335–75.

1981. "Structuralism versus Individualism, Part 2." *Social Forces* 59:627–648.

1982. "Structuralism and Ontology" *Soc. Sci. Quarterly* 63:634–9.

Mayhew, Bruce, and Roger Levinger. 1976. "On the Emergence of Oligarchy in Human Interaction." *AJS* 81:1017–49.

Mayhew, Bruce, J. M. McPherson, R. L. Levinger, and T. F. James. 1972. "System Size and Structural Differentiation in Formal Organizations: A Baseline Generator for Two Major Theoretical Propositions." *ASR* 37:629–33.

Maynard Smith, John. 1964. "Group Selection and Kin Selection." *Nature* 201: 1145–7.

1974. "The Theory of Games: The Evolution of Animal Conflict." *J. of Theor. Biol.* 47:209–21.

1976. "Group Selection." *Quar. Rev. Biol.* 51:277–83.

1982. *Evolution and the Theory of Games*. Cambridge University Press.

1984. "Game Theory and the Evolution of Behaviour." *Beh. Brain. Sci.* 7, 1: 95–126.

1986. *Problems of Biology*. New York: Oxford University Press.

Maynard Smith, John, R. Burian, S. Kauffman, P. Alderch, J. Campbell, B. Goodwin, R. Lande, D. Paup, and L. Wolpert. 1985. "Developmental Constraints and Evolution." *Quarterly Rev. Biol.* 60:265–87.

Mayr, Ernst. 1969. "Scientific Explanation and Conceptual Framework." *J. Hist. Biol.* 2:123–8.

1977. "Darwin and Natural Selection." *Am. Sci.* 65:321–27.

1982. *The Growth of Biological Thought: Diversity, Evolution, and Inheritance*. Cambridge, MA: Harvard University Press.

Mayr, E., and W. B. Provine, eds. 1980. *The Evolutionary Synthesis*. Cambridge, MA: Harvard University Press.

McAdam, Doug. 1986. "Recruitment to High-Risk Activism: The Case of Freedom Summer." *AJS* 92, 1:64–90.

McCarthy, John D., and Mayer N. Zald. 1977. "Resource Mobilization and Social Movements: A Partial Theory." *AJS* 82:1212–41.

McClelland, James, and David Rumelhart. 1985. "Distributed Memory and the Representation of General and Specific Information." *Journal of Experim. Psych.: General* 114:159–88.

McClelland, James L., David E. Rumelhart, and the PDP Research Group. 1987. *Parallel Distributed Processing: Explorations in the Microstructure of Cognition. Volume 2: Psychological and Biological Models.* Cambridge, MA: MIT Press.

McCulloch, Warren S. 1945. "A Heterarchy of Values Determined by the Topology of Nervous Nets." *Bulletin of Math Biophysics* 7:89–93.

—— 1965. *Embodiments of Mind.* Cambridge, MA: MIT Press.

McLean, Ian. 1987. *Public Choice: An Introduction.* Oxford: Blackwell.

McLellan, D. 1977. *Karl Marx: Selected Writings.* New York: Oxford University Press.

McMahon, A. M. 1984. "The Two Social Psychologies: Postcrises Directions." *Annual. Rev. Soc.* 10:121–40. Palo Alto, CA: Annual Reviews.

McPhail, Clark, and Cynthia Rexroat. 1979. "Mead vs. Blumer: The Divergent Perspectives of Social Behaviorism and Symbolic Interactionism." *ASR* 44:449–67.

Medawar, Peter. 1974. "A Geometric Model of Reduction and Emergence." In Ayala and Medawar, *Studies in the Philosophy of Biology.* Berkeley: University of California Press.

—— 1988. *The Limits of Science.* New York: Oxford University Press.

Mehan, H. 1979. *Learning Lessons.* Cambridge, MA: Harvard University Press.

Mehan, Hugh, and Houston Wood. 1975. *The Reality of Ethnomethodology.* New York: Wiley.

Meiland, Jack, and M. Krausz, eds. 1982. *Relativism: Cognitive and Moral.* So. Bend, IN: Notre Dame University Press.

Mellaart, James. 1975. *The Neolithic of the Near East.* New York: Scribner.

Menkes, Joshua. 1985. "Limits of Rationality." *The Philosophical Forum* 17, 1: 25–38.

Merton, Robert K. 1968. *Social Theory and Social Structure.* New York: Free Press.

—— 1975. "Structural Analysis in Sociology." In P. Blau, ed. *Approaches to the Study of Social Structure.* New York: Free Press.

Mesarovic, M. D., D. Macko, and Y. Takahara. 1970. *Theory of Hierarchical Multi-Level Systems.* New York: Academic Press.

Mesarovic, M., and Y. Takahara. 1989. *Abstract Systems Theory.* New York: Springer-Verlag.

Miles, John. 1984. "Strange Attractors in Fluid Dynamics." In *Advances in Applied Mathematics* 24:189–214.

Milgram, Stanley. 1967. "The Small World Problem." *Psychology Today* 22 (May): 61–7.

Milkman, R., ed. 1982. *Perspectives on Evolution.* Sunderland, MA: Sinauer Associates.

Miller, Frank C. 1973. *Old Villages and a New Town: Industrialization in Mexico.* Menlo Park, CA: Cummings.

Miller, G. A. 1956. "The Magical Number Seven Plus or Minus Two: Some

Limits of Our Capacity of Processing Information." *Psych. Rev.* 63: 81–97.

Miller, S., and L. E. Orgel. 1974. *Origins of Life on Earth.* Englewood Cliffs, NJ: Prentice-Hall.

Millikan, R. G. 1984. *Language, Thought, and Other Biological Categories: New Foundations for Realism.* Cambridge, MA: MIT Press.

Minsky, Marvin. 1975. "A Framework for Representing Knowledge." In P. Winston, ed. *The Psychology of Computer Vision.* New York: McGraw-Hill.

1985 "Communication with Alien Intelligence." *BYTE* April: 127–38.

1986. *The Society of Mind.* New York: Simon and Schuster.

Mitchell, J. C. 1974. "Social Networks." *Ann. Rev. Anthrop.* 3:279–99.

Moe, Terry. 1984. "The New Economics of Organization." *Amer. J. of Poli. Sci.* 28:739–77.

Molm, Linda. 1987. "Linking Power Structure to Power Use." In K. Cook, ed. *Social Exchange Theory.* Beverly Hills, CA: Sage.

Molotch, Harvey. 1976. "The City as a Growth Machine." *AJS* 82(2):307–30.

Moore, Barrington. 1966. *The Social Origins of Dictatorship and Democracy: Lord and Peasant in the Making of the Modern World.* Boston, MA: Beacon Press.

Moore, Wilbert E. 1978. "Functionalism." In Tom Bottomore and Robert Nisbet, eds. *A History of Sociological Analysis.* New York: Basic, pp. 321–61.

Morgan, Elaine. 1982. *The Aquatic Ape: A Theory of Evolution.* New York: Stein and Day.

Morishima, M. 1973. *Marx's Economics.* Cambridge University Press.

1974. "Marx in the Light of Modern Economic Theory." *Econometrica* 42: 611–32.

Morse, Chandler. 1961. "The Functional Imperatives." In Max Black, ed. *The Social Theories of Talcott Parsons.* Englewood Cliffs, NJ: Prentice-Hall.

Mortensen, Dale. 1982. "The Matching Process as a Noncooperative Bargaining Game." In J. J. McCall, ed. *The Economics of Information and Uncertainty.* Chicago, IL: University of Chicago Press, pp. 233–58.

1988. "Matching: Finding a Partner for Life or Otherwise." In C. Winship and S. Rosen, eds. *AJS Supplement: Organizations and Institutions,* pp. S215–S240.

Moseley, K. P., and I. Wallerstein, 1978. "Precapitalist Social Structures." *Ann. R. Soc.* 4:259–90.

Mouffe, Chantal, ed. 1979. *Gramsci and Marxist Theory.* New York: Routledge & Kegan Paul.

Mountcastle, V. B. 1978. "An Organizing Principle for Cerebral Function: The Unit Module and the Distributed System." In G. Edelman and V. B. Mountcastle, eds. *The Mindful Brain.* Cambridge, MA: MIT Press.

Mueller, Dennis C. 1979. *Public Choice.* Cambridge University Press.

Mulkay, M. J. 1971. *Functionalism, Exchange, and Theoretical Strategy.* New York: Schocken Books.

Münch, Richard. 1981. "Talcott Parsons and the Theory of Action: I. The Kantian Core." *AJS* 86:709–39.

Murphy, Raymond. 1984. "The Structure of Closure: A Critique and Development of the Theories of Weber, Collins, and Parkin." *Brit. J. Soc.* 35:547–67.

1985. "Exploitation or Exclusion?" *Sociology* 19:225–43.

Nadel, S. F. 1957. *The Theory of Social Structure.* New York: Free Press.

Nagel, T. 1955. "On the Statement the Whole is More Than the Sum of its Parts." In P. F. Lazarsfeld and M. Rosenberg, eds. *The Language of Social Research.* New York: Free Press. pp. 519–27.

1986. *The View from Nowhere.* Cambridge University Press.

Neale, R. S. 1981. *Class in English History, 1680–1850.* New York: Barnes & Noble.

ed. 1983. *History and Class.* Oxford: Blackwell.

Negandhi, A. R., ed. 1975. *Interorganizational Theory.* Kent, OH: Kent State University Press.

Nelson, Alan. 1984. "Some Issues Surrounding the Reduction of Macroeconomics to Microeconomics." *Phil. Sci.* 51:573–94.

Nelson, David. 1986. "Quasicrystals." *Sci. Amer.* August: 42.

Nelson, Richard, and S. G. Winter. 1982. *An Evolutionary Theory of Economic Change.* Cambridge, MA: Harvard University Press.

Nicolis, Gregoire. 1986. "Dissipative Systems." *Rep. Prog. Phys.* 49:873–949.

1987. *Exploring Complexity.* Munich: Piper.

Nicolis, G., and V. Altares. 1988. "Physics of Nonequilibrium Systems." In G. Caglioti, H. Haken, and L. Lugiato, eds. *Synergetics and Dynamic Instabilities.* Amsterdam: North Holland, pp. 299–328.

Nicolis, G., and F. Baras, eds. 1984. *Chemical Instabilities.* Dordrecht: Reidel.

Nicolis, G., and R. Lefever, eds. 1975. *Membranes, Dissipative Structures, and Evolution.*

Nicolis, G., and I. Prigogine. 1977. *Self-Organization in Nonequilibrium Systems: From Dissipative Structures to Order Through Fluctuations.* New York: Wiley-Interscience.

Nicolis, John S. 1986a. "Chaotic Dynamics Applied to Information Processing." *Prog. Rep. Phys.* 49:1109–96.

1986b. *Dynamics of Hierarchical Systems: An Evolutionary Approach.* New York: Springer-Verlag.

1990. *Chaos and Information Processing.* Singapore & Teaneck, NJ: World Scientific.

Ninio, J. 1983. *Molecular Approaches to Evolution.* Princeton, NJ: Princeton University Press.

North, Douglas C. 1981. *Structure and Change in Economic History.* New York: Norton.

Nowak, Leszek. 1987. "Class and Individual in the Historical Process." *Phil. Soc. Sci.* 17 (3):357–76.

Oberschall, Anthony. 1980. "Loosely Structured Collective Conflict: A Theory and an Application." *Research in Social Movements, Conflict, and Change* 3:45–68.

1986. "The California Gold Rush: Social Structure and Transaction Costs." In Lindenberg, *Approaches to Social Theory.* New York: Russell Sage Foundation, pp. 111–19.

Oberschall, Anthony, and E. M. Leifer. 1986. "Efficiency and Social Institutions: Uses and Misuses of the Economic Reasoning in Sociology." *Ann. Rev. Soc.* 12:233–53.

Odum, Howard. 1983. *Systems Ecology: An Introduction.* New York: Wiley.

Offe, Claus, and H. Wiesenthal. 1980. "Two Logics of Collective Action: Theoretical Notes on Social Class and Organizational Form." *Political Power and Social Theory.* 1:67–115.

O'Grady, R. T. 1984. "Evolutionary Theory and Teleology." *J. Theor. Bio.* 107: 563–78.

Oliver, Pamela. 1984. "If You Don't Do It Nobody Else Will: Active and Token Contributors to Local Collective Action." *American Sociological Review 49*:601–10.

Oliver, Pamela, Gerald Marwell, and Ruy Teixeira. 1985. "A Theory of the Critical Mass. I. Interdependence, Group Heterogeneity, and the Production of Collective Action." *American Journal of Sociology 91* (3): 522–56.

Olsen, L. F., and H. Degn. 1985. "Chaos in Biological Systems." *Quart. Rev. Biophysics* 18, 2:165.

Olson, Mancur. 1965. *The Logic of Collective Action: Public Goods and the Theory of Groups.* Cambridge, MA: Harvard University Press.

　1982. *The Rise and Decline of Nations: Economic Growth, Stagnation, and Social Rigidities.* New Haven, CT: Yale University Press.

　1986. "A Theory of Social Movements, Social Classes, and Castes." In S. Lindenberg et al., eds. *Approaches to Social Theory.* New York: Russell Sage Foundation, pp. 317–37.

O'Neill, John, ed. 1973. *Modes of Individualism and Collectivism.* London: Heinemann.

O'Neill, R. V., D. DeAngelis, J. Waide, and T.F.H. Allen. 1986. *A Hierarchical Concept of Ecosystems.* Princeton, NJ: Princeton University Press.

Oparin, A. I. [1938] 1953. *The Origin of Life.* Mineola, NY: Dover.

　1964. *Life, Its Nature, Origin, and Development.* New York: Academic Press.

Ouchi, William G. 1980. "Markets, Bureaucracies, and Clans." *Admin. Sci. Quarterly* 25:129–42.

　1981. *Theory Z.* Reading, MA: Addison-Wesley.

Owen, G. 1982. *Game Theory.* New York: Academic Press.

Pagels, Heinz R. 1985. "Is the Irreversibility We See a Fundamental Property of Nature?" *Physics Today*:97–8.

　1988. *The Dreams of Reason.* New York: Simon and Schuster.

Pahl, R. E. 1984. *Divisions of Labor.* Oxford: Blackwell.

Palm, G. 1982. *Neural Assemblies: An Alternative Approach to Artificial Intelligence.* New York: Springer-Verlag.

Palmer, S. E. 1980. "What Makes Triangles Point: Local and Global Effects in Configuration of Ambiguous Triangles." *Cognitive Psychology* 9: 353–83.

Parfit, Derek. 1985. *Reasons and Persons.* New York: Oxford University Press.

Parijs, P. van. 1981. *Evolutionary Explanation in the Social Sciences.* Totowa, NJ: Rowman and Littlefield.

　1984. "Marxism's Central Puzzle." In T. Ball and J. Farr, eds. *After Marx.* Cambridge University Press, pp. 88–104.

Park, Robert. 1952. *Human Communities.* New York: Free Press.

Parkin, Frank. 1979. *Marxism and Class Theory: A Bourgeois Critique.* New York: Columbia University Press.

Parsons, Talcott. 1937. *The Structure of Social Action.* New York: Free Press

　1951. *The Social System.* New York: Free Press.

1971. "Levels of Organization." In H. Turk and R. L. Simpson, eds. *Institutions and Social Exchange*. Indianapolis, IN: Bobbs-Merrill.

Pasinetti, L., ed. 1980. *Essays in the Theory of Joint Production*. New York: Columbia University Press.

Pattee, Howard H. 1970. "The Problem of Biological Hierarchy." In: C. H. Waddington, ed. *Toward a Theoretical Biology: Three Drafts*. Edinburgh University Press.

1972. "The Evolution of Self-Simplifying Systems." In E. Laszlo, ed. *The Relevance of General Systems Theory*. New York: Braziller.

1972. "Laws and Constraints, Symbols and Languages." In C. Waddington, ed. *Toward Theoretical Biology: Essays*. Hawthorne, NY: Aldine.

1973. *Hierarchy Theory: The Challenge of Complex Systems*. New York: Braziller.

1977. "Dynamic and Linguistic Modes of Complex Systems." *Int. J. Gen. Syst.* 3:259–66.

1978. "The Complementarity Principle in Biological and Social Structures." *J. Soc. Biol. Structures* 1:191–200.

1979. "The Complementarity Principle and the Origin of Macromolecular Information." *Biosystems 11*:217–26.

1988. "Simulations, Realizations, and Theories of Life." In C. Langton, ed. *Artificial Life*. Santa Fe Institute Studies in the Sciences of Complexity: Reading, MA: Addison-Wesley, pp. 105–20.

Patten, B.C. 1981. "Environs: The Superniches of Ecosystems." *Amer. Zool.* 21:845–52.

1982. "Environs: Relativistic Elementary Particles For Ecology." *Amer. Natural* 119:179–219.

Patterson, Thomas C. 1981. *Archaeology: The Evolution of Ancient Societies*. Englewood Cliffs, NJ: Prentice-Hall.

Patterson, T., and C. Gailey, eds. 1987. *Power Relations and State Formation*. Washington, DC: Amer. Anthropol. Association.

Peacock, A. R. 1983. *An Introduction to the Physical Chemistry of Biological Organization*. New York: Oxford University Press.

Penrose, Roger. 1989a. *The Emperor's New Mind*. New York: Oxford University Press.

Penrose, Roger. 1989b. "Tilings and Quasi-Crystals: A Non-local Growth Problem." In M. Jaric, ed. *Aperiodicity and Order 2*. New York: Academic Press.

Pepper, S. 1926. "Emergence." *J. of Phil.* 23:241–5.

Perkin, Harold J. 1972. *The Origin of Modern English Society 1780–1880*. London: Routledge.

Perrow, Charles. 1979/1986. *Complex Organizations: A Critical View*. Glenview, IL: Scott Foresman.

1981. "Markets, Hierarchies and Hegemony." In A. Van De Ven and W. Joyce, eds. *Perspectives on Organization Design and Behavior*. New York: Wiley, pp. 371–86, 403–4.

Perrucci, Robert, and Marc Pilisuk. 1970. "Leaders and Ruling Elites: The Interorganizational Bases of Community Power." *Am. J. Soc.* 35: 1040–57.

Perrucci, Robert, and Harry Potter, eds. 1988. *Networks of Power: Organizational Actors at the National, Corporate, and Community Levels*. New York: A. de Gruyter.

Peterson, Paul. 1981. *City Limits*. Chicago, IL: University of Chicago Press.

Peterson, R. A., and H. G. White. 1981. "Elements of Simplex Structure." *Urb. Lif.* 10:3–24.

Pettit, Philip. 1975. *The Concept of Structuralism: A Critical Analysis.* Berkeley: University of California Press.

——— 1978. "Rational Man Theory." In C. Hookway and P. Pettit, eds. *Action and Interpretation.* Cambridge University Press.

Pfeffer, Jeffrey. 1981. *Power in Organizations.* New York: Harper.

——— 1982. *Organizations and Organization Theory.* Boston, MA: Pitman.

Pfeffer, Jeffrey, and Gerald Salancik. 1973. *The External Control of Organizations.* New York: Harper and Row.

Piaget, Jean. 1970. *Structuralism.* New York: Basic.

Pianka, E. R. 1974. *Evolutionary Ecology.* New York: Harper & Row.

Pines, D., ed. 1987. *Emerging Syntheses in Science: Proceedings of the Founding Workshops of the Santa Fe Institute.* Reading, MA: Addison-Wesley.

Pinker, A., and A. Prince. 1988. "On Language and Connectionism: Analysis of a Parallel Distributed Model of Language Acquisition." *Cognition* 28:73–193.

Pinker, S. 1984. *Language Learnability and Language Development.* Cambridge, MA: Harvard University Press.

Piven, Frances Fox, and Richard A. Cloward. 1979. *Poor People's Movements: Why They Succeed, How They Fail.* New York: Vintage.

Pizzorno, Alessandro. 1985. "On the Rationality of Democratic Choice." *Telos* 63:41–69.

Platt, J. 1961. "Properties of Large Molecules That Go Beyond The Properties of Their Chemical Subgroups." *J. Theor. Bio.* 1:342–58.

Plotkin, H. C., and F. I. Odling-Smee. 1981. "A Multiple-Level Model of Evolution and Its Implications for Sociobiology." *Brain Behavior* 4:225–38.

Poggi, Gianfranco. 1978. *The Development of the Modern State.* Stanford, CA: Stanford University Press.

Polanyi, Karl. 1957. *The Great Transformation.* Boston, MA: Beacon Press.

Polanyi, Michael. 1958. *Personal Knowledge.* Chicago, IL: University of Chicago Press.

——— 1968. "Life's Irreducible Structure." *Science* 160: 1308–12.

Pollard, Jeffrey W., ed. 1984. *Evolutionary Theory: Paths into the Future.* New York: Wiley.

Ponnamperuma, C., and Hobish, M. K. 1984. "Stereochemical Approach to Genetic Code." In K. Matsuno, ed. *Molecular Evolution and Protobiology.* New York: Plenum.

Pool, Robert. 1989. "Quantum chaos: Enigma Wrapped in a Mystery." *Science* 243:893–95.

Popkin, Samuel. 1979. *The Rational Peasant.* Berkeley: University of California Press.

Popper, K. 1966. *Open Society and Its Enemies.* Princeton, NJ: Princeton University Press.

——— 1972. *Objective Knowledge: An Evolutionary Approach.* New York: Oxford University Press.

——— 1974. "Scientific Reduction and the Essential Incompleteness of All Science." In Ayala and Dobzhansky, *Studies in the Philosophy of Biology.*

——— 1976. "Darwinism as a Metaphysical Research Programme." In his *Unended Quest: An Intellectual Autobiography.* London: Fontana.

1978. "Natural Selection and the Emergence of Mind." *Dialectica* 32:339–55.

1982. *The Open Universe: An Argument for Indeterminism.* Totowa, NJ: Rowman and Littlefield.

Popper, K., and John Eccles. 1984. *The Self and Its Brain: An Argument for Interactionism.* New York: Routledge & Kegan Paul.

Porter, Michael. 1980. *Competitive Strategy.* New York: Academic Press.

Post, John F. 1987. *The Faces of Existence: An Essay in Nonreductive Metaphysics.* Ithaca, New York: Cornell University Press.

Poulantzas, Nicos. 1975. *Classes in Contemporary Capitalism.* London: New Left Books.

Poundstone, William. 1984. *The Recursive Universe.* New York: Morrow.

Pratt, John W., and Richard J. Zeckhauser, eds. 1985. *Principals and Agents: The Structure of Business.* Boston, MA: Harvard Business School Press.

Premack, D. 1988. "Minds With and Without Language." In L. Weiskrantz, ed. *Thought Without Language,* New York: Oxford University Press, pp. 46–65.

Premack, D., and A. J. Premack. 1983. *The Mind of an Ape.* New York: Norton.

Pribram, Karl. 1982. *Languages of the Brain.* New York: Random House.

Prigogine, Ilya. 1980. *From Being to Becoming: Time and Complexity in the Physical Sciences.* New York: Freeman.

Prigogine, Ilya, and C. George. 1983. "The Second Law as a Selection Principle: The Microscopic Theory of Dissipative Processes in Quantum Systems." *Proceed. Nat. Ac. Sci 80:*4590–94.

Prigogine, Ilya, and Isabelle Stengers. 1984. *Order Out of Chaos.* New York: Bantam.

Primas, H., and V. Mueller-Herold. 1978. "Quantum Mechanical System Theory." In S. A. Rice, ed. *Advances in Chemical Physics,* vol. 38.

Propp, V. 1968. *The Morphology of the Folk Tale.* Austin, TX: University of Texas Press.

Przeworski, Adam. 1977. "Proletariat Into a Class: The Process of Class Formation From Karl Kautsky's *The Class Struggle* to Recent Controversies." *Politics and Society* 7:343–401.

1980. "Social Democracy as a Historical Phenomenon." *NLR* 122:27–58. Reprinted 1985 in his *Capitalism and Social Democracy.* Cambridge University Press.

1985. *Capitalism and Social Democracy.* Cambridge University Press.

Przeworski, A., and M. Wallerstein. 1982. "The Structure of Class Conflict in Democratic Capitalist Societies." *APSR* 76:215–338.

Puccia, Charles, and Richard Levins. 1985. *Qualitative Modeling of Complex Systems.* Cambridge, MA: Harvard University Press.

Pullman, Bernard. 1979. *Catalysis in Chemistry and Biochemistry.* Reidel.

Putnam, Hilary. 1975a "Minds and Machines." In his *Philosophical Papers II:* 362–85.

1975b. "The Mental Life of Some Machines." In his *Philosophical Papers II:* 408–28.

1981. *Reason, Truth and History.* Cambridge University Press.

1982. *Philosophical Papers.* Vol. 3: *Realism and Reason.* Cambridge University Press.

1987. *The Many Faces of Realism.* LaSalle, IL: Open Court.

1988. *Representation and Reality.* Cambridge University Press.

Putnam, R., and N. Bayne. 1984. *Hanging Together: Cooperation and Conflict in The Seven Power Summits.* Beverly Hills, CA: Sage.

Pylyshyn, Zenon W. 1984. *Computation and Cognition.* Cambridge, MA: MIT Press.

Quine, W. V. 1953. *From a Logical Point of View.* Cambridge, MA: Harvard University Press.

    1960. *Word and Object.* Cambridge, MA: MIT Press.

    1969. *Ontological Relativity and Other Essays.* New York: Columbia University Press.

    1977. *Quiddities: An Intermittently Philosophical Dictionary.* Cambridge, MA: Harvard University Press/Belknap Press.

Radcliffe-Brown, A. R. 1977. "On Social Structure." In Leinhardt, *Social Networks.* New York: Academic Press.

Radner, Roy. 1968. "Competitive Equilibrium Under Uncertainty." *Econometrica* 36:31–58.

Raiffa, H. 1968. *Decision Theory.* Reading, MA: Addison-Wesley.

Rapoport, Anatol. 1966. *Two-Person Game Theory.* Ann Arbor: University of Michigan Press.

    1974. *Fights, Games, and Debates.* Ann Arbor: University of Michigan Press.

Rapoport, A., and A. Chammah. 1965. *Prisoner's Dilemma.* Ann Arbor, MI: University of Michigan Press.

Rawls, Ann W. 1985. "Reply to Gallant and Kleinman on Symbolic Interactionism vs. Ethnomethodology." *Symbolic Interaction* 8:121–40.

Redman, Charles L., ed. 1978. *Social Archaeology.* New York: Academic Press.

    1983. *Research and Theory in Current Archaeology.* Krieger.

Reeke, George N., and Gerald M. Edelman. 1984. "Selective Networks and Recognition Automata." In *Annals of the New York Academy of Sciences.* 426:181–201.

Reeke, G. N., Jr., and G. M. Edelman 1987 "Real Brains and Artificial Intelligence." *Daedalus* 117, no. 1:143–73.

Richards, D. 1988. "Order and Chaos in Strong Fields." *Nature* 336, 6199:518–20.

Richards, F., F. Cohen, M. Sternberg, and D. Phillips. 1986. "Combinatorial Tertiary Structure of Proteins." *Science*:1038–9.

Richards, R. J. 1987 *Darwin and the Emergence of Evolutionary Theories of Mind and Behavior.* Chicago, IL: University of Chicago Press.

Richardson, Jane S. 1981. "The Anatomy and Taxonomy of Protein Structure." In C.B. Anfinsen, and John Edsall, eds. *Advances in Protein Chemistry.* Vol. 34, pp. 168–340. New York: Academic Press.

Richardson, Lewis F. 1960. *Statistics of Deadly Quarrels.* Chicago, IL: Quadrangle Books.

Ricoeur, Paul. 1974. "Structure and Hermeneutics." In his *The Conflict of Interpretations: Essays in Hermeneutics.* Evanston, IL: Northwestern University Press.

Riedl, R. 1978. *Order in Living Organisms.* New York: Wiley.

Roemer, John. 1979. "Divide and Conquer: Microfoundations of a Marxian Theory of Wage Discrimination." *Bell J. of Econ.* 10:695–705.

    1981. *Analytical Foundations of Marxian Economic Theory.* Cambridge University Press.

    1982 *A General Theory of Exploitation and Class.* Cambridge, MA: Harvard University Press.

    ed. 1986. *Analytical Marxism.* Cambridge University Press.

Rogowski, Ronald. 1978. "Rationalist Theories of Politics: A Midterm Report." *World Politics* 30:296–323.

Rohfling, D. L. 1984. "The Development of the Proteinoid Model for the Origin of Life." In K. Matsuno, ed. *Molecular Evolution and Protobiology.* New York: Plenum.

Romanos, George D. 1983. *Quine and Analytic Philosophy.* Cambridge, MA: MIT Press.

Rorty, Richard. 1979. *Philosophy and the Mirror of Nature.* Princeton, NJ: Princeton University Press.

    1982. *Consequences of Pragmatism.* Minneapolis: University of Minnesota Press.

    1989. *Contingency, Irony, Solidarity.* Cambridge University Press.

Rosen, David. 1985. *Bargaining in Reality.* Princeton, NJ: Princeton University Press.

Rosen, R. 1970. *Dynamical System Theory in Biology.* New York: Wiley.

    1985. "Organisms as Causal Systems Which Are Not Mechanisms: An Essay Into the Nature of Complexity." In Robert Rosen, ed. *Theoretical Biology and Complexity.* New York: Academic Press.

    1985. "Information and Complexity." In R. Ulanowicz, and T. Platt, *Ecosystems Theory for Biological Oceanography.*

    1986. "The Physics of Complexity: Ashby Memorial Lecture." In Robert Trappl, ed. *Power, Autonomy, Utopia: New Approaches toward Complex Systems.* New York: Plenum.

Rosen, Sherwin. 1974. "Hedonic Prices and Implicit Markets: Product Differentiation in Pure Competition." *J. Pol. Ec.* 82:34–55.

Rosenbaum, D. 1987. "Hierarchical Organization of Motor Programs." In S. P. Wise, ed., *Higher Brain Function: Recent Explorations of the Brain's Emergent Properties.* New York: Wiley, pp. 45–66.

Rossi, Ino. 1974. *The Unconscious in Culture.* New York: Dutton.

    1981. "Transformational Structuralism: Lévi-Strauss's Definition of Social Structure." In Blau and Merton, eds. *Continuities in Structural Inquiry,* Beverly Hills, CA: Sage, pp. 51–80.

Rotenstreich, N. 1972. "On Lévi-Strauss' Concept of Structure." *Review of Metaphysics* 25, 3:489–526.

    1977. "An Analysis of Piaget's Concept of Structure." *Phil. and Phenom. Research* 37:368–80.

Roth, Alvin. 1984. "The Evolution of the Labor Market for Medical Interns and Residents: A Case Study in Game Theory." *Journal of Pol. Econ.* 92:991–1016.

    ed. 1985. *Game Theoretic Models of Bargaining.* Cambridge University Press.

Roth, Gerhard, and Helmut Schwegler. 1981. *Self-Organizing Systems: An Interdisciplinary Approach.* Frankfurt and New York: Campus Verlag.

Rothschild, K. W., ed. 1971. *Power in Economics.* Harmondsworth, Eng.: Penguin.

Rubinstein, David. 1986. "The Concept of Structure in Sociology." In Mark L. Wardell and Stephen P. Turner, eds. *Sociological Theory in Transition,* Boston, MA: Allen and Unwin, pp. 80–94.

Rucker, Rudy. 1987. *Mind Tools: The Five Levels of Mathematical Reality.* Boston, MA: Houghton-Mifflin.

Rudnick, Joseph, and George Gaspari. 1987. "The Shapes of Random Walks." *Science* 237:384–89.

Ruelle, David. 1980. "Strange Attractors." *Mathematical Intelligencer* 2:126–37.
  1989. *Elements of Differentiable Dynamics and Bifurcation Theory.* New York: Academic Press.
Rueschemeyer, Dietrich. 1986. *Power and the Division of Labor.* Stanford, CA: Stanford University Press.
Rule, J., and C. Tilly 1975. "Political Processes in Revolutionary France, 1830–32." In J. M. Merriman, ed. *1830 in France.* New York: New Viewpoints, pp. 41–86.
Rumelhart, David, and James McClelland. 1985. "Levels Indeed! A Response to Broadbent." *Journal of Experim. Psych.: General* 114:193–7.
Rumelhart, David, James McClelland, and the PDP Research Group. 1986. *Parallel Distributed Processing: Explorations in the Microstructure of Cognition. Volume 1:* Foundations.
Runciman, W. C., and Amartya Sen. 1965. "Games, Justice and the General Will." *Mind* 74:554–62.
Ruse, Michael. 1988. *Philosophy of Biology Today.* Albany: SUNY.
Sacks, Oliver. 1990. "Neurology and the Soul." *New York Review of Books* (November 22), 44–50.
Sailer, L. D. 1978. "Structural Equivalence: Meaning and Definition." *Soc, Networks* 1:73–90.
Salthe, Stanley N. 1985. *Evolving Hierarchical Systems: Their Representation and Structure.* New York: Columbia University Press.
Sassen-Koob, Saskia. 1984. "Growth and Informalization of the Core: The Case of New York City." In *The Urban Informal Sector: Recent Trends in Research and Theory.* Baltimore, MA: Johns Hopkins University Press, pp. 492–518
Sayer, D. 1979. *Marx's Method.* Sussex: Harvester Press.
Sayre, K. 1986. "Intentionality and Information Processing: An Alternative View." *Behavioral and Brain Sciences,* 9:121–66.
  1987. "Various Senses of 'Intentional Systems'." *Behavioral and Brain Sciences,* 10:760–65.
Scadron, M. 1985 "Spontaneous and Dynamical Symmetry Breaking in Modern Physics." *Surveys in High-Energy Physics* 5, 1–2.
Schaffer, William M. 1986. "Chaos in Ecological Systems: The Goals That Newcastle Forgot." *Trends in Ecological Systems* 1:63.
Schaffer, William M., and Mark Kot. 1985. "Do Strange Attractors Govern Ecological Systems?" *Bioscience* 35:403–27.
Schank, Roger C., and Robert P. Abelson. 1977. *Scripts, Plans, Goals, and Understandings: An Inquiry into Human Knowledge Structures.* Hillsdale, NJ: Erlbaum.
Schank, Roger C., and Peter G. Childers. 1984. *The Cognitive Computer: On Language, Learning, and Artificial Intelligence.* Reading, MA: Addison-Wesley.
Schank, R. C., and C. K. Reisbeck, eds. 1981. *Inside Computer Understanding: Five Programs Plus Miniatures.* Hillsdale, NJ: Erlbaum.
Scharpf, Fritz W. 1987. "A Game-Theoretical Interpretation of Inflation and Unemployment in Western Europe." *J. of Public Policy* 7 (3):227–57.
  1988. "The Political Calculus of Inflation and Unemployment in Western Europe: A Game Theoretical Interpretation." Unpublished paper.
Schelling, Thomas 1971. "Dynamic Models of Segregation." *J. Math. Soc.* 1: 143–86.

1978. *Micromotives and Macrobehavior.* New York: Norton.

1984. *Choice and Consequences.* Cambridge, MA: Harvard University Press.

Scherer, F. M. 1980. *Industrial Market Structure and Economic Performance.* Boston, MA: Houghton Mifflin.

Schievella, P. S. 1973. "Emergent Evolution and Reductionism." *Scientia* 108: 323–30.

Schmitt, F. O., ed. 1970. *The Neurosciences: A Study Program.* New York: Rockefeller University Press.

Schmitter, Ph. 1974. "Still the Century of Corporatism." *Review of Politics* 36: 85–131.

1977. "Modes of Interest Intermediation and Models of Societal Change in Western Europe." *Comp. Pol. Studies* 10:7–38.

Schotter, A. 1981. *The Economic Theory of Social Institutions.* Cambridge University Press.

Schotter, Andrew, and Gerhard Schwoediauer. 1980. "Economics and Game Theory: A Survey." *J. Econ. Lit.* 18:470–527.

Schrödinger, Erwin. 1944. *What is Life?* Cambridge University Press.

Schutz, Alfred. 1967. *The Phenomenology of the Social World.* Evanston, IL: Northwestern University Press.

Schutz, Alfred, and Thomas Luckmann. 1973. *The Structure of the Life World.* Evanston, IL: Northwestern University Press.

Schwartz, Barry. 1975. *Queuing and Waiting: Studies in the Social Organization of Access and Delay.* Chicago, IL: University of Chicago Press.

Schwartz, Michael, ed. 1987. *The Structure of Power in America: The Corporate Elite as a Ruling Class.* New York: Holmes and Meier.

Scott, Richard 1981. "Development in Organizations Theory, 1960–1980." *Am. Beh. Scientist* 24:407–22.

Searle, John R. 1969. *Speech Acts: An Essay in the Philosophy of Language.* Cambridge University Press.

1980. "Minds, Brains, and Programs." *Behavioral and Brain Sciences,* 3:417–57.

1984. *Minds, Brains, and Science.* Cambridge, MA: Harvard University Press.

Secord, Paul. 1982. *Explaining Human Behavior.* Beverly Hills, CA: Sage.

Sedgewick, Robert. 1983. *Algorithms.* Reading, MA: Addison-Wesley.

Sejnowski, T. J., C. Koch, and P. Churchland. 1988. "Computational Neuroscience." *Science* 241, 1299–1306.

Sen, Amartya K. 1967 "Isolation Assurance and the Social Rate of Discontent." *Quarterly J. Econ.* 80:112–24.

1970a. *Collective Choice and Social Welfare.* San Francisco, CA: Holden Day.

1970b. "The Impossibility of a Paretian Liberal." *J. of Pol. Ec. 78.* 1:152–7. Reprinted in his 1982.

1977. "Social Choice Theory. A Re-Examination." *Econometrica* 45:53–89.

1978. "Rational Fools. A Critique of the Behavioral Foundations of Economic Theory." In Henry Harris, ed. *Scientific Models of Man.* New York: Oxford University Press. Reprinted in his 1982.

1982. *Choice, Welfare, and Measurement.* Cambridge, MA: MIT Press.

Serra, R., M. Andretta, M. Zanarini, and M. Campiani, eds. 1986. *Introduction to the Physics of Complex Systems.* Elmsford, NY: Pergamon.

Sewell, William S. 1987. "Theory of Action, Dialectic, and History: Comment on Coleman." *AJS* 93, 1:166–72.

Shapere, Dudley. 1974. "On the Relations Between Compositional and Evolutiony Theories." In Ayala and Dobzhansky, *Studies in the Philosophy of Biology: Reduction and Related Problems.* Berkeley: University of California Press.

Sharrock, Wes, and Bob Anderson. 1986. *The Ethnomethodologists.* Chichester, Eng.: Ellis Horwood.

Shaw, Patrick. 1986. "Preference, Choice and Paretian Liberals." *Phil. Soc. Sci.* 16 (2):211–18.

Shaw, Robert. 1984. *The Dripping Faucet as a Model Chaotic System.* Santa Cruz, CA: Aerial Press.

Shepherd, Clovis. 1964. *Small Groups.* Scranton, PA: Chandler.

Shepherd, William. 1972. "The Elements of Market Structure." *Rev. of Econ. and Stat.* 54:25–35.

Sheridan, Alan. 1980. *Michel Foucault: The Will to Truth.* London: Tavistock.

Shubik, Martin. 1975. *Games for Society, Business, and War: Towards a Theory of Gaming.* New York: Elsevier.

1982. *Game Theory in the Social Sciences: Concepts and Solutions.* Cambridge, MA: MIT Press.

1987. *A Game-Theoretical Approach to Political Economy.* Cambridge, MA: MIT Press.

Simmel, Georg. 1955. *Conflict and the Web of Group Affiliations.* New York: Free Press.

1978. *The Philosophy of Money.* New York: Routledge & Kegan Paul.

Simon, Herbert A. 1961. *Administrative Behavior.* New York: Macmillan.

1965. "The Architecture of Complexity." *General Systems Yearbook* 10:63–76.

1973. "The Organization of Complex Systems." In H. H. Pattee, ed. *Hierarchy Theory.* New York: Braziller.

1978. "Rationality as Process and as Product of Thought." *Amer. Econ. R.* 68:1–16.

1981. *The Sciences of the Artificial.* Cambridge, MA: MIT Press.

Simons, H. 1990. *The Rhetorical Turn.* Chicago, IL: University of Chicago Press.

Skarda, C. A., and W. J. Freeman. 1987. "How Brains Make Chaos in Order to make Sense of the World." *Behavioral and Brain Sciences,* 10:161–99.

Skinner, G. W. 1977. "Cities and the Hierarchy of Local Systems." In G. W. Skinner, ed. *The City in Late Imperial China.* Stanford, CA: Stanford University Press, pp. 275–352.

Skocpol, Theda. 1979. *States and Social Revolutions.* Cambridge University Press.

Sloman, A. 1987. "Motives, Mechanisms, and Emotions." *Cognition and Emotion* 1:217–33. Reprinted in M. Boden, ed. 1990. *The Philosophy of Artificial Intelligence.* New York: Oxford University Press.

Smart, B. 1983. *Foucault, Marxism and Critique.* New York: Routledge & Kegan Paul.

1986. "The Politics of Truth and the Problem of Hegemony." In D. Couzens Hoy, ed. *Foucault: A Critical Reader.* Oxford: Blackwell.

Smelser, Neil J., ed. 1967. *Sociology: An Introduction.* New York: Wiley.

Smith, Charles W. 1981. *The Mind of the Market.* Totowa, NJ: Rowman and Littlefield.

Smith, Joseph W. 1984. *Reduction and Cultural Being: Antireductionist Critique of Positivist Programs.* The Hague: Nijhoff.

Smolensky, P. 1988. "On the proper treatment of connectionism." *Behavioral and Brain Sciences,* 11:1–23 (followed by comments 24–74).

Snow, David A. 1986. "Frame Alignment Processes, Micromobilization, and Movement Participation." *ASR* 51:464–81.

Snow, David A., Louis A. Zurcher, and Sheldon Ekland-Olson. 1980. "Social Networks and Social Movements: A Microstructural Approach to Differential Recruitment." *ASR* 45, 5:787–801.

Snyder, David, and Charles Tilly. 1972. "Hardship and Collective Violence in France, 1830–1960." *ASR* 37:520–32.

Sober, Elliott 1984a. *The Nature of Selection.* Cambridge, MA: MIT/Bradford.
ed. 1984b. *Conceptual Issues in Evolutionary Biology.* Cambridge, MA: MIT Press.

Sober, Elliott, and R. C. Lewontin. 1982. "Artifact, Cause, and Genic Selection." *Philosophy of Science* 49:157–80.

Solbrig, Otto T., and Dorothy J. Solbrig. 1979. *Introduction to Population Biology and Evolution.* Reading, MA.

Solla, S. A., G. A. Sorkin, and S. R. White. 1986. *Disordered Systems and Biological Organization.* In E. Bienenstock, ed. NATO Adv. Study Institute, vol. 20.

Soucek, Branko. 1989. *Neural and Concurrent Real-time Systems: The Sixth Generation.* New York: Wiley-Interscience.

Spence, A. Michael. 1974. *Market Signaling: Informational Transfer in Hiring and Related Screening Processes.* Cambridge, MA: Harvard University Press.
1976. "Product Selection, Fixed Costs and Monopolistic Competition." *Rev of Ec. Studies* 43:217–35.

Sperry, R. W. 1969. "A Modified Concept of Consciousness." *Psychol. Rev.* 76: 532–6.
1976a. "Changing Concepts of Consciousness and Free Will." *Perspect. Bio. Med* 20:9–19.
1976b. "Mental Phenomena as Causal Determinants in Brain Function." In G. C. Globus et al., eds. *Consciousness and the Brain: A Scientific and Philosophical Inquiry,* New York: Plenum, pp. 163–78.
1983. *Science and Moral Priority.* New York: Columbia University Press.

Spinner, Helmut. 1973. "Science Without Reduction: A Critique of Reductionism With Special Reference to Hummel and Opp's 'Sociology Without Sociology.'" *Inquiry* 16:16–44.

Stabler, E. 1983. "How are Grammars Represented?" *Behavioral and Brain Sciences,* 3:391–402.

Stanley, Steven M. 1979. *Macroevolution: Pattern and Process.* New York: Freeman.
1981. *The New Evolutionary Timetable: Fossils, Genes, and the Origins of Species.* New York: Basic.

Stauffer, Dietrich. 1979. "Computative Monte-Carlo Study of Using Spin-Glasses in 2 to 5 Dimensions." *Z. Phys. B.* 34 (1):97–105.
1985. *Introduction to Percolation Theory.* Philadelphia, PA: Taylor and Francis.

Stebbins, G. L. 1974. "Adaptive Shifts and Evolutionary Novelty: A Compositional Approach." In Ayala and Dobzhansky, *Studies in the Philosophy of Biology.* Berkeley: University of California Press.

Steeb, W. H., and J. A. Louw. 1986. *Chaos and Quantum Chaos.* Singapore: World Scientific.

Steen, L. A. 1988. "The Science of Patterns." *Science* 240, 4852:611–24.

Stewart, Ian. 1989. "Big Whorls Do Have Little Whorls." *Nature* 338:18–9.

Stich, S. 1983. *From Folk Psychology to Cognitive Science: The Case against Belief.* Cambridge, MA: MIT Press.

1990. *The Fragmentation of Reason.* Cambridge, MA: MIT Press.

Stinchcombe, Arthur. 1968. *Constructing Social Theories.* New York: Harcourt Brace.

1975. "Merton's Theory of Social Structure." In L. Coser, ed. *The Idea of Social Structure.* New York: Free Press, pp. 11–34.

1978. *Theoretical Methods in Social History.* New York: Academic Press.

1980. "Is The Prisoner's Dilemma All of Sociology?" *Inquiry* 23:187–92.

1983. *Economic Sociology.* New York: Academic Press.

Stolte, John, and Richard M. Emerson. 1977. "Structural Inequality: Position and Power in Network Structures." In R. Hamblin, ed. *Behavioral Theory in Sociology.* New Brunswick, NJ: Transaction Publishers.

Stryker, Sheldon. 1980. *Symbolic Interactionism: A Social Structural Version.* Menlo Park, CA: Benjamin-Cummings.

Studdert-Kennedy, M., ed. 1983. *Psychobiology of Language.* Cambridge, MA: MIT Press.

Suppe, Fred. 1977. *The Structure of Scientific Theories.* Urbana, IL: University of Illinois Press.

1990. *The Semantic Conception of Theories and Scientific Realism.* University of Illinois Press.

Swedberg, Richard. 1990. *Economics and Sociology: Redefining Their Boundaries.* Princeton, NJ: Princeton University Press.

Sweezy, Paul. 1968. *Theory of Capitalist Development.* New York: Monthly Review Press.

Swidler, Ann. 1986. "Culture in Action: Symbols and Strategies." *ASR* 51:273–86.

Swinney, Harry L. 1983. "Observations of Order and Chaos in Nonlinear Systems." *Physica* 7D:3–15.

Tabot, Michael. 1989. *Chaos and Integrability in Nonlinear Dynamics: an Introduction.* New York: Wiley-Interscience.

Taylor, Charles. 1975. *Hegel.* Cambridge University Press.

1979. "Interpretation and the Sciences of Man." In P. Rabinow and W. Sullivan, eds. *Interpretative Social Science: A Reader.* Berkeley: University of California Press.

Taylor, H. F. 1970. *Balance in Small Groups.* New York: Van Nostrand.

Taylor, Michael. 1976. *Anarchy and Cooperation.* New York: Wiley.

1982. *Community, Anarchy, and Liberty.* Cambridge University Press.

1987. *The Possibility of Cooperation.* Cambridge University Press.

1988. "Rationality and Revolutionary Collective Action." In *Rationality and Revolution.* Cambridge University Press.

1989. "Structure, Culture and Action in the Explanation of Social Change." *Politics and Society* 17.

Thibaut, John, and Harold Kelley. 1959. *The Social Psychology of Groups.* New York: Wiley.

Thom, René. 1984. *Structural Stability and Morphogenesis.* Elmsford, NY: Benjamin.

Thompson, E. P. 1963. *The Making of the English Working Class.* New York: Vintage.

1978. *The Poverty of Theory.* London: Merlin Press.

Thompson, James David. 1967. *Organizations in Action: Social Science Bases of Administrative Theory.* New York: McGraw-Hill.

Thompson, J. M., and B. H. Stewart. 1986. *Nonlinear Dynamics and Chaos.* New York: Wiley.

Tilly, Charles. 1973. *The Vendée: A Social Analysis of the Counter-Revolution of 1793.* Cambridge, MA: Harvard University Press.

1975a. *The Rebellious Century.* Cambridge, MA: Harvard University Press.

ed. 1975b. *The Formation of National States in Western Europe.* Princeton, NJ: Princeton University Press.

1975c. "Revolutions and Collective Violence." In Fred I. Greenstein and N. W. Polsky, eds. *Handbook of Political Science* 3:483–555. Reading, MA: Addison-Wesley.

1978. *From Mobilization to Revolution.* Reading, MA: Addison-Wesley.

1984. *Big Structures, Large Processes, Huge Comparisons.* New York: Russell Sage Foundation.

1989. *The Contentious French: Four Centuries of Popular Struggle.* Cambridge, MA: Harvard University Press.

Tilly, L., and C. Tilly, eds. 1981. *Class Conflict and Collective Action.* Beverly Hills, CA: Sage.

Torrance, Steve, ed. 1984. *The Mind and the Machine: Philosophical Aspects of Artificial Intelligence.* New York: Hulsted Press.

Touraine, Alain. 1977a. "Huit manières de se débarrasser de la sociologie de l'action." *Soc. Sci. Info* 16:879–903.

1977b. *The Self-Production of Society.* Chicago, IL: University of Chicago Press.

1988. *Return of the Actor: Social Theory in Postindustrial Society.* Minneapolis: University of Minnesota Press.

Trappl, Robert, ed. 1986. *Power, Autonomy, Utopia: New Approaches toward Complex Systems.* New York: Plenum.

Trigger, H., B. J. Kemp, D. O'Connor, and A. B. Lloyd, eds. 1983. *Ancient Egypt: A Social History.* Cambridge University Press.

Tuck, Richard. 1988. *The Free Rider Problem.* Oxford: Blackwell.

Turk, Herman. 1973. *Interorganizational Activation in Urban Communities: Deductions From the Concept of System.* Washington, DC: American Sociological Association.

Turnbull, Colin. 1962. *The Forest People: A Study of the Pygmies of the Congo.* New York: Simon and Schuster.

Turner, Jonathan H. 1983. "Theoretical Strategies for Linking Micro and Macro Processes: An Evaluation of Seven Approaches." *West. Soc. Rev.* 14, 1:4–15.

1984. "A Note on G. H. Mead's Behavioristic Theory of Social Structure." *J. Th. Soc. Beh.* 12:213–22.

1986a. "A Theory of Structuration." *AJS* 4:969–77.

1986b. *The Structure of Sociological Theory.* Fourth ed. Homewood, IL: Dorsey Press.

Turner, Jonathan, and Randall Collins. 1989. "Toward a Microtheory of Structuring." In Jonathan H. Turner, ed. *Theory Building in Sociology,* Beverly Hills, CA: Sage, pp. 118–30.

Turner, Jonathan, and Alexandra Maryanski. 1979. *Functionalism.* Menlo Park, CA: Benjamin-Cummings.

Turner, Stephen. 1977. "Blau's Theory of Differentiation: Is It Explanatory?" *Soc. Quarterly* 18:17–32.

1983. "Weber on Action." *ASR* 48:506–19.

Tversky, A., and Kahneman, D. 1974. "Judgment Under Uncertainty." *Science* 185:1124–30.

1981. "The Framing of Decisions and the Rationality of Choice." *Science* 211:453–58.

Ulanowicz, R. E. 1979. "Prediction, Chaos and Ecological Perspective." In E. Halfon, ed. *Theoretical Systems Ecology.* New York: Academic Press, pp. 107–16.

Ulanowicz, Robert, and Trevor Platt, eds. 1985. *Ecosystems Theory for Biological Oceanography.* Ottawa: Department of Fisheries and Oceans.

Vancil, Richard. 1978. *Decentralization: Managerial Ambiguity by Design.* Homewood, IL: Irwin.

van Fraassen, Bas C. 1980. *The Scientific Image.* New York: Oxford University Press.

1990. *Laws and Symmetry.* New York: Oxford University Press.

Van Gulick, R. 1988. "Consciousness, Intrinsic Intentionality, and Self-understanding Machines." In *Consciousness in Contemporary Science,* ed. A. J. Marcel and E. Bisiach, New York: Oxford University Press, pp. 78–100.

Van Parijs, Philippe. 1983. "Why Marxist Economics Needs Micro-Foundations: Postscript to an Obituary." *Review of Rad. Pol. Econ.* 15, 2: 111–24.

Venkataraman, G., D. Sahoo, and V. Bala Krishnan, eds. 1989. *Beyond the Crystalline State: An Emerging Perspective.* New York: Springer-Verlag.

Vidyasagar, M. 1978. *Nonlinear Systems Analysis.* Englewood Cliffs, NJ: Prentice-Hall.

Vol'kenshtein, Mikhail. 1970. *Molecules and Life.* New York: Plenum.

von Bertalanffy, L. 1952. *Problems of Life.* New York: Wiley.

ed. 1968. *General Systems Theory.* New York: Brazilier.

von Mises, Ludwig. 1960. *Epistemological Problems of Economics.* New York: Van Nostrand.

von Neumann, John, and Oskar Morgenstern. 1953. *Theory of Games and Economic Behavior.* Princeton, NJ: Princeton University Press.

von Wright, G. H. 1951. *An Essay in Modal Logic.* Amsterdam: North Holland Publishing Company.

Voss, Richard. 1985. "Random Fractal Forgeries: From Mountains to Music." In Sara Nash, ed. *Science and Uncertainty.* London: IBM United Kingdom.

Vrba, E. 1984. "What is Species Selection?" *Syst. Zool.* 33:318–28.

Vrba, Elizabeth, and Niles Eldredge. 1984. "Individuals, Hierarchies, and Processes: Towards a More Complete Evolutionary Theory." *Paleobiology* 10:146–71.

Wade, M. J. 1977. "An Experimental Study of Group Selection." *Evol.* 31:134–53.

1978. "A Critical Review of the Models of Group Selection." *Quarterly Rev. Biol.* 53:101–14.

Wagner, David. 1984. *The Growth of Social Theories.* Beverly Hills, CA: Sage.

Wagner, D., and J. Berger. 1985. "Do Social Theories Grow?" *AJS* 90:697–728.

Waldrop, M. Mitchell. 1988. "The Quantum Wave Function of the Universe."
    Science 242:1248–50.
    1989. "The Structure of the 'Second Genetic Code' " *Science* 246:1122.
Wallerstein, Immanuel. 1974. *The Modern World System: Capitalist Agriculture
    and the Origin of the European World-Economy in the 16th Century.*
    New York: Academic Press.
    1984. *The Politics of the World Economy: the States, the Movements and the
    Civilizations.* Cambridge University Press.
Walmsley, Julian. 1988. *The New Financial Instruments.* New York: Wiley.
Walzer, Michael. 1986. "The Politics of Michel Foucault." In David Couzens
    Hoy, ed. *Foucault: A Critical Reader.* Oxford: B. Blackwell.
Wardell, M., and S. Turner, eds. 1986. *Sociological Theory in Transition.* Bos-
    ton, MA: Allen and Unwin.
Warner, Stephen R. 1978. "Toward a Redefinition of Action Theory: Paying
    the Cognitive Element Its Due." *AJS* 83:1317–49.
Warriner, Charles. 1981. "Levels in the Study of Social Structure." In Blau and
    Merton, eds. *Continuities in Structural Inquiry,* pp. 179–90.
Warshay, Leon, and Diana H. Warshay. 1986. "The Individualizing and Sub-
    jectivizing of George Herbert Mead: A Sociology of Knowledge In-
    terpretation." *Soc. Focus* 19:177–88.
Watkins, J. W. N. 1953. "Ideal Types and Historical Explanation." In H. Feigl
    and M. Brodbeck, eds. *Readings in the Philosophy of Science.* New
    York, pp. 723–43. Reprinted in John O'Neill 1973.
    1957. "Historical Explanation in the Social Sciences." *Br. J. for Phil. Sci* 8
    (30):104–17. Reprinted in P. Gardiner, 1959 ed. *Theories of History.*
    New York: Free Press, pp. 503–14.
    1976. "The Human Condition: Two Criticisms of Hobbes." In R. S. Cohen
    et al., eds. *Essays in Memory of Imre Lakatos.* Dordrecht: Reidel, pp.
    691–716.
Watt, Donald Cameron. 1989. *How War Came: The Immediate Origins of the
    Second World War, 1938–1939.* New York: Pantheon.
Weaver, W. 1948. "Science and Complexity." *Am. Scient.* 36, 536.
Weber, Bruce, David Depew, and James Smith, eds. 1988. *Entropy, Informa-
    tion, and Evolution.* Cambridge, MA: MIT Press.
Webster, G., and B. C. Goodwin. 1982. "The Origin of Species: A Structuralist
    Approach." *J. Soc. Biol. Struct.* 5:15–47.
Webster, R. 1979. "Hierarchical Organization of Ecosystems." In E. Halfon,
    ed., *Theoretical Systems Ecology.* New York: Academic Press.
Weinberg, G. M. 1975. *An Introduction to General Systems Thinking.* New
    York: Wiley.
Weintraub, E. Roy. 1979. *Microfoundations: The Compatibility of Microecon-
    omics and Macroeconomics.* Cambridge University Press.
Weiskrantz, L., ed. 1988. *Thought without Language.* New York: Oxford Uni-
    versity Press.
Weiss, Paul. 1968. "One Plus One Does Not Equal Two." In F. O. Schmitt,
    ed., *The Neurosciences.* New York: Rockefeller University Press.
    1969. "The Living System: Determinism Stratified." In A. Koestler and J. R.
    Smythies, eds. *Beyond Reductionism.* London: Hutchinson.
    1970. *Life, Order, and Understanding: A Theme in Three Variations.* Austin:
    University of Texas Press.
    1970. "Whither Life Science?" *Am. Scientist* 58:156–63.

ed. 1971. *Hierarchically Organized Systems in Theory and Practice.* New York: Hofner.

Wellman, Barry. 1983. "Network Analysis: Some Basic Principles." In *Sociological Theory 1983.* Vol. 1:155–200.

Wellman, B., and S. D. Berkowitz, eds. 1988. *Structural Sociology: Networks of Connectivity and Power.* Cambridge University Press.

West, Candace. 1979. "Against Our Will: Male Interruptions of Females in Cross-Sex Conversations." *Annals* 327:81–97.

West, Candace, and Don Zimmerman. 1977. "Women's Place in Everyday Talk: Reflections on Parent-Child Interaction." *Soc. Problems* 24:521–9.

Wetlauter, Donald B., ed. 1984. *The Protein Folding Problem.* Boulder, CO: Westview Press.

White, David H. 1981. "A Theory for the Origin of a Self-Reproducing Chemical System by Natural Selection from Short, Random Oligomers." In Y. Wolman, ed. *Origin of Life,* Dordrecht: Reidel, pp. 399–404.

White, Harrison C. 1963. *An Anatomy of Kinship.* Englewood Cliffs, NJ: Prentice-Hall.

1970. "Search Parameters for the Small World Problem." *Social Forces* 40 (2):259–64.

1981a. "Where Do Markets Come From?" *AJS* 87:517–47.

1981b. "Production Markets, as Induced Role Structures." *Soc. Methodology*: 1–57. San Francisco, CA: Jossey-Bass.

1985. "Agency as Control." In J. W. Pratt and R. J. Zeckhauser, eds. *Principals and Agents.* Boston, MA: Harvard University Press, pp. 187–212.

1988. "Varieties of Markets." In B. Wellman and S. D. Berkowitz, eds. *Structural Sociology.* Cambridge University Press.

White, Harrison C., Scott Boorman, and Ronald Breiger. 1976. "Social Structure from Multiple Networks, part I." *Am. J. Soc.* 81:1384–1446.

White, Harrison C., and Ronald L. Breiger. 1975. "Pattern Across Networks." *Society* (July/August) 12 (5):68–73.

White, Robert W. 1989. "From Peaceful Protest to Guerrilla War: Micromobilization of the Provisional Irish Republican Army." *AJS* 94, 6:1277–1302.

Whittaker, R. H. 1970. *Communities and Ecosystems.* New York: Macmillan.

Whyte, L. L., A. G. Wilson, and D. Wilson, eds. 1969. *Hierarchical Structures.* New York: Elsevier.

Wicken, Jeffrey S. 1979. "The Generation of Complexity in Evolution: A Thermodynamic and Information-theoretical Discussion." *J. Theor. Biol.* 77:349–65.

1980. "A Thermodynamic Theory of Evolution." *J. Theor. Biol.* 87:9–23.

1985. "An Organismic Critique of Molecular Darwinism." *J. Theor. Biol.* 117: 545–61.

1986. "Evolutionary Self-organization and Entropic Dissipation in Biological and Socioeconomic Systems." *L. Soc. Biol. Structures* 9:261–73.

1987. *Evolution, Thermodynamics, and Information.* New York: Oxford University Press.

1988. "Thermodynamics, Evolution, and Emergence: Ingredients for a New Synthesis." In Bruce Weber, David Depew, and James Smith, eds. *Entropy, Information, and Evolution.* Cambridge, MA: MIT Press.

Wicksell, K. 1958. "A New Principle of Just Taxation." In Richard Musgrave and Alan Peacock. *Classics in the Theory of Public Finance.* New York: Macmillan.

Wiens, John A. 1984. "On Understanding a Non-Equilibrium World: Myth and Reality in Community Patterns and Processes." In D. Strong, Jr. and D. Strong, eds. *Ecological Communities: Conceptual Issues and the Evidence.* Princeton, NJ: Princeton University Press.

Wiley, E. O. 1988. "Entropy and Evolution." In Weber, Depew, and Smith, eds. *Entropy, Information and Evolution.* Cambridge, MA: MIT Press, pp. 173–88.

Wiley, E. O., and D. R. Brooks. 1982. "Victims of History: A Non-Equilibrium Approach to Evolution." *Syst. Zool.* 31:1–24.

Willer, David, and Bo Anderson, eds. 1981. *Networks, Exchange, and Coercion: The Elementary Theory and Its Applications.* New York: Elsevier.

Williams, George. 1966. *Adaptation and Natural Selection.* Princeton, NJ: Princeton University Press.

Williams, Simon Johnson. 1986. "Appraising Goffman." *Brit. J. Soc.* 37:348–69.

Williamson, Oliver. 1971. "The Vertical Integration of Production: Market Failure Considerations." *Am. Econ. Rev.* 61:112–23.

1975. *Markets and Hierarchies, Analysis and Antitrust Implications: A Study in the Economics of Internal Organization.* New York: Free Press.

1981a. "The Modern Corporation: Origins, Evolution, Attributes." *J. Econ. Lit.* XIX:1537–68.

1981b. "The Economics of Organization: The Transaction Cost Approach." *AJS* 87:548–77.

1985. *The Economic Institutions of Capitalism: Firms, Markets, Relational Contracting.* New York: Free Press.

Williamson, Oliver, and W. Ouchi. 1981. "The Markets and Hierarchies Program of Research: Origins, Implications, Prospects." In William Joyce and Andrew Van de Ven, eds. *Organizational Design.* New York: Wiley.

Wills, Christopher. 1989. *The Wisdom of the Genes.* New York: Basic Books.

Wilson, A. C., S. Carleton, and T. J. White. 1977. "Biochemical Evolution." *Ann. Rev. Biochem.* 46:573–639.

Wilson, D. 1969. "Forms of Hierarchy: A Selected Bibliography." In L. L. Whyte et al., eds. *Hierarchical Structures.* New York: Elsevier.

1980. *The Natural Selection of Populations and Communities.* Menlo Park, CA: Benjamin-Cummings.

Wilson, E. O. 1975. *Sociobiology.* Cambridge, MA: Belknap/Harvard University Press.

Wilson, E. O. 1978. *On Human Nature.* Cambridge, MA: Harvard University Press.

Wilson, John. 1983. *Social Theory.* Englewood Cliffs, NJ: Prentice-Hall.

Wimsatt, William C. 1972. "Teleology and the Logical Structure of Function Statements." *Stu. Hist. Phil. Sci.* 3:1–80.

1976. "Reductionism, Levels of Organization, and the Mind-Body Problem." In G. C. Globus et al., ed. *Consciousness and the Brain: A Scientific and Philosophical Inquiry.* New York: Plenum, pp. 205–67.

1980. "Reductionist Research Strategies and Their Biases in the Units of Selection Controversy." Reprinted in Elliott Sober, ed. 1984. *Conceptual Issues in Evolutionary Biology.* Cambridge, MA: MIT Press.

Winfree, Arthur. 1974. "Rotating Chemical Reactions." *Sci. Amer.* 230:82–95.

1987. *When Time Breaks Down*. Princeton, NJ: Princeton University Press.

Winograd, T. 1972. *Understanding Natural Language*. New York: Academic Press.

1980. "What Does It Mean to Understand Language?" *Cognitive Sciences* 4: 209–45.

1982. *Language as a Cognitive Process*. Reading, MA: Addison-Wesley.

Winograd, T., and F. Flores. 1986. *Understanding Computers and Cognition*. Norwood, NJ: Ablex.

Winship, C., and M. Mandel. 1983–4. "Roles and Positions." *Soc. Methodology*: 314–44.

Winship, Christopher, and Sherwin Rosen. 1988. "Introduction: Sociological and Economic Approaches to the Analysis of Social Structure." *AJS* 94 Supplement:S1–S16.

Wippler, Reinhard. 1982. "The Generation of Oligarchic Structures in Constitutionally Democratic Organizations." In Werner Raub, ed. *Theoretical Models and Empirical Analysis*. Utrecht: ES Publishers, pp. 43–62.

Wippler, Reinhard, and Siegwart Lindenberg. 1987. "Collective Phenomena and Rational Choice." In J. Alexander et al., eds. *The Micro-Macro Link*. Berkeley: University California Press.

Wisdom, J. O. 1987. "Desiderata for a Flexible Schema: Transindividualism." In his *Philosophy of the Social Sciences II: Schemata*. Aldershot, Eng.: Avebury, pp 164–70.

Wittgenstein, Ludwig. 1953. *Philosophical Investigations*. New York: Macmillan.

Woese, C. R. 1967. *Origins of the Genetic Code*. New York: Harper.

Wolf, Fred A. 1988. *Parallel Universes*. New York: Simon and Schuster.

Wolfram, Stephen. 1983a. "Cellular Automata." *Los Alamos Science* 9:2–21.

1983b. "Statistical Mechanics of Cellular Automata." *Rev. Mod. Physics* 55 (3):601–44.

1984a. "Universality and Complexity in Cellular Automata." *Physica D* 10: 1–35.

1984b. "Cellular Automata as Models of Complexity." *Nature* 311:419–24.

Wolman, Y., ed. 1981. *Origin of Life*. Dordrecht: Reidel.

Wood, Michael, and Mark L. Wardell. 1983. "G. H. Mead's Social Behaviorism vs. the Astructural Bias of Symbolic Interactionism." *Symbolic Interaction* 6:85–96.

Woolgar, Steve 1988. *Science: The Very Idea*. New York: Tavistock.

Wright, Barbara. 1973. *Critical Variables in Differentiation*. Englewood Cliffs, NJ: Prentice-Hall.

Wright, Erik O. 1980. "Varieties of Marxist Conceptions of Class Structure." *Politics and Society* 9, 3:323–70.

1985. *Classes*. London: New Left Books/Verso.

Wright, H. T. 1978. "Recent Research on the Origin of the State." *Annual Review of Anthropology*: 379–97.

Wright, S. 1956. "Modes of Selection." *Amer. Natural* 90:5–24.

1969. *The Theory of Gene Frequency*, vol. 2. Chicago, IL: University of Chicago Press.

1977. *The Theory of Gene Frequency*, vol. 3. Chicago, IL: University of Chicago Press.

1978. *The Theory of Gene Frequency*, vol. 4: *Variability within and among Populations*. Chicago, IL: University of Chicago Press.

448   Bibliography

1980. "Genic and Organizational Selection." *Evolution* 34:825–843.
Wrong, Dennis. 1961. "The Oversocialized Conception of Man." *ASR* 26:183–93.
Wu, L. L. 1983–4. "Local Blockmodel Algebras for Analyzing Social Networks." *Soc. Methodology:* 272–313.
Wynne-Edwards, V. C. 1986. *Evolution through Group Selection.* Palo Alto, CA: Blackwell-Scientific.
Yaglom, I. M. 1987. *Felix Klein and Sophus Lie.* Cambridge, CA: Birkhauser Boston.
Yamagishi, Toshio, Mary R. Gillmore, and Karen S. Cook. 1988. "Network Connections and the Distribution of Power in Exchange Networks." *AJS* 93, 4:833–51.
Yates, F. E., ed. 1984. *Self-Organizing Systems: The Emergence of Order.* New York: Plenum.
Young, Richard. 1984. "Prebiological Evolution: The Constructionist Approach to the Origin of Life." In K. Matsuno, ed. *Molecular Evolution and Protobiology.* New York: Plenum.
Zabusky, Norman. 1987. "Grappling with Complexity." *Physics Today.* 40 (10): 25–7.
Zald, Meyer N. 1987. "Review Essay: The New Institutional Economics." Review of O. Williamson, *The Economic Institutions of Capitalism. AJS* 93:701–8.
Zeeman, E. C. 1974. "Levels of Structure in Catastrophe Theory." *Proc. Intern. Congr. Mathem.* Vol.2:533–46.
Zeigler, Bernard. 1979. "MultiLevel Multiformalism Modeling: An Ecosystem Example." In E. Halfon, ed. *Theoretical Systems Ecology.* New York: Academic Press, pp. 18–54.
Zeitlin, Maurice. 1976. "Class Segments: Agrarian Property and Political Leadership in the Capitalist Class of Chile." *ASR* 41:1006–29.
1978. *Rethinking Sociology.* Englewood Cliffs, NJ: Prentice-Hall.
1981. "Class, State, and Capitalist Development: The Civil Wars in Chile." In Blau and Merton, eds. *Continuities in Structural Inquiry,* pp. 121–64.
Zeki, S. M., and S. Shipp. 1988. "The Functional Logic of Cortical Connections." *Nature* 335:311–7.
Zeleny, Milan, ed. 1980. *Autopoiesis: Dissipative Structures and Spontaneous Social Orders.* Boulder, CO: Westview Press.
ed. 1981. *Autopoiesis: The Theory of Living Organizations.* New York: Elsevier-North.
Zettlemoyer, A. C., ed. 1977. *Nucleation Phenomena.* New York: Wiley.
Zimmerman, Don, and D. Lawrence Wieder. 1970. "Ethnomethodology and the Problem of Social Order: Comment on Denzin." In J. Douglas, ed. *Understanding Everyday Life.* Chicago, IL: Aldine.
Zurcher, Louis A., and David A. Snow. 1981. "Collective Behavior: Social Movements." In M. Rosenberg and R. Turner, eds. *Social Psychology: Sociological Perspectives.* New York: Basic, pp. 447–82.
Zysman, John. 1977. *Political Strategies for Industrial Order: State, Market, and Industry in France.* Berkeley: University of California Press.
1983. *Government, Markets, and Growth: Financial Systems and the Politics of Industrial Change.* Ithaca, NY: Cornell University Press.

Index

449